Hey Ba[...]

...lists names of [...] o Hawaiian—by astrological [...] d book, you can choose a name that fits your baby in every way!

For example...

Names for Aries girls:

Alcina

Bridget

Diana

Eva

Fernanda

Jayna

Yoko

Zoe

Names for Taurus boys:

Adam

Angus

Barrett

Craig

Edward

Jared

Peter

Tyler

Names for Cancer girls:

Aileen

Cassandra

Isadora

Kamali

Lupe

Phoebe

Zara

Names for Virgo boys:

Austen

Bradley

Conrad

Hisoka

Ira

Justin

Manchu

Hey Baby, What's Your Sign?

THE ASTROLOGICAL BABY NAME BOOK

Nancy Burke

Developed by The Philip Lief Group, Inc.

BERKLEY BOOKS, NEW YORK

HEY BABY, WHAT'S YOUR SIGN?

A Berkley Book / published by arrangement with
The Philip Lief Group, Inc.

PRINTING HISTORY
Berkley trade paperback edition / November 1999

The Penguin Putnam Inc. World Wide Web site address is
http://www.penguinputnam.com

ISBN: 0-425-17046-2

BERKLEY®
Berkley Books are published by The Berkley Publishing Group,
a member of Penguin Putnam Inc.,
375 Hudson Street, New York, New York 10014.
BERKLEY and the ''B'' design
are trademarks belonging to Penguin Putnam Inc.

PRINTED IN THE UNITED STATES OF AMERICA

10 9 8 7 6 5 4 3 2 1

CONTENTS

Contents

INTRODUCTION

Who is this beautiful babe in arms? She of Grandma's curls and Daddy's dimples; he of Uncle's eyes and Mommy's smile? Will she become president? Will he colonize Mars? Will she graduate summa cum laude? Will he win the Nobel Prize?

One of the singular joys—and adventures—of parenting is discovering who our children really are and where they are heading in life. More importantly, we want to be there for them fully, to nurture and encourage them along their chosen paths in life. The world of astrology can offer us some valuable assistance as we shepherd our newborns through infancy, then toddlerhood, and school. Astrology is a fun and exciting—and amazingly accurate—tool for understanding a child's behavior and personality.

Hey Baby, What's Your Sign? is a one-of-a-kind book that satisfies two ever-popular interests: the fascination with astrology and the desire to give children singularly distinctive names.

Designed to help you understand your child's emotions and behavior from the viewpoint of astrology, this book presents brief but richly detailed astrological profiles of each of the zodiac's signs. It pays particular attention to how the sign's influences are manifested in children at home, at school, and in play. Following each discussion of a zodiac sign, an extensive list suggests suitable names—separate for girls and boys—for each particular sign.

To help you use this book most effectively, a brief primer about astrology and its origins, together with explanations of the most common terms used in this book, is contained in the following section. And to help you get started as soon as possible, the Appendix at the back of the book contains instructions for casting a shorthand version of your newborn's birth chart—something you can do right in the hospital!

Please note that *Hey Baby, What's Your Sign?* is meant to

serve as an introduction to the fascinating world of astrology, but is not an exhaustive treatment of this complex discipline. If you want to learn more about astrology, excellent reference sources are listed in the back of this book.

What Is Astrology?

For over five thousand years, people have looked to the night-time skies, to the changing patterns of the stars and planets, the Sun and Moon, for explanation and illumination of their every-day affairs. Astrology provides a richly symbolic system of studying the positions and movements of the heavenly bodies as they relate to human behavior and natural events.

Approximately five thousand to seven thousand years ago, astrological systems simultaneously sprang up in cultures as diverse as India, Egypt, and China. But the roots of modern astrology, as it is practiced today, stretch back nearly six thousand years to the first priest-astrologers of the Babylonian–Assyrian empire. Collectively these ancient Semitic people of the desert were called the Chaldeans, from the Latin *chaldaeus*, meaning "astrologer." Chaldean high priests, who were also members of the government, were the first known astrologers.

In the wide open desert expanses of ancient Babylonia, these priest-astrologers had a magnificent and unimpeded view of the night skies. Recording the movements of the stars, Sun, and Moon, they began to realize that the growth of plants and crops was somehow linked to the positioning of the heavenly bodies. They then theorized that the constantly shifting patterns of these heavenly bodies affected not only the plant world but human behavior and other natural events as well.

Over several millennia, the pioneering Chaldean astrologers made thousands of meticulous observations of the movements of the Sun, Moon, stars, and planets and linked them with corresponding events or phenomena that occurred on Earth—in weather, health, politics, human relationships, natural catastrophes, and war. These seminal astrological observations were recorded on clay tablets that could be passed down to future generations.

The Chaldean astrologers were responsible for dividing the sky into twelve equal parts to give us the twelve zodiac signs we still use today. Eventually each sign of the zodiac was associated with specific behaviors, events, and even flowers, trees, colors, animals, and gemstones.

The original twelve signs of the Chaldean zodiac were Aries, Pleiades, Gemini, Praesepe, Leo, Spica, Libra, Scorpio, Sagittarius, Capricorn, Aquarius, and Pisces. Later, when astrology was assimilated into the Greek culture, Greek astrologists renamed three of the original Chaldean signs. The Pleiades became Taurus, Praesepe became Cancer, and Spica became Virgo.

Along with formulating the twelve signs of the zodiac, the Chaldeans are also credited with devising the twelve houses of the zodiac, which are essential in drawing up and interpreting an astrological birth chart (see Appendix). Each house relates to one significant aspect of human life, including personality, wealth, school, family, love, health, marriage, death, spirituality, work, friendships and partnerships, and the metaphysical or hidden.

Astrology soon spread to the Greek and Roman empires, where it was further refined, popularized, and became entrenched in mainstream culture. Astrology's popularity dimmed for a brief period, after the fall of the Roman Empire, but it resurfaced stronger than ever in the 1200s, and has retained its great popularity and fascination ever since.

The Signs

This book focuses on the Sun signs of the zodiac. These are the traditional groupings of astrological signs that most people are familiar with because they appear frequently in the daily horoscopes featured in magazines and newspapers, as well as books.

The sign that the Sun was traveling through—or transiting—

at a child's birth (see the tables at the back of this book) is called the Sun sign, and has the most profound influence on an individual's life. The qualities and tendencies associated with a particular Sun sign uniquely characterize individuals throughout their lives and give them their distinctive approach to family, relationships, work, and the world. In many ways, the Sun sign represents the public persona of an individual.

Though Moon signs are not the focus of this book, it is interesting to look at an individual's Moon sign (see the tables at the back of this book). The sign that the Moon was traveling through, or transiting, at a child's birth is called the Moon sign and in many ways is as important as the Sun sign. The qualities and tendencies associated with a particular Moon sign may be viewed as the more emotional, instinctive, and unconscious side of an individual, or the private persona. When you cast your newborn's birth chart (see the Appendix), you will automatically record both the Sun and Moon signs.

Remember, however, that no individual can be characterized by just one zodiac sign. This is especially true of people born on the cusp of a sign (at the very beginning or the end of a sign), who invariably exhibit the qualities of two signs—their own Sun sign and the sign immediately preceding or following it.

Below is a snapshot view of the major characteristics and qualities associated with each of the zodiac's Sun signs, together with the date range for the sign. Individual Sun signs are discussed in greater detail in the body of the book.

The Sun Signs

Aries (March 21–April 20) Impulsive, proud, hot-tempered, aggressive, highly intelligent, with leadership abilities

Taurus (April 21–May 21) Down-to-earth, steady, reliable, stubborn, determined, artistic, and resistant to change

Gemini (May 22–June 21) Highly intellectual, versatile, witty, gifted with fine communication skills, opinionated, and restless

Cancer (June 22–July 23) Emotional, imaginative, home loving, extremely sensitive, moody, and loyal

Leo (July 24–August 23) Starlike persona, noble, exuberant, charismatic, arrogant, egocentric, vivacious, and charming

Virgo (August 24–September 23) Hardworking, service oriented, intellectual, analytical, obsessive, and critical

Libra (September 24–October 23) Balanced, fair-minded, peaceful, charming, adaptable, artistic, easygoing, and happy

Scorpio (October 24–November 22) Sensual, deeply emotional and imaginative, psychic, self-sacrificing, and spiritually inclined

Sagittarius (November 23–December 21) Ebullient, expansive, intelligent, freedom loving, joyful, other directed, and knowledge seeking

Capricorn (December 22–January 20) Practical, driven, inner directed, self-disciplined, assertive, responsible, and success oriented

Aquarius (January 21–February 19) Intellectual, artistic, innovative, unconventional, humanitarian, and rebellious

Pisces (February 20–March 20) Intuitive, modest, imaginative, constant, deeply emotional and sensitive, and highly adaptable

The Planets

On another level, separate from the Sun signs, are the planets. In astrology, a geocentric approach is used in the study of the planets. That is, the Earth is seen as the center of the astrological universe, and ten major planets, which seem to orbit the Earth, are considered the most significant influences in a person's birth chart. (Note: In astrology, the Sun and Moon are treated as planets, though in fact they are luminaries.)

In the geocentric system, these ten planets are the Sun, the Moon, Mercury, Venus, Mars, Jupiter, Saturn, Uranus, Neptune, and Pluto.

The innermost "planets" in our solar system—the Sun, Moon, Mercury, Venus, and Mars—are known as the "inner" or "personal" planets. They are notable for endowing individuals with their unique personality traits.

The outermost planets—Jupiter, Saturn, Uranus, Neptune, and Pluto—which are farthest from the Sun, are known as the "outer" or "impersonal" planets. These planets govern how individuals interact with others.

Uranus, Neptune, and Pluto—the most recently discovered of the planets—are also known as the "modern" or "transpersonal" planets and are strongly associated with deep and far-reaching changes.

No one planet has a singular or exclusive influence in an individual's life. Indeed, in an individual's personal birth chart, the planets cluster together or appear in patterns throughout the birth chart in ways that are unique to that individual. Many planets exert their influences in a person's life. In fact, planetary influences in general are fluid and ongoing processes, not fixed qualities.

How a planet's influence is manifested depends very much on the sign in which it appears. Thus the influence of the Moon (here considered to be a planet) is said to govern a person's home and family life; depending on what sign that person is born under, the Moon manifests its power quite differently. For example, extroverted and theatrical Leos, under the Moon's influence, turn their homes into theaters where they act out the various roles they play throughout their lives. On the other hand, the extremely sensitive and thin-skinned Pisceans, under the Moon's influence, cherish home as a quiet refuge in which they can hide from the world. Many of the reference books listed in this book contain valuable discussions of planetary influences on a sign-by-sign basis.

Below is a brief summary of the major functions and qualities associated with each planet. Further discussions of each planet can be found in the respective signs that they rule.

The Ten Planets

Sun. The most important of the planets, with the greatest influence in an individual's chart, the Sun governs life itself, ego, power, career, aggressiveness, and individuality. The Sun rules Leo.

Moon. The second most important of the planets, the Moon governs home and family life, emotions and intuition, unconscious or latent tendencies, compassion, and imagination. The Moon rules Cancer.

Mercury. Mercury governs communication and intellectual reasoning, self-knowledge, the male and female duality, and the acquiring of knowledge. Mercury rules Gemini and Virgo.

Venus. Venus governs love, romance, intimate relationships and partnerships, diplomacy, beauty, pleasure, self-indulgence, narcissism, and charm. Venus rules Taurus and Libra.

Mars. Mars governs aggression, action, energy, sexuality, drive, self-promotion, and violence. Mars rules Aries.

Jupiter. Jupiter governs great wisdom, understanding, growth, expansiveness, good luck, travel, and material abundance. Jupiter rules Sagittarius.

xvi *Introduction*

Saturn. Saturn, often called the "celestial taskmaster," governs tradition, restrictions, order, stability, religious and governmental institutions, hard work, self-discipline, and obstinacy. Saturn rules Capricorn.

Uranus. Uranus governs anarchy, revolution, radicalism, independence, progressiveness, humanitarianism, originality, change, and personal transformation. Uranus rules Aquarius.

Neptune. Neptune governs slow change, mysticism, charity, creativity, spirituality, high ideals, self-sacrifice, and disillusionment. Neptune rules Pisces.

Pluto. Pluto governs the mysterious, the deep and the dark, transformation, regeneration, profound change, magic, criminality, and spiritual healing. Pluto rules Scorpio.

The Polarities

Each sign of the zodiac is either Masculine or Feminine in polarity (also called duality). These categories should not be confused with the stereotypic characteristics often associated with the words *masculine* or *feminine*. Rather, Masculine and Feminine here refer to a broader category of fundamental and complementary positive and negative energies, similar to the Chinese concept of yin and yang.

The **Masculine** signs are outgoing, energetic, and action oriented. The six Masculine signs are: Aries, Gemini, Leo, Libra, Sagittarius, and Aquarius.

The **Feminine** signs are inner directed, sensitive, and receptive. The six Feminine signs are: Taurus, Cancer, Virgo, Scorpio, Capricorn, and Pisces.

The Qualities

Each zodiac sign is assigned one of three qualities—also called quadruplicities—that represent the essential energy of the sign and how individuals born under it interact with the environment (people, home, workplace) around them. The three qualities are: Cardinal, Fixed, and Mutable.

Cardinal signs are assertive, self-promoting, outer directed, and action oriented. They display initiative, intuition, and leadership skills. They attempt to control the environment by outthinking and outmaneuvering it. The Cardinal signs are Aries, Cancer, Libra, and Capricorn.

Fixed signs are stable, persistent, determined, and self-contained. They display consistency and reliability, and they tend to ignore the environment, being more concerned with personal goals. The Fixed signs are Taurus, Leo, Scorpio, Aquarius.

Mutable signs are adaptable, versatile, accommodating, and open. They are the most influenced by their environment—and therefore are somewhat unstable—but they are also the most adaptable of the signs. The Mutable signs are Gemini, Virgo, Sagittarius, and Pisces.

The Elements

Each zodiac sign is assigned one of four elements—also called triplicities—that characterize the fundamental nature, or personality, of individuals born under the sign. The four elements are: Fire, Earth, Air, and Water.

Fire signs are enthusiastic, energetic, charismatic, and outgoing. They are the leaders, innovators, adventurers, and explorers of the zodiac. The Fire signs are: Aries, Leo, and Sagittarius.

Earth signs are practical, conservative, down-to-earth, and reliable. They are the doers of the zodiac who implement the visions, ideas, and dreams of the other signs. The Earth signs are Taurus, Virgo, and Capricorn.

Air signs are intellectual, rational, verbally expressive, and ebullient. They are the thinkers and communicators of the zodiac. The Air signs are Gemini, Libra, and Aquarius.

Water signs are emotional, sensitive, imaginative, and compassionate. They are the lovers, nurturers, poets, and dreamers of the zodiac. The Water signs are Cancer, Scorpio, and Pisces.

How to Use This Book

Each of the twelve chapters that follows discusses in-depth each of the twelve zodiac signs. They are listed in their traditional astrological order: Aries, Taurus, Gemini, Cancer, Leo, Virgo, Libra, Scorpio, Sagittarius, Capricorn, Aquarius, and Pisces.

The chapters open with a listing of the inclusive dates covered by the sign, together with the main characteristics, symbols, and objects associated with and/or governed by the sign. These include the glyph (ideographic symbol), the pictorial symbol, the polarity, the quality, the element, the ruling planet, the birthstone, special colors, flowers, metals, animals, and the most likeable personality traits associated with the sign.

Following that is a discussion of the general personality characteristics associated with the sign, including the effects of the sign's ruling planet, the influence of the sign's polarity, quality, and element, and a description of the mythological origins of the sign's symbolism, when appropriate.

The section called "Home" discusses how children of a specific sign generally behave within the home and how they interact with parents, siblings, and friends. This section also includes lighthearted advice about how to nurture a child's astrologically endowed strengths and minimize or offset any weaknesses.

"School and Play" details how children born under a particular sign may generally respond to school, study, teachers, and classmates, what sports or extracurricular activities they may or may not be drawn to, and what their approach to play and playmates may be. Again, suggestions for managing a sign's specific strengths and weaknesses are offered.

Finally, the section on "The World" discusses the career or careers that children born under a particular sign may pursue later in life, together with a general discussion of the adult's approach to personal relationships, commitment, and marriage.

Following the discussion of the zodiac sign is an extensive listing of girls' and boys' names that may be suitable for a child born under that sign. The listing of names begins with a short introduction, "How to Choose a Name," explaining the rationale behind choosing the names. It briefly highlights the major symbols, qualities, and characteristics associated with the sign.

For each name listed, there is a pronunciation key, the linguistic derivation or origin of the name, the meaning of the name, a brief explanation of why the name is appropriate for the sign, and a listing of variations of the name. Also included in this listing, where appropriate, are famous persons who share the same name and zodiac sign under discussion.

Following each sign's list of names is an exhaustive list of famous people who were born under that sign.

The Appendix at the back of the book illustrates how to cast an astrological birth chart for your newborn in less than ten minutes—and right in the hospital if you want! You will be able to quickly determine your child's ascendant, or rising sign, one of the most profound influences in an individual's chart, as well as determine what signs are in each of your child's twelve houses, and what planets rule those houses.

The important thing to remember when using this book is to bring a light heart, an open mind, and a generous sense of humor to your readings of the signs and your casting of a birth chart. Nothing in astrology is etched in stone, and that is the beauty of the discipline. Astrology is deeply symbolic, individualistic, and interpretive; it is part art and part science. It is about potentialities and possibilities, but it is never about inevitabilities. It is rich in history and mythology, but thoroughly modern in application. In the end, astrology is but another tool to help make parenthood the joyful, rewarding, and exciting journey it is meant to be.

A Word About the Names

We have taken a very broad-based approach to selecting the names in this book. While most names have been selected because their meanings reflect characteristics associated with the signs under which they have been listed (*Kyle*, originally a Scottish name meaning "ruler," makes a great name for Ariens, who tend to be strong willed and assertive), other names have been chosen for the direct connection they bear to the symbol itself. For example, Cancer is the sign of the Moon, Leo is the sign of the Sun and the Lion, and Pisces is the sign of the Fish. As you will see, names that mean "moon," "sun," "lion," and "fish"—all words that historically, culturally, and spiritually, have had powerful and profound symbolic meaning for a variety of cultures—are abundantly represented here.

Still other names are related to aspects of a particular sign. Cancer's birthstone, for example, is the pearl, and the sophisticated name, *Margot*, derived from the Greek word for this precious gem, is a wonderful choice for a Cancer girl. We have also used the trees, colors, flowers, animals, and metals associated with a sign as inspiration in choosing names. Likewise, the elemental images of Fire, Water, Earth, and Air associated with specific signs provide another source of inspiration in choosing names.

We encourage you to be creative in choosing a name for your child. For example, if none of the names for Cancer boys resonates with you, you might want to check the names listed under Cancer's companion Water signs, Pisces and Scorpio. Likewise, if you are looking for a name for your Virgo girl, whose ruling element is Earth, you might also read over the names listed in the two other Earth signs, Taurus and Capricorn. This is also a good strategy to use if you are looking for a powerful and appropriate middle name for your child.

Choosing a name for your child is the first and perhaps most significant step you will take in beginning to help shape your child's unique personality, destiny, and place in the world. Now more than ever people attach great significance, expectations, and preconceptions to a name—the banner that singularly announces your child's entrance into the world. In this book, we have tapped the rich and powerful imagery of the ancient art and science of astrology to help you choose the most perfect and auspicious name for your child. Happy hunting!

ARIES
(March 21–April 20)

GLYPH: ♈

SYMBOL: The Ram

POLARITY: Masculine

QUALITY: Cardinal

ELEMENT: Fire

RULING PLANET: Mars

BIRTHSTONE: Diamond

SPECIAL COLOR: Red

FLOWERS: Geranium, sweet pea, and honeysuckle

METAL: Iron

ANIMALS: Sheep and Rams

MOST LIKEABLE TRAITS: Courage, enthusiasm, energy, and confidence

♈

Symbolized by the Ram, Ariens are headstrong, adventurous, and fiercely independent, never failing to leap straight into new or unfamiliar territory. Aries's parents face the constant challenge of keeping their child's boundless energy from leading him or her into various misadventures.

General Qualities

Children born under the first sign of the zodiac, ruled by fiery Mars, tend to be strong willed and energetic. At a very young age, they appear direct, driven, and possessed with a desire for independence. Being first is very important for any Aries. Their

1

competitive and dynamic personalities are frequently coupled with short attention spans, so parents may need to channel their abundant energy into a variety of creative outlets. Aries babies are subject to flash-in-the-pan temper tantrums; however, they are just as quick to calm and usually easy to pacify.

Aries children tend to be adaptable and resourceful, thus they have little trouble adjusting to change. For example, when their families move to a new town, Aries children quickly adapt. Ariens typically have no problem attracting people, due to their natural gifts of charm and vivacious energy. They tend to be very popular in school.

Generally self-assured and confident, Ariens have a natural talent for leading or guiding others. But their frequent habit of stubbornly refusing to accept the advice or ideas of others can make Ariens prone to single-mindedness and bossiness. For the thicker skinned, their directness, honesty, and no-nonsense attitudes can be refreshing: One always knows where he or she stands with an Aries.

Children born in Aries have quick, intelligent minds that thrive when given a problem to solve or an activity that involves creative innovation. Adventurous Ariens prefer the trial-and-error method for discovering solutions to problems, often adopting this experimental means of learning throughout their lives.

Home

After a busy day at school or play, your Aries child feels a special joy at the thought of returning home. Ariens, who strive for a peaceful, harmonious home life, typically enjoy the company of their families. They are quite affectionate and loving. Although they possess nearly supernatural levels of energy, Ariens need to spend time each day "recharging": Encourage your Aries child to relax while at home and make certain he or she regularly gets a good night's sleep.

If you have other children, you would be wise to give your Arien his or her own room. If you don't, more than the normal amount of sibling bickering may ensue, with your Aries child soon taking over the entire room. Ariens' rooms generally take on the bold, vivid quality that is characteristic of the sign: Don't be surprised when your child suggests painting the room bright red! The room of your Aries child must be modern and well kept—Ariens have a strong dislike for anything old or shabby. Your ever forward-looking Aries child will always want the latest and best of everything. Parents of Aries children should expect to see Christmas lists filled with requests for computers, video game systems, TV/VCRs, and the latest technological gadgets.

When they are at home, Ariens may often remain holed up in their rooms for hours at a time either with friends or alone. Parents and other family members shouldn't take this personally: Ariens just need time to experiment, create, and explore. Although even the youngest Ariens express no deep need or desire to have parents or siblings constantly around them, they still enjoy spending a few hours a day with family members, playing a game or going on an outing.

Aries children delight in playing host to their pals, serving snacks and planning activities for their guests. Ariens enjoy entertaining. As a parent, you will become accustomed to your child's friends tearing through your house on a regular basis.

Because Aries children relish having the ability to do things on their own, owning a pet allows them to take on some responsibility and to feel important. However, should you decide to get a pet for your Aries child, be prepared to take over the caretaking tasks: Once the novelty wears off, getting Aries children to clean out their hamster's cage or to feed the cat may be difficult.

Emotionally, Ariens are quite resilient, and nothing keeps them upset for long. They do have a tendency to become self-absorbed, mostly because they are so busy trying to prove themselves to the world that they forget that other people have lives, too. Still, Ariens are affectionate and intuitive, and their efforts to solve the problems of those around them make them ideal friends to turn to in times of need.

School and Play

Aries girls and boys tend to be bright, outspoken individuals. At school, their assertive, self-assured dispositions make them natural leaders and trailblazers. They may need to learn to curb their instinctive me-first attitudes, and let other children share the spotlight. Ariens, who are naturally fast learners, may have a tendency to become impatient with classmates who don't catch on quite as quickly as they do. Aries children must learn to be understanding and sensitive to the needs of others at a young age in order to offset their inclination toward selfish and domineering behavior. Regardless, Aries children pass on their enthusiastic energy to those around them, which contributes to their ability to get along with almost everyone. They are fiercely loyal to their friends, and will fight passionately for causes that touch their hearts.

Bestowed with tons of charm, energy, radiance, and a natural ability to put others at ease, Ariens are very popular and never lack friends. People are drawn to Aries's contagious enthusiasm, well-developed sense of humor, good-natured generosity, and naturally outgoing personality. However, their short attention spans may cause Aries children to jump from friend to friend, dropping someone once they become too familiar, then moving on to a new friendship, which is newer, more "mysterious"— and thus more interesting—to Aries. At an early age, try to teach your child to respect people for who they are (faults and all) and encourage your Arien to foster long-term friendships.

Often quick to anger, Ariens cool off fast and rarely carry grudges. Due to the warlike influences of their sign, Ariens are prone to fighting (verbally more than physically) and seem to thrive on challenge. Do not be surprised if your Aries child jumps into the disputes of others: Ariens enjoy conquering the obstacles presented by conflicts. As a parent of an Aries child, try to channel this quality by encouraging your youngster to take part in productive activities that make good use of the combative energy, such as debating or a team sport.

Aries children tend to be high achievers who possess a natural excitement for learning new things. They also tend to be trend setters, the first ones to come to school wearing a new style of clothing or toting a new type of toy—even starting new fads among their friends and classmates.

In the classroom, your Aries child is likely to excel. Ariens' competitive spirits encourage them to achieve high grades, and thus rise to the top of their class. Possessed of quick minds and creative talents, Ariens are also gifted at coming up with solutions to new problems.

Advanced for their age, Ariens are attracted to challenges and love to experiment. Always anxious to start something new, they become bored when the same topic is discussed in class for days on end. When information seems useless for their purposes, they often forget everything they've learned the minute the test is over. Because seeing others' point of view can be hard for them, Ariens may have slight disciplinary problems in school: They just don't see the point of following the same routine every day, which results in their questioning traditional methods of classroom learning.

At play, Ariens' overabundance of energy must be channeled in some way: They *must* become involved in physical activity from a young age. Thriving on competition, Ariens often excel in sports and leisure activities. Their take-charge attitudes and drive to win make them natural achievers in this arena. However, their low tolerance for boredom can undermine their efforts: Aries children need to learn discipline to help maximize their potential talent on and off the field. Parents should encourage their Aries children to enjoy games and sports for fun, not just as a means of competing with other children. Downplay showing off when possible.

Due to their independent natures, Ariens prefer working alone rather than as part of a group. If made to play with other children, they do best in a position of leadership. As a result, Aries children are drawn to solo sports, such as swimming, track, or tennis. They do well as captains of team sports in which they excel.

Bubbling over with excess energy, Ariens are often prone to accidents. Because the body part associated with Aries is the head, this area is especially sensitive: Make sure your Aries child wears a helmet when in-line skating, bicycling, or playing a rough contact sport like hockey. Aries children can be so consumed with winning that they would rather play a game with a painful injury than sit on the bench and miss a chance at victory. Born healthy and resilient, Ariens are quick to recover when injured.

At a young age, begin teaching your child not to take games too seriously, a typically Arien trait. While they enjoy challenges, Ariens hate to be shown up by someone else. Help them learn to be good sports. If your Aries child is given a game or toy that proves too difficult, you may find the item in the trash— or even smashed to pieces.

The World

With their minds always racing, Ariens tend to muster tons of enthusiasm for anything new—until the novelty wears off. Then they quickly move on to something else. Parents should encourage their Aries children to finish what they start and to see things through to the end, whether finishing a school project, completing weekly chores, or keeping up with piano practice.

The intrepid and corner-cutting nature of Ariens makes them want to run before they can walk, so parents will want to provide plenty of supervision (although the strong-willed, independent Aries initially resists it). Aries's boundless energy makes these children more prone to bumps and scrapes than children born under other signs, and since the head is the symbolic body area of Aries, caution should be exercised when Aries children are playing.

Children born in Aries may have a tendency to exaggerate: Their creative natures inspire overactive imaginations. Parents may want to help their Ariens see things as they are and not simply as Aries wants them to be. However, parents need to resist the temptation to push their highly intelligent and talented Aries children too hard. Too much applause from adults can put tremendous pressure on children to constantly outdo themselves in their ongoing race to be the best at everything.

As they grow older and the time comes to choose a major at college or to embark upon a career path, Ariens may have trouble focusing on just one thing: They are interested in many topics and quite talented in just as many areas too. Ariens are sure to shine if they find a field that suits their abilities and interests. But whatever they choose to do, they will do well. Ariens have a fierce desire to be successful and leave their mark on the world, a drive that propels them to achieve their goals. Aries typically excels in positions that demand leadership and/ or creative thinking and problem solving, in fields such as advertising, public relations, politics, finance, and management.

Possessed with a strong sense of self from day one, Ariens are prone to putting themselves first. The natural pride and self-esteem possessed by Aries children ensures that they grow into secure, confident adults: Nurture it. Trying to crush this self-centered tendency only causes Ariens to become more rebellious and selfish in a desperate need to prove their worth at any cost.

Though at times it may seem as if your Aries child prefers to ignore your advice, realize that this is just Aries's way of learning from their own mistakes; It is not a personal affront. Rest assured that your Aries son or daughter cares a great deal about you, as he or she will prove in the affection and love they show you, now and through the years to come. The Aries adolescent years will prove most difficult, with rebellion as the most familiar theme in your household during those years. While remaining fiercely independent throughout their lives, as they grow older Ariens also learn to appreciate the wisdom and guidance of their parents.

Parents may worry about their fearless, adventure-seeking Aries children when it's time for them to go away to college or take a trip with friends. But bear in mind that Ariens are gifted with a natural strength that skillfully guides them through life's challenges and provides them with a hardy resilience.

In the coming years, your child will display the passion, strength, and fortitude that make Ariens so successful in career endeavors. Ariens, with their zest for life and commitment to the people and causes they love, make effervescent children, attentive partners, strong parents, and invaluable contributors to society.

Choosing a Name for Your Aries Child

When you choose a name for your Aries child, first look at the major symbols and attributes of the sign. Aries is ruled by the planet Mars (the Roman god of war) and named for the god of war in Greek mythology. The metal affiliated with the sign is iron, and the imagery of fire and passion is associated with Aries, one of the three Fire signs of the zodiac. Although the diamond is Aries's official birthstone, the red-tinted ruby and bloodstone are the sign's gemstones—most appropriate, since the special color assigned to Aries is red. Aries is the first sign in the zodiac, encompassing the months of March and April—the beginning of spring. The geranium, sweet pea, and honeysuckle flowers are strongly associated with Aries, as are thorn-bearing trees. Aries's symbol is the Ram, which also is affiliated with lambs, sheep, and ewes.

Consider the most prominent personal qualities of Aries. Children born in Aries tend to be strong, courageous, and confident in all things. They have quick minds and a talent for innovation. As a result, most Arien children tend to excel in school. Ariens are driven and determined, and often drawn to competitive activities where they can prove themselves. Fiercely independent at a young age, they make natural leaders later in life. Possessed with an extraordinary zest for life, Ariens are adventurous, energetic, and enthusiastic about everything around them.

If you need further ideas when selecting a name for your Aries child, try browsing through the names listed in the sections for Leo and Sagittarius, the other Fire signs of the zodiac. Looking through those names may also be helpful when choosing a middle name for your child.

Names for Aries Girls

Abira (ah-BEE-rah) Hebrew: Powerful. This beautiful name symbolizes the strength and energy of Aries. Variations: *Abi, Adi, Adira.*

Adelle (ah-DELLE) Old German: Royal or highborn. As a natural leader—and first sign of the zodiac—Aries has often been associated with aristocratic imagery. Variations: *Addie, Adeline, Adella.*

Adesina (ah-DAY-see-nah) Nigerian: One who makes opportunities or blazes a trail for others to follow. Ariens are well known for their innovative, pioneering natures.

Agnes (AG-ness) Latin: Lamb. The sign of Aries is not only associated with the Ram, but also with the sheep and the lamb.

Akako (ah-KAH-koh) Japanese: Red. This special color associated with Aries is historically illustrative of healing and spiritual powers.

Alala (ah-LAH-lah) Latin: In Roman mythology, *Alala* is the sister of Mars. This name is appropriate to bestow upon girls born under the sign of Aries because Mars is the sign's ruler.

Alberta (al-BUR-tah) Teutonic: Noble and brilliant. This traditional name is well suited to proud, quick-minded Aries. Variations: *Allie, Berta, Bertie.*

Alcina (al-CEE-nah) Greek: Strong-minded. Ariens are notorious for their stubborn, determined ways.

Alvita (al-VEE-tah) Latin: Vivacious, animated. This ideal name connotes the zest for life found in every Arien.

April (AY-pril) Latin: Forthcoming. This pretty name suits a child born during the month of April, as many Ariens are. Variations: *Averil, Averill, Avril.*

Arden (AR-dinn) Latin: Highly excited, thrilled. Dynamic enthusiasm is a prominent characteristic of Aries.

Ardis (AR-diss) Latin: Fervent or eager. Owing to the spirit of adventure they are born with, Ariens are excited about learning and trying new things.

Asha (AH-shah) Swahili: Life. This name signifies the vibrant life force that is so obvious in Aries.

Auberta (oh-BEHR-tah) French: Noble or bright. This name suggests the intelligence and strength of Aries. Variations: *Aubrey, Aubriana.*

Audrey (AW-dree) Old English: Regal force. Strong Aries seems to exhibit qualities often found in rulers and royals. Variations: *Audra, Audrina.*

Ava (AY-vah) Hebrew: Life. This name is ideal for Ariens, who live life to the fullest every moment of every day.

Aviva (ah-VEE-vah) Hebrew: Joyful spring. This beautiful name is an appropriate choice for exuberant Aries, born in March or April.

Bahira (ba-HEE-rah) Arabic: Electrifying. Ariens are known for their high levels of energy. They are often dynamic enough to jolt even the most lethargic people into action.

Bernadette (BUR-nah-DETTE) French: Courageous like a bear. Bravery is one of the most prominent characteristics of Aries. Variation: *Bernadine.*

Bernice (bur-NEES) Greek: Bringer of victory. Highly competitive and driven Aries strives to win in everything she does.

Bertha (BUR-tha) Teutonic: Bright and shining one. This traditional name for Aries expresses her natural radiant brilliance. Variations: *Berta, Bertie.*

Bibiane (bee-bee-ANN) Latin: Lively. This name expresses the vivacious spirit found among Ariens.

Billie (BIL-lee) American: Powerful guardian. The female diminutive of *William* is ideal for the strong, courageous Aries. Variation: *Billy.* (Famous Arien: Billie Holiday, singer)

Bina (BEE-nah) Hebrew: Discernment or insight. With their bright, inquiring minds, Ariens are renowned for their discriminating judgment.

Brenda (BREN-dah) Teutonic: Firebrand. One of the three Fire signs, Aries is known to induce a passion for life.

Brianna (bree-AN-nah or bry-AN-nah) Celtic: Strength. This feminine form of *Brian* ideally represents the fortitude and courage of Aries. Variations: *Briana, Brianne, Bryana, Bryanna, Bryanne.*

Bridget (BRIHJ-itt) Celtic: Resolute strength. Determined and forceful, Ariens are extremely difficult to discourage once they set their minds on a goal. Variations: *Brighid, Brigid, Brigit, Brigitte.*

Carla (KAR-lah) Italian: Female power. This wonderful name for an Aries female reflects pride, strength, and energy in all that she does. Variations: *Carleen, Carly, Karly.*

Cassandra (kah-SAHN-drah or kah-SAN-drah) Greek: Conflicting warriors. This name suits competitive and determined Aries. Variations: *Cass, Cassie, Sandra, Sandy, Sondra.*

Casey (KAY-see) Celtic: Brave. Ariens are well known for their courage and fearlessness.

Cerella (seh-RELL-ah) Latin: Of spring. This name is often used for girls born under the signs of spring: Aries, Taurus, and Gemini.

Ceres (SEHR-ees) Latin: Of spring. This lovely name is perfect for a girl born in March or April.

Chaya (HA-yah) Hebrew: Living energy or aliveness. One of Aries' most prominent characteristics is a dynamic joie de vivre that shines through everything she does.

Cornelia (kor-NEE-lee-ah) Latin: Hornlike. This ancient Roman family name (the feminine version of *Cornelius*) suggests Aries's symbol, the Ram.

Daria (DAH-ree-ah) Greek: Queenly. *Daria* is a suitable name for a proud, successful, strong-willed Aries female. Variations: *Darian, Darienne.*

Deborah (Deh-BOR-ah or DEB-rah) Hebrew: Literally, swarm of bees. Aries is a beautiful creature of spring, but when provoked, she will attack with a series of stinging remarks. This was also the name of the biblical prophet and judge who led the Israelites to victory over the Canaanites. Variations: *Debbi, Debbie, Debi, Debora, Debra, Debrah.* (Famous Arien: Debbie Reynolds, actress)

Derica (dare-EE-kah) English: Beloved leader. A combination of intelligence, energy, charm, courage, and determination makes Aries a fine leader respected by others. Variations: *Dereka, Dericka, Derrica.*

Diamond (DI-ah-mund) English: Of high value. The April birthstone was popularized as a female name in the late nineteenth century. Variation: *Diamanda.*

Diana (DI-AN-nah) Latin: Celestial, divine. The Roman goddess of the hunt exhibits Aries's intrepid spirit and fearless leadership. Variations: *Diahann, Dian, Diane, Dianne, Dyana.* (Famous Ariens: Diana Ross, singer; Diane Arbus, photographer; Dianne Wiest, actor)

Drina (DREE-nah) Spanish: Fighter for justice. This name suits the warriorlike Aries, who devotes all her energy to fighting for what she believes is right.

Drusilla (dru-SILL-ah) Latin: Mighty. Aries is a veritable mountain of strength and determination, capable of overturning any obstacle and using it to her advantage.

Edana (eh-DAHN-ah) Gaelic: Tiny flame. Aries children exhibit a passion for life from an early age. Variations: *Aidana, Aydana, Ede.*

Edda (EDD-ah) German: With clear goals. This name is ideal for Aries, who never has trouble deciding what she wants out of life—or attaining it.

Edrea (ed-DREE-ah) Teutonic: Prosperous, powerful. The mighty Aries can rely on her many resources to gain success in any endeavor.

Eithne (ith-NEE) Irish: Fiery. This unusual name is ideal for a child born under the Fire sign of Aries.

Eloisa (ell-o-WEE-sa) Spanish/Italian: Acclaimed battler. Ariens are renowned for their love of arguing and competing, making them formidable enemies in debates or other types of battles. Variations: *Eloise, Heloise, Lois, Louisa, Louise, Louisette.*

Erica (ayr-REE-kah) Scandinavian: Ever-powerful, regal. Aries is known as the strongest, proudest sign of the zodiac. Feminine form of Eric. Variations: *Erika, Erykah, Ricki, Rickie.* (Famous Arien: Erica Jong, writer)

Eshe (EH-sheh) Swahili: Life. The vivacious, spirited nature of Aries is exemplified in this lovely name.

Etana (eh-TAHN-ah) Hebrew: Resolve or determination. Aries is the most driven, dedicated sign of the zodiac.

Eudora (yu-DORR-ah) Greek: Gift without limits. Ariens are often bestowed with many talents—often so many they have trouble picking just one extracurricular interest or career. Variations: *Dora, Dorey, Dorie*. (Famous Arien: Eudora Welty, author)

Eugenia (yu-JEEN-ee-ah) Greek: Fortunate birth. Ariens tend to be lucky people, not only because of their natural gifts, but because of their ability to get the most out of life. Variations: Eugénie.

Eva (AY-vah or EE-vah) Hebrew: She who bestows life. This name is perfect for an Aries female, who enriches life with her infectious curiosity, vivacity, and enthusiasm. Variations: *Eve, Evelyn, Evita*.

Faizah (FAH-ee-zah) Arabic: Winning. Usually quite lucky by nature, Ariens enjoy competing with others, often getting what they set out to achieve.

Fernanda (fer-NAN-dah) Spanish: Adventurous. Aries is known for her lifelong pursuit of adventure.

Fiammetta (FEE-a-MET-tah) Italian: A fluttering flame. This name reflects the fiery nature of Aries, one of the three Fire signs. Variation: *Fia*.

Fleta (FLEE-tah or FLET-ah) Teutonic: Swift. Aries is speed personified: quick thinking, physically fast, and the first to try something new or conquer new territory.

Florence (FLOR-uns) Latin: Flourishing, prosperous. Aries is well known for using her natural talents—as well as any challenges or obstacles in her way—to her advantage, ensuring success in everything she does. This name was popularized by Florence Nightingale, heroine in the Crimean War and founder of modern nursing. (Famous Ariens: Florence Blanchfield, nurse and military officer)

Folayan (faw-LAH-yahn) Nigerian: To walk in dignity. Ariens are typically proud and confident, rarely lacking in self-esteem.

Gabrielle (gah-bree-ELL or GAY-bree-ell) Hebrew: Divine heroine. This beautiful name is perfect for the brave, dynamic, well-respected Aries. Variations: *Gabbi, Gabi, Gabriella, Gigi.*

Gail (GAYL) English: Gay; lively. Aries females are charming and vivacious, often becoming the most popular personality at any gatherings. Variations: *Abigail, Gael, Gayle.*

Geraldine (JER-all-deen) French: One who rules by the spear. Thriving on adversity, Aries is known for her intense love of competition. Variations: *Geralyn, Geri, Jeraldine, Jeri.*

Gertrude (GER-trood) German, French: Power of the sword. This name is well suited to mighty, courageous Aries. Variations: *Gertie, Truda, Trude, Trudi, Trudie, Trudy.*

Gitta (GITT-ah) Gaelic: Forcefulness. Aries is adamant when it comes to something she believes in, yet at times may be too stubborn to see that others have good ideas, too.

Gudrun (goo-DROON) Scandinavian: Battle. Aries is eager to engage in competitions of all sorts, seemingly encouraged by contrary situations.

Guida (GWEE-dah) Italian: One who leads or guides. Aries daughters make natural leaders and advisors.

Gunda (GOON-dah) Norwegian: Female warrior. This name is suitable for brave and highly competitive Aries.

Haldana (HAHL-dah-na) Old Norse: Half-Danish. The name *Haldana* represents fierceness because Danes traditionally were known as fierce invaders of foreign lands, and therefore personify the forceful nature of Aries.

Harriet (HAIR-ree-ut) English: Leader. This cognate of the French *Henriette* is ideal for Aries due to the natural leadership quality that Aries inherits at birth. Variations: *Harriett, Harrietta, Harriette, Harriot, Hattie, Hatty.*

Hasana (hah-SAH-nah) Nigerian: She who enters first. As the first sign of the zodiac, Aries is known for her pioneering spirit and is often the first to try new things or create new inventions.

Hedda (HED-dah) German: One who has clear-cut aspirations. Once Ariens decide what direction they want to follow, they go to any lengths to achieve their goals. In Henrik Ibsen's play, *Hedda Gabbler*, the title character drives the play forward by her willful pursuit of her personal goals. Variations: *Heddi, Heddie, Hetta, Hettie.*

Hedwig (HED-wig) Greek: Battling. This name connotes the competitive, warriorlike drive of Aries. Variation: *Edwige.*

Heloise (HEL-oh-ees) French: Renowned fighter. Aries is famous for her ability to battle skillfully, using a combination of determination, strength, courage, and intelligence. Variations: *Eloise, Heloisa, Lois, Louisa, Louise.*

Hilda (HIL-dah) Teutonic: Woman warrior. The sign of Aries often is associated with the imagery of battles or fights. Variations: *Hilde, Hildegarde, Hildi, Hildy.*

Hillary (HIL-ah-ree) Latin: Cheerful, noisy, energetic. Aries is likely to become extremely popular, with her bounding enthusiasm, vivacious charm, and dynamic ways.

Ilka (IL-ka) Slavic: Dedicated to success. Because of her strong and competitive drive, an Aries female never has trouble motivating herself to succeed at any endeavor.

Imelda (ee-MEL-dah) Italian: One who battles forcefully. While generally good-natured, Aries can be a mighty force to reckon with when crossed.

Jaha (JAH-ha) Swahili: Dignity. Aries is among the most noble and proud signs of the zodiac.

Javiera (HA-vee-ER-ah) Spanish: Shining. This name expresses the naturally exuberant nature of Aries. Variation: *Xaviera.*

Jayna (JAY-nah) Sanskrit: Triumphant. Always up for a dare, challenge, or competition, Aries is happiest when she wins.

Jerica (JARE-ih-kah) Contemporary: Strong, gifted ruler. This blend of *Jeri* and *Erica* is ideal for the natural leader Aries. Variations: *Jerika, Jerrica, Jerrika.*

Jocasta (jo-KASS-tah) Latin: Cheerful. Naturally predisposed to an optimistic outlook, lively Aries is rarely seen downcast or depressed.

Juliana (JOO-lee-AHN-ah) Latin: Young spirit. A noteworthy characteristic of Ariens is that they often stay young at heart for their entire lives, never denouncing the simple pleasures of their youth. Variations: *Julia, Juliane, Julianna, Julianne, Julie.*

June (JOON) Latin: Young. This classic name suggests the ever-lively, youthful nature of Aries.

Karla (KAAR-la) Australian Aborigine: Fire. This pretty name is ideal for a baby born under Aries, which is one of the three Fire signs. Variations: *Carla, Carly, Karly*.

Keely (KEE-lee) Irish: Lively or aggressive. This wonderful name suits the vivacious and spirited Aries. Variations: *Keelie, Keila, Kelly*.

Keena (KEE-nah) Irish/English: Quick or brave. Speed and courage are two of the most dominant characteristics of Aries.

Kelly (KELL-ee) Gaelic: Warrior woman. The aggressive, conflict-loving Aries is a formidable opponent in debates or sports competitions. Variations: *Kelley, Kelli, Kellie*.

Kelsi (KELL-see) Gaelic: Warrior. Your Aries daughter will be brave and proud, never afraid to fight for what she believes in. Variations: *Kelsie, Kelsy*.

Kineta (kee-NET-tah) Greek: Energetic player. This unique name is ideal for Aries, who will be a dynamic addition to any team.

Lahela (lah-HAY-luh) Hawaiian: Sheep. Although the symbol of Aries is the Ram, the sign is also associated with sheep and lambs. *Lahela* is a variant of Rachel.

Latoya (lah-TOY-ya) Spanish: Victorious one. With a determination matched by no other, Aries finds success in almost every situation.

Laverne (lah-VERN) French: Springlike. This is a perfect name for a child born in March or April, as all Ariens are.

Ledah (LEE-dah) Hebrew: Born alive. An Aries daughter is a constant source of electrifying joy and enthusiasm from the moment she is born. Variations: *Leda, Letita, Lida, Lidah*.

Levana (le-VAHN-ah) Latin: Uplift. Ariens are known for their infectious zest for life, which often serves as an example to others for how to live their lives to the fullest.

Liliha (lee-LEE-huh) Hawaiian: Rebellious. Possessed with a fiercely independent streak, Aries has a tendency to believe her way is the best way and to ignore anything that might inhibit her.

Lisette (lee-SETTE) French: She who fights with honor. Although thoroughly determined when achieving a goal or winning a competition, Aries rarely acts dishonorably, preferring to gain success fairly. Variations: *Lisa, Lise.*

Lois (LO-iss) Old German: Famous warrior. As people who thrive on adversity, Ariens are often associated with warlike imagery.

Louise (loo-EEZ) Teutonic: Famous woman warrior. This honorable name symbolizes the skill Aries exhibits in battle. Variations: *Eloise, Louisa, Luisa.* (Famous Arien: Louise Lasser, actress)

Luana (lew-AHN-nah) Old German-Hebrew: Graceful woman warrior. Ariens are well known for their skill in all types of battles. Variations: *Louanna, Luane, Luann.*

Mahala (Mah-HAH-lah) Native American: Feminine power. This name suggests the strength and courage bestowed upon females born under the sign of Aries. Variation: *Mahalia.*

Maiza (MAH-ee-zah) Arabic: Discerning. Possessed with a keen intelligence, Aries knows what she wants and goes after it.

Marcella (mar-CELL-ah or mar-CHEL-ah) Latin: Of Mars. Mars is the ruling planet of the sign of Aries. Variation: *Marcelle.*

Marci (MAR-see) English: Military might. The qualities of leadership, strength, and courage make Aries a formidable opponent. Variations: *Marcie, Marcy.*

Marcia (MAR-sha) Latin: Of Mars. Marcia is an ideal name for a baby born under Aries, who is ruled by the planet Mars. The name first appeared in the Roman Empire, and was revived in the 1800s. Variations: *Marcie, Marcila, Marcy, Marsha.* (Famous Arien: Marsha Mason, actress)

Matilda (mah-TILL-dah) Old German: Chaste warrioress. This traditional name connotes the ability to fight with honor found in most Ariens. Variations: *Maddy, Mathilda, Mattie, Matty, Maud, Maude, Tilda, Tillie, Tilly.*

Megan (MEG-an, MEE-gan, or MAY-gen) Anglo-Saxon: Strong or able. This fine name suits an Aries daughter, who will stand proud and take on any challenge with zeal. Variations: *Meg, Meghan.*

Melcia (MELT-suh or MEL-shuh) Polish: Ambitious. When Ariens decide they want something, no one and nothing can keep them from getting it.

Melisande (mel-a-ZAHND) German, French: Strength or determination. Ariens are known for their unstoppable drive and ceaseless fortitude. Variations: *Millicent, Melisandra.*

Melissa (me-LISS-ah) Greek: Stinging bee. This popular and beautiful name represents the nature of Aries: attracted to every beautiful flower, yet quick to attack if challenged. Variations: *Lissa, Mel, Mellisa, Misha, Missie, Missy.* (Famous Arien: Melissa Joan Hart, actress)

Mesha (MAY-shah) Hindi: Child born under Aries. This ancient name acknowledges a long-standing awareness of when one's child is born.

Mildred (MIL-dred) English: Gentle strength. Aries generally makes use of her abundant might and energy in positive ways, often taking care of others who are less fortunate than herself.

Milica (MI-lits-uh or mi-LEE-kuh) Old Gothic: Ambitious or industrious. This name suits the hardworking Aries, who stops at nothing to achieve her goals.

Millicent (MIL-lih-sent) German: Ambitious. Your Aries daughter will need little prodding when it comes to excelling at an academic, artistic, or athletic endeavor. Variation: *Millie*.

Miranda (mir-AN-dah) Latin: Worthy of admiration. This classic name suggests the popularity of Aries, whose gifts are often simultaneously envied and acclaimed by others. In Shakespeare's *The Tempest*, the heroine Miranda is Prospero's daughter, a straightforward, headstrong girl whose love for Ferdinand blinds her to understanding her father's objections to her paramour. Variations: *Mira, Randi, Randy*.

Miriam (MIR-ee-ahm) Hebrew: She who forges her own path. Bestowed with a pioneering spirit of independence, Ariens are renowned for being natural leaders who are eagerly followed by others. Variations: *Mimi, Minnie*.

Mitzi (MIT-zee) English: She who leads or follows her own path. This name is perfect for trailblazing, innovative Aries, who is sure to set many a social trend. Variation: *Mitzy*.

Nagida (nah-GEE-dah) Hebrew: Leader or prosperous. Ariens have no trouble getting ahead at school and work, and often hold leadership positions in various arenas.

Neala (NEEL-ah) Gaelic: Victor. This ideal name for an Aries girl reflects her intense desire to win. Variations: *Neila, Neile, Neille*.

Neci (NEH-see) Latin: Passionate or without limits. One of the three Fire signs, Aries has a tendency to bubble over with enthusiasm for everything and everyone.

Neely (NEE-lee) Irish Gaelic: Victor. Highly competitive Aries always has her eye on the prize. Variations: *Nealie, Nealy, Neeli, Neelie*.

Nellie (NEL-lee) Greek: One who shines. The effervescent enthusiasm found in Aries is one of her most positive attributes. Variation: *Nelly*.

Neola (neh-OH-lah) Greek: Youthful soul. No matter how old she gets, dynamic Aries always retains a zest for life.

Nicole (nee-COLE) Greek: Triumphant march. This name suggests the desire of those born under the sign of Aries to succeed and win. Variations: *Colette, Nicholle, Nicki, Nickie, Nicola, Nicolette, Niki, Nikki, Nikky*.

Nina (NEE-nah) Native American: Powerful. This lovely name suits the strong and mighty Aries. (Famous Arien: Nina Foch, actress)

Nuria (noo-REE-ah) Hebrew: God's flames. As a Fire sign, Aries is bestowed with a burning zest for life and a fervant devotion to using her talents to their fullest.

Nyla (NYE-lah) Greek: Winner. Naturally fortunate and born with an abundance of talents, Aries constantly strives to be the best in everything she does. Variation: *Nila*.

Olabunmi (aw-lah-BOON-mee) Nigerian: Prize won through honor. This name connotes Ariens' desire to win and their noble approach to doing so.

Oma (o-MAH) Arabic: Military chief. Ariens often do well in positions of power, due to their natural leadership qualities.

Ondrea (ohn-DREE-ah) Czechoslovakian: Fierce woman. A daughter born in Aries is likely to be strong and proud, and when the wrong person crosses her, she may become a powerful force to be reckoned with.

Phaedra (FAY-dra) Greek: Glowing. This name represents the intense zest for life and brilliant energy found in every Aries. Variation: *Phadra*.

Phoebe (FEE-bee) Greek: Bright one. Many Ariens are bright and advanced for their ages, at times seeming to attain the level of genius. In Greek mythology, *Phoebe*'s daughter Leto gave birth to Artemis, goddess of the hunt, and Apollo, god of the Sun. (Famous Arien: Phoebe Cates, actress)

Posala (po-SAH-lah) Native American (Miwok): To explode. This unusual name, referring to the energy of seeds bursting into life during the springtime, is ideal for the dynamic Aries.

Prima (PREE-mah) Latin: First. *Prima* is an appropriate name for a child born under Aries, the first sign of the zodiac.

Rachel (RAY-chel) Hebrew: Ewe. The sign of Aries is associated with the Ram and the sheep. In the Bible, Rachel was the younger wife of Jacob, son of Isaac. Variations: *Rachele, Rachelle, Raquel, Raquelle, Rochelle*.

Radinka (ra-DINK-ah) Slavic: Full of life. Aries daughters are lively and vivacious, seeming to glow with enthusiasm.

Rae (RAY) Hebrew: Ewe. Although symbolized by the Ram, Aries is also associated with lambs and sheep. Variations: *Raeann, Raelene, Ray, Raye, Rayette, Raylene*.

Regan (RAY-gan or REE-gan) Gaelic: Ruling. Suggesting a capacity to lead others, this name is well suited to Aries. In Shakespeare's *King Lear*, Regan is the stormy, outspoken daughter of Lear, who meets tragedy when her father divides his kingdom among three of his daughters.

Rhonda (RON-dah) Scottish Gaelic: Strong one. This wonderful name suits Aries, who is often the one others look up to for guidance or lean on in times of need.

Roberta (ro-BER-tah) German: Bright and famous. The feminine form of *Robert*, this name expresses Aries's shining intellect and drive to succeed. Variations: *Bobbi, Bobbie, Robbie.*

Rona (ROH-nah) Teutonic: Mighty power. Ariens possess an uncanny ability to influence others and to get exactly what they set their sights on throughout life.

Sarah (SAHR-ah or SAYR-ah) Hebrew: Shining or royal. This name is ideal for spirited, effervescent Aries. The name *Sarah* has been immensely popular for centuries. In the Bible, Sarah was the wife of Abraham and mother of Isaac. Variations: *Sadie, Sally, Sara, Sarita, Sayra.* (Famous Ariens: Sarah Jessica Parker, actress; Sarah Vaughan, singer)

Scarlett (SCAR-lett) English: Bold red color. This name, associated with Aries's special color, is also the name of the dazzling heroine in Margaret Mitchell's famous novel, *Gone With the Wind.*

Scout (SKOUT) American: One who explores in order to obtain information. This name fit the dauntless protagonist in Harper Lee's *To Kill a Mockingbird*, and was further popularized after Bruce Willis and Demi Moore bestowed it upon their daughter. The name reflects Aries's love of adventure.

Shaka (SHAH-kah) English/African-American: Female defender or warrioress. This name suggests the strong, battling nature of Aries. Variations: *Chaka, Shakala.* (Famous Arien: Chaka Khan, singer)

Sigourney (sih-GUR-nee) Scandinavian: Victorious. Combining fierce determination, quick intelligence, and a drive to win, Aries rarely lose a race or fight.

Stephanie (ste-FAH-nee) Greek: Wearer of the crown. This name connotes Aries's constant vying for the top prize. Variations: *Stefani, Stefanie, Stefany, Stephany.*

Taima (tah-EE-mah) Native American: Thunderbolt. This name is indicative of the great power and might found in Aries.

Takenya (tah-KEHN-yah) Native American: Fierce falcon. This beautiful name suggests the strength and fortitude of Aries.

Tatum (TAY-tum) Scandinavian: Effervescent; energetic. Aries tend to be bubbly, vivacious, and always popular with their peers. Variation: *Tate.*

Tetsu (TET-su) Japanese: Strong as iron. This interesting name for Aries suggests strength and endurance. Iron is the metal associated with the sign.

Thelma (THEL-mah) Greek: Strong-willed. Once Aries sets her mind to something, discouraging her can be difficult. The name recently enjoyed a resurgence with the success of the 1991 film *Thelma & Louise,* in which two women accidentally become fugitives but refuse to surrender themselves or their principles.

Tracy (TRAY-cee) Latin: Courageous. This popular name suggests Aries's brave spirit. Variations: *Tracey, Traci, Tracie.*

Trudy (TROO-dee) German: Might or forcefulness. This traditional name suggests Aries's strength and determination. Variations: *Truda, Trude, Trudeliese, Trudi.*

Tyra (TEER-ah or TYE-rah) Scandinavian: Of Tyr, god of battle. This unusual name is ideal for the competitive Aries female.

Valda (VAL-dah) Old Norse: Leader. *Valda* is a popular name in Scandinavia, characterizing Aries's natural leadership ability.

Valentina (vahl-lin-TEE-nah) Latin: Powerful. This beautiful name expresses the fierce determination and bravery found in those born under the sign of Aries. Variations: *Val, Valentine*.

Valerie (VAL-ah-ree) Latin: Strong. Ariens are formidable individuals who eagerly overcome any obstacles thrown in their paths. Variations: *Val, Valeria*.

Victoria (vic-TOR-ee-ah) Latin: Victory. This traditional name suggests the competitive nature of Aries, who always plays to win. Popular with English monarchy, the name and its variations are common throughout Europe and the United States. Variations: *Vicki, Vicky, Vikki, Tori*. (Famous Arien: Vicki Lawrence, singer/actress)

Vivian (VIV-ee-an) Latin: Filled with life's energy. This lovely name suits an Aries child, who possesses a contagious zest for life. Variations: *Vivianne, Vivien, Vivienne*.

Winema (wee-NEH-mah) Native American: Female chieftain. Ariens are renowned for making admirable leaders, and this name particularly suits an Aries.

Wisia (VEE-shuh or WI-shuh) Polish: Victorious. Ariens thrive on adversity and competition, and always strive to be the best in all that they do.

Yanaba (YAH-nah-bah or yah-NAH-bah) Native American: She who meets the battle head-on. Rather than shy away from intimidating or scary situations, courageous Ariens relish any challenge in their paths.

Yoko (YO-ko) Japanese: Feminine energy. One of the most prominent characteristics of Aries is a dynamic enthusiasm, and this name refers directly to females with that energy.

Zelenka (zeh-LENN-keh) Czechoslovakian: Like a budding green plant. This name suits a child born in the spring, as all Ariens are.

Zoe (ZO-ee or ZOH) Greek: Life. This simple, pretty name for an Aries daughter represents the vivacity and animation she exudes. Variation: *Zoë*. (Famous Arien: Zoe Wanamaker, actress)

Names for Aries Boys

Abelard (AB-eh-lard) Old German: Highborn and committed. Aries is renowned for his dedication and drive.

Abraham (AY-bra-ham) Hebrew: Patriarch or ruler of many. This name is well suited to the natural leadership ability of Aries. In the Bible, Abraham was the first Hebrew patriarch. Variations: *Abe, Abram*. (Famous Arien: Abraham Maslow, psychologist)

Adir (ah-DEER) Hebrew: Noble. Aries is strong, dedicated, and honorable by nature.

Agni (AHG-nee) Hindi: Fire deity. This is an ideal name for Aries, who is one of the three Fire signs.

Akihito (ah-kee-HEE-toh) Japanese: Bright child. Ariens are advanced for their age.

Akira (ah-KEE-rah) Japanese: Intelligent. This unique name is suitable for clever Aries. (Famous Arien: Akira Kurosawa, film director)

Alaois (AY-leesh) Teutonic: Mighty battle. Ariens are well known for their love of competition and argumentative natures. Variations: *Aloys, Aloysius*.

Albert (AL-bert) German: Bright or noble. This classic name is well suited to Aries, who is possessed with a quick mind and honorable character. Variations: *Al, Bert*. (Famous Ariens: Al Gore, Vice President; Al Green, singer; Al Jolson, musician)

Alphonse (al-FONS) Old German: Prepared for war. Competitive Aries is always ready for some sort of a sparring match. Variations: *Al, Alfie, Alphonso*.

Ameer (ah-MEER) Arabic: Young ruler. Ariens exhibit leadership qualities from a young age.

Archibald (AHR-chih-bahld) German: Bold. This is a good name for Aries, who is dynamic and animated. Variation: *Archie*.

Arden (AHR-dinn or ahr-DEN) Celtic: Eager. Ariens are enthusiastic about trying new things.

Aries (ERR-eez or AHR-eez) Latin: Ram. In Greek mythology, Aries was the god of war.

Armand (AR-mahnd) Teutonic: Warrior. This name is ideal for Aries, who thrives on adversity. Variation: *Armando*.

Arthur (AR-thur) Celtic: Bold. This classic name is well suited to Aries, who is courageous and energetic by nature. King Arthur led the Round Table of Knights of the sixth century. Variations: *Art, Artie, Artur, Arturo, Arty*. (Famous Ariens: Arthur Murray, dance instructor and entrepreneur; Arturo Toscanini, conductor)

Averill (AY-ve-rill) Anglo-Saxon: Born in April. This name is ideal for an Aries boy born in April.

Bakari (bah-KAH-ree) Swahili: Of noble promise. With their gifts of intelligence, perseverance, and energy, Ariens are sure to achieve success in whatever they do.

Balin (BAH-len) Hindi: Powerful warrior. Formidable Aries is capable of winning almost any battle he is faced with.

Baron (BAHR-un or BAYR-un) Teutonic: Noble warrior. Although he loves to compete, argue, and battle, Aries never resorts to dishonorable means to win. Variation: *Barron*.

Bernard (bur-NAHRD or BUR-nahrd) Teutonic: Brave bear. This name represents the courage of Aries. Variations: *Barney, Bern, Bernardo, Bernie*.

Berto (BAIR-toh) Spanish: Bright and determined. Aries is very intelligent for his age, and once he sets his mind to something, he will let no one and nothing stand in his way.

Bodaway (bo-DAH-way) Native American: One who makes fire. This name is appropriate for those born under the Fire sign of Aries, who tend to be passionate about everything and encourage this enthusiasm in others.

Bodil (BO-del) Norwegian, Danish: Ruling with power and might. Ariens, who love instructing and guiding others, are well suited to any type of leadership position.

Bomani (boh-MAN-ee) Ngoni: Fierce soldier. In battle, Aries can be a formidable opponent.

Boris (BORE-iss) Russian: Fighter. Your Aries child will exhibit a healthy love of competing, whether debating in the classroom or playing to win on the sports field.

Caelan (KAY-lin) Irish Gaelic: Strong fighter. Ariens, who are always excited by a challenge, are fierce when it comes to winning.

Caleb (KAY-leb) Hebrew: Spontaneous, dedicated, brave. This name suggests Aries's innovative, pioneering spirit. In the Bible,

Caleb and Moses led their people through the wilderness. Variations: *Cal, Cale, Kale, Kaleb.*

Carney (CAR-nee) Celtic: Warrior. In Greek mythology, Aries was the god of war.

Casey (KAY-see) Irish: Alert or vigorous. Ariens, who seem to have more energy than they know what to do with, are enthusiastic about everything they do. (Famous Arien: Casey Stengel, baseball manager)

Charles (CHARLZ) Latin: Virile and powerful. This traditional name, used throughout the world for centuries, is ideal for strong, dynamic Aries. Variations: *Carl, Carlton, Cary, Chad, Charlie, Chas, Chuck, Karel, Karl, Karlen, Karlik, Karlin, Karol.* (Famous Ariens: Charlie Chaplin, actor; Chuck Connors, actor; Carl Reiner, actor/director; Karl Malden, actor.)

Conrad (KAHN-rad) Old German: Boldly sagacious. This name suggests Aries's bright, courageous nature. Variations: *Curt, Kurt.*

Cornelius (kor-NEE-lee-uss) Latin: Hornlike. This name connotes the features of the Ram, the symbol of Aries.

Dallin (DAY-lyn) Old English: People who are proud. This is a good name for strong, confident, and fiercely independent Aries.

Dasan (DAH-sahn) Native American: Ruler. Aries is happiest when he is in charge.

Decha (deh-CHAH) Thai: Strength. Ariens are renowned for their fortitude and courage.

Dempsey (DEMP-see) Gaelic: Proud. One of the most prominent features of Aries is a confident and fiercely proud demeanor.

Devlin (DEHV-lin) Irish Gaelic: Courageous or showing great valor. Ariens are well known for their bravery and strength.

Dima (DEE-muh) Russian: Strong soldier. Formidable Aries is a fearsome weapon in any type of battle. Your Aries child may be the first picked for sports teams at school.

Donald (DON-uld) Gaelic: Powerful ruler. Popular for centuries, this name is well suited to the mighty Aries, who is renowned for his fine leadership ability. Variations: *Don, Donnie, Donny*. (Famous Arien: Don Cheney, politician)

Duke (DOOK) Latin: Leader. Aries thrives when placed in a position where he must guide or manage others and tackle problems with innovative solutions.

Dyami (dee-AH-mee) Native American: Soaring eagle. This name connotes the strong, independent, exuberant nature of Aries.

Dylan (DIL-lun) Welsh: With great influence. This purposeful name suggests the ability of Ariens to get others to follow them. Variation: *Dillon*.

Egon (EE-gun) English: Powerful. One of the most prominent features of Aries is a fierce and mighty strength unmatched by any other sign. Variation: *Egan*.

Einar (EYE-ner) Scandinavian: Leading warrior. Aries strives to be the best in anything he does, often enjoying the challenge of competition.

Eldridge (EL-dridge) German: Wise ruler. Aries possesses an insightful intelligence that enables him to skillfully lead others in the right direction.

Eloy (eh-LOY) Old German: Famous fighter. Ariens are renowned for thriving on adversity.

Emmet (EM-it) Old German: Mighty. This name is a good choice for powerful, strong Aries.

Eric (ERR-ik) Old Norse: Enduring ruler. Due to their many natural talents and skills, Ariens often make fine leaders who are respected by all. The name has been popular in many European countries, notably England and Germany, for centuries. Variations: *Erek, Erick, Erik, Erique.* (Famous Ariens: Eric Clapton, musician; Eric Roberts, actor)

Erhard (EHR-hahrd) Teutonic: Strong resolution. Aries shows great strength of character from a young age, refusing to be discouraged from anything he believes in.

Ernest (ER-nust) German: With great vigor and conviction. When Aries becomes involved in something, he becomes filled with enthusiasm, energy, and fervor. Variations: *Ernesto, Ernie, Ernst.*

Ethan (EE-thun) Hebrew: Powerful; unswerving. The mighty Aries is not to be swayed from something he decides upon.

Evan (EV-ehn) Celtic: Young warrior. Even as a small child, your Aries son will exhibit the best qualities found in a warrior: strength, courage, determination, independence, and energy.

Fadey (fah-DAY) Russian: Bold. This is a name that suits Aries's vivacious, fierce nature.

Fagen (FAY-ginn) Irish Gaelic: Small, fiery one. From a young age, Ariens are set ablaze by new ideas.

Farley (FAR-lee) English: Sheep meadow. Because his symbol is the Ram, Aries is a sign often associated with imagery related to sheep.

Farrell (FARE-el) Irish Gaelic: Of proven courage. The challenge-loving Aries is often known for taking risks and dares in order to prove himself.

Ferdinand (FUR-dih-nand) Germanic: Courageous traveler or explorer. This name represents the brave and fearless way Aries embarks on conquering new territories. Variation: *Fernando*.

Fergus (FUR-guss) Celtic: Strong man. Suggesting strength and fortitude, this name is ideal for your Aries child.

Gautier (GOH-tyeh) French: Powerful leader. Strong, fearless, and driven, Aries is often chosen to be the one "in charge." Variation: *Gauthier*.

Gerald (JAYR-ild) Old German: He who rules by the sword. Aries often achieves positions of power through intense, battle-like competitions. Variations: *Geraldo, Gerry, Jerold, Jerry*.

Gibor (gee-BOR) Hebrew: Powerful. Strong, fierce Aries has a dynamic presence, which is sensed in any crowd.

Gideon (GIDD-ee-un) Hebrew: Mighty battler. When placed in a competitive situation, such as a sporting event, Aries is a force to be reckoned with.

Griffin (GRIFF-in) Welsh: Fierce. Strong and fearless, Ariens are tremendously powerful both inside and out. Variations: *Griff, Griffith*.

Gunther (GUN-ther) Old Norse: Brave soldier. Your Aries child will fear nothing, preferring to race right into every challenging situation. Variations: *Gunnar, Guntar, Gunter*.

Guy (GAHY) Latin: Living spirit. This wonderful name for Aries seems to embody all that it means to be truly alive.

Hale (HALE) Teutonic: Robust. This name suggests the strong, resilient nature of Aries.

Hamal (hah-MAHL) Arabic: Lamb. The animal associated with Aries is the Ram, but the sheep and the lamb are often included in this group. In astrology, *Hamal* is a star in the constellation of Aries.

Hardy (HAHR-dee) Old German: Courageous. This name, which in English translates to "bold or robust," is ideal for the brave, strong Aries.

Harold (HAYRE-ild) Old Norse: Chief of the troops. *Harold* is a fine name for the natural leader Aries. Variations: *Hal, Harry*. (Famous Ariens: Harry Houdini, magician; Harry Morgan, actor; Harry Reasoner, television journalist; Harold Lloyd, silent film actor)

Herbert (HER-burt) German: Bright soldier. The sharp intelligence of Aries is well known. Variations: *Bert, Herb, Herbie*. (Famous Ariens: Herb Alpert, musician; Herbie Hancock, musician; Herbie Mann, musician)

Henry (HEN-ree) English: Master of his domain. Used throughout the ages, frequently by nobility, this classic name exemplifies Aries's take-charge approach and regal bearing. Variations: *Enrico, Enrique, Hal, Hank, Heinrich, Hendrik, Henri, Henrik*. (Famous Ariens: Hal Linden, actor; Henrik Ibsen, playwright; Henry Mancini, composer; Henry Morgan, actor)

Herrick (HAIR-rik) German: War leader. This name is ideal for Aries, who excels not only in leadership positions, but in any combative situation.

Hillard (HIL-lahrd) Teutonic: Brave warrior. Courageous Aries relishes an opportunity to prove his worth. Variation: *Hilliard*.

Hugo (Hew-go, OO-go) Teutonic: Bright spirit or intelligent. This name, common in Spanish-speaking countries, characterizes the keen mind and dynamic energy of Aries. Variations: *Huey, Hugh, Hughie.*

Ignatius (ig-NAY-shus) English: Burning, passionate. As one of the Fire signs, Aries demonstrates a fiery zeal for everything he becomes involved in. Historically, Saint Ignatius of Loyola was the founder and leader of the Jesuits. Variations: *Ignace, Ignaz, Ignazio, Ignazo.*

Inteus (een-TAY-oos) Native American: Proud or unashamed. Aries is confident and individualistic, never afraid to stand up for what he believes in.

Jedrek (JEDD-rick) Polish: Mighty man. This name is ideal for the strong and powerful Aries image.

Jelani (jeh-LAH-nee) Swahili: Strong. Aries exhibits a powerful presence in all things, facing challenges head-on.

Jubal (JOO-bull) Hebrew: Ram. This unique name seems custom made for Aries, who is symbolized by the Ram. In the Bible, the invention of music is attributed to Jubal.

Julian (JOO-lee-un) Latin: Youthful; exuberant. The Aries child retains an everlasting enthusiasm for all of life: both its challenges and its rewards. Variations: *Jule, Jules.* (Famous Arien: Julian Lennon, singer, son of John Lennon)

Kaelan (KAY-lan) Gaelic: Mighty at war. Combining sharp intelligence, strength, and courage, Ariens excel in any situation that resembles a battle or competition.

Keahi (keh-AH-hee) Hawaiian: Flames. This name is appropriate for aggressive Aries, one of the three Fire signs of the zodiac.

Keane (KEENE) Old English: Sharp, keen. Aries is well known for his talent for innovation and his quick intelligence. Variations: *Kean, Keen, Keenan*.

Keegan (KEE-gan) Irish Gaelic: Tiny, bold flame. Born under one of the Fire signs of the zodiac, Ariens exhibit a fiery passion for life.

Keith (KEETH) Gaelic: Warrior descends. This popular name is ideal for Aries, who is always ready to compete and prove himself.

Kekoa (keh-KOH-uh) Hawaiian: Bold one. Vivacious, exuberant Aries is no stranger to risks and dares, often enjoying a chance to explore new territory.

Kellen (KELL-en) Irish Gaelic: Mighty warrior. Ariens are well known for using their natural strength and power to overcome their enemies in competitions.

Kelly (KELL-ee) Irish Gaelic: Spirited. Used for both boys and girls, *Kelly* suggests the enthusiastic, vivacious nature of those born under the sign of Aries.

Kennedy (KEN-neh-dee) Celtic: Helmeted chief. This name reflects Aries's tendency toward receiving injuries to the head.

Khalfani (kahl-FAH-nee) East African: Born to lead. Suggesting his natural ability to inspire others to follow him, this name is perfect for Aries.

Killian (KIL-ee-an) Celtic: Little and warlike. Even as infants, Ariens exhibit a strong, independent nature.

Kim (KIM) Welsh: Chief. As natural leaders, Ariens are extremely independent, thriving when placed in positions of power.

Kimball (KIM-bull) Old English: Courageous warrior. This name connotes Aries's brave, headstrong, and intensely competitive spirit.

Kincaid (kin-KAYD) Celtic: Lead warrior. Due to their intense desire to be the best at anything they undertake, Ariens excel at any type of competitive event.

Kiral (ki-RUHL) Turkish: Supreme chief. Ariens seek to be the best in whatever they do, and are gifted at inspiring others to follow in their footsteps.

Knight (NITE) Middle English: This name is appropriate for Aries, as knights are known to relish any type of battle or competition.

Kyle (KILE) Scottish: Chief. Ariens are in their natural element when taking charge and leading others. Variations: *Kile, Kye, Kylan, Kylar, Kyrell.*

Landry (LAN-dree) Anglo-Saxon: Leader. With a natural ability to influence others, Aries makes a fine leader.

Lap (LAPP) Vietnamese: Independent. This unusual name reflects Aries's individualistic nature and pioneering spirit.

Laszlo (LAHZ-loh) Hungarian: Renowned leader. Ariens are famous for skillfully leading and influencing others.

Leopold (LEE-oh-pold) German: Daring one. Adventurous Aries is often the first among his peers to try something new or come up with an innovative solution to a problem. Variation: *Leo.* (Famous Arien: Leopold Stokowski, conductor)

Li (LEE) Chinese: Strength. This simple name is well suited to the fierce and courageous sign of Aries.

Lon (LAHN) Gaelic: Strong and unflinching or potent. Once Aries has made up his mind, causing him to change his course can be difficult. Variations: *Lonnie, Lonny*. (Famous Arien: Lon Chaney, actor)

Louis (LOO-is) Teutonic: Renowned warrior. This name is appropriate for Aries, who thrives on adversity and excels in situations that require competition with others. Variations: *Lew, Lewis, Lou, Louie, Luigi, Luis*.

Luther (LOO-thir) Teutonic: Famous warrior. Ariens are renowned for their strength, bravery, and resolution—all of which are formidable weapons in competitive situations.

Malin (MAY-lin) Old English: Brave, young soldier. Aries is one of the most courageous signs of the zodiac.

Marcel (mar-SELL) French: Little and warlike. Even as infants, Ariens may display a fiercely independent nature. Derived from the Latin *Marcellus*, the name became popular after it was bestowed on several early saints in the Middle Ages. Variations: *Marceau, Marcello, Marshal, Marshall, Martial*. (Famous Arien: Marcel Marceau, mime)

Mark (MARK) Latin: Battler. This traditional and very popular name is well suited to the competitive, courageous Aries. In the Bible, Saint Mark was one of the four Evangelists; he is also known as the patron saint of Venice. Variations: *Marc, Marcus, Markus*. (Famous Arien: Marcus Allen, football player)

Maro (MAH-roh) Japanese: Myself. This name connotes the proud, self-confident, and independent aspect of Aries.

Martin (MAR-tin) Latin: Disposed to fighting; rebellious. This name is derived from that of the Roman god of war, Mars. Mars is also the ruling planet of Aries. Variations: *Marten, Marti, Marty*. (Famous Ariens: Martin Denny, composer; Martin Short, actor; Martin Lawrence, actor)

Maynard (MAY-nard) English: Strength and power. This unusual name encompasses two of Aries's most prominent characteristics.

Melvin (MEL-vin) Celtic: Chief. Ariens are extremely independent by nature, and they would much rather tell others what to do than follow orders from someone else.

Miles (MYLES) Latin: Soldier. Ariens often exhibit a courageous, challenge-loving streak, especially when it comes to competitive situations.

Nagid (nah-GEED) Hebrew: Leader. This common name in Israel represents the natural ability of Aries to influence and guide others.

Nasser (NAS-sir) Arabic: Victorious. This popular Muslim name suggests the drive to win possessed by all Ariens.

Nayati (nah-YAH-tee) Native American: He who fights. Known for their love of competition and battle, Ariens are often talented at debating and combative sports.

Nero (NEE-roh) Latin: Powerful or strict. This name, which represents the strong, determined nature of Aries, was the name of the famous Roman emperor who ruled between A.D. 54 and 68.

Ogun (oh-GOON) Nigerian (Yoruba): In the Yoruban pantheon of deities, *Ogun* is the god of war, invoked for power and fortitude.

Orson (OR-sun) Latin: Bearlike courage. Ariens are fearless and brave, never ones to run from a difficult or challenging situation.

Owen (OH-wehn) Celtic: Young warrior. Aries's eternal vigor and enthusiasm for challenges make this name perfectly appropriate for an Aries of any age. Variations: *Ewan, Ewen, Owain*.

Patrick (PA-trik) Latin: Patrician; noble. This name connotes the honorable, industrious side of Aries. The name was first popularized by Saint Patrick, the fourth-century missionary who, according to legend, drove the snakes out of Ireland and eventually became the country's patron saint. Variations: *Paddy, Padraig, Pat, Patty*. (Famous Ariens: Patrick Leahy, U.S. Senator; Patrick Manson, scientist; Pat Riley, basketball coach)

Penn (PEN) Teutonic: Commander. As naturally gifted leaders, Ariens are adept at influencing and directing those around them.

Pepin (PEP-in) German: Dedicated or diligent. Aries strives to be the best in everything he does. Variation: *Pepyn*.

Primo (PREE-moh) Italian: First or of first order. This name is suited to a child born under Aries, the first sign of the zodiac.

Quinlan (KWIN-lin) Gaelic: Powerful. Ariens are renowned for their dynamic strength and bold fearlessness.

Quinn (kwin) Gaelic: Intelligent; discriminating. Bright Aries knows exactly what he wants and goes after it.

Ramsay (RAM-see) English: Valley of the ram. The Ram is the symbol of the sign of Aries. Variation: *Ramsey*.

Rapier (RAPE-ee-air) French: Sharp or having a razor wit. Ariens possess a quick intelligence, and often are clever conversationalists.

Reece (REES) Old Welsh: Passionate or spontaneous. The impulsive, life-embracing Aries is filled with enthusiasm for life. Variation: *Reese*.

Richard (RICH-urd) German: Imposing ruler. This name, which has remained extremely popular for nearly one thousand years, suggests the innate leadership abilities that Aries possesses. Variations: *Dick, Ricard, Ricardo, Rich, Richie, Rick,*

Ricky. (Famous Ariens: Dick Ellsworth, baseball player; Richard Chamberlain, actor; Richard Kiley, actor; Richard Lugar, U.S. Senator; Rick Moranis, actor; Ricky Schroeder, actor; Richard Wagner, composer)

Ridley (RID-lee) English: Red pasture. The sign of Aries is strongly associated with the color red.

Riley (RYE-lee) Gaelic: Brave. Ariens are renowned for their fearlessness and courage, relishing any challenge or obstacle in their way. Variations: *Reilly, Rylee.*

Roald (ROH-ald) German: Marked by strength. This is a unique name for bold, courageous Aries. (Famous Arien: Roald Dahl, author)

Robert (ROB-urt) German: Bright and famous. This traditional and very popular name connotes the clever intelligence and radiant success of Aries. It was popularized in the fourteenth century by Robert the Bruce, ruler of Scotland. Variations: *Bob, Bobby, Riobard, Rob, Robard, Robbie, Roberto, Robin, Robyn, Rupert.* (Famous Ariens: Bob Costas, sportscaster; Robert Frost, poet; Rob Lowe, actor; Bobby Vinton, singer)

Rory (ROAR-ee) Gaelic: Red. This special color of Aries conjures the fiery passion found in those born under this Fire sign.

Ross (RAWSS) Old French: Red. This is a classic name for Aries, whose special color is red.

Roth (RAWTH) German: Red. Fiery Aries is associated with this bold, vivacious color.

Shandy (SHAN-dee) Old English: Energetic or lively. The meaning of this name is well suited to dynamic, enthusiastic Aries.

Shepherd (SHEP-erd) Old English: One who herds sheep. Not only is Aries associated with the Ram and sheep, but he is someone who gets others to follow him. Variations: *Shep, Shepard, Shepp, Shepperd.*

Shepley (SHEP-lee) English: Field of sheep. The sign of Aries has long been connected with imagery related to sheep, specifically the Ram.

Shipton (SHIP-tun) English: Village of shepherds. This name connotes the imagery of sheep, animals who share a special association with Aries.

Sloan (SLONE) Gaelic: Warrior. This name is appropriate for virile Aries since the ruling planet of Aries was the god of war in Greek mythology.

Stephen (STEE-vunn) Greek: Crowned. Because of their natural gifts of intelligence, strength, and confidence and their ability to achieve success in practically any arena, Ariens are often considered as one of the reigning signs of the zodiac. In the Bible, Saint Stephen stood up for his beliefs and became the first martyr in the Christian religion. Variations: *Stephan, Steve, Steven.* (Famous Ariens: Steve Martin, actor/comedian; Steve McQueen, actor; Steven Seagal, actor; Stephen Sondheim, composer)

Sultan (Sool-TAHN) Swahili: Ruler. This name is suited to an Aries individual, who makes a wonderful, well-respected leader.

Sweeney (SWEE-nee) Irish Gaelic: Brave young one. Ariens fear nothing, courageously exploring the world around them with relish.

Takeo (TAH-kay-oh) Japanese: Strong like bamboo. Ariens are renowned for their tremendous strength and fortitude.

Taro (TAH-roh) Japanese: First son. This is an appropriate name for Aries, the first sign of the zodiac.

Thaddeus (THAD-dee-us) Greek: Courageous. Aries proves fearless and strong in situations that would leave most people shaking. Variations: *Tad, Thad*.

Theobald (THEE-oh-bald) Old German: Brave kin. This fine name suits a courageous Aries, who enthusiastically meets any challenge head-on. Variations: *Theo, Tybald*.

Theodoric (THEE-oh-doh-rik) Old German: Leader of the masses. Ariens are well known for being powerful leaders, owing to their qualities of courage, intelligence, strength, and charisma.

Tracy (TRAY-cee) Latin: Courageous. This name is suitable for Aries, who is known to remain brave and strong in any situation. *Tracy* is currently used for both boys and girls.

Tristan (TRIS-tenn) Celtic: Bold. This classic name suggests the strength and power of Aries. In Gaelic legend, *Tristan* was a knight who accidentally drank a love potion intended for a king and fell in love with the princess Isolde. After being mortally wounded in battle, Tristan sent for his beloved from his deathbed, but she came too late and died of heartbreak. The myth is the subject of many medieval novels, as well as Richard Wagner's opera, *Tristan und Isolde*. Variations: *Tristram, Trystan*.

Trumble (TRUM-bull) English: Mighty. This traditional name connotes the strength and fortitude bestowed upon every Arien. Variations: *Trumball, Trumbell, Trumbull*.

Tyson (TY-sunn) French: Explosive. Nearly bursting with enthusiasm and energy, Aries is one of the most dynamic signs of the zodiac.

Ulysses (yu-LISS-ees) Greek: Wrathful. Although Aries tends to get along well with most people, when crossed he can become a force to be reckoned with.

Umi (OO-mee) Malawi, Yao: Life. This unusual name is well suited for Aries, who possesses an eternal zest for life and an intense interest in everything around him.

Valerian (Vah-LEER-ee-unn) Latin: Potent. Ariens are renowned for their power, strength, and ability to achieve almost anything. Variations: *Val, Valéry*.

Victor (VIC-tur) Latin: He who triumphs. With natural gifts of intelligence, determination, and resourcefulness, Aries is sure to succeed in any challenge he takes on. Variation: *Viktor*.

Vilmos (VEEL-mosh) Teutonic: Steadfast warrior. Named after the Greek god of war, the sign of Aries is often associated with the imagery of battling and competition.

Vincent (VIN-sent) Latin: He who embraces power. Ariens have a natural propensity toward leadership positions or roles in which they can guide others. Variations: *Enzo, Vince, Vincente, Vincenzo, Vinnie*. (Famous Arien: Vincent van Gogh, artist)

Vito (VEE-toh) Latin: Alive. This name is ideal for Aries, who seems to embody all that it means to be alive. Variations: *Vitale, Vitus*.

Vladimir (vla-DEE-mir) Slavonic: World ruler. With a strong desire to do things their own way, Ariens are often happiest when allowed to lead others.

Wakiza (wah-KEE-zah) Native American: Determined warrior. This name depicts Aries's fierce, driven way of going about getting what he desires.

Waldemar (WAHL-de-mar, VAHL-de-mar) German: Powerful and famous. Many Ariens find great success and recognition in the world due to their multitude of talents and strength of character. Variation: *Waldo*.

Walter (WAHL-tur) Teutonic: Mighty warrior. This name is perfectly appropriate for your strong, highly competitive Aries boy. Variations: *Wally, Walt*. (Famous Arien: Walter Winchell, journalist)

Warner (WAR-ner) Teutonic: Guarding warrior. Aries, named after the Greek god of war, is well known for his determination in battle. Variations: *Werner, Wernher*. (Famous Arien: Wernher von Braun, rocket engineer)

Willard (WIL-lard) German: Determination. Aries is well known for his unending drive and his resolution when he puts his mind to something.

William (WILL-yum) German: Powerful guardian. The mighty Aries is often placed in positions that require guiding others. The name is very common in its variations throughout Europe and the United States. Variations: *Bill, Billy, Guillaume, Vassily, Vilmos, Wilhelm, Will, Willie, Willy*. (Famous Ariens: William Manchester, biographer; William Shatner, actor; Billy Dee Williams, actor; William Holden, actor)

Xavier (ZAY-vee-err) Arabic: Bright. Ariens tend to possess tons of exuberance and intelligence, so it should come as no surprise that they succeed in almost everything they do. Variation: *Javier*.

Zuberi (zoo-BEH-ree) Swahili: Strong. This name suggests one of Aries's most dominant characteristics.

Famous Ariens

03-21-1685	Johann Sebastian Bach	03-22-1913	Karl Malden
03-21-1839	Modest Mussorgsky	03-22-1923	Marcel Marceau
03-21-1944	Timothy Dalton	03-22-1930	Stephen Sondheim
03-21-1962	Matthew Broderick	03-22-1931	William Shatner
03-21-1962	Rosie O'Donnell	03-22-1933	J. P. McCarthy
03-22-1887	Chico Marx	03-22-1943	George Benson

03-22-1948	Andrew Lloyd Webber
03-22-1952	Bob Costas
03-23-1908	Joan Crawford
03-23-1910	Akira Kurosawa
03-23-1912	Wernher von Braun
03-23-1923	Doc Watson
03-23-1929	Roger Bannister
03-23-1953	Chaka Khan
03-24-1874	Harry Houdini
03-24-1887	Roscoe "Fatty" Arbuckle
03-24-1919	Lawrence Ferlinghetti
03-24-1930	Steve McQueen
03-25-1867	Arturo Toscanini
03-25-1881	Bela Bartok
03-25-1908	David Lean
03-25-1920	Howard Cosell
03-25-1921	Simone Signoret
03-25-1934	Gloria Steinem
03-25-1940	Anita Bryant
03-25-1942	Aretha Franklin
03-25-1943	Paul Michael Glaser
03-25-1946	Bonnie Bedelia
03-25-1947	Elton John
03-25-1965	Sarah Jessica Parker
03-26-1874	Robert Frost
03-26-1911	Tennessee Williams
03-26-1930	Sandra Day O'Connor
03-26-1931	Leonard Nimoy
03-26-1934	Alan Arkin
03-26-1939	James Caan
03-26-1942	Erica Jong
03-26-1943	Bob Woodward
03-26-1944	Diana Ross
03-26-1949	Vicki Lawrence
03-26-1950	Teddy Pendergrass
03-26-1950	Martin Short
03-26-1954	Curtis Sliwa
03-26-1960	Marcus Allen
03-27-1899	Gloria Swanson
03-27-1924	Sarah Vaughan
03-27-1931	David Janssen
03-27-1942	Michael York
03-27-1963	Quentin Tarantino
03-27-1970	Mariah Carey
03-28-1921	Dirk Bogarde
03-28-1944	Ken Howard
03-28-1948	Dianne Wiest
03-28-1955	Reba McEntire
03-29-1867	Cy Young
03-29-1911	Philip Ahn
03-29-1918	Pearl Bailey
03-29-1918	Sam Walton
03-29-1943	John Major
03-29-1950	Bud Cort
03-29-1968	Lucy Lawless
03-29-1976	Jennifer Capriati
03-30-1853	Vincent van Gogh
03-30-1913	Frankie Laine
03-30-1930	Peter Marshall
03-30-1930	John Astin
03-30-1937	Warren Beatty
03-30-1940	Astrud Gilberto
03-30-1945	Eric Clapton
03-30-1957	Paul Reiser
03-30-1962	Hammer
03-31-1596	René Descartes
03-31-1915	Henry Morgan
03-31-1925	Leo Buscaglia
03-31-1928	Gordie Howe
03-31-1934	Shirley Jones
03-31-1935	Herb Alpert
03-31-1935	Richard Chamberlain
03-31-1943	Christopher Walken
03-31-1945	Gabe Kaplan
03-31-1948	Rhea Perlman
04-01-1908	Abraham Maslow
04-01-1920	Toshiro Mifune
04-01-1926	Anne McCaffrey
04-01-1932	Gordon Jump
04-01-1938	Ali MacGraw
04-02-1805	Hans Christian Andersen
04-02-1908	Buddy Ebsen
04-02-1914	Alec Guinness
04-02-1920	Jack Webb
04-02-1939	Marvin Gaye
04-02-1945	Linda Hunt
04-02-1947	Emmylou Harris

04-02-1954   Ron "Horshack"
             Palillo
04-02-1955   Dana Carvey
04-03-1783   Washington Irving
04-03-1916   Herb Caen
04-03-1924   Marlon Brando
04-03-1924   Doris Day
04-03-1942   Marsha Mason
04-03-1942   Wayne Newton
04-03-1958   Alec Baldwin
04-03-1961   Eddie Murphy
04-03-1972   Jennie Garth
04-04-1895   Arthur Murray
04-04-1906   John Cameron Swayze
04-04-1914   Frances Langford
04-04-1915   Muddy Waters
04-04-1928   Maya Angelou
04-04-1932   Anthony Perkins
04-04-1946   Craig T. Nelson
04-04-1963   David Gavurin
04-04-1965   Robert Downey, Jr.
04-05-1856   Booker T. Washington
04-05-1900   Spencer Tracy
04-05-1908   Bette Davis
04-05-1916   Gregory Peck
04-05-1921   Gale Storm
04-05-1926   Roger Corman
04-05-1934   Frank Gorshin
04-05-1937   Colin Powell
04-06-1866   Butch Cassidy
04-06-1929   André Previn
04-06-1937   Merle Haggard
04-06-1937   Billy Dee Williams
04-06-1941   Philip Austin
04-06-1944   Michelle Phillips
04-06-1947   John Ratzenberger
04-06-1952   Marilu Henner
04-06-1976   Candace Cameron
04-07-1897   Walter Winchell
04-07-1915   Billie Holiday
04-07-1920   Ravi Shankar
04-07-1928   James Garner
04-07-1933   Wayne Rogers
04-07-1939   Francis Ford Coppola
04-07-1939   David Frost

04-07-1951   Janis Ian
04-07-1954   Jackie Chan
04-08-1893   Mary Pickford
04-08-1912   Sonja Henie
04-08-1918   Betty Ford
04-08-1926   Shecky Greene
04-08-1963   Julian Lennon
04-09-1926   Hugh Hefner
04-09-1933   Jean-Paul Belmondo
04-09-1935   Avery Schreiber
04-09-1939   Michael Learned
04-09-1954   Dennis Quaid
04-09-1965   Paulina Porizkova
04-09-1979   Keshia Knight Pulliam
04-10-1794   Commodore Matthew
             Perry
04-10-1847   Joseph Pulitzer
04-10-1915   Harry Morgan
04-10-1921   Chuck Connors
04-10-1929   Max von Sydow
04-10-1932   Omar Sharif
04-10-1936   John Madden
04-10-1951   Steven Seagal
04-11-1913   Oleg Cassini
04-11-1932   Joel Grey
04-11-1939   Louise Lasser
04-12-1913   Lionel Hampton
04-12-1923   Ann Miller
04-12-1930   Tiny Tim
04-12-1940   Herbie Hancock
04-12-1947   David Letterman
04-12-1947   Tom Clancy
04-12-1950   David Cassidy
04-12-1956   Andy Garcia
04-12-1971   Shannen Doherty
04-12-1979   Claire Danes
04-13-1743   Thomas Jefferson
04-13-1906   Samuel Beckett
04-13-1909   Eudora Welty
04-13-1926   Don Adams
04-13-1935   Lyle Waggoner
04-13-1944   Jack Casady
04-13-1945   Tony Dow
04-13-1946   Al Green
04-13-1970   Ricky Schroder

04-13-1976	Jonathan Brandis	04-16-1955	Ellen Barkin
04-14-1904	John Gielgud	04-16-1965	Martin Lawrence
04-14-1925	Rod Steiger	04-16-1971	Selena Quintanilla
04-14-1935	Loretta Lynn	04-17-1894	Nikita Khrushchev
04-14-1941	Julie Christie	04-17-1918	William Holden
04-14-1941	Pete Rose	04-17-1923	Harry Reasoner
04-15-1452	Leonardo da Vinci	04-17-1951	Olivia Hussey
04-15-1894	Bessie Smith	04-18-1857	Clarence Darrow
04-15-1917	Hans Conried	04-18-1882	Leopold Stokowski
04-15-1933	Roy Clark	04-18-1946	Hayley Mills
04-15-1933	Elizabeth Montgomery	04-18-1956	Eric Roberts
04-15-1939	Claudia Cardinale	04-18-1963	Conan O'Brien
04-15-1959	Emma Thompson	04-18-1976	Melissa Joan Hart
04-16-1867	Wilbur Wright	04-19-1925	Hugh O'Brian
04-16-1889	Charlie Chaplin	04-19-1933	Jayne Mansfield
04-16-1920	Barry Nelson	04-19-1935	Dudley Moore
04-16-1921	Peter Ustinov	04-19-1946	Tim Curry
04-16-1924	Henry Mancini	04-19-1949	Paloma Picasso
04-16-1929	Edie Adams	04-19-1962	Al Unser, Jr.
04-16-1930	Herbie Mann	04-20-1893	Harold Lloyd
04-16-1935	Bobby Vinton	04-20-1924	Nina Foch
04-16-1939	Dusty Springfield	04-20-1941	Ryan O'Neal
04-16-1947	Kareem Abdul-Jabbar	04-20-1949	Jessica Lange

TAURUS
(April 21–May 21)

GLYPH: ♉
SYMBOL: The Bull
POLARITY: Feminine
QUALITY: Fixed
ELEMENT: Earth
PLANET: Venus
BIRTHSTONE: Emerald
SPECIAL COLORS: Soft violets, mauves, and blues
FLOWERS: Violet and poppy
METAL: Copper
ANIMAL: Cattle
MOST LIKEABLE TRAITS: Reliability, sensitivity, and kindness

♉

Competent, stalwart, strong, and dependable, Taurean children are the rock-steady foundations upon whom the other denizens of the zodiac depend to get the job done. Among all the astrological signs, pragmatic and sensible Taurus is the most driven to a life of useful production. Taureans are the penultimate seconds-in-command—the doers, builders, architects, sculptors, foot soldiers, caretakers, and landscapers of everyday affairs, giving texture and tangibility to the visions and ideals of others. Their approach to life is calm and collected, but also warm, sensual, protective, and affectionate. In a world too often colored by tension and uncertainty, Taureans cut a swift and sure path through the chaos to peace and possibility. They are among the most tenderhearted but self-sufficient of the zodiac's children—a delight and comfort to their parents.

General Qualities

Taurus is a richly layered sign of fascinating contradictions. To begin with, it is a Feminine and Fixed Earth sign governed by the planet Venus. Named for the Roman goddess of beauty, love, and springtime, Venus is the planet of romance, sensuality, sensitivity, creativity, growth, and artistic endeavors. Venus also governs wealth and, in its more negative aspects, aggression and victory in war.

Most importantly, however, Venus governs the Feminine, or yin, half of the human condition. This makes Taurus, whose duality is also Feminine, a doubly female sign. Yet Taurus is represented by the Bull, an archetypical symbol of masculine virility, potency, and aggression, which has long been worshiped in diverse cultures as a godlike creature to be both feared and venerated. Understanding how these two diverse elements in Taurus converge is key to appreciating the depth of this sign.

The Bull of Taurus is no ordinary creature of field and farm. In Greek mythology, Taurus's bull was the animal form that the great god Zeus took on Earth when he decided to lure away the young Greek maiden, Europa, as she was playing along the seashore. Zeus appeared to Europa as a beautiful, pure white bull whose eyes were made of precious jewels and whose horns were festooned with garlands of flowers. Enchanted by this stunning apparition and enticed away from her playmates, Europa jumped upon the back of the Zeus-bull, who then quickly swam across the seas and deposited the girl for safekeeping on the island of Crete, where she later became the mother of the continent of Europe.

Having achieved his aim with Europa, Zeus released the white bull to the sky, where it became the great constellation of Taurus. Soon after this, the seven daughters of Atlas came to Zeus, crying and begging that he protect them against the amorous attentions of aggressive Orion. Zeus obliged by making the sisters the stars in the small constellation of the Pleiades. Placing the Pleiades on the back of Taurus, Zeus instructed the celestial bull to protect the sisters for all eternity.

This intriguing Greek myth highlights three trademark Taurean qualities: aggressive determination (Zeus sets out to accomplish a difficult task and succeeds); an appreciation of aesthetic beauty (the white bull is adorned as an objet d'art); and a strong tendency to protectiveness (the Pleiades are rescued and their protection ensured). The Taurean character, as symbolized by the Bull, is thus equal parts aggressive masculine energy, sensual beauty, and fierce protectiveness.

The powerful, doubly Feminine Venusian nature of Taurus combines with its potent and bullish Masculine side to create a creature of enormous progenitive powers. Taureans are renowned as the most productive children of the zodiac, dedicated both to creating important, useful things and to completing the tasks that others start. They are rarely the innovators or trailblazing pathfinders of the world, as are Leos, Sagittarians, and Aquarians. Instead, Taureans form the stolid second wave of any task force. They are the ones who secure the hatches, clear the fields, throw down roots, and protect the perimeters; then they finish the jobs that others start to ensure that success is enduring and fruitful.

As the great doers of the zodiac, Taureans are single-mindedly driven, stubborn, tenacious, persevering, practical, patient, and loyal. Above all, they prize consistency and predictability. Taureans' approach to life is conservative, utilitarian, and down-to-earth, but beneath their practical demeanor lies a deep appreciation of beauty, elegance, and sensuality. Unlike Virgos and Capricorns—those other practical-minded and work-oriented children of the zodiac—once Taureans get the job done, they settle down to enjoy the fruits of their labors. Most Taureans live comfortable and somewhat self-indulgent lives, surrounded by beautiful things and fine foods and wines.

The Feminine influence in this sign endows Taureans with intuitiveness and receptiveness toward the people and the world around them, supports their inner strength and moral fiber, and amplifies the Taurean trademark quality of protectiveness. Taureans are keenly aware of their role in the world and of what others expect of them. Readily anticipating the needs of others, they are adept at focusing on the strengths and weaknesses of any argument or situation. Their tenacity and sense of purpose in the face of a challenge are unshakable. Success in all things is their single-minded goal, and they rarely fail.

The Fixed quality of the sign is responsible for Taureans' determination, practicality, reliability, resistance to change, and bullish stubbornness. No other children of the zodiac are as relentlessly determined to succeed as are Taureans. They are resolutely immovable in the face of any obstacle.

The Earth influence in Taurus supports the sign's qualities of persistence, conservatism, materialism, and stability. Taureans are quintessentially pragmatic and down-to-earth. They esteem dependability and are protective of the status quo. They have a penchant for luxury, a deep love of beauty, and are often dedicated to acquiring wealth, property, and objets d'art. Taureans are also passionate naturalists who have a keen connection to the physical environment, especially to wide-open spaces and to growing things, and they love the tactile sensuality of natural objects. Taureans also have a deeply romantic vein running beneath their sensible surface, and are themselves physically demonstrative and freely giving of affection.

While Taureans are renowned for their fiercely bad tempers, in truth they are slow burners who only explode when repeatedly challenged. They are simply too busy to engage in emotional indulgence. Together with Capricorns, Taureans have the most placid personalities in the zodiac. Stable, sensitive, and sensual, they are embodiments of the best of the earthy qualities.

Home

Taurean children are lovers of routine and predictability. They easily adapt to the flow of family life and treasure the sense of common purpose that family provides.

Like Cancers, Taureans are unduly alarmed by sudden changes at home, taking them as personal affronts. They thrive amidst stability and security and need large doses of the same to develop their trademark qualities of inner calm and practicality. In such an environment, Taureans are placid, loving, and loyal children eager to help parents and siblings.

Like Virgos, Taurean children are "low-maintenance" children of the zodiac, possessed of great emotional strength and a precocious sense of purpose. Also, they are physically robust—though sometimes emotionally tentative—and thus easily shake off the cuts and bruises of rough-and-tumble play.

Early in life, when surrounded by a secure environment, Taureans begin to demonstrate their singular inclination to stay busy and do useful things. They make eager helpers around the house and yard and have an abiding interest in how things work. While they are generally quiet and self-contained, avoiding noisy and exuberant play, Taureans rarely sit contentedly with a book, puzzle, or game. Instead, they are drawn to more practical types of play where they can build and take things apart—whether those things are household items or toys! They especially enjoy making useful items, and are frequent visitors to the sewing room or woodworking bench. Taurean children's mental focus, sense of purpose, and ability to follow a task through to its successful conclusion are remarkable traits that set them apart from other children, who tend to flit from one activity to another.

Taurean children's sensual and romantic side, though less apparent than their "busy" side, demonstrates itself in a delightful appreciation of art and other beautiful objects around the house, a love of good food, an innate sense of how to dress well, and demonstrative displays of physical affection. Taureans are huggers, touchers, and nuzzlers, and they need a great deal of affection in return. Security and continuity are overriding concerns of Taurean children. In their simple, pragmatic worlds, physical affection means they can be secure in their parents' love and loyalty.

School and Play

Like Virgos and Capricorns, Taurean children are in their element at school. They treasure routine and predictability and are rarely bored by repetition, as long as they understand the long-range purpose of a task. Taureans are often emotionally mature before other children their age, and they frequently have a greater appreciation of the simple joys inherent in a job well done. Despite their single-minded dedication to successfully completing tasks, they are not especially competitive, and work long and hard at a subject for the sheer pleasure of the challenge, not the final grade.

Taureans tend to work their way slowly and steadily through tasks—including academic studies—in a manner that is sometimes mistaken as plodding and unimaginative. In fact, instead of skimming through their work like other children might, Taureans thoroughly assimilate new information a chunk at a time until they are completely comfortable with their mastery of a subject. Hence they also tend to hold on to newfound knowledge—and see its wider applications—far better than flashier and more facile students. Taureans are especially drawn to the more practical studies of math, science, and economics. However, their strong, though often latent, sensual appreciation of the artistic can lead to gifted painters, sculptors, woodworkers, and musicians.

At play, Taureans often are drawn to activities that involve making things from scratch or discovering how things work. They enjoy making models, weaving, woodworking, and building intricate towns and cities from elaborate block sets. Like Virgos, Taureans sometimes equate play with work and may bring to play an overly serious and intense demeanor. Parents will want to discourage this tendency in young Taureans, who may benefit greatly by blowing off physical steam on a regular basis. Frequent access to the outdoors can prove extremely helpful. Because of their deep connection to nature, Taureans invariably enjoy many outdoor activities, particularly camping, gardening, climbing, and hiking. Purposeful but hard work around the yard also engages Taureans for hours, especially if they can get involved with beautifying the landscape.

Taureans are generally placid and amiable playmates who are

content to be enthusiastic members of the crowd. They are rarely the leaders of the pack, nor do they aspire to leadership, but they are consummate seconds-in-command and have firm ideas about how things should best be done. Furthermore, Taureans are stubbornly opinionated and rarely change their minds to accommodate the whims of the group, which sometimes can be daunting to their friends. Nevertheless, and despite their bullishly stubborn and opinionated streak, Taureans are cherished playmates—enthusiastic, supportive, fiercely protective, affectionate, and loyal.

The World

Adult Taureans are stable, quiet, dependable, rational, and even tempered. They possess enormous reserves of practical, productive energy, which they invariably apply to their work. Taureans are single-mindedly focused on their jobs first, family second, and possessions third, though they value consistency, fidelity, and stability in all three areas.

At work, Taureans are driven, firm, stubborn, persevering, and tenacious in pursuit of their goals. They have clear and preset ideas about how things should be done and rarely sway from their game plan. Their instincts for success are generally right on the mark, and since they are more than willing to do the hard work that ensures a common victory for all, they are among the most prized of upper-echelon executives and managers, equally adept in finance, marketing, research, science, politics, and the military arts. They are particularly adept at making and holding on to money, and at seeing difficult and problematic projects through from beginning to end. Their calm, assured, and confident work demeanors are contagious, and they are much admired bosses who inspire loyalty, dedication, and hard work in those who work for them.

Taureans who do not go into industry frequently pursue careers as creative artisans. Their deeply sensual sides, keen love of tactile sensation, and great admiration for beauty and elegance combine to make many Taureans gifted potters, sculptors, weavers, carpenters, jewelry makers, painters, gardeners, architects, and landscapers. Many Taureans also possess beautiful singing and speaking voices, and they frequently pursue careers as musical performers or public speakers. This is the sign of Ella Fitzgerald, Barbra Streisand, Ezio Pinza, and Orson Welles.

Privately, Taureans marry young, well, and usually for life. They are devoted and affectionate mates, though never overly emotional, who esteem the enduring values of faithfulness, responsibility, and consistency. Next to work, Taureans prize a stable and warm family life above all else. When they don't have to work, Taureans inevitably and happily head for home.

Home is the place where Taureans nurture their romantic and sensual sides. At home they can indulge their creative instincts by pursuing hobbies such as music, handcrafts, cabinetmaking, painting, and sculpture. Taureans are also great collectors of money, property, and valuable objects, and they like to live well and lavishly. They prize comfortable surroundings, beautiful furnishings and art, and good food and wine. Like Cancers, Taureans are also fabulous hosts and hostesses, generously spreading around their wealth and affection to loved ones and close friends.

The surprisingly complex Taurean is a remarkable blend of the pragmatic and the poetic—a rare and refreshing combination indeed. The typically Taurean qualities of practicality, fierce determination, stubbornness, and tenacity are emblematic of the stolid and forceful Bull strutting his stuff in the public arena, but sensual and softhearted Venus steps into the Taurean circle and adds a generous dollop of grace, beauty, elegance, and romance to the mix. Hence Taureans are never exactly what they appear to be. Beneath a Taurean's practical and success-driven public persona is a sensitive, sensual, and sweet-natured soul who knows better than most when to leave a job well done alone and go on to the more important pursuits of love, romance, and living life with grace and elegance.

Choosing a Name for Your Taurus Child

When choosing a name for your Taurus child, first think about the major attributes and symbols associated with the sign. Taurus is the sign of patience, stability, reliability, practicality, stubbornness, persistence, possessiveness, wealth, luxury, sensuality, and self-indulgence.

Taureans are the most dependable children of the zodiac, renowned for being the ones who follow through on the initial leads and ideas of the more fiery or dreamy signs. Taureans can always be relied upon to get the job done, whatever that job is. They are the world's builders, gardeners, artisans, guardians, caretakers, protectors, industrialists, and landowners.

Taurus is a Feminine and Fixed Earth sign governed by the planet Venus. The Feminine aspect of the sign endows Taureans with openness and receptiveness to the people and the world around them, supports their strong inner emotional resources, and feeds the Taurean trademark quality of protectiveness. The Fixed quality of the sign is responsible for Taureans' determination, practicality, reliability, resistance to change, and stubbornness. The Earth influence supports the Taurean qualities of persistence, conservatism, materialism, and stability. Taureans also have a deep connection to the natural environment, especially wide-open fields.

Taurus's ruling planet, Venus, governs romance, tender feelings, art, physical and aesthetic beauty, pleasure, self-indulgence, and vanity. Venus's potent influence gives tough, pragmatic, and stubborn Taureans a surprisingly soft and sensual side—hidden beneath their bullish demeanors, of course—and is responsible for the fact that many Taureans pursue careers in the arts, particularly in music and sculpture. Taureans also have a strong penchant for acquiring both money, property, and beautiful objets d'art, which they fiercely hoard and protect. They also love good food, fine wines, and lavishly entertaining friends.

Taurus, the second sign of the zodiac, is one of the spring signs, encompassing the months of late April and May. This is a lush and verdant time during the growing season, and Taureans are closely associated with all budding and blossoming things, particularly flowers. The violet and poppy flowers are strongly associated with Taurus, as are cypress and apple trees. Taurus's symbol is the Bull, and the sign rules all cattle. Soft light blues, mauves, and violets are the sign's symbolic colors. The emerald is the sign's official birthstone, and copper is the Taurean metal.

When you choose a name for your child, also bear in mind some of Taurean children's key personal qualities. They are ambitious, stubborn, passionate, protective, noble, dependable, dogmatic, aggressive, ethical, and indulgent. Taureans are among the most productive children in the zodiac, and they approach all tasks with conservatism and determination. They value comfort and safety and are passionately resistant to change. They love money and everything that it can buy. Many Taureans are gifted artisans—sculptors, woodworkers, gardeners, landscapers—and others are renowned for their beautiful singing and speaking voices. Above all, Taureans prize faithfulness, loyalty, and consistency.

For additional inspiration when choosing a name for your Taurus child, especially a middle name, you may want to look through the names listed in Taurus's companion Earth signs, Virgo and Capricorn.

Names for Taurus Girls

Abilene (AB-ih-leen) Hebrew: From the grass-covered place. Born under an Earth sign, Taureans feel a strong connection to the natural environment, particularly wide-open spaces. Variation: *Abbie*.

Adamina (ah-dah-MEEN-ah) Hebrew: Daughter of the red earth. Taurus is one of the three Earth signs of the zodiac. (The other two are Virgo and Capricorn.)

Aderes (ah-de-RAYS) Hebrew: Garments worn on the outside.

Aderes connotes Taureans' penchant for lavish adornments and appreciation of physical beauty. Variation: *Aderetz*.

Adia (ah-DEE-ah) African/Swahili: Present. Taureans, known for their warm, protective, ethical, and dependable natures, are considered true blessings by their loved ones.

Adonia (ah-DOH-nee-ah) Greek: The feminine variation of *Adonis*, the beautiful Greek hero who was loved by Aphrodite, the goddess of love. Venus, Taurus's ruling planet, governs romance and beauty.

Ah Kum (AH-KOOM) Chinese: Treasure. Reliable, protective, self-sufficient, sensual, and loving, Taureans are regarded as precious gifts by their friends and family.

Alane (ah-LAHN-ay) Polynesian: Flower wreath. Encompassing the spring months of April and May, Taurus is strongly associated with all budding and blossoming things, particularly flowers.

Alexandra (a-lex-AHN-drah) Greek: Protector of humankind. Taureans, who prize safety and security, are fierce protectors of their loved ones. Variations: *Alexa, Alexandria, Alexia, Alexis, Lexie*.

Algoma (ahl-GOH-mah) Native American: Flower valley. Taurus is closely affiliated with the lush and verdant growing season.

Alice (AL-iss) Greek: Truthful. Taureans are renowned for their highly virtuous natures. Variations: *Alethea, Alicea, Alicia, Alis, Alisha, Alissa, Alithia*. (Famous Taurean: Alice Faye, actress)

Alida (ah-LEED-ah) Greek: Beautifully dressed. Taureans have a great appreciation for physical and aesthetic beauty. Variations: *Aleda, Aleta, Aletta*.

Almeda (ahl-MAY-dah) Latin: Striving toward a goal. Ambitious and productive, Taureans are capable of reaching any objective they set for themselves. Variations: *Almeida, Almeta*.

Altheda (ahl-THEE-dah) Greek: Blossom. Because Taurus occurs during the months of April and May, the sign is often linked to the springtime blossoming of flowers and plants.

Alyssa (ah-LISS-sah) Greek: Sane, logical. *Alyssa* is a suitable choice for dependable, sensible, pragmatic, and down-to-earth Taurus. Variation: *Alissa*.

Amalia (ah-MAH-lee-ah) Gothic: Industrious. The most dependable children of the zodiac, Taureans can be relied on to get the job done. Variation: *Amelia*.

Amina (ah-MEE-nah) Arabic: Security. The most placid children of the zodiac, Taureans thrive in a secure and stable environment. Variation: *Aminah*.

Amoli (ah-MOH-lee) Hindu: Valuable. Hardworking, stable, sensitive, and loving, Taureans are highly esteemed by all.

An (AN; ANG) Vietnamese: Safety and security. Dependable Taureans strive to maintain stability in all things.

Andrea (AHN-dree-ah; ahn-DRAY-yah) Latin: Womanly. Taureans, born under a Feminine sign ruled by the planet Venus, possess a surprisingly soft and sensual side. Variations: *Andreana, Andria, Andriana*.

Anina (ah-NEEN-ah) Hebrew: Answer to a prayer. *Anina* is a fitting choice for strong, kindhearted, warm, and dependable Taurus.

Anthea (ahn-THAY-ah) Greek: Goddess of blossoms. Encompassing the spring months of April and May, Taurus is strongly associated with the budding and blossoming of spring.

Antonetta (ahn-toh-NETT-ah) Slavic: Beyond value. Taureans are highly esteemed for their hard work, determination, stability, sensitivity, and generosity. Variations: *Antonella, Antonette.*

April (AYE-pril) Latin: Born in the month of April. This name is an appropriate choice for a Taurus girl born in April. Variations: *Aprilette, Aprili, Aprille, Averil, Averill.*

Arcadia (ahrd-KAY-dee-ah) Greek: Pastoral. This unique name is suitable for a girl born under Taurus, an Earth sign commonly associated with wide-open fields. Variation: *Arcadie.*

Arcelia (ahr-SAY-lee-ah) Spanish: Treasure chest. *Arcelia* suggests the luxury and extravagance prized by sensual, pleasure-loving Taureans.

Ardelle (ahr-DELL) Latin: Fervent one. Although generally mild-mannered, Taureans are passionate and aggressive when it comes to achieving their goals. Variations: *Arda, Ardelia, Ardella, Ardine.*

Arete (ah-RAY-teh) Greek: Grace and beauty. Influenced by their ruling planet of Venus, Taureans have a great appreciation for the finer things in life, and enjoy being surrounded by elegant, luxurious, and aesthetically pleasing objects. Variations: *Aretha, Arethi, Aretta, Arette.*

Atara (ah-TAH-ruh) Hebrew: A crown. *Atara* suggests Taurus's penchant for beautiful and luxurious things. Variation: *Ataret.*

Audrey (AW-dree) Old English: Noble; strong. Taureans, endowed with remarkable inner strength and known for their honorable character, possess an almost regal bearing. Variations: *Audra, Audrina*. (Famous Taurean: Audrey Hepburn, actress)

Averill (AYE-vur-ill) Old English: Born in April. *Averill* is a suitable choice for a Taurus girl born during the month of April. Variations: *Averyl, Avril, Avrill*.

Aviva (ah-VEE-vah) Hebrew: Springtime. The sign of Taurus, often associated with the spring season, encompasses the spring months of April and May. Variation: *Avivah*.

Ayita (ah-YEE-tah) Native American: The worker. One of the key characteristics of Taurus is a remarkably hardworking nature.

Azami (ah-ZAH-mee) Japanese: Prickly plant. Symbolic of a stubborn and hard-nosed personality, *Azami* connotes the persistence and tenacity of Taurus.

Bakula (BAH-koo-lah) Hindu: Flower. Taurus, one of the spring signs of the zodiac, is commonly affiliated with nature's blossoming. The flowers associated with Taurus are violets and poppies.

Belinda (be-LIN-dah) Spanish: Beautiful. Taurus's ruling planet of Venus governs beauty, and Taureans are highly appreciative of exquisite objets d'art and aesthetically pleasing surroundings. Variations: *Bella, Belle, Linda*.

Blossom (BLAH-sum) Old English: Flower-like. The sign of Taurus, which encompasses the spring months of April and May, is often linked to the budding and blossoming of all things, especially flowers.

Bride (BRYDE; BRYD-ee) Irish: Power. *Bride* connotes the emotional and physical strength and resilience associated with the sign of Taurus. Variations: *Breeda, Brid, Bridey.*

Brona (BROH-nah) Greek: Coming before the victory. Taureans' ability to plan ahead in a pragmatic and sensible way almost assures them success.

Bryn (brin) Welsh: Mountain. *Bryn* suggests the formidable strength possessed by all Taureans. Variations: *Brinn, Brynn, Brynne.*

Cala (KAH-lah) Arabic: Fortress. With their feet planted firmly on the ground and their strong shoulders ready to take on any responsibility, Taureans are famous for their formidable strength.

Carla (CAHR-lah) Teutonic: Strong country woman. Born under an Earth sign, Taureans possess a special affinity for the natural environment, often choosing to live in rural areas. Variations: *Carly, Karla, Karly.*

Carling (CAHR-ling) Irish: Little champion. Ambitious, aggressive, hardworking, and pragmatic, Taureans are successful at whatever they choose to do.

Carna (KAHR-nah) Hebrew: Horn. *Carna* suggests the imagery of the Bull, Taurus's symbolic animal. Variations: *Carniela, Carnis, Carnit, Narniella.*

Cedrica (sed-REEK-ah) Welsh: Gift. Hardworking, reliable, loyal, kindhearted, and affectionate, Taureans are regarded as divine presents by their family and friends.

Cerella (se-RAY-luh) Latin: Of the spring. The sign of Taurus, encompassing the spring months of April and May, is associated with springtime. Variation: *Cerelia.*

Chloe (KLO-ee) Greek: Blooming. Taurus, one of the zodiac's spring signs, is strongly associated with all budding and blossoming flowers. Variation: *Chloë.*

Chuki (CHOO-kee) African/Swahili: A blessing among enemies. In today's chaotic, tense, often deceptive, world, Taureans shine as down-to-earth, ethical, dependable, and kindhearted treasures.

Cornelia (kohr-NEEL-ee-ah; kohr-NEEL-yah) Latin: Hornlike. Evoking the imagery of the Bull, *Cornelia* is a suitable name for a Taurus girl. Variations: *Cornela, Cornelle, Nelia.*

Courtney (KORT-nee) Old French: She who lives at the farm. Taureans, born under an Earth sign, often choose to live near the open fields with which they feel a special connection.

Dahlia (DAL-yah) Swedish: Valley. Also for the flower. One of the zodiac's three Earth signs, Taurus shares a special relationship with open spaces and the natural environment. Variations: *Dalia, Daliah, Delila.*

Davine (dah-VEEN) Hebrew: Well-loved. Taurus is highly esteemed for her kind heart, gentle ways, and giving nature. Variations: *Daveta, Davida, Davina, Davita.*

Delmelza (del-MELL-zah) English: Fortified. *Delmelza* connotes the great physical and emotional strength with which all Taureans are endowed.

Dena (DAY-nah) Native American: Low-lying meadow. Born under an Earth sign, Taureans feel a special affinity for the natural environment, especially the open fields. Variations: *Dene, Deneen, Denia, Denica.*

Denise (de-NEESE) French: Of Dionysus, the god of wine and vegetation. This popular name is a suitable choice for Taurus, who has a penchant for good food, fine wine, and luxurious surroundings. Variation: *Deniece*.

Diantha (dee-AHN-thah) Greek: Divine flower. *Diantha* is a lovely and unusual name for a girl born under Taurus, an Earth sign closely associated with the blossoming of springtime flowers. Variation: *Diandre*.

Dita (DIT-ah) Czechoslovakian: Wealth. Taureans, who are often gifted at investing, are rewarded for their hard work with great financial success. Variation: *Ditka*.

Dore (doh-RAH) French: Ornate. Taureans possess a penchant for beautiful and luxurious items. Variations: *Doretta, Dorette*.

Easter (EE-stir) Old English: For the spring holiday. *Easter* is an apt name for a Taurus girl born in April, the month during which the Easter holiday typically falls. Variation: *Pascale*.

Ediah (ee-DYE-ah) Hebrew: Decoration for God. Taureans, who have high morals and upright behavior, also show good taste in art and attire. Variations: *Edia, Ediya, Edya*.

Edwina (ed-WEEN-ah) Old English: Wealthy friend. Taureans, who often achieve financial success through their hard work and ambitious determination, are happy to share the fruits of their labor with loved ones. Variations: *Edwardine, Edweena*.

Emily (EM-ih-lee) Gothic: Industrious. Work is often the most important thing to ambitious, aggressive, and determined Taurus. Variations: *Emera, Emilie, Emlyn, Emma, Emmie*.

Erma (UR-mah) Old German: Whole one. *Erma* is an appropriate name for Taurus, who combines industriousness, pragmatism, and tenacity with the softer qualities of sensitivity, sensuality, and kindness. Variations: *Ermina, Erminia, Irma.*

Erna (UR-nah) Scandinavian: Capable. Reliable and hardworking Taureans always can be counted on to get the job done.

Ernestina (urn-ess-TEEN-ah) English: Earnest. This traditional name suits sincere and dedicated Taurus. Variations: *Ernesta, Ernestine, Ernestyna.*

Esmerelda (ez-mer-AYLD-ah) Spanish: Emerald. The emerald is the birthstone assigned to the sign of Taurus. Variations: *Emeraude, Esmaralda, Esmée, Esmeralda, Esmiralda, Ezmeralda.*

Esther (ESS-ter) Persian: Myrtle leaf. *Esther* connotes Taurus's connection to the natural environment and the budding and blossoming of all plants. Variations: *Essie, Essy, Esta, Estée, Estie.*

Fabrizia (fah-BREETZ-ee-ah) Italian: She who works with her hands. Practical yet endowed with a sensual appreciation of the artistic, Taureans often are talented painters, sculptors, and craftmakers. Variations: *Fabrice, Fabricia, Fabritzia.*

Faith (FAYTH) Latin: Faithful. Taureans are among the most reliable, loyal, and dependable children of the zodiac. Variations: *Fae, Fay, Faye.*

Felda (FELL-dah) Old German: From the field. Born under an Earth sign, Taureans feel a special connection with nature, especially wide-open fields.

Felora (fay-LOHR-ah) Hawaiian: Flower. The springtime sign of Taurus is associated with the budding and blossoming of flowers. Variations: *Felorena, Folora, Polola.*

Florence (FLORR-intz) Latin: Blossoming; prosperous. Taureans, associated with the blossoming of flowers, are renowned for creating abundance through their hard work and clear thinking. Variations: *Fiorenza, Florance, Florencia, Florinda*. (Famous Taurean: Florence Nightingale, English nurse and philanthropist)

Gerda (GAYR-dah) Old Norse: Safe barrier. Taureans cherish security and stability in all areas of their lives.

Ghislaine (gees-LANE) French: Loyal vow. This unique name is appropriate for Taurus, who shows fidelity and stability in all things. Variation: *Ghislain*.

Giborah (gee-BOHR-ah) Hebrew: Strong. The tremendous emotional and physical strength of Taurus is renowned. Variations: *Gibora, Givorah*.

Gina (GEE-nah) Hebrew: Garden. This pretty name suggests Taurus's occurrence in the spring and its association with the budding and flowering of all plants. Variations: *Geena, Gena, Ginia*.

Hana (ha-NAH) Japanese: Blossom. Encompassing the spring months of April and May, Taurus is commonly associated with all budding and blossoming plants.

Heather (HEH-thur) English: Flowering heather. Taurus, one of the zodiac's Earth signs, is strongly affiliated with the blossoming of flowers in the spring.

Helmine (HELL-meen) Old German: Unwavering protector. Taureans are fiercely protective of their loved ones. Variations: *Minchen, Minette, Minka*.

Hortencia (horr-TEN-see-ah) Latin: Garden. *Hortencia* is an apt name for a girl born under Taurus, an Earth sign with a strong connection to the growing of flowers. Variations: *Horsensia, Hortense, Ortensia.*

Ingrid (ING-rid) Old Norse: Hero's daughter. This name is appropriate for a girl born under the sign of Taurus, which often is associated with the heroic actions of the mythical Bull it was named for. Variations: *Irenka, Irini, Irisha.*

Iola (eye-OH-lah) Greek: Violet-colored dawn. The colors associated with the sign of Taurus are soft violets, blues, and mauves.

Iwilla (i-WILL-ah) African-American: "I will arise again." *Iwilla* suggests the great strength, resilience, and determination possessed by all Taureans.

Jacobina (JAK-koh-BEE-nah) Hebrew: The hard supplies. Scottish feminine variation of *Jacob*. While always pragmatic and often reserved, Taureans tend to be prepared for anything to bring wealth. Variations: *Jacoba, Jacobette.*

Janet (JAH-net) Scottish: Variation of *Jane*, meaning "God's grace." Through their upstanding morals and ideal demeanors, Taureans demonstrate the blessings of the divine. Variation: *Jan.* (Famous Taureans: Jan Hooks, comedienne/actress; Janet Jackson, singer)

Jean (JEEN) Old French: Gracious. Taureans, who tend to succeed in business and surround themselves with luxury, are happy to share their wealth and strive to make those around them comfortable. Variations: *Janine, Jeana, Jeane, Jeanetta, Jeanette, Jeanne.*

Jokla (JOH-klah) African/Swahili: Robe of adornment. Taureans, who have a penchant for beautiful things, have an innate sense of how to dress well.

Jolie (JOH-lee) French: Beautiful to look at. Venus, Taurus's ruling planet, endows the sign's children with a great appreciation for aesthetic and physical beauty. Variations: *Jolee, Joley, Joli.*

Kalani (kah-LAH-nee) Hawaiian: Chieftain. Although they rarely seek leadership positions, Taureans make excellent seconds-in-command because of their ambition, reliability, hard work, and fine instincts. Variations: *Kailani, Kalanie, Kaloni.*

Keena (KEE-nah) English: Brave and quick. *Keena* suggests the way protective and caring Taureans jump at the chance to offer their help.

Kekona (ke-KOH-nuh) Hawaiian: Second-born child. Taurus is the second sign of the zodiac.

Kelda (KELL-dah) Old Norse: Spring. The sign of Taurus encompasses the spring months of April and May. Variations: *Kelilah, Kelula, Kyla, Kyle.*

Kessie (KESS-ee) African/Ghanian: Chubby one. *Kessie* suggests the typically robust and healthy physical appearance possessed by Taureans.

Kiele (kee-ELL-ee) Hawaiian: Fragrant blossom. Encompassing the spring months of April and May, Taurus is commonly associated with all budding and blossoming plants, particularly flowers.

Kimberly (KIM-bur-lee) Old English: From the royal meadow. Born under an Earth sign, Taureans feel a strong connection to the natural environment, particularly fields. Variations: *Kimberlee, Kimberlie.*

Kuni (KOO-nee) Japanese: Country born. Taureans, born under an Earth sign, feel most at home in the natural environment. Variation: *Kuniko*.

Kyla (KYE-lah) Yiddish: Royal crown. *Kyla* suggests both Taureans' noble qualities and their love of opulence and luxury.

Kyra (KEER-rah) Greek: Enthroned; madame. Taureans, who often attain positions of success, are known for their noble actions and elegant surroundings. Variations: *Keera, Keira, Kira, Kyrene, Kyria, Kyrie*.

Lala (lah-LAH) Slavic: Flower. Among the zodiac's spring signs, Taurus is commonly affiliated with the blossoming of flowers.

Lateefah (lah-TEE-fah) Arabic: Calm. Taureans are among the most placid children of the zodiac. Variation: *Latifah*.

Leigh (LEE) English: From the pasture. Taureans, born under one of the zodiac's three Earth signs, feel a special connection to vast fields. Variations: *Lea, Leah, Lee, Leia, Lia*.

Leotie (leh-oh-TEE-e; lay-OH-tee) Native American: Prairie flower. *Leotie* is an appropriate choice for a girl born under Taurus, an Earth sign that is deeply linked to the budding of flowers and wide-open spaces.

Leya (LAY-yah) Spanish: Adherence to the law. Practical and rational Taureans, who prize security and stability, are never ones to challenge authority.

Lucretia (loo-KREESH-yah) Latin: Rewarded with wealth. *Lucretia* is a fitting name for Taurus, who often achieves great financial success through her hard work and determination. Variations: *Lucette, Lucie, Lucrecia, Lucrezia, Lucy*.

Malina (mah-LEE-nah) Hawaiian: Calm and soothing. Practical and rational Taureans prize stability and security.

Masika (mah-SEE-kah) African/Swahili: A baby who comes with the rain. *Masika* is a suitable name for a Taurus girl born during April, a month often associated with the rainy season.

Mausi (MAW-see; MOW-see) Native American: Plucking flowers. This unique name is a fitting choice for a girl born under Taurus, an Earth sign that is commonly affiliated with the flowers of spring.

Mauve (MAWVE) French: For the purple-petaled mallow plant; also for the color. The colors associated with the sign of Taurus are soft violets, blues, and mauves. Variation: *Malva*.

May (MAY) Latin: For the month. The sign of Taurus encompasses the spring months of April and May. Variations: *Mae, Mai, Mayleen, Maylene*.

Mega (MEH-gah) Spanish: Mild and peaceful. *Mega* is an appropriate name for placid, stable, and calm Taurus.

Meiko (may-EE-koh) Japanese: A blossom. Among the zodiac's three spring signs, Taurus often is affiliated with the budding and blossoming of flowers.

Melora (ma-LOHR-ah) Latin: Improve. Ambitious and pragmatic Taureans constantly strive to find ways to function more efficiently and effectively.

Miki (MEE-kee) Japanese: Stem. Often associated with the blossoming of flowers in spring, Taurus is strong and stable like a plant stem that serves as the backbone for many endeavors and successes.

Mila (MEE-lah) Slavic: Adored by the people. Dependable, loyal, sensitive, kindhearted, and generous, Taureans are cherished friends and beloved leaders. Variation: *Milla*.

Mildred (MILL-drid) Old English: Gentle strength. Taureans' determination, fortitude, and stubbornness are counterbalanced by their softer qualities of sensitivity, kindness, and grace. Variations: *Millie, Milly*.

Minna (MIN-ah) Old German: Tender affection. The influence of Venus, Taurus's ruling planet, endows the sign's children with a surprisingly soft and sensual side. Variations: *Mina, Minette*.

Mohala (moh-HAH-luh) Hawaiian: Blooming petals. One of the zodiac's spring signs, Taurus is commonly associated with all budding and blossoming plants.

Monica (MON-ih-kah) Latin: Advisor. Compassionate, wise, and stable, Taureans often offer their loved ones valuable advice. Variations: *Monika, Monique*.

Naeemah (nah-EE-mah) Arabic: Generous. Taureans, who often achieve great financial success through their hard work, readily share the fruits of their labor with close friends and family.

Nagida (nah-GEE-duh) Hebrew: Prosperous. Taurus's hard work, ambition, and determination often are rewarded with great wealth.

Nediva (neh-DEE-vuh) Hebrew: Generous. Kindhearted and luxury loving, Taureans enjoy bringing a smile to the faces of their loved ones.

Netis (NAY-tiss) Native American: One who can be trusted. Taureans can always be relied on to finish a job or help a friend.

Nicole (nee-COHL) Greek: Triumphant march. This popular name is a fitting choice for Taureans, whose hard work, ambition, and determination guarantee success in anything they attempt. Variations: *Colette, Cosette, Nicholle, Nicol, Nicola, Nicolette.*

Nizana (nee-ZAH-nah) Hebrew: Blossom. Spanning the spring months of April and May, the sign of Taurus is commonly affiliated with all blossoming plants. Variations: *Nitza, Nitzana, Zana.*

Noriko (NOH-ree-koh) Japanese: Law and order. Taureans, who prize stability and security, readily uphold rules and regulations and rarely challenge authority.

Nyssa (NISS-ah) Greek: She who begins. While Taureans may be innovative thinkers, their real strength lies in taking action to set a process in motion and get the job done. Variation: *Nissa.*

Odelia (oh-DEEL-yah) Old English: Prosperous. Taurus's hard work and tireless determination is often rewarded with great financial success. Variations: *Odella, Odile, Odilia, Othilia.*

Olwin (OHL-win) Welsh: Fair and blessed. Taurus's calm and reasonable demeanor often brings great rewards. Variation: *Olwyn.*

Onatah (oh-NAH-tah) Native American: Earth child. Taurus is one of the three Earth signs of the zodiac.

Onida (oh-NEE-dah) Native American: The anticipated one. Just as people look forward to spring, a season frequently associated with Taurus, people are always ready to welcome kind and caring Taureans. Variation: *Oneida*.

Ottilie (OT-ih-lee) Old German: Prosperous. The hard work and ambitious determination of Taurus is often rewarded with great success and wealth. Variations: *Otilie, Ottolina, Ottoline*.

Pansy (PAN-zee) French: For the flower. Taurus, one of the spring signs of the zodiac, is commonly affiliated with all of the season's blossoming flowers. Variations: *Pansey, Pansie*.

Patia (pah-TEE-uh) Spanish Gypsy: Fresh green leaf. Encompassing the months of April and May, Taurus is often linked to all budding and blossoming plants.

Peri (PER-ee) Hebrew: Blossom. One of the zodiac's three spring signs, Taurus is closely associated with the blossoming of flowers. The flowers affiliated with Taurus are the violet and the poppy.

Phyllis (FILL-iss) Greek: Green branch. Taurus, associated with the budding and blossoming of plants in spring, is like a green branch—tender yet strong. Variations: *Phillida, Phyllida, Phyllys*.

Pilar (pee-LAHR) Spanish: Pillar; foundation. Stalwart, dependable, and strong, Taureans are veritable pillars of support upon which others rely for assistance, comfort, and encouragement.

Posala (poh-SAH-lah) Native American: To burst (with seed). Connoting the annual rebirth of nature, *Posala* is a suitable name for a girl born under Taurus, one of the zodiac's spring signs.

Radmilla (RAHD-mel-luh) Slavic: Worker for the people. Driven, tenacious, and ambitious, Taureans are willing to do the hard work that ensures a common victory for all.

Randy (RAN-dee) Old English: Protectress. Taureans are fiercely protective of their loved ones. Variations: *Randene, Randey, Randi.*

Renita (ray-NEE-tah) Latin: Steady and firm. The most prominent qualities of Taurus are dependability and reliability. Variations: *Nita, Renie, Rennie.*

Resi (REH-see) German: Reaper. *Resi* connotes Taurus's Earth element as well as the sign's strong connection to the natural environment.

Risha (REE-shah) Hindu: Born during the month of Vrishabna. In Hindu astrology, Vrishabna is the month of the sign of Taurus.

Ruri (roo-REE) Japanese: Precious emerald. The emerald is the birthstone of the sign of Taurus.

Sakura (sah-KOO-rah) Japanese: Cherry blossom. In Japan, the cherry blossom is the national flower, which blooms abundantly in spring. The sign of Taurus encompasses the springtime months of April and May.

Sasa (SAH-sah) Japanese: Assistance. Taureans, generous and kindhearted by nature, always are willing to lend a helping hand.

Selima (se-LEE-mah) Hebrew: Bringing comfort and peace. Taurus, who cherishes stability and security, often soothes others with her calm and rational demeanor.

Selma (SELL-mah) Arabic: Secure. Taureans prize stability, fidelity, and consistency in all areas of their lives.

Sharon (SHAR-on) Hebrew: From the open plain. Born under an Earth sign, Taureans are endowed with a special connection to the natural environment, particularly open spaces. Variation: *Sharron*.

Shirley (SHUR-lee) English: Bright clearing. *Shirley* connotes the wide-open fields of the earth with which Taureans feel a special affinity. (Famous Taureans: Shirley Temple Black, actress; Shirley MacLaine, Academy Award-winning actress)

Shizu (SHEE-zoo) Japanese: Quiet. Taureans are among the most calm, stable, and naturally quiet children of the zodiac. Variations: *Shizuka, Shizuko*.

Signe (SIG-nee) Old Norse: Triumphant counselor. Rational, practical, and sensible, Taurus often offers wise advice and valuable assistance to those in command.

Stockard (STOCK-ird) Old English: Near the tree stump. While Taureans appreciate anything to do with nature, they especially enjoy clearings and open spaces.

Taka (TAH-kah) Japanese: Honorable one. *Taka* is a suitable name for dependable, patient, and hardworking Taurus.

Takara (tah-KAH-rah) Japanese: Beloved jewel. Taureans, whose ruling planet of Venus governs pleasure and beauty, prize the finer things in life and enjoy being surrounded by luxury and opulence.

Taree (tah-ree-EH) Japanese: Arching branch. While Taureans are willing to bend to accomplish a goal, they remain solid and secure at their essence.

Temperance (TEM-pur-antz) Latin: Moderation. Taurus is calm, stable, and dependable in all things.

Tereza (tay-RAYTZ-ah) Portuguese: Reaper. A spring Earth sign, Taurus is often associated with the growing season. Variations: *Teresa, Terry, Theresa, Therese.*

Tiara (tee-AHR-ah) Latin: Headdress; crown. *Tiara* suggests Taurus's penchant for luxurious and beautiful things. Variations: *Tiarra, Tierra.*

Tirion (TEER-ee-on) Welsh: Gentle and kind. Underneath their tough, stubborn, and pragmatic exterior, Taureans are sensitive, tender, and loving individuals who dearly cherish their friends and family.

Trava (TRAH-vah) Czechoslovakian: Fresh grasses. This unique name connotes the imagery of fields, with which Taureans feel a special affinity.

Tuwa (TOO-wah) Native American: Earth. Taurus is one of the three Earth signs of the zodiac.

Udele (oo-DELL) Old German: Prosperous and fortunate. Taureans are often rewarded for their hard work with financial success. Variations: *Uda, Ute.*

Valda (VAHL-dah) Old Norse: Governor. Highly esteemed for their hard work, stability, and natural instincts for success, Taureans do well in leadership positions.

Valerie (VAL-ur-ee) Old French: Strong. Taureans are renowned for their remarkable emotional and physical resilience and fortitude. Variations: *Valaree, Valaria, Valeria, Valerye.* (Famous Taurean: Valerie Bertinelli, actress)

Venus (VEE-nus) Latin: Lovely. Named for the planet that rules the sign of Taurus, this name is a unique choice for a Taurus girl. Variations: *Venita, Vinita.*

Vera (VEER-ah) Russian: Faithful. Loyal and reliable, Taureans make devoted and affectionate companions for life. Variations: *Verena, Verina, Verla, Viera.*

Victoria (vik-TORE-ee-ah) Latin: Victorious. Aggressive, hard-working, and ambitious, Taureans often attain the high goals they set for themselves. Variations: *Tori, Vicky, Victoriana, Victorina, Victorine, Vikki, Vittoria.* (Famous Taurean: Tori Spelling, actress)

Violet (VYE-oh-let) Latin: For the flower. The violet is one of the flowers affiliated with the sign of Taurus. Also, the special colors assigned to Taurus are soft violets, blues, and mauves. Variations: *Violetta, Violette.*

Wiara (VEE-ahr-ah) Polish: True and faithful. *Wiara* connotes the loyalty and dependability associated with the sign of Taurus. Variation: *Wiera.*

Xenia (ZEEN-ee-ah) Greek: Hospitable. Taureans, who possess a decidedly self-indulgent streak, enjoy entertaining friends and family while surrounded by good food, fine wine, and beautiful objects. Variations: *Xena, Zena, Zenia, Zina.*

Yamka (YAHM-kah) Native American: Time for blossoms. Taurus, which encompasses the months of April and May, is strongly associated with the flowering of spring.

Yarmilla (YAHR-mil-luh) Slavic: She who sells in the marketplace. Taureans are known to have a good head for business and investing. Variation: *Jarmilla.*

Yemena (yeh-MEE-nah) Hebrew: Capable. The most dependable children of the zodiac, Taureans can be counted on to get any job done.

Yolanda (yoh-LAHN-dah) Greek: The violet. The flowers associated with the sign of Taurus are the violet and the poppy. Variations: *Iolanda, Iolande, Iolanthe, Yolande, Yolane.*

Yori (YOO-ree) Japanese: Trustworthy. Taureans make reliable friends and workers who always can be counted on in times of need.

Yusra (YOOS-rah) Arabic: Affluent. Taurus's virtuous work ethics and determined ambition often are rewarded with great financial success.

Zea (ZAY-uh) Latin: Grain. Taureans, born under a spring Earth sign and endowed with a deep connection to nature, are commonly associated with the growing of plants and flowers.

Zohra (ZOH-rah) Arabic: Blooming. Taurus is associated with the blossoming of plants in spring. *Zohra* also is another name for the planet Venus, which rules the sign of Taurus. Variation: *Zora*.

Names for Taurus Boys

Abdul (ahb-DOOL) Arabic: Servant. Dependable, caring, and productive, Taureans are always willing to offer their assistance. Variations: *Abdalla, Abdel, Abdullah*.

Adadel (A-dah-del) Arabic: Prosperous one. Taureans' hard work and determined ambition often are rewarded with great financial success.

Adam (ADD-um) Hebrew: Man of the red earth. Taurus is one of the three Earth signs of the zodiac. (The other two are Virgo and Capricorn.) Variations: *Adamec, Adamko, Adan, Ade, Adem, Damek*.

Addison (ADD-iss-un) Old English: Adam's son. Any name that connotes a close connection to the earth and environment is appropriate for a boy born under Taurus, one of the zodiac's three Earth signs.

Alcott (AL-cot) Old English: From the old cottage. This old-fashioned name is suited for Taureans, who tend to have a traditional yet romantic outlook on the world and enjoy living near the great outdoors. Variation: *Alcot.*

Aloysius (al-oh-ISH-uss) Old German: Illustrious warrior. Brave, fiercely protective, and strong, Taureans will go to any lengths to protect the people or causes they care about. Variations: *Alois, Aloys.*

Alton (AHL-tin) Old English: One who resides in the old town. Traditional and sociable Taureans prefer to establish longtime friends and lifelong roots. Variations: *Alten, Altin.*

Amon (AYE-mon) Hebrew: Builder. Strong, practical, and competent, Taureans are the quintessential "doers" of the zodiac. Variation: *Ammon.*

Andrew (AN-droo) Greek: Manly and strong. This classic name is suitable for Taurus, who is renowned for his power and strength. Variations: *Anders, Andor, André, Andrius, Andy.* (Famous Taurean: Andre Agassi, champion tennis player)

Angus (ANG-gus) Scottish: Only choice. *Angus* was a Celtic god renowned for his wisdom and intelligence. The practical, rational, and insightful advice offered by Taurus is highly valued by others. Variation: *Aengus.*

Antoan (AN-twan) Vietnamese: Safe and secure. Taureans cherish safety, security, and stability in all things.

Anton (AHN-ton) Latin: Inestimable. Taureans are highly regarded for their perseverance, stability, sensitivity, and kindness. Variations: *Antinka, Antonin, Antosha, Tosya.*

Archibald (AHR-chih-bahld) Old German: Genuine and simple. This traditional name is appropriate for Taurus, who is practical, rational, and stable in all things. Variations: *Archibaldo, Archie.*

Ardley (AHRD-lee) Old English: From the land of the home lover. Taureans, who possess a deep connection to the natural environment, treasure the stability and security their home offers. Variations: *Ardleigh, Ardlie.*

Aric (AYRE-ik) Norse: Merciful ruler. Taurus, whose hard work, ambition, dedication, and fine instincts may earn him positions of authority, is renowned for his sensitivity and kindness. Variations: *Arek, Arick, Asric.*

Arthur (AHR-thur) Irish: Stonelike. This traditional name is apt for Taurus, whose stability, determination, and strength make him a veritable rock upon which others rely for support. Variations: *Artair, Arte, Artur, Arturo.* (Famous Taurean: Arthur Sullivan, composer)

Arve (AHR-veh) Scandinavian: Inheritor of property. *Arve* is a suitable name for Taurus, who has a penchant for acquiring property, wealth, and luxurious objects.

Atworth (AT-wurth) English: Farm. Taureans are deeply linked to the land and to the natural environment. As one of the zodiac's spring signs, Taurus is also associated with the growing season.

Aubrey (AW-bree) Old French: Leader of the elves. Hardworking, practical, and fair, Taureans make capable and accessible leaders.

Auriel (OR-ee-ell) Hebrew: Lion of god. *Auriel* is the name of the archangel who protects those born under the sign of Taurus. Variation: *Ariel.*

Baron (BAYR-un) Old English: Baron. Taureans often become successful leaders of business and industry through their ambition and determination.

Barrett (BARE-it) Old English: Strong and mighty as a bear. One of the key characteristics of the sign of Taurus is great physical and emotional strength.

Barth (BAHRTH) Hebrew: Son of the earth. Taurus is one of the three Earth signs of the zodiac. Variations: *Bart, Bartel, Barto, Bartz.*

Bartholomew (bahr-THOL-oh-MYOO) Hebrew: One who farms. This traditional name is suitable for a boy born under Taurus, an Earth sign strongly associated with the growing season and the glory of the outdoors. Variations: *Bart, Barth, Bartholome, Bartlett, Bartley, Barton.*

Beldon (BELL-dun) Old English: Man of the beautiful glen. Taureans possess a deep appreciation for the natural environment. Variations: *Belden, Beldin.*

Bergen (BEHR-gen) Scandinavian: From the mountain. Born under an Earth sign, nature-loving Taureans relish time spent outdoors surrounded by the earth's glorious gifts. Variations: *Berg, Berger, Bergren.*

Berger (BUR-ger) French: Shepherder. *Berger* connotes Taurus's skill at leading and guiding others.

Berwin (BUR-win) Middle English: Friend of the harvest. An Earth sign encompassing the spring months of April and May, Taurus is commonly affiliated with the growing season.

Bonar (BOHN-ahr; BOHN-ayr) Old French: Kind and courteous. Underneath their often stubborn and tough exteriors, Taureans are surprisingly gentle, sensitive, and caring. Variation: *Bonnar.*

Bond (BOND) Old English: Tiller of the soil. Taurus, born under an Earth sign, enjoys working with the land. Variations: *Bondon, Bonds*.

Boyce (BOYSE) Old French: Son of the forest. Born under an Earth sign, Taureans feel a special connection to the natural environment.

Bryan (BRY-an) Celtic: Virtuous and strong. Taureans are esteemed for their dependability, loyalty, and highly ethical natures. Variations: *Brian, Bryant, Bryon*.

Byron (BYE-rin) Old English: Cow barn. Symbolized by the Bull, the sign of Taurus rules all cattle.

Calvert (KAL-vurt) Old English: Calf herder. *Calvert* is a suitable name for a boy born under Taurus, the sign associated with all cattle. Variation: *Calbert*.

Carl (KAHRL) Old German: Farmer. Taureans, born under an Earth sign and endowed with a great appreciation for the natural environment, enjoy working outdoors. Variations: *Car, Karl*. (Famous Taurean: Karl Marx, German socialist and political philosopher)

Carlin (KAHR-lin) Irish: Little champion. Driven, strong-minded, and hardworking, Taureans are capable of achieving any goal and overcoming any obstacle. Variation: *Carling*.

Carlisle (KAHR-lyle) Old English: From the castle tower. Taureans often try to turn their homes into veritable "castles": safe, secure, and luxurious. Variation: *Carlyle*.

Carlos (KAHR-los) Spanish: Strong and manly. Like the Bull that symbolizes their sign, Taureans are powerful, aggressive, protective, and proud.

Carter (KAHR-ter) Old English: Cart driver. Strong and dependable, Taureans are good at taking charge and guiding any situation to a safe and prosperous conclusion.

Cass (KAS) Contemporary: Keeper of the riches. Particularly adept at making—and holding on to—money, many Taureans pursue careers in finance.

Castel (kas-TEL) Latin: Of the castle. Possessing a regal and refined bearing, Taureans love to fill their homes with the most luxurious decor and beautiful objects.

Chasin (hah-SIN; CHAH-sin) Hebrew: Strong and mighty. Endowed with great emotional and physical resilience, Taureans are capable of overcoming any obstacle. Variations: *Chason, Hason.*

Che (chay) Spanish: He will increase. Taureans, who are among the most productive and hardworking children of the zodiac, have a penchant for creating wealth and prosperity.

Chen (chen) Chinese: Vast. *Chen* suggests Taurus's openness to others and his affinity for wide-open fields.

Chester (CHESS-tir) Old English: From the fortress. Taurus, who prizes security and stability, often strives to ensure the safety of his home. Variations: *Cheston, Chet.*

Clune (KLOON-ee) Irish: From the open fields. Born under an Earth sign, Taureans have a special affinity for the natural environment, particularly open spaces. Variations: *Cluney, Cluny.*

Cornelius (kohr-NEEL-ee-us) Latin: Horn. *Cornelius* connotes the horns of the Bull, Taurus's symbolic animal. Variations: *Cornel, Cornell, Cornnall.*

Craig (KRAYG) Scottish Gaelic: From the craggy rocks. This popular name suggests Taurus's affinity for the natural environment.

Dagan (day-GON) Hebrew: Grain. Encompassing the spring months of April and May, Taurus is commonly affiliated with the growing of all plants and flowers. Variation: *Dagon*.

Dallin (DAY-lyn) Old English: People who are proud. Honorable and virtuous Taureans take great pride in their work. Variations: *D'Alan, Dalan, Dallan, Dalon*.

Darius (DAYR-ee-us) Persian: He who manages his holdings well. Taureans, who are dedicated to acquiring wealth, property, and luxurious things, are often wise investors with a talent for making money. Variations: *Dario, Derry*.

Dayton (DAY-ton) Middle English: From the friendly town. Often appearing tough and stubborn on the outside, Taureans are genuinely kind, loyal, sensitive, and caring individuals who make wonderful friends.

Dennis (DEN-iss) English: Of Dionysus, the god of wine and vegetation. *Dennis* is a suitable name for Taurus, who has a penchant for good food, fine wine, and luxurious surroundings. Variations: *Denis, Denys*. (Famous Taureans: Dennis Hopper, actor; Dennis Rodman, professional basketball player)

Devlin (DEHV-lin) Irish: Showing great valor. Taurus is renowned for his stalwart, tenacious, and honorable character. Variations: *Devland, Devlen, Devlyn*.

Dobry (DO-bree) Polish: Good. Ethical, sensitive, and kind, Taureans are highly esteemed by others.

Drake (DRAYKE) Middle English: Dragonlike. *Drake* is a fitting choice for stalwart, formidable, and protective Taurus. Variation: *Drayke*.

Dreng (DREHNG) Norwegian: Farmhand. Taureans, who are associated with the earth and growing plants, have a reputation for being strong and dependable workers.

Dunixi (doo-NEE-shee) Greek: God of wine. Taureans, who possess a decidedly self-indulgent streak, have a penchant for beautiful objects, good food, and fine wine.

Ebisu (EE-bih-soo) Japanese: From Japanese mythology, this Japanese god of work and good luck was the son of Daikoki, a god of wealth. *Ebisu* is an apt choice for Taurus, whose hard work is often rewarded with great financial success.

Edik (ED-ick) Russian: Prosperous guardian. *Edik* suggests Taurus's protective nature and his talent for making money.

Edward (EDD-wurd) Old English: He who guards his wealth. This classic and ever-popular name is appropriate for Taurus, who esteems money and all it can buy. Variations: *Edouard, Eduardo, Edvard, Ewart, Ned, Ted.* (Famous Taureans: Eddy Arnold, actor/country-and-western singer; Edward R. Murrow, journalist; Eddie Albert, actor)

Eker (EE-kur) Hebrew: Root. This name connotes not only the earth, with which Taurus is deeply linked, but also the rock-steady support Taureans offer to the other children of the zodiac.

Eldridge (ELL-drij) German: Wise counselor. Rational, practical, and sensible, Taurus readily offers sage and insightful advice or valuable assistance to those who need it.

Erdman (URD-men) German: Man of the earth. Taurus is one of the three Earth signs of the zodiac. Variations: *Erdmann, Hartman.*

Ernest (UR-nest) German: Earnest and intent. *Ernest* suggests Taurus's ambitious determination and dedication to hard work. Variations: *Earnest, Ernesto, Ernst.*

Fadey (fah-DAY) Russian: Bold. With his strong and determined approach to any challenge, Taurus bravely stands behind his beliefs. Variation: *Faddei*.

Farleigh (FAHR-lee) Old English: From the bull's meadow. The Bull is the symbolic animal of the sign of Taurus. Variations: *Fairlay, Farlay, Farlee, Farley, Farly*.

Farrell (FARE-el) Irish: Courageous and heroic. *Farrell* suggests Taurus's fiercely protective nature and his great strength. Variations: *Farr, Farrel, Farris, Ferrell, Ferris*.

Ferdinand (FUR-dih-nahnd; FUR-dih-nand) Old German: Bold adventurer. Taureans take on any challenge bravely and openly. Variations: *Ferd, Ferdie, Ferdinando, Fernando, Hernando*.

Fergus (FUR-gis) Irish: Manly vigor. Formidable and stalwart Taureans are the quintessential "doers" of the zodiac, always capable of getting the job done. Variations: *Ferghus, Ferguson*.

Ferrand (FAYR-ahnd) Old French: One with an iron temperament. Taureans tend to be stable, tenacious, persistent, and stubborn. Variations: *Farrand, Farrant, Ferrant*.

Florian (FLOR-ee-in) Latin: Flourishing; flowering. Encompassing the spring months of April and May, Taurus is commonly associated with the budding and blossoming of flowers. Variations: *Florent, Flory*.

Forbes (forbs) Irish: Owner of the fields. Taureans are possessed of a deep appreciation for the natural environment, particularly fields.

Galton (GAHL-tin) English: Landlord. Taureans are known to be excellent caretakers, as well as investors who gain ownership in many business opportunities.

Gardner (GAHRD-nur) Middle English: A gardener. This name is an obvious and appropriate choice for Taurus, who is born under an Earth sign and enjoys the tactile sensations of nature. Variations: *Gard, Gardener, Gardiner*.

Garner (GAHRN-ur) Old English: Fighter who shelters and protects. Taureans are fiercely protective of their loved ones. Variation: *Garnett*.

Garth (GAHRTH) English: Gardener. Encompassing the spring months of April and May, Taurus is deeply linked to all budding and blossoming plants.

Gibor (gee-BOHR) Hebrew: Strong. Taureans are endowed with great emotional and physical strength.

Gregory (GREG-or-ree) Greek: Watchman. Taureans, who value safety and security, often keep a constant and fiercely protective eye on their loved ones. Variations: *Greg, Greggory, Gregor*.

Haig (HAYG) Dutch: He who tends the hedges. This unique name suggests Taurus's meticulous attention to detail and great love of the land and growing plants. Indeed, landscaping is a vocation that many Taureans find satisfying.

Harcourt (HAHR-kort) Old French: From the fort. A great desire to protect and a strong will are among the key qualities associated with Taurus. Variation: *Court*.

Harding (HAHRD-ing) Old English: Hardy. Taureans are famous for their resilient and strong natures. Variation: *Hardy*.

Harith (HAH-rith; hah-REETH) Arabic: Ploughman. One of three Earth signs in the zodiac, Taurus is considered a hard and determined worker who makes certain that the most essential job is done, and done well.

Hector (HEK-tor) Greek: Perservering and steadfast. The persistence and determination possessed by Taureans invariably leads them to great success. Variations: *Heck, Hektor*.

Holt (HOHLT) Old English: Forests. Taureans possess a keen appreciation for the natural environment.

Horst (HORST) Old German: Dense grove. *Horst* is a suitable name for Taurus, who feels a special affinity for nature.

Howard (HOW-ird) Old English: Protector. Taurus is fiercely protective of his loved ones. Variation: *Ward*.

Isas (i-SAHS) Japanese: Valuable one. Taurus is highly esteemed for his dependability, sensitivity, kindness, and practicality.

Jagger (JAG-ur) English: He who carts things around. Symbolized by the strong-backed Bull, Taurus often shoulders the responsibility of moving a difficult situation or task forward, slowly but surely ensuring progress in all its forms.

Jared (JAR-id) Hebrew: Down to earth. *Jared* is a suitable name for practical, rational, and stable Taurus.

Jelani (jeh-LAH-nee) African/Swahili: Strong. Taureans are renowned for their emotional and physical resilience.

Jerzy (JUR-zee or YEHR-zhee) Polish: He who works the land. One of three Earth signs of the zodiac, Taurus has a close connection to the land.

Jesse (JESS-ee) Hebrew: Wealthy one. Taurus's hard work and ambitious determination are often rewarded with great financial success. Variations: *Jesiah, Jess, Jessie*.

Jethro (JETH-roh) Hebrew: Abundance. *Jethro* suggests the great wealth Taureans strive so hard to acquire. Variations: *Yitran, Yitro*.

Joji (JOH-jee) Japanese: Farmer. Born under one of the zodiac's Earth signs, Taureans have a deep connection to the land and growing plants.

Jonathan (JON-a-thun) Hebrew: Gift from God. Taureans are dearly cherished by friends and family for their generosity, kindness, dependability, and sensitivity. Variations: *Jon, Natan, Nathan*.

Joseph (JO-sef) Hebrew: God will increase. This classic and ever-popular name suggests the abundant prosperity and remarkable success with which Taurus's hard work is rewarded. Variations: *Jody, Joe, Joey, Jojo, Jose, Josef*. (Famous Taureans: Joe Louis, professional boxer; Joe Cocker, singer; Joseph Cotten, actor)

Kale (KAH-lay; KAYL) Hawaiian: Strong and manly. Like the Bull that symbolizes their sign, Taureans are powerful, aggressive, protective, and proud.

Kare (KAW-reh) Norwegian: Enormous. *Kare* suggests the robust and formidable physical appearance possessed by many Taureans.

Keane (KEEN) Old English: Sharp. This traditional name connotes Taurus's keen appreciation of beauty and pleasure. Variations: *Kean, Keen, Keenan, Keene, Kenney, Kienan*.

Kenan (KEE-nan) Hebrew: To acquire or possess. Taureans are avid collectors who prize lavish surroundings and beautiful objects.

Kendrick (KEN-drik) Welsh: Royal chieftain. With their noble ethics and lavish tastes, Taureans make natural, and even regal, leaders. Variations: *Kendric, Kendrik, Kendrix*.

Kenton (KEN-tun) Old English: Castle estate. Taureans, who prize security, stability, and luxury, are dedicated to making their homes lavish fortresses where they truly can feel comfortable.

Kingman (KING-men) English: The king's man. Although they rarely aspire to leadership positions, Taureans are the penultimate seconds-in-command who see that the job gets done. Variation: *Kinsman*.

Kiyoshi (kee-YOH-shee) Japanese: Quiet one. Taureans are among the most placid and reserved children of the zodiac. Variation: *Yoshi*.

Knox (NOHKS) Old English: He who hails from the hills. Prizing stability and security and deeply appreciative of the natural environment, Taurus often chooses to make his home in rural areas, surrounded by the earth's glorious gifts.

Koresh (koh-RESH) Hebrew: To dig in the earth. Taurus is one of the three Earth signs of the zodiac. Variation: *Choresh*.

Kuper (KOO-pir) Yiddish: Copper. Copper is the precious metal associated with the sign of Taurus.

Laird (LAYRD) Scottish: He who owns lands. Endowed with a special affinity for wide-open fields, wealthy Taureans often purchase land.

Lander (LAN-der) Middle English: Owner of property. Prosperous Taureans are often dedicated to "collecting" land, luxurious objects, and wealth. Variations: *Landan, Landen*.

Landry (LAN-dree) Anglo-Saxon: Leader. Ambitious, reliable, hardworking, and tenacious, Taureans are naturals in leadership positions.

Liam (LEE-um) Irish: Firm protector. Determined Taurus is fiercely protective of his loved ones.

Mando (MAHN-doh) Spanish: Army man. *Mando* suggests Taurus's dependability, strength, and willingness to do the hard work that ensures a common victory for all.

Manley (MAN-lee) English: The man's meadow. Born under an Earth sign, Taureans feel a special connection to fields. Variation: *Manleigh.*

Manton (MAN-ton) English: The man's town. In addition to possessing many "manly" traits attributed to the Masculine side of their sign, Taureans are known as excellent architects and craftsmen, the builders of civilization. Variations: *Mannton, Manten.*

Maska (MAHS-kah) Native American: Powerful. Taureans, who possess remarkable physical and emotional strength, are capable of overcoming any obstacle.

Mather (MA-thur) Old English: Advancing troops. In addition to governing love, beauty, and pleasure, Taurus's ruling planet, Venus, is strongly associated with aggression and victory in war.

Mato (MAH-toh) Native American: Brave. Taureans are among the most stalwart, persistent, and strong children of the zodiac.

Mayfield (MAY-feeld) English: The strong man's field. Taurus, noted for his bull-like physical and emotional strength, is often associated with vast pastures.

Mead (MEED) English: Meadow. Endowed with a deep appreciation for the natural environment, Taurus feels a special affinity for open fields. Variations: *Meade, Meed.*

Merrick (MAYR-ick) Old English: Hardworking ruler. Stable, reliable, ambitious, determined, and industrious, Taureans often make widely respected leaders who inspire loyalty and dedication in those who work for them. Variations: *Mayrick, Merick.*

Montgomery (mont-GUM-ur-ee) English: The rich man's mountain. Taurus, whose hard work is often rewarded with great wealth, is deeply appreciative of the natural environment. Variations: *Monte, Monty.*

Morley (MORR-lee) English: Meadow on a moor. Born under an Earth sign, Taureans have a strong association with open fields. Variations: *Moorley, Moorly, Morlee.*

Nelek (NELL-ik) Polish: Like a horn. *Nelek* connotes the horns of the Bull, Taurus's symbolic animal.

Nibaw (NEE-baw) Native American: "I stand up." Sometimes called stubborn, Taureans often stand up for their beliefs, which tend to be highly ethical.

Nicanor (nee-kah-NOHR) Spanish: Victorious. Aggressive, ambitious, and hardworking, Taureans usually reach the high goals they set for themselves.

Nicholas (NIH-ko-las) Greek: Triumph of the people. This classic name reflects Taureans' willingness to do the hard work that ensures a common victory for all. Variations: *Nick, Nicky.*

Onan (oh-NUHN) Turkish: Prosperous. The hard work and relentless determination of Taurus is often rewarded with great wealth.

Paris (PAYR-iss) Greek: Journeyman. This old-fashioned name refers to workers who are experienced and reliable, traits that often describe the work habits of Taureans. Variation: *Parris*.

Parlan (PAHR-lun) Scottish: Son of the earth. Taurus is one of the three Earth signs of the zodiac. (The other two are Virgo and Capricorn.)

Parr (PAHR) Old English: Garden in the park. The sign of Taurus is associated with budding and blossoming plants, as well as open spaces in the great outdoors.

Pascal (PAHS-cull; pahs-CAL) French: Eastertide's infant. *Pascal* is a suitable name for a Taurus boy born on or near the Easter holiday, which typically occurs during the month of April. Variations: *Pascale, Pascual, Pasquale*.

Patrin (PA-trin) English Gypsy: Leaf trail. Wherever Taurus goes, he leaves behind the evidence of the productive tasks he has accomplished.

Pattin (PAT-tin) English Gypsy: Leaf; freshness. Encompassing the spring months of April and May, Taurus is commonly associated with the lush and verdant growing season.

Payne (PAIN) Latin: From the country. Endowed with a deep affinity for nature and cherishing stability and security, many Taureans choose to live in rural areas. Variation: *Paine*.

Peter (PEE-tur) Greek: Rock. Stalwart and dependable, Taureans are the foundations upon whom others rely for support. Variations: *Pete, Petey*. (Famous Taureans: Peter Benchley, author; Peter Frampton, singer; Pete Townsend, musician; Pete Seeger, folk singer; Peter Ilich Tchaikovsky, composer)

Pitney (PIT-nee) Old English: Island of the strongman. Taurus is renowned for his great physical and emotional resiliency. Variation: *Pittney*.

Proctor (PROK-tir) Latin: One who manages. Aggressive, determined, hardworking, and ethical, Taureans excel in leadership positions. Variation: *Procter.*

Prosper (PROS-pir) Latin: Prosperous. *Prosper* is an obvious and apt choice for ambitious and hardworking Taurus, who is capable of achieving great wealth through his determined efforts. Variation: *Prospero.*

Quinlan (KWIN-lin) Irish: Great strength. The remarkable resilience and power of Taurus is well known. Variations: *Quinley, Quinlin, Quinlyn.*

Reeve (REEV) Middle English: Manager of the farm. This traditional name represents both Taurus's deep connection to the natural environment and his aptitude for leadership. Variations: *Reave, Reeves.*

Rez (REHZ) Hungarian: Copper. Copper is the precious metal associated with the sign of Taurus.

Riki (REE-kee) Estonian: Ruler of an estate. *Riki* suggests both Taureans' capability as leaders and their great love of the comfort, stability, and security that they find at home.

Rodman (ROD-mun) Old English: Heroic. The great strength and protectiveness of Taurus is capable of reaching heroic proportions. Variations: *Rod, Rodd, Roddy, Roderic, Roderick, Roderich, Rodrick.*

Sayer (sayr) Welsh: Carpenter. Greatly appreciative of aesthetic beauty, Taureans are often drawn to careers as creative artisans. Variations: *Sawyer, Sayre, Sayres.*

Sean (shawn) Hebrew: Heavenly generosity. Also Irish form of *John. Sean* is an apt name for Taurus, who is always willing to share the fruits of his labor with loved ones. Variations: *Shane, Shawn.*

Segel (SEE-gul) Hebrew: Treasure. This name is appropriate for Taurus on two levels: Considered great gifts by those who love them, Taureans return this love by generously providing for their loved ones and sharing their prosperity with them.

Sholto (SHOHL-toh) Scottish: Sower of seeds. Taurus is associated with the spring, a time when many types of seeds are planted.

Slevin (SLAY-vin) Irish: Mountaineer. Born under an Earth sign, Taureans are happiest when engaging in outdoor activities. Variations: *Slaven, Slavin.*

Spark (SPAHRK) Middle English: Happy and gallant. *Spark* is a unique choice for even-tempered and honorable Taurus. Variations: *Sparke, Sparky.*

Squire (SQUYE-er) English: Medieval landlord. Taureans are known to make strong leaders and overseers, as well as to control great wealth.

Sweeney (SWEE-nee) Irish: Young brave one. Taureans are among the most stalwart, strong, and fiercely tenacious children of the zodiac.

Talbot (TAL-but) Middle English: Wood sculptor. Lovers of tactile sensations who are endowed with a deep appreciation for aesthetic beauty, Taureans often pursue careers as creative artisans. Variations: *Tal, Talbert, Tally.*

Talmi (TAHL-mee) Hebrew: My hill. This unusual name reflects Taurus's closeness to the land, as well as his ability to climb and conquer any mountain.

Tatanka (tah-TAHNK-ah) Native American: Bull. The Bull is the symbolic animal of the sign of Taurus.

Tedmund (TED-mond) English: Watcher over the land. Endowed with a great appreciation for the earth, Taureans often become involved in environmentalism and conservation. Variation: *Tedmond*.

Terence (TAYR-ince) Latin: Tender. Underneath their tough, stubborn, and pragmatic exteriors, Taureans are sensitive, tender, and loving individuals who dearly cherish their friends and family. Variations: *Terance, Terrence, Terry*. (Famous Taurean: Terry Southern, author/screenwriter)

Teva (TAY-vah) Hebrew: Nature. Born under an Earth sign, Taureans possess a special affinity for the natural environment.

Tem (TEM) Gypsy: Country. Born under an Earth sign and deeply linked to the natural environment, Taureans find comfort, stability, and security in rural areas.

Thorne (THORN) English: Thorn. *Thorne* connotes the difficult and obstinate side of Taurus, who is tenacious and determined in all things. Variation: *Thorn*.

Thornton (THORN-tun) English: Thorny town. Taureans, sometimes referred to as the builders of civilization, are willing to overcome any obstacles in order to triumph at a task, particularly when it involves the comfort of their loved ones.

Thorpe (THORP) English: Village. Due to their mastery of architecture and carpentry, Taureans can be called ''the builders of civilization.'' Variation: *Thorp*.

Tilford (TILL-furd) Old English: Prosperous dale. This old-fashioned name is apt for Taureans, who tend to be wealthy and sociable. They also prefer the intimacy of smaller groups in social situations. Variation: *Tilden*.

Timur (tee-MOOR) Hebrew: Imposing height. *Timur* suggests the often formidable physical appearance possessed by many Taureans.

Tirion (TEER-ee-in) Welsh: Kind and gentle. Underneath their often tough, pragmatic, and obstinate exteriors, Taureans possess a surprisingly soft and sensitive side.

Tito (TEE-toh) Spanish: To honor. Taureans are highly moral, patient, loyal, and sensitive—all qualities that make them endeared and respected leaders.

Toal (TOH-ahl) Irish: Strong people. Taureans are among the most formidable, stalwart, and tenacious children of the zodiac. Variations: *Tuathal, Tully.*

Trumble (TRUM-bil) Old English: Strong and brave. *Trumble* is a fitting choice for courageous and formidable Taurus. Variations: *Trumball, Trumbull.*

Turner (TURN-ur) English: Woodworker. Practical yet endowed with a great appreciation for aesthetic beauty, Taureans often make talented and creative artisans.

Tyge (TEEG) Greek: He who hits the mark. Dependable, stable, and productive, Taureans can always be counted on to get the job done. Variations: *Tycho, Tyko.*

Tyler (TYE-lur) English: Tile maker. Keen lovers of tactile sensation, Taureans are often drawn to creative and practical careers as fine craftsmen. Variations: *Ty, Tylar.*

Tyson (TYE-sun) Old French: Explosive. Generally placid and mild mannered, Taureans are capable of becoming enraged when repeatedly challenged. Variations: *Tison, Ty, Tycen, Tysen.*

Upton (UP-tin) English: Hill town. While enjoying the company of others, Taureans also appreciate the open spaces and views provided on the hilltops.

Vadin (VAH-din) Hindu: Educated orator. Many Taureans are renowned for their powerful and captivating speaking voices.

Varick (VAR-ik) Old German: Chief who defends honorably. When Taureans take on the tasks of leadership, they remain strong, yet caring, which earns them great respect from all. Variations: *Waric, Warrick.*

Vasu (vah-SOO) Hindu: Prosperous. Taureans are adept at making money—and greatly enjoy the luxuries it affords.

Vilmos (VILL-mohs) German: Steady soldier. Taurus is renowned for his stability, reliability, and dependability.

Volker (VOHL-ker) German: Protector of the people. Fiercely protective Taureans are passionate about shielding their loved ones from harm.

Volney (VOLL-nee) German: Spirit of the people. Although Taureans often remain quiet in social situations, they have an intuitive understanding of people's emotions and their circumstances.

Wakeman (WAYK-man) English: Watchman. Taurus, who prizes stability and security, goes to any lengths to shield his loved ones from harm.

Walton (WAHL-tun) Old English: Reinforced village. Taureans are known for protecting their possessions and those of their loved ones.

Walworth (WALL-wirth) English: Walled farm. Lovers of the land, Taureans appreciate cultivated and controlled surroundings rather than wild woodlands.

Wardell (WAHR-dell) English: Watchman's hill. Taureans, known for their fiercely protective natures, cherish safety and security and always keep a close eye on their loved ones.

Wardley (WAHRD-lee) English: Watchman's meadow. Taurus feels a special connection to wide-open fields. Variations: *Wardlea, Wardleigh.*

Ware (WAYR) English: Observant. By nature, Taureans are watchful and fiercely protective of their loved ones.

Wayne (WAYN) Old English: One who drives wagons. Strong and reliable, Taureans are adept at taking charge and guiding any situation to a safe and prosperous conclusion.

Webley (WEB-lee) English: Weaver's meadow. Born under an Earth sign, Taureans feel a deep affinity for the natural environment, particularly wide-open fields. Variations: *Webbley, Webly.*

Wenceslaus (WENN-sih-sloss) Old Slavic: Marvelous garland of honor. Taureans are highly esteemed for their virtuous natures. Variations: *Wenceslas, Wenzel.*

Werner (WUR-nur or VEHR-ner) German: Defending army. *Werner* suggests both Taurus's strength as well as his fiercely protective nature. Variations: *Warner, Wernher.*

Winthrop (WIN-throp) Old English: Village of friends. Placid, affectionate, supportive, and loyal, Taureans never lack for friends.

Worth (WIRTH) English: Enclosed farm. Taureans, who often choose to live in rural areas, cherish stability and security.

Wright (RYTE) English: Carpenter. Deeply sensual and possessed of a keen love of tactile sensation, Taureans often are drawn to professions in which they can work with their hands to create beautiful objects.

Yasir (yah-SEER) Arabic: Wealthy one. Taureans, who determinedly and tenaciously pursue their goals, often achieve high levels of financial success. Variations: *Yasah, Yasser, Yusra.*

Yitro (YEE-troh) Hebrew: Plenty. Taureans, who work long and hard to gain success and wealth, readily enjoy the fruits of their labor, surrounding themselves with beautiful objects, good food, and fine wine. Variation: *Yitran.*

Zan (ZAN; ZAHN) Hebrew: Well fed. *Zan* connotes the healthy and robust physical appearance possessed by many Taureans.

Zion (ZYE-on) Hebrew: Guarded land. Born under an Earth sign and naturally protective, Taureans are eager conservationists and environmentalists.

Famous Taureans

04-21-1838	John Muir	04-23-1942	Sandra Dee
04-21-1915	Anthony Quinn	04-23-1949	Joyce DeWitt
04-21-1926	Elizabeth II, Queen of	04-23-1957	Jan Hooks
	England	04-23-1960	Valerie Bertinelli
04-21-1932	Elaine May	04-23-1970	Scott Bairstow
04-21-1935	Charles Grodin	04-24-1934	Shirley MacLaine
04-21-1951	Tony Danza	04-24-1936	Jill Ireland
04-21-1958	Andie MacDowell	04-24-1942	Barbra Streisand
04-22-1870	Vladimir Ilyich Lenin	04-25-1908	Edward R. Murrow
04-22-1899	Vladimir Nabokov	04-25-1918	Ella Fitzgerald
04-22-1908	Eddie Albert	04-25-1930	Paul Mazursky
04-22-1916	Yehudi Menuhin	04-25-1932	Meadowlark Lemon
04-22-1928	Aaron Spelling	04-25-1940	Al Pacino
04-22-1936	Glen Campbell	04-25-1945	Bjorn Ulvaeus
04-22-1937	Jack Nicholson	04-25-1946	Talia Shire
04-22-1950	Peter Frampton	04-26-1785	John James Audubon
04-23-1564	William Shakespeare	04-26-1933	Carol Burnett
04-23-1928	Shirley Temple Black	04-26-1938	Duane Eddy
04-23-1940	Lee Majors	04-26-1942	Bobby Rydell

04-27-1822	Ulysses S. Grant	05-03-1937	Frankie Valli
04-27-1922	Jack Klugman	05-03-1947	Doug Henning
04-27-1932	Casey Kasem	05-03-1951	Christopher Cross
04-27-1932	Anouk Aimee	05-04-1919	Heloise
04-27-1937	Sandy Dennis	05-04-1929	Audrey Hepburn
04-27-1959	Sheena Easton	05-04-1941	George F. Will
04-28-1758	James Monroe	05-04-1956	Pia Zadora
04-28-1937	Saddam Hussein	05-05-1818	Karl Marx
04-28-1941	Ann-Margret	05-05-1913	Tyrone Power
04-28-1950	Jay Leno	05-05-1915	Alice Faye
04-28-1981	Jessica Alba	05-05-1927	Pat Carroll
04-29-1863	William Randolph Hearst	05-05-1942	Tammy Wynette
		05-05-1973	Tina Yothers
04-29-1899	Duke Ellington	05-05-1981	Danielle Fishel
04-29-1909	Tom Ewell	05-06-1856	Sigmund Freud
04-29-1919	Celeste Holm	05-06-1856	Robert E. Peary
04-29-1936	Zubin Mehta	05-06-1895	Rudolph Valentino
04-29-1955	Jerry Seinfeld	05-06-1915	Orson Welles
04-29-1957	Daniel Day-Lewis	05-06-1931	Willie Mays
04-29-1958	Michelle Pfeiffer	05-06-1945	Bob Seger
04-29-1970	Andre Agassi	05-06-1953	Tony Blair
04-29-1970	Uma Thurman	05-06-1961	George Clooney
04-30-1912	Eve Arden	05-07-1833	Johannes Brahms
04-30-1926	Cloris Leachman	05-07-1840	Peter Ilich Tchaikovsky
04-30-1933	Willie Nelson	05-07-1885	Gabby Hayes
04-30-1940	Burt Young	05-07-1901	Gary Cooper
04-30-1944	Jill Clayburgh	05-07-1919	Eva Peron
04-30-1961	Isiah Thomas	05-07-1922	Darren McGavin
05-01-1909	Kate Smith	05-07-1931	Teresa Brewer
05-01-1916	Glenn Ford	05-07-1933	Johnny Unitas
05-01-1918	Jack Paar	05-08-1884	Harry S Truman
05-01-1924	Terry Southern	05-08-1895	Bishop Fulton Sheen
05-01-1939	Judy Collins	05-08-1926	Don Rickles
05-01-1945	Rita Coolidge	05-08-1940	Peter Benchley
05-02-1892	Baron von Richthofen	05-08-1940	Rick Nelson
05-02-1903	Dr. Benjamin Spock	05-08-1943	Toni Tennille
05-02-1904	Bing Crosby	05-08-1964	Melissa Gilbert
05-02-1924	Theodore Bikel	05-09-1918	Mike Wallace
05-02-1925	Roscoe Lee Browne	05-09-1936	Albert Finney
05-02-1945	Bianca Jagger	05-09-1936	Glenda Jackson
05-02-1946	Lesley Gore	05-09-1940	James L. Brooks
05-03-1898	Golda Meir	05-09-1946	Candice Bergen
05-03-1919	Pete Seeger	05-09-1949	Billy Joel
05-03-1928	James Brown	05-09-1960	Tony Gwynn
05-03-1936	Engelbert Humperdinck		

05-10-1899	Fred Astaire	05-16-1801	William Seward
05-10-1902	David O. Selznick	05-16-1905	Henry Fonda
05-10-1922	Nancy Walker	05-16-1919	Liberace
05-10-1936	Gary Owens	05-16-1952	Pierce Brosnan
05-10-1946	Donovan	05-16-1955	Debra Winger
05-10-1960	(Paul Hewson) Bono	05-16-1966	Janet Jackson
05-11-1888	Irving Berlin	05-16-1973	Tori Spelling
05-11-1904	Salvador Dali	05-17-1900	Ayatollah Khomeini
05-11-1912	Phil Silvers	05-17-1911	Maureen O'Sullivan
05-11-1927	Mort Sahl	05-17-1936	Dennis Hopper
05-11-1933	Louis Farrakhan	05-17-1956	Sugar Ray Leonard
05-12-1820	Florence Nightingale	05-17-1956	Bob Saget
05-12-1907	Katharine Hepburn	05-18-1897	Frank Capra
05-12-1925	Yogi Berra	05-18-1912	Perry Como
05-12-1929	Burt Bacharach	05-18-1919	Margot Fonteyn
05-12-1936	Tom Snyder	05-18-1920	Pope John Paul II
05-12-1937	George Carlin	05-18-1930	Pernell Roberts
05-12-1948	Steve Winwood	05-18-1931	Robert Morse
05-12-1962	Emilio Estevez	05-18-1934	Dwayne Hickman
05-13-1842	Arthur Sullivan	05-18-1946	Reggie Jackson
05-13-1914	Joe Louis	05-19-1890	Ho Chi Minh
05-13-1926	Beatrice Arthur	05-19-1925	Malcolm X
05-13-1939	Harvey Keitel	05-19-1939	James Fox
05-13-1941	Richie Valens	05-19-1941	Nora Ephron
05-13-1950	Stevie Wonder	05-19-1945	Pete Townshend
05-13-1961	Dennis Rodman	05-19-1952	Grace Jones
05-14-1933	Laszlo Kovacs	05-20-1908	Jimmy Stewart
05-14-1936	Bobby Darin	05-20-1919	George Gobel
05-14-1944	George Lucas	05-20-1940	Stan Mikita
05-14-1951	Robert Zemeckis	05-20-1944	Joe Cocker
05-15-1905	Joseph Cotten	05-20-1946	Cher
05-15-1909	James Mason	05-20-1959	Bronson Pinchot
05-15-1918	Eddy Arnold	05-21-1904	Fats Waller
05-15-1936	Anna Maria Alberghetti	05-21-1916	Harold Robbins
05-15-1937	Trini Lopez	05-21-1917	Raymond Burr
05-15-1953	George Brett	05-21-1924	Peggy Cass
05-15-1969	Emmitt Smith	05-21-1952	Mr. T

GEMINI
(May 22–June 21)

GLYPH: ♊
SYMBOL: The Twins
POLARITY: Masculine
QUALITY: Mutable
ELEMENT: Air
RULING PLANET: Mercury
BIRTHSTONE: Agate
SPECIAL COLOR: Yellow
FLOWERS: Lavender and lily of the valley
METAL: Mercury
ANIMALS: Brilliantly colored birds and butterflies
MOST LIKEABLE TRAITS: Exuberance, versatility, and joy

♊

Like the mythological Twins who symbolize their sign, Geminis are two personalities in one. They show a mercurial combination of ebullient high spirits and brooding earthiness, commanding intellect and base instincts, materialism and idealism, substance and shadow. This is the sign of perpetual duality and sharp, sudden contrasts. Change, excitement, and intellectual stimulation make up Gemini's credo, and no other children of the zodiac use their minds—and sometimes their bodies—to such extraordinary effect as Geminis do. Alternately brilliant, restless, joyful, intriguing, challenging, and sometimes exhausting, Geminis are the indefinable rara avises of the zodiac. Perpetually young at heart, they are possessed with such bedazzling charisma that their impact is often felt for generations. Raising a Gemini child is an intoxicating and enthralling experience.

General Qualities

Gemini is a Masculine and Mutable Air sign governed by the planet Mercury. In Roman mythology, Mercury was the god who served as messenger to the other gods and governed business, travel, eloquence, and cunning. The planet Mercury rules all forms of communication, intellectual pursuits, and personal transformation through self-knowledge.

Geminis are powerful communicators, equally adept at the written and spoken word. Their facile intellects perpetually run at high speed as they question, debate, process, and synthesize all the information, viewpoints, and impressions they absorb like sponges from the people and world around them. As Mercury-ruled children whose elemental nature is Air—the quality that governs intellect and communication—Geminis live a life almost exclusively of the mind. They require a great deal of intellectual stimulation just to feel connected with the world and often seem somewhat cut off from, or uncomfortable with, their emotional sides.

Many Geminis, particularly when young, engage in a feverish kind of information gathering merely for the mental exercise it provides. These same Geminis then delight in parading their knowledge—often during verbal sparring matches—with anyone close at hand. Geminis in full verbal swing are remarkable to behold—all mind, mouth, and hands; simultaneously thinking, orating, and gesturing; each action going faster than the other to drive home a point. The Masculine influence in Gemini feeds this intellectual aggressiveness, endowing Geminis with their trademark qualities of full-throttled enthusiasm, nonstop energy, engaging charm, and indiscriminate expansiveness. They enjoy being the centers of attention amidst crowds of people and are eminently comfortable around a wide cast of characters. The Mutability of the sign contributes to this comfortableness, enabling Geminis to quickly adapt to new people and new situations—a critical talent for this sign, since Geminis crave change and rarely stay in one place, or with one person, for long.

Some more intellectually driven Geminis are more circum-spect about how they utilize their formidable minds. They may store the vast amounts of information they gather for future use, refine and update it over the course of time, and then pull out just the right nugget of wisdom or bon mot necessary to command a situation or meet a challenge. A Gemini lawyer, politician, or crusading journalist is nearly unstoppable after a win or coup, able to move a crowd emotionally, intimidate an opponent thoroughly, and command a room completely.

Invariably Geminis use their stores of knowledge and consummate verbal skills for personal advantage to augment their mental prowess, gain an edge in a close relationship, or enhance their status and careers. Geminis frequently become esteemed writers, orators, attorneys, and teachers who use words powerfully and eloquently to sway and instruct their audiences. They are fast on their feet, verbally and physically expressive, emotionally persuasive, and naturally funny—easily making riveting and mesmerizing impressions in any field they choose to enter.

The list of famous Geminis who have left indelible marks on the public landscape in fields as varied as music, football, politics, poetry, finance, and philosophy includes such diverse personalities as Bob Dylan, Henry Kissinger, the Marquis de Sade, John F. Kennedy, Ralph Waldo Emerson, Judy Garland, Igor Stravinsky, Jacques Cousteau, Donald Trump, Joe Namath, Jean-Paul Sartre, Marilyn Monroe, Sir Laurence Olivier, Paul McCartney, and William Butler Yeats.

Publicly Geminis are upbeat, optimistic, endearing, and engaging. They genuinely enjoy the company of others, though they are most comfortable when they are the centers of attention and rarely connect one-on-one with others. The private, emotional side of Gemini—the shadow self of the dual-natured extrovert—may be underdeveloped or hidden behind the verbal gymnastics and charismatic public persona, often remaining a mystery that's difficult to fathom.

The duality inherent in Gemini is far more complex than that observed in other signs. It is not the conflict of love of work versus love of home that is occasionally observed in Taureans, nor is it the dilemma of sexuality versus spirituality with which Scorpios sometimes grapple.

The Gemini duality is a far more fundamental one than those, as basic and as profound as human nature itself. It is about the primal versus the evolved, light versus shadow, spirit versus matter, idealism versus baseness. It is also about combining those elements into a magnificent human whole, a challenge all individuals face. In many ways, then, Gemini may be the most human of the zodiac's signs, its duality encompassing all the best and the worst in humankind.

The brilliant Gemini poet William Butler Yeats alludes to the origins of this duality in one of his most renowned poems, "Leda and the Swan." In that poem, Yeats exquisitely describes the seduction of a mortal by a god, a mating that would result in the birth of the Gemini Twins who symbolize this sign. The mortal was Leda, the beautiful queen of Sparta who was seduced by the Greek god Zeus when he came to her in the form of a giant swan. From their union, Leda bore two eggs, each containing a set of twins, two boys and two girls. Miraculously— and mysteriously—one boy, Castor, was the son of the queen's mortal husband, but the other boy, Pollux, was Zeus's son.

The two boys were identical twins, though emotionally and spiritually as different as heaven and Hades. Castor was mortal; Pollux was immortal. Castor, who was amiable and peaceful, tamed horses as a hobby. Pollux, who was rash and aggressive, taught boxing. Yet the brothers were inseparable and grew up devoted to one another, each playing off the other's unique strengths. When Castor died prematurely, the grieving Pollux was inconsolable and even offered to sacrifice his own immortality to be with his brother in the underworld. Instead, Zeus took pity on his brokenhearted son and reunited the brothers for all eternity as the brilliant constellation Gemini. There in the night sky, they guide and protect sailors, and are often observed as the mysterious golden glow known as Saint Elmo's fire.

Many astrologers have observed that of all the signs, Geminis seem to struggle most mightily throughout their lives to reconcile their two opposing natures. And people have a tendency to focus only on the Pollux side of Gemini—brilliant intellect but shallow soul. This depiction of these gifted children is unfair, because only the most immature of Geminis allow the Pollux twin to run wild through life. The great majority of Geminis are largely successful in combining and using to great advantage the two unique sides of their personalities: the high-minded idealist and the earthy realist; the gentle spirit and the fierce intellectual; the sensitive altruist and the aggressive self-promoter.

A successful synthesis of the Castor and Pollux elements in Gemini makes for an extraordinary individual. Two incomparable Geminis, Anne Frank and Norman Vincent Peale, made phenomenal personal successes out of dreadful circumstances: she suffered a young adolescence spent in fear and confinement, then cut miserably short by death; he survived an early career crippled by low self-esteem, doubt, and shyness. Yet through the power of their singular spirits and words, Frank and Peale have changed lives and lived on in the memories of millions of people. That kind of success and impact is quintessentially Gemini.

Home

Without a doubt, Gemini children are a challenge. Intellectually and physically precocious, they often walk and talk at a very young age, and once they start walking and talking, they never stop, except to sleep and eat. They are on a perpetual quest, and that quest is for knowledge.

After infancy and toddlerhood, Geminis don't need a great deal of traditional nurturing because they are eminently capable of caring for themselves and don't like a lot of emotional fussiness. What Geminis do need—and demand—is feeding of their minds. More than most children, Geminis must have challenging mental stimulation on a regular basis. They are the zodiac's penultimate information gatherers, thinkers, and rationalizers— the ones who later become the world's quintessential communicators—and they require huge amounts of raw information to start the process. Parents become the banquet of knowledge from which Gemini children partake, again and again.

A veritable Greek chorus of "Whys?" and "But hows?" and "What ifs?" greet the parents of Gemini children on a daily basis. Geminis question everything and everyone. Infinitely curious, they are determined to learn the who, why, what, when, where, and how of the people, ideas, and objects they encounter every day. Sometimes this can feel like a benevolent form of intellectual vampirism, and in many ways it is. Geminis grow and gather enormous inner strength and confidence through feeling that they are the intellectual masters of their worlds. Ideas and reasoning are their major preoccupations, making them mightily different from other children in the zodiac.

Young Geminis are not concerned with feelings and with nurturing, as are the Water signs. Nor do they care about being useful and making things work, as do the Earth signs. Geminis are more similar to the aggressive Fire signs, but don't really want to be stars, as children of the Fire element do. Geminis want to influence—to be heard, esteemed, and respected. Their instruments of influence are their minds and voices.

Next to asking questions, Gemini children love nothing more than providing answers. Verbal wizards, they are emphatic and often relentless debaters, orators, and raconteurs. Verbosity is how Geminis test their mastery of all the knowledge they've absorbed. They eloquently spin out their intellectual interpretations of the world to anyone who will listen, and then they carefully assess the effect their words have. The Gemini communication style might be exhausting, if it weren't so charming, witty, and insightful. Geminis are marvelous storytellers as well, even at a young age. They also can be gifted mimics and often develop distinctive speech patterns.

The Gemini child's mind is also extraordinarily facile, able to focus on several things at once and move from one task to another with lightning speed and deft competence. This quality is unique to Geminis, who are renowned for their capacity to manage many tasks simultaneously and often make genuine jacks- and jills-of-all-trades, rather than dabblers and dilettantes. The challenge in parenting multitalented Geminis is to be sure that they are stimulated enough by something to stick with it long enough to actually learn meaningful and lasting lessons.

Getting Geminis to stay in one place for any extended amount of time can be next to impossible if their minds aren't fully engaged. Geminis have absolutely no tolerance for the boring and mundane, and when faced with it are constantly looking over their shoulders for the nearest exit.

Sophisticated computer games, intricate verbal and mental board games and puzzles may all engage the Gemini child's interest for a time. Even the challenge of learning a second language appeals to these children, who can easily handle being bilingual. Developing focus and tolerance within the learning process is crucial for Geminis, who later struggle with these same issues in school.

Ironically, despite their prodigious mental skills, Geminis are frequently slow to mature emotionally and socially. Indeed, some astrologers view Gemini as the sign of perpetual youth, and many Geminis seem not to want to grow up. They often retain a childlike capacity and propensity for mischievousness, restlessness, and reckless naïveté. They abhor being pinned down and more often than not would rather flee than fight when faced with a challenge. They are notorious for leaving home early to set off for a life of adventures, though they invariably remain loving and loyal children throughout their lives, even if they love from a distance.

While Geminis are at home, however, they are among the most astonishing of creatures, who can dazzle and bewitch anyone with their gifted minds and exuberant approach to living. At their best, they possess an uplifting joyfulness and optimism that touches everyone in their orbit. Geminis are dynamic reminders of the extraordinary heights the human mind can achieve.

School and Play

Predicting how any one Gemini will do in school is difficult. Academic achievement depends, to a large extent, on how well the Gemini child has learned to focus mentally and tolerate boredom and on just what kind of school he or she attends.

The good news is that Geminis genuinely love learning and, indeed, crave it. The bad news is that they generally detest school because of its regulations, limitations, and demands that learning be compartmentalized. Ideally Geminis need a very fluid method of learning. They prefer to move from one subject to another at their own pace and in their own way, and they are happiest when they can see the interrelatedness of different tasks.

A large, traditional school is perhaps not the best choice for Geminis, though they can learn much about self-discipline, patience, and tolerance in such an environment. Also, Geminis may be happy to meet the great variety of children available in a large, public school setting. Nevertheless, Geminis may fare better in smaller, progressive, "no walls" schools where the subjects covered are more diverse and liberal, and where learning is holistic, rather than segmented.

Oddly enough, the biggest problem Geminis may face in school is being good at many subjects, but never excelling in any one. That peculiarly Gemini propensity encourages these children to skim through subjects easily, acquiring a surface kind of knowledge on many topics, but never learning how to work hard at and enjoy mastering one special skill. Not getting a handle on this tendency early in life can create serious consequences for adult Geminis, who may flounder in a series of careers before they find one genuine life path that uniquely engages them.

At play, Geminis may be as agile and adept physically as they are mentally. This combination is rare, as most children sacrifice one strength for the other. Yet Geminis often make gifted athletes, particularly in sports that require running and endurance. In fact, they need regular and hard physical exercise to balance out the intensely furious workings of their minds.

Geminis immensely enjoy the company of other children. Peers, another great source of information for Geminis, also make terrific sounding boards. Gemini children possess abundant charm and energy, and usually are quite popular. However, they also can be demanding and opinionated, and often may struggle to be the center of attention. They are not happy when ignored or left on the sidelines. Indeed, more than any other children of the zodiac, Gemini children—powerfully affected by the influence of the Twin duality in their sign—purposely avoid being alone with themselves. They always seem to need an "other" to feel energized and complete.

The World

Because Geminis are preeminent jacks- and jills-of-all-trades, they can achieve great success in any number of fields, but they are strongly drawn to writing, journalism, law, education, politics, and the performing arts. As performers, many Geminis have achieved fame as uniquely distinctive singers and songwriters. This is the sign of Patti LaBelle, Al Jolson, Peggy Lee, Stevie Nicks, Gladys Knight, Melissa Etheridge, Bob Dylan, Judy Garland, Paul McCartney, and the Artist Formerly Known as Prince. Other Geminis naturally use their tremendous minds and verbal gifts to become powerful and influential writers. Gemini is also the sign of Sir Arthur Conan Doyle, Ralph Waldo Emerson, Walt Whitman, Allen Ginsberg, Thomas Mann, Saul Bellow, Anne Frank, and William Butler Yeats.

Romantically, Geminis are cautious about committing themselves to one mate. First of all, they cherish intellectual freedom and the ability to come and go as they please. They will not give up, or compromise on, those privileges easily. Second, Geminis are not particularly emotional creatures. Despite their energy, ebullience, and enjoyment of others' company—aspects of their Masculine expansiveness that are sometimes mistaken for genuine warmth—Geminis in fact are rather shut off from their emotional resources. The world of ideas enthralls them; the world of feelings intimidates and confuses them. Feelings can't be conveniently analyzed, synthesized, and repackaged to one's advantage—the very things that Geminis do with information and knowledge. In the end, Geminis often avoid marriage and other intimate commitment.

Yet Geminis were meant to be "Twins." When they choose solitude, they are metaphorically opting to be just half of what could be a more powerful whole. Perhaps many Geminis delay romance and marriage for so long because they are really searching for their lost Twin, their true soul mate.

Geminis seem to have an unending urge to search. Questions around the fundamental duality of the universe—and the human animal's place in it—haunt Geminis throughout their lives. Singularly gifted with great reserves of those very qualities that separate humans from animals—extraordinary minds, the gift of communication, and the ability to change—Geminis continually search for the ultimate point of possessing these prizes.

Whatever paths Geminis choose to take in the world, they seem to carry along with them an especially heightened awareness of the extraordinary potentialities of the human soul, together with a firsthand knowledge of the struggle between all that is great and noble in us, and all that is base and self-absorbed. That most Geminis can masterfully straddle both sides of the human equation, and be brilliant, enlightening, entertaining, and optimistic in the bargain, is a testament to their unique brand of endurance.

Choosing a Name for Your Gemini Child

When choosing a name for your Gemini child, first think about the major attributes and symbols associated with the sign. Gemini is the sign of versatility, exuberance, wit, inconsistency, quicksilver changeability, restlessness, high intelligence, adaptability, and keen communicative skills.

The sign of Gemini governs communication and invention. Geminis make superbly gifted writers and public speakers. They are naturally clever, verbally expressive, and often irrepressibly high-spirited as well as occasionally high-strung. Born under the sign of singular intellectual energy, Geminis live a life almost exclusively of the mind. Thus they sometimes are cut off from, or uncomfortable with, their emotional selves.

Geminis abhor rules and routine. Instead, they crave diversity, challenge, and constant change. They get bored easily and are always on the move, looking for new people and new territory that will stimulate and engage their formidable intellects. Geminis, who take great pleasure in influencing the people around them, are enormously persuasive and charismatic. Indeed, they often possess starlike, mesmerizing personas.

Gemini is a Masculine and Mutable Air sign governed by the planet Mercury. The Masculine aspect of the sign endows Geminis with their hallmark qualities of enthusiasm, energy, and expansiveness. Assertive Geminis are always on the go and relentlessly upbeat. The Mutable quality of the sign enables Geminis to be highly adaptable to changing environments, a critical ability for this sign that craves constant change. The Air influence supports the sign's keen intellectual and communication skills and contributes to Geminis' exuberant and optimistic personalities. Geminis are perennially young at heart and often have a breezy, carefree attitude toward life, which is sometimes mistaken for superficiality. Yet they can be formidable intellectual opponents in the public arena, particularly in politics and law.

Gemini's ruling planet, Mercury, governs all forms of communication, intellectual pursuits, and personal transformation through self-knowledge. Geminis are powerful communicators with facile intellects that constantly process information and impressions and search for ways to utilize new knowledge to personal advantage.

Gemini is the third sign of the zodiac and the first of the summer signs, encompassing the months of May and June. Bright yellow is Gemini's color. The agate, a multicolored jewel, is the sign's birthstone, but the pearl, beryl, and aquamarine are also associated with the sign. Mercury is the Gemini metal. Lavender and lily of the valley are the flowers that are strongly associated with Gemini, as are all nut-bearing trees. The sign governs brilliantly colored birds and butterflies.

When you choose a name for your child, bear in mind some of Gemini children's key personal qualities. Expressing perpetual youth, Geminis are vivacious, upbeat, verbal, inquisitive, opinionated, humorous, unpredictable, imaginative, innovative, and restless. They value the power of the mind over the heart and soul, but are exuberantly charming and lighthearted, making them a joy to be around.

For additional inspiration when choosing a name for your Gemini child, especially a middle name, you may want to browse through the names listed in Gemini's companion Air signs, Libra and Aquarius.

Names for Gemini Girls

Abigail (AB-bih-gayl) Hebrew: A source of great joy. With their boundless energy, unlimited enthusiasm, overwhelming exuberance, and eternal optimism, Geminis illuminate the lives of their loved ones. Variations: *Abby, Gail.*

Agate (A-get) Greek: For the agate stone, the precious gem associated with the sign of Gemini. The agate is believed to make its wearer independent and eloquent, both qualities strongly present in Geminis.

Aida (ah-EE-dah) Latin: She arrives. With their formidable intellects and mesmerizing communication skills, Geminis often show a powerful presence and a dynamic ability to influence others. Variation: *Ada.*

Akhila (ah-KEEL-ah) Hindu: Total; complete. Geminis, born under the sign of the Twins, exhibit a duality that encompasses the best and worst human qualities yet combines to make an extraordinarily complex and brilliant whole.

Akwete (ah-KWEE-teh) African/Ghanian: Firstborn of twins. The sign of Gemini is symbolized by the Twins.

Alana (ah-LAHN-ah) Hawaiian: To float. Born under one of the zodiac's Air signs, Geminis possess a carefree and breezy approach to life. Variations: *Alaina, Alani, Alanis, Alanna, Alayne.* (Famous Gemini: Alanis Morissette, singer)

Aleela (ah-LEE-lah) African: Girl who cries. *Aleela* suggests the perpetual youth—and, at times, immaturity—associated with the sign of Gemini, who sometimes seem to show their emotions publicly and influence others in doing so.

Aleta (ah-LAY-tah) Spanish: Little winged one. This name is appropriate for a girl born under Gemini, the sign associated with butterflies and brilliantly colored birds.

Alhena (ahl-HEE-nuh) Arabic: Ring. *Alhena* is the name of a star in Pollux, which is part of the Gemini constellation.

Almond (AH-mund) English: Nut. The sign of Gemini is strongly affiliated with all nut-bearing trees.

Alnaba (ahl-NAHB-ah) Native American: Two wars fought at the same time. Born under the sign of the Twins, Geminis possess a decidedly dualistic nature that often creates a conflict of interest within themselves.

Alvita (al-VEET-ah) Latin: Energetic. *Alvita* is a lovely and appropriate name for exuberant, enthusiastic, and vivacious Gemini.

Amani (ah-MAHN-ee) Arabic: To desire. More than anything, Geminis hunger for knowledge, often spending their lives gathering vast amounts of information to feed their formidable intellects.

Andeana (ahn-dee-AHN-ah) Spanish: A walker or goer. *Andeana* suggests Geminis' tendency to wander from one thing, person, or place to the next, constantly in search of new stimulation and excitement. Variation: *Anda*.

Anemone (ah-NAY-moh-nee) Greek: Wind flower. Gemini is one of the three Air signs of the zodiac. (The other two are Libra and Aquarius.) Variations: *Annamone, Annemone*.

Angela (AN-jel-lah) Greek: The heavenly messenger. The element of Air in Gemini endows the sign's children with powerful communication skills. Variations: *Angel, Angelica, Angeline, Angelique, Angie.*

Anila (ah-NEEL-ah) Hindu: Children of the wind. *Anila* is a suitable choice for a girl born under the Air sign of ever-changing Gemini.

Apona (ah-POH-nah) Hawaiian: Encompassing. Gemini's complex dual nature encompasses the best and worst of human qualities, yet creates a mesmerizing and keenly intelligent whole.

Aponi (ah-POH-nee) Native American: Butterfly. The sign of Gemini is closely affiliated with butterflies.

Ardelle (ahr-DELL) Latin: Enthusiastic. Geminis are renowned for their contagious exuberance and boundless energy. Variations: *Ardelia, Ardella, Ardia, Ardra.*

Arlene (ahr-LEEN) Irish: Pledge. This name is a form of *Arline*, a name invented by M. W. Balfe for the title character in his opera, *The Bohemian Girl*—an apt description of many carefree and restlessly wandering Gemini girls. Variations: *Arleen, Arlena, Arlina, Arline.*

Ashira (ah-SHEER-ah) Hebrew: Wealthy. Highly intelligent Geminis often possess abundant talent in virtually all fields, which enables them to achieve great success in anything they pursue.

Asmee (as-MEE) Hindu: Confident. Knowledge-hungry Geminis gather great inner strength and confidence through feeling that they are the intellectual masters of their worlds.

Astra (AHS-trah) Greek: Star. *Astra* suggests not only Geminis' mesmerizing and starlike personas, but the constellation of the

Gemini Twins who symbolize the sign. Variations: *Astraea, Astrea.*

Audra (AWE-drah) Lithuanian: Thunderstorm. Generally exuberant and high-spirited, Geminis possess a fierce rage that can erupt if they are challenged or betrayed. Variation: *Audrey.*

Aura (AW-rah) Greek: Gentle breeze. *Aura* is a fitting choice for a girl born under Gemini, one of the zodiac's three Air signs. Variations: *Aurea, Auria.*

Balbina (bal-BEEN-ah) Italian: Stammerer. Highly charged and extremely intelligent, Geminis often speak at breakneck speeds in order to get out all of their racing thoughts. Variation: *Balbine.*

Barbara (BAR-bah-rah) Latin: The stranger. Geminis, who keep their inner personas hidden behind a charming, intelligent, and outgoing exterior, often remain mysteries to their closest loved ones. Variations: *Barbie, Barbra.* (Famous Gemini: Barbara Bush, former First Lady of the U.S.)

Barran (BAR-an) Irish: Little top. *Barran* suggests Gemini's prominent qualities of remarkable exuberance and high energy.

Beryl (BURL; BEH-rel) Sanskrit: For the gemstone. Gemini's gemstones are the pearl, the aquamarine, and the beryl.

Blasia (BLAH-see-ah) Latin: Stutterer. *Blasia* is a suitable name for Gemini, who often speaks so quickly others have a hard time catching up.

Bobina (boh-BEE-nah) Czechoslovakian: Brilliantly famous. Charismatic, mesmerizing, and persuasive, Geminis often possess starlike personas. Variation: *Roba.*

Breezy (BREE-zee) English: Breezy. Geminis, born under an Air sign, are renowned for their lighthearted and carefree approach toward life. Variations: *Brisa, Brisha, Brisia, Brissa, Briza.*

Caltha (CAHL-thah) Latin: Yellow flower. Yellow is the color assigned to the sign of Gemini. Variation: *Kaltha.*

Carol (KARE-ol) Old French: Song of joy. Exuberant Geminis, who are endowed with exceptional verbal skills, often go on to careers as successful singers and songwriters. Variations: *Carola, Carole, Caroline, Carolyn.* (Famous Geminis: Carol Kane, actress; Carroll Baker, actress)

Celandine (SELL-ahn-deen) Greek: Yellow flower. Gemini is strongly associated with the color yellow.

Chandi (CHAHN-dee) Hindu: Mad. Although they are usually happy-go-lucky and joyful, Geminis can reveal a furiously wrathful side when crossed or challenged.

Charde (CHAHR-dee) Arabic: One who leaves. Gemini, whose mind needs constant, fresh stimulation, often finds it difficult to stick to the same task for long periods of time before moving on to a new challenge.

Chimalis (chee-MAH-lis) Native American: Bluebird. The sign of Gemini is closely affiliated with all brightly colored birds.

Clytia (CLY-tee-ah) Greek: Splendid. Most people find Gemini's enthusiasm, clever wit, charisma, and zest for life enthralling and inspiring. Variations: *Clyte, Clytie.*

Colleen (kol-EEN) Irish: Girl. *Colleen* is a fitting choice for a girl born under Gemini, the sign of perpetual youth. Variations: *Coleen, Colene, Colline.* (Famous Gemini: Colleen Dewhurst, actress)

Dagmar (DAG-mahr) Old German: Famous thinker. Gemini is the sign of singular intellectual energy. Variations: *Daga, Dagagi, Dagmara*.

Daisy (DAY-zee) Old English: Day's eye. For the flower. With their bright and impulsive moods, Geminis reflect the cheerful-looking daisy, which commonly blooms in the months overseen by the sign. Variations: *Daisey, Daisi, Daizy, Dasie*.

Dede (dee-dee) African: Firstborn daughter. This cheerful name is appropriate for a girl born under the sign of Gemini, the zodiac's first summer sign.

Deirdre (DEE-drah, DAYR-drah, or DEER-dree) Irish: Complete wanderer. *Deirdre* suggests Gemini's desire for constant change, which often leads her to move from one place to another in search of new challenges, adventures, and experiences. Variations: *Deidra, Deidre*.

Desiree (DEZZ-ir-ay) French: Desire. Intelligent and inquisitive Geminis constantly search for an ever-elusive conclusion to their great yearning for knowledge. Variations: *Desarae, Desira, Dezarae, Diziree*.

Dory (DOHR-ee) French: Yellow-haired girl. Yellow is the color assigned to Gemini. *Dory* is a particularly apt choice for a blond girl born under the sign. Variations: *Dora, Dori, Dorrie, Dorry*.

Dusana (doo-SAHN-ah) Czechoslovakian: Spirit. Geminis are among the most exuberant, enthusiastic, and vivacious children of the zodiac. Their Air sign lends them an ethereal quality. Variations: *Dusa, Duska*.

Effie (EFF-ee) Greek: Singing talk. The element of Air in Gemini endows the sign's children with powerful communication skills; many Geminis go on to successful careers as singers and songwriters. Variations: *Effi, Effy, Ephie*.

Ehina (ay-HEEN-ah) Hindu: Desire. Geminis are driven by a deep but undefinable force to pursue answers to life's mysteries.

Erlinda (ayr-LIN-dah) Hebrew: Spirit. *Erlinda* connotes Geminis' natural ebullience, vivacity, and zest for life.

Evelyn (EV-ih-lin; EEV-ih-lin) French: Hazelnut. This classic name is a fitting choice for a girl born under Gemini, the sign associated with all nut-bearing trees. Variations: *Eveline, Evelyne, Evelynne, Evlin, Evlun, Evlynn.*

Ewalina (ay-wah-LEEN-ah) Hawaiian. Hazelnut. The sign of Gemini is affiliated with all nut-bearing trees. Variation: *Ewa.*

Fineeva (fin-EEV-ah) Polynesian: Talkative woman. Geminis are the most verbally gifted—and inclined—children of the zodiac.

Finlay (FINN-lee) Irish: Fair-haired heroine. *Finlay* is an appropriate name for a blond girl born under Gemini, the sign associated with the color yellow. Variations: *Findlay, Finley.*

Flavia (FLAH-vee-ah) Latin: Yellow hair. Gemini is closely affiliated with the color yellow, making *Flavia* an apt choice for a blond Gemini girl. Variations: *Flavie, Flaviere.*

Gauri (GO-ree) Hindu: Yellow. The special color assigned to the sign of Gemini is bright yellow.

Gemini (GEM-in-eye) Greek: Twin. This name is an obvious choice for a girl born under the sign of Gemini, symbolized by the Twins. Variations: *Gemella, Gemelle, Gemina.*

Gita (GEE-tah) Hindu: Song. Verbally gifted, naturally exuberant, and often attention seeking, many Geminis go on to successful careers as singers and songwriters. Variations: *Geeta, Geetika.*

Gypsy (JIP-see) English: Gypsy. Carefree, wandering, and spirited, Geminis have a decidedly distinct approach to life.

Hansa (HAHN-sah) Hindu: Swan. The original Gemini twins were born to the queen of Sparta after she was seduced by Zeus, who appeared to her in the guise of a large swan. Variations: *Hansika, Hansila*.

Hazel (HAY-zill) Old English: For the hazelnut tree. *Hazel* is an appropriate name for a girl born under the sign of Gemini, which is affiliated with all nut-bearing trees. Variations: *Hazal, Hazell, Hazelle, Hazle*.

Hedda (HED-ah) Old German: She who quarrels and debates. Keenly intelligent and gifted with excellent communication skills, Geminis delight in verbal sparring matches in which they can demonstrate their vast knowledge. Variations: *Heda, Heddi, Hedvig, Hedy*. (Famous Gemini: Hedda Hopper, gossip columnist)

Huberta (yoo-BUR-tah or hew-BER-tah) German: Intelligent. Those born under Gemini, the sign of singular intellectual energy, value the power of the mind over the heart and soul. Variation: *Huette*.

Iuana (ee-oo-AHN-ah) Native American: Wind blowing over a stream. Gemini, one of the three Air signs of the zodiac, is known for her whimsical, ever-changing ways.

Jae (jay) Latin: Jay bird. The sign of Gemini is affiliated with all brilliantly colored birds. Variations: *Jaya, Jaylee, Jaylene*.

Japera (jah-PAYR-ah) African/Zimbabwean: Complete. Just as the original Gemini Twins successfully played off each other's unique strengths, Geminis combine their vastly diverse qualities to create consummate and well-rounded individuals.

Jasmine (JAZ-min) Persian: Jasmine flower. The lusciously fragrant jasmine plant is associated with the sign of Gemini. Variations: Yasmeen, Yasmin.

Jaylene (jay-LEEN) English: Blue jay. The animals affiliated with the sign of Gemini are butterflies and brightly colored birds. Variations: *Jaye, Jayline, Jaynell.*

Joan (JONE) Hebrew: God's gracious gift. Geminis charm their friends and family with their inspiring exuberance, eternal optimism, and dynamic intelligence. (Famous Geminis: Joan Collins, actress; Joan van Ark, actress; Joan Rivers, comedienne/talk show host)

Jocelyn (JOSS-ah-lin) Latin: Playful one. Geminis never seem to want to grow up, forever maintaining a penchant for mischief and humorous antics.

Julia (JOO-lee-ah) Latin: Youthful. Gemini is known as the sign of perpetual youth. Variations: *Juliana, Julianna, Julianne, Julie, Juliet, Juliette.* (Famous Gemini: Juliette Lewis, actress)

June (JOON) English: The month. The sign of Gemini encompasses the months of May and June. Variations: *Junae, Junel, Junella, Junelle, Juno.*

Kanara (kah-NAHR-ah) Hebrew: Canary. Gemini is associated with all brilliantly colored birds. Variation: *Kanarit.*

Kane (KAH-ne) Japanese: Doing two things at once. Geminis, born under the sign of the Twins, are strongly associated with all forms of duality. Variation: *Kaneru.*

Kimama (kee-MAH-mah) Native American: Butterfly. *Kimama* is a lovely and unique choice for a girl born under Gemini, the sign linked to all butterflies and brightly colored birds.

Kuri (KOO-ree) Japanese: Chestnut. The sign of Gemini is affiliated with all nut-bearing trees.

Kylie (KYE-lee) Australian/Aboriginal: Boomerang. Naturally exuding joie de vivre, nothing keeps Geminis down for long. Variations: *Kye, Kyla, Kylene*.

Lalage (lah-LAH-yeh) Greek: Talkative. Highly gifted at verbal communication, Geminis often pursue careers in which public speaking plays a large role. Variations: *Lallie, Lally*.

Lalita (lah-LEE-tah) Hindu: Mischievous. Perennially young at heart and often restless, Geminis have a playful inclination toward mischief.

Leda (LEE-dah or LAY-dah) Hebrew: Birth; lady. In Greek mythology, *Leda* was the queen of Sparta who was seduced by Zeus in the form of a swan. From this meeting, Leda gave birth to twin sons, who later became the constellation of Gemini. Variations: *Leida, Leta, Lida, Lyda*.

Lenis (LAY-nis) Latin: Smooth and silky. Comfortable in any group and capable of adapting instantly, Geminis easily handle any social situation with eloquence and grace.

Levia (leh-VEE-uh) Hebrew: To join. The sign of Gemini is symbolized by the Twins of Greek mythology, who were joined eternally as the Gemini constellation. Variation: *Lia*.

Liberty (LIB-ur-tee) English: Freedom. *Liberty* is an apt choice for carefree Gemini, who abhors rules and routines. Variations: *Libertina, Librada*.

Lilia (lil-LEE-ah) Hawaiian: Lilies. Gemini is closely associated with the flowers of lavender and lily of the valley.

Lirit (leer-RIT) Hebrew: Lyrical; poetic. *Lirit* suggests the exceptional verbal gifts bestowed upon all Geminis.

Lisandra (lih-SAHN-drah) Greek: Liberator. Geminis skillfully use their powers of persuasion and innovative ideas to open the minds of others to new concepts. Variations: *Lissandra, Lizandra, Lizanne, Lysandra.*

Livanga (lee-VAHN-gah) African: Think before you act. *Livanga* is an apt choice for fast-talking Gemini, who sometimes loses sight of the consequences of her words and her whimsical ways.

Mahanga (mah-HAHN-gah) Polynesian: Twins. The Twins symbolize the sign of Gemini.

Makani (mah-KAHN-ee) Hawaiian: The wind. Gemini is one of three Air signs of the zodiac. (The other two are Libra and Aquarius.)

Mamo (MAH-moh) Hawaiian: Yellow bird. *Mamo* is an apt choice for a girl born under Gemini, the sign associated with both the color yellow and brightly colored birds.

Marini (mah-REE-nee) African/Swahili: Fresh and healthy. Geminis are as agile and adept physically as they are mentally— a rare combination in people.

Marmara (mah-MAHR-ah) Greek: Sparkling. Others are mesmerized by Gemini's natural exuberance, clever wit, endearing charm, and perpetual enthusiasm. Variation: *Marmee.*

May (MAY) Latin: For the month. The sign of Gemini encompasses the months of May and June. Variations: *Mai, Mayleen, Maylene.*

Mehira (meh-HEER-ah) Hebrew: Quick. *Mehira* is a fitting name for fast-talking, fast-thinking, and fast-acting Gemini.

Mei (MAY) Hawaiian: The great one. Bright and talented Geminis enjoy creating a sensation, as well as being the center of attention.

Melia (may-LEE-ah) Spanish: Yellow. Bright yellow is the color assigned to the sign of Gemini.

Minowa (mi-NOH-wah) Native American: Stirring voice. Geminis, who are endowed with exceptional communication skills, often make mesmerizing public speakers. Many Geminis also are gifted singers.

Mohana (moh-HAHN-ah) Hindu: Engaging. Renowned for their remarkable intellects and considerable communication skills, Geminis make fascinating and witty companions. Variations: *Mohini, Mohonie.*

Moray (mor-AYE) Scottish: Great. *Moray* is a suitable name for Gemini, who is capable of success in any endeavor she pursues.

Nadida (nah-DEE-dah) Arabic: Equal. Named after the Twins, Gemini is known for having two distinctly separate but equal sides. Variation: *Nadidah.*

Nashota (nah-SHOH-tah) Native American: Twin. The sign of Gemini is symbolized by the Twins.

Nasnan (NAHS-nan) Native American: Embraced by music. Although they often have difficulty getting in touch with their emotions, verbally gifted Geminis often make mesmerizing singers and songwriters.

Nelia (neh-LEE-ah) Spanish: Yellowish. Bright yellow is the special color of Gemini. Variations: *Neelia, Neelie, Nela, Nila.*

Nurita (noo-REE-tah) Hebrew: Yellow-blossomed flower. Gemini is affiliated with the color yellow. Variations: *Nurice, Nurit.*

Odessa (oh-DESS-ah) Greek: Long journey. Because Geminis crave constant change and stimulation, they are often drawn to the experiences and adventures offered by travel.

Odette (oh-DETT) French: Wealthy. Skilled communicators, gifted singers, and powerful thinkers, Geminis possess a rich array of talents. Variation: *Odetta.*

Oona (OO-nah) Irish: Unity. Oona is a name well suited to a girl born under Gemini, the sign of the Twins. The original Twins in Greek mythology were so devoted to each other that Zeus joined them eternally as the Gemini constellation. Variations: *Oonagh, Oonah.*

Oriole (OH-ree-ohl) Latin: Fair-haired; gold-speckled bird. The special color assigned to Gemini is yellow, and the sign governs all brightly colored birds. Variations: *Auriel, Orella, Oriel, Oriola.*

Pearl (PURL) Latin: For the jewel. The pearl is one of the gemstones associated with the sign of Gemini.

Pualani (poo-ah-LAH-nee) Hawaiian: Heavenly flower; a reference to the colorful bird-of-paradise flower. Gemini is strongly associated with bright yellow color and all brilliantly colored birds.

Raphaela (ra-fee-ELL-ah) Hebrew: God has healed. This name is the feminine variation of *Raphael*, the archangel of healing who protects those born under the sign of Gemini. Variation: *Rafaela.*

Rebecca (re-BECK-ah) Hebrew: Joined together. A biblical name, *Rebecca* suggests the imagery of the Twins who symbolize the sign of Gemini. Variations: *Becca, Becky, Reba, Rebeca, Rebecka, Rebeka, Rebekka, Rebi, Reby, Rheba.*

Sally (SAL-ee) Hebrew: Princess. Geminis, whose keen intelligence and renowned communication skills lend them a feeling of superiority, often possess a somewhat regal bearing. (Famous Geminis: Sally Ride, first female astronaut; Sally Kellerman, actress)

Sora (SOH-rah) Native American: Soaring songbird. With their considerable gifts of verbal communication, Geminis often pursue highly successful careers as singers and songwriters.

Stephanie (STEF-ah-nee) Greek: Wearer of the crown. Highly intelligent, multitalented, and full of energy, Geminis are capable of success in any endeavor they pursue. Variations: *Stefanie, Steffi, Stevie.* (Famous Geminis: Steffi Graf, tennis champion; Stevie Nicks, singer/musician)

Tamah (tah-MAH) Hebrew: Marvel. In full verbal swing, highly intelligent Geminis are a wonder to behold—thinking, gesturing, and speaking, all at breakneck speeds. Variation: *Tama.*

Tamasine (tah-mah-SEEN) English: Twin. The sign of Gemini is symbolized by the Twins. Variations: *Tamasin, Tamsin, Tamsyn.*

Tasmine (TAZ-min) English: Twin. The sign of Gemini is represented by the Twins. Variation: *Tasmin.*

Tate (TAYT) Scandinavian: Bubbly. *Tate* is a fitting choice for ebullient, energetic, and vivacious Gemini.

Thelma (THELL-mah) Greek: Willful. Free spirited and exuberant, Geminis detest rules and regulations of any kind, often rebelling against things with which they disagree. Variation: *Telma.*

Thomasina (tom-ah-SEEN-ah) English: Twin. The Twins symbolize the sign of Gemini. Variations: *Tamasin, Tamasine, Tamsin, Tamsyn, Thomasa, Thomasine, Toma, Tommi.*

Tonya (TOHN-yah) Russian: Priceless. With their exuberant spirits and tremendous talents, Geminis impress everyone they meet with their irreplaceable and invaluable abilities.

Tosia (TOH-shuh) Polish: Inestimable. Geminis' boundless energy, exceptional communication powers, and keen intelligence earn them great respect and high esteem.

Twyla (TWYE-lah) English: Meaning unknown, but possibly, "two threads woven together." *Twyla* evokes the imagery of the Twins, who symbolize the union of two halves into a whole. Variation: *Twila.*

Uda (OO-dah) English: Wealthy. Geminis possess an abundance of charm, energy, and talent. Variations: *Udele, Udella, Udelle.*

Una (OO-nah) Latin: The one. Born under the sign of the Twins, Geminis often spend their lives searching for the person who will complete them and make them whole—their soul mate and other "Twin." Variations: *Ona, Oona.*

Unity (YOO-nih-tee) English: Oneness. This unique choice suggests the Greek imagery of the original Gemini Twins, Castor and Pollux, who were so devoted to each other that the god Zeus joined them eternally as the Gemini constellation. Variation: *Unita.*

Vanessa (vah-NESS-ah) Greek: Butterflies. This classic name is suitable for a girl born under Gemini, the sign associated with butterflies. Variations: *Vanesa, Vanesse, Vannessa, Venesa, Venesso, Nessa, Nessi, Nessie.*

Veronica (ver-RON-ni-kah) Latin: True face. *Veronica* reflects Gemini's tendency to show an outer persona that hides their inner emotions. Variations: *Verona, Veronika, Veronike, Ronnie.*

Wanda (WAHN-dah) Old German: Wanderer. Geminis, who crave constant change, are always on the move, looking for new places, people, or experiences that will stimulate their renowned intellects. Variations: *Wandie, Wandis, Wonda, Wonnda.*

Waneta (wah-NAY-tah) Native American: One who pushes forward. Though Geminis tend to flit from one cause to another, they constantly strive to reach a final goal. Variation: *Wanneta.*

Wendy (WEN-dee) Old German: She who wanders. Highly intelligent and bursting with energy, Geminis often wander from one thing to the next in order to keep their minds busy. Variations: *Wende, Wendeline, Wendelle, Wendi, Wendye.*

Winola (win-OHL-ah) German: Enchanting friend. Witty, exuberant, charismatic, vivacious, and charming, Geminis make wonderful companions who are a joy to be around.

Xanthe (ZAN-thah) Greek: Yellow. Bright yellow is the color assigned to Gemini. Variations: *Xantha, Xanthia.*

Yuriko (yoo-REE-koh) Japanese: Lily child. The flowers affiliated with the sign of Gemini are the lavender and the lily of the valley.

Zephira (ze-FEER-ah) Greek: Westerly wind. Versatile Gemini is one of the three Air signs of the zodiac. Variations: *Zefir, Zephyr, Zephyra.*

Zoe (ZOH or ZOH-ee) Greek: Life. Geminis are renowned for their natural exuberance, eternal optimism, and inspiring joie de vivre. Variation: *Zoë.*

Names for Gemini Boys

Abel (AY-bel) Hebrew: Vaporlike. This traditional name is appropriate for ephemeral and ever-changing Gemini. Variation: *Abele*.

Achates (ah-KAY-teez) Greek: Agate. The agate is the birthstone of Gemini.

Acher (AH-ker) Hebrew: Other. *Acher* connotes Gemini's eternal search for his soul mate—his "Twin" who makes him complete. Variation: *Asher*.

Adamya (ah-DAHM-yah) Hindu: Difficult and formidable. Highly opinionated Geminis can become resistant and unyielding when their ideas are challenged.

Akela (AH-kay-lah) Hawaiian: Lucky. Whimsical and winsome Gemini tends to be greeted by good fortune. Variation: *Asera*.

Amycus (AM-ih-kus) Greek: Friendly. Outgoing and vivacious, Geminis usually are popular and enjoy being surrounded by groups of people.

Ananya (ah-NAHN-yah) Hindu: Unique. Never afraid to follow the beat of a different drummer, Geminis express distinct styles and viewpoints.

Anoki (ah-NOH-kee) Native American: Actor. Endowed with outstanding communication skills, many Geminis pursue successful careers in the performing arts.

Apara (ah-PAH-rah) African/Nigerian: Child that comes and goes. Geminis, who find it challenging to occupy their busy minds, often wander from one place to another in search of new challenges and adventures.

Aquilo (ah-KWIH-loh) Latin: The north wind. Whimsical Gemini is one of the three Air signs of the zodiac. (The other two are Libra and Aquarius.)

Astraeus (as-TRAY-us) Greek: Starry one. In Greek mythology, *Astraeus* was the father of the Winds. *Astraeus* suggests Gemini's element of Air, as well as the charismatic, starlike quality evident in many of the sign's children. Variation: *Astreus*.

Ata (AH-tah) African/Ghanian: Twin. The sign of Gemini is symbolized by the Twins.

Awan (AH-wahn) Native American: Somebody. Possessing the most unique and distinct personalities of all the children in the zodiac, Geminis always stand out in social situations.

Balder (BAHL-der) Old Norse: White god. In Norse mythology, the wisest and kindest of the Norse gods is *Balder*, who was born under the sign of Gemini. Variations: *Baldur, Daudier*.

Berdy (BAYR-dee) Russian: Very smart. Gemini is the sign of great intellectual energy.

Blaze (BLAYZ) Latin: One who stammers. *Blaze* connotes Gemini's trouble in getting his mouth to keep up with his rapidly racing thoughts. Variations: *Blaise, Blase, Blayze*. (Famous Gemini: Blaise Pascal, French mathematician and philosopher)

Botan (BOH-tan) Japanese: Peony. In Japan, the peony is the flower associated with the month of June. *Botan* is a fitting choice for a June-born Gemini boy.

Bowie (BOO-ee; BOH-ee) Scottish: Yellow-haired. The special color associated with the sign of Gemini is yellow, making *Bowie* an apt name for a blond Gemini boy. Variations: *Bow, Bowen, Boyd*.

Brady (BRAY-dee) Irish: High-spirited. *Brady* is a suitable choice for ebullient, vivacious, and upbeat Gemini. Variation: *Brad*.

Brock (BRAHK) Old English: To badger. Keenly intelligent and endowed with excellent communication skills, Geminis often delight in verbal sparring matches that allow them to demonstrate their vast knowledge.

Burr (BURR) Scandinavian: Youthful. Irrepressible Geminis are perennially young at heart.

Byrd (BIRD) English: Like a bird. The animals affiliated with the sign of Gemini are butterflies and brilliantly colored birds.

Camey (KAM-ee) Irish: Champion. Geminis' remarkable intellect and abundant energy assures them success in any endeavor they choose to pursue. Variation: *Camy*.

Campbell (KAM-bull) Irish: Mouth askew. This traditional name is a suitable choice for Gemini, who has a penchant for talking—and expressing unusual viewpoints. Variations: *Cam*, *Camp*.

Castor (KASS-tur) Greek: Beaver. *Castor* was one of the original Twins who, along with his brother Pollux, creates the Gemini constellation.

Chal (KAL) Gypsy: Boy. Born under the sign of perpetual youth, Geminis tend to retain a playful, exuberant, and mischievous streak throughout their lives.

Chen (CHEN) Chinese: Tremendous. *Chen* suggests the remarkable abundance of energy, intelligence, and enthusiasm possessed by Gemini.

Chenzira (chen-ZEE-rah) African/Zimbabwean: Born while traveling. From the moment they leave the womb, Geminis are restless, energetic, and full of eternal wanderlust.

Chesmu (CHESS-moo) Native American: Abrasive. Some people may be irritated by Gemini's opinionated demeanor and tendency to show off his vast stores of knowledge.

Chumo (CHOO-moh) Spanish: Twin. The sign of Gemini is represented by the Twins.

Cibor (sih-BORR) Hebrew: Strong. Renowned for their formidable intelligence, Geminis gain enormous confidence and strength through feeling that they are the intellectual masters of their worlds.

Clovis (KLOH-viss) German: Famous fighter. Though naturally happy-go-lucky and ebullient, Geminis can become powerful forces to be reckoned with if they are crossed or challenged.

Cowan (KOH-an or KOW-an) Irish: Twin. This name is an apt choice for a boy born under Gemini, the sign symbolized by the Twins.

Danior (DAH-nee-or) English Gypsy: Born with teeth. *Danior* suggests Geminis' well-known love of talking, which they combine with their keen intelligence to become gifted public speakers.

Darby (DAHR-bee) Irish: Free man. Carefree Geminis have a distaste for rules and routines of any kind. Variations: *Darbee, Derby*.

David (DAY-vid) Hebrew: Beloved one. Geminis are adored by their loved ones for their inspiring exuberance, eternal optimism, and dynamic intelligence. Variations: *Dave, Davie, Davy*.

Dempsey (DEMP-see) Irish: Proud. The keen intelligence of Geminis often lends them a feeling of confident superiority.

Didier (dee-DYAY) French: Desire. Born under the sign of the Twins, Geminis have a deep and constant longing to find their missing half in order to feel complete.

Doherty (DOW-ur-tee) Irish: Wicked. Perennially youthful, Geminis often retain a penchant for mischief. Variation: *Dougherty*.

Doran (DOHR-an) Irish: Stranger. Because they devote so much energy to improving their keen minds, many Geminis feel uncomfortable with their inner emotions, often remaining unsure of their "real" selves. Variations: *Doron, Dorran, Dorren*.

Douglas (DUG-liss) English: Dark water. This classic name suggests the deep mystery that Gemini's inner persona presents to others—and perhaps even to himself. Variation: *Douglass*.

Duman (DOO-mahn) Turkish: Misty. This unique name suggests the ephemeral nature of ever-changing and evasive Geminis.

Dusan (DOO-shahn) Czechoslovakian: Spirit; soul. Geminis are among the most exuberant, upbeat, and high-spirited children of the zodiac. Variations: *Dusa, Dusanek*.

Dwyer (DWY-ur) Irish: Dark wisdom. *Dwyer* connotes Geminis' keen intelligence, which they often use to shield their inner personas from public view.

Edzard (EDD-zahrd; AYD-zahr) Scandinavian: Strong edge. Geminis often use their exceptional verbal skills and stores of knowledge to gain an edge over others in their careers or relationships.

Egil (EH-gl) Scandinavian: Edge. Geminis' sharp wit and keen insight offers them an advantage in social interactions.

Ellery (EL-luhr-ee) Greek: One who speaks cheerfully. Geminis are renowned for both their exuberant natures and their considerable—and often exercised—verbal communication skills. Variations: *Ellary, Ellerey.*

Elvet (ELL-vet) English: Stream of swans. The original Gemini twins, Castor and Pollux, were born to the queen of Sparta after she was seduced by Zeus, who disguised himself as a large swan.

Elvis (EHL-vis) Scandinavian: One who knows all. Born under the sign of keen intellect, Geminis often devote themselves to gaining knowledge about a vast array of subjects.

Fareed (fah-REED) Hindu: Unique. Displaying distinct ideas and styles, Geminis stand out as extremely individualistic. Variation: *Farid.*

Fekitoa (fay-kee-TOH-ah) Polynesian: Two men gather. *Fekitoa* suggests the Twins who make up the symbol of the sign of Gemini.

Filbert (FILL-burt) English: Hazelnut; smart. The sign of Gemini governs all nut-bearing trees.

Flavian (FLAH-vee-an; FLAY-vee-an) Latin: Yellow hair. The color yellow is strongly associated with the sign of Gemini, making *Flavian* an apt choice for a blond Gemini boy. Variations: *Flavien, Flavio.*

Fremont (FREE-mont) Old German: He who guards his freedom. Bohemian and free spirited by nature, Geminis refuse to be confined by the restrictions of others. Variations: *Free, Freeman, Monty.*

Gage (GAYJ) Old French: Token of defiance. Breezy and care-free, Geminis abhor—and often rebel against—rules and routines. Variation: *Gaige*.

Gaylord (GAY-lord) French: Lively. Geminis are naturally exuberant, optimistic, and high spirited. Variation: Gaelord.

Gemini (GEM-in-eye) Latin: Twins. This name is an obvious choice for a boy born under Gemini, the sign of the Twins.

Gershom (GUR-shem) Hebrew: Sojourner. In order to satisfy their need for constant mental stimulation, many Geminis are drawn to travel and the challenges, experiences, and adventures it brings. Variation: *Gerson.*

Guthrie (GUHTH-ree) Irish: Place where the wind blows. Gemini, one of the three Air signs of the zodiac, presents an ever-changing force. Variation: *Guthrey*.

Hahnee (HAH-nee) Native American: Beggar. *Hahnee* suggests Gemini's tendency to feed on others' knowledge, always begging for more answers to their countless and constant questions.

Hardy (HAHR-dee) Old German: Audacious. Keenly intelligent Geminis are prone to showing off their vast stores of knowledge, often in order to gain an edge in business or relationships.

Hartman (HAHRT-min) German: Hard man. Geminis are renowned for their opinionated natures and refusal to adhere to the rules and regulations imposed on them by others.

Haslett (HAYZ-let) English: Land of hazel trees. The sign of Gemini governs all nut-bearing trees.

Hassel (HAHS-el) Teutonic: One who lives by a hazel tree. Nut-bearing trees are closely affiliated with the sign of Gemini. Variations: *Hassall, Hassell*.

Hernando (hur-NAHN-doh) Spanish: Brave traveler. Constantly craving new experiences, Geminis often find that travel offers the adventures and mental stimulations they desperately seek.

Hobart (HOH-bahrt) Old German: Highly brilliant. Born under the sign of high intelligence, many Geminis value the power of the mind rather than the heart and soul. Variations: *Hobard, Hobie*.

Hod (HOHD) Hebrew: Splendid. Most people find vivacious, witty, charismatic, and keenly intelligent Geminis to be delightful companions.

Hogan (HOH-gan) Irish: Youthful. Exuberant and irrepressible, Geminis are perennially young at heart.

Hugh (HEW) Old English: Spirited one. Geminis are among the most outgoing, upbeat, energetic, and enthusiastic children of the zodiac. Variations: *Hewett, Hewitt, Huey, Hugo, Ugo*.

Idris (ID-riss) Welsh: Impulsive. *Idris* is an appropriate choice for a boy born under Gemini, the sign of quicksilver changeability.

Ilom (EE-lohm) African/Nigerian: "I have enemies." Gemini's highly opinionated nature and tendency to show off his knowledge may lead others to regard him as arrogant and shallow.

Inar (EE-nahr) English: Individual. Confident of his ideas and expressive in his style, Gemini often appears unique and distinct.

Inteus (ee-TAY-oos) Native American: Unashamed. With their carefree and breezy approach to life, Geminis often are not concerned with the opinions of others or the rules society imposes.

Janus (JAY-nus) Latin: Gate. In Roman mythology, *Janus* was the god of beginnings and endings, depicted as having two faces.

This name suggests the duality associated with Gemini, the sign of the Twins.

Jareb (JAYR-eb) Hebrew: He struggles. Born under the sign of the Twins, Gemini often goes through life struggling to reconcile the two opposing sides of his nature. Variations: *Jarib, Yariv.*

Jay (JAY) Latin: Blue jay; one who chatters like the bluejay. *Jay* suggests not only Gemini's affiliation with brightly colored birds, but also his affinity for speaking. Variations: *Jae, Jai, Jaye, Jeye.*

Jett (JET) English: Airplane. This unusual name, an apt choice for a Gemini boy, connotes not only the sign's Air element, but also the attraction to travel possessed by most Geminis.

John (JON) Hebrew: God's precious gift. Geminis dazzle their loved ones with their inspiring exuberance, eternal optimism, and dynamic intelligence. Variations: *Ian, Iannis, Jack, Jan, Jean, Johann, Johannes, Johnny, Jon, Juan, Sean.* (Famous Geminis: Ian Fleming, writer; John F. Kennedy, thirty-fifth president of the United States; Johnny Depp, actor; John Goodman, actor; John Wayne, actor; Johnny Paycheck, country-and-western artist; Johnny Weissmuller, actor/original Tarzan)

Kadar (KAH-dahr) Arabic: Imposing presence. The formidable intellect possessed by all Geminis is their greatest weapon.

Kaliq (KAH-leek) Arabic: Creative. Because all Geminis are endowed with remarkable verbal skills, many embark upon highly successful careers as writers, singers, and songwriters.

Kasim (kah-SEEM) Arabic: Divided. Geminis, born under the sign of perpetual duality, encompass both the best and worst of human qualities. Variation: *Kaseem.*

Kennedy (KEN-a-dee) Irish: Helmet head. *Kennedy*, an increasingly popular name in this country, suggests the often hardheaded nature possessed by Geminis. Variations: *Cinneide, Cinneidid, Cinneidigh.*

Kerey (KEH-ree) English Gypsy: Homeward bound. Tending toward wanderlust, Geminis constantly search for that part of themselves that feels comfortable and complete. Variations: *Keir, Keri.*

Kermit (KUR-mit) Irish: He who is free. Carefree and breezy Geminis have a strong dislike for restrictive rules and regulations. Variations: *Kermie, Kermy.*

Kilian (KIL-ee-an) Irish: Problems. Due to the two opposing sides of their natures, Geminis often struggle to reconcile their "good" and "bad" sides throughout their lives, often with remarkable results. Variations: *Killian, Killie, Killy.*

Kontar (KOHN-tahr) African/Ghanian: Only child. Exuberant and energetic, Geminis remain forever young and childlike.

Kuzih (KOO-zih) Native American: Fast or skillful talker. Endowed with superb communication skills, Geminis are often drawn to careers that involve public speaking.

Lado (LAH-doh) Arabic: Second-born twin. The sign of Gemini is symbolized by the Twins.

Lamond (lah-MOND) African-American: Lawyer. Endowed with keen intelligence and powerful communication skills, many Geminis are drawn to careers in law. Variations: *La Mond, Lammond.*

Levi (LEE-vye) Hebrew: Joined. *Levi* suggests the imagery of the Twins, who represent the sign of Gemini.

Liu (LEE-oo) African/Nalawi: Voice. Geminis, whose element of Air endows them with exceptional communication skills, make gifted public speakers and singers.

Lorcan (LORR-kan) Irish: Little fierce one. Even as children, Geminis are aggressive, energetic, and headstrong, capable of using their formidable intellects as weapons.

Louis (LEW-iss) Teutonic: Renowned warrior. Although generally good-natured and happy-go-lucky, Gemini is a force to be reckoned with when he is challenged or crossed. Variations: *Lew, Lewis, Lou, Louie, Luigi, Luis*. (Famous Geminis: Lou Gehrig, baseball legend; Louis Gossett, Jr., actor)

Luke (LUKE) Greek: Illuminating. Geminis enjoy educating others with their vast stores of knowledge, and their boundless effervescence often inspires the lives of many. Variations: *Luc, Lucas, Lukas*.

Maas (MAHS) Dutch: Twin. The Twins represent the sign of Gemini.

Mamo (MAH-moh) Hawaiian: Yellow bird. The animals affiliated with the sign of Gemini are butterflies and all brightly colored birds.

Mander (MAHN-der) English Gypsy: From me. Possessing a strong awareness of their ability to influence others, Geminis enjoy being the catalyst in social situations.

Maro (MAH-roh) Japanese: Myself. *Maro* suggests Geminis' need to be the center of attention, which often leads them to pursue careers in the performing arts.

Marshall (MAHR-shil) French: He who cares for horses. Castor, one of the original Gemini twins from Greek mythology, was famed as a tamer of horses.

Masio (MAH-see-oh) African-American: Twin. *Masio* is a suitable name for a boy born under the sign of Gemini, the sign of the Twins. Variation: *Macio*.

Maslin (MAHS-lin) Old French: Little twin. The Twins symbolize the sign of Gemini.

Methodios (may-THOH-dee-ohs) Greek: Fellow traveler. Geminis, constantly in search of excitement and mental stimulation, are often drawn to the adventures of travel.

Narcissus (nahr-SIS-sus) Greek: Filled with self-love; also the yellow daffodil flower. Those born under the sign of Gemini, which is strongly associated with the color yellow, may have a tendency to place their own needs over those of others. Variations: *Narcis, Narcisco, Narcisse*.

Nestor (NESS-tir) Greek: Traveler. Geminis, who crave constant mental stimulation, are often drawn to the new experiences and adventure offered by travel.

Odion (OH-dee-ohn) African/Nigerian: First of twins. Gemini is the sign of the Twins.

Orban (OR-ben) Hungarian: Urbanite. Strongly attracted to excitement and adventure, Geminis often choose to live in or near large cities.

Oz (AHZ) Hebrew: Power. Gemini's formidable intellect is his most dangerous and potent weapon.

Peretz (per-RETZ) Hebrew: Burst forward. *Peretz* connotes the abundant energy and vitality that Geminis possess. Variations: *Perez, Pharez*.

Pili (PEE-lee) African/Swahili: Second-born son. Symbolized by the Twins, Gemini oversees both the first- and second-born twins equally.

Pitney (PITT-nee) English: Isle of the headstrong man. Geminis, famous for their strong opinions, tend to rebel against rules and regulations that restrict their independence in any way. Variation: *Pittney*.

Pollux (POL-ux) Greek: Crown. In Greek mythology, *Pollux* was one of the Twins that formed the original Gemini constellation. He was the brother of Castor and immortal son of Zeus. Variations: *Pollack, Polloch, Pollock*.

Raphael (rah-FAY-ell; RAH-fee-ell) Hebrew: God has healed. *Raphael* is the archangel who protects those born under the sign of Gemini. Variation: *Rafe*.

Rider (RYE-der) English: Horseman. Castor, one of the original Gemini twins, was famed in Greek mythology as a horse tamer. Variations: *Ridder, Ryder*.

Riordan (REER-den) Irish: Royal poet. Gifted in all forms of communication, many Geminis gain success for their skillful dexterity with the written word. Variations: *Reardan, Rearden*.

Ripley (RIP-lee) Old English: From the shouter's pasture. Many Geminis, who are endowed with exceptional communication skills, make powerful and influential public speakers. Variations: *Lee, Rip, Ripleigh*.

Rodney (ROD-nee) Old English: Great power. Gemini's greatest weapon is his formidable intellect, which enables him to attain any goal he wholeheartedly pursues. Variations: *Rodnee, Rodnie*.

Samir (sah-MEER) Arabic: Entertainer. Endowed with exceptional communication skills, many Geminis pursue successful careers in the performing arts.

Sivan (SEE-vahn) Hebrew: Born in the ninth month. The ninth month of the Jewish calendar corresponds to the sign of Gemini.

Sorley (SORR-lee) Scandinavian: Summer traveler. Geminis, born under the first of the summer signs, often are drawn to the new people, places, and experiences that travel offers.

Sprague (SPRAYG) Old French: Spirited one. *Sprague* suggests Geminis' exuberance, optimism, energy, and vitality.

Stannard (STAN-urd) English: Hard as stone. Although they are adept at influencing others, Geminis are highly opinionated and refuse to be swayed in their beliefs.

Steele (STEEL) English: Resistant. Geminis, who abhor any rules or regulations that restrict them, possess a decidedly rebellious streak. Variation: *Steel*.

Stig (STEEG) Scandinavian: Wanderer. Inquisitive but easily bored, Geminis often move from one idea to the next in search of new challenges to engage their minds. Variations: *Styge, Stygge*.

Stoddard (STAHD-urd) English: Protector of horses. Castor, one of the original Gemini Twins in Greek mythology, was a famed horse tamer.

Tadi (TAH-dee) Native American: The wind. Ever-changing Gemini is one of the three Air signs of the zodiac. Variation: *Tadewi*.

Tavish (TAH-vish) Scottish: Twin. Represented by the Twins of Greek mythology, Gemini is the sign of perpetual duality. Variations: *Tavis, Tevis*.

Thomas (TAHM-us) Aramaic: Twin. This classic name is a fitting choice for a boy born under Gemini, the sign of the Twins. Variations: *Tam, Tameas, Thom, Thompson, Tomas, Tomaso, Tomcio, Tomelis, Tomsen, Tomson, Tooman, Tuomas*. (Famous Geminis: Tommy Chong, actor/ "Chong" of Cheech and Chong; Thomas Mann, author; Tom Jones, singer)

Todd (TAHD) Middle English: Fox. Like the fox, Geminis are clever, quick thinking, and fast acting. Variation: *Tod*. (Famous Gemini: Todd Bridges, actor)

Tomlin (TAHM-lin) English: Little twin. *Tomlin* is a suitable name for a boy born under Gemini, the sign symbolized by the Twins. Variation: *Tomlinson*.

Twain (twayn) English: Split in two. Geminis often spend their lives struggling to reconcile the two opposing sides of their nature. Variations: *Twaine, Twayn*.

Twyford (TWIFF-ird) English: The place where rivers converge. Born under the sign of perpetual duality, Geminis often possess both the best and worst qualities of man.

Ulan (OO-lahn) Arabic: Firstborn twin. This unusual name is ideal for a child born under Gemini, the sign of the Twins.

Uzoma (oo-ZOH-mah) African/Nigerian: Born during a trip. Restless, thrill seeking, and possessing eternal wanderlust, Geminis are drawn to travel from the moment they leave the womb.

Waban (wah-BAHN) Native American: Easterly breeze. Born under an Air sign, Geminis possess a breezy and carefree approach to life.

Walkara (wahl-KAHR-ah) Native American: Yellow. Bright yellow is the color assigned to the sign of Gemini. Variation: *Wakara*.

Wendell (WEN-del) German: Wanderer. Geminis, who crave constant change, are often drawn to travel. Variations: *Wendel, Wendle*.

Wildon (WILL-den) Old English: From the wild valley. *Wildon* connotes Geminis' prominent qualities of enthusiasm, vitality, unpredictability, and restlessness.

Wiley (WHY-lee) Old English: Charming. Exuberant, upbeat, witty, and charismatic, Geminis make entertaining and delightful companions. Variations: *Wye, Wylie*.

Yamal (yah-MAHL) Hindu: One of twins. Symbolized by the Twins, Gemini is the sign of perpetual duality.

Zesiro (zeh-SEE-roh) African/Ugandan: Elder twin. *Zesiro* is an appropriate name for a boy born under Gemini, the sign of the Twins.

Famous Geminis

05-22-1813	Richard Wagner	05-26-1907	John Wayne
05-22-1859	Sir Arthur Conan Doyle	05-26-1908	Robert Morley
05-22-1907	Laurence Olivier	05-26-1913	Peter Cushing
05-22-1938	Richard Benjamin	05-26-1920	Peggy Lee
05-22-1938	Susan Strasberg	05-26-1923	James Arness
05-22-1941	Paul Winfield	05-26-1939	Brent Musburger
05-21-1970	Naomi Campbell	05-26-1948	Stevie Nicks
05-23-1910	Scatman Crothers	05-26-1949	Philip Michael Thomas
05-23-1920	Helen O'Connell	05-26-1949	Hank Williams, Jr.
05-23-1928	Rosemary Clooney	05-26-1951	Sally Ride
05-23-1933	Joan Collins	05-27-1837	Wild Bill Hickock
05-23-1952	Marvin Hagler	05-27-1878	Isadora Duncan
05-24-1938	Tommy Chong	05-27-1894	Dashiell Hammett
05-24-1941	Bob Dylan	05-27-1911	Hubert H. Humphrey
05-24-1943	Gary Burghoff	05-27-1911	Vincent Price
05-24-1944	Patti LaBelle	05-27-1922	Christopher Lee
05-24-1945	Priscilla Presley	05-27-1923	Henry Kissinger
05-24-1955	Rosanne Cash	05-27-1936	Louis Gossett, Jr.
05-24-1963	Joe Dumars	05-27-1965	Todd Bridges
05-25-1803	Ralph Waldo Emerson	05-28-1888	Jim Thorpe
05-25-1918	Claude Akins	05-28-1908	Ian Fleming
05-25-1925	Jeanne Crain	05-28-1931	Carroll Baker
05-25-1926	Miles Davis	05-28-1944	Gladys Knight
05-25-1927	Robert Ludlum	05-29-1736	Patrick Henry
05-25-1929	Beverly Sills	05-29-1903	Bob Hope
05-25-1943	Leslie Uggams	05-29-1917	John F. Kennedy
05-25-1955	Connie Sellecca	05-29-1932	Paul Erlich
05-26-1886	Al Jolson	05-29-1939	Al Unser

05-29-1956	LaToya Jackson	06-04-1928	Dr. Ruth Westheimer
05-29-1958	Annette Bening	06-04-1936	Bruce Dern
05-29-1961	Melissa Etheridge	06-04-1971	Noah Wyle
05-30-1908	Mel Blanc	06-05-1928	Tony Richardson
05-30-1909	Benny Goodman	06-05-1934	Bill Moyers
05-30-1936	Keir Dullea	06-05-1949	Ken Follett
05-30-1939	Michael J. Pollard	06-05-1971	Marky Mark
05-30-1964	Wynonna Judd	06-06-1875	Thomas Mann
05-31-1819	Walt Whitman	06-06-1939	Gary U.S. Bonds
05-31-1894	Fred Allen	06-06-1955	Sandra Bernhard
05-31-1898	Norman Vincent Peale	06-06-1956	Bjorn Borg
05-31-1908	Don Ameche	06-07-1848	Paul Gauguin
05-31-1922	Denholm Elliott	06-07-1909	Jessica Tandy
05-31-1930	Clint Eastwood	06-07-1940	Tom Jones
05-31-1938	Peter Yarrow	06-07-1952	Liam Neeson
05-31-1941	Johnny Paycheck	06-07-1958	The Artist Formerly
05-31-1943	Sharon Gless		Known As Prince
05-31-1943	Joe Namath	06-07-1981	Larisa Oleynik
05-31-1950	Gregory Harrison	06-08-1867	Frank Lloyd Wright
05-31-1961	Lea Thompson	06-08-1918	Robert Preston
05-31-1965	Brooke Shields	06-08-1925	Barbara Bush
06-01-1921	Nelson Riddle	06-08-1929	Jerry Stiller
06-01-1926	Andy Griffith	06-08-1933	Joan Rivers
06-01-1926	Marilyn Monroe	06-08-1940	Nancy Sinatra
06-01-1930	Edward Woodward	06-08-1944	Boz Scaggs
06-01-1934	Pat Boone	06-09-1892	Cole Porter
06-01-1937	Morgan Freeman	06-09-1910	Robert Cummings
06-01-1940	Rene Auberjonois	06-09-1934	Jackie Mason
06-01-1974	Alanis Morissette	06-09-1940	Dick Vitale
06-02-1890	Hedda Hopper	06-09-1961	Michael J. Fox
06-02-1904	Johnny Weissmuller	06-09-1963	Johnny Depp
06-02-1937	Sally Kellerman	06-09-1981	Natalie Portman
06-02-1941	Stacy Keach	06-10-1915	Saul Bellow
06-02-1944	Marvin Hamlisch	06-10-1922	Judy Garland
06-02-1948	Jerry Mathers	06-10-1928	Maurice Sendak
06-03-1808	Jefferson Davis	06-10-1933	F. Lee Bailey
06-03-1906	Josephine Baker	06-10-1966	Elizabeth Hurley
06-03-1915	Leo Gorcey	06-10-1982	Tara Lipinski
06-03-1925	Tony Curtis	06-11-1910	Jacques Cousteau
06-03-1926	Colleen Dewhurst	06-11-1935	Gene Wilder
06-03-1926	Allen Ginsberg	06-11-1936	Chad Everett
06-03-1942	Curtis Mayfield	06-11-1945	Adrienne Barbeau
06-04-1919	Robert Merrill	06-11-1956	Joe Montana
06-04-1922	Gene Barry	06-12-1924	George Bush
06-04-1924	Dennis Weaver	06-12-1928	Vic Damone

06-12-1929	Anne Frank
06-12-1932	Jim Nabors
06-12-1941	Chick Corea
06-13-1865	William Butler Yeats
06-13-1913	Ralph Edwards
06-13-1926	Paul Lynde
06-13-1935	Christo
06-13-1943	Malcolm McDowell
06-13-1951	Richard Thomas
06-13-1953	Tim Allen
06-13-1962	Ally Sheedy
06-13-1969	Jamie Walters
06-13-1986	Mary-Kate and Ashley Olsen
06-14-1909	Burl Ives
06-14-1925	Pierre Salinger
06-14-1931	Marla Gibbs
06-14-1933	Jerzy Kosinski
06-14-1961	Boy George
06-14-1969	Steffi Graf
06-15-1921	Erroll Garner
06-15-1932	Mario Cuomo
06-15-1937	Waylon Jennings
06-15-1954	Jim Belushi
06-15-1963	Helen Hunt
06-15-1964	Courteney Cox
06-16-1890	Stan Laurel
06-16-1937	Erich Segal
06-16-1943	Joan van Ark
06-16-1971	Tupac Shakur
06-17-1882	Igor Stravinsky
06-17-1904	Ralph Bellamy
06-17-1917	Dean Martin
06-17-1943	Newt Gingrich
06-17-1946	Barry Manilow
06-17-1951	Joe Piscopo
06-18-1898	M. C. Escher
06-18-1903	Jeanette MacDonald
06-18-1908	Bud Collyer
06-18-1910	E. G. Marshall
06-18-1942	Roger Ebert
06-18-1942	Paul McCartney
06-18-1952	Carol Kane
06-18-1952	Isabella Rossellini
06-19-1623	Blaise Pascal
06-19-1897	Moe Howard
06-19-1902	Guy Lombardo
06-19-1903	Lou Gehrig
06-19-1917	Pat Buttram
06-19-1919	Pauline Kael
06-19-1934	Gena Rowlands
06-19-1948	Phylicia Rashad
06-19-1954	Kathleen Turner
06-19-1962	Paula Abdul
06-20-1924	Chet Atkins
06-20-1931	Martin Landau
06-20-1933	Danny Aiello
06-20-1942	Brian Wilson
06-20-1945	Anne Murray
06-20-1949	Lionel Richie
06-20-1952	John Goodman
06-20-1953	Cyndi Lauper
06-21-1905	Jean-Paul Sartre
06-21-1921	Jane Russell
06-21-1925	Maureen Stapleton
06-21-1940	Mariette Hartley
06-21-1947	Meredith Baxter
06-21-1947	Michael Gross
06-21-1967	Nicole Kidman
06-21-1973	Juliette Lewis

CANCER
(June 22–July 23)

GLYPH: ♋
SYMBOL: The Crab
POLARITY: Feminine
QUALITY: Cardinal
ELEMENT: Water
RULING PLANET: Moon
BIRTHSTONE: Pearl
SPECIAL COLORS: Violets, blue-greens, and silver
FLOWERS: Larkspur and acanthus
METAL: Silver
ANIMALS: Crab and other crustaceans
MOST LIKEABLE TRAITS: Devotion to family and friends, loyalty, and compassion

♋

Like the Crab that symbolizes their sign, Cancers possess a complex dual nature—hard and crusty on the surface, fragile and vulnerable beneath. This daunting combination can be a special challenge to parents of Cancer children.

General Qualities

Cancers frequently present a tough, defensive front to the world, with which they often have an adversarial relationship. Cancer's hidden but delicate sensibilities are easily offended, and the world offers just too many opportunities for hurt feelings. With strangers especially, Cancers may appear cold, withdrawn, moody, and sharp-tongued. Quick to snap when they feel threatened or hurt, Cancers are also fierce defenders of their personal home turf, striking fast and wounding deeply when challenged. They are equally adept at nursing their wounds and tenaciously regrouping for the next assault. Like the Crab, Cancers are resilient survivors, equally at home on firm land or shifting waters.

Beneath their defensive shells, however, Cancers are a web of complicated and intense feelings. The first of the emotional Water signs, with a strongly Feminine aspect, Cancer is the only sign ruled by the Moon. Its powerful and mysterious influence intensifies Cancer's deeply emotional nature.

Cancer children are keenly sensitive—indeed, often oversensitive—to the slightest hurts life throws their way. This extreme vulnerability to the vagaries of the world frequently leaves Cancers captives of their feelings, and they may try to shut out the world as much as possible. Early in life, most Cancers decide that home is the best and safest place to be.

Home

More than any other sign of the zodiac, home and family are where Cancer's heart lies. Cancers are rarely the adventurers, explorers, or innovators of the zodiac. Instead, Cancers are the keepers of the home fires. Only in the security of home and in the embrace of family can Cancers feel happiest and safest, and they never stray far from home for most of their lives.

As the zodiac's quintessential homebodies, Cancers appreciate—indeed, need—a warm, stable, and more traditional home and family life than do other signs of the zodiac. In fact, Cancers' deep need for stability and security is often why they have problems with the "real" world and head for home at the first sign of trouble. Cancers believe that change of any kind is a direct threat to their happiness and well-being. They especially don't like surprises at home—the one place they expect to always remain the same—and just rearranging the furniture in their rooms may cause them alarm. Cancers especially need to be prepared long and well for major life changes, such as a new sibling, a move to another town, or the first day of kindergarten.

Parents can assuage much of Cancer's fear of change and the outside world by providing their child with a safe and comfortable "nest" within the home. A room of one's own is especially important to Cancers, who return to these safe harbors again and again for rest and renewal. Paint their rooms in the soothing blues, violets, and greens of the sea, for which Cancers have such an affinity.

Within a stable and loving home, Cancers are at their absolute best. The sign of fertility and reproduction, Cancer makes its children wildly passionate about family life. Whether boy or girl, they possess many of the qualities of the archetypical Great Mother. They are deeply loving and loyal champions of their family and friends, consummately protective and nurturing of those they care about. Even as young children, Cancers frequently put the needs of family and friends before their own, often worrying more about others than they do about themselves. This tendency to be more concerned about others is one of Cancer's most admirable qualities—and Cancer children often grow up to be outstanding teachers, social workers, and political activists. But unchecked, this tendency can backfire on them later in life. Putting their own needs last may cause Cancers to neglect their health, lose out on a plum job opportunity, or simply miss much of the fun that life has to offer.

Cancer children are emotionally and physically demonstrative in their love for family and friends. They freely and frequently offer up their affection in eloquent words and gestures. Cancers are adept at anticipating people's needs and understanding how others feel, and they also possess an innate ability to perceive the hidden agendas beneath the everyday surface of things. This innate awareness is heightened by the influence of the Moon, which endows Cancers with various intuitive gifts and uncanny powers of observation. In later life, many Cancers display remarkable psychic abilities.

Because they are so "other" directed, Cancers are especially sensitive to subtle changes in the behavior and emotions of those around them, particularly in the home. They are quick to read body language and vocal cues for signs of trouble. And since maintaining a peaceful status quo at any price is critical to their sense of well-being, Cancers will go to great lengths to try to "fix" any and all situations. They are dedicated peacekeepers in the pursuit of a stable homefront, even subjugating their own needs to keep the peace.

Cancer is also the sign of procreation and nurturing. Just as Cancers are natural peacekeepers, they are also are instinctive caretakers. Indeed, an alternate interpretation of the glyph, or written symbol, associated with the sign of Cancer—♋—which is commonly thought to represent a crab's pincers, is that it illustrates the female breasts, perennial symbols of nourishment and the maternal instinct.

Whether boy or girl, Cancers do seem to relish having some-one to care for. The same sense of security and belonging that Cancers experience in being loved and cared for by family is intensified when Cancers themselves become the caretakers. They are natural parents and eager caregivers, and they need regular outlets early on for their nurturing instincts, or they may try to "mother" the people around them—sometimes in inap-propriate and annoying ways.

Assuming the role of "parent" too soon and too intensely can also trigger Cancer's innate tendency to sacrifice self for the sake of others. And Cancer children, who are particularly at risk for becoming "old" before their time, need to enjoy the carefree aspects of childhood as long as possible.

Providing Cancer children with the responsibility of a family pet satisfies the young Cancer's need to care for someone. A turtle—another sensitive but sturdy shell-covered animal—is a good choice for a first pet.

The downside to Cancers' deep reserves of love, loyalty, and nurturing instincts is their equally ardent demand for constant love and attention in return. They repeatedly look for reassur-ances that they are number one in the hearts of their families and friends. In the absence of that reassurance, Cancers can turn the tiniest of slights, imagined or real, into a mountain of hurt feelings. Rather than talk about their hurt feelings, Cancers pre-fer to withdraw into their shells, scuttle away to a dark corner, and sulk. Cancers can hold on to their darker feelings with as much tenacity as their more loving ones.

School and Play

Ideally, Cancers fare better in small schools and classrooms where they can have a closer, one-on-one relationship with teachers. But being great survivors, Cancers also adapt quickly to larger schools by forming strong subgroups of close friends and favorite teachers who provide the safe "family" feelings that Cancers crave. In a rocky school environment, Cancers often show their unhappiness through sudden poor grades or minor illnesses, particularly of the stomach, where Cancer is most prone to illness.

In a stable school environment, however, Cancer children usually excel, academically and socially. They are renowned for their prodigious memories and keen powers of observation. Those qualities, together with their Moon-related gift of intuition and their eagerness to please others, serve them well. Cancers also love learning, show a great respect for education, and possess a special passion for the classics and history. They often seem able to simply absorb information and make excellent test takers.

Socially, Cancers' great eagerness to please, even at the expense of their own needs, makes them popular with both teachers and classmates. But their equally ardent desire for attention and affection in return can be off-putting to people outside the family. Cancers have to be reminded that people need some private space and room to breathe. Cancers also need to be told that they are worthwhile in their own right, just as they are, and that it's not necessary to make everyone happy all the time. Indeed, one of the hardest social lessons Cancers must learn is that some people are not worth all that loving and pleasing. If they don't learn this lesson, Cancers can get into some serious trouble. These most passionate people pleasers of the zodiac are especially susceptible to peer group pressure, particularly when they are children.

At play, Cancers usually don't enjoy traditional school sports like soccer, softball, basketball, or football. Being a team player is not one of their innate strengths; it's an acquired skill. Cancers try to keep the peace at all costs, and may even attempt to control people and situations mightily to further that aim. That kind of manipulation doesn't work on the playing field (though later in life, the same qualities help Cancers to become outstanding athletic coaches). As young children, Cancers will benefit greatly by being exposed to play groups, scout troops, and other group activities. Team playing is a vital skill for succeeding later in life.

What young Cancers often do excel at are the more solitary sports like track and field, swimming, gymnastics, and figure skating. They also enjoy the one-on-one camaraderie of challenging board games like chess, which especially engages their powers of intuition and observation. At a very young age, Cancers also enjoy building imaginary homes of their own—playhouses, castles, forts, and farms—where they can act out their need to be the ruler of the domain.

Cancer children especially enjoy being alone with their parents, engaged in quiet and sensual pursuits: learning to bake bread in the kitchen; watching a lunar eclipse from the backyard, wrapped in a blanket; strolling the seashore on a perfect July day, searching for shells and sea glass.

The World

The emotional bond between Cancers and their parents is uniquely complex, deep, and passionate. Cancers happily and eagerly choose spending time with family over time with friends.

Indeed, long after other children have struck out for college, jobs, and families of their own, Cancers may still be living contentedly at home. Their lifelong commitment and devotion to parents and siblings is unique among the signs of the zodiac, and is one of Cancer's most charming qualities. But all children need to leave the nest sometime, and Cancers in particular may need a firm nudge out the door and into a world that they sometimes see as cold, dangerous, and unmanageable.

As young adults, Cancers may be frightened by the prospect of living alone for a while. In fact, they may feel an urgent need to create a brand-new family of their own, a place where they can nestle down again and be safe. But Cancers must be particularly cautious about marrying and having a family at too young an age. More than any other sign of the zodiac, Cancers see marriage and family as sacred and eternal obligations. A mistake made early on in that arena of life could haunt Cancers for the rest of their lives.

From infancy to old age, home is the only place where Cancers feel 100 percent safe and alive. Home is the rock-steady base from which they sally forth to meet the world. More importantly, home is the safe harbor to which Cancers retreat again and again, to soothe and restore their sensitive souls.

Assure young Cancers that home, family, love, and attention are always there for them when they need it. But also strongly encourage Cancers to sample what the world has to offer, and to have some fun before they settle down. Young Cancers may get a much-needed dose of independence by spending a college semester abroad, doing volunteer work in the inner city, or interning in the career of their choice on the other side of the country.

Many Cancers do learn to healthfully combine their natural gifts of compassion and understanding with their intense need to connect with others by pursuing outstanding careers in education, the social services, or psychotherapy. The arts also offer Cancers a way to connect with others: This sign is abundantly represented by performers, writers, painters, and designers.

Cancers who learn to hook into the more pragmatic, hard-hitting, and assertive Cardinal qualities of their sign can combine those tougher characteristics with their intuitive skills of observation and become formidable successes in business. Cancer is the sign of the Rockefellers—John *and* Nelson—and many self-styled entrepreneurs.

Despite their many achievements, Cancer children always let feelings rule their lives in one way or another. Indeed, one of

the greatest challenges faced by Cancers' parents is teaching
their children that deep feelings, even good and honorable ones,
aren't necessarily facts, and everything bad that happens in the
world isn't personally directed at them. Cancer children need to
learn early on how to discern which things are worth feeling
deeply about, and which things need to be shrugged off.

When Cancers discover that the world isn't such a bad place
after all, they can come home again to roost, throw down roots
of their own, and become the passionate, loving mates and parents they are destined to be.

Choosing a Name for Your Cancer Child

When choosing a name for your Cancer girl or boy, first think
about the major attributes and symbols associated with the sign.
Cancer is the sign of fertility and procreation: Home and family
are the driving themes of this sign. Cancer is one of three Water
signs, and the only zodiac sign ruled by the Moon. Thus Cancers
have a strong affinity for both the ocean and the night, particularly because the Moon exerts such a strong influence on the
ocean and its tides. Cancer is also associated with the colors of
the sea—deep violets, blues, greens, and blue-greens—*and* with
the color of the Moon—silver. The pearl is the official birthstone
of Cancer, but the sign also governs several gemstones: emer-
alds, moss agates, and rubies. Cancer is a summer sign, encompassing the months of June and July. The larkspur and acanthus
flowers are strongly associated with Cancer, as are all trees rich
in sap. The sign's animal symbol is the Crab, and it also has a
strong association with other shell-covered creatures.

When you choose a name for your child, bear in mind some
of Cancer children's key personal qualities. They are extremely
sensitive and emotional, but often hide this side of themselves
under a gruff exterior. They are wildly passionate about family
and home, deeply loving and committed to parents and siblings.
They often extend these passionate feelings to their friends as
well. Considered the archetypical parents of the zodiac, Cancers
are penultimate defenders of the homefront, eager to nurture,

protect, and preserve the family line. They are deeply compassionate, quick to sense how others are feeling, and eager to offer help. Cancers also have a great love of learning and education, and are drawn to history and antiquity.

For additional inspiration when choosing a name, especially a middle name, for your Cancer child, you may want to consider the names listed in Cancer's two companion Water signs, Pisces and Scorpio.

Names for Cancer Girls

Abra (AH-brah) Hebrew: Mother of many children. Feminine version of *Abraham*. For Cancers, who hold family and ancestry in such high esteem, this beautiful and popular Hebrew name is a marvelous choice. Cancer is also the sign of fertility.

Achala (AH-cha-lah) Hindu: Steady. Cancers are renowned for their unswerving loyalty to family and friends. Variation: *Achalaa*.

Adelpha (ah-DELL-fah) Greek: Caring sister. This name suits a Cancer daughter, who will exhibit kindness and generosity toward any and all of her siblings.

Ae-Cha (ay-CHA) Korean: Loving daughter. Cancers are born with an intense devotion to family, and Cancer children demonstrate eternal respect for their parents.

Ahilya (ah-HIL-yah) Hindu: Compassionate. Deep compassion for those around them is a noted quality of Cancer children.

Aileen (eye-LEEN) Greek: Celestial ray. Popularly called the "Moon Children" of the zodiac, Cancers often have a luminous, otherworldly quality about them. Variations: *Aila, Ailene, Ailey, Aili, Eileen, Elene, Ilene.*

Aisling (ASH-ling) Irish: Dream. Cancers, with their close affinity to the Moon, are comfortable denizens of the night and the world of dreams. Variations: *Aislinn, Ashling, Isleen.*

Alaina (ah-LANE-ah) Greek: Bright or luminous. This name, connoting the luminescent qualities of the Moon, is a good choice for Cancer, the "Moon Child." Variations: *Alayna, Alena, Allayna.*

Alamea (ah-luh-MAY-uh) Hawaiian: Ripe. This name represents the nurturing and abundant nature of Cancer's love. Cancer is also the sign of fertility.

Alea (ah-LEH-ah) Arabic: Honorable. Cancers possess a strong sense of morality, often compromising their own needs in order to make others happy or do the right thing. Variation: *Aleah.*

Alexandra (a-lex-AHN-dra) Greek: One who defends. Cancers are ferocious defenders of their home fronts. Variations: *Aleka, Aleksasha, Aleksi, Alex, Alexa, Alexis.*

Alma (AHL-mah) Latin: Nourishing. This name connotes the natural tendency of Cancer to nurture and care for others.

Althea (al-THEE-ah) Greek: Healer. Acutely sensitive to the wounded feelings of others, Cancers are quick to comfort and soothe. Variations: *Altha, Althaea, Althaia, Altheta, Althia.*

Am (UHM) Vietnamese: Moon-empowered. Cancer is the only sign of the zodiac ruled by the Moon, and its children are keenly aware of its dynamic force.

Amarjaa (am-AR-jah) Hindu: Everlasting. Famous for their steadfast devotion, Cancers believe that love, marriage, family, and friendship are all lifetime commitments.

Ambika (am-BEE-kah) Hindu: God of fertility. This name is well suited to Cancer, the sign affiliated with procreation.

Amica (ah-MEE-cah) Italian: Close friend. Cancers are well known for making sensitive, loyal friends.

Amity (AM-ih-tee) English: Friendship. Cancers bring to friendship the same depth of devotion that they bring to family. Variations: *Ami, Amy, Mitty*.

Amma (AH-mah) Hindu: Mother goddess. Cancer is the sign of fertility and procreation, with its nurturing, strong, even archetypical, Feminine aspect.

Andrea (AN-dree-ah) Greek: Womanly or feminine. This ideal name for Cancer reflects the sign's strongly Feminine aspect. Variations: *Andie, Andra, Andria, Andrine, Ondrea*.

Anthea (an-THEE-ah) Greek: Goddess of blossoms. In Greek mythology, *Anthea* is an alternate name for Hera, the goddess of women and marriage. Cancer is associated with fertility and family life.

Aolani (ow-LAH-nee) Hawaiian: Celestial home. Home is where every true Cancer's heart lies.

Argenta (ar-GENT-ah) Latin: Silver. Silver is the precious metal associated with the sign of Cancer.

Ariana (ar-ee-AN-nah) Welsh: Silver. Silver, the metal associated with the sign of Cancer, is also the color of the Moon, Cancer's ruling planet. Variations: *Arene, Argana, Ariane, Arianie, Arianna*.

Artemis (AR-te-miss) Greek: In Greek mythology, the name of the goddess of the Moon. This interesting name suits a child born in Cancer, the only sign of the zodiac ruled by the Moon.

Atifa (ah-TEEF-ah) Arabic: Sympathetic. Even at a young age, Cancers display an instinctive compassion toward others. Variation: *Atifah*.

Ava (AY-vah) Hebrew: Life. As the sign of fertility and pro-creation, Cancer is known for exhibiting a strong life force. Variations: *Avah, Avia, Aviana, Avis, Aviva.*

Ayda (AY-dah) Arabic: Help. Compassionate Cancer is quick to offer aid when needed.

Badriyyah (bah-DREE-yah) Arabic: Full moon. This unusual name is well suited to Cancer, the only sign of the zodiac ruled by the Moon. Variation: *Budur.*

Beryl (BURL or BEHR-il) Greek: A sea-green-colored jewel. The emerald, one of Cancer's gemstones, is derived from this gem. Variations: *Beryla, Beryle.*

Bhavika (bah-VEE-kah) Hindu: Devoted. Intensely loyal and committed to those they care about, Cancers make committed friends, parents, and spouses.

Billie (BILL-lee) English: Constant protector. Loyal and nurturing, Cancers are quick to come to the aid of those in need. Variations: *Billa, Billee, Billey, Billi, Billy.*

Brigit (BRIJ-it) Gaelic: In Celtic mythology, the Irish goddess of home and fertility. Cancers, born under the sign of fertility, possess an intense devotion to their homes and families. Variations: *Biddy, Bride, Bridget, Bridie.*

Brina (BREE-na) Slavic: Defender. Although they are naturally sensitive and peace-loving, Cancers rise to the occasion when the well-being of anyone they care about is threatened. Variations: *Breena, Brena, Brinna, Bryn, Bryna, Brynne.*

Cala (KAH-lah) Arabic: Castle or fortress. A strong home base is crucial to Cancer's sense of security and well-being.

Calypso (kah-LIP-soh) Greek: Girl in hiding. Cancers are adept at hiding their softer, vulnerable sides, frequently presenting a tough facade to the world.

Candra (KAHN-drah) Latin: Luminescent. This rare and beautiful name suggests the quality of the moon's light.

Cara (KAR-ah) Gaelic: Friend. Possessed with intense loyalty and devotion, Cancers often make ideal, ever-reliable friends. *Cara* is commonly used as a pet name for *Caroline* and *Charlotte*.

Cassandra (kah-SAHN-drah) Greek: Protector. In Greek mythology, *Cassandra* possesses the gift of prophecy. The Moon's strong, Feminine influence in their sign often endows Cancers with remarkable intuitive, even psychic, gifts. Variations: *Cass, Cassie, Casson, Kasandra, Kass, Kassie.*

Chandra (CHAHN-drah) Hindu: Moonlike. This beautiful name is ideal for a baby girl born in Cancer, the only sign of the zodiac ruled by the Moon. Variations: *Chandaa, Chandrakanta.*

Channary (CHAN-nah-ree) Cambodian: Moon-faced girl. This unique name is suitable for Cancer, a Feminine sign ruled by the Moon.

Chantrea (chan-TREE-ah) Cambodian: Moonlight. Cancer, the only sign of the zodiac ruled by the Moon, often affords individuals a luminescent quality to their bearing.

Chau (CHOW) Vietnamese: Pearl. The pearl, a precious gem that resembles the Moon, is Cancer's birthstone.

Chava (HA-vah) Hebrew: Life. This name is appropriate for a girl born under Cancer, the sign of fertility and procreation. Variations: *Chabah, Chaya, Eva, Hava.*

Cherish (CHER-ish) English: To cherish. Cancers revere and honor the close ties found in family and friendship.

Chloe (KLOH-ee) Greek: Fresh blooming, fertile. This lovely name suits a daughter born in Cancer, which is the sign of procreation and fertility. Variations: *Clo, Cloe.*

Christine (kriss-TEEN) English: Anointed one. Cancers often view their deep commitment to family as a sacred, preordained role. Variations: *Chrissy, Christa, Christi, Christina, Christy, Kristi, Kristine, Teena, Tina.* (Famous Cancer: Kristi Yamaguchi, figure-skating Olympic medalist)

Clarice (klah-REES) Latin: Bright, clear. This traditional name suggests the light of the Moon, Cancer's ruling orb. Variations: *Chiara, Clara, Clarissa, Clarisse, Klarissa.*

Constance (KON-stans) Latin: Constancy. This wonderful name suits Cancer females, who frequently seek stability in all things. Variations: *Connie, Constanza.*

Cordelia (kor-DEEL-yah) Celtic: Daughter of the sea. In Shakespeare's play, *King Lear*, Cordelia was the king's only faithful daughter. Cancers, who are devoted and loyal children, also have a special affinity for the sea. Variations: *Delia, Lia.*

Cybele (se-BELL) Greek: Mother. Loving, protective, and compassionate, Cancers are the archetypical parents of the zodiac. Variations: *Cybil, Sybil, Sybille, Sibyl.*

Cynthia (SINN-thee-ah) Greek: Goddess of the moon. This name is a classic choice for Cancer, whose ruling planet is the Moon. Variations: *Cindi, Cindy, Cinthia, Cintia, Cyndi, Cynth.*

Dana (DAY-nah) Gaelic: Great womb. In Celtic mythology, the goddess *Dana* was the mother of all things. This pretty name is ideal for a Cancer female, who will display a tendency to nurture and protect others.

Darda (DAR-dah) Hebrew: Pearl of wisdom. This beautiful and traditional name suits Cancer, who reveres history, especially ancient history, and whose birthstone is the pearl.

Davida (da-VEE-dah or DAY-vid-ah) Scottish: Cherished friend. Cancers, who are kind, loyal, and compassionate, make wonderful, lifelong friends. Variations: *Davia, Davianna, Davina, Davita, Davonna.*

Dayaa (day-YAH) Hindu: Sympathy. Compassion and sensitivity are prominent qualities found in Cancers. Variation: *Dyanita.*

Deanna (dee-AN-nah) English: Ocean lover. As one of the three Water signs of the zodiac, Cancer shows a strong affinity for the ocean. Variations: *Deanne, Deeanna, Deena, Deondra.*

Delia (DEE-lee-ah) Greek: Of Delos. Delos is the island birthplace of—and an alternate name for—Artemis, Greek goddess of the Moon, Cancer's ruling symbol. Variations: *Dede, Dee.*

Diana (dye-AHN-ah) Greek: Goddess of the Moon and the night. This classic name is wonderful for those born in Cancer, who, as the only sign of the zodiac ruled by the Moon, have a strong affinity for the night. Variations: *Deanna, Di, Dianne.* (Famous Cancers: Princess Diana; Diana Rigg, English actress)

Divine (deh-VINE) English: Beloved friend. Loyal, nurturing, and loving, Cancers make wonderful friends who inspire adoration from those they love. Variation: *Divinia.*

Donna (DAHN-ah) Italian: Woman of the home. Cancers are the most domestic of all the zodiac's signs, possessing a deep passion for their families and homes. Variations: *Dahna, Dona, Donielle, Donni, Donya.*

Duscha (DOO-shah) Russian: Soul. Many Cancers—whose deep feelings emerge close to the surface and frequently motivate all their actions—epitomize the word *soulful*. Variation: *Dusha*.

Edwardine (EDD-wer-dyne) English: Rich protector. Because of their natural tendencies to nurture and defend, Cancers are extremely protective of those they care about. Variations: *Edwarda, Edwardeen, Edwardyne*.

Eibblin (ebb-LINN) Gaelic: Luminescent glow. This name represents the light of the Moon, Cancer's ruling orb, and the gentle light that Cancers bestow on those around them.

Eirian (AIR-ahn) Welsh: Silver. Ideal for Cancer, this name represents the color of the Moon, Cancer's ruling celestial body, as well as the metal associated with the sign. Variation: *Erin*.

Eleanor (ELL-ah-nor) Greek: Shining one. Like their ruler, the Moon, Cancers exhibit a luminous, glowing quality. *Variations: Eleanora, Elinore, Elle, Nell.* (Famous Cancer: Eleanor Parker, 1940s film star)

Ellama (ELL-ah-mah) Hindu: She who rules her children. Cancers are passionate, tenacious, and wholly involved parents who remain strong influences throughout their children's lives. Variation: *Elamma*.

Ellen (ELL-in) Greek: Luminous light. This name conjures the imagery of the Moon, Cancer's ruling celestial orb. Variations: *Elan, Elene, Elin, Elly, Lene*.

Emma (EMM-ah) Old German: All-embracing one. Considered the quintessential parents of the zodiac, Cancers are known for their extremely nurturing and compassionate spirits. Variations: *Ema, Emmalynn, Emmeline, Emmy*.

Emerald (EM-mer-uld) English: A type of beryl. The emerald is a rare stone, one of the gemstones associated with the sign of Cancer. Variations: *Emarald, Emmarald, Emmerald, Esmée, Esmeralda, Esmerelda.*

Enid (EE-nid) Old Welsh: Soul. This traditional name is well suited to the thoughtful, intense, and deeply passionate Cancer.

Eun (YOON) Korean: Silver. The metal associated with Cancer is silver, as is the color.

Eva (AY-vah or EE-vah) Hebrew: She who bestows life. This name is appropriate to Cancer, the sign of fertility and procreation. Variations: *Evaine, Eve, Evi, Evita, Evy.*

Fallon (FA-linn) Gaelic: Of a ruling family. Cancers, who revere family, are fascinated with family lineage and often make a point of tracing their ancestry. Variation: *Falon.*

Freya (FREE-ya or FRAY-ah) Scandinavian: Norse goddess of fertility. This unique name is an ideal choice for Cancer, the sign of reproduction and fertility. Variation: *Fraya.*

Fulla (FOO-lah) Scandinavian: Mythological fertility goddess. Cancer is the sign of fertility and procreation.

Gabriel (gah-bree-ELL or GAY-bree-el) Hebrew: "God is my strength." In astrology, *Gabriel* is the archangel who watches over those born under the sign of Cancer, making this name a classic choice for a girl or boy. Variations: *Gabbie, Gabby, Gabriella, Gabrielle.*

Ghita (GEE-tah) Italian: Pearl-like. The pearl is the birthstone of Cancer.

Gin (JIN) Japanese: Silver. This unique name is well suited to Cancer, which is associated with the metal and color silver.

Greer (GREER) Latin: Watchful. Cancers' powers of observation are a hallmark of the sign. Cancers, who rapidly discern the undercurrents in many social and business situations, are adept at rising to any occasion and anticipating people's needs.

Greta (GRETT-ah) Greek: Pearlescent. This classic name is appropriate for Cancer, whose birthstone is the beautiful pearl. Variations: *Grete, Gretel.*

Gretchen (GRETT-shin) German: Pearl-like. This traditional name is well suited to a Cancer female, whose birthstone is the pearl.

Guida (GYE-dah) Italian: Guide or teacher. Cancers, who revere education and learning, are also naturally gifted with children—both qualities that make them fine, often one-of-a-kind, teachers.

Hang (HAHNG) Vietnamese: Full Moon. Because Cancer's ruling heavenly body is the Moon, this name is well-suited to a child born under Cancer.

Harriet (HARE-ee-et) French: One who rules the home. Cancers possess an intense devotion to home and family life. Variations: *Harriette, Hattie, Hatty.* (Famous Cancer: Harriet Nelson, 1950s television star)

Helen (HELL-in) Greek: Illuminated one. Like their ruler, the Moon, Cancers possess a glowing, luminous quality. (Famous Cancer: Helen Keller, writer, lecturer, and subject of the award-winning play and film, *The Miracle Worker*)

Henrietta (HEN-ree-ETT-ah) French: Ruler of the home. Cancers are passionate about their homes and typically enjoy playing guardian to friends and family. Variations: *Etta, Hattie, Hettie, Yetta.*

Hera (HARE-ah) Greek: Goddess of women and marriage. Cancers are renowned for their fierce devotion to family.

Hesper (HESS-per) Greek: Evening star. Ruled by the Moon, the sign of Cancer has a strong affiliation with all things of the night.

Ina (EYE-nah) Latin: One who is motherlike. Females born in Cancer have a strong gift for nurturing others.

Indigo (IN-dee-go) Latin: Dark blue. The deep blues, violets, and greens of the sea are colors associated with the sign of Cancer.

Indu (IN-doo) Hindu: Moon. Cancer is the only sign of the zodiac ruled by the Moon.

Inga (ING-ah) Scandinavian: Norse goddess of fertility and peace. This name is a wonderful choice for a girl born under Cancer, the sign of fertility and procreation. Variations: *Ingaar, Inge.*

Iolanthe (ee-oh-LAHNTH or eye-oh-LAHNTH) English: Violet. This beautiful name suggests one of the special colors associated with Cancer. Variation: *Yolanda.*

Ione (ee-OH-nee or eye-OH-nee) Greek: Violet. As one of the three Water signs of the zodiac, Cancer is associated with the colors of the ocean: deep blues, greens, and violets. Variations: *Ionia, Ionie.*

Irisa (ee-REE-sah) Greek: In astrology, the irisa is the symbolic flower of the Moon, which is Cancer's ruling planet. Variations: *Iris, Irisha.*

Isadora (iz-ah-DORR-ah) Greek: Literally, "Gift from Isis." Isis was an Egyptian fertility goddess. This name is a beautiful and apt choice for a child born in Cancer, the sign of fertility and procreation. Variations: *Dora, Dori, Dory, Isidora.*

Jelena (yay-LAY-nah or juh-LAY-nah) Russian: Illumination. This unusual name is ideally suited to Cancer, whose ruling planet is the luminescent Moon. A variation of *Helena*.

Joline (yo-LEEN) Hebrew: She whose fortunes shall multiply. Cancers, who love children, frequently have huge, flourishing families. Variations: *Joleen, Jolene*.

Julia (JOO-lee-ah) Latin: Young or freshly sown. The sign of Cancer is characterized by qualities that suggest fertility, growth, and nourishment. Cancers are passionate caretakers and often become avid gardeners. Variations: *Juliana, Juliet, Julietta, Juliette*. (Famous Cancer: Julia Duffy, television actress)

Jumana (joo-MAH-nah) Arabic: Pearl. The pearl is Cancer's birthstone. Variation: *Jumanah*.

June (JOON) English: One born in June. This lovely and traditional name suits Cancers who are born at the beginning of their zodiac cycle. Variations: *Junette, Junia, Juniata, Junieta*. (Famous Cancers: June Lockhart, 1950s television actress; June Carter, country-and-western singer)

Juno (JOO-noh) Latin: The Roman goddess of marriage. Cancers, who are passionate about family and home, consider marriage a sacred, eternal union. Variation: *Junita*.

Jyoti (ji-OH-tee) Hindu: Light of the moon. Cancer is the only sign of the zodiac ruled by the Moon.

Kamali (KAH-mah-lee or kah-MAH-lee) African/Mahana: Protector. One of the most prominent characteristics of Cancer is an intense desire to nurture and protect loved ones.

Kamaria (ka-MAHR-ree-ah) African/Swahili: Like the Moon. Like their ruler, the Moon, Cancers possess a mysterious, luminous quality.

Kameko (KA-may-ko) Japanese: Child of the tortoise. Cancers, whose animal symbol is the Crab, have a special affinity for other shell-covered creatures. The tortoise, like the Crab, appears shy and withdrawn, hiding behind its hard outer shell, but snapping sharply when threatened.

Kay (KAI) English: Keeper of the keys. Home-loving Cancers, who are affectionate but firm rulers of their domains, are the ultimate "gatekeepers." Variations: *Caye, Kai, Kayana*.

Keilani (kay-LAH-nee) Hawaiian: Glorious chief. This choice is appropriate for Cancer, who thrives when in a position to nurture and protect others.

Kenda (KEN-dah) English: Child of clear, cool water. This name is wonderful for Cancer, one of the three Water signs of the zodiac. Variations: *Kendi, Kendy, Kennda, Kenndi, Kenndy*.

Kishi (KEE-shee) Japanese: Beside the shore. Any name that connotes the imagery of the ocean is ideal for Cancer, one of the zodiac's three Water signs.

Konane (koh-NAH-nee) Hawaiian: Lunar glow. The sign of Cancer is ruled by the luminous Moon.

Ladonna (lah-DAHN-ah) French: Lady of the house. This name is well suited to Cancer, who is passionate about family and home. Variations: *Ladonne, Ladonya*.

Laila (LAY-lah) Persian: Night's child. Cancers, the only children of the zodiac who are ruled by the Moon, have a special affection for the night. Variations: *Layla, Laylah, Leila*.

Lavinia (lah-VIN-ee-ah) Latin: Cleansed. In Roman mythology, *Lavinia* was the last wife of Aeneas and considered to be the mother of all Roman people. This classical name is an apt choice for Cancers, who celebrate the notion of a pure home and long lineage. Variation: *Lavina*.

Lena (LEE-nah) Hebrew: Dwelling. The sign of Cancer is strongly associated with home and family. Variations: *Lenah, Liene, Lina*. (Famous Cancer: Lena Horne, singer)

Leonora (lee-ah-NOR-ah or lay-ah-NOR-ah) Greek: Light or torch. Like their ruler, the Moon, Cancers possess a glowing quality that lights up the lives of those around them. Variations: *Lennora, Lennorah, Lenora, Lenorah, Lenore*.

Leta (LEE-tah) African/Swahili: Creating. This apt name for Cancer evokes the sign's affiliation with fertility and procreation. Variation: *Lita*.

Lilith (LIL-ith) Hebrew: From the darkness. This classic and beautiful name, with mystical overtones, evokes the Moon's image as it changes from darkness to fullness. In Jewish mythology, *Lilith* was the first wife of Adam (before Eve) and mother of humankind who challenged his male authority and thus was cast out of Eden—a plight causing great empathy among motherly Cancers. Variation: *Lillith*.

Lissa (LIS-sah) African: In African/Dahoman mythology, the mother goddess of the Sun and the Moon. This lovely name connotes both the "mothering" quality found in Cancers and the symbolism of the Moon, the sign's ruling heavenly body. Variations: *Alissa, Alyssa, Lisa*.

Liv (LIV or LEEV) Scandinavian: Full of life. This name is well suited to a female born under Cancer, the sign of fertility and procreation. Variations: *Livvy, Olive, Olivia*. (Famous Cancers: Liv Tyler and Liv Ullman, film actresses)

Livana (lee-VAH-nah) Hebrew: Moon glow. Cancer is the only sign of the zodiac ruled by the mysterious, luminous Moon. Variations: *Levana, Levanna, Lewana*.

Lucy (LOO-see) Latin: Light. Just as their ruling planet, the Moon, emanates a luminous glow, so do Cancers radiate a warm, shining quality that lights up the lives of those around them. Variations: *Lucetta, Lucinda.*

Lujayn (loo-JANE) Arabic: Silver. This name represents not only the metal associated with Cancer, but also the color of the sign's ruling orb, the Moon.

Lulu (LOO-loo) African/Swahili: Pearl. Cancer's birthstone is the precious and beautiful pearl.

Luna (LOO-nah) Latin: Roman Moon goddess. This lovely name for a girl born under Cancer is directly connected to the Moon, ruler of the sign. Variations: *Lunetta, Lunette, Lunneta.*

Lupe (LOO-pay) Hawaiian: Ruby. The ruby is one of the precious gemstones associated with the sign of Cancer.

Madonna (mah-DON-nah) Latin: My lady. A regal, and currently very popular, name for a ruling "lady of the house." This name also evokes the image of motherhood, a trait that is strong in the sign of Cancer.

Magena (mah-GEE-nah) Native American: New moon. This name is appropriate for Cancer, whose ruling planet is the Moon.

Mahina (mah-HEE-nah) Hawaiian: Moon. Cancer is the only sign of the zodiac ruled by the luminous Moon.

Maia (MY-ah) Greek: One who tenderly nurses. In Greek mythology, *Maia* is a Greek fertility goddess. This beautiful name is ideal for Cancer, the sign of fertility and procreation, known for a strong tendency to nurture and care for others. Variations: *Maiah, Maya, Mya.*

Maisie (MAY-zee) Scottish: Pearl. Cancer's birthstone is the pearl. Variations: *Maisey, Maisy, Maizie.*

Maj (MY) Scandinavian: Pearl. This name is an apt one for Cancer, whose birthstone is the beautiful pearl. Variations: *Mae, Mai, Maia, Maja.*

Makaleka (mah-kah-LEE-kah) Hawaiian: Pearl. The pearl, Cancer's birthstone, also resembles the sign's ruling planet, the shining Moon.

Margaret (MAHR-gah-ret) English: Pearl. This traditional name is ideal for Cancer, whose birthstone is the shining pearl. Variations: *Maggie, Maire, Marge, Margie, Margret, Marjorie, Meg, Peggy.*

Matrika (mah-TREE-kah) Hindu: Divine Mother. With their intense desire to nurture and care for others, Cancer females often make wonderful mothers who fiercely love, protect, and support their children.

Megan (MEG-an, MEE-gan, or MAY-gan) Welsh: Pearl-like. Cancer's birthstone is the beautiful, precious pearl. Variations: *Maegen, Meagan, Meg, Megeen, Meghan.*

Mei-Zhen (MAY-zhen) Chinese: Beautiful pearl. This unique name suits a Cancer, whose birthstone is the pearl.

Meredith (MARE-eh-dith) Old Welsh: Protector of the seas. This name is wonderful for a girl born in Cancer. As one of the three Water signs of the zodiac, Cancer shares a special affinity for the sea; Cancers are also known for possessing a protective nature.

Merla (MER-lah) Old Welsh: Fortress by the sea. This lovely old name suggests two of Cancer's outstanding characteristics: the desire for a strong home base and an affinity for the ocean.

Mi-Ok (MEE-ok) Korean: Lovely pearl. Just as their birthstone, the precious pearl, is hidden inside a hard, protective shell, Cancers are prone to hiding their sensitive, vulnerable sides from the world by displaying only a guarded, outer layer.

Mitena (mih-TEN-ah) Native American: Born during the new Moon. This name is a perfect fit for a girl born under Cancer, the only sign of the zodiac ruled by the Moon.

Midori (mee-DO-ree) Japanese: Green. The green and blue colors of the sea are associated with the sign of Cancer.

Migina (mee-GEE-nah) Native American: New Moon. Like their ruler, the Moon, Cancers emit a warm, luminescent glow.

Mika (MEE-kah) Japanese: New Moon. This lovely name is well suited for Cancer, who is ruled by the Moon, in all its phases.

Mikazuki (mee-kah-ZOO-kee) Japanese: New Moon. This name is well suited for Cancer, ruled by the dark of the Moon as well as the light.

Mimiteh (mih-MIH-teh) Native American: New Moon. Cancers, ruled by the Moon, have a special affinity for the night and its darkness.

Moran (mor-AN) Hebrew: Teacher. Due to their love of education and a desire to help others, Cancers often make outstanding teachers.

Munirah (moo-NEE-rah) Arabic: Teacher. Compassionate, patient, and wise, those born in Cancer are well suited to a career in teaching.

Murasaki (moo-rah-SAHK-ee) Japanese: Purple. The sign of Cancer is affiliated with the colors of the sea: deep blues, greens, and purples.

Myrna (MER-nah) Gaelic: Beloved or affectionate. Cancer children are likely to shower love and devotion on their family and close friends. Variation: *Morna*.

Nata (NAH-tah) Native American: Voice of creation. This traditional Native American name echoes the Mother Goddess qualities of Cancer.

Nelia (neh-LEE-ah) Spanish: Womanly. This name is well suited to a girl born in Cancer, which is one of the Feminine signs of the zodiac. Variations: *Cornelia, Neile, Neilla, Nela, Nila*.

Nerissa (ner-RISS-ah) Greek: Sea snail. Like the crab that symbolizes Cancer, the snail is another shell-covered creature who is hard on the outside, fragile within. Variations: *Nerisa, Nerise*.

Nguyet (NOO-et) Vietnamese: Moon. Cancer is the only sign of the zodiac ruled by the Moon.

Niranjana (nee-ran-JAN-ah) Hindu: Full Moon. Ruled by the Moon, Cancers have a special connection with the night.

Odharnait (OR-nat or OR-nah) Irish: Green. As one of the three Water signs of the zodiac, Cancer is associated with the colors of the sea: deep blues, violets, and greens. Variations: *Orna, Ornat*.

Ozera (o-ZER-ah) Hebrew: Help. Extremely sensitive toward the feelings of others, those born in Cancer are often quick to come to the aid of someone in need.

Pearl (PURL) Latin: Pearl. This lovely name is ideal for a Cancer female, whose birthstone is the luminescent pearl. Variations: *Pearley, Perl, Perla, Perlena, Perlie*.

Penelope (pen-EL-o-pee) Greek: Worker of the loom. In Greek mythology, *Penelope*, the wife of Odysseus, faithfully waited twenty years for his return. Steadfast Cancers will identify with the story of *Penelope*, whose home-loving name has both classic and contemporary appeal. Variations: *Pennie, Penny*.

Pepita (pe-PEE-tah) Spanish: One who is fruitful. The sign of Cancer is affiliated with fertility and procreation. Variations: *Pepi, Peta, Pipi, Pippi*.

Philana (fee-LAHN-ah) Greek: Lover of men. Cancers have a deep love for their families, and as a result, Cancer women are extremely devoted to and supportive of their husbands. Variations: *Philene, Philina, Phillidia*.

Phoebe (FEE-bee) Greek: Bright one. *Phoebe* was a Greek goddess of the Moon, Cancer's ruling planet. (Famous Cancerian: Phoebe Snow, singer)

Pomona (poh-MOHN-ah) Latin: One who is fruitful. Cancer is the sign of fertility and procreation.

Poppy (POP-ee) Latin: From the name for the poppy flower. In astrology, the red poppy flower is associated with the Moon, which governs Cancer.

Purnima (poor-NEE-mah) Hindu: Full Moon. Cancer is the only sign of the zodiac ruled by the Moon.

Queta (KAY-tah) Spanish: Mistress of the house. Cancers are passionate about their family and home and, even as children, they would rather be at home than anywhere else in the world.

Radinka (ra-DINK-ah) Slavic: Full of life. This name suggests the generous and nurturing emotional qualities of Cancer.

Rea (RAY or RE-ah) Greek: Red poppy flower. According to the Greek tradition, this flower is associated with the Moon, Cancer's ruling planet.

Rhiannon (ree-AHN-nun) Welsh: A Celtic goddess of fertility. This lovely name is ideal for a girl born in Cancer, which is the sign of procreation and fertility. Variations: *Reannon, Rheannon*.

Rita (REE-tah) English: Pearl. The birthstone of Cancer is the pure, beautiful pearl. Variations: *Reeta, Reta, Rheta, Rhetta*.

Ruby (ROO-bee) English: The red jewel. The ruby is one of the gemstones associated with the sign of Cancer. Variations: *Rubey, Rubie, Rubye*.

Selda (SEL-dah) Old English: Companion. Cancers make devoted and lifelong friends. Variations: *Selde, Zelda*.

Selene (seh-LEH-neh or seh-LEE-nee) Greek: The Moon. Cancer is the only sign of the zodiac ruled by the Moon. This name also belongs to a Greek Moon goddess. Variations: *Salena, Selena, Selina*.

Sesheta (sih-SHEET-ah) Egyptian: An Egyptian goddess of the stars and patroness of literature and writing. Cancers are passionate lovers of books, particularly the classics, and many writers are represented by this sign. Variation: *Seshat*.

Shahar (sha-HAHR) Arabic: Moonlight. This name represents Cancer's luminescent glow, as well as the connection the sign has to its ruling planet, the Moon.

Shenandoah (shen-an-DOH-ah) Native American: Beautiful girl from the stars. This name is apt for a child born in Cancer, a sign possessing a strong connection to the mysterious, luminescent night.

Silver (SIL-ver) English: The precious metal. The metal associated with the sign of Cancer, silver is also the color of the Moon, Cancer's ruling planet.

Siv (SIF) Old Norse: A variation of the name *Sif*, a Norse goddess of fertility. This name is appropriate for a female born in Cancer, the sign of fertility and procreation.

Soma (SO-mah) Hindu: Moon. Cancer is the only sign of the zodiac ruled by the Moon.

Taini (tah-EE-nee) Native American: New Moon. Like their ruling planet, the Moon, Cancers' moods range from mysterious reserve to brilliant vigor. Variation: *Tainee*.

Tale (TAH-leh) African/Botswanan: Green. One of the special colors assigned to Cancer is green.

Taliba (tah-LEE-bah) Arabic: Seeker of knowledge. Cancers hold education in high esteem, often making gifted teachers. Variation: *Talibah*.

Teal (TEEL) English: Green-blue. Cancer, one of the three Water signs of the zodiac, is associated with the colors of the ocean.

Tracy (TRAY-cee) English: Summer. This modern-sounding name is a classic choice for Cancer, the first sign of the zodiac to occur in summer. Variations: *Tracee, Tracey, Traci, Tracie, Treacy, Treesy*.

Tuki (TOO-kee) Japanese: Moon. Cancer is the only sign of the zodiac ruled by the Moon. Variation: *Tukiko*.

Uma (oo-MAH) Hindu: Flax. This name, one that belongs to the Hindu fertility goddess Parvati, suggests Cancers' ties to fertility and procreation.

Vesta (VESS-tah) Latin: Roman goddess of the home. Cancers are well known for their fierce devotion to family and home life. Variation: *Vessy*.

Violet (VI-oh-let) Latin: The purple flower. The sign of Cancer is associated with the darker, cooler colors of blue, green, and deep violet. Variations: *Viola, Violetta, Violette.*

Willa (WIL-lah) German: Protector. Cancers are renowned for fiercely protecting their loved ones. Variation: *Wilma.*

Winema (wee-NEH-mah) Native American: Female chief. Cancers are at their best when in a position where they can oversee, protect, and care for others.

Yoshina (YO-shee-nah) Japanese: Fertile land. This name is appropriate for a baby girl born in Cancer, the sign of fertility and procreation.

Zara (ZAR-ah) Arabic: To blossom. Though they often keep their feelings hidden from the world, once Cancers come out of their shells, they become wonderful, loving friends, parents, and spouses.

Zina (ZEE-nah) English: Hospitable. Cancers, who celebrate the home above all else, are adept at making guests feel welcome and make gifted hostesses. Variations: *Xena, Zena.*

Names for Cancer Boys

Abbott (ABB-it) Arabic: Father. A Muslim variation of the Hebrew name *Abba*, which means "father of all," this classic name celebrates family and children above all else. Variations: *Abba, Abban, Abbey, Abbie.*

Abdal-Fattah (ahb-DAHL-fah-TAH) Arabic: One who serves the one who nourishes. Cancers are devoted and enthusiastic mates who relish the lifelong commitment to partnership and caretaking that marriage provides. Variation: *Abdel-Fattah.*

Abner (AB-ner) Hebrew: Father of light. This traditional name, with its connotations both of progeny and illumination, is a marvelous choice for Cancers, the "Moon Children" of the zodiac. Variations: *Ab, Avner, Eb, Ebner.*

Abraham (ABE-rah-ham) Hebrew: Father of many. This classic name connotes the fertility associated with the sign of Cancer. Variations: *Abe, Abrahan, Abram, Abran, Avraham, Avran.*

Adam (AD-am) Hebrew: He who sprang from the earth. In the Bible, *Adam* was the progenitor of the human race. Cancers have a keen and special reverence for their ancestors. Variations: *Ad, Adamek, Adamo, Adan, Ade.*

Adri (AH-dree) Hindu: Fortress or rock. In Hindu mythology, *Adri* was the god who protected mankind. Cancers are renowned for fiercely defending home, family, and friends.

Alden (AHL-den) English: Old friend. Cancers bring to their friendships the same passionate devotion and deep loyalty that they hold for family.

Amos (AY-muss) Hebrew: One with many responsibilities. Amos was an Old Testament prophet. Cancer's keen sense of responsibility to others is apparent at an early age.

Andrew (AN-drew) Greek: Manly. Cancer is the sign of virility and fertility. Variations: *Anders, André, Andre, Andy, Drew, Dru.* (Famous Cancer: Andrew Wyeth, painter.)

Anselm (AN-selm) Old German: Divine guardian. Cancers often take their roles as guardians or parents as "holy" tasks. Variations: *Ansel, Ansen, Hansel, Hansen.*

Anwar (AHN-wahr) Arabic: Shafts of light. This extremely popular name for Muslim boys suggests the luminous qualities of the Moon, Cancer's ruling planet.

Apekaloma (ah-peh-kah-LO-mah) Hawaiian: Peaceful father. Cancers, who make wonderful parents, are dedicated peacekeepers. Hawaiian version of *Absalom*. Variation: *Abesaloma*.

Apelahama (ah-peh-lah-HAH-mah) Hawaiian: Father of many. Cancers are known as the archetypical parents of the zodiac, willing to fight to protect anyone in need. Variation: *Aberahama*.

Arsenio (ar-SEH-nee-oh) Greek: Manly. Cancer is the sign of virility and procreation.

Artemus (AHR-teh-mos) Greek: "One who follows Artemis." In Greek mythology, *Artemis* was goddess of the Moon, Cancer's ruling celestial body.

Asa (ACE-ah) Hebrew: Healer or physician. Cancers, keenly attuned to the hurt feelings of others, are quick to soothe and offer comfort.

Atmar (AHT-mahr) Hindu: Soul. Despite their sometimes gruff and cold exteriors, Cancers have complex and driving emotions that run close to the surface, ready to spill over at the slightest provocation.

Austin (AU-sten) Latin: Great and venerable. Cancers often view the roles of parent and mate as preordained and sacred tasks—and they often expect "veneration" in return.

Avery (AY-ve-ree) English: Counselor. Cancers are keen observers, careful listeners, and eager peacemakers. Later in life, they often shine in the fields of politics and social services. Variations: *Ave, Averel, Averell, Avrel, Avrell, Avryll*.

Avi (AH-vee) Hebrew: Divine father. Cancers, with their natural tendency to nurture and their passion for family, make highly sensitive and responsive parents.

Avinoam (ah-vee-NO-ahm) Hebrew: Pleasant father. Passionate about family and home, Cancers make supportive, nurturing, loving parents who strive to make their children happy.

Axel (AX-ul) Old German: Father of peace. Cancers are considered the archetypical parents of the zodiac, and they are dedicated to maintaining a peaceful atmosphere. Variations: *Axell, Axl.*

Badar (BAH-der or bah-DAR) Arabic: Full Moon. Any name that connotes the Moon is an appropriate choice for Cancer, the only zodiac sign ruled by the Moon.

Badru (BAH-droo or bah-DROO) Arabic: Full Moon. Cancer's ruling planet is the Moon.

Baha (bah-HAH) Arabic: Brilliance. Like their ruler, the Moon, Cancers emit a shining glow that lights up the lives of everyone around them.

Bahir (bah-HEER) Arabic: Luminous. This name suggests the light of the Moon, Cancer's ruling planet.

Baldric (BAHL-drik) German: Brave ruler. Ideal for a Cancer boy, this name suggests the natural tendency of Cancers to protect those around them.

Baldwin (BAHLD-win) Old German: Brave defender. When their home or family is threatened, Cancers exhibit a courageous strength. Variations: *Baldovino, Baldvin, Baldwinn, Baldwyn, Baudoin.*

Balraj (bah-lah-RAJ) Hindu: King of strength. Because of their natural tendency to protect and watch over others, Cancers are often associated with the imagery of royalty or leadership.

Baram (BAH-ram) Hebrew: Son of the people, or, a nation's heir. This name suggests Cancers' tendency to do as much as they can to protect and help their communities. Cancers often are drawn to careers in social services.

Barnabas (BAHRN-ah-bas) Hebrew: Comfort. Filled with compassion, concern, and empathy, Cancers are ideal friends to turn to in times of need. Variations: *Barnabus, Barnaby, Barney*.

Baruti (bah-ROO-tee) African/Botswanan: Teacher. Cancers, who have a great respect for education and a desire to reach out to others, often make excellent teachers.

Baul (BALL) English: Snail. This traditional and unique English name is particularly apt for Cancers, whose sign is associated with the Crab and other shell-covered creatures.

Benaiah (ben-nah-EE-ah or ben-AYE-ah) Hebrew: God builds. This name suggests Cancer's desire for a large, flourishing family.

Benjamin (BEN-jah-min) English: Son of my right hand. *Benjamin* is a classic choice for Cancers, who are especially devoted children and eager helpmates. Variations: *Ben, Benjaman, Benji, Benny*.

Bert (BURT) English: Bright light. This name connotes Cancer's ruling planet, the Moon. Variations: *Bertie, Bertolde, Burt, Burtt*. (Famous Cancer: Bert Convy, actor/singer)

Bertil (ber-TEEL) Scandinavian: Bright. Like their ruler, the Moon, Cancers light up the lives of those around them. Variation: *Bertel*.

Blake (BLAYKE) Old English: Pale, shining one. This traditional name conjures imagery of the Moon, Cancer's ruling planet.

Boone (BOON) Old French: One who is good and bounteous. This hearty, old-fashioned name—with its suggestion of the

American West—appeals to Cancer's love of the past and reverence for family lineage, along with Cancer's generous concern for others.

Brady (BRAY-dee) Old English: One with broad eyes. Cancers are keen and perceptive observers of the social world around them, often able to discern the hidden agendas of many a business and social situation.

Burchard (BERK-hart) English: Strong castle. For Cancer, the home truly is his castle. Variation: *Burkhart.*

Burke (BERK) French: Fortress dweller. A strong home base is vital to Cancer's sense of well-being, creating a haven where he feels safe and can recover from the rigors of the outside world. Variations: *Berk, Berke, Birke, Burk.*

Burl (BURL) Old English: One who serves the wine. Cancers, who celebrate home and hospitality, make superlative hosts. Variations: *Burle, Burleigh, Burlie, Byrle.*

Burton (BER-tun) Old English: Stronghold or fortress. Cancers, who crave security and stability, often find a place in which they can hide from the world.

Callister (KAL-uh-ster) Irish: Derived from the Gaelic for *Alastair*, a form of *Alexander*, meaning helper or defender of mankind. This unique name suits Cancers, who never fail to go out of their way to help someone in need.

Cam (KAHM) Gypsy: One who is deeply loved. Cancers, who are warm, compassionate, and loving, are usually greatly appreciated by others.

Carlisle (KAHR-lyl) English: Protected tower. Sensitive and vulnerable by nature, Cancers try to shield themselves from the harshness of the outside world. Variation: *Carlyle.*

Carter (KAHR-ter) English: Driver of the cart. Always willing to shoulder responsibility on the homefront, Cancers take charge and get the task done when carrying the weight of their loved ones.

Casey (KAY-see) Irish: Derived from the Gaelic word *cathasach*, meaning watchful or vigilant. Cancers are always on their guard, ready to protect those they love from any sudden perils.

Casper (KAS-per) Persian: Keeper of the riches. Cancers, who highly value security and stability, would rather save their money than spend it, always prepared for a possible emergency. Variations: *Cas, Caspar, Cass, Gaspar, Jasper, Kasper.*

Chad (CHAD) English: Protector. One of Cancer's key characteristics is a strong desire to nurture and protect others. Variation: *Chadwick.*

Chalmers (CHAHM-erz) Scottish: Head of the household. This name is suitable for Cancer, who is happiest when protecting and caring for others, especially on the homefront. Variation: *Chalmer.*

Chand (CHAND) Hindu: Shining moon. Cancer is the only sign of the zodiac ruled by the Moon. Variation: *Chanda.*

Chau (CHAH-oo) Vietnamese: Pearl. Cancer's birthstone is the shining pearl. Variation: *Chepito.*

Cid (SEED) Spanish: Lord. This name suggests Cancer's desire to protect and oversee his family and friends. Variation: *Cyd.*

Colin (KOL-in or KOH-lin) Irish: One who is young and virile. Cancer is the sign of virility and reproduction. Variations: *Cole, Collin.*

Conrad (KAHN-rad) Old German: Brave, wise counselor. With their keen senses of intuition and insight, Cancers are often looked to for advice or consolation. Variations: *Con, Conney, Cort, Konrad, Kort.*

Cook (COOK) English: A cook. Hospitable and home-loving Cancers love all the rituals that surround cooking and dining, and they are especially fond of rich foods. (Indeed, the stomach is considered the most vulnerable area of the body for Cancers, who are prone to bad bouts of indigestion and weight gain later in life.) Variation: *Cooke.*

Corey (KOR-ee) Irish: Dweller in a hollow pool. The Crab, who often hides in shallow waters, is the animal symbol for Cancers, who frequently conceal their softer, more emotional sides beneath a crusty exterior. Variations: *Corie, Correy, Cory, Kory.*

Cosmo (KOZ-moh) Greek: One in harmony with their surroundings. Peace-loving Cancer is most comfortable in his own home. Variations: *Cos, Cosimo, Cosme.*

Curtis (KUR-tis) French: Courteous. Because they possess intuitive understanding and compassion, Cancers are polite and ever conscious of the feelings of others. Variations: *Curt, Kurt.*

Dabir (dah-BEER) African: Teacher or record keeper. Cancers show a keen respect for the past, prove eager students with prodigious memories, and often become gifted teachers.

Dai (DAY) Welsh: To shine. Like their ruling planet, the Moon, Cancers display an illuminating inner light to all those close to them.

Damon (DAY-mun) Greek: Loyal friend. Cancers bring to their friendships the same depth of feeling and commitment that they share with their family. Variations: *Damone, Daymon.*

Dante (DAHN-tay) Latin: Everlasting. Loyalty and steadfast devotion are considered two of Cancer's most outstanding qualities.

Dar (DAR) Hebrew: Pearl. The pearl is the precious jewel associated with the sign of Cancer.

Daren (DAH-rehn) African/Nigerian: Night child. Ruled by the Moon, Cancers have a special affinity for things of the night. Variations: *Darren, Darrin*.

Darnell (DAHR-nell) English: Hidden area. Children born in Cancer often seek out secret nooks and crannies to play in. Variation: *Darnel*.

Darrick (DARE-ik) English: Ruler of the land. Cancers are renowned for their passion and devotion to maintaining and overseeing their homestead. Variations: *Del, Derek, Derick, Derrick*.

Davin (DAH-vin) Scandinavian: Shining. This name conjures the luminous imagery of the Moon, Cancer's ruling orb.

Devin (DEV-un) Irish: Derived from the Gaelic *dámh*, meaning poet. Cancers often use the written word as a vehicle for their deeply felt and complex emotions. Variations: *Devan, Deven, Devon*. (Among the famous writers represented by the sign of Cancer are Pearl Buck, Helen Keller, Antoine de Saint-Exupéry, Hermann Hesse, Franz Kafka, Tom Stoppard, Neil Simon, Jean Cocteau, E. B. White, Erle Stanley Gardner, and Marianne Williamson.)

Deacon (DEE-ken) English: One who serves. Cancers have a natural desire to please others, and often put the needs of others above their own. Variations: *Deke, Dekel*.

Demetrius (dee-MEE-tree-us) Greek: Belonging to Demeter, Greek goddess of fertility. This name is well suited to a child born in Cancer, the sign of procreation and fertility. Variations: *Demeter, Demetre, Demetri, Demetrio, Dimitri*.

Dillon (DIL-lun) Irish: Loyal. The most dominant characteristics of Cancers include intense loyalty and unwavering commitment. Variations: *Dilon, Dilyn, Dylan.*

Dinos (DI-nos) Latin: Continuous support. As parents, friends, or spouses, Cancers are steadfast sources of encouragement. Variations: *Costa, Gus, Kastas, Kostas.*

Diya (dee-YAH) Arabic: To shine. Like their ruling planet, the Moon, Cancers have a special glow that illuminates the lives of those around them.

Dominic (DOM-ih-nik) Latin: Lord and master. This name suggests Cancer's love of watching over and protecting his family. Variations: *Domenic, Dominick, Dominique, Dominyck.*

Duran (der-RAN) Latin: Long lasting. Cancers are renowned for their unending devotion and their ability to see things through to the very end. Variations: *Durand, Durant.*

Eamon (EH-mon) Old English: Affluent protector. This name is suitable for Cancers, who are sure to be good providers for their families.

Edmund (ED-muhnd) Old English: Rich defender. Cancers have a strong need to take care of and protect others. Variaton: *Edmond.*

Edric (ED-rik or EED-rik) English: Powerful man who holds property. When their homestead is threatened, Cancers can become formidable guardians. Variation: *Edrick.*

Edward (EDD-ward) English: Guardian of property. Cancer goes to any lengths to keep his home and family from any type of harm. Variations: *Ed, Eddie, Edgard, Edouard, Edouardo, Eduard, Eduardo, Edvard.* (Famous Cancers: Ed Bradley, journalist; Ed Ames, television actor)

Einri (en-REE) Irish: Ruler at home. Cancers are passionate about their homes and home lives. Gaelic for *Henry*. Variations: *Anrai, Hanraoi*.

Emery (EH-mur-ee) German: Leader of the house. Even as children, Cancers find great pride, comfort, and strength in their homes. Variations: *Emerson, Emmery, Emmo, Emory*.

Enoch (EE-nok) Hebrew: Devoted or scholarly. Cancers are great lovers of learning and make enthusiastic students.

Enrico (en-REE-ko) Italian: Leader of the house. Possessed with a need to nurture and protect, Cancers make strong, involved parents. Variations: *Enric, Enrique, Rico*.

Enzio (EN-zee-o) Italian: Ruler at home. Cancers, who are passionate about their family and home, are considered the archetypical parents of the zodiac.

Epelaima (eh-peh-lah-EE-mah) Hawaiian: Fertile. Cancer is the sign of fertility and reproduction.

Ephraim (EFF-ram or eff-REYE-im) Hebrew: Fertile. This traditional name suggests Cancer's role as the sign of procreation and fertility. Variations: *Efraim, Efrem, Ephrayim*.

Esmond (EZ-mund) English: Rich protector. Cancers are noted for being particularly thrifty and good with finances, preferring to hoard their money rather than spend it.

Eustace (YOOS-tiss) Greek: Fertile. Those born under Cancer, the sign of fertility, often desire big families. Variation: *Eustazio*.

Falan (FAL-an) Hindu: Fertile. Cancer is the sign associated with fertility and procreation. Variations: *Faleen, Falit*.

Feivel (FYE-full) Hebrew: Bright one. This name suggests the imagery of the Moon, Cancer's ruling celestial force.

Gabriel (GAY-bree-el) Hebrew: "God is my strength." In astrological traditions, *Gabriel* is the angel who watches over those born under the sign of Cancer. Variations: *Gabby, Gabe, Gabie, Gabriello, Gavi, Gavril.*

Garridan (GAH-rih-duhn) Gypsy: He who hides. Cancers are not only adept at hiding their emotional natures, they also frequently remove themselves altogether when threatened or confronted by a situation (much like the sign's token animal, the Crab).

Garth (GARTH) Old Norse: Defender of the homestead. Fiercely devoted to their homes, Cancers go to any means to protect or maintain the comfort, security, and harmony of their favorite place in the world. Variations: *Gareth, Garrett.*

Gifford (GIF-ferd) English: Brave provider. Inclined to put the needs of others above their own, Cancers often go to any lengths to keep their loved ones happy and safe.

Goodwin (GOOD-win) Old English: Good friend. This name is well suited to the loyal and compassionate Cancer.

Graham (gram or GRAY-um) Old English: Derived from *ham*, meaning home. This traditional name is ideal for those born in Cancer, who possess an intense love of family and home life. Variations: *Ghramm, Graeme, Grahame, Gram.*

Hafiz (hah-FIZ) Arabic: Protector. One of the most prominent qualities found in Cancer is an intense desire to keep loved ones from harm. Variation: *Hafez.*

Hagan (HAY-gan) Irish: Home ruler. Cancers relish being safe at home, where they are able to care for and closely guard their family. Variation: *Hagen.*

Hale (HALE) English: From the Old English *halh*, meaning nook or remote place. Outside the safety net of family and close friends, Cancers are uncomfortable with strangers and may appear cold and unfriendly. When threatened, they retreat into a world that is all their own.

Hall (HAHL) English: Worker at the manor. Any name associated with home is a good choice for Cancer, who is passionate about his family and home life.

Hallward (HAHL-ward) English: Protector of the manor. This unique name is ideal for Cancer, who will go to any lengths to protect his home and family. Variation: *Halward*.

Hamlin (HAM-lin) German: One who loves to stay at home. This unusual name is perfectly apt for the ultimate homebody, Cancer. Variations: *Hamlen, Hamlyn*.

Hammond (HAM-mund) English: Chief guardian. Cancers possess a natural instinct to nurture and protect others. Variation: *Hammand*.

Harry (HAR-ree) English: Ruler at home. Cancers, considered the quintessential parents of the zodiac, are passionate about family and home. (Famous Cancer: Harry Dean Stanton, film actor)

Harrison (HAYR-ih-sun) English: Son of Harry. (See *Harry*, above.) If possible, *Harrison* reflects an even deeper commitment to home life than his father, *Harry*. Variations: *Harris, Harrisen*. (Famous Cancer: Harrison Ford, film actor)

Haven (HAY-ven) English: Secure, safe place. Sensitive and emotionally vulnerable, Cancers often seek refuge from the chaos and turmoil of the outside world.

Hemachandra (hem-ah-CHAND-rah) Hindu: Golden Moon. The ruling planet of Cancer is the Moon.

Henry (HEN-ree) German: Ruler of the house. This classic name suggests Cancer's passion for home and family. Variations: *Enrico, Enzio, Hal, Hank, Heinrich, Hendrik, Henri, Henric*. (Famous Cancer: Henry David Thoreau, writer and naturalist)

Hesperos (HEH-sper-os) Greek: Evening star. Cancer has a special connection not only with the Moon, its ruling orb, but with all things of the night. Variation: *Hespero*.

Hewney (HEW-nee) Irish: Green. The deep blue, green, and violet colors of the ocean are associated with the sign of Cancer. Variations: *Aney, Oney, Owney*.

Hillel (hye-LEL) Arabic: New or quarter Moon. Cancer is the only sign of the zodiac ruled by the Moon. Variation: *Hilel*.

Hirohito (hee-ro-HEE-toh) Japanese: Emperor. This name suggests Cancer's desire to protect and oversee others.

Humphrey (HUM-free) Old German: Warrior of peace. Although gentle and sensitive by nature, Cancer fights with mighty strength when his home or family is threatened. Variation: *Humphry*.

Ingemar (ING-geh-mar) Scandinavian: Norse fertility god. Cancer is the sign of fertility and reproduction. Variations: *Ingamar, Ingmar*.

Jabbar (jah-BAHR) Hindu: One who comforts. Keenly sensitive to others' feelings and empathetic by nature, Cancers are quick to offer help and comfort.

Jacob (JAY-kob) Hebrew: Supplanting one. In the Bible, Jacob was the father of twelve sons whose progeny became the twelve tribes of Israel. This name suggests Cancer's traits of fertility and procreation. Variations: *Jake, Jakov, Yakov*.

Jacy (JAY-cee) Native American: Moon. Cancer is the only sign of the zodiac ruled by the Moon. Variation: *Jace*.

Jared (JARE-ed) Hebrew: Descent or down to earth. Cancers, who are lovers of the past, have a special respect for their ancestors. Variations: *Jarrod, Jerod, Jerrod*.

Jason (JAY-son) Latin: To heal. Because of their deep compassion, Cancer children possess a strong desire to fix the problems of others and to restore peace in turbulent situations. Variation: *Jayson*.

Javier (hah-vee-AIR) Basque: New homeowner. Any name that suggests the imagery of home is well suited to Cancer. Variation: *Xavier*.

Jericho (JARE-a-ko) Arabic: City of the Moon. Cancer is associated with the imagery of the Moon, which is the sign's ruling planet. Variation: *Jerico*.

Jindrich (YEEN-der-zheech) Czech: Home ruler. Any name that suggests the importance of the home is ideally suited to Cancers. Variations: *Jindrik, Jindrisek*.

Jordan (JOR-dun) Hebrew: To flow or descend. This name evokes the Cancerian quality of flowing and changing like Water, the element that describes those born under the sign of Cancer. Variations: *Jordon, Jordyn, Jory, Judd*.

Joseph (JO-seph) Hebrew: God will increase. This classic and ever-popular name for a boy born under Cancer reflects his many successes. Variations: *Giuseppe, Jody, Joe, Joey, Jojo, Jose, Josef, Josip*. (Famous Cancer: Joseph Papp, American theatrical producer)

July (ju-LYE) Latin: From *Julius*, for the seventh month of the year. A unique choice for a Cancer boy born during the month of July, this name is a popular character in Larry McMurtry's novel *Lonesome Dove*.

Kalani (kah-LAH-nee) Hawaiian: Chieftain. Just as Cancers make strong leaders within their own homes, they make successful rulers of larger clans as well.

Karel (KAHR-el) Old French: Virile. Cancer is the sign of fertility, reproduction, and virility. Variations: *Carl, Carroll, Karl, Karol*. (Famous Cancer: Karl Menninger, psychiatrist)

Kasib (KA-sib or ka-SEEB) Arabic: Earthy, productive. Cancer is the sign of fertility and reproduction. Variation: *Kaseeb*.

Kemikilio (kay-mee-kee-LEE-o) Hawaiian: Fertile. Cancer is the sign of fertility and procreation. A variation of the Greek *Demetrios*, for Demeter, a Greek fertility god.

Keenan (KEE-nun) Irish: From the Gaelic *cian*, meaning ancient, or in the past. Passionate about learning and education, Cancers are drawn to the study of history. Variations: *Kenan, Kienan*.

Keo (KEH-o) Hawaiian: God will increase. Cancer is the sign of fertility. This name is a Hawaiian variation of *Joseph*.

Kibbe (KEEB-beh) Native American: Night bird. Cancers possess a special affinity for all things of the night.

Konane (ko-NAH-nee) Hawaiian: Bright moonlight. This name is an interesting choice for a boy born in Cancer, the only sign of the zodiac ruled by the Moon.

Kyle (KILE) Scottish: Chief. Due to their intensely protective and loyal natures, Cancers are often associated with leadership. Variations: *Kye, Kylan, Kylar, Kyler, Kyrell*.

Laird (LAYRD) Scottish: Lord of the manor. Cancers are known to be conscientious leaders in their own homes, with their strong integrity deserving of respect and honor.

Leif (LEEF or LYFE) Scandinavian: Loved one. Cancers are renowned for their lifelong devotion to parents, mates, and children, which brings them great love in return.

Logan (LO-gun) Irish: From the Gaelic, literally, "dweller at a little hollow." This traditional name evokes the image of the home-loving Cancer Crab, tucked discreetly away in his comfortable dwelling place.

Lucian (LOO-shan) Latin: Illumination. This unusual name connotes the light of the Moon, Cancer's ruling planet. Variations: *Luciano, Lucien, Lucio.*

Manco (MAHN-ko) Spanish: Supreme leader. For those in their intimate circle of influence, Cancers are known as the ultimate protectors and suppliers.

Maon (MAY-on) Hebrew: House. Cancers are in their element when enjoying their homes with family and friends.

Maxwell (MAX-wel) Scottish: Great pool or spring. Cancers, like the other Water signs—Scorpio and Pisces—have a special affinity for seas, lakes, rivers, and streams. Variation: *Max.*

Meir (MY-urr) Hebrew: One who gives light. Like their ruling orb, the Moon, Cancers illuminate the lives of everyone around them. Variations: *Mayer, Meyer, Myer.*

Merril (MER-il) Gaelic: Sea bright. As one of the three Water signs in the zodiac, Cancer has a strong association with the sea. Masculine form of *Muriel.* Variation: *Merrill.*

Millard (MIL-erd) Old English: Caretaker of the mill. As the central source for converting grain to flour, the miller enabled people to nourish their most basic needs, just as Cancers are devoted to providing emotional and physical nurturing for all of their loved ones. Variations: *Miller, Milo, Myles.*

Morgan (MORE-ginn) Welsh: Great and bright. This name suggests Cancer's ruling planet, the Moon. Variation: *Morgen.*

Mortimer (MOR-tih-mer) French: Still water. Cancer's often tough facade is a protective device to hide the deep feelings that easily well up to the surface.

Munir (moo-NEER) Arabic: Bright light. As the only sign of the zodiac ruled by the Moon, Cancer is associated with the intense lunar glow.

Mwai (MWAH-ee) African: Prosperity. When it comes to handling money, Cancers—who are keenly concerned about protecting home and family both now and in the future—are particularly talented, being wise investors and long-term savers.

Namid (NAH-meed) Native American: Star dancer. Ruled by the Moon, Cancers share a special affinity for all things of the night.

Ned (NED) English: Guardian of one's wealth. Because of their naturally protective tendencies, Cancers often put their money away for a potential future emergency, rather than spend it frivolously. Variation of *Edward.* (Famous Cancer: Ned Beatty, film and television actor)

Neil (NEEL) Irish: Champion. Cancers, enthusiastic promoters of those they love, are great defenders of their loved ones' rights. Variations: *Neal, Neils, Nels, Nigel, Niles, Nils.* (Famous Cancer: Neil Simon, playwright)

Nelson (NEL-sun) Scandinavian: Son of the champion. Even through his role as offspring, the Cancer child proves to be an important supporter of the family. Variations: *Nealson, Nels,*

Nils, Nilson. (Famous Cancers: Nelson Rockefeller, industrialist and politician; Nelson Mandela, South African civil rights activist, politician, and president of South Africa)

Nigel (NIGH-jel) Irish: Champion. Just as Cancers are cherished as leaders of their families, they are also known and valued as defenders and protectors of their families.

Niram (NEE-rum) Hebrew: Fertile meadow. Cancer is the sign of procreation and fertility.

Noah (NO-ah) Hebrew: Rest and comfort. In the Bible, Noah was the great patriarch who saved two of every animal from the Flood. He is considered the second father of the human race, after Adam. A traditional name for boys, *Noah* has increased in popularity in recent years.

Nuru (NOO-roo) African/Swahili: Illumination. Like their ruler, the Moon, Cancers tend to light up the lives of those around them.

Obike (o-BEE-kay) African/Nigerian: A strong family. This unique name reflects the passion Cancer possesses for his family.

Odhran (OHD-rahn) Irish: Green. As one of the three Water signs of the zodiac, Cancer is associated with the colors of the sea: deep blues, violets, and greens. Variation: *Odran.*

Oran (OH-ran) Irish: Green life. This name connotes the color green and the quality of fertility, both associated with Cancer. Variations: *Oren, Orin, Orran, Orren, Orrin.*

Oren (O-ren) Hebrew: Pine tree. The pine and other sap-rich trees are associated with the sign of fertile Cancer. Variations: *Orin, Orren, Orrin.*

Osbert (OZ-burt) Old English: Luminescent divinity. This name conjures the imagery of the Moon, Cancer's ruling planet, and the sign's highly spiritual quality. Variations: *Bert, Ossie, Ozzie.*

Otto (Ah-to) Old German: Wealthy one. Owing to their abundant loyalty, wisdom, and passion, Cancers tend to prosper both financially and emotionally. Variations: *Odon, Othello, Tilo.*

Ozni (OZ-nee) Hebrew: To listen. Great troubleshooters and keepers of the peace, Cancers are eager to listen to the problems of others.

Pila (PEE-lah) Hawaiian: Constant protector. Cancer never fails to keep his loved ones from harm. Variation of *Bill.*

Porter (PORR-tir) Latin: Gatekeeper. *Porter* is a traditional and apt choice for Cancer, the ultimate homebody and keeper of the hearth.

Qamar (KAH-mahr) Arabic: Moon. Cancer is the only sign of the zodiac ruled by the Moon.

Rajnish (rahj-NEESH) Hindu: Ruler of the night. Born under the sign of the Moon, Cancers have a strong affinity for the night. Variation: *Rajneesh.*

Raymond (RAY-mund) German: Counselor and protector. Possessed with the gifts of intuition, sensitivity, and compassion, Cancers often make wonderful counselors, teachers, and advisers. Variations: *Ramon, Ray, Raymonde, Reimond.*

Regan (RAY-gan) Irish: Little king. Respected as rulers in their own homes, Cancers can extend this leadership ability to other areas of life when necessary. Variations: *Reagan, Reagen, Regen.*

Reginald (REJ-ih-nuld) Old German: Wise ruler. Known for their deep care and concern as heads of their families, Cancers make safe and successful family leaders. Variations: *Reg, Reggie, Reynold.*

Reynard (reh-NARD) Old French: Strong counselor. Possessed with a compassionate nature and desire to help others, Cancers are wonderful at offering comfort and advice to those in need. Variation: *Renny.*

Richard (RICH-urd) German: Strong ruler. This ever-popular and traditional name is ideal for Cancer, who is loyal, protective, and wise. Variations: *Dick, Dickie, Rich, Richie, Rick, Ricky.* (Famous Cancers: Richard Simmons, diet guru; Dick Button, Oscar-winning film and television actor; Ringo [Richard] Starr, musician and ex-Beatle)

Richmond (RICH-mond) Old German: All-powerful guardian. Cancers are known to be unstoppable defenders, especially when protecting those they love. Variation: *Richman.*

Rip (RIP) Dutch: Ripe. This classic "American" name suggests Cancer's renown as the sign of fertility.

Roderick (ROD-rik) German: Famous ruler. Generously involved in the lives of their families, Cancers are worthy of—and highly regarded for—their great success as parents and spouses. Variations: *Rod, Roddy, Rodrick, Rodrigo, Rurik.*

Ryan (RYE-an) Irish: Little king. *Ryan* is a popular name that connotes both the protective quality found in Cancer and the aristocratic imagery associated with the sign. Variation: *Rian.*

Schuyler (SKY-ler) Dutch: Shield. Cancers hide their true feelings deep inside, protecting themselves by showing only a protective, outside layer to the world. Variations: *Schuylar, Sky, Skylar, Skyler.*

Scott (SKOT) Old English: Scotsman. This popular name that reflects its heritage is appropriate for Cancer, who esteems history and is greatly interested in family lineage. Variations: *Scot, Scottie, Scotty.*

Selby (SELL-bee) English: Manor in the village. Cancers, who celebrate the home above all other possessions, often have the most beautiful home in the neighborhood.

Somerset (SUM-ur-set) Old English: Residence for summer. This traditional English name, with its connotation of home, is an ideal choice for Cancer, the first summer sign of the zodiac. Variations: *Sommerset, Summerset.*

Spencer (SPEN-ser) Middle English: Host. By combining their passionate love for their homes and their intense desires to please others, Cancers make outstanding hosts. Variations: *Spense, Spenser.*

Sterling (STER-leen or STER-ling) English: Silver of excellent quality. Silver is the metal associated with the sign of Cancer.

Stuart (STOO-ert) English: Steward. Old English: Dark blue. With its double meaning suggestive of both home and hospitality and the color of the sea, *Stuart* makes a classic name for a Cancer boy. Variations: *Stew, Steward, Stewart, Stu.*

Tale (TAH-leh) African/Tswana: Green. Cancer is often associated with the color green.

Trevor (TREV-ur) Welsh: Large homestead. This name connotes Cancer's deep love for his home and family. Variations: *Trev, Trevar, Trever, Trevis.*

Truman (TROO-mun) English: Loyal one. Steadfast devotion is one of Cancer's most prominent characteristics. Variations: *Trueman, Trumain, Trumann.*

Umar (oo-MAHR) Arabic: To bloom. Cancer is the sign of fertility, positioned in the summer when plants present their blooms in preparation for creating offspring.

Varick (VAR-ik) Old German: Chief who defends honorably. Cancers are known to make excellent and particularly honorable leaders. Variations: *Waric, Warrick.*

Vassily (vah-SEE-lee) Russian: Definitive guardian. Protective and nurturing, Cancers are seen as the archetypical parents of the zodiac. Variations: *Vas, Vasja, Vassi, Vasya.*

Vea (VAY-ah) Polynesian: Chief. Although they do not crave the power associated with leadership positions, Cancers often thrive when able to protect and take care of others.

Verrill (VER-il) Old French: True one. By nature, those born under the sign of Cancer are extremely loyal and trustworthy. Variations: *Verrall, Verrell, Veryl.*

Vitale (vee-TAH-lay) Latin: Life giving. Cancer is the sign of virility and fertility.

Ward (WARD) Old English: Guardian or watchman. This name is well suited to Cancer, who has a strong desire to take care of others and protect them from harm. Variations: *Warden, Worden.*

Wilfred (WIL-frid) Old English: A desire for peace. Known for their eagerness to keep the peace around them, Cancers are quick to mediate squabbles and disagreements. Variation: *Wilfrid.*

William (WILL-yum) German: Constant protector. Cancers will go to any means to ensure that those they love never come to harm. Variations: *Bill, Billy, Guillaume, Guillermo, Wilhelm, Will, Willem, Willis, Willy, Wilson.* (Famous Cancers: Billy Wilder, film director; Bill Haley, pioneering rock-and-roll musician of the 1950s; Bill Cosby, television entertainer, educator, and entrepreneur)

Wray (RAY) English: From the Old Norse, meaning dweller in the nook. Cancers are known for hiding their intense feelings deep inside themselves, showing only their hard, protective, outside layer to the world.

Wyatt (WHY-it) Old French: He who fights little. This classic name, with deep roots in the American West, is a marvelous choice for Cancer, who always prefers to keep the peace. Variations: *Wiatt, Wye*.

Xavier (ZAY-vee-ayre) Spanish: New house. Cancers are passionate about their homes, and often are the quintessential "homebodies." Variations: *Javier, Saverio, Xaver*.

Xayvion (ZAY-vee-on) African-American: New house. Any name praising the homefront suits Cancer's love of the home, and nothing feels purer to a Cancer than spreading his roots to establish a brand new home. Variations: *Savion, Xavion*.

Yair (YAH-eer) Hebrew: He will instruct. Cancers are gifted teachers, often choosing a career in education. Variation: *Jair*.

Yazid (YAH-zid) Arabic: Ever increasing. Cancer is the sign of fertility and reproduction. Variation: *Zaid*.

Yosef (YO-sef) Hebrew: God increases. Cancers possess a sacred sense of the importance of creating and supporting a flourishing family. Variations: *Yosif, Yusef, Yuzef, Zif, Ziff*.

Zakur (ZAK-kur) Hebrew: Masculine. The sign of Cancer is associated with virility and procreation.

Zan (ZAN) Hebrew: Well nourished. This name connotes the abundance of nurturing concern and skill found in every Cancer. Variation: *Zane*.

Zeus (ZOOS) Greek: In Greek mythology, the father of the gods and the great father of all. This powerful name is ideal for Cancer, who is the archetypical parent of the zodiac.

Zindel (ZIN-dell) Hebrew: Protector of mankind. Cancers have a strong need to take care of others and to shield them from any harm. Variation of *Alexander*.

Ziv (ZIV) Hebrew: To shine. This name connotes the imagery of the Moon, Cancer's ruling planet. Variations: *Zivan, Zivi*.

Famous Cancers

06-22-1906	Billy Wilder	06-27-1930	Ross Perot
06-22-1921	Joseph Papp	06-27-1951	Julia Duffy
06-22-1936	Kris Kristofferson	06-28-1902	John Dillinger
06-22-1941	Ed Bradley	06-28-1926	Mel Brooks
06-22-1949	Meryl Streep	06-28-1933	Pat Morita
06-22-1949	Lindsay Wagner	06-28-1946	Gilda Radner
06-22-1954	Freddie Prinze	06-28-1948	Kathy Bates
06-23-1894	Alfred Kinsey	06-28-1960	John Elway
06-23-1927	Bob Fosse	06-29-1900	Antoine de Saint-Exupéry
06-23-1929	June Carter		
06-24-1895	Jack Dempsey	06-29-1930	Robert Evans
06-24-1899	Chief Dan George	06-29-1944	Gary Busey
06-24-1942	Michele Lee	06-29-1948	Fred Grandy
06-24-1944	Jeff Beck	06-30-1917	Lena Horne
06-25-1903	George Orwell	06-30-1919	Susan Hayward
06-25-1924	Sidney Lumet	06-30-1934	Harry Blackstone, Jr.
06-25-1925	June Lockhart	06-30-1966	Mike Tyson
06-25-1945	Carly Simon	07-01-1916	Olivia DeHavilland
06-25-1949	Jimmie Walker	07-01-1931	Leslie Caron
06-25-1949	Phyllis George	07-01-1934	Jamie Farr
06-25-1963	George Michael	07-01-1934	Jean Marsh
06-26-1892	Pearl S. Buck	07-01-1941	Twyla Tharp
06-26-1904	Peter Lorre	07-01-1942	Karen Black
06-26-1922	Eleanor Parker	07-01-1942	Genevieve Bujold
06-26-1961	Greg LeMond	07-01-1945	Deborah Harry
06-26-1970	Chris O'Donnell	07-01-1952	Dan Aykroyd
06-27-1880	Helen Keller	07-01-1961	Princess Diana of England
06-27-1927	Bob Keeshan		

07-01-1967	Pamela Anderson	07-08-1973	Kathleen Robertson
07-01-1977	Liv Tyler	07-09-1927	Ed Ames
07-02-1877	Hermann Hesse	07-09-1947	O. J. Simpson
07-02-1908	Thurgood Marshall	07-09-1952	John Tesh
07-02-1922	Dan Rowan	07-09-1956	Tom Hanks
07-02-1951	Cheryl Ladd	07-09-1957	Kelly McGillis
07-03-1878	George M. Cohan	07-09-1958	Jimmy Smits
07-03-1883	Franz Kafka	07-09-1964	Courtney Love
07-03-1927	Ken Russell	07-09-1976	Fred Savage
07-03-1937	Tom Stoppard	07-10-1920	David Brinkley
07-03-1952	Alan Autry	07-10-1921	Jake La Motta
07-03-1962	Tom Cruise	07-10-1926	Fred Gwynne
07-04-1872	Calvin Coolidge	07-10-1943	Arthur Ashe
07-04-1883	Rube Goldberg	07-10-1947	Arlo Guthrie
07-04-1902	George Murphy	07-11-1767	John Quincy Adams
07-04-1911	Mitch Miller	07-11-1899	E. B. White
07-04-1918	Abigail Van Buren	07-11-1920	Yul Brynne
07-04-1918	Ann Landers	07-11-1931	Tab Hunter
07-04-1924	Eva Marie Saint	07-11-1934	Giorgio Armani
07-04-1927	Neil Simon	07-11-1953	Leon Spinks
07-04-1928	Gina Lollobrigida	07-11-1959	Suzanne Vega
07-04-1930	George Steinbrenner	07-12-1817	Henry David Thoreau
07-04-1943	Geraldo Rivera	07-12-1895	Buckminster Fuller
07-05-1810	P. T. Barnum	07-12-1895	Oscar Hammerstein
07-05-1889	Jean Cocteau	07-12-1908	Milton Berle
07-05-1951	Huey Lewis	07-12-1917	Andrew Wyeth
07-06-1915	Laverne Andrews	07-12-1934	Van Cliburn
07-06-1921	Nancy Reagan	07-12-1937	Bill Cosby
07-06-1925	Merv Griffin	07-12-1948	Richard Simmons
07-06-1925	Bill Haley	07-12-1971	Kristi Yamaguchi
07-06-1927	Janet Leigh	07-13-1928	Bob Crane
07-06-1932	Della Reese	07-13-1940	Patrick Stewart
07-06-1937	Ned Beatty	07-13-1942	Harrison Ford
07-06-1946	Sylvester Stallone	07-13-1946	Cheech Marin
07-07-1922	Pierre Cardin	07-14-1912	Woody Guthrie
07-07-1927	Doc Severinsen	07-14-1913	Gerald R. Ford
07-07-1940	Ringo Starr	07-14-1918	Ingmar Bergman
07-07-1949	Shelley Duvall	07-14-1923	Dale Robertson
07-08-1839	John D. Rockefeller	07-14-1926	Harry Dean Stanton
07-08-1908	Nelson Rockefeller	07-14-1930	Polly Bergen
07-08-1914	Billy Eckstine	07-14-1932	Rosie Grier
07-08-1935	Steve Lawrence	07-15-1606	Rembrandt
07-08-1951	Anjelica Huston	07-15-1935	Alex Karras
07-08-1952	Marianne Williamson	07-15-1944	Jan-Michael Vincent
07-08-1958	Kevin Bacon	07-15-1946	Linda Ronstadt

07-15-1973	Brian Austin
07-16-1821	Mary Baker Eddy
07-16-1907	Barbara Stanwyck
07-16-1911	Ginger Rogers
07-16-1924	Bess Myerson
07-16-1968	Barry Sanders
07-17-1889	Erle Stanley Gardner
07-17-1899	James Cagney
07-17-1912	Art Linkletter
07-17-1917	Phyllis Diller
07-17-1934	Donald Sutherland
07-17-1935	Diahann Carroll
07-17-1952	David Hasselhoff
07-17-1952	Phoebe Snow
07-18-1911	Hume Cronyn
07-18-1913	Red Skelton
07-18-1914	Harriet Nelson
07-18-1918	Nelson Mandela
07-18-1921	John Glenn
07-18-1929	Dick Button
07-18-1939	Hunter S. Thompson
07-18-1941	Martha Reeves
07-19-1834	Edgar Degas
07-19-1860	Lizzie Borden
07-19-1922	George McGovern
07-19-1941	Vikki Carr
07-20-1938	Diana Rigg
07-20-1938	Natalie Wood
07-20-1946	Kim Carnes
07-20-1947	Carlos Santana
07-21-1911	Marshall McLuhan
07-21-1920	Isaac Stern
07-21-1922	Kay Starr
07-21-1924	Don Knotts
07-21-1926	Norman Jewison
07-21-1948	Cat Stevens
07-21-1952	Robin Williams
07-21-1957	Jon Lovitz
07-22-1898	Alexander Calder
07-22-1923	Robert Dole
07-22-1928	Orson Bean
07-22-1934	Louise Fletcher
07-22-1940	Alex Trebek
07-22-1947	Albert Brooks
07-22-1947	Danny Glover
07-22-1947	Don Henley
07-22-1949	Alan Menken
07-23-1893	Karl Menninger
07-23-1934	Bert Convy
07-23-1936	Don Drysdale
07-23-1961	Woody Harrelson

LEO
(July 24–August 23)

GLYPH: ♌
SYMBOL: The Lion
POLARITY: Masculine
QUALITY: Fixed
ELEMENT: Fire
RULING PLANET: Sun
BIRTHSTONE: Ruby
SPECIAL COLORS: Red, gold, and orange
FLOWERS: Sunflower and marigold
METAL: Gold
ANIMALS: Cats of all types
MOST LIKEABLE TRAITS: Exuberance, magnetism, self-confidence, and generosity

♌

Like the Lion that symbolizes their sign, Leos cut a powerful and commanding figure—regal, dominating, aristocratic, dramatic, self-confident, and flamboyant. These qualities help to make Leos the consummate superstars of the zodiac, born performers who crave the spotlight from early childhood on. Parents of Leo children can expect to be held captive and enchanted audiences of their dramatic, talented, magnetic, and ego-driven cubs.

General Qualities

Leo is ruled by the Sun, the most potent celestial influence in all of astrology. The Sun imbues Leos with a powerful sense of self, enormous vitality, and a commanding personality. Sun-ruled Leos light up the world. They are born leaders and easily draw people into their golden circle. The Sun's dramatic effects in Leo are intensified by the fact that Leo is also a Masculine and Fixed Fire sign.

The Masculine influence in this sign endows Leos with tremendous reserves of physical and emotional energy that Leos easily tap into—for their legendary stamina and creative leaps of inspiration—and then just as easily channel outward, frequently in very public arenas, to entertain, dazzle, lead, and command. The Fixed quality of Leo directs all that energy with single-minded determination and resourcefulness. The influence of Fire in Leo's chart adds a considerable measure of impulsiveness, aggressiveness, and enthusiasm to the mix.

Clearly, Leos are the high-voltage stars of the zodiac and astrology's bonafide royalty. They command attention, and they revel in it. Indeed, the roll call of well-known Leos may be the most impressive in the zodiac, including some of modern history's most famous and infamous movers and shakers. In fact, many Leos make such powerful public impressions that they go on to achieve icon status.

In politics, science, business, and the military, notable Leos include: Bill Clinton, Menachem Begin, Fidel Castro, Napoleon Bonaparte, Norman Schwarzkopf, Henry Ford, Malcolm Ford, and Carl Jung. In the arts, innovative Leo directors, producers, and writers include: Alfred Hitchcock, Stanley Kubrick, John Huston, Gene Roddenberry, Cecil B. DeMille, George Bernard Shaw, Herman Melville, James Baldwin, Ray Bradbury, Dorothy Parker, and Percy Bysshe Shelley. Famous Leo actors and performers include: Peter O'Toole, Dustin Hoffman, Robert DeNiro, Sean Penn, Robert Redford, and Antonio Banderas, as well as superstars Madonna, Whitney Houston, Tony Bennett, and Mick Jagger. Among the famous Leos who have made an indelible mark on the cultural landscape and achieved icon status are Annie Oakley, Jacqueline Kennedy Onassis, Mae West, Julia Child, Lucille Ball, Amelia Earhart, Andy Warhol, and Jerry Garcia.

What these and all Leos have in common is a driving need to be the rulers of their particular domains. They want to be the absolute best in whatever they do, regardless of challenges or public opinion. And Leos combine this driving need to succeed with an unshakable belief in themselves and in their ability to have and do it all. Naturally, large measures of egotism and self-absorption, together with an innate desire to be the center of people's attention and devotion, are hallmarks of this flamboyant, Sun-driven sign. Such qualities may appear off-putting at first glance, but they are the stuff of every great success story—and the secret envy of many.

While imbuing Leo with such a magnificent ego and single-minded drive, the brilliant Sun also endows Leo with less self-centered qualities. Leos are wonderfully warmhearted and generous to family, friends, and associates. They are emotionally expansive and uninhibited in showing their affection. They are wholehearted optimists who have a glorious zest for living that is downright infectious, and they are delightfully magnanimous about taking everyone along on their exhilarating ride through life. Leos are a joy to be around—once you catch your breath and pay them the homage they believe they're due!

Home

First and foremost, and from early on in life, Leos demand attention, attention, and then more attention. As the reigning royalty of astrology and the zodiac's consummate entertainers, Leos need spectators. One way or another, these lion kings and queens are always "on," and they are most comfortable and happy holding court or performing center stage. Home provides young Leos with their first royal arena, and family provides them with their first adoring subjects.

Most children thrive on the simple attention—nurturing, caretaking, playing, and displays of affection—they receive in their everyday interactions with family and siblings. But Leo children demand a more compelling and proactive kind of attention. Leos need a captive and enthusiastic audience—and not because they need to be reassured they are loved (as do their nearest cousins, Cancers). Leos know they are eminently lovable, and they naturally assume you think them wonderful too. What these quintessential stars need from family and friends is critique and feedback, validation that they are on the right road to becoming the unqualified successes that they are destined to be.

More than any other sign in the zodiac, Leos regard home as a critical dress rehearsal for real life. Early on, they begin to search for the one unique role that will guarantee them "stardom" and set them apart from the ordinary masses. Home becomes the testing ground where Leos can experiment with and parade their talents, essay the roles of a variety of characters, try on costumes, language, and postures, and rewrite and restage their life scripts. What Leos desperately need from their parent-audience is unqualified confirmation that they are getting their "parts" right and wholehearted affirmation that they are "performing" well.

Be prepared to give your Leo child an extra measure of your undivided attention and an extra round of appreciative applause. Consciously affirming the Leo child's burgeoning ego, considerable pride, and precocious sense of self-mastery goes far to helping a Leo learn how to be healthfully self-seeking and not autocractically self-serving.

Provide Leo children with a multidimensional, brightly colored, artistic, and well-equipped playing ground that gives them ample mental stimulation and all the tools they need to explore their great and varied creative gifts. Such an arena will engage Leo's considerable emotional and mental energy and prevent— what in Leo's book is the cardinal sin in life—boredom. When Leos are bored, they often shut down and do nothing at all. Laziness is the frequent and unattractive response of an under-stimulated and underappreciated Leo.

Give your Leo cubs plenty of safe space in which to romp, tumble, dance, fly, and simply flex their muscles. Not only do Leos possess great physical energy, but they also need a healthful outlet for all the excess emotional energy they generate in any single day. This activity outlet may give parents a much-needed break from their Leo child's insistent demands for attention, affirmation, and applause.

The rewards for giving gifted Leos all the extra time and attention they demand are great and long lasting. Well-nurtured Leos are remarkably joyous, golden children with a healthy, abundant sense of self. Because they have an abiding belief in their ability to endure and succeed, they can shake off hurts, large and small, and nobly get on with their lives. They constantly move forward, and rarely have time to hold a grudge. Indeed, Leos view life as a wondrous amusement park ride, and are always eager to invite the rest of the world along. They never forget the early attention and favors they are paid, and remain passionately loyal and generous to those who gave them. And because Leos so fervently believe that anything is possible and achievable if one wants it badly enough, they easily transmit this belief to others around them who may not be so self-assured. Like the life-sustaining Sun that governs them, Leos radiate their own unique and irresistible warmth, one that draws many willingly to their sides.

School and Play

Leos, naturally bright and self-directed, have very strong ideas about, and preferences for, what's worth their time and energy. Leos want to be the superstars of their classrooms, and they invariably throw themselves into tasks that draw on their considerable creative talents and spotlight their individuality—writing, oration, music, debate, and art. They show less interest in abstract or "dry" subjects, like math, science, and history, and if they are to succeed in these challenging areas, they often need the one-on-one guidance of an attentive teacher who flatters and cajoles them into believing they can meet the challenge. Left to their own devices, Leos may have the tendency to just give up when they feel they're not succeeding. They may even pretend they're simply not interested in a subject, when in fact they are feeling frustrated and defeated.

Leos often excel in group tasks and projects when they are allowed to take the lead. Given Leo's warmth, confidence, energy, and generosity, most other children (with the exception of feisty Aries) gladly turn over the reigns of command to Leo, who can be counted on to get the project done with flair and make it fun in the process.

With their great physical energy and grace, Leos make natural athletes, often choosing to play the more flashy and dangerous sports, such as football, soccer, and hockey. But sports usually remain just a hobby for Leo, and a childhood hobby at that, because Leo's great creative instincts and drive to be number one are simply not satisfied in the sports arena.

At play, when Leos aren't performing for their family, they often withdraw to their rooms or backyards, with a few friends in tow, and weave elaborate stories and dramas in which they direct all the action and play all the leading roles, complete with background music and changes of costume, dialect, props, and scenery. Any challenging and creative task, in fact, will absorb Leo's attention, often for hours at a time. Parents of Leo children must encourage and validate the richness and worth of these quiet creative pursuits, so that Leos can learn the joy to be found outside the limelight as well as in it.

The World

The world is Leo's oyster, plain and simple. Leos joyfully march out from the testing grounds of family and school, confident of their unique gifts and determined to make an indelible impression on their own particular patch of Earth. And they have all the ego, talent, and energy to do it—they've been practicing for years! Whether their patch of Earth is politics, industry, or the arts, Leos know they have an invaluable role to play and stop at nothing to reach center stage.

Along the way, Leos ably demonstrate that they are the zodiac's natural leaders, with their innately commanding and magnetic personalities that radiate a mesmerizing kind of charisma. They are eloquent and moving speechmakers who are adept at working the emotional pulse of any crowd. Leos know how to give the people exactly what they want, which may be why the sign is so abundantly represented by politicians and world leaders.

With their deep creative gifts and enormous emotional energy, Leos love the spotlight, luxuriate in attention, and blossom with adulation. In grabbing center stage, they may be alternately dramatic and flamboyant, sinuous and seductive, aristocratic and aloof. Whatever they do, they command respect, and even adoration. Leo is the sign of the performer, hence many Leos become consummate performing artists.

In return for the attention, authority, and adulation that others freely give them, Leos give much in return. They are gloriously optimistic, fiercely loyal, warm and generous, passionate, life affirming, and eager to please. Once Leos get your attention, they don't just rest on their laurels and bask in it. Leos strive to *hold* your attention, too. And they work long and hard to do just that, lighting up the world around them, helping to make it a more joyous and fascinating place.

Choosing a Name for Your Leo Child

When choosing a name for your Leo girl or boy, consider the major attributes and symbols associated with the sign: Leo is the sign of nobility, leadership, flamboyance, and creativity. Leos are commanding and influential, energetic and extravagant, and they love to be the center of attention.

Leo is also one of three Fire signs and the only zodiac sign ruled by the Sun, the most powerful planetary influence in astrology. Leos are warm and generous, enthusiastic and impulsive, and they frequently have magnetic personalities. They are natural leaders who enjoy the spotlight and are adept at drawing others into their circle of influence.

Leos have a vital and burning quality about them, and the colors associated with this sign—red, gold, and orange—reflect that flamboyant quality. The fiery ruby is the official birthstone of Leo, but the diamond is also strongly associated with the sign. Gold is the sign's precious metal. Sunflowers and marigolds, with their bright and showy blossoms, are Leo's official flowers, and orange and other citrus trees also are affiliated with the sign. Its animal symbol is the regal Lion, and the sign governs all types of felines. Leo is a summer sign, touching the hot months of July and August.

When you choose a name for your child, also bear in mind some of Leo children's key personal qualities. Vivacious, entertaining, magnanimous, extroverted, and inherently attractive—even beautiful—they are born actors and actresses. They are considered the archetypical performers of the zodiac and have a tremendous love for all things creative. Leos have great strength of will and a single-minded determination to excel at whatever they do.

For additional inspiration when choosing a name for your Leo child, especially a middle name, you may want to look over the listings in Leo's two companion Fire signs, Aries and Sagittarius.

Names for Leo Girls

Aceline (ay-suh-LEEN) French: Of noble birth. This lovely and aristocratic French name is a beautiful choice for a girl born under Leo, the sign of nobility and high birth. Variation: *Ascelin*.

Ada (AYE-dah) Old English: Of noble birth. Leo females are the reigning queens of the zodiac, making this classic English name an excellent choice for a Leo girl. Variations: *Adda, Addie, Adi, Aida*.

Adelaide (ADD-eh-lade) Old German: Noble. This fanciful and musical old name is an apt choice for regal and creative Leo.

Adelle (ah-DELL) Old German: Highborn. This classic and popular name—or one of its beautiful variations—is suitable for aristocratic Leo, the queen of the zodiac. Variations: *Adelia, Adelita, Dela, Lela*.

Ah Kum (AH-KOOM) Chinese: Good as gold. Gold is the precious metal associated with the sign of Leo.

Aidan (AYD-uhn) Irish: Fire. Leo is one of three Fire signs and the only sign ruled by the Sun. *Aidan* is also a suitable name for a boy. Variations: *Aidana, Aydana, Edana*.

Akahana (ah-kah-HAH-nah) Japanese: Red flower. The color red is strongly associated with the sign of Leo.

Akaula (ah-kah-OO-lah) Hawaiian: Red sunset. Both the color red and the Sun are uniquely associated with Leo.

Alake (ah-lah-KAY) African/Nigerian: One to be fussed over. Leo children have well-developed egos and often expect to be the center of everyone's attention.

Alberta (ahl-BUR-tah) Old English: Noble and brilliant. This classic royal name—celebrated by Eric Clapton in a song of that title—is enjoying a comeback. Variations: *Albertina, Albertine, Berta, Berti, Elbertina, Elby*.

Alcinda (ahl-SIN-dah) Latin: Light. Leos are ruled by the Sun and share many of that star's bright and shining qualities.

Aleka (ah-LEH-kah) Hawaiian: Noble. Aristocratic and outstanding Leo princesses are well suited to this melodic and unusual Hawaiian name.

Alepeka (ah-leh-PEE-kah) Hawaiian: Bright and noble. As children who are ruled by the Sun, regal Leos have a luminous and commanding persona. Variation: *Alebeta*.

Alesa (ah-LEH-sah) Hawaiian: Noble one. This lyrical name is a lovely choice for regal Leo. Variations: *Aleka, Alika*.

Ali (ah-LEE) Arabic: Greatest. Leos are famous for their healthy and well-developed egos. Variations: *Allie, Ally*.

Alice (AL-lis) Middle English: Nobility. This classic English name is perfect for a girl born under Leo, the sign of nobility and high birth. Variations: *Alicia, Alys, Alyssa*.

Alike (ah-LEE-keh) African/Nigerian: Nobility. This name is an unusual but powerful choice for aristocratic Leo, the Lion queen.

Alina (ah-LEE-nuh) Russian: Nobility. Leo children are the reigning kings and queens of the zodiac, making this popular Russian name—or one of its beautiful variations—an apt choice for a Leo girl. Variations: *Aleen, Aleena, Aline, Leena, Leenah, Lena*.

Alita (ah-LEE-tah) Spanish: Nobility. Traditional Leos are innately regal, often cutting a commanding figure in the public arena. Variation: *Alida*.

Alzubra (ahl-ZOO-brah) Arabic: For the name of a star in the constellation Leo. *Alzubra* is an ideal name for Leos, the superstars of the zodiac.

Amelia (ah-MEEL-ya) Latin: Hard worker. This classic name is most appropriate for success-conscious Leo, who can be single-mindedly determined in pursuit of her chosen goals. Variations: *Amalea, Amalia, Amalies, Amelita*. (Famous Leo: Amelia Earhart, aviatrix)

Amira (ah-MEE-ruh) Arabic: Leader. Leos, with their magnetic personalities and supreme self-confidence, are born leaders. Variations: *Ameerah, Amirah, Meerah, Mira*.

Anala (ah-NAH-luh) Hindu: Fire. Leo is one of three Fire signs, and the only sign ruled by the powerful Sun.

Aonani (ow-NAH-nee) Hawaiian: Beautiful light. *Aonani* is a lovely and lyrical Hawaiian name for the sunny-dispositioned Leo.

Ariel (ah-ree-AYL) Hebrew: Lioness of God. This classic name, most recently popularized in Disney's *The Little Mermaid*, is a marvelous choice for a girl born under the sign of Leo, whose animal symbol is the Lion. Variations: *Ari, Ariela, Ariella, Arielle*.

Asa (AH-sah) Japanese: Starting life at dawn. This name is a lovely and unusual choice for a Leo girl, whose ebullient personality is as bright and warming as the Sun.

Audrey (AW-dree) Old English: Regal. *Audrey* is a classic and aristocratic name for a royal Leo girl. Variations: *Audie, Audra, Audree, Audreen, Audria*.

Augusta (aw-GUSS-tah) Latin: Grand. This ancient Roman name is an impressive and commanding choice for regal and expansive Leo. Variation: *Augustina*.

Aurelia (aw-REE-lya or aw-RAY-lya) English: Gold. Gold is the precious metal associated with the sign of Leo, and *Aurelia*, with its suggestion of rosy, golden light, is a lovely choice for a Leo girl. Variations: *Arella, Aurene, Auriel, Aurielle*.

Aurora (oh-ROHR-ah) Latin: The Roman goddess of the dawn. *Aurora* is wonderfully suitable for a Leo Sun child.

Awendela (ah-wayn-DAY-lah) Native American: Sunrise. The Sun is the single most potent influence in the sign of Leo.

Ayah (EYE-ah) African/Swahili: Bright. Like the Sun, Leos spread warmth and light wherever they go.

Bahira (ba-HEE-rah) Arabic: Electrifying. Leos are noted for their bright and energetic personalities.

Bella (BEL-lah) Old English: Noble and bright; Italian: Beautiful. This newly popular English name is perfect for a regal and exuberant Leo girl. Variations: *Bela, Belle*.

Bertha (BUR-thah) German: Bright. This traditional German name—or one of its lovely variations—is a good choice for radiant and magnetic Leo. Variations: *Berta, Berthe, Bertina, Bird, Birdie, Birtha.*

Beryl (BURL or BEH-ril) Sanskrit: Cat's eye. The sign of Leo governs all felines, and this classic name well suits a Leo lioness. Variations: *Berri, Berrie, Berry, Beryle.*

Bonita (bah-NEE-tah or bo-NEE-tah) Spanish: Beautiful. All Leos, with their sunny and larger-than-life personalities, have an inherent, often unique, beauty. Variations: *Bonni, Bonnie, Bunnie, Bunny.*

Brenda (BREN-dah) English: On fire. This is a classic choice for Leo, who is powerfully influenced by the Sun and is one of three Fire signs. Variations: *Bren, Brenn, Brennda, Brenndah.*

Caltha (KAHL-thah) Latin: Marigold. The brilliantly colored marigold is one of the two flowers associated with the sign of Leo. *Callie*, a variation of *Caltha*, is currently one of the most popular names for girls in America. Variations: *Cal, Callie, Kal, Kallie, Kaltha.*

Chamania (kah-mah-NEE-ah) Hebrew: Sunflower. The large-blossomed and warm-colored sunflower is one of the two flowers associated with the sign of Leo.

Chao-xing (chow-TSEENG) Chinese: Morning star. Sun-kissed Leo is renowned for her ability to light up the world around her.

Charisma (kah-RIZ-mah) American: Magnetic personality. Fiercely exuberant and radiant Leo, who excels in drawing people toward her, personifies the word *charisma.*

Chrisann (kriss-AHN) English: Golden flower. Gold is one of the colors associated with Leo, and marigolds and sunflowers, with their brilliant and showy summer blossoms, are the flowers of the sign. Variations: *Chrisanne, Chrysandra, Chrysann, Chrysanta.*

Clara (KLAH-rah) English: Bright. This traditional name is a splendid choice for a sunny Leo girl. Variations: *Clair, Clairine, Clare, Claresta, Clarissa.*

Dagna (DAG-nah) Scandinavian: New day. The Sun's influence in Leo imbues children born under that sign with a magnetic warmth and energy. Variations: *Dagney, Dagny.*

Dai (DYE) Japanese: Grand. Noble Leos have an aristocratic and commanding presence.

Damita (dah-MEE-tah) Spanish: Baby princess. From her earliest days, a Leo female reflects the sign's affiliation with royalty and high birth.

Danica (DAN-i-kah) Slavic: Morning star. Leo, who is ruled by the Sun, often seeks fame in the public eye. Variations: *Danika, Dannika.*

Darah (DAH-rah) African-American: Princess. This name, a modern variation of *Sarah*, is perfect for a girl born under Leo, the sign of nobility.

Dawn (DAWN) English: Sunrise. *Dawn* is a classic choice for Leo, for whom the Sun is such a strong influence. Variations: *Dawna, Dawne, Dawnelle, Dawnette, Dawnn.*

Dea (DAY-ah) Latin: Goddess. Aristocratic and magnetic Leos often achieve superstar status in the public arena.

Della (DEL-ah) Old German: Of the nobility. *Della*, a recently popular name, is perfect for Leo, the sign of nobility and high birth. Variation: *Dell.*

Derry (DARE-ee) Irish: Red haired. Red is a classic Leo color, and many Leo children are born redheads. Variations: *Deri, Derrie*.

Dior (dee-ORR) French: Golden. Gold is one of Sun-kissed Leo's primary colors. Variation: *D'or*.

Dona (DON-nah) English: Mighty. Like the Lion that symbolizes their sign, many Leos have an autocratic and commanding presence. Variations: *Dominica, Dominika*.

Donelle (don-EL) Irish: Ruler of the world. This classic Irish name suits Leo, the sign of royalty.

Donoma (doo-NO-mah) Native American: Sun. The Sun rules the sign of Leo.

Dory (DORR-ee) French: Golden. Golds, reds, and oranges are the colors associated with Leo.

Drisana (dree-SAH-nah) Hindu: Daughter of the Sun. This classic name is a perfect choice for Sun-driven Leo. Variation: *Drisa*.

Edana (eh-DAHN-ah) Irish: Tiny flame. Leo is one of the zodiac's three Fire signs.

Edeline (EDD-ah-leen) German: Noble. Leo is the sign of nobility, aristocracy, and high birth.

Eibblin (ebb-LIN) Irish: Shining. A Fire sign and the only sign of the zodiac ruled by the Sun, Leo is renowned for her exuberance, warmth, and zest for life.

Eileen (eye-LEEN) Irish: Shining. This name is a brilliant choice for a girl born under the Sun-rich sign of Leo. Variations: *Aileen, Ailene, Aline, Ayleen, Ilene*.

Elaine (ee-LAYNE) French: Bright, shining. This traditional name maintains modern appeal for an energetic and magnetic Leo girl. Variations: *Alayne, Elaina, Elana, Elayne, Eleni, Ellaine, Ellen.*

Elata (eh-LAH-tah) Latin: Held in high regard. Royal Leos are natural leaders in business, politics, and the arts.

Eldora (ell-DORR-ah) Spanish: Coated by gold. Gold is the precious metal associated with the sign of Leo. Variations: *Eldoria, Eldoris.*

Electra (eh-LEK-trah) Greek: Shining one. Charismatic Leo, with her confident and energetic personality, is a born star. Variation: *Elektra.*

Eli (ELL-ee) Scandinavian: Light. This popular and classic Scandinavian name is a terrific choice for a girl born under Leo, the only zodiac sign ruled by the Sun. *Eli* is also a good choice for a Leo boy. Variations: *Ellie, Elly.*

Elidi (eh-LEE-dee) Greek: Gift from the Sun. The Sun rules the sign of Leo and imbues Leo children with great warmth, energy, and magnetism.

Elsa (ELL-sah) Spanish: Noble. Leo is the sign of nobility and high birth. Variations: *Else, Elsie, Ilse.*

Ena (EE-nah) Irish: Bright. Like their ruler, the Sun, Leos are warm, sunny, and brilliant.

Erica (eyr-REE-kah or EH-ri-kah) Scandinavian: Ever powerful, regal. Leos, born under the sign of nobility, possess great strength and often make natural leaders. Variations: *Erika, Erykah.*

Etain (ay-TAHN) Irish: Irish Sun goddess. Royal and aristocratic Leos, the monarchs of the zodiac, are governed by the Sun.

Eugenia (yoo-GEHN-ee-ah or yoo-JEEN-ee-ah) Greek: Well born. *Eugenia* is a beautiful and fitting name for the noble Leo girl. Variations: *Eugena, Eugenie*.

Faline (fah-LEEN) Latin: Catlike. The sign of Leo, symbolized by the Lion, also governs all other types of felines.

Flannery (FLAN-uhr-ee) Irish: Red hair. Red is the color most strongly associated with the sign of Leo, and many Leos are born redheads. This classic Irish name, popularized by one of America's great writers, Flannery O'Connor, is an apt choice for a creative Leo. Variation: *Flanna*.

Galiena (gah-lee-AYN-yah) German: High one. Leo is the sign of nobility and high birth.

Galina (gah-LEE-nah) Russian: Shining one. Sun-driven Leos are the superstars of the zodiac and easily secure a favored spot in the public eye.

Gilda (JILL-dah or GEEL-dah) English: Golden. Gold is the precious metal associated with the sign of Leo, making this lovely old English name a wonderful choice for a magnetic Leo girl.

Gillian (JIL-lee-un) Latin: Derived from *Julius* for July (the month in which many Leos are born). This classic name is currently enjoying a renewed popularity, due in part to the many fans of actress Gillian Anderson of *The X-Files*. Variations: *Jill, Jillian, Jilly*. (Famous Leo: Jill St. John, actress)

Golda (GOLD-ah) Old English: Of gold. Gold is the precious metal associated with the sign of Leo. Variations: *Goldarina, Goldi, Goldia, Goldie, Goldina*.

Gurice (goo-REES) Hebrew: Lion cub. The Lion is the animal symbol for the sign of Leo. This very popular Hebrew name is perfect for a Leo cub, with her abundant energy and need for attention.

Halina (hahl-EEN-ah) Russian: Shining one. The Sun imbues Leo with great reserves of warmth, exuberance, and simple joie de vivre.

Helia (HEH-lee-ah or HEE-lee-ah) Greek: The Sun. The sign of Leo is ruled by the Sun.

Honour (ON-ur) Latin: Esteemed or dignified. Leo is the sign of nobility and high birth, and Leos have a naturally command-ing presence. Variations: *Honor, Honoria.*

Ilka (ILL-kah) Slavic: Committed to success. Leos possess a single-minded determination to succeed at whatever they do. Variations: *Elke, Ilke.*

Imperia (eem-PARE-ee-ah) Latin: Imperial. Inherently noble and aristocratic, Leo women are the reigning monarchs of the zodiac.

Jacqueline (JAK-ka-lin or zhahk-LEEN) French: One who re-places others. This classic English and French name is particu-larly suited to charismatic Leo, who so often is driven to be center stage in the public eye. Variations: *Jacalyn, Jackalin, Jackelyn, Jacki, Jackie, Jaclyn, Jacolyn, Jacquelynne, Jacqui.* (Famous Leo: Jacqueline Kennedy Onassis, former First Lady and cultural icon)

Jamila (jah-MEE-lah) Arabic: Beautiful. Leos possess a com-manding and magnetic energy that lends them an inherent, and often unique, beauty. Variations: *Jamilah, Jamillah, Jamillia.*

Juliana (joo-lee-AN-nah) Latin: From *Julianus*, for July (the month in which many Leos are born). This name is a classic choice for a Leo girl born in July. Variations: *Juliann, Julianna, Julianne*.

Kalala (kay-LAH-lah) Hawaiian: Bright. Sun-kissed Leos spread warmth and light wherever they go. Variation: *Kalara*.

Kalama (kuh-LAH-muh) Hawaiian: Flaming torch. Charismatic Leo, ruled by the Sun, is one of three Fire signs.

Kalinda (kay-LIN-dah) Hindu: The Sun. The Sun has a potent influence in Leo, greatly magnifying Leo's natural warmth and energy. Variation: *Kaleenda*.

Kaliona (kah-lee-O-nah) Hawaiian: Lion. The king of the jungle is the symbol for Leo: Just as the Lion reigns over other beasts, Leos are known as rulers of the zodiac.

Kamea (kah-MEH-ah) Hawaiian: The one and only. Leos, with their abundantly healthy egos and supreme self-confidence, are the superstars of the zodiac.

Karla (CAHR-lah) Australian/Aborigine: Fire. A classic name with an unusual origin, this is a perfect choice for Leo, one of the three Fire signs of the zodiac. Variation: *Carla*

Kaulana (kow-LAH-nuh) Hawaiian: Famous one. Leos naturally seek the limelight and are frequently leaders in their chosen fields.

Kenna (KEN-nah) Welsh: Beauty born of fire. Leo is one of the three Fire signs, and the only sign in the zodiac that is ruled by the Sun. Variation: *Kenina*.

Kimi (KEE-mee) Japanese: Superb. *Kimi* is a classic and popular Japanese name that is eminently suitable for a self-confident and charismatic Leo. Variations: *Kimie, Kimiko*.

Kin (keen) Japanese: Gold. Gold is the precious metal associated with the sign of Leo.

Kineta (kee-NET-tah) Greek: Dynamic. Leos, brimming with physical and emotional energy, always cut a commanding figure.

Kisa (KEE-sah) Russian: Kitten. Leo governs all felines, and this delightful, classic Russian name is a charming choice for a Leo girl. Variations: *Keesa, Kysa.*

Lady (lady) English: A royal title, befitting aristocratic Leo.

Lara (LAR-ah) English: Famous. This beautiful and traditional name, popularized in the film *Dr. Zhivago*, is a wonderful choice for success-driven Leo, who craves the spotlight. Variations: *Lari, Larina, Larinda, Larita.*

Lareina (la-RAIN-ah) Spanish: Queen. Leo is the sign of nobility and high birth. Variations: *Lareine, Larena, Larraine, Lorena.*

Leandra (lee-AHN-drah) English: Like a lioness. The Lion symbolizes the sign of Leo. Variations: *Leodora, Leoline, Leonelle, Leonissa.*

Leanore (LEE-ah-nor) English: Bright one. Sun-kissed Leos frequently have a charismatic and burning quality about them that draws wide attention in the public arena. Variations: *Lenora, Lenorah, Lenore, Leonara, Leonora, Leonore.*

Lena (LEE-nah) English: Bright one. Self-confident and success-driven Leos often achieve widespread fame. Variations: *Leni, Lenia, Lina, Linah.*

Lenna (LEHN-ah) German: The strength of a lion. The sign of Leo, one of whose characteristics is great physical energy, is symbolized by the Lion. Variations: *Lenda, Lennah.*

Leonarda (lay-o-NAHR-dah) German: Roar of the lion. Born under the symbol of the Lion, Leos always make certain that their voices are heard. Variations: *Lenda, Leonora*.

Leonie (LAY-o-nee or lay-OH-nee) French: Lioness. The Lion is the symbol of the sign of Leo. Variations: *Leonda, Leondra, Leondrea, Leonia, Leonine, Leonissa*.

Leora (LEE-or-ah) Greek: Light. This is a lovely name for a Leo girl that suggests the brightness of the Sun, Leo's ruler. Variations: *Leorah, Liora, Liorah*.

Levana (leh-VAHN-ah) Latin: Rising sun. The Sun rules the sign of Leo.

Leviah (leh-VEE-ah) Hebrew: God's lioness. The Lion is the symbol of the sign of Leo. Variations: *Levia, Liviya*.

Liona (lee-OH-nah) Hawaiian: Roaring lion. The symbol of Leo, the Lion in this Hawaiian name, exemplifies the exuberance of outspoken Leos.

Lucinda (loo-SIN-dah) Latin: Beautiful light. This lyrical name is a classic choice for Sun-burnished Leo.

Lucy (LOO-see) English: Light. This English name is a brilliant option for Leo's superstar girls. Variations: *Lucia, Lucie, Lucienne, Lucilla, Lucille, Lucita*. (Famous Leo: Lucille Ball, actress and comedienne)

Lupe (LOO-pay) Hawaiian: Ruby. The ruby is the birthstone of Leo.

Madonna (mah-DON-nah) Italian: My lady. *Madonna* is a commanding name for regal and charismatic Leo. (Famous Leo: Madonna, singer, actress, and pop icon)

Majesta (mah-JESS-tah) Latin: Royal. Leo is the sign of nobility and high birth. Variations: *Maja, Majesty.*

Malama (mah-LAHM-ah) Polynesian: Shine. Sun-driven Leos often light up the world for those around them.

Marigold (MARE-ih-gold) English: Flower. The marigold is one of the two flowers associated with the sign of Leo. (The other is the sunflower.)

Marisol (mah-ree-SOLE) Spanish: Bitter Sun. The usually sunny Leo can show a dark and sulky side on occasion—particularly when she's not getting the attention she wants. Variation: *Marizol.*

Martha (MAHR-thah) English: Lady. This old and traditional name—with several beautiful variations—is a fitting "title" for the regal and commanding Leo princess. Variations: *Marit, Marlet, Marta, Marthe, Matti.*

Marvel (MAR-vell) Old French: Deserving of awe. Charismatic Leo, with her exuberant personality and amazing energy, impresses all who meet her. Variations: *Marva, Marvela, Marvella, Marvelle, Marvis.*

Maura (MAUR-ah or MOR-ah) Irish: Great. This traditional Irish name underscores Leo's superstar qualities.

Maxine (MAX-een or max-EEN) Latin: The greatest. A strong ego and abundance of self-confidence are Leo trademarks. Variations: *Max, Maxie.*

Meira (meh-EE-rah) Hebrew: Light. Energetic and commanding Leo is the brightest star in the zodiac. Variations: *Meora, Meorah.*

Mona (MOHN-nah) Greek: Regal. Leo is the sign of nobility and high birth.

Morgan (MOR-gin) Welsh: Great and bright. This old Welsh name, now enjoying a new popularity in America, is a perfect choice for the magnetic and exuberant Leo. Variations: *Morgana, Morganne, Morgen.*

Moina (MOYN-ah) Irish: Little noble one. This recently popularized classic Gaelic name wonderfully suits the regal Leo girl. Variations: *Moyna, Muadhnait.*

Nanala (nah-NAH-lah) Hawaiian: Sunflower. The brilliantly colored sunflower is one of two flowers associated with the sign of Leo. (The other flower is the marigold.)

Nani (NAH-nee) Hawaiian: Beautiful. Star-powered Leos, with their magnetic and driving personalities, have a supreme beauty.

Natsu (NAHT-soo) Japanese: Summer. Leo, one of the zodiac's summer signs, encompasses the months of July and August. Variation: *Natsuko.*

Neci (NEH-see) Latin: On fire. Sun-ruled Leo is the second—and probably the most flamboyant—of the three Fire signs of the zodiac. (Aries and Sagittarius are the other two Fire signs.)

Nemera (nah-MER-ah) Hebrew: Leopard. The sign of Leo governs all felines.

Nitsa (NIT-sah) Greek: Shining girl. This popular Greek name is a suitable choice for a Sun-born Leo girl.

Nora (NOR-ah) Greek: Light. *Nora* is a classic name for a bright personality born under the sign of Leo. Variation: *Norah.*

Nova (NOH-vah) Latin: A bright star. Unique yet wonderfully appropriate. *Nora* is an ideal choice for a Leo girl, born under the most powerful star in this solar system.

Nuria (noo-REE-ah) Hebrew: Fire of the Lord. This classic Hebrew name is appropriate for Leo, one of the three Fire signs. Variation: *Nuriel*.

Nuru (NOO-roo) African/Swahili: Daylight. As the Sun brings light and warmth to the new day, so Leos spread warmth and light to those around them.

Oralie (OR-ah-lee) French: Golden. The color gold is symbolic of the sign of Leo. Variations: *Oralee, Oralia, Oriel, Orielle, Orlena*.

Oriana (oh-ree-AHN-ah) Latin: Sunrise. Like the Sun, which rules their sign, Leos are always up-and-coming, constantly striving to move forward. Variations: *Oralia, Orania, Orelle, Oriane*.

Oriole (OH-ree-ole) Latin: Golden. Golds, reds, and oranges are the colors associated with the fiery sign of Leo. Variations: *Orella, Oriel, Oriola*.

Owena (OH-en-ah) Welsh: Wellborn. Leo is the sign of nobility and high birth.

Paka (PAH-kah) African/Swahili: Kitten. The sign of Leo governs all felines.

Pandora (pan-DOR-rah) Greek: Bestowed with talents. This marvelous mythological name is perfect for Leos, who are abundantly creative and fiercely determined to succeed. Variations: *Panda, Pandy*.

Patricia (pah-TREE-shah) English: Noble. This ever-popular, classic English name is a perfect choice for regal Leo. Variations: *Patria, Patrica, Patrice, Patricka, Patti, Tricia, Trisha*.

Pazia (pah-ZEE-uh) Hebrew: Full of gold. Gold is the precious metal associated with the sign of Leo. Variations: *Paz, Paza, Pazia, Pazice, Pazit, Pazya*.

Phaedra (FAY-drah) Greek: Glowing. This classic name, with its origins in mythology, is a marvelous choice for Sun-born Leo. Variations: *Fedra, Phadra, Phedre*.

Pyrrha (PYE-rah) Greek: Red. The color red is most strongly associated with Leo, boldest of the three Fire signs.

Queenie (KWEEN-ee) Old English: Queen. This whimsical name is an obvious choice for a girl born under Leo, the sign of royalty. Variation: *Queena*.

Quenby (KWEN-bee) Old English: Queen's settlement. Commanding and noble Leo relishes being the ruler of her own domain.

Quinn (KWIN) Old English: Queen. This name is a rare and regal choice for a Leo girl's commanding nature.

Quintina (kwin-TEEN-ah) English: Fifth. Leo is the fifth sign of the zodiac. Variations: *Quinetta, Quintana, Quintessa*.

Rane (RAH-neh) Polish: Queen. Leos are the reigning monarchs of the zodiac.

Raomi (ray-OH-mee) Hebrew: Lofty. Regal Leos often have an aristocratic and dominating persona. Variation: *Reuma*.

Reanna (ree-AHN-ah) Welsh: Great queen. This old Welsh name, currently enjoying a renewed popularity, is wonderfully apt for a noble Leo girl. Variations: *Rheanna, Rheanne, Rhiann, Rhiannon, Riane, Rianna*.

Regina (reh-JEEN-ah) Latin: Queen. This classic name is a marvelous choice for regal and commanding Leo. Variations: *Raina, Raine, Rayna, Regena, Reggi, Regine.*

Rhonda (RON-dah) Welsh: Grand. Noble Leos have a commanding and often autocratic presence. Variation: *Rhonnda.*

Riona (ree-OH-nah) Irish: Queen. This traditional and popular Irish name offers an appealing ring for Leo, the sign of royalty. Variation: *Rioghnach.*

Roberta (ruh-BUR-tah) English: Bright fame; feminine version of *Robert.* Leos are born entertainers who are driven to seek center stage. Variations: *Bobbi, Bobby, Bobina, Robbi, Robena, Robertha.* (Famous Leo: Bobbie Gentry, singer)

Robyn (RAH-bin) English: Famous. *Robyn* is a suitable choice for vivacious, attention-loving, and tremendously talented Leos, the born superstars of the zodiac. Variation: *Robin.*

Roderica (RO-day-REE-kah) German: Famous ruler. Leo is the sign of nobility and leadership. Variations: *Rica, Roderiqua.*

Rostislava (ros-tee-SLAH-vah) Czech: One who seizes fame. Leos have an inborn drive to seek the limelight. Variations: *Rosta, Rostina, Rostuska.*

Roxanne (roks-AHN) Greek: Dawn of day. *Roxanne* is a classic choice for ever-rising Leos. Variations: *Roxane, Roxanna.*

Ruby (ROO-bee) English: The name of the precious gem that is Leo's birthstone. Variations: *Rubey, Rubie.*

Sahar (sah-HAR) Arabic: Sunrise. This lovely and popular Muslim name is perfect for the expansive, Sun-ruled Leo.

Sally (SAL-lee) Hebrew: Princess. Originally derived from *Sarah*, this name, which now has its own entity in its own right, is a modern choice for the zodiac's reigning royalty. Variation: *Sal*. (Famous Leo: Sally Struthers, actress)

Sana (sah-NAH) Arabic: To shine. Sun-born Leos show a magnetic and luminous quality.

Sanura (sah-NOO-rah) African/Swahili: Like a kitten. While all felines are governed by the sign of Leo, this youthful name adds a special charm to Leo's feline qualities.

Sarah (SAYR-uh) Hebrew: Princess. This name is a classic choice for Leo, the sign of royalty. Variations: *Sadie, Saleena, Salena, Sara, Sarai, Sarita, Sarra*.

Saura (SOW-rah) Hindu: Devoted to the sun. Leo is the only sign in the zodiac that is governed by the Sun.

Scarlett (SKAR-litt) English: Red. Red is the color most strongly associated with the sign of Leo. Scarlett O'Hara, the fiery heroine of *Gone With the Wind*, is a classic Leo princess.

Seraphina (sare-ah-FEE-nah) Hebrew: Burning one. Leo is one of the three Fire signs in the zodiac, and the only sign ruled by the Sun. Variations: *Fina, Serafina, Seraphine*.

Sidra (sid-RAH) Latin: Star directed. Exuberant and creative Leos are born actors who frequently are driven to seek public fame.

Solana (soh-LAH-nah) Spanish: Sunshine. This classic Spanish name—or one of its beautiful variations—is an ideal choice for Sun-blessed Leo. Variations: *Solina, Soline, Soulle, Zelena, Zelia, Zelie*.

Sona (SO-nah) Hindu: Gold. Gold is the precious metal associated with the sign of Leo. Variations: *Sonala, Sonika, Sonita*.

Stephanie (STEH-fan-ee) Latin: Crown. This classic name, which has recently gained great popularity, is perfectly suited for a girl born under Leo, the sign of royalty. Variations: *Stefanie, Steffany*.

Sunniva (soo-NEE-vah) Scandinavian: Gift of the sun. Leo is ruled by the Sun and draws from that great star many of her finest qualities—charisma, exuberant energy, and magnanimous warmth.

Sunshine (SON-shine) English: Sun. The Sun is the greatest influence in the sign of Leo. Variations: *Sunni, Sunnie, Sunny*.

Surya (SOOR-yah) Hindu: Sun god. Innately aristocratic Leos are governed by the Sun.

Talutah (tah-LOO-tah) Native American: Red. Reds, golds, and oranges are the colors associated with the brilliant sign of Leo.

Tama (TAH-mah) Japanese: Gleaming. Sun-ruled Leos have a magnetic warmth that is distinctly their own. Variation: *Tamae*.

Tara (TAR-ah or TARE-ah) Gaelic: The place name for the ancient seat of Irish royalty. The Irish kingdom's name later became that of the famed plantation owned by *Gone With the Wind's* Scarlett O'Hara, herself a quintessential Leo lioness.

Tiara (tee-AR-ah) Latin: Crown. Leo is the sign of royalty and high birth.

Tigris (TIH-gris) Irish: Tiger. The sign of Leo governs all cats, and this name bears the distinctly feminine quality of one of the most irresistible of felines.

Tora (TORR-ah) Japanese: Tiger. All types of felines are ruled by the sign of Leo, symbolizing both prowess and graceful strength.

Usha (oo-SHAH) Hindu: Dawn. This unique Eastern name is an appropriate choice for Sun-ruled and expansive Leos.

Valentina (vahl-lin-TEE-nah) Latin: Powerful. Inherently aristocratic, Leos often have a commanding and dominating persona. Variation: *Valentine.*

Valerie (VAL-ah-ree) Old French: Fierce one. Leos are renowned for their fierce and single-minded determination to succeed. Variations: *Val, Valaree, Valaria, Valery, Valli.* (Famous Leo: Valerie Harper, actress)

Vanalika (van-ah-LEE-kah) Hindu: Sunflower. The sunflower is one of two flowers associated with the sign of Leo. (The other flower is the marigold.)

Vanna (VAH-nah) Cambodian: Golden. Gold is the precious metal associated with the sign of Leo.

Vivian (VIVE-ee-ahn) Latin: Alive. *Vivian* is a classic choice for exuberant and energetic Leo, who lives life at full tilt. Variations: *Viv, Viviana, Viviene, Vivienne.*

Xanthe (ZAN-tha or ZAN-thee) Greek: Sun kissed. The Sun's influence in Leo is stronger than in any other sign. Surely Leos are favored by the radiant strength of the Sun.

Xiao-Xing (zhow-zhing) Chinese: Morning star. Leos, who are ruled by the Sun, lose no time in beginning to establish their warmth and radiance.

Zahara (zah-HAH-rah) Hebrew: Shine. Consummate performers, Leos love to live in the spotlight.

Zahava (zah-HAH-vah) Hebrew: Golden. Gold is the precious metal associated with the sign of Leo, as are the colors gold, red, and orange.

Zara (ZAH-rah) Hebrew: Dawn. The Sun rules the sign of Leo, and this classic name—with its suggestion of a soft and golden sunrise—is a beautiful choice for a Leo girl. Variations: *Zarah, Zaria.*

Zerlinda (zuhr-LINN-dah) Hebrew: Beautiful dawn. Magnetic and electrifying Leos, who possess a unique beauty, are strongly influenced by the Sun from the very beginning of their lives. Variation: *Zerlina.*

Zora (ZORR-ah) Slavic: Dawn. The Sun is the single greatest influence in the sign of Leo, establishing its brilliance and increasing this force throughout Leo's days. Variation: *Zorah.*

Zorina (zor-EEN-ah) Slavic: Golden. Golds, reds, and oranges are the bright, flamboyant colors associated with the brilliant sign of Leo.

Zubaida (zoo-bay-DAH) Arabic: Marigold. The marigold, with its showy yellow, orange, or maroon blossoms, is one of two flowers associated with the sign of Leo. (The other is the sunflower.) Variation: *Zubeda.*

Names for Leo Boys

Aaron (AYR-un) Hebrew: Illuminated. This classic and popular name is a fitting choice for exuberant and Sun-powered Leo, who radiates warmth and brightness wherever he goes. Variations: *Aharon, Arek, Aronne, Aronos.*

Abelard (ah-beh-LARD or AH-beh-lard) Old German: Highborn. Leo is the sign of nobility and high birth. Variations: *Ab, Abbie, Avner, Eb, Ebbie, Ebner.*

Adar (ah-DAHR) Syrian: Ruler or prince. Leo children are the reigning royalty of the zodiac.

Addae (ah-DAH-eh) African/Ghanian: Morning sun. The Sun rules the sign of Leo.

Adir (ah-DEER) Hebrew: Majestic. Leos, known as aristocratic and commanding figures, are naturally drawn to leadership roles.

Afi (AH-fee) Polynesian: Fire. Leo is a doubly energized sign: powerfully influenced by the Sun and also one of the zodiac's three Fire signs. (The other two are Aries and Sagittarius, with whom Leo shares many traits.)

Agni (AHG-nee) Hindu: Fire deity. Kingly Leo, a Fire sign energized by the Sun, easily commands the attention and admiration of those around him.

Aidan (AYE-duhn) Irish: Little fiery one. Sun-driven Leo is renowned for his enormous energy and determination to succeed. *Aidan*, a traditional Irish name that is enjoying a newfound popularity, is also appropriate for a Leo girl. Variations: *Aedan, Aiden, Edan.*

Akihito (ah-kee-HEE-toh) Japanese: Bright child. Sun-fueled Leos light up the lives of those around them.

Ala (AH-LAH) Arabic: Supreme. This revered Arabic name is an appropriate choice for a majestic Leo.

Alain (ah-LAYN) French: Handsome. *Alain* is a classic French name that is perfect for a charismatic Leo boy whose exuberant personality endows him with an innate attractiveness. Variations: *Alan, Allan, Allen.*

Albert (AL-burt) Old English: Noble and brilliant. The variations of this old-fashioned name are all perennial favorites, and any one of them is a suitable choice for the royal and charismatic Leo. Variations: *Al, Albie, Bert, Berto, Burt.* (Famous Leos: Burt Convey and Bert Lahr, actors)

Ali (AHL-ee) Arabian: The greatest. Leos are famous for their healthy egos and larger-than-life personalities. This name is also suitable for a Leo girl in its most popular feminine variation— *Allie*.

Alroy (AHL-roy) Spanish: King. Leos are the reigning royalty of the zodiac.

Ameer (ah-MEER) Arabic: Prince. This very popular Middle Eastern name is a fitting choice for royal Leo.

Amon (AY-muhn) Hebrew: Of the Sun. Leo is the only sign of the zodiac governed by the powerful Sun.

Anoki (ah-NO-kee) Native American: Performer. Charismatic Leos are born entertainers who eagerly seek the limelight.

Anshu (ahn-SHOO) Hindu: Sunbeam. Energetic and brilliant Leo is a Fire sign ruled by the Sun. Variation: *Anshul*.

Anthony (ANN-thuhn-ee or ANN-ton-ee) Latin: Priceless. This traditional favorite is a classic choice for magnetic and one-of-a-kind Leo. Variations: *Anders, Antoine, Anton, Antonin, Antonio, Tony*. (Famous Leos: Antonio Banderas, actor; Tony Bennett, singer)

Arden (ahr-DEN or AR-den) Celtic: Lofty. Leo is the sign of aristocracy and high birth. Variations: *Ardie, Ardin, Ardy*.

Ari (AR-ree) Hebrew: Lion. The Lion, the animal symbol for the sign of Leo, embodies many of Leo's most striking qualities—magnetism, majesty, and a commanding personality. *Ari* is also an appropriate choice for a girl.

Ariel (ahr-ee-EHL) Hebrew: Lion of god. This classic name choice for the Lion king of the zodiac is also suitable for a Leo girl. Variations: *Airel, Airyel, Aryel, Auriel*.

Aristotle (ah-ree-STOT-uhl) Greek: Superior. Leos, who rarely suffer from low self-esteem or shaky egos, have an indefatigable belief in their supreme self-worth. Variations: *Ari, Ary.*

Arpiar (ahr-pee-ARH) Armenian: The Sun reigns down. Leo is ruled by the Sun, the most powerful planetary influence in astrology. This greatest of stars endows Leos with a fiery intensity and enormous reserve of energy.

Asad (ah-SAHD) Arabic: Lion. The stately Lion symbolizes the sign of Leo. Variations: *Alasid, Aleser, Asi, Assad, Assid.*

Ashon (ah-SHON) African/Ochi: Seventh-born son. This unique name is fitting for Leos born in July, the seventh month of the calendar year.

August (AW-gust) Latin: Exalted one. This dual-purpose name is wonderfully appropriate for a regal and commanding Leo born in the month of August. Variations: *Agustin, Agustino, Augie, Augustine, Augy.*

Aulelio (ah-oo-leh-LEE-oh) Hawaiian: Golden. Gold is the precious metal associated with the sign of Leo. Variation: *Aurelio.*

Austin (AWE-stuhn) English: Majestic. This traditional English surname, recently enjoying a renewed popularity as a first name, is a fitting choice for aristocratic Leo.

Aviur (ah-VEE-uhr) Hebrew: Father of fire. Leo is one of the zodiac's three Fire signs.

Bakari (bah-KAH-ree) African/Swahili: Of noble promise. Royal Leo, ruled by the Sun, is born sizzling with star power. From early in life, he generates a commanding presence that presages great things to come.

Ballard (BAY-lerd or BAL-lard) German: Mighty. Leos are known for their great strength and power.

Bartram (BAHR-trahm) English: Brilliant renown. The Leo tendency to shine brightly in any setting often brings them great fame and success. Variation: *Bart*.

Basil (BAZZ-il, BASS-il, or BAZE-il) English: Royal. Like the Lion that symbolizes them, Leos are considered the reigning kings of the zodiac. Variations: *Basile, Basilio, Bazil, Bazyl*.

Bay (BEH) Vietnamese: Seventh-born child. This unusual name suits a Leo born in July, the seventh month of the calendar year.

Beau (BOH) French: Very attractive. Leos are often associated with great physical beauty. Variations: *Beal, Beale, Bo*.

Berdy (BAIR-dee) Russian: Brilliant spirit. With their bright personalities and flamboyant natures, Leos are perceived as possessing powerful souls.

Bodaway (boh-DAH-way) Native American: Fire maker. With the Sun as their guiding sphere, Leos are known to have fiery and creative natures.

Bu (BOO) Vietnamese: Leader. Naturally strong and innovative, Leos are born to lead without scheming or effort.

Cam (KHAM) Gypsy: Sun. The Sun rules the sign of Leo.

Cham (HAM) Hebrew: Hot. This popular Middle Eastern name makes a fitting choice for the fiery Leo. Variation: *Ham*.

Charles (CHARHLZ) Latin: Masculine and powerful. Leos, with their Masculine polarity, often are associated with strength and force. Variations: *Carlton, Cary, Chad, Charlie, Chas, Chip*. (Famous Leo: Charles Bronson, actor)

Clarence (KLARE-ince) Latin: Acclaimed. More than any other sign in the zodiac, Leo is attributed with fame and public adoration. Variations: *Clarance, Clarrance*.

Cleon (KLEH-on) Greek: Famous. Once a Leo sets his mind on gaining success in the public realm, he is certain to achieve the recognition he desires. Variations: *Cleo, Leon.*

Coman (ko-MAHN) Arabic: Noble. Regal Leos are perceived as kingly and high ranking.

Conall (KON-ahl) Irish: High and mighty. Leos often reach the utmost ranks of success, particularly in endeavors involving the public eye. Variation: *Connell.*

Cullen (KUL-len) Irish: Handsome. Majestic Leo, with his brilliant and magnetic personality, great warmth, and joyful disposition always cuts an attractive figure. Variations: *Cullan, Cullin.*

Cyril (SIRR-il) Greek: Lord. Just as Leo's Lion is the lord of the animal world, Leos themselves often are seen as supreme leaders. Variations: *Cyrill, Cyrille, Cyrillus, Kyril.*

Cyrus (SYE-rus) Latin: Sun. Leo's reigning celestial force is the Sun. Variation: *Cy.*

Dag (DAHG) Scandinavian: Light of day. Leos, brilliant in their mental and physical appearances, often are associated with the bright light of the full Sun. Variations: *Daeg, Daegan, Dagen, Deegan, .*

Darren (DARE-in) Irish: Great. Filled with self-assurance and garnering the adoration of those surrounding them, Leos are viewed as simply supreme. Variations: *Darin, Darran, Darrin, Darron, Darryn, Daryn.*

Daudi (dah-OO-dee) African/Swahili: Adored friend. Leos make passionate and magnanimous friends, but their need for constant praise and admiration sometimes can be daunting. Variation: *Daudy.*

Delbert (DELL-burt) English: Sunny day. Typically bright and cheerful, Leos bring all the assurance of a warm, sunny day when they enter a room. Variations: *Bert, Del.*

Derek (DEH-rehk) English: Leader. With a strong ego and a stunning physical presence, Leo is a natural-born leader. Variations: *Dereck, Derick, Derik, Derrek, Derrik, Deryck.*

Derry (DARE-ree) Irish: Red haired. Fiery reds are the colors of the sign of Leo, making this popular Irish place name a fitting choice for a redheaded Leo prince. Variations: *Darrie, Darry, Derrie.*

Devendra (dayv-EN-drah) Hindu: God of the sky. With their high aims and strong connection to the Sun, Leos are ideally suited to bear this unique name.

Eagan (EE-gin) Irish: Extremely mighty. Leos are known for their great strength and power. Variations: *Egan, Egon.*

Earl (URL) English: Nobleman. Natural-born leaders with high-minded goals, Leos are considered the reigning class of the zodiac. Variations: *Earle, Earlie, Erie, Erl, Errol.*

Elbert (EL-burt) English: Shining. Leos are associated with the Sun and its brilliant force.

Elmer (EL-muhr) Old English: Famous. Leos are considered the "most likely to succeed" when it comes to living in the limelight. Variations: *Ellmer, Elmir, Elmo, Elmore.*

Eloni (aye-LO-nee) Polynesian: Lofty or exalted one. Polynesian form of *Aaron*. Associated with the kingly Lion, Leos often are high ranking and adored.

Engelbert (EHN-guhl-burt) Old German: Bright as an angel. With their high ideals and brilliant bearing, Leos can be compared to the glowing celestial beings. Variations: *Englebert, Ingelbert, Inglebert*.

Esteban (ay-STAY-bahn) Spanish: Crown. Leos are the reigning monarchs of the zodiac. Variations: *Esteben, Estefan, Estiban, Stephen, Teb*.

Etu (ay-TOO) Native American: The sun. The Sun rules all those born under the sign of Leo.

Eugene (YOO-jeen or yoo-JEEN) English: Highborn. Leo is regarded as the sign that reigns supreme above the rest of the zodiac. Variations: *Egen, Eugenio, Eugenios, Eugenius, Gene, Yergeny*. (Famous Leo: Gene Roddenberry, *Star Trek* creator; Gene Kelly, actor/singer/dancer).

Finley (FIN-lee) Irish: Golden ray of sun. Leos are affiliated with the Sun, its ruling celestial body, and the kingly color of gold. Variations: *Fin, Findlay, Finlay, Finn*.

Flynn (FLIN) Irish: Son of the red-haired one. Red is among the colors strongly associated with the sign of Leo. Variations: *Flin, Flinn, Flyn*.

Golding (GOLD-ing) English: Little gold one. Gold is the precious metal associated with the sign of Leo.

Goldwin (GOLD-win) English: Golden friend. Leos, who often are associated with the color gold, make magnanimous friends that tend to be "good as gold." Variations: *Goldewyn, Goldwinn, Goldwyn, Goldwynn*.

Grant (GRANT) Old English: Great. Leos reign supreme in every endeavor.

Griffin (GRIFF-in) Welsh: Fierce. The gryphon was a legendary creature that was half-lion and half-eagle. Leo, who is symbolized by the Lion, is renowned for his fierce determination to succeed. Variations: *Griff, Griffen, Griffith.*

Gur (GOOR) Hebrew: Baby lion. Leos are symbolized by the Lion. Variations: *Guri, Guriel, Gurion.*

Haidar (high-DAHR) Arabic: Lion. The king of beasts matches the strength and bearing of regal Leos.

Hakan (HAK-ahn) Native American: Fiery. Leos are ruled by the fiery strength of the earth's most powerful celestial influence, the Sun.

Hari (HAH-ree) Hindu: Hindu Sun god. This appealing name suits charismatic Leo, who is ruled by the Sun and displays the bearing of a god.

Harkin (HARK-en) Irish: Dark red. Reds, golds, and oranges are the colors associated with the sign of Leo. Variations: *Harkan, Harken.*

Howell (HOW-ell) Welsh: Exceptional. Leos always manage to stand out in a crowd. Variations: *Howe, Hywel.*

Hubert (YOO-burt or HEW-bert) Old German: Brilliant spirit. Associated with the fiery and fleeting Sun, Leos convey a powerful and supreme bearing. Variations: *Hobart, Hubbard, Hube, Huber, Hubie, Huey, Hugh, Hugo, Hugoberto.*

Ignatius (ig-NAY-shus) English: On fire. Leos are affiliated with the Sun and its fiery force. Leo is also one of the three Fire signs of the zodiac. Variations: *Iggy, Ignace, Ignacio, Ignatz, Ignaz, Inigo, Nacek.*

Isha (ISH-ah) Hindu: Lord. Leo is considered the reigning sign of the zodiac.

Ishaan (ISH-ahn) Hindu: Sun. Leo's ruling celestial body is the Sun.

Jakeem (ya-KEEM) Hebrew: Exalted. Often perceived as the reigning class of the zodiac, Leos frequently manage to achieve high rank and public adoration. Variations: *Jakim, Yakim.*

Jalal (jah-LAL) Arabic: Great. Leos reign supreme, both in the eyes of others and themselves.

Jamal (jah-MAHL) Arabic: Attractive. Leos often gain recognition for their good looks, as well as for their appealing warmth and vitality. Variations: *Jamaal, Jameel, Jamel, Jamelle, Jamiel, Jamil, Jhamal.*

Jin (JEEN) Chinese: Gold. Gold is the precious metal associated with the sign of Leo.

Jitendra (jih-TANE-drah) Hindu: One who wins over the lord of the sky. This name is well suited to Leos, who are known for their tremendous successes.

Jomei (joh-MAY) Japanese: Light. Leos are associated with the bright and shining force of the Sun.

Judah (JOO-dah) Hebrew: Praised one. This name is likely to apply to the Leo lad, who easily earns adoration from an early age. Variations: *Jud, Juda, Judd, Jude, Judson.*

Jules (JOOLZ) Latin: From *Julius*, for the month of July. This name is appropriate for Leos who are born in the hot, summer month of July.

Kadar (ka-DAHR) Arabic: Imposing presence. The regal and powerful Leo always makes his presence known.

Kakana (kah-KAH-nah) Hawaiian: Powerful. *Kakana* is the Hawaiian form of the name *Tarzan*, for virility and manliness.

Leo is known for his unstoppable energy and strength.

Kalino (kah-LEE-noh) Hawaiian: Brilliant. With the Sun as his ruling sign, Leo shines brightly in all of his endeavors.

Kane (KA-neh) Japanese: Golden. This name carries a double meaning for Leo: Gold is the sign's precious metal, as well as one of its assigned colors.

Kang-Dae (KANG-day) Korean: Powerful. Leo is associated with strength and force.

Keahi (keh-AH-hee) Hawaiian: Flames. This popular Hawaiian name evokes the fiery image of the Sun's favorite sign.

Keahilani (keh-ah-hee-LAH-nee) Hawaiian: Heavenly fire. Leo, ruled by the Sun, is subject to its celestial guiding force. Leo is also one of the three Fire signs of the zodiac.

Keegan (KEE-gan) Irish: Bold flame. Leo is the most passionate of the zodiac's three Fire signs. Variations: *Kagen, Keagan, Keegen, Kegan.*

Kefir (KEE-fer) Hebrew: Lion cub. The young Leo is as attractive, yet resourceful, as the sign's powerful symbolic animal, the Lion.

Kelii (ke-LEE) Hawaiian: Chief. Leos are considered the ultimate rulers of the zodiac.

Kenneth (KENN-ith) Irish: Sprung from fire. This name is well suited to Leo, whose ruling celestial source is the hot and fiery Sun. Variations: *Ken, Kendall, Kennie, Kenny, Kenyon.* (Famous Leo: Kenny Rogers, singer)

Keon (key-ON) Irish: Wellborn. Often viewed as lordly and high ranking, Leos are considered the reigning class of the zodiac.

Khalfani (kahl-FAH-nee) African/Swahili: Born to lead. Leos often prove to be natural-born leaders.

Kilchii (kil-CHEE-ee) Native American: Red boy. This name is apt for a Leo boy, as the color of red is strongly associated with the fiery and passionate sign of Leo.

Kim (KIM) Vietnamese: Golden ore. The precious metal assigned to Leo is gold.

Kingston (KING-stun) Old English: From the king's estate. Leo is considered the ruling sign of the zodiac. Variations: *King, Kinston*.

Kiran (kir-AHN) Hindu: Ray of light. Leos, like the Sun, spread their warmth and light to all those around them wherever they go.

Koren (KO-ren) Hebrew: Shining. Leos are associated with the Sun and reflect its warmth and strength in themselves.

Kwayera (kwah-YEH-rah) African/Malawian: Sunrise. Leo's flamboyance is well represented by the Sun's magnificent entry into the sky.

Lais (LAYS) Hindu: Lion. Leo's presence, like the Lion's, is noble and commands immediate attention.

Lani (LAHN-nee) Hawaiian: Sky. The sky's lofty stature and broad influence are indicative of Leos.

Lapidos (LAH-pee-dos) Hebrew: Torches. As torches light the way for travelers in the night, Leos serve as leaders in dark times. Variation: *Lapidoth*.

Lasairian (lay-SAYR-ee-an) Irish: Flame. People gather around Leos for their generous warmth and light. Variation: *Laserian*.

Lave (LAH-vee) Hebrew: Roaring lion. The Lion's roar is a symbol of Leo's dominance and masculinity. Variations: *Leib, Leibel*.

Leander (lee-AN-dir) Greek: Leonine. Leo's attributes are like those of the Lion—noble, strong, and commanding attention. Variations: *Ander, Leandre, Leandro, Lee, Leo*.

Leibel (LEE-bil) Hebrew: My Lion. *Leibel* is an appropriate name for a mother's young Leo "cub." Variation: *Leib*.

Lennor (LEH-nohr) Gypsy: Summer. Leo is a summer sign, touching the months of July and August.

Leo (LEE-oh) Latin: Lion. The Leo namesake calls to mind the royalty of the sign. Variations: *Lee, Lev*.

Leon (LEE-on) Latin: Powerful like a Lion. Leo's potent spirit helps him attain a lofty status. Variations: *Leonas, Leos, Lion, Lyon*.

Leonard (LEN-ard) Old German: Lion hearted. Leos posses the great inner strength of the Lion. Variations: *Len, Lenny, Leonardo, Lon, Lonnie*.

Leor (leh-OHR) Hebrew: "I have light." Leos are often associated with sources of light, such as Fire (which is their element) and the Sun (which is their ruler). *Leor* is also appropriate for a girl.

Leroy (LEE-roy) French: The king. Just as the Lion is the ruler of the wild, Leos have great influence over their environment. Variations: *Le Roy, LeeRoy, Leeroy, LeRoi, LeRoy*.

Lionel (LYE-ah-null) Latin: Lion cubs. Like Lion cubs, young Leos need plenty of space in which to romp and play. Variations: *Lionell, Lionello, Lonell, Lonnell*.

Lisimba (lee-SEEM-bah) Malawi/Yao: Lion. Both Lions and Leos command attention with their regal stature.

Llewellyn (loo-ELL-an) Welsh: Leonine. Leos posses the charisma and vitality of a Lion, which is their symbol. Variations: *Lew, Llewllyn*.

Lopati (lo-PAY-tee) Polynesian: Bright fame. Leos' intense personalities help them achieve high social status.

Lucius (LOO-shus) Latin: Light. Generous Leos are eager to share their inherent light with those around them. Variations: *Luca, Lucan, Luce, Luciano, Lucio*.

Mahendra (mah-HEN-drah) Hindu: Great god of the sky. Leos are represented by the Sun, the ruling body of the astrological sky.

Majid (mah-JEED) Hindu: Magnificent. This name represents the nobility and flamboyance of Leo. Variations: *Magid, Majeed*.

Malki (MAL-kee) Hebrew: My king. Leos often attain the most lofty positions of leadership.

Mehtar (meh-TAHR) Hindu: Prince. Like a prince, the young Leo can expect a rise in power as he grows.

Miloslaw (MEE-lo-swahv) Polish: Lover of glory. Leos love the spotlight and will do anything in their power to be the center of attention. Variations: *Milo, Miloslav*.

Ming-Hoa (ming-HWA) Chinese: Prestigious. Leos are often associated with positions of nobility and prestige.

Minh (MIN) Vietnamese: Brilliant. Leos are represented by the brightest of all celestial bodies, the Sun, and the most brilliant metal, gold.

Mohammed (moh-HAH-mid) Arabic: Greatly praised. One of the most common male names in the world, this is a magnificent choice for glory-seeking Leos. Variations: *Ahmad, Amad, Hamid, Hammad, Mohamed, Muhammad.*

Myung-Ki (MY-UNG-KEE) Korean: To rise up shining. Resilient, energetic Leos are renowned for their burning and charismatic personalities.

Nagid (nah-GEED) Hebrew: Kingly. Regal Leos strive to be the rulers of their domains.

Namir (nah-MEER) Hebrew: Swift cat. This popular Israeli name is a fitting choice for a boy born under Leo, the sign that rules all cats.

Napoleon (nah-POH-lee-in) African-American: Lion in a new city; French, Italian: Fierce one from Naples. This historic name represents the immediate impact Leos bring to any new situation. (Famous Leo: Napoleon Bonaparte)

Nolan (NOH-lahn) Irish: Noble and famous. Leos draw others to them with their regality and influence.

Numair (noo-MARE) Arabic: Panther. The sign of Leo governs all felines.

Nuri (NOO-ree) Hebrew: Flaming lights. A very popular name in Israel, *Nuri* is an ideal choice for a fiery Leo. Variations: *Nur, Nuria, Nuriel, Nurit, Nury.*

Oba (AW-bah) African/Nigerian: King. This name is appropriate for boys born under the royal sign of Leo.

Orion (oh-RYE-in) Greek: Sun or fire; sunrise. The presence of a Leo can light up any occasion.

Oro (OR-o) Spanish: Gold. Gold is the precious metal associated with the sign of Leo.

Oron (OH-ron) Hebrew: Light. Leos are represented by the Sun, the giver of light.

Othniel (OTH-nee-el) Hebrew: Lion of God. Leo, the sign of the Lion, is the most powerful and commanding of all astrological signs.

Pakile (pah-KEE-leh) Hawaiian: Royal. Leos are born with a strong sense of leadership and nobility.

Patrick (PAT-trick) Latin: Noble one. *Patrick* is a perfect name for the regal Leo child. Variations: *Paddy, Padraig, Patrice, Patricio*. (Famous Leo: Patrick Swayze, actor and dancer)

Pirro (PEER-ro) Greek: Red hair. Leos often share their brilliant hair color with the bright mane of the Lion, their symbolic animal.

Prince (PRINTZ) Latin: Son of a king. Young Leos are sure to ascend to greatness. Variations: *Prinz, Prinze*.

Quentin (KWEN-tin) Latin: The fifth. Leo is the fifth sign of the zodiac. Variations: *Quent, Quinn, Quinten, Quintus*.

Quillan (KWILL-uhn) Irish: Baby Lion. Leos are impulsive and enthusiastic like young Lion cubs.

Quincy (KWIN-see) French: Fifth son's place. This popular contemporary name is a fitting choice for Leo, the fifth sign of the zodiac. Variations: *Quin, Quincey*.

Raby (RAY-bee) Scottish: Famous and bright. This name represents two common traits of Leos. Variations: *Rab, Rabbie, Rabi*.

Radborne (RADD-born) English: Red stream. The color red is often used in association with Leo. Variations: *Rad, Radbourn, Radburn, Radd.*

Ravi (RAV-vee) Hindu: Sun. Leos strive to be as bright and high as the Sun.

Ravindra (rav-IN-drah) Hindu: Sun power. To others, Leos seem to give off the gold light of the Sun.

Ray (RAY) English: King or royal. Leos possess the influence and extravagance of the ruling class. Variations: *Raydell, Raydon, Raylce, Raylen, Raynell.* (Famous Leo: Ray Bradbury, writer)

Read (REED) English: Red haired. Leos are often born with hair the color of a Lion's mane. Variations: *Reade, Reed, Reid, Reyd.*

Reece (REES) Welsh: Fiery. This name symbolizes Leos' inner passion and drive. Variations: *Reese, Rhys.*

Reed (reed) Old English: Auburn. The name *Reed* is indicative of a common Leo hair color. Variations: *Read, Reade, Reid, Reide.*

Regan (RAY-gan) Irish: Would-be king. This popular Irish name calls to mind the princely attributes of Leo. Variations: *Reagan, Reagen, Regen.*

Rex (REX) Latin: King. This name suggests the regal, proud nature of Leo. Variations: *Rexford, Rey.*

Robert (ROB-burt) Old English: Shining with fame. This classic name embodies two of Leo's most striking qualities—charisma and a desire for the limelight. Variations: *Bob, Bobbie, Bobby, Rob, Robb, Robbie, Robin.* (Famous Leos: Robert Plant, singer; actors Robert Mitchum, Robert Culp, Robert DeNiro, and Robert Redford)

Rogan (RO-gan) Irish: Redhead. Red is the color most strongly associated with the sign of Leo, and many Leos are born redheads.

Rohan (RO-an) Irish: Red. Red is the color of Leo, and it is also the color of many Leo symbols, such as Fire and the mane of a Lion, Leo's animal symbol.

Rooney (ROO-nee) Irish: Auburn. This name describes a common hair color for Leos. Variations: *Rowan, Rowen, Rowney*.

Rory (ROAR-ee) Irish: Red. Brilliant reds are the colors most strongly associated with the sign of Leo. This name, which echoes the sound of a Lion's roar, is especially apt for kingly Leo, who is symbolized by the Lion. (Famous Leo: Rory Calhoun, actor)

Ross (RAWSS) Scottish: High station. Kingly Leos often achieve lofty status. Variations: *Rosse, Rossell*.

Roth (RAWTH) German: Red. Leo is represented by the color red.

Roy (ROY) French: King. Leo is the reigning sign of astrology.

Royce (ROYSS) French: Son of the king. Leo is the sign of royalty and noble lineage.

Rufus (ROO-fuss) Latin: Red haired. Reds, golds, and oranges are the symbolic colors of Leo. Variations: *Rufo, Rufous*.

Rurik (RUHR-ick) Slavic: Red king. *Rurik* is a strikingly bold name for royal Leo, one of whose symbolic colors is red.

Rush (rush) English: Red haired. Many Sun-powered Leos are born with red hair.

Russell (RUS-sil) French: Red haired. This name, which is currently making a strong comeback, is a classic choice for a Leo boy. Variations: *Rus, Russ, Russel, Rusty.* (Famous Leo: Russell Baker, writer and journalist)

Ryan (RYE-ann) Irish: Little king. This very popular Gaelic name is a fitting title for a little Lion king. Variation: *Ryon.*

Sakima (sah-KEE-mah) Native American: King. Leo is the sign of nobility and high birth.

Samson (SAM-son) Hebrew: Sun. The luminous Sun rules the sign of magnetic Leo. Variations: *Sam, Sammie, Sammy, Sampson, Simson.* (Famous Leo: Sam Elliott, actor)

Saraph (SAR-af) Hebrew: Burn. Ruled by the Sun and one of the Fire signs, Leo is a whirling dervish of fiery energy. Variations: *Saraf, Seraf, Seraph.*

Sean (SHAWN) Gaelic: Heavenly generosity. This ever popular name, an Irish derivative of *John*, is an appealing choice for Leo, who is renowned for his great generosity. Variations: *Shaine, Shan, Shandon, Shane, Shawn, Shayne.* (Famous Leo: Sean Penn, actor and director)

Sef (SEF) Egyptian: Yesterday. *Sef* is also the name of the Egyptian Lion god immortalized in *The Book of the Dead.* The sign of Leo is symbolized by the Lion.

Simba (SEEM-bah) African/Swahili: Lion. This traditional African name is symbolic of Leo's powerful and influential personality. Leo's animal symbol is the Lion.

Stephen (STEE-vehn) Greek: Crowned. This name is perfect for the royal Leo. Variations: *Steffen, Steph, Stephan, Steve,*

Steven, Stevie. (Famous Leo: Steve Martin, actor and comedian)

Tab (TABB) German: Brilliant. Leo is represented by the bright and shining symbols of the Sun and gold. Variation: *Tabb.*

Tank (TANK) Polynesian: God of the sky. The Sun is the most potent star in the solar system, and Leos are the reigning stars of the zodiac.

Tau (TAH-oo) African/Tswana: Lion. The stately and majestic Lion is the symbol of the sign of Leo.

Tawa (tah-WAH) Native American: The Sun. The powerful and life-sustaining Sun rules the sign of expansive and flamboyant Leo.

Thor (THORE) Scandinavian: King. This exceedingly popular and traditional Scandinavian name is an appropriate choice for kingly Leo. *Thor* was the mythological Norse god of thunder. Variation: *Tor.*

Tiernan (TEER-nan) Irish: Little lord. Another traditional Gaelic surname that is enjoying renewed popularity as a first name, *Tiernan* is a delightful choice for the little king of the zodiac. Variation: *Tierney.*

Tipu (tee-POO) Hindu: Tiger. The sign of Leo, symbolized by the Lion, also governs all other wild and domestic cats.

Trumble (TRUM-bull) Old English: Mighty. Kingly Leo is gifted with supreme self-confidence and an unshakeable belief in his ability to succeed. Variations: *Trumball, Trumbell, Trumbull.*

Tyrone (TIE-rohn) Greek: Sovereign one. Leo is the sign of royalty and leadership. Variations: *Ty, Tye.*

Vidal (vee-DOLL) Latin: Life. Sun-kissed Leos have warm, vivacious, and commanding personalities and great reserves of physical and emotional energy.

Victor (VIK-ter) English: Winner. This always popular traditional name reinforces Leo's single-minded determination to be the leader in everything he does. Variations: *Vic, Viktor.*

Vito (VEE-toh) Latin: Lively. Supremely self-confident and wildly exuberant, all Leos live life to the hilt. Variations: *Veit, Vitas, Vite, Wit.*

Waldemar (WAHL-de-mahr or VAL-de-mar) German: Strong and famous. Leos possess abundant physical energy and an inborn drive to be the center of attention. Variations: *Valdemar, Waldo.*

Yaphet (YAH-fet) Hebrew: Good-looking. Charismatic Leos, with their Sun-endowed attributes of magnetism, enthusiasm, and expansiveness, are inherently beautiful creatures. Variations: *Japhet, Japheth.*

Zeheb (ze-HEB) Turkish: Gold. Gold is the precious metal associated with the sign of Leo.

Ziven (ZYE-ven) Slavic: Vigorous and alive. A widely popular name in Czechoslovakia, Poland, and Russia, *Ziven* is an ideal choice for a supercharged Leo boy. Variations: *Ziv, Zivon.*

Famous Leos

07-24-1898	Amelia Earhart	07-25-1954	Walter Payton
07-24-1936	Ruth Buzzi	07-26-1856	George Bernard Shaw
07-24-1951	Lynda Carter	07-26-1875	Carl Jung
07-24-1982	Anna Paquin	07-26-1902	Gracie Allen
07-25-1894	Walter Brennan	07-26-1912	Vivian Vance
07-25-1924	Estelle Getty	07-26-1922	Blake Edwards
07-25-1935	Barbara Harris	07-26-1922	Jason Robards, Jr.

07-26-1928	Stanley Kubrick	08-03-1940	Martin Sheen
07-26-1943	Mick Jagger	08-03-1941	Martha Stewart
07-26-1956	Dorothy Hamill	08-03-1950	John Landis
07-26-1959	Kevin Spacey	08-03-1951	Jay North
07-26-1965	Sandra Bullock	08-04-1792	Percy Bysshe Shelley
07-27-1922	Norman Lear	08-04-1901	Louis Armstrong
07-27-1931	Jerry Van Dyke	08-04-1912	Raoul Wallenberg
07-27-1944	Bobbie Gentry	08-04-1962	Roger Clemens
07-27-1948	Peggy Fleming	08-05-1906	John Huston
07-27-1948	Betty Thomas	08-05-1930	Neil Armstrong
07-27-1949	Maureen McGovern	08-05-1946	Loni Anderson
07-28-1866	Beatrix Potter	08-06-1911	Lucille Ball
07-28-1901	Rudy Vallee	08-06-1917	Robert Mitchum
07-28-1902	Richard Rogers	08-06-1928	Andy Warhol
07-28-1929	Jacqueline Onassis	08-07-1876	Mata Hari
07-28-1940	Phil Proctor	08-07-1904	Ralph Bunche
07-28-1945	Jim Davis	08-07-1926	Stan Freberg
07-28-1948	Sally Struthers	08-07-1928	"The Amazing" James Randi
07-29-1883	Benito Mussolini	08-07-1942	Garrison Keillor
07-29-1907	Melvin Belli	08-08-1922	Rory Calhoun
07-29-1938	Peter Jennings	08-08-1923	Esther Williams
07-30-1863	Henry Ford	08-08-1927	Carl "Alfalfa" Switzer
07-30-1891	Casey Stengel	08-08-1932	Mel Tillis
07-30-1930	Thomas Sowell	08-08-1937	Dustin Hoffman
07-30-1933	Ed "Kookie" Byrnes	08-08-1938	Connie Stevens
07-30-1939	Peter Bogdanovich	08-08-1949	Keith Carradine
07-30-1941	Paul Anka	08-08-1953	Donny Most
07-30-1947	Arnold Schwarzenegger	08-09-1896	Jean Piaget
07-30-1956	Delta Burke	08-09-1944	Sam Elliott
07-31-1912	Milton Friedman	08-09-1957	Melanie Griffith
07-31-1919	Curt Gowdy	08-09-1963	Whitney Houston
07-31-1944	Geraldine Chaplin	08-09-1967	Deion Sanders
07-31-1962	Wesley Snipes	08-10-1874	Herbert Hoover
07-31-1966	Dean Cain	08-10-1923	Rhonda Fleming
08-01-1819	Herman Melville	08-10-1928	Jimmy Dean
08-01-1933	Dom DeLuise	08-10-1928	Eddie Fisher
08-01-1936	Yves Saint Laurent	08-10-1933	Rocky Colavito
08-01-1942	Jerry Garcia	08-10-1947	Ian Anderson
08-01-1973	Tempestt Bledsoe	08-10-1959	Rosanna Arquette
08-02-1905	Myrna Loy	08-10-1960	Antonio Banderas
08-02-1924	James Baldwin	08-11-1925	Mike Douglas
08-02-1924	Carroll O'Connor	08-11-1928	Arlene Dahl
08-02-1932	Peter O'Toole	08-11-1933	Reverend Jerry Falwell
08-02-1950	Judge Lance Ito	08-11-1950	Steve Wozniak
08-03-1926	Tony Bennett		

08-11-1953	Terry "Hulk" Hogan
08-12-1881	Cecil B. DeMille
08-12-1912	Jane Wyatt
08-12-1931	William Goldman
08-12-1939	George Hamilton
08-13-1860	Annie Oakley
08-13-1895	Bert Lahr
08-13-1899	Alfred Hitchcock
08-13-1919	George Shearing
08-13-1926	Fidel Castro
08-13-1929	Pat Harrington, Jr.
08-13-1930	Don Ho
08-13-1951	Dan Fogelberg
08-14-1925	Russell Baker
08-14-1941	David Crosby
08-14-1945	Steve Martin
08-14-1946	Susan St. James
08-14-1947	Danielle Steel
08-14-1959	Earvin "Magic" Johnson
08-14-1968	Halle Berry
08-15-1769	Napoleon Bonaparte
08-15-1879	Ethel Barrymore
08-15-1912	Julia Child
08-15-1919	Huntz Hall
08-15-1924	Phyllis Schlafly
08-15-1925	Mike Conners
08-15-1944	Linda Ellerbee
08-15-1948	Jim Webb
08-16-1913	Menachem Begin
08-16-1920	Charles Bronson
08-16-1925	Fess Parker
08-16-1930	Robert Culp
08-16-1930	Frank Gifford
08-16-1932	Eydie Gorme
08-16-1946	Lesley Ann Warren
08-16-1953	Kathie Lee Gifford
08-16-1958	Madonna
08-16-1960	Timothy Hutton
08-17-1892	Mae West
08-17-1920	Maureen O'Hara
08-17-1943	Robert DeNiro
08-17-1960	Sean Penn
08-18-1922	Shelley Winters
08-18-1927	Rosalynn Carter
08-18-1933	Roman Polanski
08-18-1937	Robert Redford
08-18-1943	Martin Mull
08-18-1954	Patrick Swayze
08-18-1969	Christian Slater
08-18-1970	Malcolm-Jamal Warner
08-19-1871	Orville Wright
08-19-1902	Ogden Nash
08-19-1919	Malcolm Forbes
08-19-1921	Gene Roddenberry
08-19-1931	Willie Shoemaker
08-19-1940	Jill St. John
08-19-1946	Bill Clinton
08-19-1963	John Stamos
08-20-1833	Benjamin Harrison
08-20-1890	H. P. Lovecraft
08-20-1921	Jacqueline Susann
08-20-1942	Isaac Hayes
08-20-1946	Connie Chung
08-20-1948	Robert Plant
08-21-1872	Aubrey Beardsley
08-21-1904	Count Basie
08-21-1923	Chris Schenkel
08-21-1924	Jack Weston
08-21-1932	Melvin Van Peebles
08-21-1936	Wilt Chamberlain
08-21-1938	Kenny Rogers
08-22-1862	Claude Debussy
08-22-1917	John Lee Hooker
08-22-1920	Ray Bradbury
08-22-1934	Norman Schwarzkopf
08-22-1939	Carl Yastrzemski
08-22-1940	Valerie Harper
08-22-1947	Cindy Williams
08-22-1963	Tori Amos
08-23-1912	Gene Kelly
08-23-1930	Vera Miles
08-23-1932	Mark Russell
08-23-1934	Barbara Eden
08-23-1949	Shelley Long
08-23-1949	Rick Springfield
08-23-1970	River Phoenix

VIRGO
(August 24–September 23)

GLYPH: ♍

SYMBOL: The Virgin

POLARITY: Feminine

QUALITY: Mutable

ELEMENT: Earth

RULING PLANET: Mercury

BIRTHSTONE: Sapphire

SPECIAL COLORS: Navy blue and gray

FLOWERS: Morning glory and pansy

METAL: Mercury

ANIMALS: Small domestic pets

MOST LIKEABLE TRAITS: Conscientiousness, service to others, modesty, and industriousness

♍

Like the archetypical Virgin that symbolizes their sign, Virgos are esteemed for their purity, modesty, refinement, rationality, perfectionism, self-containment, and fastidiousness. Yet the belief that these cool, passive, and pristine qualities are all there is to Virgo is a common fallacy. This sign has a robust, emotional, and earthy side. In ancient times, the Virgin was a manifestation of the Feminine divine and an Earth mother-goddess who ruled the regeneration and growth of all living things. Today's Virgos are also hardworking, purposeful, sensitive, kindly, and strongly drawn to serving others. Parents of Virgo children will marvel at their incisive intelligence, precocious self-possession, and quiet devotion and loyalty. Without a doubt, Virgos are the low-maintenance children of the zodiac.

General Qualities

Virgo is ruled by Mercury, the planet that governs intelligence, logic, communication, and business. Mercury is also the planet of reconciliation or resolution between conflicting sides, achieved through the application of knowledge, truth, and understanding. Mercury endows Virgos with deep intelligence, rational and analytical thinking, deft communication skills, and a reverence for wisdom, learning, and truth.

Virgos are the doers and organizers of the zodiac. They are highly esteemed in business and the social services, where they are renowned for their no-nonsense commitment to hard work, their dedication to finding answers, and their willingness to work behind the scenes.

The Feminine influence in this sign gives Virgos sensitivity, receptiveness, a meditative approach to problems, considerable inner resourcefulness, and a strong moral fiber. The mutable quality of the sign allows Virgos to calmly adapt to new or challenging situations and accommodate or put into action the desires and directives of others. The strong influence of Earth in this sign serves to anchor Virgos in the here and now, making them dependable, practical, industrious, and physically and mentally robust. Indeed, remarkably good health is a hallmark of the sign of Virgo.

Virgos invariably shun the limelight, abhor self-indulgence, and rarely care to make flamboyant public statements like their near cousins, the Leos. Instead, Virgos consciously choose to work in strong supporting roles, where they view themselves as the problem solvers, essential to holding together the fabric of an organization or group. They are consummate managers, analysts, troubleshooters, and organizers.

Above all, Virgos prize intelligence, rationality, and intellectual activity. Their minds are always working overtime—cogitating, analyzing information, sifting through data, searching for answers. In a crowd, quiet and self-possessed Virgos may appear aloof and uninvolved. Instead, they are probably mentally involved in working through a long and complicated problem. Virgos live through their work and rarely rest. Despite their good health, they must be cautious about a tendency to become workaholics.

In public, Virgos are often quite shy and withdrawn, qualities that can be mistaken for coldness or snobbery. In fact, Virgos are gentle and kindly souls who care deeply about serving others. Hence, they often choose careers in the social services, where they shine in one-on-one relationships and make wise, compassionate listeners who are eager to use their considerable intelligence and practicality to help find solutions to any type of problem. Virgos can be depended on to stay the course until the very end, when an answer is finally found. They are renowned for their strong sense of responsibility.

Home

As the "low-maintenance" characters of astrology, Virgo children sometimes seem capable of raising themselves! Compared to other children in the zodiac, Virgo's surface maturity and self-possession make them appear wise beyond their years.

From early on in life, Virgos are methodical and organized, ready to follow the rules. They are the first to pick up their own rooms. They rarely make demands, are quiet and kind, respectful of authority, unfailingly polite, eager helpers, and naturally self-disciplined. They always favor mental activities over physical ones, and almost never get themselves into the kind of rough-and-tumble accidents that other children do. Virgos simply don't like to get dirty or make messes. They appreciate a subdued, pristine, and orderly environment. Even the colors associated with the sign of Virgo—gray and navy blue—are the classic colors of refinement and good taste.

Virgos, with their fertile and facile minds that dominate all their waking hours, need little outside stimulation, or anyone else's input, to keep themselves amused. Virgos are content to sit quietly off to the side, keenly observing the environment around them, and furiously working out one stratagem or another. The intellectual life fully engages and excites Virgos: They may stay with the same challenging project for hours at a time, then resolutely put it away to quietly go and set the dinner table, without being asked.

If this sounds too good to be true, it is. All children learn valuable life lessons by frivolously playing, physically acting out, making mistakes, getting dirty, bucking the system, and testing the limits of their parents' indulgence. No children need to enjoy a little mischief as much as Virgos do.

Living a life only of the mind is stressful and unhealthy, particularly in the young. Virgos especially need to learn the benefits of balancing work and play, if only to blow off some intellectual steam and give their minds a break. Virgos also may have underdeveloped imaginations, and free-form and fantastical play can teach them much about how to strengthen and nurture their imaginative abilities.

Most importantly, young Virgos need to be around their peers as much as possible to build up their social skills. Because they are so self-contained and comfortable being alone, Virgos sometimes come up short on some of the basic interpersonal skills that others learn in simple, social give-and-take situations: flexibility, tolerance, and patience. Learning about others' sensitivities and limits is also vital to Virgo's social development. Virgos, particularly, need to learn the difference between critique and criticism, discernment and judgment.

School and Play

Virgo children's traits of keen intelligence, dedication to hard work, and strong self-discipline serve them very well at school. They are outstanding students academically and behaviorally, who relish the orderly routines, clear goals, and daily intellectual challenges that school can offer. Without any prodding from parents or teachers, Virgos instinctively know how to study efficiently, organize and prepare material well, and budget their time and energy. They are the ones whose homework and projects are handed in ahead of time.

Virgos especially excel in subjects that call on their gifts of observation, analysis, discrimination, and information gathering:

science, mathematics, history, social studies, research, and essay writing. They particularly relish the challenges of long-term projects that require independent study, research, and analysis.

Virgos are less confident with unstructured tasks that require large infusions of imagination—creative writing, art, and drama, for example—and they often require some individual coaching and coaxing to get started. Once Virgos do get going, however, they apply their hallmark traits of intelligence, discernment, self-discipline, and hard work to these more imaginative tasks, often with considerable success. Virgos, who are keen observers and analysts of the world around them, frequently become successful writers and journalists. Both Edgar Rice Burroughs, the creator of the fantastical *Tarzan* series, and Agatha Christie, the grande dame of mystery fiction, are classic Virgos.

Virgos rarely get involved in competitive school sports, though they certainly have the mental focus to excel as athletes. This lack of involvement is unfortunate since Virgos, more than any other sign, need to let off mental steam. Nevertheless, Virgos invariably favor the life of the mind over that of the body, and they are more inclined to join after-school computer, science, and chess clubs.

At play, Virgos are content to amuse themselves for hours on end with a challenging game or project that fully engages their classic traits of concentration, absorption, and analysis. Virgos can become so lost in this kind of activity that they need to be consciously prodded into taking mental time off and just having some purely physical fun. Young Virgos benefit greatly from becoming a part of an informal play group, particularly if they are thrown in with more rambunctious children who can challenge them to act completely out of character.

The World

Virgos truly come into their own through work, where they are among the most esteemed of employees. Virgos are rarely the leaders in their chosen fields, not because they aren't suited for leadership roles, but because they simply aren't interested. Instead, Virgos find the role of being the power behind the throne far more challenging and suitable to their talents. Don't let that deceive you: The impact of Virgo's incomparable gifts is felt throughout any organization.

Virgos are the ones who set and maintain the impeccably high standards that others are expected to follow. Their dedication to hard work, long hours, and finding solutions to impossible dilemmas is legendary. More importantly, their crystal-clear intelligence, critical analytical skills, and quiet commitment to serving the interests of others (rather than promoting themselves) are the very stuff from which success is born. In the end, Virgos are the ones who give form, purpose, and direction to the half-realized dreams and nebulous desires of their more flashy, but less hardworking, contemporaries. Thus Virgos shine in management positions of any kind, but particularly in the fields of science, finance, publishing, and communication, where critical thinking and an ability to cut quickly through extraneous details and get to the crucial bottom line are key requirements for success.

Many Virgos who have a strong desire to serve others in a more direct, one-on-one fashion enter some branch of social service. This field enables them to use their intuitive intelligence, practicality, and compassion to become extraordinary counselors, therapists, and client advocates.

Outside the office, Virgos, who are naturally shy and self-effacing, are sometimes socially inept and often reticent about establishing intimate relationships. Work always takes precedence over anything else in a Virgo's life, which can cause conflicts between Virgos and potential mates. Many Virgos postpone marriage until later in life, when their work is well established, or they simply never marry at all. Instead, Virgos may fill their lives with important work and rich friendships, to which they bring their considerable gifts of intelligence, discernment, practicality, and compassion.

Choosing a Name for Your Virgo Child

When choosing a name for your Virgo girl or boy, first think about the major attributes and symbols associated with the sign. Virgo is the sign of the archetypical Virgin, who embodies the qualities of purity, chastity, modesty, industriousness, conscientiousness, and service to others. Virgos are modest, self-possessed, self-effacing, practical, hardworking, intelligent, analytical, truthseeking, and concerned about others. They shun the limelight and prefer taking secondary but crucial, roles behind the scenes.

Virgo is a Feminine, Mutable Earth sign governed by the planet Mercury. The Feminine aspect endows Virgos with sensitivity and a meditative, inner-directed quality. The Mutable aspect allows Virgos to adapt easily to new or changing environments. The Earth influence anchors Virgos in reality, makes them dependable and practical, and endows them with robust and down-to-earth dispositions.

Virgo's ruling planet, Mercury, governs all forms of communication, intelligence, and logic. Virgos are adept communicators, good listeners, and have sharp analytical skills. They value learning and higher education.

Virgo is the last of the summer signs, encompassing the months of August and September. The sapphire is Virgo's official birthstone, and the refined and classic colors of gray and navy blue are strongly associated with the sign. Mercury is Virgo's symbolic metal. Morning glories and pansies are Virgo's official flowers and the sign is also associated with the ash tree and all nut-bearing trees. Virgo governs all domestic animals.

When you choose a name for your child, also bear in mind some of Virgo children's key personal qualities. They are sensitive, determined, committed to high ideals, highly intelligent and logical, discriminating and self-contained. They are loyal and supportive friends, but frequently shy and reserved, qualities that are often mistaken for coldness. They are the doers and the organizers of the zodiac, and have a great need to understand problems and dilemmas and get to the truth of the matter. They are rarely self-indulgent, but can be inclined to being workaholics, overly critical, and obsessed with cleanliness.

For additional inspiration when choosing a name, or a middle name, for your Virgo child, you may want to browse through the names listed in Virgo's companion Earth signs, Taurus and Capricorn.

Names for Virgo Girls

Achala (ah-CHA-lah) Hindu: Steady. Reserved, modest, and rational in their approach to life, Virgos are noted for their dependability.

Adara (AH-dah-rah) Arabic: Chaste one. The qualities of purity and modesty are strongly associated with the sign of Virgo.

Adiba (AH-dee-bah) Arabic: Refined. Virgos are reserved and self-possessed.

Adila (AH-dee-lah) Arabic: Just. Virgo's calm and practical approach to problems enhances her ability to make wise and meaningful assessments of most situations. Variation: *Adilah*.

Agatha (AH-ga-thah) Latin: Virtuous. High-mindedness and a strong code of ethics are hallmarks of the sign of Virgo. (Famous Virgo: Agatha Christie, mystery writer)

Agnes (AG-ness) Latin: Pure and chaste. This traditional name and its modern variations is a classic choice for Virgo, who is symbolized by the archetypical symbol of the Virgin. Variations: *Aga, Aggie, Agna, Angella, Nessa, Nesta.*

Aida (ah-EE-dah) Latin: Help. Virgo is also the sign of service to others. Virgos are noted for their strong desire to help others and to make a difference in the world. Variation: *Ada*.

Akamai (ah-kah-MAH-ee) Hawaiian: Wise. Intelligence and analytical thinking are key qualities of the Virgo child.

Akanesi (ah-kah-NAY-see) Polynesian: Pure. Purity is the most prominent characteristic associated with the sign of Virgo.

Akilah (AH-kee-lah) Arabic: Logical. Rationality and crystal-clear thinking are key qualities of Virgo.

Alaia (ah-LAY-ah) Arabic: Virtuous. Purity, modesty, practicality, and self-denial are all characteristics of the Virgo child.

Albina (ahl-BEE-nah) Latin: White. The color white has long been a symbol of purity, the quality most strongly associated with the sign of Virgo. The many traditional names that have "white" as their root word are fitting choices for a Virgo girl. Variations: *Alba, Albinia, Alvina, Alvinia*.

Alethea (ahl-uh-THEE-ah or ah-LEE-thee-ah) Greek: Truth. Virgos, with their analytical and practical approach to life, are concerned with finding the truth in all situations and doing the right thing. Variation: *Aletea*.

Alexis (ah-LEX-iss) Greek: Helper. Virgos enjoy working hard and quietly behind the scenes, where they are renowned for putting in motion the ideas, dreams, and directives of the more aggressive signs of the zodiac.

Alma (AHL-mah) Hebrew: Maiden. The Virgin is the symbol of the sign of Virgo.

Almeda (ahl-MAY-dah) Latin: Determined. Hardworking Virgo thrives on turning chaos into order, bringing a measured practicality and cautiousness to all her tasks. Variations: *Allmeda, Allmeta, Almedah, Almeida, Almeta, Almida, Almita*.

Almena (ahl-MEEN-ah) English: Constant protector. Virgo has a strong desire to place her gifts of wisdom, rationality, and dependability in the service of others, and she is noted for her steadfast loyalty. Variations: *Almeena, Almina, Elmena, Elmina*.

Almera (ahl-MARE-ah) Arabic: Refined. Refinement, understatement, and good taste are key characteristics of the Virgo girl. Variations: *Allmeera, Almeria, Almira, Meera, Mira, Mirah, Myra*.

Amelia (ah-MEEL-ya) English: Hardworking. Virgos are renowned for their industrious determination. Variations: *Amalea, Amalia, Amalie, Amelie, Amelina, Amelinda, Amella*.

Amina (ah-MEE-nah) Arabic: Beyond reproach. Modesty and caution are hallmarks of Virgos, who rarely make waves and always have an innate understanding of how to behave in any situation. Variations: *Ameena, Aminah, Amineh*.

Amita (ah-MEE-tah) Hebrew: Truth. High-minded Virgo is committed to finding the truth in all problematic situations.

Andromeda (an-DRAH-mee-dah) Greek: One who ponders. Virgos are ruled by Mercury, the planet that governs the acquisition of knowledge and all forms of communication. Virgo uses her great intelligence and sharp analytical skills to quietly dissect and rationally explain any problem.

Anezka (ah-NEHZH-kah) Czech: Pure. Purity is the most dominant characteristic of the sign of Virgo. Variations: *Anesa, Neska*.

Ann (ahn) English: Grace. One of the most popular names in the world, *Ann* is a classic choice for modest and reserved Virgo. Variations: *Ana, Anita, Anitra, Anna, Annah, Anne, Annella, Annie, Hannah, Hannelore*. (Famous Virgos: Anne Bancroft, Oscar-winning actress; Anne Meara, actress and comedienne)

Annis (AN-iss) English: Chaste. Symbolized by the Virgin, or Maiden, Virgos are renowned for their modesty, reserve, and discrimination. Variation: *Annys*.

Annora (ahn-NORR-ah) English: With honor. Pure and virtuous, Virgos tend to follow strict inner moral codes. Variations: *Anora, Anorah, Nora, Norah, Onora*.

Antonia (an-TOH-nee-ah) Latin: Of exceptional worth. This lovely name suits highly intelligent, virtuous, and refined Virgo. Variations: *Antoinette, Antonella, Antonie, Antonina, Toni, Tonya*.

Anura (an-OO-rah) Hindu: Information. Virgo is ruled by the planet Mercury, which governs all forms of communication. Virgos are singularly adept at communicating new ideas and information.

Areta (ah-RAY-tah) Greek: Virtuous. Virgos are honorable, ethical, and disciplined in all things. Variations: *Aretha, Arethi, Aretina, Aretta, Arette*.

Arista (ah-REE-stah) Latin: Sowing the fields. In astrology, the long-standing tradition of using this name for a girl born under the sign of Virgo harks back to the image of a maiden in spring.

Astraea (as-TREE-ah or as-TRAY-ah) Greek: Greek goddess of justice and innocence. The goddess *Astraea* is famed for leaving earth to become the constellation Virgo. Variation: *Astrea*.

Athena (ah-THEE-nah) Greek: Goddess of wisdom. This classic name distinguishes itself for Virgo maidens, who are esteemed for their deep intelligence.

Augusta (aw-GUSS-tah) Latin: Highly respectable. This name is a traditional choice for rational and discriminating Virgos who are born in the month of August. Variations: *Gussie, Gusta*.

Azra (ahz-rah) Hindu: Virgin. The Virgin is the symbol of the sign of Virgo.

Bailey (BAY-lee) English: Public servant. This increasingly popular name is fitting for Virgo, the sign of service to others. Many Virgos pursue careers in social service and have a deep desire to help others and make a difference in the world. Variations: *Bailee, Baylee, Bayley, Baylie*.

Betula (beh-TOO-luh) Hebrew: Maiden. This lovely name suits a girl born under the sign of Virgo, whose symbol is the Virgin, or Maiden. Variations: *Betulia, Petula*.

Bianca (bee-YAHN-kah; BYAN-kah) Italian: White. White is the color most often associated with purity, Virgo's most prominent characteristic. Variations: *Biancha, Bionca, Bionka, Blanca, Blancha, Blanche*.

Bibi (bee-bee) Arabic: Lady. This charming name is a fitting title for the reserved and refined Virgo.

Bina (BEE-nah) Hebrew: Discernment. Virgos are esteemed for their quiet intelligence, good taste, and modest approach to life. Variation: *Bena*.

Caitlin (KATE-lin) Irish: Chaste. *Caitlin*, which began as a variation of *Cathleen*, has now achieved independent status and is currently one of the most popular names bestowed on girls. Its meaning makes it a perfect choice for the Virgo maiden. Variations: *Caitlan, Caitlyn, Catlin, Kaitlan, Kaitlin, Katelyn*.

Camilla (kah-MIL-lah) Latin: Unblemished; virginal. The Virgin, or Maiden, is the symbol of the sign of Virgo. Variation: *Camille*.

Candace (KAN-diss) Latin: White. Bestowed frequently upon girls during the 1950s and 1960s and due for a comeback, this classic name is a fitting choice for Virgo, the sign of purity, which is signified by the color white. Variations: *Candee, Candi, Candice, Candis, Candy, Dacey, Kandace*.

Candida (kan-DEE-dah) Latin: Dazzling whiteness. The color white is a traditional symbol of purity, Virgo's most esteemed quality. Variations: *Candee, Candi, Candy, Kandi, Kandie, Kandy*.

Carissa (kah-RISS-ah) Greek: Refined. The characteristic Virgo is quiet, refined, reserved, and self-effacing. Variations: *Carisa, Carisse*.

Caroline (KARE-oh-line) Latin: Womanly one. In ancient times, the Virgin was also celebrated for her potential to become another form—the Earth Mother or fertility goddess, esteemed for her fertile and life-affirming strength. Variations: *Carolyn, Ina, Karlinka, Karoline, Lina, Linka*.

Casey (KAYE-see) Irish: Observant. With their calm, rational, and intelligent approach to life, Virgos, known as gifted observers of the social landscape, can rapidly and objectively assess any problem and offer practical solutions. Variations: *Cacia, Casie, Cassie, Kacey, Kacia, Kasie*.

Charissa (KARE-iss-ah; KAR-iss-ah) Greek: Grace. Virgo, who is quiet, reserved, and self-possessed, embodies the qualities of gracefulness. Variation: *Charis*.

Charumati (char-oo-MAH-tee) Hindu: One with wisdom and intelligence. This name is well suited to the sign of wise and rational intelligence.

Chasida (kah-SEE-dah) Hebrew: Ethical. High-mindedness, honesty, and a no-nonsense code of right and wrong are key qualities of the sign of Virgo. Variation: *Hasida*.

Chastity (CHASS-tah-tee) Latin: Purity. Virgo's most prominent characteristic is purity. Variations: *Chasta, Chastina, Chas-
tine*.

Chenoa (chay-NO-ah) Native American: White dove. The color
white and the dove are traditional symbols of purity and peace,
key characteristics of Virgo children.

Cloris (KLORH-iss) Latin: Pure. The most prominent characteristics of Virgo are innocence and purity. Variation: *Chloris*.

Corinna (kor-RIN-nah; kor-REE-nah) Greek: Maiden. This
newly popular name is perfect for Virgo, who is symbolized by
the archetypical Virgin or Maiden. Variations: *Corrina, Corrine,
Corrinne*.

Dagmar (DAHG-mar) Scandinavian: Brilliant mind. Virgo is
the sign of deep intelligence and life-long learning. Variations:
Daga, Dagi, Dagmara, Dasa.

Danielle (dan-YELL) French: Divine judgements. This classic
French name has returned to popularity and suits Virgo's calm
and practical approach to problems, which enables her to make
meaningful assessments of most situations. Variations: *Daniela,
Daniele, Daniella, Danika, Danyelle, Donielle*.

Dara (DARE-rah or DAR-ah) Hebrew: Wise. Deep and practical wisdom is a key characteristic of the sign of Virgo. Variations: *Dahra, Darah, Dareen, Darice, Darissa, Darra, Darrah*.

Drew (dru) Greek: Wise. This classic Greek name, popularized
by actress Drew Barrymore (and suitable for a boy as well), is
a perfect choice for Virgo, the sign of great intelligence. Variation: *Dru*.

Duena (DWAY-nah) Spanish: Protector. Virgos are noted for
protecting the interests of others and for their fierce devotion to
high ideals.

Eadoin (eh-DEEN) Irish: Blessed with many friends. Virgos are loyal and devoted friends, which earns them many friends in return.

Eartha (UR-thah) Old English: Earth's daughter. This classic Old English name, popularized in recent times by singer Eartha Kitt, is a wonderful choice for Virgo, one of the zodiac's three Earth signs. Variations: *Erta, Ertha, Herta, Hertha.*

Edda (EHD-ah) German: With clear goals. Virgos are noted for their crystal-clear thinking. They are admired for their rational and measured approach to any problem and for their ability to come up with practical solutions. Variation: *Eda.*

Edwina (ed-WEE-nah) Old English: Prosperous friend. Virgos are quietly loyal and steadfast friends who avoid self-indulgence and remain practical in money matters. Variations: *Edina, Edween, Edwena, Edwyna.*

Effie (EFF-ee) Greek: Well-spoken. Mercury, Virgo's ruling planet, governs all forms of communication, making Virgos gifted at both communicating new ideas and listening to others.

Eirene (ee-REH-nee; eye-REE-nee) Scandinavian: Eternal calm. Virgos, poised and self-possessed in the face of any challenge, thrive on creating order out of chaos.

Eloise (ELL-oh-weez) French: Wise. A lovely old French name, immortalized in the twelfth century by the tragic love story of Eloise and Abelard and in recent history by the mischievous heroine of the popular children's books of the same name, *Eloise* is a marvelous choice for Virgo, the sign of deep intelligence. Variations: *Eloisa, Eloiza, Elouise, Heloise.*

Elvira (ell-VYE-rah; ell-VEER-ah) Latin: White. The color white is a traditional symbol of purity, Virgo's most prominent characteristic. This lovely and lyrical name, which enjoyed a renewed popularity in the late 1960s with the release of the critically acclaimed film *Elvira Madigan*, deserves a comeback. Variations: *Ela, Elvire, Wira, Wirke.*

Emily (EMM-ah-lee) English: Industrious. This traditional English name has a refined ring to it. Virgos also are renowned as industrious, determined, loyal, and hardworking. Variations: *Amalia, Amalie, Amelia, Amelie, Amy, Emalee, Emelda, Emelia.*

Emma (EMM-ah) English: Complete or whole. A traditional English name that is enjoying a renewed popularity, *Emma* is a marvelous choice for self-possessed and quietly dignified Virgo. Variations: *Em, Ema, Emeline, Emmaline, Emmalyn.*

Engracia (enn-GRAH-see-ah) Spanish: Grace. Dignified and refined, yet virtuous and compassionate, Virgo is the epitome of grace. Variation: *Graciella.*

Enid (EE-nid) Welsh: Pure. This name is ideal for a girl born under Virgo, whose key quality is purity.

Ernestine (air-nay-STEEN-eh or ER-neh-steen) German: Earnest. The success Virgos so often achieve can be attributed to their commitment to getting a job done right and their enthusiasm for honest, hard work. Variations: *Ernesta, Ernestina.*

Etana (eh-TAHN-ah) Hebrew: Dedicated. Virgos are renowned for their patience and unwavering determination.

Faith (FAYTH) Latin: Conviction. Renowned for their resolute commitment to finding solutions to difficult problems, Virgos are fueled by a clear-minded intelligence and strong inner moral code. Variations: *Fae, Fay, Faye, Fayth.*

Fatima (FAH-tee-mah) Arabic: Chastity. This very popular Middle Eastern name is an apt choice for Virgo, the sign of purity and modesty. Variations: *Farimah, Fatma, Fatuma.*

Fidelia (fee-DAYL-yah) Latin: Faithful. Virgos are loyal friends and workers.

Fukayna (foo-KEH-ee-nah) Arabic: Scholarly. Virgo is ruled by the planet Mercury, which governs the acquisition of knowledge.

Gitel (gih-TEL) Hebrew: Good. Virgos exemplify the simple essence of goodness and purity. Variations: *Gitel, Gitela, Gitele*.

Glenda (GLEN-dah) Welsh: Mild and kind. Virgos are gentle and calm, compassionate and benevolent.

Glenys (GLEN-iss) Welsh: Pure and holy. This name is suitable for a girl born under Virgo, whose most prominent characteristics are purity and innocence. Variations: *Glenice, Glenis, Glynis, Glynnis*.

Grace (GRAYSE) Latin: Grace. This traditional name is a popular choice for modest and discriminating Virgo. Variations: *Gracey, Graci, Gracia, Graciana, Gracie, Graciella, Grazia, Graziella*.

Greer (GREER) Scottish: Ever watching. Virgos are keen and objective observers of the social landscape, adept at perceiving the truth of a situation.

Guida (GWEE-dah) Italian: One who guides. The discerning and emotionally self-possessed Virgo child, often wise beyond her years, is able to offer clear and rational advice.

Gwyneth (GWEN-ith or GWINN-eth) Welsh: White. This old Welsh name is in vogue again, in part due to the popularity of actress Gwyneth Paltrow. The color white is a traditional symbol of purity, Virgo's most dominant characteristic. Variations: *Gwen, Gweneth, Gwenyth*.

Hagne (HAHG-nee) Greek: Pure. Symbolized by the Virgin, the sign of Virgo's key quality is purity.

Haidee (HAY-dee) Greek: Modest. This unique name is a wonderful choice for virtuous and humble Virgo. Variation: *Haydee*.

Hannah (HAH-nah) Hebrew: Grace. Through her natural sense of goodness and serenity, Virgo always exudes a graceful air. Variations: *Ann, Anna, Hana, Hanah, Hanna, Hannele, Hannie, Johanna*.

Hermia (HEHR-mee-ah) Greek: In Greek mythology, the messenger of the Greek gods. Virgos—ruled by the planet Mercury, which governs all forms of communication—are gifted communicators. Variations: *Herma, Hermaine, Hermina, Hermione*.

Hikmat (hik-MAHT) Arabic: Wise. Virgo is the sign of wisdom and higher learning.

Hilda (HILL-dah) German: Virgin warrior. The Virgin is the symbol of the sign of Virgo. While Virgos are quiet and reserved on the surface, they possess a fierce and unwavering inner moral code. Variations: *Hilde, Hildegard, Hildi, Hildie, Hildy*.

Honor (AH-ner) Latin: Integrity. Virgos are noted for their honesty and simplicity. Variations: *Honora, Honore, Honoria*.

Immaculada (ee-mahk-yoo-LAH-dah) Spanish: Innocent. Innocence and purity are key characteristics of Virgo. Variation: *Immaculata*.

Imogen (EYE-mah-jeen; IM-oh-geen) Latin: Innocent. Symbolized by the pure Maiden, Virgo's outlook is innocent and unassuming. Variations: *Imogene, Imogenia*.

Ina (EYE-nah) Greek: Pure. Virgo exemplifies the quality of pure innocence and idealized purity. Variation: *Ena*.

Inez (eye-NEZ) Spanish: Unadulterated. This name suggests purity and innocence, Virgo's most prominent qualities. Variations: *Ines, Inessa, Inetta, Ynes, Ynez.*

Inocencia (ee-no-SEN-see-ah) Spanish: Innocent. The symbol of Virgo is the Virgin, which exalts both innocence and purity. Variations: *Inocenta, Inocentia.*

Iuginia (ee-oo-JEE-nee-ah) Hawaiian: Well-bred. Modesty, refinement, and reserve characterize Virgo. Variation: *Iugina.*

Jaha (JAH-hah) African/Swahili: Dignity. Those born under the sign of Virgo are known for their calm reserve and dignified bearing.

Jena (jay-nah) Hindu: Patience. Virtuous Virgo is known for her dedication, commitment, and patience.

Jennifer (JEN-nih-fur) Welsh: Fair lady. Virgo is known for her clear reasoning and solid integrity. Variations: *Jennie, Jenny.*

Jezebel (JEZ-ah-bell) Hebrew: Virginal. Contrary to the popular concept of Jezebel in the Old Testament, this name actually translates into "Virgin," the symbol for the sign of Virgo. Variations: *Jez, Jezzie.*

Joline (yo-LEEN) Hebrew: She whose fortunes shall multiply. Virgo's calm reasoning and patient planning often lead her to success and prosperity. Variations: *Joleen, Jolene.*

Justine (jus-TEEN) Latin: Just and proper. Virtuous Virgos adhere to their own strict moral codes and take pride in following rules. Variation: *Justina.*

Kacie (KAY-see) Irish: Eagle-eyed. Perceptive and highly intelligent, Virgos are always attuned to their environment and are highly aware of what's going on around them. Variations: *Kacey, Kaci, Kacia, Kacy, Kaesha, Kaycie, K.C.*

Kane (KAH-neh) Japanese: Two right hands; able to do many things at the same time. Virgos are renowned for their industriousness in business, and for their willingness to work long, hard hours behind the scenes until the job is done.

Kanya (KAHN-yah) Hindu: Virgin. In astrology, this traditional Hindu name is often given to a child born under the sign of Virgo. It is also another name for the dynamic Hindu goddess *Sakti*.

Karen (KARE-inn) Greek: Immaculate. This name evokes the purity and cleanliness of spirit inherent in all Virgos. Variations: *Caron, Caryn, Karin, Karina, Karrin, Karyn, Katina.*

Karida (KA-ree-dah) Arabic: Virginal. This lovely name connotes purity and innocence, as well as Virgo's symbol, the Virgin.

Katherine (KATH-rin) Greek: Chaste. With a long and esteemed history, *Katherine*—or one of its many beautiful variations—is a wonderful choice for Virgo, the sign of purity. Variations: *Cass, Cassie, Catarina, Catherine, Kate, Kathryn, Katrina, Katya, Kit, Kitty.*

Kaya (KAY-yah) Native American: Wise child. The translation of this name combines two of Virgo's most noted qualities—wisdom and innocence.

Kayla (KAY-lah) English: Pure. Originally a variant of *Katherine*, *Kayla* and its many variations have achieved independent status. Virgo is the sign of purity and modesty. Variations: *Kaela, Kaeleigh, Kaeli, Kaelin, Kailey, Kalen, Kalie, Kaylea, Kayleigh, Kayley, Kayli.*

Keke (KEH-keh) Hawaiian: Pure. Virgo is known for its quality of purity.

Kiska (KISS-kah) Russian: Chaste. This very popular Russian variant of *Katherine* is perfect for the Virgo maiden.

Kolina (ko-LEE-nah) Swedish: Chaste; a Swedish variant of *Katherine*. Chastity is a keen characteristic of the Virgo maiden.

Korina (kor-REEN-ah) English: Maiden. Virgo's maiden is known as pure and innocent. Variations: *Korinna, Korinne, Korrina*.

Kostya (KAH-stya) Russian: Persistent. With their intense dedication and strong work ethic, Virgos can achieve any goal they set their sights on.

Lara (LAR-ah) Latin: Protection. Virgo's are known for their undeterred concern and loyal care. Variations: *Laralaine, Laramae, Lari, Larina, Larinda, Larita*.

Lavinia (lah-VEEN-ee-ah or lah-VIN-ee-ah) Latin: Purified. The sign of Virgo exemplifies all that is open, innocent, and pure. Variations: *Lavina, Lavinie*.

Leslie (LEZ-lee) Scotch: One who lives in the gray fortress. Virgos are noted for their inner strength and determination, and gray is among Virgo's traditional colors. Variations: *Lesley, Lesli, Lezli, Lezlie, Lezly*.

Li Hua (LEE-HWAH) Chinese: Pear blossom. In China, the pear blossom is the flower of August and the symbol of longevity. Many Virgos are born in the latter part of August.

Lilly (LIL-ee) Middle English: Pure. This name connotes the flower, a traditional symbol of purity and peace—key qualities of the sign of Virgo. Variations: *Lili, Lily*.

Maiba (MAY-bah) African/Zimbabwean: Serious. Virgos are known for their sincerity and earnestness.

Maikai (mah-ee-KAH-ee) Hawaiian: Good. Those born under the sign of Virgo exemplify inner purity and exude kindness.

Maiza (MAY-sah) Arabic: Discerning. The clear-headed thinking and fair judgment of Virgos make this name highly appropriate.

Matilda (mah-TILL-dah) Old German: Chaste warrioress. While connoting the purity of the Virgo maiden, this name also reveals her strength and determination. Variations: *Mat, Mathilda, Matilde, Mattie, Matty, Maude, Tilda, Tildy, Tillie.*

Melba (MELL-bah) Latin: From *malva*, for the mallow flower, which is associated with the month of September. Many Virgos are born in September. Variations: *Malva, Melva.*

Mercy (MER-see) Old English: Compassion. Virgos have a deep concern for the welfare of others and often pursue work in the field of social services. Variations: *Mercedes, Merci, Mercie, Mersey.*

Mildred (MILL-dred) Old English: Gentle strength. This traditional name evokes Virgo's childlike gentility and determined willpower. Variations: *Mil, Mildrid, Millie, Milly.*

Milica (MI-lits-uh; mi-LEE-kuh) Old English: Hardworking. Virgos are esteemed for their determination and industriousness, and for their willingness to work long and hard hours behind the scenes.

Minerva (mi-NER-vah) Latin: Wisdom. In Roman mythology, *Minerva* is the goddess of wisdom, one of Virgo's prevalent qualities. Variations: *Min, Minda, Minnie, Minny.*

Miwa (MEE-wah) Japanese: Wise eyes. With their sharp analytical skills and calm, rational approach to life, Virgos are gifted and objective observers of the social landscape.

Modesty (MAH-dess-tee) Latin: Without conceit. Modesty and self-effacement are qualities associated with the sign of Virgo. Variations: *Modesta, Modestine.*

Monica (MAHN-ee-kah) Latin: Adviser. This classic name is well suited to self-possessed Virgo, who is esteemed for her ability to analyze difficult problems and come up with clear and practical solutions. Variations: *Monika, Monique.*

Morwenna (mor-WENN-ah) Welsh: Maiden. The Virgin, or Maiden, is the symbol of the sign of Virgo.

Nahiba (nah-HEEB-ah) Arabic: Smart. Virgo is the sign of deep intelligence and logical thinking.

Nancy (NAN-see) Latin: Full of grace. This variant of *Ann* has achieved independent status and, though not as popular as it was during the 1950s, is still a classic choice for Virgo, the sign of poise, modesty, and self-possession.

Nariko (NAH-ree-koh) Japanese: Child who is humble. Virgos are generally quiet and self-effacing, shunning the limelight and preferring to work behind the scenes.

Nathifa (nah-THEE-fah) Arabic: Pure. Virgo's prominent trait is purity, of both body and mind. Variations: *Nathifah, Natifa, Natifah.*

Nazihah (nah-ZEE-hah) Arabic: Trustworthy. Always honorable and virtuous, Virgos set high ethical standards for themselves.

Neva (NEH-vah) Spanish: Extremely white. The color white is a traditional symbol of purity, Virgo's most pronounced characteristic.

Neza (NEH-zhuh) Slavic: Pure. Among traits such as intelligence, order, and kindness, purity stands out as Virgo's supreme strength.

Nina (NEE-nah) Russian: Full of grace. Virgo's calm reserve and rational consideration evoke her quality of gentleness and grace. Variation: *Nena*.

Nona (NOH-nah) Latin: Nine. This name is ideal for Virgos born in September, the ninth month of the calendar year.

Nuha (NOO-hah) Arabic: Smart. Virgo is esteemed for her intelligence and clear-thinking.

Olga (OL-gah) Old Norse: Holy one. A commitment to high ideals and a strong moral fiber are noted qualities of the sign of Virgo. Variations: *Ola, Olli, Ollyl, Olya*.

Ona (OH-nah) Lithuanian: Full of grace. The Virgo Maiden is acknowledged for her quiet reserve and kind dignity.

Pavana (pah-VAH-nah) Hindu: Pure. Purity and modesty characterize the sign of Virgo.

Pandita (pahn-DEE-tah) Hindu: Scholar. Virgos are esteemed for their deep, rational intelligence and commitment to higher learning.

Pandora (pan-DOR-rah) Greek: Bestowed with talents. Among Virgo's many gifts are poise, calm, rationality, logic, industriousness, and practicality. Variations: *Panda, Pandy*.

Pansy (PAN-zee) English: For the flower. The pansy is one of two flowers associated with the sign of Virgo. (The other is the morning glory.) Variations: *Pansey, Pansie*.

Parthenia (par-THEEN-ee-ah) Greek: Virginal. The Virgin, or Maiden, symbolizes the sign of Virgo. Virgos are renowned for their modesty and commitment to higher aims. Variations: *Parthania, Parthena, Parthina, Parthine, Pathania, Pathenia, Pathina*.

Patience (PAY-shentz) English: For the virtue of patience and derived from the Latin *pati* (to suffer). Virgos approach all challenging tasks slowly, calmly, and rationally. Variations: *Paciencia, Patient*.

Pilar (pee-LAHR) Spanish: Foundation. Virgos are unconcerned with being the center of attention. Instead, they are the committed worker bees behind the throne, the ones who give form and direction to others' ideas, dreams, directives, and fancies.

Prudence (PROO-dens) Latin: For the virtue of prudence and derived from the Latin *prudens* (providence). Virgos are blessed with an inborn distaste of self-indulgence and extravagance. Variations: *Prudy, Prue*.

Questa (KWES-tah) French: Seeking. Noted for their gifts of logic and clear thinking, Virgos are adept at sifting through mounds of complicated information and getting to the heart and truth of a problem.

Radmilla (rahd-MILL-ah) Slavic: Hard worker. Virgos are renowned for their committed and industrious work habits.

Rane (RAH-neh) Latin: Chaste. Modesty and purity characterize the sign of Virgo.

Raphaela (ra-fee-ELL-ah) Hebrew: God has healed. This feminine variation of *Raphael* refers to the archangel of healing, who also oversees the sign of Virgo. Variation: *Rafaela*.

Rawnie (RAW-nee) Gypsy: Fine lady. The Virgin, or Maiden, who symbolizes the sign of Virgo, is a highly esteemed ancient Earth goddess.

Rehema (reh-HEH-mah) African/Swahili: Compassion. Though their quiet reserve is often mistaken for coldness, Virgos, who are dedicated to truth and justice, have a deep concern for the welfare of others. They often choose work in the field of social services.

Riju (REE-joo) Hindu: Pure. Purity is the most prominent characteristic of all Virgos.

Rokuko (ro-KOO-ko) Japanese: Sixth born. Virgo is the sixth sign of the zodiac.

Ronni (ROHN-ee) English: Strong counsel. This Old English name is an ideal choice for thoughtful Virgo, who uses her gifts of analysis and logic to attack complex issues and get to the heart of a problem. Variations: *Ronnette, Ronney, Ronnica, Ronny.*

Ruth (ROOTH) Hebrew: Companion. A traditional name with biblical origins, *Ruth* is a classic choice for Virgos, who are loyal and devoted friends. Variations: *Rue, Rut, Ruthie.*

Sabriyya (sah-BREE-yah) Arabic: Patience. Virgo's invariable approach to all challenges and problems is slow, calm, cautious, and practical. Variations: *Sabira, Sabirah, Sabriyyah.*

Sada (SAH-dah) Japanese: Virginal. The Virgin is the archetypical symbol of the sign of Virgo.

Safa (sah-FAH) Arabic: Pure. Purity is the most potent characteristic associated with the sign of Virgo.

Sage (SAYJE) English: Wise one. This traditional English name is a lovely choice for Virgo, the sign of wisdom and higher learning.

Salha (SAHL-hah) Arabic: Ethical. High-mindedness and inner moral strength are key qualities of Virgo.

Salihah (SAH-lee-hah) Arabic: Virtuous. Refined and practical Virgos have a built-in defense against self-indulgence.

Samantha (sah-MAN-thah) Aramaic: Listener. Practical, intuitive, and compassionate, Virgos make wonderful friends who are always willing to listen to the problems of others and offer wise advice. Variations: *Sam, Sammi.*

Sandra (SAN-drah; SAHN-drah) Greek: Helper. Virgos shine in supporting roles, deftly executing the dreams and directives of their more aggressive cousins. Variations: *Sanda, Sandee, Sandi, Saundra, Sondra.*

Sapphire (SAF-ire) Arabic: Gorgeous. The sapphire is the birthstone of Virgo. Variations: *Safira, Saphira, Sapphira, Sephira.*

Serena (seh-REE-nah) Latin: Calm and peaceful. Reserve and equanimity are key characteristics of Virgo. Variations: *Sarena, Sarene, Sarina, Sereena, Serenah, Serina.*

Shimona (shi-MO-nah) Hebrew: Listen. Mercury, Virgo's ruling planet, governs all forms of communication, and Virgos understand the value of being good and objective listeners. Variations: *Simeona, Simona, Simone.*

Shizu (SHEE-zoo) Japanese: Quiet. Virgos rarely display either the electrifying flamboyance or ebullient good humor of their two nearest cousins, Leo and Libra. Yet their keen intelligence, heartfelt loyalty to friends and coworkers, and deep reserves of inner moral strength are equally impressive and highly esteemed. Variations: *Shizuko, Shizuyo.*

Shura (SHOO-rah) Russian: Protector. Virgos, who often seek work in the field of social services, are noted for protecting the interests of others and for their fierce devotion to high ideals.

Sofronia (so-FRO-nee-ah) Greek: Wise. A deep and measured intelligence characterizes the sign of Virgo. Variation: *Sophronia*.

Solange (soh-LANZH) French: Dignified. Modesty, high-mindedness, inner moral strength, and refinement characterize the actions of Virgo.

Sonia (SOHN-jah) English: Wisdom. Virgo is the sign of great intelligence, cool rationality, and razor-sharp logic. Variations: *Sonal, Sonala, Sonali, Sonika, Sonita, Sonya*.

Sophia (soh-FEE-ah) Greek: Wisdom. This classic and time-honored name personifies the notion of wisdom, one of Virgo's major characteristics. Variations: *Sofi, Sofia, Sophey, Sophie, Sophy, Zofia*.

Sumi (SOO-mee) Japanese: One who sees clearly. Virgo's calm thinking and undeterred intelligence give them great insight into—and solutions to—many problems.

Tacey (TAY-see) English: Quiet. Unlike their gregarious, extroverted Leo cousins, Virgos are reserved and self-possessed. Variations: *Tace, Tacita*.

Teriah (teh-REE-ah) Hebrew: Fresh. The image of Virgo evokes the Maiden and her ever youthful and open approach to looking at life. Variations: *Tari, Taria, Teria*.

Terra (TERR-ah) Latin: For the planet Earth. Virgo is one of three Earth signs. In astrology, this name is often bestowed on a child born under an Earth sign.

Vera (VAR-ah or VEER-ah) Latin: Truth. Virgo is known for her open and perceptive insight into reality.

Verdad (ver-DAD) Spanish: Truth. Despite her innocence, Virgo's quest is always inspired and rewarded by the truth.

Verena (var-EEN-ah) Latin: True. This lovely name exemplifies Virgo's graceful pursuit of justice and truth. Variations: *Vereena, Verene, Verina, Verine, Veruschka.*

Verity (VER-ih-tee) Latin: Truth. This name contains an obvious reference to one of the most prominent of Virgo's fine qualities. Variations: *Verita, Veritie.*

Virginia (ver-JIN-yah) Latin: Chaste. Although commonly heard, this name is seldom associated with its direct derivation: the Virgin maiden that signifies the sign's innocence and purity. Variations: *Gina, Ginger, Ginia, Ginny, Vergie, Virginai, Virgy.*

Virtue (VER-choo) Latin: Virtue. While Virgo is a sign of many fine qualities, this unique name sums them up in one concise word.

Winifred (WIN-ih-fred) Welsh: Blessed peace. This name conveys the sense of the sacred and serene that is seen in many Virgos. Variations: *Win, Winnie.*

Wynne (WIN) Welsh: White. Traditionally, the color white is a symbol of purity, Virgo's key characteristic. Variation: *Wynn.*

Xenia (ZAYN-yah or ZEEN-yah) Greek: Gracious. This unique name evokes the image of the benevolent and innocent maiden. Variation: *Xena.*

Yamina (yah-MEE-nah) Arabic: Ethical. In her concern with fairness and moral valor, Virgo reflects a deep conviction in the importance of high ethical standards. Variations: *Yaminah, Yemina.*

Yasu (YAH-soo) Japanese: Calm. In her rational and serene approach to every situation, the Virgo maiden proves herself calm and in control. Variations: *Yasuko, Yasuyo.*

Yoshiko (YO-shee-koh) Japanese: Quiet. Virgo is known for her calm demeanor and silent strength. Variations: *Yoshi, Yoshie, Yoshiyo*.

Zakah (zah-KAH) Hebrew: Pure. Purity is considered Virgo's greatest virtue. Variations: *Zaka, Zakia, Zakiah*.

Zakiya (zah-KEE-yah) African/Swahili: Pure. Purity is the most prominent trait attributed to those born under the sign of Virgo. Variation: *Zakiyah*.

Zarifa (zah-REE-fah) Arabic: Moves with grace. Symbolized by the image of the pure young Maiden, Virgos are the quintessence of graceful strength.

Zilpah (ZILL-pah) Hebrew: Dignity. Credited with great intelligence and admirable self-control, Virgos earn their well-deserved reputations as dignified and highly principled. Variations: *Silpha, Zillpha, Zulpha*.

Zocha (ZO-kah) Polish: Wisdom. Virgos are known to be highly intelligent and emotionally insightful, qualities that lead to great wisdom.

Zulema (zoo-LEE-mah; zoo-LAY-mah) Hebrew: Peace. In their calm thought processes and serene demeanors, Virgos reflect a sublime sense of peace. Variation: *Zulima*.

Names for Virgo Boys

Akil (ah-KEEL) Arabic: Intelligent. Intelligence and analytical thinking are key qualities of the Virgo child.

Akio (AH-kee-o) Japanese: Smart child. Virgo is ruled by the planet Mercury, which governs all forms of learning. Variation: *Akira*.

Alban (ALL-ban) Latin: White. The color white is a traditional symbol of purity, the most prominent characteristic associated with the image of the Virgin, who symbolizes the sign of Virgo. Variations: *Albek, Albin, Albinek, Alby, Aubin.*

Alfred (AL-fred) English: Wise listener. Virgo—ruled by the planet Mercury, which governs all forms of communication—wisely understands the value of being a good listener. Variation: *Alfredo.*

Alister (AL-iss-tur) Scottish: Helper. Virgo is also the sign of service to others, and Virgos are noted for their strong desire to help others and to make a difference in the world.

Apenimon (ah-PEE-nih-mohn) Native American: Reliable. Reserved, modest, and practical in their approach to life, Virgos are noted for their dependability.

Archimedes (ahr-kee-MEH-des or ahr-kih-MEE-dees) Greek: To think about. Virgos, gifted with sharply analytical minds, are able to calmly view problems and challenges from all angles.

Arif (ar-EEF) Arabic: Knowledgeable. Virgo is the sign of wisdom and higher learning.

Austen (AWE-stin) Latin: Venerable. This name is a classic and popular choice for high-minded and supremely ethical Virgo. Variation: *Oisten.*

August (AW-gust) Latin: Highly respectable. This name is a traditional choice for a rational and discriminating Virgo born in the month of August. Variations: *Auguste, Augustus.*

Baruti (bah-ROO-tee) African/Tswana: Tutor. With their love of knowledge, practical approach to problems, and keen communication skills, Virgos make excellent teachers.

Basir (buh-SEER) Turkish: Discriminating. Modest and cautious in their approach to life, Virgos tend to make purposeful and calculated choices.

Bello (BELL-oh) African: Assistant. Virgos enjoy working hard behind the scenes, putting in motion the ideas, dreams, and directives of the more aggressive signs of the zodiac.

Berdy (BAIR-dee) Russian: Genius. Intelligence is the hallmark of the sign of Virgo.

Berwin (BUR-win) Middle English: Harvest son. Virgo is one of the three Earth signs of the zodiac. (The other two are Taurus and Capricorn.) Its positioning in the months of August and September mark the time of year when harvesting begins.

Blair (BLAYR) Irish: Meadow child. This classic Gaelic name, which continues to be popular for both boys and girls, is a wonderful and contemporary choice for the Earth sign Virgo. Variations: *Blaire, Blayre.*

Boden (BOH-den) French: One who delivers the news. Mercury, the planet that governs all forms of communication, rules the sign of Virgo. Variations: *Bodin, Bowden, Bowdoin.*

Bradley (BRAD-lee) Old English: From the expansive field. Virgo is one of the zodiac's three Earth signs, and Virgos themselves are renowned for their practical and down-to-earth demeanors. Variations: *Brad, Bradlee, Bradshaw, Brady, Lee.*

Calum (KAL-um) Irish: Dove. The dove is the symbol of purity and peace, qualities that are strongly associated with the sign of Virgo. Variation: *Callum.*

Carlin (KAR-len) Irish: Little champion. Virgos, noted for their steadfast loyalty to friends and causes, have a heartfelt desire to serve others. Variations: *Carling, Carly, Carolan.*

Casey (KAY-see) Irish: Alert. Crystal-clear thinking is one of Virgo's principal characteristics.

Caton (kah-TOHN or KAY-ton) Latin: Knowing. Mercury, which rules the sign of Virgo, governs the acquisition of all types of knowledge. Variation: *Cato*.

Clark (KLARK) Old French: One committed to studies. Virgos, with their discerning intelligence and love of learning, are committed to life-long education. Variations: *Clarke, Clerc, Clerk*.

Cleary (CLEER-ee) Irish: Educated man. Virgo is the sign of intelligence and wisdom.

Clement (KLEM-int) Latin: Accommodating. Virgos rarely aspire to leadership roles. They prefer to work in the background, where they are noted for their industrious loyalty. The strongly Mutable quality of their sign allows them to adapt easily to most situations Variations: *Clem, Clemens, Clemmons*.

Conrad (KAHN-rad) German: Brave adviser. With their keen analytical skills and their facility for communication, Virgos can rapidly hone in on the heart of a problem and offer clear and practical solutions. Variations: *Conn, Connie, Conrade, Conrado, Konrad*.

Conroy (KAHN-roy) Irish: Wise man. Virgo is the sign of higher learning.

Curtis (KUR-tehs) Old French: Imbued with courtesy. Modest, reserved, and often quite shy, Virgos are usually unfailingly polite. Variations: *Curt, Kurt, Kurtis*.

Dabir (dah-BEER) Arabic: Tutor. Virgos are dedicated to acquiring knowledge and are gifted at communicating their enthusiasm for learning.

Dakota (dah-KOH-tah) Native American: Ally, partner. Virgos particularly shine in one-on-one partnerships and make steadfast friends.

Dan (dan) Hebrew: Judge. Virgo's rational and practical approach to problems enhances his ability to make meaningful assessments of most situations.

Darius (DARE-ee-us) Latin: He who defends the good. Virgos have an innate drive to be of service to others and often pursue careers in the field of social justice.

Davin (DAH-vin) Old Scandinavian: Brilliant Finn. A popular name in Finland, literally referring to the high intelligence purportedly enjoyed by all Finns, makes an apt choice for the deeply intelligent Virgo boy.

Dema (DEEM-ah) Russian: Calm. Virgos are noted for their reserve and calm in the face of chaos.

Dimitri (dih-MEE-tree) Russian: Lover of the Earth. Virgo is one of the three Earth signs of the zodiac, reflected in Virgo's close connection to his natural environment. Variations: *Demeter, Dimitre, Dmitri, Dimitrios, Dimitry.*

Din (DIN) Vietnamese: Calm. Quiet intelligence and a reserved demeanor are hallmarks of the sign of Virgo.

Dominick (DAHM-ih-nik) Latin: Sunday's child. This traditional and wonderfully appropriate choice for a Virgo boy embodies all the qualities of a child born on Sunday: "... fair and wise and good and gay." Variations: *Dom, Domingo, Dominic, Dominik, Dominique, Domo, Mingo.*

Duc (YUKE) Vietnamese: Upright. Virgos, who possess great inner discipline and self-control, are noted for their ethical behavior.

Eldred (ELD-red) English: Elderly counselor. The discerning and emotionally self-possessed Virgo child is often wise beyond his years.

Elvis (EHL-viss) Scandinavian: Wise. This very popular Scandinavian name, immortalized by rock-and-roll icon Elvis Presley, is a delightful choice for the intelligent Virgo boy.

Enoch (EE-nok) Hebrew: Scholarly. Virgo is the sign of wisdom and higher learning.

Ernan (UR-nan) Irish: One who is wise. Virgo governs intelligence and the acquisition of knowledge. Variation: *Earnan*.

Ernest (UR-nest) German: Serious. Virgos bring a sober and discriminating eye to all their tasks. Variations: *Ernestas, Ernesto, Ernie, Erno, Ernst*.

Esmé (EZZ-may) French: Esteemed. Virgos are renowned and highly valued both for their great inner strength and for their high work ethics.

Ethan (EE-than) Hebrew: Permanence. This beautiful and traditional biblical name, with its suggestion of constancy, is an ideal choice for steadfast and loyal Virgo. Variation: *Etan*.

Ezra (EZZ-rah) Hebrew: Helper. Virgos are renowned for their loyalty and industriousness in business, and for their willingness to work hard behind the scenes.

Farouk (fah-ROOK) Arabic: Truth; moralist. Virgos, with their analytical and practical approach to life, are concerned with finding the truth and doing the right thing in all situations. Variations: *Faraq, Faraqh, Farook*.

Feivel (FYE-full) Hebrew: Bright. Virgo is the sign of wisdom and rational thinking.

Festus (FESS-tuhs) Latin: Steadfast. Virgos are noted for their hardworking determination and their loyalty to friends and business associates. Variation: *Fess*.

Galen (GAY-len) Greek: Calm. Reserve, quiet, and inner calm are key qualities associated with the sign of Virgo. Virgos are also renowned for their deep desire to serve others. Galen is the name of the famed second-century Greek physician who founded the school of experimental physiology called Galenism. Variations: *Gale, Galeno, Gayle*.

Gomer (GO-mur) Hebrew: Accomplish. Virgos, with their high work ethics and single-minded determination to finish any task put before them, are renowned for getting the job done.

Gordon (GORR-din) Old English: Round hill. This earthy reference applies to Virgo because it is one of the three Earth signs of the zodiac. Variations: *Gordie, Gordy*.

Graham (GRAY-um) English: Gray house. Gray, a refined and classic color, is one of the two colors strongly associated with the sign of Virgo. (Navy blue is the other.) Variations: *Graeham, Graem, Graeme, Grahame, Gram*.

Gray (GRAY) English: Gray. Gray is one of Virgo's symbolic colors. Variations: *Graydon, Grey*.

Greeley (GREE-lee) English: Gray meadow. This traditional place name is an apt choice for Virgo, an Earth sign that is strongly associated with the color gray. Variations: *Greeleigh, Greely*.

Gregory (GREG-a-ree) Greek: Observant. Rational and clear-minded Virgos are keen and objective observers of any situation. Variations: *Greg, Gregg, Gregoire, Gregor, Gregorio*.

Griswold (GRIZ-wahld) English: Gray forest. This traditional place name is suitable for Virgo, with its close connection to the Earth and its symbolic color of gray.

Grover (GROH-vur) English: Gardener or grove dweller. This whimsical but traditional English name is an apt choice for Virgo, an Earth sign that is keenly attuned to the natural surroundings.

Hakeem (hah-KEEM) Arabic: Wise. Virgo is the sign of intelligence and analytical thinking. Variations: *Hakem, Hakim.*

Halim (hah-LEEM) Arabic: Mild. Most Virgos possess quiet, refined, and reserved personalities.

Hanbal (HAHN-bal) Arabic: Purity. One of the original virtues, purity is the quality most prominently associated with the sign of Virgo. Variation: *Hannibal.*

Hanley (HAN-lee) Old English: Meadow on a cliff. The natural image evoked by this name links it to Virgo, one of the zodiac's three Earth signs. Variations: *Handleigh, Handley, Henley.*

Harith (hah-REETH) Arabic: Capable. Multi-talented Virgo brings an abundance of skills—including intelligence, practicality, discrimination, and perseverance—to any task.

Harley (HAHR-lee) Old English: Spacious meadow. Born under an Earth sign, Virgos are closely connected to the natural environment around them. Their sound judgment is often referred to as down-to-earth. Variations: *Arleigh, Arley, Harleigh, Harly.*

Hector (HEK-torr) Greek: Persevering. Virgos are renowned for their industriousness and determination. Variations: *Heck, Heitor, Hektor.*

Hideaki (hee-day-AH-kee) Japanese: Wise. Virgo is the sign of intelligence and learning.

Hikmat (HEEK-maht) Arabic: Knowledge. Mercury, which rules the sign of Virgo, governs the acquisition of all knowledge.

Hillel (hih-LELL) Hebrew: Highly praised. Virgos, the singular workhorses of any business, are greatly esteemed for their high work ethics.

Hisoka (hee-SO-kah) Japanese: Restrained. Modesty and caution are hallmarks of the sign of Virgo.

Holden (HOLD-en) Old English: Deep valley. Virgo, an Earth sign, is quiet, reserved, and inner-directed. Variation: *Holman*.

Horton (HORR-tun) English: Gray town. This traditional English name, immortalized by Dr. Seuss, is a fitting choice for fastidious Virgo, whose symbolic color is gray.

Howell (HOW-ell) Welsh: Exceptional. In this results-oriented era of quick results, Virgo brings the refreshingly old-fashioned—and increasingly rare—virtues of hard work, high-mindedness, and determination to any task presented him.

Hoyt (HOYT) Irish: Mind. This classic Gaelic name is an appropriate choice for keenly intelligent Virgo.

Hubert (HYOO-burt) German: Bright mind. This old-fashioned name, now enjoying a renewed popularity (particularly in several of its more contemporary variations), is an apt choice for clear-thinking Virgo. Variations: *Hubbard, Hube, Huberto, Huey, Hugh, Hughes, Hugo, Uberto*.

Hywel (HYOO-ell) Welsh: Famous. While Virgos never seek the spotlight like their more fiery cousins, they are just as highly esteemed for their tremendous behind-the-scenes energy.

Igasho (ee-GAH-sho) Native American: Seeker. High-minded Virgo is committed to finding the truth in all situations.

Innocenzio (ee-no-CHEHN-tsee-o) Italian: Innocent. Purity and innocence are the most powerful characteristics of the sign of Virgo. Variation: *Ince*.

Ira (EYE-rah) Hebrew: Observant. With their sharp analytical skills and calm and rational approach to problems, Virgos are gifted observers of the social landscape.

Jahi (JAH-hee) African/Swahili: Honor. Virgo is renowned for his well-developed sense of ethics and commitment to working hard and honestly.

Jaja (JAH-jah) African/Nigerian: Honored. Because they are known for holding positions of responsibility and trust, Virgos earn their reputations for having integrity and are honored for it.

Jaspal (JAHS-pahl) Pakistani: Virtuous. Virgos are beloved for their upright and honest principles.

Jonah (JOH-nah) Hebrew: Dove. Virgos are known for their mild-mannered, peace-loving ways. Variation: *Jonas*.

Jun (JOON) Chinese: Wisdom. In their thoughtful and perceptive approach to any problem, Virgos prove themselves wise beyond their years.

Justin (JUS-tin) Old French: Just and righteous. This classic—and recently revived—name combines two of Virgo's finest qualities. Variations: *Just, Juste, Justen, Justino, Justis, Justo*.

Keli (KEH-leh) Hawaiian: Observer. With their keen perception and receptive spirits, Virgos are extremely aware of the emotions and actions of those around them.

Keller (KELL-ur) Irish: Dear companion. This classic Gaelic name is an appropriate choice for loyal and committed Virgo.

Kevin (KEH-vin) Irish: Gentle one. Calm, self-effacing, and quietly committed to the service of others, Virgos are the gentle souls of the zodiac. Variation: *Kevan*.

Ladd (LAD) English: Assistant. Virgos invariably take strong supporting roles in any endeavor and are renowned for their committed and industrious work habits. Variations: *Lad, Laddie, Laddy*.

Langundo (lahn-GOON-doh) Native American: Calm. Well regarded for their serene and rational approach to any situation, Virgos are known for their sense of calm.

Latimer (LAH-tih-mer) English: Interpreter. Virgos are noted for utilizing their exceptional gifts of analysis and logic to dissect complex issues and get to the crux of the problem.

Leslie (LEZ-lee) Scottish: Gray castle. Gray is one of the symbolic colors of the sign of Virgo, and this traditional name (also very popular for girls) is a good choice for steadfast and dependable Virgo. Variations: *Les, Lesley*.

Macaulay (mah-KAW-lay) Scottish: Son of righteousness. This popular and classic Scottish surname is an appropriate choice for high-minded Virgo.

Magnus (MAHG-nus) Latin: Excellent. A fierce commitment to excellence sets Virgos apart from the rest. Variations: *Magnes, Manus*.

Mahir (mah-HEER) Hebrew: Industrious. This unusual name is well suited to the hardworking, behind-the-scenes dedication of faithful Virgo.

Malachi (MA-la-kye) Hebrew: Messenger. Often responsible for resolving conflicts between others, Virgos are known to excel in the area of communication. Variations: *Malachai, Malachie, Malachy, Malechy.*

Man (MAHN) Vietnamese: Sharp mind. Their strong reasoning abilities and keen insight put Virgos among the most intelligent individuals in the zodiac.

Manchu (MAN-chew) Chinese: Pure. Virgos are considered pure in thought and action, as well as in their moral stance.

Manfred (MAN-freed) Old English: One who bestows peace. Virgos are the acknowledged peacemakers of the zodiac. Variations: *Manfrede, Manfrid, Manfried, Mannfred.*

Mendel (MEN-del) Hebrew: Wisdom. Virgo is the sign of high intelligence. Variation: *Mendell.*

Moran (MORE-ahn) Hebrew: Guide. Known as thoughtful and gentle teachers, Virgos often help others gain a stronger foothold and reach higher ground.

Najib (nah-JEEB) Arabic: Smart. Virgos are placed among the most brainy signs of the zodiac. Variations: *Nagib, Najeeb.*

Neto (NEY-toh) Spanish: Earnest one. Virgos are loved for their sincerity and honesty.

Nhean (NEE-ahn) Cambodian: All-seeing. This unusual name recognizes Virgo's ability to observe and understand life on many levels.

Nibaw (NEE-baw) Native American: Upright. This unique name connotes Virgo's strong sense of doing what is right.

Noah (NOH-ah) Hebrew: Calm. This newly revived biblical name is a complementary choice for the quiet and reserved Virgo. Variations: *Noach, Noak, Noel*.

Noble (NOH-bell) Latin: Well-bred. Refinement and discrimination are key qualities of the sign of Virgo.

Oved (OH-vehd) Hebrew: Devotee. Virgos, who often see work and school as holy tasks, are renowned for their single-minded devotion to doing the best job possible under any circumstances.

Ozni (OZ-nee) Hebrew: To listen. Mercury, Virgo's ruling planet, governs all forms of communication. Virgos are gifted at both communicating their ideas and listening to others.

Padget (PAG-ett) English: Young assistant. Virgos excel at supporting roles in which they are highly esteemed for their extraordinary work ethics. Variations: *Padgett, Paget, Pagett*.

Paki (PAH-kee) South African: Witness. Virgos are great observers of the social climate and are adept at perceiving the truth of any situation.

Peleke (peh-LEH-kee) Hawaiian: Wise counselor. Virgos are well respected for their supporting roles as givers of sage advice.

Pepin (PEP-in) German: Persevering. Virgos are renowned for their resolute commitment to hard work. Variations: *Pepi, Peppi, Peppie, Peppy, Pepyn*.

Placido (PLAH-si-doh) Spanish: Peaceful and calm. This beautiful name expresses Virgo's most admirable qualities. Variation: *Placidus*.

Pravin (PRAH-ven) Hindu: Capable. This interesting name describes Virgo's industrious and trustworthy nature.

Prentice (PREN-tiss) English: Apprentice. Virgos are willing students, content to remain behind the scenes and lend support when needed. Variations: *Prent, Prentis, Prentiss*.

Primo (PREE-moh) Italian: Premier quality. Virgos set the standard for fine character and outstanding principles. Variations: *Preemo, Premo*.

Quinn (KWIN) Irish: Discerning. This unique name suggests Virgo's ability to observe others and distinguish the purest path to pursue in any situation.

Quon (KWON) Chinese: Bright. Virgo is the sign of high intelligence and rational thinking. Variation: *Kwan*.

Rad (RAHD) Old English: Counselor. Virgos, with their brilliant minds and supportive stance, make excellent advisors. Variation: *Radd*.

Raghnall (RAHG-nahl) Irish: Powerful judgment. This rare name alludes to Virgo's ability to decisively sum up any situation.

Ragnar (RAHG-nahr) Scandinavian: Warrior of judgment. Once Virgo discerns the correct path, his determination to follow it cannot be shaken.

Rainart (RAYNE-art) German: Great judgment. Virgos are known to be fair and upstanding observers of human behavior. Variations: *Rainer, Rainhardt, Reinart, Reinhard, Reinhardt, Reinhart*.

Ramiro (rah-MEE-roh) Portuguese: Supreme judge. This handsome name is well suited to Virgo's ability to assess many facts and sum them up with keen accuracy. Variation: *Ramirez*.

Raphael (RAH-fee-el) Hebrew: God has healed. *Raphael*, the archangel of healing, is also the angel who protects both Virgos and Geminis. Variations: *Rafael, Rafe, Rafi, Refael, Refi, Rephael.*

Rapier (RAPE-ee-air) French: Sharp. Virgos are renowned for their razor-sharp analytical skills.

Rashid (rah-SHEED) Turkish: Righteous. High-mindedness and inner moral strength are key characteristics of the sign of Virgo. Variations: *Rasheed, Rasheyd.*

Raymond (RAY-mund) Old French: Wise protection. Virgo, with a strong desire to place his gifts of wisdom, rationality, and dependability at the service of others, is noted for his steadfast loyalty. Variations: *Raimundo, Ramón, Raymonde, Ray-Monde, Raymund.* (Famous Virgo: Ray Charles, jazz musician)

Redmond (RED-mund) Irish: Counselor. Virgos are esteemed for their ability to give logical, practical advice to others. Variations: *Radmond, Radmund, Redmund.*

Regin (REH-gin) Scandinavian: Judgment. Virgos' keen insight and calm reasoning make them excellent judges of both characters and circumstances.

Reginald (REH-gin-ahld) English: Counselor. Virgos are known as loyal supporters with insightful offerings. Variations: *Reg, Reggie.*

Renaud (ruh-NOH or RAY-noh) Teutonic: Sagacious strength. Virgo's great personal strength is largely drawn from his superior mental skills and high-minded morality.

Renjiro (ren-JEE-roh) Japanese: Virtuous. Purity, modesty, practicality, and self-denial are key virtues associated with the sign of Virgo.

Renny (REHN-ee) Irish: Compact strength. Reserved Virgo may not cut a flamboyant and commanding public persona like his close cousin, Leo, but his great intelligence and inner fortitude pack a powerful punch behind the scenes.

Reynold (REN-old) English: Powerful adviser. Virgos shine in the supporting roles of any endeavor, ably executing the dreams and directives of their more aggressive contemporaries. Variations: *Renaldo, Renault, Reynaldo, Reynolds, Rinaldo, Ron, Ronald, Ronny.*

Rohin (roh-HEEN) East Indian: Striving. Virgos, remarkably determined to finish any job set before them, can become absorbed in the minutest of tasks for hours at a time.

Saad (sah-AHD) Hebrew: Assistance. Virgos are renowned for working hard and determinedly behind the scenes.

Salah (sah-LAH) Arabic: Virtuous. The qualities of purity and modesty are strongly associated with Virgo. Variations: *Saladdin, Saladin, Saleh, Salih.*

Santo (SAHN-toh) Italian: Pious one. Refined and practical Virgos have a built-in defense mechanism against self-indulgence and often lead pristine and ascetic lives.

Sebastian (seh-BASS-chun) Latin: Reserved. This classic male name, due for a comeback, is a perfect choice for calm and discriminating Virgo. Variations: *Seb, Sebastien.*

Serge (SEHRG) Latin: Servant. Hardworking Virgo shines behind the scenes, where he is renowned for implementing the ideas and directives of others. Variations: *Serg, Sergei, Sergi, Sergio, Sergius.*

Seth (SETH) Hebrew: Appointed. Virgos, particularly those who work in social services, approach work as a holy task—with devotion and fervor.

Sextus (SEKS-tuss) Latin: Sixth. Virgo is the sixth sign of the zodiac. Variation: *Sixtus*.

Shanahan (SHAH-nah-han) Irish: Wise and discerning. This unique but traditional Gaelic surname is an apt choice for practical and rational Virgo.

Sherwin (SHUR-win) English: Smart friend. Keenly intelligent and sensitive to others, Virgos make loyal friends. Variation: *Sherwyn*.

Siegfried (SIG-freed) Old German: Calm. Quiet refinement and practicality are key qualities of Virgo. Variations: *Sig, Sigfried, Ziggy, Zygi*.

Simon (SYE-mun) Hebrew: He listens. Their ruling plant, Mercury, endows Virgos with the gift of communication. Most Virgos appreciate the importance of being a good listener. Variations: *Chimone, Shimon, Sim, Simeon, Simone, Siomon, Ximon*.

Sterne (STURN) Old English: Unwavering and strict. Virgos possess deft analytical skills that allow them to accurately size up problematic situations and offer solutions, but they must avoid a tendency to expect others to meet their own tremendously high standards. Variations: *Stearne, Stearns, Stern*.

Stewart (STOO-art) English: Steward. Virgos prefer working behind the scenes, where they are renowned for their industriousness, determination, and loyalty to superiors. Variations: *Stew, Steward, Stu, Stuart*.

Stillman (STILL-mahn) English: Silent man. Virgos are reserved and shy in public, qualities that may be unfairly mistaken for coldness.

Tab (TABB) Old German: Genius. Virgos are esteemed for their keen analytical skills. Variations: *Tabb, Taber, Tabor*.

Tahir (tah-HEER) Arabic: Pure. Purity is the key quality associated with the sign of Virgo. Variation: *Taheer*.

Talib (tah-LEEB) Arabic: One who searches. Virgos, who are renowned for committing themselves wholeheartedly to finding solutions to complicated problems, welcome the challenge of creating order out of chaos.

Tedmund (TED-mund) Old English: Guardian of the land. Virgo, an Earth sign deeply rooted in the natural environment, is highly committed to protecting the interests of the world around him. Variation: *Tedmond*.

Tin (TIN) Vietnamese: Think. Virgo is the sign of crystal-clear and unemotional analysis.

Tivon (tee-VOHN) Hebrew: Nature lover. Virgo, an Earth sign, is closely attuned to the natural environment around him.

Toshiro (toh-SHEE-roh) Japanese: Skillful. Self-controlled, rational, practical, and hardworking, Virgo is adept at any task he sets for himself.

Tov (TOHV) Hebrew: Good. Virgos are calm, pleasant, and self-contained, eager to please and maintain the status quo. Variations: *Tovi, Toviel, Tuvia, Tuviah*.

Truman (TROO-mun) English: Loyal one. Known for their steadfast morals and undaunted devotion to others, Virgos are extremely loyal friends and workers. Variations: *Trueman, Trumaine, Trumann*.

Tully (TULL-ee) Irish: Calm. Quiet reserve and a discriminating nature are key qualities of Virgo. Variations: *Tull, Tulley, Tullie*.

Tzach (TZAK) Hebrew: Clean. Virgos pride themselves on presenting a refined and pristine public image.

Vadin (VAH-deen) Hindu: Scholar. Virgo is the sign of intelligence and higher learning.

Verrill (VER-rihl) Old French: Faithful. Virgos are renowned for their steadfast loyalty. Variations: *Verill, Verrell, Verroll, Veryl*.

Vimal (vee-MAHL) Hindu: Pure. Purity is the characteristic most strongly associated with the sign of Virgo.

Virgil (VURR-jill) Latin: Flourishing. This name is the masculine equivalent of Virgin, the symbol of the sign of Virgo. Variations: *Vergil, Virge, Virgilio*.

Vivek (vih-VECK) Hindu: Wisdom. Virgo is the sign of great intelligence and higher learning. Variation: *Vivekananda*.

Waite (WAYT) English: Watchman. With their calm, rational, and intelligent approach to problematic situations, Virgos are noted for being keen and informed observers who can rapidly get to the heart of a problem and offer practical solutions. Variation: *Waits*.

Ward (WARD) Old English: One who guards. Virgos, who often seek work in the field of social services, are noted for protecting the interests of others and remaining fiercely devoted to their own high ideals. Variations: *Warde, Warden, Worden*.

Warner (WAR-nuhr) Old German: Determined defender. Virgos have a strong desire to help others and are known for their steadfast loyalty. Variations: *Werner, Wernher*.

Warren (WAR-rihn) Old English: Warder of an animal enclave. Considered protectors of the innocent, this name suits Virgo, a loyal friend to all people and animals. Variations: *Ware, Waring, Warrin, Warriner*.

Washington (WASH-ing-tuhn) English: Town of smart men. Intelligence is a hallmark of the sign of Virgo.

Wendell (WEN-duhl) Old German: Seeker. Noted for their logical thinking and sharp analytical skills, Virgos are adept at wading through mounds of information until they reach the heart and truth of the matter. Variations: *Wendall, Wendel.*

Whitby (WHIT-bee) Old English: Farm with white walls. The color white has long been a symbol of purity, the quality most strongly associated with the sign of Virgo. Also an Earth sign, Virgo is noted for its robust and down-to-earth personalities. Variations: *Whitbey, Whitbie.*

Whitcomb (WHIT-cum) Old English: Valley of white light. This old-fashioned name suggests the purity for which Virgo is so well known.

Whitfield (WHIT-feeld) Old English: White fields. Virgos often are associated with both the purity of the color white and the earthiness of the open fields.

Whitford (WHIT-furd) Old English: White ford. The color white, in any form, is appropriate to use for the sign of Virgo.

Whitley (WHIT-lee) Old English: White meadow. The color white typically summons thoughts of Virgo, and the open meadow further connects this name to the sign's Earth imagery.

Whittaker (WHIT-tah-kur) Old English: White acre. With its reference to the color white, this classic name also connotes Virgo's pure connection to the Earth. Variation: *Whitaker.*

Willard (WILL-ahrd) Old German: Determined. Hardworking Virgo thrives on turning chaos into order, bringing a measured practicality and cautiousness to all his tasks.

Yana (yah-NAH) Hebrew: He answers. Virgo is ruled by the planet Mercury, named for the mythological god of communication, linking the sign of Virgo to all forms of communication. Variations: *Janai, Jannai, Yan, Yannai.*

Yeoman (YO-mahn) English: Servant. Practical and shy, Virgos prefer working behind the scenes, where they are noted for being the ones who can always get the work done.

Zaccheus (zak-EE-uhs) Hebrew: Pure. Symbolized by the archetypical Virgin, Virgos are noted for their modesty, reserve, and discrimination. Variations: *Zakai, Zaki.*

Zeki (ze-KEE) Turkish: Smart. Virgos, born under the sign of keen intelligence and logic, are renowned for their crystal-clear thinking.

Famous Virgos

08-24-1912	Durward Kirby	08-26-1980	Macaulay Culkin
08-24-1958	Steve Guttenberg	08-27-1908	Lyndon B. Johnson
08-24-1960	Cal Ripken, Jr.	08-27-1910	Mother Teresa
08-24-1965	Marlee Matlin	08-27-1916	Martha Raye
08-25-1905	Clara Bow	08-27-1942	Daryl Dragon
08-25-1909	Ruby Keeler	08-27-1943	Tuesday Weld
08-25-1916	Van Johnson	08-27-1947	Barbara Bach
08-25-1917	Mel Ferrer	08-27-1952	Pee-wee Herman
08-25-1918	Leonard Bernstein	08-28-1899	Charles Boyer
08-25-1923	Monty Hall	08-28-1925	Donald O'Connor
08-25-1930	Sean Connery	08-28-1930	Ben Gazzara
08-25-1933	Regis Philbin	08-28-1943	David Soul
08-25-1946	Rollie Fingers	08-28-1957	Daniel Stern
08-25-1949	Gene Simmons	08-28-1969	Jason Priestley
08-25-1954	Elvis Costello	08-29-1898	Preston Sturges
08-25-1961	Billy Ray Cyrus	08-29-1915	Ingrid Bergman
08-25-1970	Claudia Schiffer	08-29-1917	Isabel Sanford
08-26-1904	Christopher Isherwood	08-29-1920	Charlie Parker
08-26-1921	Ben Bradlee	08-29-1923	Richard Attenborough
08-26-1935	Geraldine Ferraro	08-29-1928	Dick O'Neill

08-29-1938	Elliott Gould
08-29-1939	William Friedkin
08-29-1941	Robin Leach
08-29-1958	Michael Jackson
08-30-1898	Shirley Booth
08-30-1908	Fred MacMurray
08-30-1947	Peggy Lipton
08-30-1951	Timothy Bottoms
08-30-1972	Cameron Diaz
08-31-1870	Maria Montessori
08-31-1903	Arthur Godfrey
08-31-1908	William Saroyan
08-31-1924	Buddy Hackett
08-31-1928	James Coburn
08-31-1935	Eldridge Cleaver
08-31-1945	Van Morrison
08-31-1945	Itzhak Perlman
08-31-1949	Richard Gere
08-31-1970	Debbie Gibson
09-01-1875	Edgar Rice Burroughs
09-01-1922	Yvonne DeCarlo
09-01-1933	Conway Twitty
09-01-1935	Seiji Ozawa
09-01-1939	Lily Tomlin
09-01-1946	Barry Gibb
09-01-1957	Gloria Estefan
09-02-1948	Christa McAuliffe
09-02-1951	Mark Harmon
09-02-1952	Jimmy Connors
09-02-1964	Keanu Reeves
09-03-1913	Alan Ladd
09-03-1914	Kitty Carlisle Hart
09-03-1943	Valerie Perrine
09-03-1965	Charlie Sheen
09-04-1908	Richard Wright
09-04-1917	Henry Ford II
09-04-1918	Paul Harvey
09-04-1930	Mitzi Gaynor
09-04-1970	Ione Skye
09-05-1847	Jesse James
09-05-1929	Bob Newhart
09-05-1934	Carol Lawrence
09-05-1940	Raquel Welch
09-05-1950	Cathy Guisewaite
09-05-1969	Dweezil Zappa
09-06-1937	Jo Anne Worley
09-06-1944	Swoosie Kurtz
09-06-1947	Jane Curtin
09-07-1533	Elizabeth I, Queen of England
09-07-1860	Grandma Moses
09-07-1909	Elia Kazan
09-07-1936	Buddy Holly
09-07-1942	Richard Roundtree
09-07-1951	Julie Kavner
09-07-1954	Corbin Bernsen
09-08-1900	Claude Pepper
09-08-1922	Sid Caesar
09-08-1925	Peter Sellers
09-08-1932	Patsy Cline
09-08-1981	Jonathan Taylor Thomas
09-09-1925	Cliff Robertson
09-09-1941	Otis Redding
09-09-1946	Billy Preston
09-09-1951	Michael Keaton
09-09-1952	Angela Cartwright
09-09-1960	Hugh Grant
09-09-1971	Henry Thomas
09-10-1907	Fay Wray
09-10-1929	Arnold Palmer
09-10-1934	Charles Kuralt
09-10-1934	Roger Maris
09-10-1945	Jose Feliciano
09-10-1953	Amy Irving
09-11-1862	O. Henry
09-11-1940	Brian DePalma
09-11-1943	Lola Falana
09-11-1962	Kristy McNichol
09-11-1967	Harry Connick, Jr.
09-12-1888	Maurice Chevalier
09-12-1901	Ben Blue
09-12-1902	Margaret Hamilton
09-12-1913	Jesse Owens
09-12-1940	Linda Gray
09-12-1943	Maria Muldaur
09-12-1944	Barry White
09-12-1954	Peter Scolari
09-12-1957	Rachel Ward
09-13-1903	Claudette Colbert
09-13-1916	Roald Dahl

09-13-1925	Mel Torme	09-18-1940	Frankie Avalon
09-13-1942	Bela Karolyi	09-19-1933	David McCallum
09-13-1944	Jacqueline Bisset	09-19-1940	Paul Williams
09-13-1948	Nell Carter	09-19-1941	"Mama" Cass Elliott
09-13-1980	Ben Savage	09-19-1948	Jeremy Irons
09-14-1849	Ivan Pavlov	09-19-1949	Leslie "Twiggy"
09-14-1914	Clayton Moore		Hornby
09-14-1933	Harve Presnell	09-19-1950	Joan Lunden
09-14-1938	Nicol Williamson	09-20-1878	Upton Sinclair
09-14-1944	Joey Heatherton	09-20-1890	Ferdinand "Jelly Roll"
09-15-1857	William H. Taft		Morton
09-15-1889	Robert Benchley	09-20-1928	Dr. Joyce Brothers
09-15-1890	Agatha Christie	09-20-1929	Anne Meara
09-15-1903	Roy Acuff	09-20-1934	Sophia Loren
09-15-1922	Jackie Cooper	09-20-1957	Gary Cole
09-15-1940	Merlin Olsen	09-21-1866	H. G. Wells
09-15-1946	Tommy Lee Jones	09-21-1931	Larry Hagman
09-15-1946	Oliver Stone	09-21-1934	Leonard Cohen
09-15-1961	Dan Marino	09-21-1935	Henry Gibson
09-16-1914	Allen Funt	09-21-1947	Stephen King
09-16-1924	Lauren Bacall	09-21-1950	Bill Murray
09-16-1925	B.B. King	09-21-1962	Rob Morrow
09-16-1927	Peter Falk	09-21-1968	Ricki Lake
09-16-1949	Ed Begley, Jr.	09-21-1983	Joseph Mazzello
09-16-1955	Robin Yount	09-22-1927	Tommy Lasorda
09-16-1956	David Copperfield	09-22-1954	Shari Belafonte-Harper
09-16-1956	Mickey Rourke	09-22-1956	Debby Boone
09-17-1928	Roddy McDowall	09-22-1960	Joan Jett
09-17-1931	Anne Bancroft	09-22-1961	Scott Baio
09-17-1935	Ken Kesey	09-22-1961	Eric Stoltz
09-17-1948	John Ritter	09-23-1920	Mickey Rooney
09-17-1951	Cassandra "Elvira"	09-23-1930	Ray Charles
	Peterson	09-23-1943	Julio Iglesias
09-18-1905	Eddie "Rochester"	09-23-1945	Paul Petersen
	Anderson	09-23-1947	Mary Kay Place
09-18-1905	Greta Garbo	09-23-1949	Bruce Springsteen
09-18-1920	Jack Warden	09-23-1959	Jason Alexander

LIBRA
(September 24–October 23)

GLYPH: ♎

SYMBOL: The Scales

POLARITY: Masculine

QUALITY: Cardinal

ELEMENT: Air

RULING PLANET: Venus

BIRTHSTONE: Opal

SPECIAL COLORS: Blue and lavender

FLOWERS: Rose, cosmos, and hydrangea

METAL: Copper

ANIMALS: Snakes and lizards

MOST LIKEABLE TRAITS: Charm, diplomacy, and sociability

♎

True to the Scales that symbolize their sign, Libras strive to create harmony, balance, and justice in their environment and in their relationships with others. Libra is the sign of artful partnership and diplomacy, ideals that require large measures of charm, sensitivity, equanimity, consideration, and optimism. And Libras possess all of these qualities in abundance. They are among the most naturally pleasant, happy, sociable, and easygoing children of the zodiac. Parents will find them enchanting companions and deceptively easy to raise.

General Qualities

Libra is a Masculine and Cardinal Air sign that is ruled by the powerful planet Venus. In Roman mythology, Venus was the

308

supreme goddess of love and beauty, and this planet naturally governs the areas of love, romance, beauty, grace, art, pleasure, sociability, and adornment. Libras are romantic and sensitive social animals who prize beautiful people, objects, and surroundings. They are naturally artistic and are especially drawn to music and to fashion.

Venus is the planet that rules marriages, intimate relationships, and partnerships—all areas of deep interest and concern to harmony-conscious Libras, the zodiac's born diplomats. Venus also rules the feminine or "yin" aspects of human endeavors, an important planetary influence in this sign because it adds softness, sensitivity, intuition, and receptivity to the strong Masculine, Cardinal, and Air qualities.

The Masculine influence in this sign gives Libras a positive, animated, and extroverted approach to life, qualities that contribute to Libras' great sociability and popularity with others. Libras are among the most likeable children of the zodiac. The Cardinal quality of this sign adds to Libras' extroversion an edge of assertiveness and an occasional need to control, but also inspires Libras' deep interest in creating change and promoting harmonious partnerships.

The element of Air in Libra is critically significant. Without the influence of Air, Libras might be nothing more than people-pleasing social animals with an occasional penchant for doing good with limited intellectual ability to follow through on their intentions. Indeed, Venus-ruled Libras run the risk of being dilettantes, albeit charming ones. But Air, the element that rules the mind, endows Libras with sharp and facile intellects and the gifts of discernment and clear communication. These qualities are crucial to Libras' success as the diplomats of the zodiac.

Throughout their lives, Libras are driven by three recurring themes that are key to understanding what's going on beneath their charming and happy-go-lucky facades.

First and foremost, Libras fervently want to bring resolution and peace to all the chaos, conflict, and dissension that they see between people in the world around them. Libras believe that by asserting their considerable gifts of charm, diplomacy, tact, and sensitivity, they can help find the perfect, happy middle ground for everyone and every situation. However elusive such a tailor-made peace may be in reality, peace nevertheless remains Libra's ultimate goal. And Libras are willing to subjugate their own needs and personal dreams, often beneath a smiling face, to further their larger goal of making peace for others.

Pursuing peace also requires compromises, which usually are reached by exhaustively sorting through a myriad of confounding options, possibilities, and opportunities. This sorting through possibilities is another recurrent theme in the sign of Libra. Despite the fact that the only constant in life is change, Libras fervently believe that by weighing and measuring everything very carefully, they can find the one true and fair solution to any problem and thus make everyone happy. When this doesn't happen—and it rarely does in the real world—Libras may view themselves as personally responsible for the dissensions and problems they see around them. Their self-confidence and self-worth may seriously erode and, when faced with future problems or conflicts, Libras may become paralyzed by indecision and unable to make other, more critical, life choices for themselves.

Thirdly, no other sign in the zodiac needs the company of people more than Libra. Libras are not concerned with personal freedom and independence like the fiery signs of Leo and Aries, or the self-possessed signs of Virgo and Scorpio. Libra is the sign of meaningful partnership and relationship, and of peace and harmony *through* relationships. All their lives, Libras are driven to connect happily and harmoniously with other people: They derive their self-validation and sense of worth through the approving eyes of others. And they go to extraordinary lengths to get that approval.

Home

Charming, accommodating, and tuned into the feelings of others, Libras are delightful and entertaining children who do anything and everything to keep the peace at home. If they sense any unhappiness or discord around them, Libras perform for, flirt with, and joyfully cajole adults and children alike until everyone is happy again. Libras also go out of their way to avoid arguments and confrontations. They can artfully hide any personal problems they're experiencing, even affecting a happy indifference when asked what *they* need or want.

On the surface these are laudable qualities, especially in children, who are often naturally selfish. But sometimes Libras push down their own feelings—especially anger—and subjugate their personal desires, all in an effort to keep the homefront peaceful. Parents should be alert to this overly accommodating tendency in their Libra children. Unchecked, Libras can be ready targets for emotional manipulation and easily set up to sacrifice their personal happiness for the greater good. Remind them that sometimes the best course of action is to put themselves first, or they'll have no reserves to go on in the long run.

Parents also need to be mindful about Libra children's strong tendency, when faced with making decisions, of laboriously weighing and measuring all the options they believe available to them. Tempered with time, maturity, and experience, this is one of Libra's great qualities and the reason why they are born diplomats and mediators. In young Libras, however, this type of rumination can be unhealthy—not to mention exasperating—and create an opposite and unintended effect: absolute indecision! Carefully limiting Libras' choices when they are very young may go far in helping them learn the value of solid, insightful decision making later.

Parents of Libra children need to be particularly clear and consistent about rules and discipline. The Scales of Balance that symbolize the sign of Libra are also the Scales of Justice. Libra's abiding desire for peace and harmony is wedded with a deep concern for justice and fairness to all. The one sure thing that can turn Libra children's trademark charm to simmering anger is unjust treatment—even if it's only in their own eyes. With their gifted communication skills, Libras are capable of debating long and eloquently about just *how* unfairly they've been treated.

Other than occasional flare-ups about issues of fairness or periodic bouts of indecision, Libras are among the happiest and most endearing of the zodiac's children. They are bright, witty, and easygoing spirits who easily adapt to any family situation and are both eager and easy to please. Libras genuinely love people, are wonderfully accommodating to parents' and siblings' feelings, and are rarely the ones to rock the family boat.

School and Play

Because Libras love being with people, cherish harmony and order, and are disarmingly easygoing and accommodating, they naturally shine in the ordered social environment of a school—though they may first demonstrate more proficiency in social skills than in academic achievements.

Libras are certainly bright enough. The sign's strong Air element, which governs mental acuity, intuition, and communication, guarantees that Libras are naturally intelligent. They are especially good with creative writing, essays, and oral presentations that require a sensitive and balanced view of opposing arguments. They also have an aptitude for the social sciences, to which they bring their strong powers of intuition. Libras always excel in artistic endeavors, particularly painting and music.

Libra is also powerfully influenced by Venus, the planet that rules relationships, romance, and beauty. In school, Libras invariably place more importance on their friendships than on their academics, wanting to spend more time in the schoolyard than in study hall. Without firm study rules at home, and without a demanding teacher who isn't susceptible to their disarming flattery, Libras may try to get by with just the bare essentials as far as homework and studies are concerned. If this tendency to shortchange school is caught early on, however, accommodating Libras will work hard to upgrade their study habits and work performance, if only to please their parents and teachers.

At play, Libras are happiest and most comfortable when surrounded by a group of their peers. Libras thrive on companionship and revel in the give and take of relationships—almost always on the giving end. Libras bring to friendship all their gifts of charm, joyfulness, equanimity, caring, accommodation, and fairness. Their easygoing and deferential ways invariably make them the most popular people in their groups but, again, Libras must be careful not to sacrifice their own needs and uniqueness for the sake of the group's common good.

Libras especially revel in organized group activities, scout troops, hobby clubs, playgroups, and the like. They are thrilled with the prospect of a big party or family reunion, where they can thrive on the many-textured "vibes" of people enjoying themselves and interrelating. But Libras should never be expected to amuse themselves alone, as Leos and Virgos are known to do. Libras almost always shun solitary play and search out at least one partner with whom to interact. Finding ways to keep Libras amused when their friends aren't around can be a daunting task for busy parents. Luxury-loving Libras do enjoy creative projects that involve making beautiful things, particularly clothes, jewelry, paintings, and sculptures. Keeping a rainy-day box of brightly colored beads and stones, ribbons, fabric, clay, paper, and paint is a particularly good idea for Libras. Learning to play a musical instrument is another solitary pursuit that many Libras enjoy because they enjoy a special affinity for music.

The World

Well-integrated Libras wed their genuine need to relate to others with their considerable gifts of charm, equanimity, fairness, and creative intelligence. The resulting mix makes them excellent candidates for work in diplomacy, mediation, psychoanalysis, human services, counseling, and statesmanship. The same qualities that make Libras excellent diplomats and mediators also make them gifted parents and teachers.

More creatively inclined and ego-driven Libras may pursue careers in the performing arts, especially in music, for which they have a particular aptitude. Other Libras, who have a Venus-driven love for beauty, luxury, and adornment, favor careers in fashion and design, but they must be careful that their genuine love of the beautiful doesn't degrade into artifice or self-indulgence. Libras who love beautiful objects and self-adornment must also be cautious about how they spend their money: These individuals show a decided tendency toward becoming spendthrifts.

Libras also must be cautious about another potentially disastrous tendency for which their ruling planet of Venus is responsible: Libras, often in love with the idea of romance and intimacy, can be driven to connect intimately with others at an astonishingly early age. This urge makes them prime candidates for early marriages, long before they are emotionally mature enough for such partnerships. Libras' penchant for accommodating others first and sacrificing their own needs in the process indicates that they value others before they learn to value themselves. In intimacy, this makes for dangerously lopsided partnerships.

Aside from the tendency to marry early and unwisely, Libras shine above all the other children of the zodiac for the extraordinary gifts they bring to friendships, partnerships, and relationships. Warmhearted and charming, guilelessly accommodating, joyful and optimistic, fun-loving and easygoing, just and fair . . . Libras are incomparable companions on the road through life.

Choosing a Name for Your Libra Child

When choosing a name for your Libra girl or boy, first think about the major attributes and symbols associated with the sign. Libra, symbolized by the Scales, is the sign of balance, harmony, and partnership. Libras are highly sociable, charming, artistic, sensitive, and easygoing.

Libra is a Masculine and Air sign ruled by the planet Venus. The Masculine quality gives Libras a bright and outgoing personality. The element of Air endows Libras with quick intellects and great powers of communication, qualities they share with their nearest cousin, Virgo. But the influence of Venus in Libra has a softening effect on the sign's strong Air and Masculine qualities. Venus governs love, pleasure, and beauty, and Libras are generally loving, gentle, creative, and diplomatic.

Libras are naturally attractive, personable, and romantic, and the colors associated with their sign—blue and lavender—suggest harmony and refinement. The opal is the official birthstone of Libra, but the diamond is also associated with the sign. Copper is the sign's precious metal. Roses, cosmos, and hydrangeas are the official flowers of Libra, which also has a strong association with cypress and ash trees. Libra heralds the start of autumn and encompasses the months of September and October. The animals most closely associated with the sign are snakes and lizards.

When you choose a name for your child, also bear in mind some of Libra children's key personal qualities. They are extroverted, charming, and flirtatious. They are at their best in intimate personal relationships and constantly seek balance and harmony in all their affairs. Libras are also great listeners who are genuinely interested in others. Considered the diplomats of the zodiac, they cherish peace, justice, order, and natural beauty. On the downside, Libras have a tendency toward laziness and self-indulgence. Since they are rarely good with money, their penchant for self-adornment and buying beautiful things, when combined with their self-indulgence, may get them into financial difficulties.

For additional inspiration when choosing a name for your Libra child—especially a middle name—you may want to look over the listings in Libra's two companion Air signs, Gemini and Aquarius.

Names for Libra Girls

Abelia (ah-bel-LEE-ah) Hebrew: Breath. This charming and melodic name is a perfect choice for Libra, one of the zodiac's three Air signs. Variation: *Abella*.

Adie (ah-dee-AY) Hebrew: Decoration. Libras are renowned for their love of beautiful things and their penchant for adorning themselves. Variations: *Ada, Adiella*.

Adila (AH-dee-lah) Arabic: Equal. The sign of Libra is symbolized by the Scales of Balance, and Libras esteem peace, harmony, and justice.

Ailaina (ah-LAYN-ah) Irish: Harmony. Libra is the sign of harmony and justice. Variation: *Alaine*.

Aisha (eye-EESH-ah) Arabic: Alive and well. This newly popular name is a wonderful choice for vivacious and easygoing Libra. Variations: *Asha, Ashia, Asia, Ayesha*.

Allegra (ah-LAYG-rah) Italian: Cheerful. Ebullient Libra is a joy to be around.

Aloha (ah-LOH-hah) Hawaiian: Love, affection, mercy, and kindness. This well-known Hawaiian word has a multitude of meanings, all of them qualities associated with the sign of Libra.

Alethea (ah-leh-THEE-ah or ah-LEE-thee-ah) Greek: Truth. Libra, symbolized by the scales of Justice, places high value on truth and honesty.

Amanda (ah-MAN-dah) Latin: Worthy of love. People find it easy to like enchanting, charming Libras. Variations: *Amandine, Amenda, Manda, Mandi, Mandie, Mandita, Mandy*.

Amabel (AHM-ah-bell) Latin: Lovable. This is a delightful choice for charming and gentle Libra.

Amara (ah-MAHR-ah) Greek: Eternal beauty. Venus, Libra's ruling planet, governs love, pleasure, and beauty. Variations: *Amarinda, Mara*.

Amaryllis (ah-mah-RILL-iss) Greek: Sparkle. Libras are attracted to luxury and refinement, and sometimes must learn to resist the temptation to spend more money than they have.

Amina (ah-MEE-nah) Arabic: Peace. This popular and cherished Middle Eastern name was also the name of Muhammad's mother. Libras seek peace and balance in all their affairs. Variations: *Ameena, Aminah.*

Amissa (ah-MEE-suh) Hebrew: Friend of truth. Libras are joyfully loving friends who cherish the truth. Variation: *Amisa.*

Amity (AM-a-tee) Latin: Friendship. Libras, who are charming, outgoing, and peaceful, tend to have many friends.

Amy (AY-mee) French: Beloved. This popular name is suitable for naturally pleasant, charming, generous Libra. Variations: *Aime, Aimee, Amada, Amata, Amatia, Amia.* (Famous Libras: Amy Jo Johnson, actress/"Pink" Power Ranger; Aimee Semple McPherson, evangelist)

Andromeda (ahn-DROM-eh-dah) Greek: Meditator; ponderer. Symbolized by the Scales of Balance, Libras are the thinkers of the zodiac. Variation: *Meda.*

Angela (AHN-jell-ah) Greek: Angel, angelic, or messenger. Gentle-hearted and peace-loving Libras possess great powers of communication. Variations: *Angel, Angele, Angelina, Angelique, Angie.* (Famous Libras: Angie Dickinson, actress; Angela Lansbury, actress)

Arella (ah-RAY-luh) Hebrew: Angel or messenger. As one of the three Air signs of the zodiac, Libras' great powers of communication have earned them their reputation as peace-makers. Variation: *Arela.*

Asela (ah-SEH-lah) Spanish: Slim ash tree. The ash tree is strongly associated with the sign of Libra.

Ashley (ASH-lee) Old English: Meadow of ash trees. This lovely name suits a girl born under Libra, which is associated with the ash tree. Variations: *Ashlea, Ashlee, Ashleigh, Ashlie, Ashly*.

Autumn (AWE-tum) Latin: The season. Libra is the sign that heralds the start of autumn.

Aziza (ah-ZEE-zah) African/Swahili: Exquisite. This beautiful name is an appropriate choice for Libra, who is attracted to luxury and refinement. Variation: *Azize*.

Beatrix (bee-AH-trix; BEE-ah-trix) English: She who brings happiness. Charming, easygoing, and pleasure loving, Libras spread joy wherever they go. Variations: *Bea, Beata, Beatrice, Trixie*.

Belinda (beh-LIN-dah) German: From *betlindis*, meaning snake or serpent. The sign of Libra governs snakes and lizards.

Bella (BELL-ah) Latin: Beautiful. Charming and lighthearted Libras, who are genuinely interested in pleasing others, have a unique and shining beauty. Variations: *Bel, Belinda, Bell, Belle, Isabel*.

Bibiane (bee-bee-AHN) French: Alive. Enchanting Libras possess a natural joie de vivre.

Bliss (blis) Old English: Bliss; joy. This name is an obvious choice for a buoyant, happy Libra girl. Variations: *Blisse, Blyss, Blysse*.

Blythe (BLYTH) Old English: Carefree and joyous. This beautiful name is ideal for a lighthearted, happy-go-lucky Libra. Variation: *Blithe*.

Bonnie (BAH-nee) English: Good. This delightful, traditional English name, with its joyous and lyrical lilt, is an excellent choice for even-tempered Libra. Variations: *Boni, Bonita, Bonne, Bonnee, Bonnibel, Bonnibelle, Bonny*.

Calandra (kah-LAHN-drah) Greek: Beautiful one. Venus, Libra's ruling planet, governs love, pleasure, and beauty. Variation: *Kalandra*.

Callidora (kah-lee-DORR-ah) Greek: Beauty's gift. Libras are often beautiful both inside and out.

Calliope (kah-LYE-eh-pee) Greek: Beautiful voice. Libras are renowned for their eloquent and often precocious speech. Variation: *Kalliope*.

Calumina (KAL-um-EE-nah) Scottish: Dove. Feminine form of *Calum*. The dove is a traditional symbol of peace, one of the qualities closely associated with the sign of Leo. Variation: *Mina*.

Carey (KARE-ee) English: Loving. Libras, whose ruling planet Venus is strongly associated with love, are often caring, generous, and eager to please those they care about. Variations: *Careem, Carreem, Carrie*. (Famous Libra: Carrie Fisher, actress)

Caruta (cah-REE-tah) Latin: Charity. Gentle and sensitive Libra is genuinely concerned about others' feelings.

Charmaine (shar-MANE) Old French: To charm. Libra is known for her charming, effervescent personality.

Cherie (SHARE-ee) French: Beloved. Generous, charming, peaceful Libras never lack for friends. Variations: *Cher, Chere, Cheri, Cheryl, Sherry*.

Concordia (kon-KOR-dee-ah) Latin: Harmony and union. This name belonged to the mythological Roman goddess of concord and harmony, two qualities that are powerfully associated with the sign of Libra.

Cosima (ko-SEE-mah) Italian: Order and harmony. Feminine version of the Greek *Cosmo*. Cosmos are among the flowers associated with Libra, the sign of balance and harmony.

Dakota (dah-KOH-tah) Native American: Friend. This unusual name is a fitting choice for carefree Libra, who is at her best in intimate relationships.

Daria (DAH-ree-ah) Greek: Luxurious. This lovely name is well suited to Libra, who enjoys refined opulence. Variations: *Darian, Darianna, Darielle, Darienne, Darrelle*.

Darlene (dahr-LEEN) Old English: Darling. Libras are naturally charming and enchanting. Variations: *Darla, Darleen, Darline, Daryln*.

Davina (dah-VEE-nah; dah-VIN-ah) Scottish: Beloved. Venus, Libra's ruling planet, governs love and beauty. Feminine form of *David*. Variation: *Davinia*.

Dayo (DAH-yoh) African/Nigerian: Joy arrives. Pleasant, happy-go-lucky Libras often spread joy wherever they go.

Dee Dee (dee dee) Hebrew: Beloved. Libras, naturally pleasant, sweet, and generous qualities make them popular and adored. Variation: *Didi*.

Deka (DEE-kah) Somalian: Pleasing. Peace-loving Libras are eager to satisfy the needs of those around them.

Delicia (de-LEE-shah) Latin: Pleasure giver. Not only do Libras relish self-indulgence and pleasure, but they love spoiling and pampering others. Variations: *Dalisha, Delight, Delisa, Delisha, Delissa, Deliza, Delyssa*.

Delilah (dee-LYE-lah) Hebrew: Craving love. Ruled by Venus, the planet that governs love, beauty, and pleasure, Libras are caring individuals who constantly aspire to bring their loved ones happiness. Variations: *Dalila, Delia.*

Denise (de-NEES) French: Dionysian. Libras are famous for their love of beautiful and decorative things, and for their leanings toward extravagant self-indulgence. Variations: *Denice, Deniece, Denisa, Dennisha.*

Dina (DEE-nah) Hebrew: Judgment. The sign of Libra is symbolized by the scales of Justice. Variation: *Dinah.*

Dionne (dee-ON) Greek: Devotee of Dionysus. Libras have a tendency toward the Dionysian qualities of self-indulgence and laziness. Variations: *Deonne, Diona, Dione, Dionia, Dionna.*

Dodie (DOH-dee) Hebrew: Beloved. Venus, the ruling planet of Libra, governs love, beauty, and pleasure. Libras are adored by others for their charming, congenial, and pleasant ways. Variations: *Dodee, Dodey, Dodi, Dody.*

Dove (DUV) Greek: For the bird, the symbol of peace. Libras, who cherish harmony and balance, are considered the "diplomats" of the zodiac.

Dulcie (DOOL-cee) Latin: Sweet. Libras possess an endearing and pleasant nature. Variations: *Dulce, Dulci, Dulcia, Dulcy.*

Eda (EHD-ah) Old English: Rich. Libras express a love of luxury and refinement, which may flow to excess. Variations: *Edda, Ede.*

Eden (EE-den) Hebrew: Pleasing delights. This lovely name, with its biblical connotations, is ideal for Libra, who has a penchant for pleasure and indulgence. Variations: *Edana, Edenia.*

Edith (EE-dith) Old English: Precious treasure. Libras have a strong attraction to luxury and refinement. Variations: *Editha, Ediva, Edyth, Eyde.*

Edmée (ed-MAY) Scottish: Beloved or valued. This Scottish variant of the French Esmée suits the pleasing, generous, and charming nature of Libra and makes her adored by all. Variations: *Edmé, Esmée.*

Edna (EDD-nah) Hebrew: Delight. Fun-loving, friendly, and happy-go-lucky Libras are always a delight to be around. Variations: *Eddie, Eddy.*

Eliska (ELL-izh-kah) Czechoslovakian: Truthful. Symbolized by the Scales of Justice, Libras always seek the truth.

Elsa (ELL-suh) Swedish or Spanish: Truthful. Libras are highly honorable and ethical by nature. Variations: *Else, Ilsa, Ilse.*

Evangelia (eh-vahn-GEE-lee-ah) Greek: Angel or bearer of good news. This unique name suggests Libra's great powers of communication. Variations: *Evangeline, Lia, Litsa.*

Felicia (feh-LEE-shah) Latin: Happy. *Felicia* is an ideal name for Libra, who exudes high spirits. Variations: *Felice, Felicie, Felicija, Felicity, Felizia, Licia, Phylicia.*

Fiona (fee-OH-nah) Irish: Pretty. Venus, Libra's ruling planet, governs beauty, making Libras beautiful inside and out. Variation: *Fionna.*

Fortunata (for-tyoo-NAH-tah) Italian: Prosperous; lucky. Libras tend to be fortunate in all things.

Freyja (FREE-ya; FRAY-ah) Old Norse: Mythological goddess of love, beauty, and marriage. Libra is born under the planet that governs love, beauty, and relationships. Variations: *Freya, Freyja.*

Frida (FREE-duh) Hungarian: Peaceful ruler. Libra is the sign of harmony and balance. Variation: *Frieda.*

Gay (GAY) Old French: Joyful. Libras possess a special joie de vivre. Variation: *Gaye*.

Gelya (GAYL-yah) Russian: Angel or bringer of good news. As one of the three Air signs of the zodiac, Libra is endowed with excellent communication skills.

Gilana (jee-LAHN-ah) Hebrew: Happiness. A key characteristic of Libra is a perpetually cheerful nature.

Gioconda (jee-oh-KON-dah) Latin: Delight. This name is an appropriate choice for pleasant, ebullient Libra.

Harmony (HAHR-moh-nee) Greek: Agreement. *Harmony* is well suited to Libra, who cherishes equality and peace among everyone.

Heidi (HYD-ee) Old German: Cheerful. Happy-go-lucky Libras are rarely in a down mood, and their jovial high spirits are often contagious.

Hedy (HEDD-ee) Greek: Sweet and pleasant. *Hedy* is an ideal choice for gentle, good-natured Libra.

Hilary (HILL-ah-ree) Latin: Cheerful. One of the most prominent characteristics of Libra is a naturally happy-go-lucky, buoyant disposition. Variations: *Hilaria, Hilarie, Hillary, Hillery*.

Irene (eye-REEN) Greek: Peace. Libras, who avoid discord at any cost, are considered the peacemakers of the zodiac. Variations: *Eirene, Irena, Irina, Rena, Rene, Renie, Rina*.

Jafit (ya-FEET) Hebrew: Lovely. Gentle, pleasant, and good-natured, Libras are a delight to spend time with. Variations: *Jaffa, Jaffice*.

Jamila (jah-MEE-lah) Arabic: Beautiful. *Jamila* is a lovely name for a girl born under Libra, whose ruling planet governs pleasure and beauty. Variations: *Jamala, Jamilah, Jamillah, Jamillia.*

Jane (JAYNE) Hebrew: God's gracious gift. This classic name—or one of its popular variations—is a fitting choice for Libra, who is generous, compassionate, congenial, and kind. Variations: *Jan, Jana, Janeane, Janet, Janette, Janice, Janine, Janis, Jean, Jeanette, Jeanne, Jeannine, Joan.* (Famous Libras: Janeane Garofalo, actress/comedienne; Jayne Meadows, actress; Jean Arthur, actress/comedienne; Jeannie C. Riley, singer; Joan Fontaine, actress)

Jessica (JESS-sah-kah) Hebrew: Wealthy. This popular name is an appropriate choice for Libra, who adores luxury and refinement. Variations: *Gessica, Jess, Jessalyn, Jessi, Jessie, Jesslyn, Jessy.*

Jonina (yo-NEE-nah; jo-NEE-nah) Hebrew: Dove of peace. Harmony-loving Libras are the "diplomats" of the zodiac. Variations: *Jona, Jonati.*

Justina (juss-TEEN-ah) Latin: Just. Libra is symbolized by the Scales of Justice. Variations: *Justine, Justyna, Jusztina.*

Kalila (kah-LEE-lah) Arabic: Sweetheart. *Kalila* is a lovely and apt choice for Libra, who is charming, loving, and gentle. Variations: *Kaleela, Kaylee, Kaylil.*

Kalyca (ka-LEE-kah) Greek: Budding rose. The rose is one of the symbolic flowers of Libra. Variations: *Kali, Kalica, Kalika, Kaly.*

Kelly (KELL-ee) Irish: Defender of justice. This popular name is an apt choice for a girl born under Libra, who is symbolized by the Scales of Justice. Variations: *Keli, Kelia, Kellen, Kelley,*

Kelli, Kellie, Kellina, Kellisa. (Famous Libra: Kellie Martin, actress)

Keshia (KEESH-ah) African-American: Favorite one. Libras are often adored for their peaceful, gentle ways and their charming, effervescent spirit.

Kioko (kee-OH-koh) Japanese: Happy child. Easy to please, Libra children often seem the easiest to raise.

Lana (LAH-nah) Hawaiian: Buoyant. Libra's high spirits often lift others out of bad moods.

Larrissa (lah-RIH-sah) Greek: Happy girl. *Larrissa* is an ideal choice for pleasant Libra, who is typically in high spirits. Variations: *Laressa, Larisa, Larissa, Laryssa.*

Lavita (lah-VEE-tah) Latin: Life. Happy-go-lucky Libras enjoy every second of every day, never taking their life for granted. Variation: *Laveeda.*

Leanna (lee-AHN-ah) Irish: Great affection. Sweet-natured, generous Libras often demonstrate their appreciation of loved ones in thoughtful ways. Variations: *Leana, Leann, Leanne, Leeanne, Leianna.*

Linda (LIN-dah) Spanish: Beautiful. Venus, Libra's ruling planet, governs love, pleasure, and beauty. Variations: *Belinda, Lin, Lindy, Lynda, Melinda.* (Famous Libras: Linda Lavin, actress; Linda McCartney, author, musician, photographer, and wife of Paul McCartney; Linda Hamilton, actress)

Lokelani (loh-kay-LAH-nee) Hawaiian: Rose blossom from the heavens. The beautiful rose is one of the flowers associated with the sign of Libra.

Mabel (MAY-bell) Latin: Amiable. Easygoing, sociable, and pleasant, Libra never lacks for friends. Variations: *Amabel, Mabelle, Mable, Maible, Maybelle*.

Malana (mah-LAH-nah) Hawaiian: Buoyant. Libras always share an abundance of high spirits with those around them.

Manda (MAHN-dah) Spanish: Harmony. Libra is the sign of balance and harmony.

Mandisa (mahn-DEE-sah) South African: Sweet. Libras are pleasant, charming, and good-natured.

Mega (MEH-gah) Spanish: Peaceful. Libra is the sign of harmony and balance.

Megan (MEG-an; MEE-gan; MAY-gan) Irish: Gentle. By nature, Libras are calm and peaceful. Variations: *Maygan, Meagan, Meaghan, Meeghan, Meggan*.

Melinda (me-LINN-dah) Greek: Calm. Libras, who cherish harmony and peace, have a soothing effect on others. Variations: *Linda, Lynda, Malina, Malinda, Melina, Melli, Melynda*. (Famous Libra: Melina Mercouri, politician and actress)

Melisande (mel-a-ZAHND) French: Determination. When it comes to defending a loved one, Libras are strong and forceful. Variations: *Melisandra, Millicent*.

Merrill (MARE-ell) English: Merry hill. With its connotations of joy, *Merrill* is an ideal name for happy-go-lucky Libra. Variation: *Meryl*.

Merry (MARE-ee) Old English: Merry. This delightful name is an obvious choice for exuberant and fun-loving Libra. Variations: *Meredith, Merri, Merrie*.

Mieko (mee-EH-koh) Japanese: Prosperous. Libras are known to appreciate a luxurious and opulent lifestyle filled with the good things in life.

Milada (mi-LAH-dah) Czech: My love. *Milada* is the name of a mythological Slavic goddess of youth, fertility, and love. Libras make adored and cherished friends and intimates. Variation: *Mila*.

Mirabelle (meer-ah-BELL or MIR-ah-bell) Latin: Wondrous. This lovely name is ideal for Libra, who amazes others with her invariable high spirits.

Myrna (MURR-nah) Irish: Loved one. Libra, whose planetary ruler governs love and beauty, never takes her family and friends for granted. Variations: *Merna, Mirna, Moina, Morna*.

Nagida (nah-GEE-dah) Hebrew: Prosperous. Libra brings an abundance of love and good feelings to all those in her circle and, when she is careful, uses her good fortune to express the best of tastes.

Nani (NAN-nee) Greek: Charming. One of the most charismatic signs of the zodiac, Libra is sociable, ebullient, good-natured, and fun-loving.

Naomi (nay-OH-mee) Hebrew: My joy, my delight. Libras are among the most happy and charming children of the zodiac. Variation: *Noemi*.

Nissa (NIS-suh) Scandinavian: Friendly elf. This popular Scandinavian name is perfect for charming, helpful, and vivacious Libra.

Nunzia (NUN-zee-ah) Italian: Messenger. As one of the three Air signs of the zodiac, Libra possesses wonderful communication skills. Variation: *Annunzia*.

Ogin (oh-GEEN) Native American: Wild rose that grows in the fields. The rose is one of the flowers associated with Libra.

Olina (oh-LEE-nah) Hawaiian: Filled with happiness. Libras are among the most ebullient, pleasant, and jubilant children of the zodiac.

Olive (AH-liv) Latin: For the olive tree. The olive branch is a traditional symbol of peace, a quality strongly associated with the sign of Libra.

Opal (OH-pul) Sanskrit: For the gem. The opal is the birthstone of Libra. Variation: *Opaline.*

Pacifica (pah-SIH-fee-kah) Latin: To make peace. Libras are considered the "diplomats" of the zodiac.

Paloma (pah-LOH-mah) Spanish: Dove of peace. This lovely name suggests Libra's gently striving toward harmony and balance.

Rabi (rah-BEE) Arabic: Sweet wind. This unique name is well suited to charming Libra, one of the three Air signs of the zodiac.

Radhiya (rah-THEE-yah) African/Swahili: Agreeable. Peace-loving Libras do anything in their power to avoid discord and maintain harmony.

Raisa (rah-EE-sah) Russian: Rose. Roses, cosmos, and hydrangeas are the flowers of the sign of Libra. Variations: *Raisie, Raissa, Raiza, Raizel, Rasia, Rayzil.*

Rena (RAY-nah or REE-nah) Greek: Peace. Libra is the sign of harmony and balance.

Renny (REN-nee) Irish: Little prosperous one. This name reflects the luxury-loving Libra, who brings a wealth of love and peace to all those around her.

Rez (REHZ) Hungarian: Copper. Copper is the precious metal associated with the sign of Libra.

Rhoda (ROH-dah) Greek: Rose. The rose, often considered the most beautiful of all flowers, is one of the flowers associated with Libra, the sign of beauty and harmony. Variations: *Rho, Rhodia, Rhody.*

Rose (ROHZE) Latin: Rose. The official flowers of Libra are cosmos, hydrangeas, and roses. Variations: *Rosa, Rosabel, Rosabella, Rosabelle, Rosaleen, Rosalia, Rosaline, Rosalyn, Rosella, Rosette, Rosi, Rosie, Rosina, Rosy.*

Roselani (roh-suh-LAH-nee) Hawaiian: Rose from the heavens. This name is a beautiful choice for Libra, an Air sign whose official flowers are cosmos, hydrangeas, and roses.

Rozene (roh-ZAY-nuh) Native American: Rose blossom. The sign of Libra is closely associated with love, due to the influence of Venus, Libra's ruling planet. The rose, one of Libra's official flowers, is often given as a symbol of love.

Ruth (ROOTH) Hebrew: Companion or friend. Generous, gentle Libra makes a wonderful friend.

Salome (SAL-oh-may) Hebrew: Peace. Libra is the sign of harmony and balance. Variations: *Salima, Saloma, Selima, Selma.*

Scout (SKOUT) American: A person sent out to explore an area and obtain information. Libra, symbolized by the Scales of Justice, is concerned with maintaining peace, order, and harmony. This ideal Libra name was first popularized by the appearance of the feisty, precocious, and justice-seeking child heroine,

Scout Finch, in Harper Lee's Pulitzer Prize-winning novel, *To Kill a Mockingbird*.

Selda (SEL-dah) Old English: Friend; Hebrew: Joy. Both of *Selda*'s meanings suit Libra, whose naturally pleasant and charming personality gains her many friends. Variation: *Zelda*.

Shaina (SHAY-nah) Yiddish: Beautiful. Libra's ruling planet of Venus governs love, beauty, and pleasure. Variations: *Shana, Shayna*.

Shireen (shir-EEN) Persian: Charming. Libras are naturally pleasant, sociable, and gracious.

Shoshannah (show-SHAHN-nah) Hebrew: Rose. The beautiful rose is one of the official flowers of Libra. Variations: *Shanna, Shosha, Sue, Susan, Susie, Suzannah, Suzanne*.

Shumana (SHOO-mah-nah) Native American: Rattlesnake girl, a name used by the Hopis of the rattlesnake cult. The sign of Libra governs all snakes and lizards. Variations: *Chuma, Chumana, Shuma*.

Sita (SEE-tah) Spanish: Rose. The flowers associated with the sign of Libra are cosmos, hydrangeas, and roses.

Sky (skye) American: The upper atmosphere. *Sky* is a classic American name for Libra, one of three Air signs. Variation: *Skye*.

Solana (soh-LAH-nah) Latin: Wind from the east. Libra, an Air sign, brings a constant and refreshing breath of joyful vitality.

Suletu (soo-LEH-too) Native American: Soaring without warning. This unusual name reflects Libra's element, Air.

Susan (SOOZ-in) Hebrew: Rose or lily. This ever-popular name—or one of its lovely variations—is an ideal choice for

Libra, who is associated with the rose. Variations: *Sue, Suka, Suke, Suki, Susannah, Susanne, Suse, Suzanna, Suzanne, Suzette, Zuska, Zuza.* (Famous Libras: Suzanne Somers, actress; Susan Anton, actress; Susan Sarandon, actress)

Tatum (TAY-tuhm) Scandinavian: Ebullient. This name is an appropriate choice for Libras, who are lively, fun-loving, and bubbly. *Tatum* is also an appropriate name for a Libra boy. Variation: *Tate*.

Themis (THEE-miss or TEE-miss) Greek: In Greek mythology, *Themis* was the goddess of justice and prophecy, who is depicted as holding a scale for weighing opposite claims. From the Greek word, *thema*, meaning law or justice. The sign of Libra is symbolized by the Scales of Justice.

Tirza (TEER-zah) Hebrew: Cypress tree; desirable. The cypress is another tree associated with the sign of Libra.

Tomiko (TOH-mee-koh) Japanese: Child of riches. Luxurious Libras love to spend money on beautiful and tasteful objects.

Tonya (TOHN-yah) Russian: Priceless. Libras often have no limits when it comes to buying the best of something they admire. Variation: *Tanya*. (Famous Libra: Tanya Tucker, country-and-western singer)

Estrella (ess-TRAY-lah) Spanish: Little star. *Trella* suggests Libra's shining, sparkling personality.

Tula (TOO-lah) Hindu: Libra. In Hindi astrology, this name is traditionally given to a child born under the sign of Libra.

Unity (YOO-nih-tee) Latin: Harmony; united. Libra is the sign of harmony in all things.

Vardis (vahr-DEES or VAR-diss) Hebrew: Rose. The official flowers of Libra are cosmos, hydrangeas, and roses.

Venus (VEE-nuss) Latin: Beloved. Named for the Roman goddess of love and beauty, the planet Venus rules the sign of Libra.

Vevina (veh-VEE-nah) Irish: Sweet lady. This name is a perfect choice for always pleasant Libra.

Wilhelmina (will-hell-MEEN-ah) Old German: Defender of justice. This name is appropriate to Libra, who is symbolized by the Scales of Justice. Variations: *Billie, Mina, Minna, Minnie, Valma, Velma, Wiletta, Wilette, Willi, Willie, Willamina*.

Wynne (WINN) Welsh: Fair and blessed. High-minded Libra is honorable and just in every matter. Variation: *Wynn*.

Yasu (YAH-soo) Japanese: Bestower of peace and calm. Constantly in search of harmony and balance, Libras are considered the "diplomats" of the zodiac.

Yoninah (yoh-NEE-nah) Hebrew: Little dove. The dove is a traditional symbol of peace, a quality strongly associated with the sign of Libra. Variations: *Yona, Yonit, Yonita*.

Zanna (ZAN-nah) Hebrew: Rose. The rose is one of three flowers associated with the sign of Libra. *Zanna* has now achieved independent status as a name, but it was originally a variant of the beautiful *Shoshannah*.

Zina (ZEE-nah) African/Swahili: Beautiful. Gentle and pleasant Libra is naturally beautiful both inside and out.

Zita (ZEE-tah) Spanish: Little rose. The beautiful rose is one of Libra's official flowers.

Zuleika (zoo-LAY-kah) Arabic: Beautiful. Venus, Libra's ruling planet, is associated with love and beauty. Variation: *Zula*.

Names for Libra Boys

Abel (AY-bel) Hebrew: Breath or evanescent. This classic and ever-popular name with biblical origins is a fitting choice for Libra, one of three Air signs.

Absalom (AB-sa-lom) Hebrew: Peace bringer. This traditional biblical name is suitable for Libra, symbolized by the Scales of Justice. Libras cherish peace, order, and harmony.

Ace (AYCE) Latin: Unity. A quintessential American name with a surprisingly profound meaning, *Ace* is a wonderful choice for ebullient Libra, who prizes peace and order.

Adiv (ah-DEEV) Hebrew: Pleasant. Libras are naturally easy-going, friendly, and charming.

Adlai (ADD-lay) Hebrew: Justice of the Lord. Libra is symbolized by the Scales of Justice. Variation: *Adley.*

Ahmed (ah-MED) Arabic: Most highly adored. Individuals born under the sign of Libra often inspire adoration and praise from all who know them. Another name for *Muhammad.* Variation: *Ahmad.*

Aikane (ah-ee-KA-nee) Hawaiian: Friend or friendly. Sociable and pleasant, Libras always have many friends and companions.

Ailill (AYE-lil) Irish: Sprite. While he cherishes peace and harmony, Libra's fun-loving side enjoys the humor provided by innocent mischief.

Aksel (AHK-sel) Hebrew: Father of peace. One of Libra's key characteristics is a strong desire to maintain harmony. Variations: *Axel, Axl.*

Alan (A-lin) Celtic: Harmony. Symbolized by the Scales, Libra is the sign of harmony and balance. Variations: *Alain, Allan, Allen, Allin*.

Albin (AHL-bin) Russian: Everyone's friends. Libras are known to create peace and harmony among all those they encounter. Variations: *Alban, Alben*.

Alexander (al-ig-ZAN-der) Greek: Protector of humanity. Symbolized by the Scales of Justice, Libra is quick to defend those who have been wronged. Variations: *Alastair, Alec, Alejandro, Aleksander, Alessandro, Alex, Alexandre, Sandor*.

Alf (ALF) Old Norse: Elfin. Known for their magical sense of humor, Libras bring joyful fun to any occasion.

Alvin (AL-vin) Old English: Friend of the elves. While Libras are known as friends to everyone, their sense of the magic and charm they see in everyone they meet can bring them special friends and inspired insight. Variations: *Alwyn, Aylwin*. (Famous Libra: Alvin Toffler, author and influential social thinker)

An (AHN) Chinese: Peace. More than anything, Libras cherish peace, balance, and harmony.

Anael (ah-NAY-ell) Hebrew: Name of an archangel. This angel is attributed to being the protector of Libras.

Angus (AYN-gus) Scottish: Choice. Libras are recognized for their ability to see many options and ponder them with care. Variation: *Gus*.

Anthony (AN-thuh-nee or AN-ton-ee) Latin: Priceless. Lovers of luxury and fine things, Libras rarely are concerned with how much something they want costs. Variations: *Anton, Antonio, Tonio, Tony*. (Famous Libra: Anthony Newley, singer/actor)

Arden (AHRD-in) Celtic: Eager. Full of life and energy, Libras throw themselves into any commitment without reserve.

Asher (ASH-urr) Hebrew: Lucky and happy. This unique name connotes the wondrously open and joyful aspect of Libras. Variations: *Acher, Ashur.*

Ashley (ASH-lee) Old English: One from the ash-tree meadow. Ash and cypress trees are closely associated with the sign of Libra. *Ashley* is also a very popular name for a girl. Variations: *Ash, Ashleigh, Ashlen.*

Ashlin (ASH-linn) Old English: From the pool surrounded by ash trees. Libra is affiliated with the ash tree. Variation: *Ashlen.*

Ashton (ASH-tun) Old English: Grove of ash trees. Libra is associated with beauty and grace, as is the beautiful ash tree.

Baird (BAYRD) Scottish: Poet and singer of epic poems. Libras are endowed with great gifts of communication and make eloquent speakers. Variation: *Bard.*

Bellamy (BELL-lah-mee) Old French: Beautiful friend. Libras are revered for both their beauty and their friendship.

Benedict (BEN-eh-dikt) Latin: Blessed. With a keen sense of the sacred in life, Libra realizes the importance of appreciating and enjoying one's blessings. Variations: *Ben, Bendix, Benedick, Bennet, Benny.*

Benjiro (ben-JEE-roh) Japanese: Be in peace. Libras cherish peace, harmony, and serenity.

Bennett (BEN-et) Scottish: Blessed. Libras have a fine sense of life's gifts and glories.

Bertin (BAIR-ten) Spanish: Distinguished friend. This name of a popular Spanish saint reflects Libra's outstanding ability to be loyal and lifelong friends and partners.

Beval (BAY-vahl) Gypsy: Like the wind. Libra is one of three Air signs.

Boye (BOY-yeh) Dutch: Lad or knave. This name is an appropriate choice for ever-youthful, fun-loving, and innocently mischevious Libra.

Brady (BRAY-dee) Irish: Spirited. This name is well-suited to Libras, who show effervescent energy and have a strong sense of the divine. Variation: *Bradie*.

Broder (BROH-der) Old Norse: Brother. Libras, who thrive in intimate, one-on-one relationships, make devoted and affectionate friends.

Bud (BUD) English: Buddy, brother, or friend. One of Libra's prominent qualities is longstanding and trustworthy friendship. Variation: *Buddy*. (Famous Libra: Bud Abbott, comedian)

Calum (KAL-um) Scottish: Dove, symbol of peace. One of Libra's key characteristics is a love of peace and harmony. Variation: *Callum*.

Carthage (KAR-thaj) Irish: Loving. Libra's ruling planet is Venus, which governs love, pleasure, and beauty. Variations: *Cartagh, Carthach, Carthy*.

Casimir (KAH-zah-meer) Old Slavic: He commands peace. Libras are masters at establishing communication and creating peace in every situation. Variations: *Cachi, Cashi, Casimiro, Castimer, Kazimir, Kazio*.

Chance (CHANSS) English: Good fortune. This name is ideal for naturally lucky Libras, who have good fortune in all things.

Clement (KLEM-int) Latin: Kind or accommodating. Libras, who are quick to put others at ease, make excellent hosts. Variations: *Clem, Clemens, Clemmie, Clemmons*.

Cody (KO-dee) Irish: Cushion. A traditional Gaelic name that is growing in popularity, *Cody* is a wonderful choice for harmony-loving Libra. Variations: *Codey, Codie, Coty, Kodey, Kodie, Kody*.

Colman (KOL-mahn) Irish: Little dove. *Coleman* is the name of several Irish saints, and the dove is a traditional symbol of peace, one of the qualities often associated with the sign of Libra. Variations: *Cole, Coleman*.

Conan (KOH-nahn) Irish: Counsel or wisdom. Showing strong diplomacy skills, Libras have an innate ability to resolve any struggle. Variation: *Conant*.

Conn (KONN) Irish: Wisdom or sense. Libra's contented and balanced ways actually reveal an underlying wisdom about the true meaning of life.

Corliss (KORR-lis) English: Generous. Gentle Libras are quick to please others. Variation: *Corley*.

Courtney (KORT-nee) English: One who lives in the court. Libras, born diplomats who love to charm and flatter, have a strong penchant for luxurious surroundings. Variations: *Cortney, Cortenay, Courteney, Courtnay*.

Culver (KULL-vur) English: Dove. The dove is the universal symbol of peace, one of the key qualities associated with harmony-loving Libra. Variations: *Colver, Culley, Cully*.

Darryl (DARE-ell; DARR-ell) Old French: Dear or beloved. Libras are known to inspire devotion in their family members and many friends. Variations: *Darel, Darrel, Darrell, Daryl*.

Daudi (dah-OO-dee) African/Swahili: Beloved. Libras naturally evoke love from all who know them.

David (DAY-vid) Hebrew: Beloved. This classic name reflects one of Libra's most remarkable characteristics: the ability to inspire love and devotion. Variations: *Daoud, Dawud*. (Famous Libra: David Lee Roth, rock singer)

Dennis (DENN-is) English: Variation of *Dionysus*, for the god of wine. Libras are renowned for their self-indulgence and love of beautiful, decorative things. Variations: *Den, Denis, Denney, Denny, Deon, Dion, Dwight*. (Famous Libra: Dwight Eisenhower, former U.S. president)

Dewey (DOO-ee) Old Welsh: Beloved. This old-fashioned name refers to one of Libra's strongest traits: evoking love in all they meet. Welsh form of *David*.

Dexter (DEKS-tur) Latin: Right-handed. Libra is symbolized by the Scales of Justice. Variation: *Dex*.

Dillon (DILL-in) Irish: Faithful. Libras, who highly value relationships, are loyal friends for life. Variation: *Dylan*.

Donato (doh-NAH-toh) Latin: A gift. Full of charm, optimism, beauty, and love, Libras are often considered divine blessings. Variations: *Donatello, Donati, Donatus, Dontat*.

Dorek (DOH-rek) Polish: Gift. Bestowed with the gifts of charm, diplomacy, sensitivity, optimism, good looks, and excellent communication skills, Libras are among the luckiest children of the zodiac. Polish form of *Theodore*.

Drury (DREW-ree) French: Cherished. Due to their generous, serene, and loving spirits, Libras are dearly treasured by family and friends.

Duran (der-RAN) Latin: Enduring, long lasting. Generous, loving, and caring, Libras make wonderful lifelong companions. Variations: *Durand, Durant*.

Edwin (ED-win) Old English: Brimming with friends. Naturally pleasant, generous, and charming, Libras are always quite popular. Variation: *Edwyn*.

Elan (EH-lahn) Native American: Friendly. Libras, who have a natural interest in people and relationships, are outgoing and sociable.

Emil (AY-meel; ay-MEEL) Latin: Seeks to please. Driven by their need to maintain harmony, Libras often go out of their way to please others. Variations: *Amal, Emile, Emilek, Emilio, Emils, Milko, Milo*.

Esmé (EZ-may) French: Beloved. Libras' great love for their family and friends is often returned tenfold.

Esmond (EZ-mund) Old English: Graceful protection. *Esmond* is an apt name for Libra, who is quick to come to the aid of someone who has been treated unfairly.

Evan (EV-an) Irish: Little swift one. This traditional name suggests the grace and speed of the wind. Libra, one of the three Air signs of the zodiac, is quick to smooth things over when any disharmony occurs. Variations: *Evin, Ewan*.

Evander (ee-VAN-der) Greek: Good man. Libras, symbolized by the Scales of Justice, are honorable, just, and ethical in all things.

Ewald (EE-wahld) English: Powerful in the law. Justice, order, and peace are key qualities of the sign of Libra. Variation: *Evald*.

Ewing (YOU-ing) English: Friend of the law. The sign of Libra is symbolized by the Scales of Justice.

Ezra (EZ-rah) Hebrew: Help. People-pleasing Libras are eager to offer assistance to others. Variations: *Esdras, Esra.*

Fagan (FAY-gan) Irish: Eager child. *Fagan* is an ideal name for ebullient and enthusiastic Libra. Variation: *Fagin.*

Fane (FAYNE) English: Happy. Libras are always pleasant, easygoing, and cheerful.

Farquhar (FAHR-kwar) Scottish: Dear man. This unusual name is a great choice for generous, good-hearted Libra. Variation: *Fearchar.*

Felix (FEE-lix) Latin: Happy. One of the most prominent characteristics of Libra is a naturally cheerful and bright disposition.

Fiorello (fee-oh-RELL-oh) Italian: Little flower. Happy-go-lucky and attractive Libras, lovers of all beautiful things, are a delight to be around.

Fortune (FOR-tuyne) French: Lucky. Optimistic, easygoing Libras tend to be fortunate in most things. Variations: *Fortunato, Fortunatus, Fortunio.*

Frederick (FRED-rik) Old German: One who leads peacefully. Libras are the diplomats and peacekeepers of the zodiac. Variations: *Fred, Freddie, Freddy, Rick, Rickie, Ricky.*

Frodi (FROH-dee) Old Norse: The name of a mythical Danish king who proclaimed universal peace—the Peace of Frodi—for thirty years. Libras have a strong desire for harmony and peace in all things.

Gale (GAYL) Old English: Gay and lively. This name is well suited to happy-go-lucky, ebullient Libra. *Gale*, with its connotations of wind, is ideal for an Air sign. Variations: *Gael, Gail, Gayle*.

Gaylord (GAYE-lord) Old German: Joyous and hardy. Ebullient and happy-go-lucky by nature, Libras spread laughter wherever they go. Variations: *Gallard, Gayelord*.

Gillespie (gill-ESS-pee) Gaelic: Servant of the bishop. Libras make great adjuncts to anyone in a position of power. Born diplomats, they are adept at restoring peace and harmony in contentious situations.

Gyasi (JAH-see) African/Ghanian: Wonderful child. With their strong desire to please others, Libras are remarkably well behaved children who are eager to win approval from family and friends.

Habib (hah-BEEB) Arabic: Beloved. This popular Arabic name is a fine choice for Libra, whose family and friends cherish his generous ways and enchanting laughter.

Hasin (hah-SEEN) Hindu: Laughing. *Hasin* is an attractive name for Libra, whose bubbly charm and zest for life are contagious.

Hayden (HAY-dinn) Old English: The rosy meadow. The rose is one of the flowers associated with the sign of Libra. This newly popular, but quite old and traditional English place name, is an apt choice for luxury-loving Libra. Variations: *Haydn, Haydon*.

Heman (HAY-man) Hebrew: Faithful. Libras, who are among the most social children of the zodiac, make wonderful, lifelong friends.

Hilary (HILL-ah-ree) Latin: Cheerful. Happy-go-lucky Libra spreads his high spirits. *Hilary* also makes a good name for a girl. Variations: *Hilery, Hillary, Hillery*.

Holleb (HOLL-ib) Polish: Dovelike. The dove is the universal symbol of peace, a quality strongly associated with Libra. Variations: *Hollub, Holub*.

Hopkin (HOP-kin) English: Bright renown. Libra's naturally happy-go-lucky, ebullient nature is famous. Variation of *Robert*. Variation: *Hopkins*.

Isaac (EYE-zak) Hebrew: Laughter. Libras are quick to brighten the spirits of others with their genuine effervescence and lively exuberance. Variations: *Isaak, Yitzhak*.

Jasper (JAS-per) English: Treasure master. Extravagant Libra loves luxurious things.

Jesse (JESS-ee) Hebrew: Gift. Peaceful, generous, and kindhearted Libras are thought of by family and friends as a divine gift. Variations: *Jess, Jessie*. (Famous Libras: Jesse Jackson, political activist; Jesse Helms, politician)

Justin (JUS-tin) Latin: Just. Libra is symbolized by the Scales of Justice. Variations: *Jusa, Just, Justen, Justis, Justyn*.

Kacey (KAY-see) English: He announces peace. The most prominent characteristic of Libra is a desire for harmony and balance.

Kadin (kah-DEEN) Arabic: Companion and confidant. Charming and animated, sensitive and diplomatic, Libras make wonderful friends. Variation: *Kadeen*.

Kalil (kah-LEEL) Arabic: Faithful friend. Libras, who greatly cherish their personal relationships, are loyal and trustworthy companions. Variations: *Kahlil, Kalee, Khaleel, Khalil*.

Kane (KAYNE) Celtic: Beautiful. Libra's ruling planet of Venus governs love and beauty. Variations: *Kaine, Kayne*.

Kantu (kahn-TOO) Hindu: Happy. For the Hindu god of love. This name is a fine choice for cheerful, vivacious Libra, whose ruling planet, Venus, governs love and beauty. Variations: *Kama, Kami.*

Karif (kah-REEF) Arabic: Born in the fall. Libra is the sign that heralds the start of autumn. Variation: *Kareef.*

Keefe (KEEF) Irish: Lovable. Libras, who highly value their friends and family, are greatly loved in return. Variation: *Keeffe.*

Keith (KEETH) Scottish: The wind. Libra is one of three Air signs.

Keller (KEL-ler) Irish: Companion dear. Bubbly, good-hearted Libras make cherished friends.

Kenneth (KENN-ith) Irish: Appealing. This classic and popular name suggests Libra's natural charm, good-natured spirit, and physical attractiveness. Variations: *Ken, Kennett, Kenney, Kennith, Kenny, Kenya, Kesha.*

Kevin (KEH-vin) Irish: Little gentle one. A popular name, *Kevin* is a classic choice for harmony-loving Libra. Variation: *Kevan.*

Knoton (K'NO-ton) Native American: The wind. Libra is one of the three Air signs of the zodiac. Variation: *Nodin.*

Kuper (COO-pur) Yiddish: Copper. Copper is the precious metal associated with the sign of Libra.

Kwende (KWEHN-deh) African/Ngoni: Let's go. Vivacious and outgoing Libra is always on the move.

Kyle (KEY-el) Irish: Good-looking. Libra's ruling planet of Venus governs love and beauty, often making Libras physically attractive and appealing. Variation: *Kiel.*

Ladd (LAD) Middle English: An attendant. People-pleasing Libras go to any lengths to make their loved ones happy. Variations: *Lad, Laddey, Laddie, Laddy*.

Lal (LAHL) Hindu: Loved one. Libras, who have a special interest in human relationships, dearly cherish their friends and family.

Lamont (luh-MONT) Scottish: Man of law. Libras, symbolized by the Scales of Justice, are often drawn to careers in law. Variations: *Lammond, Lamond, Lamonte, Monty*.

Langundo (lahn-GOON-do) Native American: Peaceful. Gentle Libras cherish balance and harmony.

Leif (LEEF, LAYF, or LIFE) Old Norse: Beloved. Charming, pleasant, good-natured Libras are generally popular and well-liked. Variation: *Lief*.

Levi (LEE-vye) Hebrew: Joined in harmony. Libra is the sign of harmony, peace, and balance. Variation: *Levy*.

Linfred (LIN-freed) Old German: Gentle peace. The most prominent characteristic of Libra is an intense desire to maintain harmony and balance.

Lucky (luk-ee) American: Having good fortune and good luck. Pleasant, outgoing Libras tend to be lucky in every endeavor.

Makani (mah-KAH-nee) Hawaiian: The wind. Libra is one of the three Air signs of the zodiac.

Malcolm (MAL-cum) English: Servant. Libras have an ardent desire to satisfy others' needs. Variations: *Malcom, Malkolm*.

Malu (mah-LOO) Polynesian: Breeze. Lighthearted Libras are one of the Air signs of the zodiac.

Mandel (MAN-dull) German: Almond. Almond, cypress, and ash trees are strongly associated with the sign of Libra. Variation: *Mandell*.

Mannix (MAN-nix) Irish: Little monk. This classic Gaelic name is a great choice for easygoing Libra, who cherishes peace, harmony, truth, and justice. Variation: *Mainchin*.

Meldan (MELL-dan) Irish: Little pleasant one. Gentle and good-natured Libras have a soothing effect on others. Variations: *Meallan, Mellan*.

Milo (MY-loh) Old German: Mild and peaceful. Libras, the "diplomats" of the zodiac, seek harmony in all things.

Mohan (MO-hahn) Hindu: Delightful. *Mohan*, another name for the most celebrated Hindu God, Krishna, suggests the cheerful nature of Libra.

Mojag (MOH-yahg) Native American: Never quiet. Sociable, outgoing Libras are known for their lively conversation and infectious laughter.

Naldo (NAHL-doh) Spanish: Good advice. Genuinely interested in helping others and seeing justice served, Libras make wonderful counselors or lawyers.

Nathan (NAY-thin) Hebrew: Gift. Libras, who possess considerable charm, sensitivity, optimism, intellect, beauty, and inner peace, are among the most fortunate of the zodiac's children. Variations: *Nat, Natan, Nate, Nathon, Natt*.

Nesbit (NES-bit) Old English: Curving like a rose. The flowers associated with the sign of Libra are hydrangeas, cosmos, and roses. Variations: *Naisbit, Nesbitt, Nisbet, Nisbett*.

Nitis (NEE-tes) Native American: Good friend. Sensitive and generous Libras often maintain cherished, lifelong friendships. Variation: *Netis*.

Noam (NOH-ahm) Hebrew: Pleasantness. This masculine version of *Naomi* is an appropriate choice for amiable, good-natured Libra.

Nodin (NOH-dinn) Native American: Windy day or spirit that blows the trees. Libra is one of the three Air signs of the zodiac. Variation: *Noton*.

Nuncio (NOON-zee-oh) Italian: Messenger. This name connotes the wonderful communication skills with which Libras are endowed. Variation: *Nunzio*.

Paxton (PAX-tun) Old English: Village of peace. The most prominent characteristic of Libra is a desire to maintain harmony and balance. Variations: *Pax, Paxon*.

Paz (pahz) Spanish: Peace. Peace and justice are qualities strongly associated with the sign of Libra. This name is also applicable for a girl.

Placido (PLAH-si-doh) Spanish: Placid or calm. Libra is the sign of balance and harmony. Variations: *Placidus, Placyd, Placydo*.

Prosper (PRAHS-per) Latin: Fortunate or lucky. Charming and people-pleasing Libras are so welcoming that prosperity and good fortune often come their way. Variation: *Prospero*.

Rabi (ra-BEE) Arabic: Soothing breezes. Harmony-loving Libra is one of the three Air signs of the zodiac. Variations: *Rabbi, Rabee*.

Rafi (RAHF-ee) Hindu: Friend. Charming, generous Libras are among the most sociable children of the zodiac. Variations: *Raafiki, Rafee, Rafiq*.

Ram (RAHM) Hindu: One who pleases others. In order to satisfy their desire to maintain harmony, Libras do all they can to make others happy. Variations: *Rama, Ramananda*.

Regin (REE-ghin) Old Norse: Advice or judgement. Genuinely interested in helping others, Libras make wonderful counselors, often offering excellent guidance to their friends and family.

Rez (REHZ) Hungarian: Copper. Copper is the metal associated with the sign of Libra.

Rhodes (ROADZ) Greek: Field of roses. The rose is one of the flowers associated with the sign of Libra. Variations: *Rhoades, Rhodas, Rodas*.

Rodas (ROH-dahs) Spanish: Place of roses. Libras, who prize beauty, are closely associated with the exquisite rose.

Roni (RO-nee; RAH-nee) Hebrew: My joy. Possessing a mixture of charm, sensitivity, generosity, and true inner beauty, Libras bring pleasure and happiness into the lives of everyone they come in contact with. Variations: *Ron, Ronel, Ronli*.

Roosevelt (ROO-zeh-velt) Dutch: Field of roses. The official flowers of Libra are roses, hydrangeas, and cosmos.

Roswell (ROZ-well) Old English: Springtime of roses. The beautiful rose is one of the flowers associated with ebullient, ever-youthful Libras.

Sacha (SAH-shah) Russian: Helper of mankind. People-pleasing Libras are quick to assist others in need, often choosing careers in social service. Variation: *Sasha*.

Salim (sah-LEEM; SA-lim) Arabic: Peace. Libras desire harmony and balance in all matters. Variation: *Saleem*.

Sarad (SAH-rahd) Hindu: Born in autumn. This name is an apt one for a child born under the sign of Libra, which heralds the start of autumn.

Scully (SKULL-ee) Irish: Town crier. Considered the sign of communication, Libra shows an innate strength in relaying information and protecting the interests of others.

Shandy (SHAN-dee) Old English: Energetic or noisy. Although gentle and harmonious by nature, fun-loving Libra can become boisterous when he becomes involved in a game or sport. Variations: *Shandey, Shandie*.

Shanon (SHA-nun) Hebrew: Peaceful. Libra is the sign of harmony and balance. Variation: *Shanan*.

Sheehan (SHEE-han) Irish: Little peaceful one. Gentle Libras are known for their love of peace and serenity.

Sherwin (SHUR-win) English: Bright friend. Generous, fun loving, and pleasant, Libras make wonderful friends who light up the lives of those around them. Variations: *Sherwinn, Sherwyn, Sherwynne*.

Sigfrid (SIG-freed) Old German: Peaceful. Gentle Libras cherish harmony in all things. Variations: *Siegfried, Sig, Sigfried, Zygfryd, Zygi*.

Simon (SYE-munn) Hebrew: To be heard. As an Air sign, Libras have great powers of communication and make eloquent speakers. Variations: *Shimon, Si, Simeon, Symon*.

Skelly (SKELL-ee) Irish: Storyteller. Born under the sign of communication, Libras are naturally gifted at all forms of public speaking. Variations: *Skelley, Skellie*.

Solomon (SOL-oh-mahn) Hebrew: Peaceful. Libra is the sign of balance and harmony. Variations: *Salamun, Salom, Selim, Sholom, Sol, Solly, Soloman.*

Spiro (SPEE-roh) Latin: To blow. Libra is one of three Air signs.

Storm (STORM) American: An atmospheric disturbance or high winds. Although life with Libra is far from stormy, those born under the Air sign of Libra can react vehemently when they witness great injustice.

Sweeney (SWEEN-ee) Irish: Small hero. Symbolized by the Scales of Justice, Libras are quick to come to the aid of those who have been treated unfairly or injustly. Variation: *Sweeny.*

Tadi (TAH-dee) Native American: Wind. Libra is one of the three Air signs of the zodiac.

Talib (TAH-lib) Arabic: Seeker of the truth. Symbolized by the Scales of Justice, Libra is known to be honorable and ethical in all things.

Tate (TAYT) Native American: Windy or a great talker. Libra, an Air sign, is renowned for his exceptional communication skills. Variations: *Tait, Taite, Taitt, Tayte.*

Terence (TER-uns) Latin: Soft and tender. All Libras possess a warm, gentle, and loving inner spirit. Variations: *Terrance, Terrence.*

Theodore (THEE-oh-dor) Greek: A gift. Charming, peaceful, and loving, Libras bring joy to the lives of their loved ones. Variations: *Ted, Theodor.*

Vadin (vah-DEEN) Hindu: Speaker. As one of the Air signs, Libra is gifted with excellent communication skills.

Vartan (VAHR-tahn) Armenian: Rose. The rose is one of the flowers associated with the sign of Libra.

Waban (wah-BAHN) Native American: The east wind. Libra is one of the three Air signs of the zodiac.

Webster (WEB-stir) English: Weaver. Eloquent Libra is a gifted communicator and storyteller who realizes the importance of maintaining harmony and balance in everything he creates. Variations: *Web, Webb, Webber, Weber.*

Wilfred (WIL-fred) Old English: A wish for peace. Libras, who desire harmony and balance in all things, are considered the "diplomats" of the zodiac. Variation: *Wilfrid.*

Yadid (yah-DEED) Hebrew: Friend. Generous, pleasant, and fun loving, Libras make wonderful friends and companions.

Yakez (YAH-kehz) Native American: Divine skies. Libra is an Air sign ruled by the planet Venus, who governs love, beauty, and pleasure.

Yeoman (YO-man) English: Servant. This name is a suitable choice for Libra, who always seeks to make others happy.

Yunus (YOO-nus) Turkish: Dove of peace. Libra is the sign of harmony, balance, and serenity.

Famous Libras

09-24-1896	F. Scott Fitzgerald	09-25-1931	Barbara Walters
09-24-1921	Jim McKay	09-25-1932	Glenn Gould
09-24-1924	Sheila MacRae	09-25-1936	Juliet Prowse
09-24-1931	Anthony Newley	09-25-1944	Michael Douglas
09-24-1936	Jim Henson	09-25-1951	Mark Hamill
09-24-1942	Linda McCartney	09-25-1952	Christopher Reeve
09-24-1948	Phil Hartman	09-25-1961	Heather Locklear

09-25-1965	Scottie Pippen	10-01-1928	George Peppard
09-25-1968	Will Smith	10-01-1933	Richard Harris
09-26-1888	T. S. Eliot	10-01-1935	Julie Andrews
09-26-1898	George Gershwin	10-01-1945	Rod Carew
09-26-1914	Jack LaLanne	10-01-1950	Randy Quaid
09-26-1926	Julie London	10-02-1869	Mahatma Gandhi
09-26-1948	Olivia Newton-John	10-02-1890	Groucho Marx
09-26-1956	Linda Hamilton	10-02-1895	Bud Abbott
09-27-1920	William Conrad	10-02-1928	George "Spanky"
09-27-1922	Arthur Penn		McFarland
09-27-1926	Jayne Meadows	10-02-1938	Rex Reed
09-27-1934	Wilford Brimley	10-02-1945	Don McLean
09-27-1934	Greg Morris	10-02-1948	Donna Karan
09-27-1948	Meat Loaf	10-02-1951	Sting
09-27-1947	Cheryl Tiegs	10-03-1916	James Herriot
09-27-1949	Mike Schmidt	10-03-1925	Gore Vidal
09-27-1958	Shaun Cassidy	10-03-1941	Chubby Checker
09-28-1901	Ed Sullivan	10-03-1954	Stevie Ray Vaughn
09-28-1909	Al Capp	10-04-1822	Rutherford B. Hayes
09-28-1924	Marcello Mastroianni	10-04-1884	Damon Runyon
09-28-1925	Arnold Stang	10-04-1895	Buster Keaton
09-28-1934	Brigitte Bardot	10-04-1923	Charlton Heston
09-28-1964	Janeane Garofalo	10-04-1928	Alvin Toffler
09-28-1967	Moon Unit Zappa	10-04-1941	Anne Rice
09-28-1973	Gwyneth Paltrow	10-04-1946	Susan Sarandon
09-29-1547	Miguel de Cervantes	10-04-1976	Alicia Silverstone
09-29-1907	Gene Autry	10-05-1829	Chester A. Arthur
09-29-1908	Greer Garson	10-05-1902	Larry Fine
09-29-1913	Stanley Kramer	10-05-1902	Ray Kroc
09-29-1931	Anita Ekberg	10-05-1919	Donald Pleasence
09-29-1935	Jerry Lee Lewis	10-05-1923	Glynis Johns
09-29-1942	Madeline Kahn	10-05-1951	Karen Allen
09-29-1943	Lech Walesa	10-05-1951	Bob Geldof
09-29-1948	Bryant Gumbel	10-05-1965	Mario Lemieux
09-30-1921	Deborah Kerr	10-05-1975	Kate Winslet
09-30-1924	Truman Capote	10-06-1908	Carole Lombard
09-30-1931	Angie Dickinson	10-06-1942	Britt Ekland
09-30-1935	Johnny Mathis	10-06-1963	Elisabeth Shue
09-30-1943	Marilyn McCoo	10-06-1970	Amy Jo Johnson
10-01-1903	Vladimir Horowitz	10-07-1885	Niels Bohr
10-01-1920	Walter Matthau	10-07-1905	Andy Devine
10-01-1921	James Whitmore	10-07-1911	Vaughn Monroe
10-01-1924	Jimmy Carter	10-07-1917	June Allyson
10-01-1927	Tom Bosley	10-07-1927	R. D. Laing

10-07-1931	Bishop Desmond Tutu
10-07-1951	John Cougar Mellencamp
10-07-1955	Yo-Yo Ma
10-08-1895	Juan Peron
10-08-1936	Rona Barrett
10-08-1939	Paul Hogan
10-08-1941	Jesse Jackson
10-08-1943	Chevy Chase
10-08-1949	Sigourney Weaver
10-08-1956	Stephanie Zimbalist
10-09-1890	Aimee Semple McPherson
10-09-1899	Bruce Catton
10-09-1908	Jacques Tati
10-09-1940	John Lennon
10-09-1948	Jackson Browne
10-10-1813	Giuseppe Verdi
10-10-1900	Helen Hayes
10-10-1924	Edward D. Wood, Jr.
10-10-1917	Thelonious Monk
10-10-1930	Harold Pinter
10-10-1946	Ben Vereen
10-10-1955	David Lee Roth
10-10-1958	Tanya Tucker
10-11-1884	Eleanor Roosevelt
10-11-1918	Jerome Robbins
10-11-1925	Elmore Leonard
10-11-1961	Steve Young
10-11-1966	Luke Perry
10-12-1932	Dick Gregory
10-12-1935	Luciano Pavarotti
10-12-1947	Chris Wallace
10-12-1950	Susan Anton
10-12-1970	Kirk Cameron
10-13-1915	Cornel Wilde
10-13-1921	Yves Montand
10-13-1924	Nipsey Russell
10-13-1925	Lenny Bruce
10-13-1925	Margaret Thatcher
10-13-1941	Paul Simon
10-13-1959	Marie Osmond
10-13-1962	Jerry Rice
10-13-1969	Nancy Kerrigan
10-14-1644	William Penn
10-14-1890	Dwight Eisenhower
10-14-1894	e.e. cummings
10-14-1896	Lillian Gish
10-14-1910	John Wooden
10-14-1927	Roger Moore
10-14-1939	Ralph Lauren
10-14-1949	Harry Anderson
10-15-1908	John Kenneth Galbraith
10-15-1917	Arthur Schlesinger, Jr.
10-15-1920	Mario Puzo
10-15-1924	Lee Iacocca
10-15-1937	Linda Lavin
10-15-1942	Penny Marshall
10-15-1945	Jim Palmer
10-16-1758	Noah Webster
10-16-1854	Oscar Wilde
10-16-1888	Eugene O'Neill
10-16-1925	Angela Lansbury
10-16-1946	Suzanne Somers
10-16-1958	Tim Robbins
10-16-1962	Flea
10-16-1975	Kellie Martin
10-17-1893	Spring Byington
10-17-1905	Jean Arthur
10-17-1915	Arthur Miller
10-17-1918	Rita Hayworth
10-17-1920	Montgomery Clift
10-17-1927	Tom Poston
10-17-1930	Jimmy Breslin
10-17-1938	Evel Knievel
10-17-1948	Margot Kidder
10-17-1948	George Wendt
10-17-1950	Howard Rollins
10-18-1900	Lotte Lenya
10-18-1921	Jesse Helms
10-18-1925	Melina Mercouri
10-18-1926	Chuck Berry
10-18-1927	George C. Scott
10-18-1939	Mike Ditka
10-18-1939	Lee Harvey Oswald
10-18-1947	Laura Nyro
10-18-1951	Pam Dawber
10-18-1956	Martina Navratilova
10-18-1960	Jean-Claude Van Damme

10-18-1961	Wynton Marsalis	10-21-1956	Carrie Fisher
10-19-1922	Jack Anderson	10-22-1811	Franz Liszt
10-19-1931	John Le Carré	10-22-1844	Sarah Bernhardt
10-19-1937	Peter Max	10-22-1903	Curly Howard
10-19-1945	Divine	10-22-1917	Joan Fontaine
10-19-1945	John Lithgow	10-22-1920	Timothy Leary
10-19-1945	Jeannie C. Riley	10-22-1938	Christopher Lloyd
10-20-1854	Arthur Rimbaud	10-22-1939	Tony Roberts
10-20-1882	Bela Lugosi	10-22-1942	Annette Funicello
10-20-1925	Art Buchwald	10-22-1943	Catherine Deneuve
10-20-1931	Mickey Mantle	10-22-1952	Jeff Goldblum
10-20-1953	Tom Petty	10-23-1925	Johnny Carson
10-21-1772	Samuel Taylor Coleridge	10-23-1940	Pele
10-21-1833	Alfred Nobel	10-23-1942	Michael Crichton
10-21-1917	Dizzy Gillespie	10-23-1959	"Weird" Al Yankovic
		10-23-1965	Al Leiter

SCORPIO
(October 24–November 22)

GLYPH: ♏

SYMBOL: The Scorpion

POLARITY: Feminine

QUALITY: Fixed

ELEMENT: Water

RULING PLANET: Pluto

BIRTHSTONE: Topaz

SPECIAL COLORS: Crimson red, burgundy, and black

FLOWERS: Chrysanthemum and rhododendron

METAL: Plutonium

ANIMALS: Insects and crustaceans

MOST LIKEABLE TRAITS: Passion, imagination, and persistency

♏

Scorpios are the deepest, most complex, and often most misunderstood of the zodiac's signs. Theirs is the sign of dramatic and sweeping extremes, and Scorpios have been characterized as both wildly sensual and rigidly withdrawn, fiercely independent and desperately clinging, deeply spiritual and wantonly amoral, keenly sensitive and callously cold. In some ways, Scorpios epitomize both the noblest and the basest of human traits. Because of this, many devotees of astrology tend to focus only on Scorpio's darker traits, ignoring their astonishingly intuitive, deeply loving, and genuinely caring natures. Scorpio children's darker side may confound and mystify their parents from time to time, but the bond between Scorpios and their parents is one of the most fervently passionate and long lasting in the zodiac.

General Qualities

The key to understanding Scorpio lies in the dual meaning of its symbolic glyph (♏). In contemporary astrology, the glyph is a representation of the stinger of the Scorpion, the ''animal'' that symbolizes this sign. Scorpions are solitary, stealthy, venomous arachnids who prefer the dark, possess a ferocious aspect, and react with a sudden sting when provoked. For many people, scorpions are synonymous with pain and death. Children born under the sign of Scorpio also have a dark and fierce side, are quick to anger when challenged, and are renowned for their notoriously bad tempers that drive them to strike back when hurt. These dark and fierce qualities lurk in the unconscious side of every Scorpio, just below the surface.

The golden and conscious side of Scorpio, however, is illustrated in the other meaning of the sign's glyph. In ancient astrology, this glyph was the symbol of the Phoenix, the mythological bird of immortality who lived for five hundred years, burned itself to ashes in a fiery pyre, and then was reborn from the ashes to live another five hundred years. Thus, Scorpio is also the sign of regeneration, transformation, and healing— the reason why Scorpio also is known as the sign of the physician.

These dark and dual-sided elements are key influences in the sign of Scorpio. All their lives, Scorpios are on a quest to discover their unique purpose, place, and destiny in life. More than anything, they want to be the conduits of change. To that end, they are keenly attuned to the creative and healing potentials in the elemental life-energies around them—what the Chinese would call *qi*—and to their own progenitive, elemental energies. Their ultimate goal is to harness the energy within and around them, and then use this energy to affect profound and transcendent changes in themselves and in others. These changes may be spiritual, physical, or emotional in nature—the reason why Scorpio is not only the sign of the physician, but the sign of spirituality, science, religion, and the occult.

Scorpios are aided in their life missions by several unique influences in their sign. Scorpio is a Feminine and Fixed Water sign, ruled by the planet Pluto. Pluto is the planet of profound change and, to that end, it governs the underworld, birth, death, regeneration, and transformation. Pluto also rules all things that are deep, dark, and mysterious. It is strongly associated with healing, mysticism, psychology, and criminality. Pluto's influence sustains and encourages Scorpio's abiding passion in spirituality, religion, and the occult. And Pluto also accounts for Scorpio's compulsive and obsessive qualities.

The Feminine quality in Scorpio gives children of this sign their great inner strength, receptivity, intuitiveness, and deep emotion. The element of Water endows Scorpios with imagination, sensitivity, and a strong interest in things religious or mystical. Scorpio is also a Fixed sign, which adds the famed Scorpio determination and obstinacy to the mix.

Remembering that Scorpios are naturally a bundle of contradictory qualities can help one go far to understanding and accepting these extraordinarily complicated creatures. On the one hand, Scorpios can be open, imaginative, intuitive, passionate, witty, committed, and idealistic, particularly when they are happily in pursuit of a well-chosen goal. They often see themselves as heroic figures on a picaresque quest. Indeed, they possess great vision, courage, and strength in pursuit of their ideals. They also are adept at intuiting others' feelings, especially fear, and offering a compassionate ear and shoulder. Scorpios are innately gifted healers, soothsayers, and mentors, and people are naturally drawn to Scorpio's high-minded visions of what life can be.

On the other hand, Scorpios who see themselves as thwarted or betrayed, or who are forced to do something they don't want to do, may turn into fierce, vindictive, and angry creatures from whom people want to flee. At their darkest, Scorpios are rigid and unyielding, cold and withdrawn, stormy and uncommunicative. They strike first, and think later.

Much of this behavior is unconscious: More than any other sign of the zodiac, including labile Cancer (with whom Scorpio has much in common), Scorpios are ruled by their emotions. Indeed, some might say that Scorpio is the emotional life personified. However, being naturally secretive and self-protective, Scorpios invariably frame their emotionalism with a tough edge.

Home

The key to living peaceably with Scorpio children—and fully enjoying their unusual gifts—is to understand from the outset that Scorpio is a creature of contradictions who has an intensely black-or-white view of the world. For instance, acutely sensitive to what others have to say about them, Scorpios nevertheless can be sharp-tongued and brutally insensitive when they are doing the communicating. This has nothing to do with manners. Rather, Scorpios don't seem to have any inner censor.

Scorpios' lack of self-censorship often accounts for their doing and saying whatever they want, whenever they want, often with disastrous results. What sometimes comes out of their mouths as young children can be harsh and hurtful to those on the receiving end. Realizing that Scorpios are truly astonished when they discover that they have hurt you—and are desperately eager to make amends—offers little consolation. Scorpios need to be reminded that other people are just as sensitive as they are. They also need to learn at a young age how to take a deep breath, stop, and think before they open their mouths!

Another key to understanding Scorpio children is realizing that they often mask their deepest feelings, including their fears and insecurities, beneath a deceptively cool and brave facade. Never ones to cling, and always determined to present a strong and independent front, Scorpios are cautious about letting others see the chinks in their armor. Scorpios need to be repeatedly encouraged to express their feelings openly and honestly, and they need to be reassured that being fearful and insecure from time to time is natural, not a failing.

The upside to life with Scorpio children is their deeply passionate and devoted love of family, which they share without much self-censorship! Many parents are initially astounded by their Scorpio child's decidedly sensual approach to life and relationships.

Scorpio children also possess some of the most fascinating and precocious minds in the zodiac, displaying deep and mystical powers of intuition and discernment, together with an uncanny ability to see the real truth behind artifice and guile. They have marvelously deft verbal skills and a genuine interest in surprisingly sophisticated topics. Despite their sometimes dark and stormy natures, Scorpios are devoted, engaging, and always fascinating additions to any family.

School and Play

Scorpios bring their classic all-or-nothing approach to life right into the classroom, where it can become either an asset or a hindrance. As with everything else, Scorpios want to do *what* they want to do, *when* they want to do it, and *how* they want to do it. If they are interested in a subject, Scorpios bring to it their gifts of intuitive intelligence, heroic self-determination, and vision-driven hard work. In the end, Scorpios want to succeed and make a difference, and these desires affect much of what they do, in school and out.

However, when Scorpios are not interested in a particular subject, that's another situation entirely. Scorpios frequently do not see the purpose in wasting precious energy on something that doesn't engage them or isn't part of their heroic vision. They may simply refuse to do the work required of them. Needless to say, this laissez-faire attitude toward academics doesn't go over well in the structured and bureaucratic environment of school. Early on, parents and teachers of Scorpio children can expect some battles of the will about the necessity of their doing what is expected of them, and not simply what they think is worth their time and effort.

Scorpios also bring their all-or-nothing approach to athletics. If they are drawn to a particular sport, they'll throw themselves into it wholeheartedly and typically excel at it. Scorpios love the sense of belonging that being part of a team affords, and they are naturally strong and fiercely competitive.

In informal play, Scorpios bring their powers of imagination, persuasion, and creativity to any group activity. They often become the leaders of games and adventures that they themselves invent from scratch. Creative Scorpios also are quite comfortable pursuing any solitary play that engages their imaginations, and they particularly excel at writing and handicrafts.

The World

Scorpios have an abiding interest in the dark, the mysterious, the mystical, and the fantastical, and they bring to these interests their keen imaginative skills, single-minded passion, and visionary sense of purpose. All these qualities make them excellent candidates for careers in the more arcane fields of history, astronomy, astrology, and archeology.

Surprisingly, these same qualities are responsible for endowing many Scorpios—who are astute observers of the murky undercurrents of life—with a consummate and often innovative gift for writing. The sign of Scorpio includes some of the finest and most influential writers, including: Michael Crichton, Dylan Thomas, Ezra Pound, John Keats, Kurt Vonnegut, Robert Louis Stevenson, Victor Hugo, Goethe, and Voltaire.

Even more than history, exploration, or writing, the topics of spirituality or medicine appeal to many Scorpios. Whether pursued as vocations or avocations, these two fields seem to uniquely satisfy Scorpio's drive to be the instrument of profound and transformational change in others. Possessed with a penetrating mind, emotional magnetism, single-minded strength of purpose, physical stamina, and visionary ideals, Scorpios fully come into their own in the fields of religion and science. Scorpio also is the sign of notables such as Jonas Salk, Christaan Barnard, Marie Curie, Martin Luther, and Carl Sagan.

Compared to other children of the zodiac, from a very young age Scorpios march to the beat of a decidedly different drummer. They develop deep, passionate, and highly noble goals to which they often give a lifelong commitment. They possess a heroic sense of destiny and purpose, and an unshakable belief that they, and they alone, can make a profound difference in the world. If Scorpios sometimes go about achieving their noble goals too fiercely and darkly, they can be forgiven. They are among the few genuine idealists in the world.

Choosing a Name for Your Scorpio Child

When choosing a name for your Scorpio girl or boy, first think about the major attributes and symbols associated with the sign. Scorpio is the sign of deep passion, mystery, destiny, sensuality, imagination, intensity, healing, spirituality, and the occult.

Scorpio is a Feminine and Water sign ruled by the planet Pluto. The Feminine quality gives Scorpios great inner strength and a receptive and emotional disposition. The element of Water endows Scorpio with imagination and sensitivity and a strong inclination toward things of religion or the occult. Scorpio is also a Fixed sign, which adds a layer of determination and obstinacy to the mix.

Scorpio's ruling planet, Pluto, enhances and intensifies all of Scorpio's qualities. Pluto governs the underworld, all forms of regeneration and transformation, and all things deep, dark, and mysterious. It is Pluto's influence that accounts for Scorpio's sometimes compulsive and obsessive qualities, and Pluto sustains and encourages Scorpio's abiding passion for spirituality, religion, mysticism, and/or the occult. Pluto is also associated with all forms of healing, as well as with criminal behavior.

Scorpios are deep, subtle, complex, persistent, emotional, motivated, and unyielding. The passionate colors of Scorpio are maroon, crimson red, and black. The topaz is the official birthstone of the sign, and plutonium is its precious metal. Chrysanthemums and rhododendrons are Scorpio's official flowers, and the sign rules the blackthorn and bushy trees. Insects and crustaceans are Scorpio's "animals."

When you choose a name for your child, also bear in mind Scorpio's key personal qualities. They love deeply, and sometimes foolishly, and expect to be loved deeply in return. They are renowned for their passionate energy and endurance and have a great sense of their own destiny in life. They are deep thinkers, interested in history, in ancestral legacies, and in transformations. They are natural healers, psychologists, historians, spiritual leaders, and scientists.

For additional inspiration when choosing a name for your Scorpio child—especially a middle name—you may want to browse through the names listed in Scorpio's companion Water signs: Cancer and Pisces.

Names for Scorpio Girls

Abida (ah-BEE-dah) Arabic: Worshiper. Scorpios are deeply drawn to religious or mystical experiences.

Abira (ah-BIR-ah) Hebrew: Strong. Scorpios are renowned for their determination, obstinacy, and mental and emotional endurance. Variation: *Adira*.

Aditi (ah-DEE-tee) Hindu: Without chains. In Hindu mythology, *Aditi* was the mother goddess of compassion and protection who gave birth to all the gods. Freedom-loving Scorpios are nonconformists, determined to do things their own way or not at all.

Adoette (ah-do-AY-tuh) Native American: Big tree. This name was given to children who were believed to be tree spirits in disguise. Scorpios have an abiding interest in the magical and occult.

Adrienne (AY-dree-in) Latin: Dark one. Scorpio is the "deepest" sign of the zodiac, ruled by the planet Pluto which was named for the mythological god of the underworld and the dead. Scorpios are drawn to the deep, the dark, and the mysterious. Variations: *Adri, Adria, Adrian, Adriana, Adrie, Adrien, Adriena*.

Akako (ah-KAH-koh) Japanese: Red. This magical name is believed to be a charm that cures diseases. Mystical Scorpio is strongly drawn to any of the healing arts, and crimson red is one of the colors of Scorpio.

Aki (ah-KEE) Japanese: Born in autumn. Scorpio is the last of the autumn signs, touching the months of October and November.

Alamea (ah-luh-MAY-uh) Hawaiian: Ripe. Pluto, the planet that rules the sign of Scorpio, governs all regenerative and transformational energies.

Alike (ah-LEE-keh) African/Nigerian: She who drives out beautiful women. Scorpios are fierce, passionate, and relentless competitors on the field of romance. Variations: *Aleeka, Alika*.

Alma (AHL-mah) Italian: Spiritual essence. Scorpio is the sign of intensity and spirituality.

Alumit (ah-loo-MEET) Hebrew: Sacred mystery. This popular Israeli name is a fitting choice for Scorpio, a deep spiritual seeker. Variation: *Alumice*.

Alzbeta (ahlz-BAY-tah) Czechoslovakian: Consecrated to God. Scorpios are devoted to spirituality and religion.

Amarantha (ah-mar-AN-thah) Greek: Beyond death. In mythology, the amaranth plant was believed to be immortal. Scorpio is ruled by Pluto, the planet of regeneration, birth, and death. Variations: *Amarana, Amarande, Amarante*.

Anaba (ah-NAH-bah) Native American: She returns from war. Scorpios are fierce and relentless competitors, likely to be the survivors in any conflict they undertake. Variation: *Alnaba*.

Ananda (ah-NAHN-dah) Hindu: Bliss. This revered Hindu word has profound spiritual resonance and frequently is used in the names and titles of Eastern spiritual masters. Scorpios frequently become religious or spiritual leaders.

Anastasia (AHN-ah-STAH-see-ah) Greek: Reborn from the dead. Scorpio's ruling planet, Pluto, is associated with regenerative and transformational energies. Variations: *Anastace, Anastasie, Anastazia, Nastasya, Nastusha, Stacy, Stasa, Tasia, Taska.*

Ariadne (ah-ree-ODD-nee) Greek: Very holy or devout. In Greek mythology, *Ariadne* rescued Theseus from the center of a dark, underground labyrinth. Scorpios are the psychologists of the zodiac who feel at home maneuvering the hidden pathways of the mind. Variations: *Ariana, Arianie, Arianna, Arianne.*

Arnina (àhr-NEE-nah) Middle Eastern: One who delivers God's words. Deeply interested in spirituality, Scorpios are often drawn to careers in religion. This name, always popular in Israel, is now gaining popularity in America as well. Variations: *Arnice, Arnie, Arnit.*

Asisa (ah-SEE-sah) Hebrew: Ripe. Scorpio's ruling planet, Pluto, governs all regenerative and transformational energies.

Astrid (ah-STREED or AH-strid) Old Norse: Beautiful goddess or divine strength. *Astrid* is a fitting choice for Scorpio, who possesses great inner strength and determination. Variations: *Asta, Astrud, Astyr, Sassa.*

Atida (ah-TEE-duh) Hebrew: The future. Scorpios are strongly drawn to psychic exploration and have an abiding interest in the notions of destiny and fate.

Barbara (BAR-bah-rah) Greek: Not from here. Deep, intense, and mysterious, Scorpios often have an otherworldly aura. Variations: *Babs, Barb, Barbette, Barbie, Barbra.* (Famous Scorpio: Barbara Bel Geddes, actress)

Batini (bah-TEE-nee) African/Swahili: Innermost thoughts. This name is appropriate for deep and intense Scorpio.

Bian (BEE-uhn) Vietnamese: Hidden or secretive. Getting to know mysterious Scorpio, who often keeps her feelings hidden deep inside, can be a difficult task.

Birjit (BEER-jit) Norwegian: Protecting power. Passionate Scorpio uses her great strength to defend those she loves. Variations: *Bergitte, Birgit, Birgitta.*

Brandy (BRAN-dee) Dutch: Burnt wine. In ancient times, burnt offerings were often made to appease the gods. Scorpio has a keen interest in occult and mystical practices. Variations: *Brandi, Brandie.*

Bua (BOO-uh) Vietnamese: Magical chant. The sign of Scorpio is associated with spirituality, mysticism, and the occult.

Camille (kah-MEEL) French: Born free. Passionate, intense Scorpios refuse to live their lives according to the rules of others. Variations: *Cam, Cama, Cami, Camilia, Camilla, Kamilka, Milla, Millie.*

Capucine (kah-poo-CHEEN) French: Hood. This name was originally derived to describe the hooded cloaks worn by monks and other religious clerics. Scorpios have a special interest in spirituality, and many are drawn to careers in religion. Variations: *Cappucine, Capucina.*

Carmen (KAHR-min) Spanish: Crimson. Crimson red is one of the colors of Scorpio. Variations: *Carmia, Carmina, Carmine, Carmita, Charmaine.*

Cella (CHELL-lah) Italian: Free one. Scorpios are endowed with great imagination and passion, and often are drawn to creative pursuits.

Cerise (sah-REES) French: Cherry red. Deep, cherry red is one of the colors of Scorpio. Variations: *Cherise, Sarise, Sharise, Sheriz.*

Chandi (CHAHN-dee) Hindu: Fierce. One of the names of the powerful Hindu goddess Sakti, *Chandi* is a suitable name for Scorpio, who is determined and unwavering in her actions. Variation: *Chanda.*

Chika (CHEE-kah) Japanese: Intimate. Deep, intense Scorpio only shares her true feelings with a select few.

Cho (CHOH) Japanese: Butterfly. Scorpio governs all insects and crustaceans.

Choomia (CHOO-mee-ah) Gypsy: Kiss. Scorpio is the sign of sensuality and deep passion.

Christa (KRISS-tah) Greek: Anointed one. Many Scorpios have an innate sense of the sacred, and are drawn to vocations in religion. Variations: *Christa, Christine, Chrysta, Crista, Crysta.*

Cocheta (co-SHAY-tah) Native American: That which cannot be fathomed. *Cocheta* is an ideal name for Scorpio, who is fascinated by religion, mysticism, the occult, and the paranormal. Many people also find it difficult to figure out mysterious and secretive Scorpio.

Dagny (DAG-nee) Old Norse: Release from darkness. The sign of Scorpio is often associated with dark, mysterious imagery and the quest to understand it.

Darcy (DAR-see) Irish: Dark man's descendant. One of the colors associated with the sign of Scorpio is black. Variations: *Darcelle, Darcey, Darci, Darcia, D'Arcy.*

Dasha (DAH-shah) Greek: Divine display. Scorpios often possess a special interest in religion. Variation of *Dorothy.*

Deborah (DEH-bor-ah) Hebrew: Stinger or bee. Deborah is a classic name denoting great and penetrating power. This traditional name suits deep and powerful Scorpio, whose sign also rules all insects. Variations: *Debbie, Debby, Debora, Deboran, Debra, Debrah, Devora.*

Deidre (DEE-dra) Gaelic: Sadness. *Deidre* was a legendary Irish heroine comparable, in beauty and in fate, to the Greek Helen of Troy. Mythological and mystical names are apt choices for Scorpio who is strongly drawn to the notions of fate, legacy, and destiny. Variations: *Dee, Deedee, Deedra, Deidra, Deirdre.*

Desiree (dez-ih-RAY) French: Ardently desired. Scorpio is the sign of deep passion and intensity. Variations: *Desarae, Desirae, Desire, Desirée, Desyre.*

Devaki (dah-vah-KEE) Hindu: Black. In Hindu mythology, *Devaki* is the name of the goddess who gave birth to Krishna, the greatest of the Hindu gods. Black is one of the colors associated with Scorpio.

Devany (DEV-a-nee) Gaelic: Dark haired. Many Scorpios are born with brown or dark hair. Variations: *Davanie, Devaney, Devenny, Devony.*

Devi (DAY-vee) Hindu: Goddess. *Devi* is one of the many names of the Hindu goddess Sakti, who represents the feminine divine.

Durva (DURE-vah) Hindu: durva grass, a holy grass used in worship. Scorpios cherish religious or mystical relics.

Duscha (DOO-shah) Russian: Soul. Emotionally and spiritually complex Scorpios often embody the word *soul.* Variation: *Dusha.*

Ebony (EBB-ah-nee) Greek: Black; for the dark, black wood. Black is one of the colors of the sign of Scorpio. Variations: *Ebonee, Eboni, Ebonique.*

Edna (EDD-nah) Hebrew: Rejuvenation. Pluto, the ruling planet of Scorpio, governs regeneration and transformation. Variation: *Edena.*

Elizabeth (ee-liz-ah-BETH) Hebrew: Oath of God. Scorpios, who possess a special interest in spirituality, often pursue religious vocations. Variations: *Bess, Beth, Betsy, Betty, Eliza, Elsbeth, Elyse, Lisa, Lisbeth, Liz, Liza, Lizzie.*

Ellama (ELL-lah-mah) Hindu: Mother goddess. *Ellama* is another name that connotes the fascination Scorpios have with all types of spirituality and religion. Variation: *Elamma.*

Enid (EE-nid) Welsh: Living soul. This name is appropriate for Scorpio, who possesses a deeply emotional, intensely active spirit. Variations: *Eanid, Enidd, Enyd.*

Erma (ER-mah) Greek: Cosmic whole. This name suggests Scorpio's contradictory personality elements, which continue to create a deep, yet enigmatic whole. Variations: *Ermina, Erminia, Erminie, Hermia, Hermine, Hermione, Irma, Irminia.*

Fayina (figh-EE-nah) Russian: Free one. Born under a Fixed sign, Scorpios' obstinate determination helps them to stand up for their beliefs and persistently follow their dreams.

Femi (FEH-mee) African/Nigerian: Love me. Scorpios love deeply and expect to be loved deeply and devotedly in return.

Frances (FRAN-siss) Latin: Free one. *Frances* is a fitting name for Scorpio, who stubbornly follows her own path through life. Variations: *Fannie, Fanny, Fran, Frankie, Frannie, Franny.* (Famous Scorpio: Ziegfeld star Fanny Brice)

Galatea (gah-lah-TEE-ah or gah-lah-TAY-ah) Greek: Ivory-colored, for the statue of *Galatea*. In Greek mythology, *Galatea* was the beautiful statue brought to life through the sculptor Pygmalion's ardent prayers to the goddess Aphrodite. Scorpios are renowned for their deeply sensual and passionate natures. Variations: *Gal, Gala, Galatee, Galatée*.

Gali (gah-LEE) Hebrew: A spring. Scorpio, a Water sign, governs the processes of regeneration, birth, and death. Variations: *Gal, Galice, Galit*.

Ganesa (guh-NAY-shuh) Hindu: For the Hindu elephant god who bestows good luck and wisdom. Scorpios are intrigued by different forms of religion and spirituality.

Gavrilla (gahv-REE-luh) Hebrew: Heroine. This name suggests Scorpio's ability to conquer the enemy by using her passion, strength, intensity, and determination.

Genevieve (JEN-ah-VEEV) Celtic: Female lineage. Scorpio is the sign of destiny, inheritance, birth, and death. Variations: *Gena, Genavieve, Geneva, Gennie, Genny, Gina, Janeva, Jenevieve*.

Gitana (hee-TAHN-ah) Spanish: Gypsy girl. Intuitive, unconventional, and passionate, Scorpios often possess a "gypsy" quality.

Gunda (GOON-dah) Scandinavian: Warrior. Intense, emotional Scorpio can be a formidable enemy when crossed or betrayed. Variation: *Gundula*.

Habibah (hah-BEE-bah) Arabic: Beloved. Scorpios, who love deeply (and sometimes to extremes), expect to be loved deeply in return. Variation: *Haviva*.

Haley (HAL-ee) Irish: Scientific or ingenious. Scorpios are deeply drawn to medicine and the healing arts. Variations: *Hali, Halie, Halli, Hallie, Hally.*

Halima (hah-LEE-mah) African/Swahili: Caressing nature. Scorpios are among the most sensual children of the zodiac.

Hara (HAH-rah) Hindu: Seizer. The feminine form of the Hindu name, *Hari*, one of the many sacred names for the powerful god Siva, *Hara* suggests Scorpio's deep power and energy.

Hedda (HED-ah) Old German: Strike in battle. When betrayed or wronged in some way, Scorpios may attack quickly and fiercely. Variations: *Heda, Heddi, Heddy, Hedi, Hedy.* (Famous Scorpio: Hedy Lamarr, actress)

Hedia (hay-DEE-ah) Hebrew: The echo of God. This name connotes Scorpio's strong inclination toward religion. Variation: *Hedya.*

Helga (HEL-gah) Old German: Religious or devout. Scorpio is the sign of religion, healing, and spirituality.

Ima (EE-mah) Japanese: In the moment; eternal present. Scorpio's great powers of endurance make *Ima* a fitting name for those born under the stalwart sign.

Indira (in-DEER-ah) Hindu: Beauty and splendor. Also the name of a Hindu goddess of heaven and thunderstorms, Indira is a beautiful choice for passionate Scorpio. Variations: *Indra, Indria.* (Famous Scorpio: Indira Gandhi, Indian prime minister)

Iphigenia (iff-ah-ZHEEN-ee-ah) Greek: Of royal birth. Princess Iphigenia was a true daughter of destiny whose sacrifice resulted in the transformation of ancient Greece. Scorpios are associated with transformation and a strong sense of destiny. Variations: *Iffy, Iphigene.*

Isabel (ee-sah-BELL) Spanish: Dedicated to God. Scorpios, who are drawn to religion and spirituality, often devote their lives to God. Variations: *Bella, Belle, Isa, Isabella, Isabelle, Isobel*.

Isadora (iz-ah-DORR-ah) Latin: Gift of Isis. In Egyptian mythology, the goddess Isis granted Osiris the gift of rebirth. Scorpio rules regeneration and the transformation of death into life. Variation: *Isidora*.

Jennifer (JENN-ah-fer) Welsh: Pale ghost. Scorpios have a special fascination with the supernatural. *Jennifer* has achieved independent name status, but it was originally a Cornish variant of *Guinevere*. Variations: *Genn, Genny, Jen, Jeni, Jeniffer, Jenni, Jennica, Jennie, Jenny*. (Famous Scorpio: Jenny McCarthy, MTV personality)

Jora (YO-rah) Hebrew: Autumn mists. Encompassing the months of October and November, Scorpio is an autumn Water sign. Variation: *Jorah*.

Kala (KA-la) Hindu: Black, or time. One of the names for the god Siva. Black is one of the colors associated with dark, mysterious Scorpio. *Kala* is also an appropriate choice for a boy.

Kali (ka-LEE; KAH-lee) Hindu: Black one. *Kali* is the fierce and avenging form of the divine mother goddess Sakti. Scorpios are renowned for their deep and retaliating anger when crossed.

Kama (KAH-mah) Hindu: Love. *Kama* is an apt name for Scorpio, who loves deeply and expects to be loved deeply in return.

Kamali (KA-mah-lee; ka-MAH-lee) African/Rhodesian: Spirit. *Kamali* is a divine spirit who protects newborn children. This name is a wonderful choice for Scorpio, who is associated with healing and spirituality.

Kanika (ka-NEE-ka) African/Kenyan: Black cloth. The special colors associated with Scorpio are maroon, crimson red, and black.

Kapua (ka-POO-uh) Hawaiian: Blossom. The newly flowering bud is a perfect symbol of Scorpio's connection with transformation and all forms of regeneration.

Karma (KAHR-mah) Hindu: Fate, destiny. This name is ideal for Scorpio, who places high value on the power of destiny.

Kaula (KOW-luh) Hawaiian: Prophet. Scorpios are intrigued by religion, mysticism, the future, and the occult.

Kaveri (kah-VAIR-ee) Hindu: For the Indian Kaveri River, a sacred river where devoted Hindus cleanse their souls by taking ritual baths. Scorpios, born under a Water sign, are intrigued by religious rituals and ceremonies.

Kei (KAY) Japanese: Rapture or reverence. This popular Japanese name is a great choice for Scorpios, who are strongly attracted to religion and other types of spirituality. Variation: *Keiko*.

Kenda (KEN-dah) American: Child of clear, cool water. This very popular contemporary name is suitable for Scorpio, a Water sign. Variations: *Kendi, Kendie, Kendy, Kennda, Kenndy*.

Kenisha (ke-NEE-shah) African-American: Gorgeous woman. This lovely, unusual choice suits Scorpio, who is attractive and passionate. Formed from *Ken* and *Iesha*. Variations: *Keneisha, Keneshia, Kennesha*.

Kerry (KER-ee) Irish: Dusky. Mysterious Scorpio is associated with dark imagery. Variations: *Kera, Keri, Kerianne, Kerra, Kerri, Kerrie*. (Famous Scorpio: Kerri Strug, Olympic gymnast)

Kiku (kee-KOO; KEE-koo) Japanese: Chrysanthemum. One of the flowers that symbolize the sign of Scorpio, the chrysanthemum is believed to bestow longevity.

Kimana (ke-MAH-nah) Native American: Butterfly. In Native American mythology, God traveled across the earth in the form of a butterfly looking for the most beautiful and ideal place to create the first human. The sign of Scorpio rules all insects and crustaceans. Scorpios also are associated with regeneration and rebirth.

Kismet (KISS-met or KIHZ-met) American: Fate, destiny. This name is an ideal choice for Scorpio, who has an intuitive sense of her own destiny in life.

Klesa (KLAY-sah) Hindu: Pain. In many cultures, negative names are deliberately given to children in an attempt to trick wrathful or mean-spirited gods. *Klesa,* one of these names, is an appropriate choice for deep and dark Scorpio.

Kostya (KO-stya; KOSS-stya) Russian: Constant. Scorpios are passionate and devoted lovers, even when they choose their loves foolishly.

Krishna (KREESH-nah) Hindu: Delightful. *Krishna* is the greatest of all Hindu gods. Scorpios intensely enjoy the exploration of all types of spirituality.

Laka (LAH-kah) Hawaiian: Seduce. *Laka* is the name of a mythological Hawaiian goddess who created the hula dance. Scorpios are the most sensual of the zodiac's children.

Lalita (lah-LEE-tuh) Hindu: Charming. Another of the many names given to the great Hindu goddess Sakti, *Lalita* suggests Scorpio's inspired and unpretentious search for the divine.

Leeba (LEE-bah) Hebrew: Full of emotion. This very popular Israeli name is wonderfully suited to deeply passionate Scorpio.

Lisa (LEE-sah) English: Dedicated to God. Scorpios, who are associated with healing and spirituality, often find religion to be a motivating power in their lives. Variation: *Lisette*. (Famous Scorpio: Lisa Bonet, actress)

Lissa (LISS-ah) Arabic: From the name of the melissa plant, which symbolizes sympathy and rejuvenation. Scorpio's ruling planet, Pluto, is associated with regeneration and transformation.

Litonya (li-TOHN-yah) Native American: A name derived to suggest the darting movements of the hummingbird. In mythology, the hummingbird is believed to be a love charm. This name suits Scorpio, who approaches all things, including love, with a sense of passionate enchantment.

Livona (li-VOH-nah) Hebrew: Divine spices. *Livona* is an ideal name for spiritual Scorpio, who enjoys exploring the variety in both spiritual and emotional ways. Variation: *Levina*.

Liza (LY-zah) Russian: Devoted to the Lord. Many Scorpios search passionately for deep spiritual meaning, and even pursue religious vocations.

Lolita (loh-LEE-tah) Spanish: Of the sorrows. Scorpio's ruler, Pluto, governs all things deep, dark, and mysterious. As a result, many Scorpios possess a darker side, with emotions that fluctuate, even toward depression. Variation: *Lola*.

Lynn (LINN) Old English: Waterfall. Scorpio is one of the three Water signs of the zodiac. Variations: *Lin, Linelle, Linette, Lyn, Lyndell, Lyndelle, Lynnette*.

Madeline (MAD-ah-lin) Greek: Of Magdala, village of Mary Magdalene. This biblical heroine suggests a quintessential Scorpio woman who loved deeply and did things her own way while pursuing a decidedly spiritual course. Variations: *Lena, Lina, Madalena, Maddy, Madeleine, Madelina, Madge, Magda, Magdalena*.

Maeve (MEHV) Irish: Mythological name of the first-century queen of Ireland who was known for her deep and strong will. Scorpios, too, are famous for their firm, passionate beliefs and unwavering determination.

Mahira (mah-HEE-rah) Hebrew: Quick or energetic. *Mahira* is a fitting name for Scorpio, who possesses almost supernatural levels of energy and passion. Variation: *Mehira*.

Mana (MAH-nuh) Hawaiian: Supernatural power. Scorpios are fascinated by—and intuitive about—all things unexplained: religion, mysticism, the occult, the future, and the supernatural.

Mani (MAH-nee) Hindu: Derived from the ancient Buddhist prayer, *om mani padme hum*, *Mani* is a sacred word believed to ward off evil and to bestow wisdom. Scorpios possess a special reverence for religious customs and rituals.

Mary (MARE-ee) Hebrew: Bitter heart or rebelliousness. This ever-popular, classic name is well suited to obstinate, determined Scorpio, who prefers to live life according to her own rules. Variations: *Mame, Mara, Marabel, Maria, Marian, Mariana, Marianne, Marie, Mariel, Marilyn, Marla, Marlo, May, Meri, Meriel, Mimi, Minni, Minny, Molly, Muriel*. (Famous Scorpios: Marlo Thomas, actress; Mary Travers, folksinger; Minnie Pearl, country-and-western singer; Maria Shriver, newscaster; Mary Hart, television personality; Mariel Hemingway, actress; Marie Curie, scientist)

Matrika (mah-TREE-kah) Hindu: Mother goddess. *Matrika* is one of the names of the divine goddess Sakti, whose dual nature exemplifies Scorpio's wide range of emotional extremes. (See *Sakti*.)

Maureen (maw-REEN) French: Dark or bitter child or baby *Mary*. While Scorpios can overflow with happiness and pleasure, their emotions may flow to equal extreme on the darker side. Variations: *Marina, Marine, Maura, Moira, Mora, Moreen, Morena*.

Meda (MAY-duh) Native American: Prophet or priestess. Many Scorpios seek spiritual insight and may even pursue careers in religion.

Mel (MAYL) Portuguese: Honey. Scorpio governs all insects, including the honey-making bee.

Mela (MAY-lah) Hindu: Sacred encounter. *Mela* is an apt name for a child born under Scorpio, the sign of religion, healing, and spirituality.

Melanie (MEL-uh-nee) Greek: Dark. This name is a lovely and popular choice for Scorpio, whose ruling planet Pluto governs the underworld and is associated with all things deep, dark, and mysterious. Variations: *Mel, Mela, Melaney, Melani, Melania, Melanney, Melantha, Mella, Melli*.

Melantha (me-LANN-tha) Greek: Dark blossom. Also the name of a dark violet Mediterranean lily, *Melantha* is an ideal choice for Scorpio, who is associated with all things dark and mysterious.

Melissa (me-LISS-sah) Greek: Bee. The sign of Scorpio rules all insects and crustaceans, and the bee is an ancient symbol of immortality and the eternal life. Variations: *Melessa, Melisa, Melisse*.

Melosa (meh-LOH-sah) Spanish: Honeylike. Scorpio's birthstone is the honey-colored topaz, and the sign rules all insects, including the bee.

Mia (MEE-ah) Hebrew: Who is like God? Scorpios, who seek spirituality throughout their lives, often use their healing powers and emotional sensitivity to help others.

Michelle (mih-SHELL) Hebrew: Who is like the Lord? *Michelle* is a lovely and fitting choice for spiritually inclined Scorpio. Variations: *Michele, Micki.*

Michi (MEE-chee) Japanese: The righteous way. Scorpio's visionary ideals, coupled with their great determination, lead to divine insight when they pursue the spiritual path.

Minda (MIN-dah) Hindu: Wisdom. Their keen intuition and spiritual sensitivity often lead Scorpios to great wisdom.

Minette (min-ETT) French: Unwavering protector. Determined, strong, and passionate, Scorpios go to any lengths to defend their loved ones. Variation: *Minna.*

Mirella (mir-ELL-ah) Hebrew: Jehovah spoke. Religion and spirituality are key forces in Scorpio's life. Variations: *Mireille, Mirelle, Myrelle.*

Miri (MEE-ree) Gypsy: Mine. Scorpios often have a strongly possessive, even jealous, side. Scorpios must learn the value of sharing at an early age to lessen this tendency.

Miriam (MIR-ee-ahm) Hebrew: Rebellious or bitter. As a Fixed sign, Scorpios have a tendency to become determined, obstinate, even adamant about their own beliefs. Variations: *Meryem, Mimi, Minni, Minnie, Mitzi.*

Misty (MISS-tee) English: Full of mist. *Misty* is a suitable name for mysterious Scorpio, one of the three Water signs of the zodiac. Variations: *Misti, Mistie, Mystee, Mysti.*

Miwa (MEE-wah) Japanese: Farseeing. Scorpios are fascinated by the future and the unknown. Variation: *Miwako.*

Miya (MEE-yah) Japanese: Sacred house. Scorpio's great passion for all things spiritual makes this a most appropriate name.

Morena (mo-RAY-nah) Portuguese: Brunette. Many Scorpios are brown haired or dark haired. Variation: *Morella.*

Moriah (moh-RYE-ah) Hebrew: God is my tutor. Scorpio holds a sacred respect for religion and spirituality. Variations: *Moria, Morice, Moriel, Morit.*

Mozelle (moh-ZEH-le; moh-ZELL) Hebrew: Lifted from the dark seas. This name is a perfect choice for deep and dark Scorpio, a Water sign. Variation: *Moselle.*

Myrta (MIR-tah) Latin: In Roman mythology, the evergreen shrub *myrta* symbolized love. Passionate Scorpios take the subject of love very seriously. Variation: *Myrtle.*

Naida (NAY-dah) Latin: Water nymph. This name is a mystical choice for a girl born under Scorpio, one of the three Water signs of the zodiac.

Nari (NAHR-ee) Japanese: Thunder peal. The awe-inspiring power of thunder echoes Scorpio's strength, bravery, and emotional intensity.

Nata (NAH-tah) Native American: Creator. Pluto, Scorpio's ruling planet, governs transformation and regeneration. Scorpios are skilled at evaluating their lives and recreating themselves if necessary.

Neci (NEH-see) Latin: Intense. *Neci* is an apt name for passionate, deep, and serious Scorpio.

Nenet (neh-NET) Egyptian: For the Egyptian goddess of the deep. The sign of Scorpio is associated with all things deep, dark, and unknown.

Nepa (NEH-pah) Arabic: Walking backward. In Middle Eastern astrology, *Nepa* is another name for the sign of Scorpio.

Nika (NEE-kah) Russian: Belonging to God. Scorpios experience a special connection to the divine.

Nirveli (neer-VAY-li) Hindu: Water child. Scorpio is one of the three Water signs of the zodiac.

Nitara (ni-TAHR-ah) Sanskrit: Connected to the source. This name suggests the powerful connection many Scorpios have with divine or higher powers.

Nova (NOH-vah) Native American: Butterfly. The sign of Scorpio governs all insects and crustaceans. Like the butterfly, Scorpio is a symbol of transformation.

Nuria (noo-REE-ah) Hebrew: Fire of God. Scorpio's passion for the mystical is fiery in its intensity. Variations: *Nuri, Nuriel, Nurit*.

Oba (oh-BAH) African/Nigerian: Goddess who rules the rivers. As one of the three Water signs of the zodiac, Scorpio is associated with all types of water.

Odelia (oh-DELL-yah) Hebrew: I will praise God. A strong awareness of the divine is central to the lives of many Scorpios.

Olga (OHL-gah) Old Norse: Holy one. The realms of mysticism, religion, and the occult appeal most strongly to Scorpios, who often become spiritual leaders. Variations: *Ola, Olia, Olina, Olli, Olva*.

Oni (OH-nee) African/Nigerian: Born on holy ground. All things related to mysticism and religion hold fascination for those born under Pluto's sign.

Ophelia (oh-FEEL-yah) Greek: Aid. *Ophelia* is the name of Shakespeare's tragic young woman who passionately loved Hamlet. Passionate Scorpios love deeply, but sometimes focus their intentions on the wrong people. Variation: *Ofelia*.

Orenda (oh-REN-dah) Native American: Spirit force or mystical powers. This name connotes Scorpio's fascination with spirituality and mysticism.

Pamela (PA-muh-lah) Greek: Honey coated. *Pamela* is a pretty name for Scorpio, who governs all insects, including the honey-making bee.

Pinga (PEEN-gah) Hindu: Dark. *Pinga* is one of the names of the goddess Sakti, whose traits range between many extremes. (See *Sakti*.)

Questa (KWES-tah) French: Ever seeking. Restless, passionate, and intense, Scorpios often pursue religion in their quest to find meaning in their lives.

Ramla (RAHM-lah) African/Swahili: Fortune-teller. Scorpios are obsessed with and fascinated by all things unknown, including the future. They often seem to have powers of intuition and divination.

Ratri (rah-TREE) Hindu: Night. *Ratri* is one of the names of the goddess Sakti, known for her dual nature and extremes between light and darkness. (See *Sakti*.)

Renee (reh-NAY) French: Reborn. Pluto, Scorpio's ruling planet, governs transformation and regeneration. Variations: *Rene, René, Renée, Renelle, Rennie*.

Sachi (SAH-chee) Japanese: Bliss. Scorpios are uniquely receptive to spiritual feelings, enabling them to attain a state of bliss.

Sakti (SAHK-tee) Hindu: The greatest of the Hindu goddesses, *Sakti* represents both regeneration and destruction. This name suggests highly complex Scorpio's two extremes: an inclination toward religion and great inner strength, and a passion for things deep, dark, and mysterious. Variation: *Shakti*.

Sharissa (shah-RISS-ah) African-American: Honey princess. This name is fitting for Scorpio, who rules all insects, including the honey-making bee. *Sharissa* is a combination of *Melissa* and *Sharon*. Variations: *Shari, Sharice, Sharie, Sharine, Sherice, Sherissa*.

Sidra (SID-rah) Latin: Star borne. A deep-seated affinity for the mystical makes *Sidra* an appropriate name for otherworldly Scorpio.

Taima (tah-EE-mah) Native American: Sound of thunder. When crossed or betrayed, Scorpio is ready to strike her enemy with roaring power.

Taipa (tah-EE-pah) Native American: Spreading one's wings. Scorpios relish freedom and independence.

Taki (TAH-kee) Japanese: Waterfall. Scorpio is one of the three Water signs of the zodiac.

Tallulah (tah-LOO-lah) Native American: Water leaps to the sky. This name is a good choice for Scorpio, one of the zodiac's three Water signs. Its imagery suggests Scorpio's tendency to move to extremes. Variations: *Talli, Tallie, Talula*.

Tempest (TEHM-pist) English: Stormy. Passionate Scorpios feel all things intensely and deeply, and can be prone to turbulent eruptions when hurt or angered.

Topaz (TOH-paz) Latin: For the gem. The topaz is the birthstone of the sign of Scorpio.

Vanessa (vah-NESS-ah) Greek: Butterfly. *Vanessa* is a fitting choice for a girl born under Scorpio, which rules all insects and crustaceans, and is associated with transformation and regeneration. Variations: *Ness, Nessa, Nessie, Vanna, Vannie*.

Veda (VAY-dah) Sanskrit: Divine understanding. Scorpios seem to have special insight into all things spiritual.

Wakanda (wah-KAHN-dah) Native American: Magical power. Scorpios are fascinated by spirituality, mysticism, and the occult. Variations: *Kanda, Kenda, Wakenda.*

Zera (ZAY-rah) Hebrew: Seeds. This name suggests Scorpio's regenerative and transformational qualities.

Zina (ZEE-nah) African/Nsengan: Secret spirit name. *Zina* is a lovely name that connotes Scorpios' fascination with the mysteries of spirituality and magic. Variations: *Xena, Zena.*

Names for Scorpio Boys

Abban (A-bahn) Irish: Abbot. Scorpios, who have a passionate interest in things of religion or the occult, often become spiritual leaders.

Abbud (ah-BOOD) Arabic: Devoted. This popular Arabic name is suitable for Scorpio, who possesses great inner strength and determination.

Abdul (ahb-DOOL) Arabic: Servant of Allah. An extremely popular Middle Eastern name, *Abdul* is an appropriate choice for spiritually inclined Scorpio. Variations: *Abdalla, Abdel, Abdullah.*

Adrian (AY-dree-inn) Latin: Black. Black is one of the colors of the sign of Scorpio. Variations: *Adriano, Adrien, Adrik, Andri, Hadrian.*

Agathon (AG-ah-thon) Greek: Godly. Scorpios, who are deeply interested in religion and spirituality, often dedicate their lives to God's will.

Alein (ah-LIGHN or ah-LAYN) Yiddish: Alone. Unlike some of the more gregarious, outgoing signs, Scorpios are independent and free-spirited by nature, happy alone or in a small group of friends.

Alf (ALF) Norwegian: One who lives in the world beyond. Deep, intense, mysterious Scorpio often seems tuned to another time or place.

Amadeus (ah-mah-DAY-us) Latin: Lover of God. This name is a terrific choice for spiritually inclined Scorpio. Variations: *Amado, Amando*.

Ambrose (AM-broze) Greek: Immortal. Pluto, the planet that rules the sign of Scorpio, governs birth and death. Variations: *Abrosi, Ambroise, Ambrosio, Brose*.

Amin (AH-min or ah-MEEN) Hindu: Faithful. Scorpios, who possess great inner strength and determination, dedicate themselves wholly to people or causes they care about. Variations: *Ameen, Amitan, Amnon*.

Antares (an-TARE-ees) Greek: The name of the giant red star in the constellation of Scorpio. Its red color gives it special significance as one of Scorpio's symbolic colors.

Apollo (ah-POL-oh) Greek: Destroyer. *Apollo* was the beloved Greek and Roman god of poetry, prophecy, music, and medicine. This name is an intriguing choice for imaginative and creative Scorpio, who also is associated with healing and the unknown. Variations: *Apollos, Apolonis*.

Asa (ACE-ah) Hebrew: Healer or physician. Scorpios are deeply drawn to the healing arts and often become doctors or scientists.

Aswad (ahs-WAHD) Arabic: Dark. Scorpio's ruling planet, Pluto, governs the underworld and all things dark and mysterious.

Atman (AHT-muhn) Hindu: Soul. Deep, emotional, complex, and intense, Scorpios epitomize the word *soul*.

Aubrey (AWE-bree) Old German: Elfin king of the supernatural. Scorpios hold a special fascination for all things unknown, including the supernatural.

Azrael (AZ-ree-ell) Hebrew: *Azrael* is the name of the archangel who protects those born under the sign of Scorpio. *Azrael* is said to separate the individual's soul from the body at the time of death.

Baruch (bah-ROOK) Hebrew: Blessed. Scorpios, often very interested in religion, seem to have a special relationship with the divine.

Benjamin (BEN-jah-min) Hebrew: Son of the right hand. A classic reference to one born close to the divine, this is a traditional choice for spiritually inclined Scorpio.

Bertram (BAIR-tram) Old German: Brilliant raven. *Bertram* is a traditional and powerful name for independent and passionate Scorpio, whose symbolic colors include black. Variations: *Bartram, Bertrand.*

Biral (BEER-uhl) Aborigine: *Biral* is an ancient Australian mythological character who taught tribal customs and lore to the people of northern Australia. Mystical Scorpio has a deep reverence for religious and mythological symbols.

Bishop (BISH-up) English: Clergyman. This name, with its religious connotation, is perfect for a child born under Scorpio. Many Scorpios pursue careers in religion.

Blackburn (BLAK-burhn) Old English: Brook of black water. Scorpio is a Water sign, and black is among Scorpio's colors.

Brishen (BREE-shen) Gypsy: Storm baby. Even as children, Scorpios are tempestuous and ever changing.

Bruns (BROONS) German: Dark. Pluto, Scorpio's ruler, is associated with all things dark and mysterious.

Christian (KRIS-chin) Greek: Follower of the anointed one. This increasingly popular name is ideal for Scorpio, who often gravitates toward religion and spirituality. Variations: *Christen, Christiano, Christo, Christophe, Kristian, Kristos.*

Christopher (KRIS-toh-fuhr) Greek: He who carries Christ. Scorpios, innately drawn to spiritual experiences, may often align themselves with charismatic spiritual leaders. Variations: *Christofer, Christoforo, Kristofer, Kristofor.*

Clark (klark) Old English: Cleric in a religious order. Many Scorpios decide to pursue religious vocations. Variation: *Clarke.*

Colby (KOHL-bee) Old English: Dark haired. Scorpios are often born dark haired and dark eyed. Variations: *Colbert, Colbey.*

Cole (KOLE) Old English: Darkly complexioned. In appearance, Scorpios are typically dark skinned with dark eyes and hair.

Constant (KON-stahn) Latin: Constant and steadfast. Though their moods may change rapidly, Scorpios never waver when it comes to their beliefs.

Daniel (DAN-yul) Hebrew: God is my judge. This classic name is a fitting choice for spiritually inclined Scorpio. Variations: *Dan, Daniele, Danny, Danyel.* (Famous Scorpios: Dan Rather, news anchor; Danny DeVito, actor)

Dante (DAHN-tay) Italian: Eternally enduring. Suitable for Scorpio, this name suggests his passionate endurance.

Darby (DAHR-bee) Irish: Free. Scorpios are renowned for their fierce commitment to living life their own way. They are the archetypical nonconformists of the zodiac. Variation: *Derby*.

Darcy (DAHR-see) Irish: Dark skinned. Scorpio, symbolized by the color black, are fascinated by the mysterious darkness. Variations: *Darcey, D'Arcy, Darsey, Darsy*.

Daren (DAH-rehn) African/Nigerian: Child born at night. Pluto, Scorpio's ruling planet, governs all things dark and mysterious. Thus, Scorpios have a special affinity for the night. Variation: *Darren*.

Delano (de-LAHN-oh) Irish: Healthy black man. Black is one of the colors associated with the sign of Scorpio.

Destin (DESS-tin; dess-TEEN) French: Destiny. Scorpios are strong believers in controlling their own destiny in life. Variation: *Deston*.

Didier (dee-DYAY) Latin: Desire, longing. Also the name of several early saints, *Didier* connotes the passion of Scorpio.

Dion (DEE-on) Greek: Of Dionysus. Dionysus was the Greek god of wine, revelry, and passion. This name is an apt choice for emotional and passionate Scorpio, who possesses an indulgent, and even, decadent side. Variations: *Dinos, Dionysios*.

Dominic (DOM-in-ik) Latin: Belonging to the Lord. Scorpio's natural love of spirituality makes this name an attractive choice for natives of the sign. Variations: *Dominick, Dominique*.

Donahue (DOHN-ah-yoo) Irish: Dark warrior. When angered or betrayed, Scorpio can become a fearsome force to be reckoned with. Variations: *Don, Donnie, Donny, Donohue*.

Donnelly (DOHN-nell-ee) Irish: Brave dark man. *Donnelly* is an ideal name for those born under Scorpio, one of the most fearless signs of the zodiac and one that also is associated with darkness.

Donovan (DOHN-oh-van) Irish: Dark. Pluto, Scorpio's ruling planet, governs all things dark and mysterious.

Doron (DOHR-on or dor-OHN) Hebrew: Divine gift. Scorpio's brilliant mind and religious insight are truly gifts from above.

Dougal (DOO-gal) Celtic: Mysterious stranger. This name is an apt choice for dark, enigmatic Scorpio, who may remain a mystery even to his closest friends. Variations: *Dougald, Duggal.*

Douglas (DUG-liss) Scottish: From the black river. *Douglas* is an excellent choice for Water sign Scorpio, who is strongly associated with the color black. Variations: *Doug, Douglass.*

Dowan (DOH-wan) Irish: Black or dark. Scorpio's special colors are maroon, crimson red, and black.

Doyle (DOY-el) Irish: Descendant of the dark stranger. Scorpios often appear to be dark and mysterious creatures who reveal little.

Duane (DWAYNE) Irish: Richly dark. Scorpios are attracted to deep, lush, and dark colors, fabrics, and textures. Variations: *Dewain, Dewayne, Dwain, Dwayne.*

Duff (DUF) Irish: Black haired. Many Scorpios are born with dark or black hair.

Dugan (DOO-gin) Irish: Dark colored. Linked with the color black and with all forms of mystery, this name is well suited to Scorpio. Variations: *Doogan, Dougan, Duggan.*

Dukker (DOOK-kuhr) Gypsy: To tell fortunes or bewitch. Scorpios' metaphysical abilities often lead them to an occupation in the arts of the occult. Variation: *Duke*.

Dunham (DUNN-ahm) Irish: Dark man. Often physically dark, Scorpios also are fascinated by the dark mysteries of the unknown. Variations: *Dun, Dunam*.

Dunstan (DUN-stun) Old English: Dark stone. *Dunstan* was the name of an archbishop of Canterbury who became a saint. Darkness is an attribute of Pluto, Scorpio's ruling planet; together with the Scorpion's interest in religion, this name becomes a particularly apt choice for those born under the sign.

Dwyer (DWYE-ir) Irish: Dark wisdom. Scorpios enjoy an intuitive grasp of mystical knowledge.

Elliott (EL-lee-ut) Hebrew: Jehovah is God. Any name with religious connotations is ideal for Scorpio, who is intensely spiritual by nature. Variations: *Eliot, Elliot, Ellis, Ellison*.

Eloi (EE-loy) Latin: To choose. *Eloi* is the name of a sixth-century saint who founded a monastery and worked among the poor. The sign of Scorpio is associated with healing powers, and many Scorpios follow an independent path in deciding to pursue careers in either medicine or religion.

Enoch (EE-nok) Hebrew: Dedicated. Strong and determined, Scorpios devote all their passionate energy to things they believe in.

Ethan (EE-than) Hebrew: Unwavering. Scorpios, who possess great inner strength, can sometimes be obstinate and stubborn. Variation: *Etan*.

Ferdinand (FUR-dih-nahnd; FUR-dih-nand) German: Courageous explorer. Imaginative, passionate, energetic, and deep-thinking, Scorpios are often seasoned travelers who enjoy immersing themselves in foreign cultures. Variations: *Ferde, Ferdie, Ferdinando, Fernando, Hernando*.

Foster (FOSS-ter) Middle English: To nurse or heal. Scorpios, who have an abiding interest in the healing arts, make excellent doctors.

Gilchrist (GIL-kreest) Irish: Christ's servant. A natural affinity for religion and a willingness to explore the rigors of the spiritual path are key ingredients in Scorpio's makeup. Variations: *Gil, Gilley*.

Gitano (hee-TAHN-oh) Spanish: Gypsy. Passionate, emotional, and unconventional, Scorpios possess a gypsylike quality.

Guy (GYE) Latin: Living spirit. Intense Scorpio is one of the most spiritual signs of the zodiac. Variations: *Gui, Guido, Guyon*.

Hanif (HAH-neef or ha-NEEF) Arabic: True believer. Scorpios are blessed with unwavering faith and natural strength in their convictions.

Hercules (HER-kyoo-leez) Greek: Splendid gift; Hera's servant. *Hercules* is an unusual name for Scorpio, who possesses great strength and power. Variation: *Hercule*.

Hinun (hee-NOON) Native American: Spirit of the storm. This name suggests both Scorpio's spiritual side and stormy nature.

Homer (HOH-mur) Greek: Pledged. When Scorpio dedicates himself to someone or something, nothing can dissuade him. Variations: *Homere, Homeros, Homerus, Omer, Omeros*.

Ian (EE-an) Scotch: Gracious gift of God. Scorpio's sensitivity and commitment to visionary change makes him truly "heaven-sent." Variation of *John*. Variation: *Ion*.

Ingram (ING-ram) English: Raven. Black is one of the special colors associated with the sign of Scorpio. Variation: *Ingraham.*

Ishmael (ISH-mah-eh or ISH-mayl) Hebrew: God listens. This name suggests Scorpio's natural openness to religion and spirituality. Variations: *Ismael, Ismail.*

Isidore (IZ-eh-dorr) Greek: Isis's blessing. In Egyptian mythology, the goddess Isis granted Osiris the gift of rebirth. Scorpio rules regeneration and the transformation of death into life. Variations: *Isadore, Isidor, Isidoro, Izzy.*

Iye (EE-yeh) Native American: Smoky clouds. Scorpios are often associated with the dark imagery of their ruler, Pluto, who governs the underworld.

Jadon (JAY-don) Hebrew: God has heard. This popular name is indicative of Scorpio's special bond with the spiritual world. Variations: *Jaden, Jaedon, Jaydon.*

Jahi (JAH-hee) African/Swahili: Honor. Courageous, determined, and idealistic, Scorpio easily earns high respect from others.

Jason (JAY-son) Greek: One who heals. The sign of Scorpio is associated with religion and healing. Variations: *Jace, Jaison, Jasen, Jay, Jayce, Jayson.*

Jedediah (je-deh-DYE-ah) Hebrew: God's beloved. Attuned to religious principles and to the divine, Scorpio is truly a child of God. Variations: *Jebediah, Jed, Jedd.*

Jedrek (JEDD-rick) Polish: Mighty man. The great inner strength and power of Scorpio is famous. Variations: *Jedrick, Jedrus.*

Jeremiah (jeh-ah-MYE-ah) Hebrew: God exalts. *Jeremiah* was the old testament prophet who believed that true religion was found in the human heart. Names with religious connotations are ideal for spiritually inclined Scorpio. Variations: *Jem, Jeremias, Jeremiya, Jeremy, Jerimiah, Jerry.*

Jerome (jer-ROHM) Greek: Calling. *Jerome* is the patron saint of archeologists and scholars. Scorpios, who esteem history, legacy, and inheritance, often pursue careers in archeology. Variations: *Gerome, Gerry, Jeremy, Jerrome, Jerry.*

Jordan (JORR-den) Hebrew: Flowing down. This name is given to those baptized in the holy waters of the Jordan River. *Jordan* is an appropriate name for Water sign, Scorpio, who is fascinated by religion and spirituality.

Joshua (JOSH-oo-ah) Hebrew: God saves. With a deep understanding of spiritual truths, Scorpio merits the special attention of the divine. Variations: *Josh, Josua, Jozua.*

Juro (joo-ROH) Japanese: Tenth son. Many Scorpios are born in October, the tenth month of the calendar year.

Kabil (kah-BEEL) Turkish: Possessed. Scorpio's ruling planet, Pluto, often influences Scorpio's obsessive and compulsive qualities.

Kade (KAYD) Scotch Gaelic: From the wetlands. *Kade* is a unique choice for Water sign Scorpio.

Kado (KAH-doh) Japanese: Gateway. Scorpio is the sign of the dark and the mysterious, of regeneration and transformation. Many Scorpios, who often become spiritual or mystical leaders, see themselves as conduits of transformational, life-changing energy.

Kalkin (kahl-KEEN) Hindu: *Kalkin* is the name of a Hindu god who, it is believed, will arrive during a future Age of Darkness. This name is doubly apt for Scorpios, who possess visionary insight into the future and are associated with the period of darkness that eventually results in rebirth.

Kearn (KURN) Irish: Dark. Pluto, Scorpio's ruling planet, governs all things dark and mysterious.

Keb (KEBB) Egyptian: *Keb* is a god immortalized in the Egyptian Book of the Dead, where it is said he laid an egg from which the world hatched. This name suggests the regenerative and transformational qualities associated with Scorpio.

Keir (KEER) Gaelic: Black. Black is one of the colors of the sign of Scorpio. Variations: *Keiron, Kerr, Kieran, Kieron.*

Kern (KURN) Irish: Dark-haired boy. Scorpios are commonly born with dark hair. Variations: *Kearn, Kerne.*

Kerr (KIR or KAR) Irish: Black. Black is one of the special colors associated with the sign of Scorpio.

Kerry (KER-ree) Irish: Father's dark child. This name is ideal for a deep and intense Scorpio child. Variations: *Keary, Kerrigan.*

Kerwin (KUR-win) Irish: Baby with dark eyes. This name is appropriate for a brown-eyed Scorpio boy. Variations: *Kervin, Kervyn, Kerwen, Kirwin.*

Kibbe (KEEB-beh) Native American: Night bird. Because of the influence of Pluto, their ruling planet, Scorpios have a special affinity for the dark, mysterious night.

Killian (KIL-ee-an) Irish: Problems. Scorpio's strong emotions and fierce determination to do things his way often offend those around him. Variations: *Kilian, Killie, Killy.*

Kirk (KURK) Old Norse: Church. Scorpio is drawn to all things spiritual, mystical, or occult. Variations: *Kerk, Kirke.*

Kirkley (KURK-lee) Old English: Meadow by a church. Scorpios have a close connection with religion and its imagery. Variations: *Kirklee, Kirklie*.

Kirkwood (KURK-wood) Old English: Forest by a church. This unusual name suggests Scorpio's ties to religion, along with the darker shades of the sign's mysterious side.

Kistna (KIST-nah) Hindu: For the name of the sacred river in India. Scorpios revere religious and mystical rituals and relics.

Lazarus (LAH-zah-rus) Hebrew: God will help. This traditional name, with biblical origins, is fitting for Scorpio, the sign of spiritual energy, birth, death, and regeneration. In the New Testament, *Lazarus* was raised from the dead by Jesus Christ. Variations: *Eleaser, Laza, Lazare, Lazaro*.

Lemuel (LEMM-you-el) Hebrew: Devoted to God. This name is an appropriate choice for Scorpio, who is committed to the pursuit of divine truths. Variations: *Lem, Lemmie*.

Leor (leh-OHR) Hebrew: Light descends into me. Mystical Scorpio may become a vessel for spiritual illumination.

Leron (leh-ROHN) Hebrew: Song of my soul. This popular Hebrew name suggests Scorpio's intensely emotional spirit. Variations: *Lerone, Liron, Lirone*.

Lev (LEHV) Hebrew: Heart. Passionate and emotional Scorpio loves deeply and feels everything intensely. Variation: *Leb*.

Li Ko (LEE-koh) Chinese: Buddhist nun. This traditional Chinese Buddhist name is given to a child for protection by Buddha. Scorpios are interested in all types of religion and spirituality.

Lukman (look-MAHN) Arabic: Seer. Scorpios are fascinated by the future.

Macdougal (mac-DOOG-ahl) Irish: The dark stranger's son. Darkness and mystery are strongly associated with the sign of Scorpio. Variations: *Dougal, Mack.*

Makarios (Ma-KA-rios) Greek: Anointed. This name is a fitting choice for Scorpio, who possesses the qualities required for spiritual greatness. Variations: *Macario, Maccario, Maccarios, Marcarios.*

Malachi (MA-la-kye) Hebrew: God's messenger. Because they are so attuned to the mystical, Scorpios often serve as a conduit for metaphysical truths. Variations: *Malachai, Malachy.*

Malcolm (MAL-kum) Gaelic: Servant of Saint Columba. Saint Columbia was a fifth-century Irish missionary who founded several monasteries. Scorpios are frequently drawn to the religious life.

Maloney (mal-LOH-nee) Irish: Church-going. Scorpios have a strong association with religion and spirituality. Variations: *Malone, Malony.*

Manuel (mahn-WELL) Hebrew: God is with us. A love of the divine is a deep-seated part of the Scorpio character. Variations: *Emanuel, Immanuel, Manny, Mano.*

Marcus (MAHR-kuss) Latin: Rebellious. Scorpios are the passionate nonconformists of the zodiac. Variations: *Marc, Marco, Marcos, Mark, Marko, Markos, Marqus.*

Matthew (MATH-yoo) Hebrew: Divine present. Scorpio is the sign of the courageous visionary who is dedicated to the healing of humankind—truly a gift from God. Variations: *Mathew, Mathias, Mathieu, Matt, Matteo, Matty.*

Maurice (maw-REESE; MORE-iss) English: Black Moor. The colors associated with Scorpio are maroon, crimson red, and black. Variations: *Maurie, Maury, Morey, Moris, Morrill, Morris, Morrison, Morry, Moss.*

Maynard (MAY-nahrd) Old English: Hard strength. Scorpios are renowned for their obstinacy and emotional endurance. Variations: *Maynhard, Meinhard, Mendar.*

Merlin (MUR-len) French: Blackbird. The name of the great and wise wizard of Arthurian legend is an intriguing choice for mystically inclined Scorpio. Also, black is one of Scorpio's symbolic colors. Variations: *Merle, Merlyn.*

Micah (MY-kah) Hebrew: Who is like God? With their delight in the divine, Scorpios look to spiritual means for inspiration in their own lives. Variation: *Micaiah.*

Michael (MY-kul) Hebrew: Who compares to God? This immensely popular name, with its religious connotations, is ideal for spiritual Scorpio. Variations: *Micah, Michel, Michele, Mick, Micky, Migael, Mikael, Mike, Mikhail, Mikie, Misha.* (Famous Scorpios: Michael Landon, actor; Mike Nichols)

Munchin (MUN-chin) Irish: Little monk. Many Scorpios find themselves drawn to the religious life. Variation: *Mainchin.*

Murdock (MUR-dock) Scotch Gaelic: Warrior-sailor. This name is a marvelous choice for the Water sign Scorpio, which is renowned for passionate loyalty and fierce commitment to those served. Variations: *Murdoch, Murtaugh.*

Murphy (MUR-fee) Irish: Soldier of the seas. As a Water sign, Scorpio has a deep affinity for the ocean.

Nen (NENN) Egyptian: Ancient waters. Scorpio is one of the three Water signs of the zodiac. In Egyptian mythology, *Nen* (half-man and half-frog) was the spirit of the primal seas from which life sprung.

Nevan (NEH-van) Irish: Little holy one. Religion and spirituality appeal to Scorpios, who make great efforts to live according to their ideals. Variations: *Naomhan, Nev, Nevan, Nevin.*

Nicabar (nee-kah-BAHR) Gypsy: Secret taking. Although mysterious and deep Scorpio reveals little, he loves to know the secrets of others.

Nigel (NYE-jehl) Latin: Dark. Pluto, Scorpio's ruling planet, governs all things dark and mysterious.

Nikita (nee-KEE-tah) Greek: Unconquered. Scorpios passionately cherish their independent and nonconformist ways.

Nissim (nee-SEEM) Hebrew: Heavenly omen. This popular Hebrew name is ideal for Scorpio, who strongly believes in the power of divine prophecy.

Octavius (ahk-TAH-vee-us) Latin: Eighth. Scorpio is the eighth sign of the zodiac. Variations: *Octave, Octavian, Octavio, Octavo.*

Okon (oh-KOHN) African/Efik: Born at night. Scorpios have a fascination with all things dark and mysterious.

Oleg (OH-legh) Russian: Sacred. Scorpio is in tune with the awesome force of the divine as it is expressed in earthly life.

Omar (OH-mahr) Arabic: Supreme devotee; also means astrologer. Scorpios have a keen, intuitive sense of astrology. Variation: *Omarr.*

Oscar (OSS-ker) Old English: Sacred sword. This name reflects Scorpio's fierce valor and deep commitment to divine beliefs. Variations: *Oskar, Ossie, Ozzy.*

Osmond (OZ-mund) Old English: Godly defense. Daunting intellectual powers combined with strong spiritual convictions make this name an ideal choice for heroic Scorpio. Variation: *Osman.*

Oswin (OZ-winn) Old English: Friend in spirit. Although Scorpios often seem distant and reveal little about themselves, they make wonderful, compassionate, and devoted friends to those they trust. Variations: *Osvin, Oswinn, Oswyn.*

Oved (OH-vehd) Hebrew: Devotee. Possessed with great inner strength, Scorpios dedicate themselves wholly to what they believe in.

Peregrine (PER-reh-grin) Latin: Pilgrm. While Scorpios are drawn to religion, some wander from one denomination to another in search of what has the greatest meaning for them. Variations: *Peregin, Peregryn.*

Phineas (FINN-ee-us) Hebrew: Prophecy. Scorpios, who are fascinated by the future, are credited with having gifts of divination.

Phoenix (FEE-niks) Greek: The name of the bird that regenerated and arose from the ashes. The phoenix became the symbol of immortality and rebirth, qualities deeply associated with the sign of Scorpio. Variation: *Phenix.*

Pillan (pee-LAHN) Native American: God of stormy weather. Scorpios are prone to turbulent mood swings.

Price (PRYCE) Welsh: Passion's son. One of the most prominent characteristics of Scorpio is an intensely passionate nature. Variations: *Brice, Bryce, Pryce.*

Ragner (RAG-nur) Old Norse: Powerful forces. This popular Scandinavian name connotes Scorpio's great inner strength and power. Variations: *Ragnor, Rainer, Rainier, Rayner.*

Rees (REES) Welsh: Passion. Scorpio is the most passionate and intense of all the zodiac's signs. Variations: *Reese, Rhys.*

Rene (reh-NAY) French: Reborn. Pluto, Scorpio's ruling planet, is associated with regeneration and transformation. Variations: *Renato, René, Renne, Rennie, Renny.* (Famous Scorpio: René Magritte, painter)

Rudo (ROO-doh) African/Zimbabwean: Love. Passionate Scorpios love deeply and expect to be loved deeply in return.

Salvador (sahl-vah-DOHR; SAL-vah-dor) Spanish: The savior. The sign of Scorpio is strongly associated with healing. Variations: *Javier, Salvidor, Xavier.*

Samuel (SAM-yu-ull) Hebrew: God's word. *Samuel* is a fitting choice for a boy born under Scorpio, the sign most strongly affiliated with religion. Variations: *Sam, Sammy.* (Famous Scorpios: Sam Shepherd, actor and Pulitzer Prize-winning playwright; Sam Waterston, actor)

Santo (SAHN-toh) Spanish: Sacred. Scorpios revere all things religious and spiritual.

Seth (SETH) Hebrew: Appointed. Scorpios, who revere religion and spirituality, often feel a special connection to God.

Shen (SHEN) Chinese: Spirit or contemplation. Scorpios are renowned for their deep thinking and spiritual inclinations.

Shen (SHEN) Egyptian: The *shen* is a sacred amulet described in the Egyptian Book of the Dead. It symbolizes eternal life, or immortality, a quality closely associated with the sign of Scorpio.

Shiloh (SHY-loh) Hebrew: He who is sent. *Shiloh,* another name used to describe the Messiah, is also the name of a town that became a safe sanctuary for the tribes of Israel. Names with religious connotations are wonderful choices for Scorpio, who is attuned to religion and spirituality.

Smokey (SMOH-kee) English: Smoky or the color of smoke. Scorpios are associated with all things dark and mysterious.

Sterne (STURN) Old English: Unwavering. Scorpios possess great inner strength and determination. Variations: *Stearne, Stern*.

Sullivan (SULL-ih-venn) Irish: Dark and burning eyes. Many Scorpios are born dark haired and dark eyed. Variation: *Sully*.

Thanos (THAHN-ohs) Greek: Eternal existence. Pluto, Scorpio's ruler, is associated with life and death, as well as immortality. Variations: *Athanasios, Thanasis*.

Theodore (THEE-oh-dorr) Greek: Divine present. The sign of Scorpio is strongly associated with religion and spirituality, and those born under the sign are said to be blessed with spiritual gifts. Variations: *Ted, Teddy, Teodor, Teodoro, Theo, Theodor*. (Famous Scorpios: Theodore Roosevelt, American president; Ted Turner, media giant)

Titus (TYE-tuss) Greek: Of the giants. This name is suitable for formidable Scorpio, who at times can seem larger than life. In Greek mythology, *Titus* was a giant who was slain by the god Apollo. *Titus* is also the name of a Greek saint.

Toussaint (too-SAHN) French: All saints. Those born on All Saints' Day, November first, are governed by the spiritually inclined sign of Scorpio.

Tristan (TRIS-tenn) Celtic: Melancholy. Scorpios may be prone to moodiness and depression. Variations: *Tris, Tristram*.

Uriah (you-RYE-ah) Hebrew: Jehovah is my light. Scorpios possess a keen interest in religion.

Valerian (vah-LEER-ee-unn) Latin: Potent. Passionate and intense, Scorpios possess great inner strength and determination. Variations: *Valerio, Valery.*

Vincent (VIN-sent) Latin: Embraces powerfully. Scorpios may become extremely attached when they are committed to something that fascinates them. Variations: *Vin, Vince, Vincence, Vincenz, Vincenzo.*

Zachary (ZAH-ka-ree) Hebrew: Remembered by the Lord. *Zachary* is a suitable choice for a boy born under Scorpio, the sign strongly associated with religion and spirituality. Many Scorpios are drawn to religious vocations. Variations: *Zach, Zachariah, Zachery, Zack, Zeke.*

Famous Scorpios

10-24-1904	Moss Hart	10-27-1939	John Cleese
10-24-1936	David Nelson	10-27-1946	Carrie Snodgress
10-24-1939	F. Murray Abraham	10-27-1951	Jayne Kennedy
10-24-1947	Kevin Kline	10-28-1927	Cleo Laine
10-25-1881	Pablo Picasso	10-28-1936	Charlie Daniels
10-25-1886	Leo G. Carroll	10-28-1944	Dennis Franz
10-25-1912	Minnie Pearl	10-28-1949	Bruce Jenner
10-25-1924	Billy Barty	10-28-1955	Bill Gates
10-25-1941	Helen Reddy	10-28-1967	Julia Roberts
10-25-1944	Jon Anderson	10-29-1891	Fanny Brice
10-25-1963	Tracy Nelson	10-29-1947	Richard Dreyfuss
10-26-1911	Mahalia Jackson	10-29-1948	Kate Jackson
10-26-1914	Jackie Coogan	10-29-1971	Winona Ryder
10-26-1942	Bob Hoskins	10-30-1735	John Adams
10-26-1947	Hillary Rodham Clinton	10-30-1885	Ezra Pound
10-26-1947	Pat Sajak	10-30-1893	Charles Atlas
10-26-1947	Jaclyn Smith	10-30-1896	Ruth Gordon
10-26-1954	Lauren Tewes	10-30-1912	Gordon Parks
10-27-1858	Theodore Roosevelt	10-30-1932	Louis Malle
10-27-1872	Emily Post	10-30-1937	Claude Lelouche
10-27-1914	Dylan Thomas	10-30-1939	Grace Slick
10-27-1920	Nanette Fabray	10-30-1945	Henry Winkler
10-27-1923	Roy Lichtenstein	10-30-1951	Harry Hamlin
10-27-1924	Ruby Dee		

10-30-1960	Diego Armando Maradona	11-06-1854	John Philip Sousa
		11-06-1861	James Naismith
10-31-1632	Jan Vermeer	11-06-1887	Walter Perry Johnson
10-31-1795	John Keats	11-06-1931	Mike Nichols
10-31-1860	Juliette Lowe	11-06-1946	Sally Field
10-31-1887	Chiang Kai-shek	11-06-1955	Maria Shriver
10-31-1900	Ethel Waters	11-07-1867	Madame Curie
10-31-1912	Dale Evans	11-07-1903	Dean Jagger
10-31-1922	Barbara Bel Geddes	11-07-1918	Billy Graham
10-31-1931	Dan Rather	11-07-1922	Al Hirt
10-31-1936	Michael Landon	11-07-1926	Joan Sutherland
10-31-1942	David Ogden Stiers	11-07-1943	Joni Mitchell
10-31-1950	John Candy	11-07-1959	Keith Lockhart
10-31-1950	Jane Pauley	11-08-1900	Margaret Mitchell
11-01-1871	Stephen Crane	11-08-1927	Patti Page
11-01-1957	Lyle Lovett	11-08-1931	Morley Safer
11-01-1972	Jenny McCarthy	11-08-1933	Esther Rolle
11-02-1795	James K. Polk	11-08-1949	Bonnie Raitt
11-02-1901	Paul Ford	11-08-1951	Mary Hart
11-02-1913	Burt Lancaster	11-09-1913	Hedy Lamarr
11-02-1914	Ray Walston	11-09-1918	Spiro Agnew
11-02-1938	Pat Buchanan	11-09-1934	Carl Sagan
11-02-1942	Stefanie Powers	11-09-1936	Mary Travers
11-02-1961	k.d. lang	11-09-1952	Lou Ferrigno
11-03-1921	Charles Bronson	11-10-1483	Martin Luther
11-03-1952	Roseanne	11-10-1889	Claude Rains
11-03-1953	Dennis Miller	11-10-1925	Richard Burton
11-03-1954	Adam Ant	11-10-1932	Roy Scheider
11-04-1879	Will Rogers	11-10-1944	Tim Rice
11-04-1916	Walter Cronkite	11-10-1949	Donna Fargo
11-04-1918	Art Carney	11-10-1956	Sinbad
11-04-1919	Martin Balsam	11-10-1959	MacKenzie Phillips
11-04-1937	Loretta Swit	11-11-1885	General George Patton
11-04-1950	Markie Post	11-11-1899	Pat O'Brien
11-04-1954	Yanni	11-11-1904	Alger Hiss
11-04-1962	Ralph Macchio	11-11-1922	Kurt Vonnegut, Jr.
11-05-1905	Joel McCrea	11-11-1925	Jonathan Winters
11-05-1911	Roy Rogers	11-11-1935	Bibi Andersson
11-05-1913	Vivien Leigh	11-11-1962	Demi Moore
11-05-1931	Ike Turner	11-11-1974	Leonardo DiCaprio
11-05-1940	Elke Sommer	11-12-1840	Auguste Rodin
11-05-1941	Art Garfunkel	11-12-1918	Jo Stafford
11-05-1943	Sam Shepard	11-12-1929	Grace Kelly
11-05-1959	Bryan Adams	11-12-1934	Charles Manson
11-05-1963	Tatum O'Neal	11-12-1943	Wallace Shawn

11-12-1944	Al Michaels	11-17-1944	Tom Seaver
11-12-1945	Neil Young	11-18-1908	Imogene Coca
11-12-1961	Nadia Comaneci	11-18-1923	Alan Shepard, Jr.
11-12-1970	Tonya Harding	11-18-1939	Brenda Vaccaro
11-13-1850	Robert Louis Stevenson	11-18-1942	Linda Evans
11-13-1856	Louis Brandeis	11-19-1905	Tommy Dorsey
11-13-1915	Nathaniel Benchley	11-19-1917	Indira Gandhi
11-13-1922	Oskar Werner	11-19-1933	Larry King
11-13-1938	Jean Seberg	11-19-1936	Dick Cavett
11-13-1949	Whoopi Goldberg	11-19-1938	Ted Turner
11-14-1765	Robert Fulton	11-19-1942	Calvin Klein
11-14-1840	Claude Monet	11-19-1961	Meg Ryan
11-14-1889	Jawaharlal Nehru	11-19-1962	Jodie Foster
11-14-1900	Aaron Copland	11-19-1977	Kerri Strug
11-14-1904	Dick Powell	11-20-1908	Alistair Cooke
11-14-1909	Senator Joseph McCarthy	11-20-1925	Robert F. Kennedy
		11-20-1926	Kaye Ballard
11-14-1910	Rosemary DeCamp	11-20-1927	Estelle Parsons
11-14-1921	Brian Keith	11-20-1932	Richard Dawson
11-14-1929	McLean Stevenson	11-20-1939	Dick Smothers
11-14-1948	Prince Charles	11-20-1943	Veronica Hamel
11-15-1887	Georgia O'Keeffe	11-20-1956	Bo Derek
11-15-1929	Ed Asner	11-21-1694	Jean Francois Voltaire
11-15-1932	Petula Clark	11-21-1785	William Beaumont
11-15-1940	Sam Waterston	11-21-1898	René Magritte
11-15-1945	Frida Lyngstad	11-21-1920	Stan Musial
11-16-1908	Burgess Meredith	11-21-1927	Joseph Campanella
11-16-1916	Daws Butler	11-21-1938	Marlo Thomas
11-16-1964	Dwight Gooden	11-21-1941	Juliet Mills
11-16-1967	Lisa Bonet	11-21-1944	Harold Ramis
11-17-1901	Lee Strasberg	11-21-1945	Goldie Hawn
11-17-1925	Rock Hudson	11-21-1966	Troy Aikman
11-17-1938	Gordon Lightfoot	11-22-1899	Hoagy Carmichael
11-17-1942	Martin Scorsese	11-22-1921	Rodney Dangerfield
11-17-1943	Lauren Hutton	11-22-1932	Robert Vaughn
11-17-1944	Danny DeVito	11-22-1943	Billie Jean King
11-17-1944	Lorne Michaels	11-22-1958	Jamie Lee Curtis
		11-22-1961	Mariel Hemingway

SAGITTARIUS
(November 23–December 21)

GLYPH: ♐
SYMBOL: The Archer
POLARITY: Masculine
QUALITY: Mutable
ELEMENT: Fire
RULING PLANET: Jupiter
BIRTHSTONE: Turquoise
SPECIAL COLOR: Purple
FLOWERS: Holly, narcissus, and dandelion
METAL: Tin
ANIMAL: Horse
MOST LIKEABLE TRAITS: Enthusiasm, optimism, and friendliness

♐

Much like the soaring arrow associated with their sign, Sagittarians are the unstoppable highfliers of the zodiac—sharp, insightful, and freedom-loving adventurers with wildly curious minds and effervescent personalities. Sagittarians are always on an exhilarating quest for new ideas, experiences, and relationships. This is the sign of wisdom and philosophical ideas, but also the sign of the hunt or chase, and many Sagittarians seem to spend their lives in perpetual pursuit of some elusive truth or ideal. If they never seem to quite reach their goals, however, this typical trait of the sign should not come as a surprise. Sagittarians are not really interested in arriving at a final destination or in capturing some final prize. Rather, the thrill of the journey itself, and the adventures that exploration brings, motivate Sagittarians. And because they bring to their unique life quests a bubbling optimism, fabulous good humor, innate joyfulness, and utter lack of guile, Sagittarians are among the most exciting, adored, and charmed—if sometimes impulsive—children of the zodiac.

General Qualities

Sagittarius is a Masculine and Mutable Fire sign that is ruled by the largest of the planets, Jupiter. In Roman mythology, Jupiter (or Jove) was the chief of the Roman gods who governed wisdom, philosophy, justice, the heavens, light, and affairs of state. But the god Jupiter also governed more sensual and bacchanalian pursuits and was renowned for his love of women and good food.

This seemingly disparate duality between the higher ideals of the mind and the earthly desires of the body is very much present in those children born under the sign of Sagittarius. For this reason, the sign is symbolized by one of the most unusual of the zodiac's icons—the Archer.

Sagittarius's Archer is, in fact, a representation of the mythological Roman centaur, Chiron, a creature who was half-human and half-horse. The human side of the Archer—the arms poised with bow and arrow and the head and eyes lifted to the sky— symbolizes the Sagittarian love of wisdom, philosophy, high ideals, and the pursuit of truth: The archer and the arrow aim high and far toward lofty goals. But the animal side of the Archer—the horse's powerful torso—represents the Sagittarian love of the hunt, the outdoors, the sensual, and the practical and immediate: The feet of the archer are always firmly planted on the ground and in the here-and-now.

This unique double nature of Sagittarius is often hidden and deceptively complex. In fact, many Sagittarians spend their lives attempting to reconcile the more esoteric side of their personalities with their earthier side. Fortunately, Sagittarians have such wonderfully energetic and optimistic natures that they are more than able to rise to the challenge.

The jovial influence of the planet Jupiter endows the Sagittarian child with one of the most sparkling personalities in the zodiac. Jupiter governs opportunity, good luck, material bounty, expansiveness, and optimism, and it rules all types of travel, exploration, and adventure.

Jupiter-ruled Sagittarians are invariably happy and free spirits who throw themselves, body and soul, into the banquet of life. They cherish freedom and new experiences, relish the challenge of the open road, and rarely let temporary obstacles and setbacks get them down. In fact, their physical and emotional resiliency is astonishing and, like Virgos, Sagittarians are robustly healthy. They thrive on adventure, remain invariably upbeat and cheerful, and make generous, ardent, and amusing friends. Indeed, the Sagittarian sense of humor and keen appreciation of the comic absurd is legendary. Among the more brilliant "fools" born under this sign are Woody Allen, Harpo Marx, Charles Schulz, Bette Midler, James Thurber, Mark Twain, Richard Pryor, Tim Conway, Garry Shandling, Redd Foxx, Dick Van Dyke, Emmett Kelly, and Flip Wilson.

The Masculine influence in this sign endows Sagittarians with their trademark optimism, energy, and expansiveness. Sagittarians are among the great doers of the zodiac, wholeheartedly throwing all their energies into whatever project or adventure comes their way. Their sparkling and magnanimous personalities make them adept at recruiting others to help them get a job done.

This ability to recruit others to help them complete tasks is an especially important strength of Sagittarians, because beneath their great energy and pursuit of lofty goals is a decided tendency toward restlessness, impatience, and impulsiveness. In fact, they are often accused of being fickle and having little staying power. But the truth is that life is so rich and challenging to adventure-seeking Sagittarians that they constantly feel they don't have enough time to do everything they want—and then frequently crowd too much into their agendas. With this tendency to overdo, Sagittarians show an inclination to procrastinate about completing projects until the very last minute, or to abandon tasks halfway through, simply because something more interesting comes along. It is not uncommon to find Sagittarians juggling many projects and tasks at one time and, under the gun—and with some help—they eventually bring everything to a happy closure.

The Mutable quality of this sign underscores the Sagittarian tendency to do many things at once. Mutability endows Sagittarians with highly adaptable natures and the ability to throw themselves into new situations with utter and joyful aplomb. Sagittarians are open to any challenge, rarely hold a grudge, never take criticism to heart for long, and always have their eyes on tomorrow, not yesterday. Yet their approach to life is rarely frenetic or aggressive unlike the other Masculine Fire signs, Leo and Aries.

Sagittarius's great driving energy to understand, explore, and interpret all the varied flavors that the world has to offer is remarkably self-controlled and directed. Sagittarians are not dabblers or social butterflies. They are genuine free spirits with fully formed and healthy egos. They know who they are and what they want, but they always hold the reins of life loosely. The expansive good cheer of Jupiter and the Mutable adaptability of the sign combine to make Sagittarians among the most relaxed and even-tempered children of the zodiac.

The influence of Fire in Sagittarius helps fuel the trademark Masculine energy of the sign and endows Sagittarians with tremendous verve, enthusiasm, and high hopes. Their infectious and joyous personalities are surefire magnets for other people's attention and admiration, but unlike Leos, who often use their Fire-fueled magnetism to further their personal goal of being number one, Sagittarians rarely have any hidden agendas. Remarkably straightforward and guileless, they are genuine people lovers. With Sagittarians, what you see is what you get.

Home

Sagittarius is the child who simply refuses to be confined. Rigid schedules, fancy clothes, and pointless rules are not for him or her. Absolute freedom—physical, mental, and emotional—and the opportunity to roam, wander, explore, and investigate the outer boundaries of their small worlds are the primary directives of happy Sagittarians. If parents can understand and accept the Sagittarian child's compelling need for independence and exploration even at a very young age, the reward is one of the most joyful, fun loving, and funniest of the zodiac's children.

Sagittarian children's natural and simple happiness, together with their straightforward and frank approach to life, make them among the most enjoyable and easygoing of children. Like their near cousins, Libras, Sagittarians are "low-maintenance" children. They require very little in the way of outside stimulation, and they don't need a lot of things or toys to hold their attention or teach them about the world. Sagittarians learn about the world by living and experiencing it firsthand, head-on. Eminently resourceful, imaginative, and upbeat, Sagittarians view all of life as an opportunity for fun and games, and anything or anyone that the world throws their way is an opportunity for adventure, exploration, and learning.

Young Sagittarians feed their need to hunt, explore, challenge, and understand the environment around them through hard and challenging play. From this playful initial understanding of the world, Sagittarians go on to construct a formidable and one-of-a-kind approach to tackling life's challenges that is equal parts confidence, courage, humor, joy, and bravado. Provide Sagittarian children with lots of wide-open playing space (preferably outdoors), opportunities to make as many friends as possible, and the time and freedom to play long and hard without too much parental interference.

With Sagittarian children, be prepared to answer many, many questions about anything and everything. Along with an almost insatiable curiosity about life, free-spirited and independence-loving Sagittarians also have an innate need to challenge the status quo—any status quo! They want to know the whys and wherefores of every rule and regulation put before them.

Sagittarians aren't purposely obstreperous; on the contrary, they are remarkably accommodating and adaptable. But this is the sign that governs both wisdom and pushing the envelope to its absolute limit. Sagittarians need to know not only the how, but the why of the world around them, and they are persistent and gifted verbal duelists. Their constant need to know can sometimes be exasperating, and no one understands this better than wise and intuitive Sagittarians, who genuinely care about the happiness—and the limits—of those around them. Thus, they are adept at diffusing tense situations with ample doses of good humor (as Sagittarius is also the sign of the clown), and can be downright hilarious and even ribald.

School and Play

Despite the fact that Sagittarius is ruled by Jupiter, the planet of wisdom and higher learning, the urge to play and explore is very strong in young Sagittarians and remains the singular leit-motif throughout most of their primary school years. Long after other children have settled down and become serious about their studies, Sagittarians are still bedazzled by all the opportunities for fun, adventure, and learning that the real world has to offer. And in the real world, unlike school, Sagittarians are unfettered by stultifying rules and requirements.

When Sagittarians happen to find a particular subject that consumes their interest they invariably excel in it. And they are also enormously popular with students and teachers alike. But academic excellence is not usually a primary goal of the young Sagittarian, so parents who cherish academic achievement should not despair. Children born under this sign are renowned for pursuing higher learning later in life, when they have put behind them the adventurous forays of their youth. Then Sagittarians apply to their studies all of their driving need to explore, understand, and illuminate the ultimate truths of life.

At play, young Sagittarians are natural athletes who frequently excel on the playing field in almost any competitive team sport. They shine in track and field and make excellent equestrians. Few things intimidate insatiably curious Sagittarians, and physical obstacles are embraced head-on. Sagittarians therefore experience more than their fair share of minor accidents and mishaps. But their great physical resilience and high-spirited optimism get them back in the saddle in no time, fearless as ever.

Sagittarians have a keen affinity for the outdoors. Nature in all its forms and all its abundance is the Sagittarian child's natural milieu. Any form of physical activity—climbing, hiking, swimming, running, and horseback riding, among others—captures and engages the Sagittarian's attention and imagination. And with their engaging and forceful personalities, Sagittarians easily organize large armies of friends for any number of wild expeditions around the neighborhood.

Sagittarians also relish camping out in the wild and really roughing it. While other young children may be frightened in the wilderness, surrounded only by the dark and wide expanse of the night sky and the shrill and mysterious calls of wild animals, Sagittarians are in their element, thrilled by all the spectacle that nature has to offer.

The World

Given unconventional Sagittarius's love of the wild and predilection for adventure and intrigue, many are surprised to discover that this is also the sign of high intellectual achievement, philosophy, and Socratic discourse. Strongly influenced by Jupiter, the planet that above all else rules wisdom, many Sagittarians later in life turn their keen love of exploring the natural delights of the world into an equally enthusiastic pursuit of higher learning and philosophical ideals. Sagittarians often make gifted teachers, particularly in one-on-one mentor-student relationships. They particularly shine in the areas of philosophy and theology. Alternately, with their sharp minds and considerable communication skills, Sagittarians also make formidable prosecuting attorneys, who are relentless in their pursuit of truth and justice.

Writing, communication, and publishing are all key Sagittarian fields. Inspired by wise and expansive Jupiter, making them clearheaded, single-minded, and utterly frank in their view of life, Sagittarians are sharp and able craftsmen of the written word and inspired interpreters of the vagaries of the world. This sign includes many fine writers, such as Eugene Ionesco, James Agee, Louisa May Alcott, Jonathan Swift, Mark Twain, David Mamet, Joseph Conrad, James Thurber, John Milton, Emily Dickinson, Shirley Jackson, Noel Coward, and William Blake.

Given their natural intelligence, abundant good spirits, and considerable ability to inspire people to work together for a common cause, Sagittarians can excel in almost any field that fully engages their curious, unconventional, and inquiring hearts and minds and offers them a wide variety of interesting and challenging tasks. Although publishing is a quintessential Sagittarian career, the fields of natural science, travel, archeology, and history also hold a strong appeal.

Socially Sagittarians are among the most popular people of the zodiac: joyful, enthusiastic, easygoing, optimistic, funny, and endearing. They are ardent and devoted friends who give freely of their time, attention, and energy, and demand little in return.

Romantically, however, Sagittarians are reluctant to settle down and make a commitment. Their lifelong wanderlust, love of adventure, and fierce need for independence make them unlikely candidates for marriage. If they do marry, they often do so later in life and often to another Sagittarian, with whom they are the most compatible.

No wonder Sagittarians ultimately seek out their own kind with whom to finally nestle down. Few signs can match Sagittarius's irrepressible joy, enthusiasm, optimism, and good humor. Sagittariaus's relationship with and response to the world is nothing less than extraordinary—they fear little, love passionately, forgive easily, and embrace wholeheartedly. They are truly one-of-a-kind free spirits, whose ebullient personalities inspire those around them.

Choosing a Name for Your Sagittarius Child

When choosing a name for your Sagittarius child, first think about the major attributes and symbols associated with the sign:

410 HEY BABY, WHAT'S YOUR SIGN?

Sagittarius is the sign of wisdom and higher learning, exploration and adventure, philosophy and earthiness, travel and nature. Sagittarians are free spirited, energetic, freedom loving, unconventional, courageous, and optimistic. They are innately joyful, humorous, and genuine lovers of people and life. Their generosity and lack of guile make them enormously popular. They love the outdoors, travel, and adventure, but later in life they grow keenly interested in pursuing lofty and philosophical ideals.

Sagittarius is a Masculine, Mutable Fire sign governed by the planet Jupiter. The masculine aspect endows Sagittarians with expansiveness, energy, and an extroverted personality. The Mutable quality allows Sagittarians to easily adapt to new or changing environments. The Fire influence fuels Sagittarians's trademark qualities of enthusiasm, optimism, and adventurousness.

Sagittarius's ruling planet, Jupiter, governs wisdom, higher learning, exploration, travel, philosophy, humor, good fortune, and material bounty. Sagittarians are frequently struck by wanderlust at a young age and develop a lifelong yen for travel and exploration. They are also gifted communicators who often turn their talents to writing and publishing. The jovial aspect of Jupiter also endows Sagittarians with a marvelous and often ribald sense of humor. They are natural comedians with a keen eye for the comic absurdities of life.

The Archer, as represented by the centaur, a mythological creature that was half-human and half-horse, is the symbol of the sign of Sagittarius. Sagittarians are great lovers of nature, of the hunt and of the chase. They are naturally gifted athletes who excel at outdoor activities.

Sagittarius, the ninth sign of the zodiac, is the first of the winter signs, encompassing the months of November and December. The turquoise is the sign's official birthstone, and tin is Sagittarius's metal. The color purple is assigned to Sagittarius. Its flowers are the holly, narcissus, and dandelion, while the oak, mulberry, and birch trees are also strongly associated with the sign. Its animal is the horse.

When you choose a name for your child, also bear in mind some of Sagittarian children's key personal qualities. They are happy, energetic, optimistic, and expansive. Like the arrow of the Archer, they also are direct and to the point; Sagittarians are among the most frank and guileless children of the zodiac. They cherish their independence and easily allow others their freedom. Sagittarians, invariably cheerful, upbeat, laid-back, and relaxed, have great physical and emotional resiliency—very little gets them down for long.

For additional inspiration when choosing a name for your Sagittarius child—especially a middle name—you may want to browse through the names listed in Sagittarius's companion Fire signs, Leo and Aries.

Names for Sagittarius Girls

Abigail (AB-bih-gayl) Hebrew: My father rejoices. This classic name is suitable for the joyful and easygoing Sagittarian, one of the most delightful of children to raise. Variations: *Abbe, Abbie Abby*.

Agalia (ah-gah-LEE-ah) Greek: Brightness and joy. Ruled by Jupiter, the planet of expansive and good fortune, Sagittarians are naturally upbeat and optimistic.

Aida (AYE-dah or ah-EE-dah) Old English: Happy. A guileless infatuation with and enthusiasm for all that life has to offer is a trademark quality of Sagittarians. Variation: *Ada*.

Aiyana (eye-YAH-nah) Native American: Eternal bloom. Ever-optimistic Sagittarians always look for the bright side of life's occasional clouds.

Alana (ah-LAHN-ah) Gaelic: Buoyant. Naturally ebullient, Sagittarians are renowned for easily shaking off small hurts and obstacles. Variations: *Alaina, Alanna, Alayne, Allayne*.

Alauda (ah-LOWD-ah) Gaelic: Lark. Among the most relaxed and carefree of the zodiac's children, Sagittarians are renowned for their happy dispositions.

Aleeza (ah-LEETZ-ah) Hebrew: Joyful. This classic name is a marvelous choice for the innately enthusiastic and optimistic Sagittarian. Variations: *Alitza, Aliza, Alizah*.

Aleta (ah-LAY-tah) Spanish: Little winged one. Like the straight-shooting arrow of the Archer who symbolizes their sign, Sagittarians are uncomplicated and inveterate free spirits who aim high in all their endeavors. Variation: *Alida*.

Almeda (al-MAY-dah) Spanish: Avenue for strolling. Ruled by Jupiter, the planet of adventure and travel, Sagittarians are born with a lifelong case of wanderlust. The simple pleasures of the journey, not the destination, excites them. Variation: *Almeida*.

Alona (ah-LOH-nah) Hebrew: Oak tree. Oak, birch, and mulberry trees are associated with the sign of Sagittarius.

Amanda (ah-MAHN-dah) Latin: Lovable. A lovely name with many beautiful variations, *Amanda* is a splendid choice for endearing and easygoing Sagittarius. Variations: *Amandine, Amata, Manda, Mandaline, Mandi, Mandy*.

Amira (ah-MEE-rah) Hebrew: One who speaks. Influenced by Jupiter, the planet of wisdom and philosophy, Sagittarians frequently make deft communicators. Variations: *Ameera, Amirah*.

Andeana (ahn-dee-AHN-ah) Spanish: A walker. Lovers of nature, the outdoors, and rugged physical activity, many Sagittarians enjoy hiking and climbing. Variation: *Anda*.

Apara (ah-PAH-rah) African/Nigerian: One who comes and goes. Ruled by Jupiter, the planet of travel, Sagittarians are happy and carefree wanderers who are most content when they are on a new and exciting journey.

Arden (AHR-dinn) Latin: Excited. Naturally enthusiastic and possessed of a great zest for life, Sagittarians are among the most joyfully buoyant of the zodiac's signs.

Atida (ah-TEE-duh) Hebrew: She that comes tomorrow. This popular Israeli name is a wonderful choice for optimistic Sagittarians who rarely worry about what happened yesterday, and instead joyfully anticipate tomorrow's new adventures.

Aulii (OW-lee) Hawaiian: Delicious. Warmhearted, generous, funny, and joyous, Sagittarians are among the most endearing children of the zodiac.

Ayla (AY-lah) Hebrew: Oak tree. The oak is one of three trees associated with the sign of Sagittarius. (The birch and the mulberry are the other two.) Variation: *Ayala*.

Ayoka (ah-YO-kah) African/Nigerian: Joy giver. Optimistic and high-spirited, Sagittarians love to share their happiness with others.

Barika (bah-REE-kah) Arabic: Successful. Like their symbol, the Archer, Sagittarians aim high, and usually get what they desire.

Bayo (BAH-yoh) African/Nigerian: Joy is found. While they may wander restlessly throughout their lives, Sagittarians find great happiness in life's journey and the adventures they encounter along the way.

Beatrice (BEE-ah-triss or BAY-ah-triss) Latin: Bringer of joy. Humorous, optimistic, and high-spirited, Sagittarius is a positive and uplifting influence on all around her. Variations: *Bea, Beata, Beatrisa, Beatrix, Beatriz, Bebe, Bee*.

Bertille (bur-TEEL) Teutonic: Heroine. *Bertille* connotes the adventurous spirit of Sagittarius.

Bibiane (bee-bee-ANN) Latin: Lively. Sagittarians possess an innate joie de vivre.

Blythe (BLITHE) Old English: Free spirited. Independent Sagittarius compromises her dreams for no one. Variation: *Blithe*.

Bona (bow-NAH) Hebrew: Creator of dreams. Blessed with a spirit of adventure, Sagittarians spend their lives following their desires and aspirations.

Buo (BOO-uh) Vietnamese: Written charm. Imaginative and unconventional, Sagittarians have a special talent for writing.

Cadence (KAY-dintz) Latin: Rhythmic flow. This musical name is well suited to effervescent, whimsical Sagittarius. Variations: *Cadena, Cadenza, Kadena*.

Calida (kah-LEE-dah) Spanish: Warm and loving. Sagittarians, who are sincerely interested in others, embrace their loved ones wholeheartedly.

Caprice (kah-PREESE) Italian: Whimsical and fanciful. *Caprice* is a perfect choice for Sagittarius, who is known for her refreshingly unconventional and free-spirited nature. Variations: *Capriana, Capricia, Caprie*.

Carina (kah-REE-nah) Italian: Little darling. Sagittarius, who genuinely cares about others, loves passionately and forgives easily. Variations: *Carena, Cariana, Carin, Carinna, Karina*.

Carissa (kah-RISS-ah) Greek: Very precious. This beautiful name is perfectly suited to honest, endearing, and loving Sagittarius. Variations: *Carisa, Carisse*.

Carly (KAHR-lee) English: Female strength. *Carly* is an ideal name for a highly resilient, independent Sagittarius girl. Variations: *Carlee, Carleen, Carley, Carli, Carlina, Carlita*.

Cedrica (SEDD-rih-kah) Welsh: Gift of splendor. Sagittarians, who cherish wisdom, freedom, relationships, and adventure, are truly one of a kind.

Celeste (seh-LEST) Latin: From the heavens. *Celeste* is a beautiful choice for free-spirited, joyful Sagittarius. Variations: *Celesta, Celestina, Celestine.*

Chelsea (CHEL-see) Old English: Ship's port or harbor. This lovely name suits Sagittarius's intense love of travel. Variations: *Chelsey, Chelsi.*

Cholena (ko-LEE-nah) Native American: She who soars. Free-spirited Sagittarius always aims high, refusing to let anything confine her.

Damhnait (DEV-nat) Irish: Poet. This name is ideal for insightful Sagittarius, who is a naturally gifted writer. Variations: *Devnet, Downet, Dympha.*

Darlene (dahr-LEEN) English: Darling. Sagittarians are renowned for their inspiring enthusiasm, good humor, and genuine interest in the welfare of others. Variations: *Darla, Darleen, Darleena, Darlena, Darlina, Darline.*

Daryl (DARE-il) Old French: Small and precious. Daryl is a lovely choice for Sagittarius, whose zest for life, insatiable curiosity, and truly loving nature endears her to all. Variations: *Darrell, Darill, Darolyn, Darryll.* (Famous Sagittarian: Daryl Hannah, actress)

Daryn (DARE-inn) Greek: Gift. Loving, optimistic, and fun loving, Sagittarians are considered gifts from above by their family and friends.

Decembra (dee-SEM-brah) Latin: For the tenth month of the calendar year. This name is a distinctive choice for a December-born Sagittarian.

Degula (deh-GOO-lah) Hebrew: Marvelous. *Degula* is an apt name for Sagittarius, who is famous for her effervescence, independence, wisdom, humor, and sincerely caring nature.

Derica (DEH-rih-kah) English: Beloved leader. All Sagittarians possess a pioneering spirit and a love of adventure, bravely taking risks that others fear. Variations: *Dereka, Dericka, Derrica*.

Derora (de-ROH-rah) Hebrew: Free bird. Independent-minded Sagittarius compromises her dreams for no one. Variations: *Derorice, Derorit*.

Dessa (DESS-ah) Greek: Roaming nomad. Restless and free spirited, Sagittarians adore the thrill of travel and exploration.

Deva (DEE-vah or DAY-vah) Hindi: Heavenly spirit. Like *devas*, beings who bestow blessings in Hindu tradition, Sagittarians bestow happiness and enthusiasm upon all.

Dita (DEE-tah) Czechoslovakian: Rich gift. Loved ones consider endearing, enthusiastic, inquisitive, and free-spirited Sagittarius a divine blessing.

Dora (DORR-ah) Greek: Talent. When they combine their wisdom, enthusiasm, and unconventional ways, Sagittarians can achieve just about anything. Variations: *Dodee, Dodie, Dody, Dorabella, Doralia, Doralynn, Doreen, Dorelia, Dorelle*.

Duci (DOO-tsee) Hungarian: Rich girl. Sagittarius's abundance of wisdom, enthusiasm, and optimism help her to achieve any goal.

Eberta (ee-BUR-tah) Teutonic: Shiny. Ebullient and effervescent Sagittarius seems to emit a radiant glow.

Echo (EK-oh) Greek: Sound returned. In Greek mythology, *Echo* was the nymph whose passionate and unrequited love for Narcissus caused her body to disappear and left only her voice behind. Inveterate gabbers, Sagittarians are often in love with the sound of their own voices. Variation: *Ekko*.

Edrea (ed-DREE-ah) Old English: Wealthy and strong. This name is an apt choice for naturally resilient and fortunate Sagittarius. Variations: *Edra, Eidra, Eydra*.

Effie (EFF-ee) Greek: Musical talk. Effervescent Sagittarians are endowed with excellent communication skills. Variations: *Effi, Effy, Ephie, Euphemia, Euphemie, Euphie*.

Elvira (ell-VYE-rah) Teutonic: Sprite or fairy. This unique name suggests the free-spirited and whimsical nature of Sagittarius. Variations: *Elva, Elvera, Elvia, Elvina, Elvinia, Elvita*.

Elysia (ee-LEE-see-ah) Latin: From Elysium Fields, the mythological place of eternal joy that exists at the end of the world. Happy and carefree Sagittarians are inveterate explorers who often search for an elusive and ultimate truth. Variations: *Elise, Elisia, Elissa, Elyse, Ilise, Ilysa, Ilyse, Ilysia*.

Esperanza (ess-per-AHN-zah) Spanish: Hope. One of Sagittarius's key characteristics is an eternal optimism.

Estrella (ess-TRELL-ah) Latin: Girl of the stars. *Estrella* is an appropriate choice for Sagittarius, who always shoots for the stars. Variation: *Stella*.

Eudora (yu-DORR-ah) Greek: Gift without limits. Endowed with unending optimism and enthusiasm, free-spirited Sagittarians let nothing get in the way of their dreams. Variations: *Eudore*.

Eugenia (yu-JEEN-ee-ah) Greek: Fortunate birth. Sagittarius's ruling planet Jupiter governs opportunity and good luck. Variations: *Eugena, Eugenie, Eugina*.

Faizah (FAH-ee-zah) Arabic: Winning. Sagittarians, who always set their goals high, use their unconventional blend of wisdom, curiosity, imagination, and enthusiasm to achieve the results they desire.

Fanya (FAHN-yah) Russian: Free one. Adventurous and exuberant Sagittarians cherish their independence and live life according to their own rules.

Farrah (FAIR-uh) Middle English: Delightful. Sagittarians are known for their infectious laughter, eternal optimism, and tremendous zest for life. Variations: *Fara, Farah, Farra.*

Faustine (faws-TEEN) Latin: Lucky. Sagittarians, who willingly take risks, are fortunate by nature. Variations: *Fausta, Fauste, Faustina.*

Fay (faye) Old French: Fairy. *Fay* suggests the free-spirited, whimsical ways of Sagittarius. Variations: *Fae, Faye.*

Fayette (faye-ETT) Old French: Little fairy. This beautiful name is an ideal choice for Sagittarius, who possesses a magical quality. Variations: *Fae, Fay.*

Felcia (FELL-shuh) Polish: Happy. Sagittarians are among the most cheerful children of the zodiac. Variations: *Fela, Felka.*

Fernanda (fer-NAHN-dah) Spanish: Adventurous. Free-spirited Sagittarius has a great love for exploration and travel.

Fiala (fee-AH-lah) Czechoslovakian: Violet. Purple is the color of the sign of Sagittarius.

Flo (flow) Native American: Like an arrow. The Archer and his bow and arrow are symbols of the sign of Sagittarius. This name is also appropriate for a boy.

Fortuna (for-TOO-nah) Latin: Roman goddess of fortune and chance. Sagittarians are typically lucky by nature.

Frances (FRAN-siss) Latin: Free and without fetters. Sagittarians cherish freedom above all other things. Variations: *Fancy, Fannie, France, Francesca, Francie, Francine, Francoise, Frankie, Franny.*

Gada (GAH-dah) Hebrew: Good luck. This popular Middle Eastern name suits a Sagittarian girl, whose ruling planet, Jupiter, governs good luck and material abundance.

Gari (GAR-ee) Teutonic: Spear maiden. Symbolized by the archer, with his bow and arrow, Sagittarian children are lovers of the hunt and chase, who are often relentlessly single-minded in their pursuit of adventure.

Gay (GAYE) Old French: Happy and carefree. Happiness and a carefree attitude toward life are noted characteristics of Sagittarians. Variations: *Gae, Gai, Gaye.*

Geela (GEE-lah) Hebrew: Joy. This popular Israeli name suits the naturally happy Sagittarian.

Geraldine (JER-all-deen) French: She who rules by the spear. A classic name with many beautiful variations, *Geraldine* is a fitting choice for Sagittarius, the sign of the hunter. Variations: *Deena, Dina, Geralda, Geraldeen, Geralyn, Geri, Jeraldeen, Jeraldine, Jeralee, Jeri.*

Ginger (JIN-jer) English: Full of spice. Strongly influenced by the quality of Fire and governed by Jupiter, the planet of pleasure and adventure, Sagittarians have a uniquely zestful approach to life. Variations: *Gineen, Ginelle, Ginna, Ginnelle, Ginnette, Ginnie.*

Gleda (GLAY-dah) Icelandic: Makes happy. The Sagittarian child's joyful and expansive approach to life is wonderfully infectious.

Halona (hah-LOH-nah) Native American: Happy fortune. Sagittarians are governed by Jupiter, the planet of good luck and opportunity.

Hanako (hah-NAH-koh) Japanese: Flower child. Free-spirited Sagittarians are great lovers of nature.

Holly (HAH-lee) English: For the holly tree. The holly, one of three flowers that symbolize the sign of Sagittarius, is also strongly associated with December, the month in which many Sagittarians are born. Variations: *Hollee, Holli, Hollie, Hollis, Hollyann.*

Hope (hope) English: Great expectation. Optimism, in the face of all challenges, is a hallmark of the sign of Sagittarius.

Hoshi (HOH-shee) Japanese: Shining star. Sagittarians are among the most popular and sought after children of the zodiac. Variations: *Hoshi, Hoshiko.*

Iantha (ee-AHN-thah) Greek: Purple-colored flower. The color purple is strongly associated with the sign of Sagittarius.

Idelle (eye-DELL) Welsh: Bountiful. Sagittarius is ruled by Jupiter, the planet of good fortune and great bounty. Variations: *Idelisa, Idella.*

Ilka (EEL-kah) Slavic: Flattering. Genuine lovers of life and people, Sagittarians are ardent and guileless friends who offer praise and encouragement without expecting anything in return. Variation: *Ilke.*

India (IN-dee-ah) Indian: For the country. Governed by Jupiter, the sign of travel, adventure, and exploration, Sagittarians are bitten by the wanderlust bug at an early age. Any of the exotic place names that also serve as given names are wonderful choices for travel-loving Sagittarians. Variations: *Inda, Indee, Indiana.*

Ituha (ee-TOO-hah) Native American: Strong and sturdy oak. The oak tree is strongly associated with the sign of Sagittarius.

Jafit (ya-FEET) Hebrew: Wonderfully attractive. Overflowing with joie de vivre, a great deal of Sagittarius's appeal can be attributed to her exuberant charm. Variations: *Jaffi, Jaffice.*

Jamaica (jah-MAY-kah) English: The place name for the West Indian island. Jupiter, Sagittarius's ruling planet, governs travel and adventure, and Sagittarians are renowned for their search for new and intriguing places to explore.

Jin (JIN) Japanese: Better than the best. Sagittarians, who aim to excel at all they do, approach life with a firm belief that everything turns out well in the end.

Jocasta (joh-KASS-tah) Latin: Cheerful. This classic name is a unique choice for the joyful Sagittarian. In mythological literature, Jocasta was the mother of Oedipus, who unknowingly marries her.

Jocelyn (JOSS-lin; JOS-sah-lin) French: Lighthearted. Remarkably easygoing and laid-back, Sagittarians are among the most accommodating signs of the zodiac. Variations: *Jocelina, Joceline, Jocelynn, Josalyn, Joslin, Joslyn, Jozlin.*

Jodi (JOH-dee) Hebrew: Much praised. Due to their joyful nature, delightful sense of humor, wondrous curiosity, endearing ways, and sincere interest in others, Sagittarians are immensely popular and greatly respected. Variations: *Jodie, Jody.*

Jolan (YOH-lahn; jo-LAHN) Greek: Purple flower. Purple is the color of the sign of Sagittarius. Variation: *Yolanda.*

Joyce (joice) Latin: Joyous. Joyce is an appropriate choice for happy and high-spirited Sagittarians, who spread joy wherever they go. Variations: *Joi, Joice, Joie, Jovita, Joy, Joya, Joyann, Joye, Joyoua.*

Kalli (ka-LEE) Greek: Singing lark. This name is an apt choice for perpetually cheerful, fun-loving Sagittarius. Variations: *Callie, Kal, Kallie, Kally.*

Karissa (kah-RISS-ah) Greek: Very precious. Sagittarian children's abundance of appealing personal qualities makes them unique among the children of the zodiac.

Kavindra (kah-VEEN-drah) Hindu: Mighty poet. Ruled by Jupiter, the planet that governs not only wisdom but the interpretation of it, many Sagittarians are gifted writers.

Kaya (KA-ya) African/Ghanian: "Don't leave, live!" This beautiful African name is quintessentially Sagittarian. Sagittarius is the sign that celebrates facing life head-on and living it to its fullest.

Keely (KEE-lee) Irish: Lively. Enthusiastic and optimistic, Sagittarius embodies the meaning of joie de vivre. Variations: *Keelie, Keila, Keilah, Kelley.*

Kenzie (KEN-zee) Scottish: Light and buoyant one. *Kenzie* is a lovely choice for optimistic, fun-loving Sagittarius.

Keshia (KEESH-ah) African: Beloved. Family and friends find it easy to love Sagittarius, who possesses a bright personality, individualistic spirit, and loving nature. Variations: *Kesha, Shia.*

Kora (KOH-rah) Greek: Lithe maid or lass. Great lovers of the outdoors, many Sagittarians are gifted athletes. Variations: *Cora, Corie, Corrie, Cory, Korie, Korrie, Kory.*

Lacey (LAY-see) English: Joyous girl. *Lacey* is an old English name that is eminently suitable for happy-go-lucky and always young-spirited Sagittarians. Variations: *Lacee, Lacie.*

Lana (LAN-ah; LAHN-ah) Hawaiian: Attractive to the eye. Happy, carefree, optimistic, and genuinely interested in the world around her, the Sagittarian girl is innately attractive. Variations: *Lanae, Lanice, Lanna, Lannette, Lanni.*

Ledah (LEE-dah) Hebrew: Born lively and happy. Enthusiasm and joy are hallmarks of the sign of Sagittarius. Variations: *Leda, Lida, Lidah.*

Letitia (le-TEE-shah) Latin: Great happiness. This beautiful name suits optimistic and effervescent Sagittarius. Variations: *Latisha, Leticia, Letisha, Letizia, Letty.*

Levana (le-VAHN-ah) Latin: Uplifting. In mythology, *Levana* was the Roman goddess of newborns. This unusual name reflects the cheer and ebullience that Sagittarius inspires in those around her.

Liberty (LIB-ur-te) English: Freedom. The love of independence is a key characteristic of those born under the sign of Sagittarius. Variations: *Libertina, Librada.*

Limber (LIMB-ur) African/Nigerian: Joyful. Sagittarians, who have a naturally joyous and optimistic approach to life, are great lovers of physical activities and arts.

Linda (LIN-dah; LEEN-dah) Spanish: Pretty. This classic name, and its many beautiful variations, never goes out of style. It's a fitting choice for innately beautiful Sagittarius, who has one of the most endearing personalities of the zodiac. Variations: *Belinda, Lin, Lindee, Lindey, Lindi, Lindy, Lynda, Lynde, Lyndy, Lynn, Melinda.*

Lirit (leer-RIT) Hebrew: Lyrical, musical, poetic. This popular Israeli name is suitable for Sagittarians who often have a poetic gift for writing and storytelling.

Lisandra (le-SAN-drah) Greek: One who frees others. No other children of the zodiac love freedom and independence as much as do Sagittarians, who in turn keenly respect the freedom and independence of those around them. Variations: *Lissandra, Lizandra, Lysandra.*

Maemi (mah-AY-mee) Japanese: Honest smile. Renowned for their lack of guile, Sagittarians rarely have hidden agendas. Their approach to the world is direct and joyful.

Makana (mah-KAN-nah) Hawaiian: A prize. This unique name suggests the appealing gifts that Sagittarius offers, with her incomparable good humor, spirit of adventure, and endless enthusiasm.

Malka (MAL-kah) Hebrew: Spritely. *Malka* is a whimsical name for fun-loving and free-spirited Sagittarians.

Mandisa (mahn-DEE-sah) African/Xhosa: Sweet as sugar. People warm to Sagittarius's honest and sincere nature and her enthusiastic interest in others.

Marni (MAHR-nee) Hebrew: Proclaim with joy. Full of life, Sagittarians spread happiness wherever they go. Variation: *Marinna.*

Melcia (MELT-shuh; MEL-shuh) Polish: Admirer. Sagittarians are ardent and generous friends who rarely ask for anything—other than friendship—in return for their devotion.

Melica (MI-lits-uh; mi-LEE-kuh) Old Gothic: Ambitious. Sagittarius's ruling planet, Jupiter, also governs opportunity and ambition. Despite their happy and carefree natures, Sagittarians can be single-mindedly ambitious when they find a special cause or project that stirs them.

Melosa (meh-LOH-sah) Spanish: Sweet and tender. Endearing Sagittarius loves passionately, forgives easily, and embraces wholeheartedly.

Merry (MERR-ee) Old English: Cheerful. *Merry* is an obvious choice for a girl born under Sagittarius, one of the most lively and brilliant signs of the zodiac. Variations: *Merri, Merrie, Merrilee, Merrily.*

Michiko (MEE-chee-koh) Japanese: Beautiful and wise child. Ruled by Jupiter, the planet of wisdom, and endowed with a joyful disposition, Sagittarians have an innate beauty.

Mitzi (MIT-see) English: A mind of her own. Freedom loving and unconventional, Sagittarians often eschew rules and regulations, joyfully marching to the beat of their own inner drummer. Variation: *Mitzy.*

Naavah (nah-VAH) Hebrew: Delightful. Enthusiastic and upbeat, imaginative and free-spirited, Sagittarians make enchanting friends. Variations: *Nava, Navah.*

Nadia (NAHD-ee-ah) Russian: Looks to the future. Optimistic by nature, Sagittarians rarely get bogged down in the past. Variation: *Natka.*

Nailah (NAH-ee-lah) Arabic: Successful woman. Bright, eager, and possessed of one of the most ebullient personalities in the zodiac, Sagittarian women find success in anything they undertake with great commitment.

Naomi (nay-OH-mee) Hebrew: Cordiality. Sagittarians, who have a genuine interest in people, are unfailingly friendly and pleasant. Variations: *Neoma, Neomi, Noemi, Noemy.*

Nara (NAHR-ah) Japanese: Strong oak tree. Oak trees are strongly associated with the sign of Sagittarius. Variations: *Nareen, Nareena, Nareene.*

Narcissa (nahr-SISS-ah) Greek: Daffodil. The narcissus is one of three flowers that symbolize the sign of Sagittarius. (The other two are the holly and the dandelion.) Variations: *Narcisa, Narcisse, Narcyssa.*

Navit (nah-VEET) Hebrew: Beautiful and pleasant. Sagittarius's joyous and easygoing approach to life gives them an endearing and unique appeal. Variations: *Nava, Navice.*

Neith (NEETH) Egyptian: For the goddess. *Neith,* a mythological Egyptian goddess who governed the domestic arts as well as war, is often portrayed carrying a bow and arrows. This unusual but stunning choice suits a girl born under Sagittarius, the sign of the archer. Variation: *Neit.*

Nellie (NELL-ee) Greek: She who shines. This name is appropriate for Sagittarius, whose sunny personality spreads its light to others. Variations: *Nella, Nelly, Nelya.*

Netis (NAY-tis) Native American: Trusted friend. Genuine and sincere, Sagittarians make truly endearing friends who embrace their loved ones wholeheartedly.

Numa (NOO-mah) Arabic: Attractive and pleasant. With their zest for life, curiosity about the world, sharp sense of humor, and genuine interest in others, Sagittarians are among the most popular children of the zodiac.

Nyla (NYE-lah) Greek: A winner. Sharp, enthusiastic Sagittarius always aims high—and typically achieves her goals. Variation: *Nila.*

Olisa (oh-LEE-sah) African/Ibo: Great spirit. *Olisa* suggests the inimitable exuberance and zest for life possessed by Sagittarius.

Omusa (oh-MOO-sah) Native American: To miss with arrows. This charming Native American name, referring to a hunting expedition, is an apt choice for those born under the sign of the Archer.

Orane (oh-RAHN) French: Rising. Like the soaring arrow that symbolizes their sign, Sagittarians are noted for their ever ebullient optimism. Variations: *Orania, Oriane*.

Oseye (oh-SEH-yeh) African/Nigerian: Happy person. Joy and genuine happiness are hallmarks of the sign of Sagittarius.

Papina (pah-PEE-nuh) Native American: For a vine that grows on the oak tree. The sturdy oak is one of the trees associated with the sign of Sagittarius.

Pelipa (peh-LEE-pah) Native American: Lover of horses. The horse is the special animal governed by Sagittarius, the sign that symbolizes the love of the hunt.

Phillipa (fill-LEE-pah or FILL-ih-pah) Greek: Horse lover. The Horse is the animal symbol for the sign of Sagittarius. Variations: *Philipa, Philippine, Phillie, Pippa, Pippy*.

Radinka (rah-DINK-ah) Slavic: Brimming with life. Freedom-loving Sagittarians throw themselves into living with infectious zest and good humor.

Ranita (rah-NEE-tah) Hebrew: Happy noise. Joyful and enthusiastic Sagittarians love to talk and often make gifted communicators. Variations: *Ranice, Ranit, Ranith, Ranitra, Ranitta*.

Resi (REH-zee) German: She who reaps. This German variant of *Theresa* suits a girl born under the sign of Sagittarius, ruled by Jupiter, the planet of abundance and good fortune.

Risa (REES-ah) Latin: Laughter. Sagittarians, endowed with fabulous senses of humor, frequently entertain friends and family with their comic tales.

Ronli (rohn-LEE) Hebrew: My joy. Happy Sagittarius is a joy to be around. Variations: *Rona, Roni, Ronia, Ronice, Ronlia.*

Sakari (sah-KAH-ree) Hindu: Sweetness. Naturally happy and carefree, Sagittarians are endearing souls to whom people naturally gravitate.

Sami (SAH-mee) Arabic: Highly praised. Undemanding, entertaining, and often captivating friends and coworkers, Sagittarians are among the most popular signs of the zodiac. Variations: *Samia, Samina, Sammar, Sammie, Sammy.*

Sarah (SAYR-uh) Hebrew: She who laughs. A highly attuned and even clownish sense of humor is a hallmark of the sign of Sagittarius. Variations: *Sadie, Sally, Sara, Sarene, Sarine, Zaidee, Zara, Zarah, Zaria.*

Seki (SEH-kee) Japanese: Wonderful. Never ones to get bogged down in past mistakes or little hurts and slights, Sagittarians are noted for their ability to see the bright side in every situation.

Sarolta (SHAW-rohl-tah) Hungarian: She who laughs. Sagittarians are renowned for their abundant good humor and keen sense of the comically absurd.

Shaina (SHAY-nah) Yiddish: Beautiful to look at. Innately attractive Sagittarians have one of the most endearing and infectious personalities of the zodiac. Variation: *Shana.*

Shani (SHAH-nee) African/Nigerian: Wonderful. For Sagittarians, all of life is an astounding journey to be explored and relished. Relentlessly optimistic, the art of living is always exciting for the classic Sagittarian.

Suletu (soo-LEH-too) Native American: To fly around. Like the arrow of the Archer who symbolizes their sign, Sagittarians are highfliers who love the thrill of adventure, travel, and the chase.

Sunki (SHOON-kee; SOON-kee) Native American: To overtake. This Native American term refers to the traditional hunt. Sagittarius is the sign of the Hunter.

Tadita (tah-DEE-tah) Native American: A runner. Great lovers of the outdoors and of physical exercise, many Sagittarians are natural athletes. Variation: *Tadeta.*

Tamika (TAH-mee-kah; tah-MEE-kah) Japanese: A girl born for the people. This lovely and unusual name, currently very popular in the United States, is perfect for people-loving Sagittarians, who are natural-born leaders. Variations: *Tami, Tamiko, Tamiya.*

Tasida (tah-SEE-dah) Native American: Riding on top of a horse. The Horse is the animal ruled by Sagittarius, the sign that celebrates travel, the outdoors, and the hunt.

Tatum (TAY-tum) Middle English: Cheerful. This modern classic is eminently suitable for the ever optimistic Sagittarian girl. Variations: *Tate, Tayte.*

Tassos (TAH-sohs) Greek: One who reaps. Sagittarius is ruled by Jupiter, the planet of good luck and material bounty.

Teagan (TEE-gan) English: Attractive. This classic name is well suited to a Sagittarian whose genuine good spirits and optimism about life makes her innately attractive to those around her. Variations: *Teague, Tegan, Teige.*

Thalia (THAYL-yah) Greek: Flowering. This name of the Greek muse of comedy is a superb choice for an ever-joyful Sagittarian, noted for her flourishing sense of humor. Variation: *Talia.*

Tisa (TEE-sah) African/Swahili: Ninth born. This beautiful and contemporary name is fitting for a girl born under Sagitarrius, the ninth sign of the zodiac.

Tivona (tee-VOH-nuh) Hebrew: Nature lover. This popular Israeli name is a splendid choice for Sagittarians, noted for their great love of the outdoors.

Trixie (TRIK-see) Latin: She who brings happiness. The Sagittarian's genuine and enthusiastic joy for living is remarkably contagious.

Ulani (oo-LAH-nee) Hawaiian: Optimistic. Jupiter, the planet of heavenly ideals and earthly pleasures, endows Sagittarians with ever-present enthusiasm.

Vanda (VAHN-dah) Slavic: Wayfarer. Consumed by wanderlust all their lives, Sagittarians are happiest when on the move.

Varina (vah-REE-nah) Slavic: Unknown or still to be discovered. Ruled by Jupiter, the planet of adventure, Sagittarians thrill to the task of exploring new and uncharted territory.

Vesta (VESS-tah) Greek: She who tarries. *Vesta,* the name of a Roman goddess of the hearth and fire, is a whimsical choice for the Fire-influenced Sagittarian. Among Sagittarius's flaws is the tendency to procrastinate. Variation: *Hestia.*

Wanda (WAHN-dah) German: Traveler. Sagittarius is the sign of travel and exploration. Variations: *Wandi, Wandie, Wenda, Wendi, Wendy.*

Willow (WILL-oh) Middle English: Free spirit. Sagittarians cherish personal freedom above all else.

Yepa (YAY-pah) Native American: Winter princess. Sagittarius is the first of the zodiac's winter signs.

Yovela (yo-VAY-luh) Hebrew: Joyful heart. Invariably upbeat, Sagittarians are among the happiest and most openhearted of the zodiac's children.

Yvette (ee-VETT) French: Arrow's bow. This classic French name is a beautiful choice for Sagittarius, the sign symbolized by the Archer. Variations: *Ivona, Ivone, Yvonne*.

Zada (ZA-dah) Arabic: Good luck. Jupiter, the planet that governs Sagittarius, rules good luck, opportunity, and abundance. Popular variations: *Zaida, Zayda*.

Zigana (ZEE-gah-nah) Hungarian: Gypsy girl. Born with a wandering heart and free-spirited soul, the life of the caravan gypsy is wonderfully suitable to the Sagittarian nature.

Names for Sagittarius Boys

Abejide (ah-beh-JEE-deh) African/Nigerian: Winter's child. This musical-sounding name is well suited to Sagittarius, the first of the zodiac's winter signs.

Adeben (ah-deh-BEHN) African/Ghanian: Twelfth-born son. *Adeben* is a fitting choice for a December-born Sagittarian boy.

Adiv (ah-DEEV) Hebrew: Soothing. This popular Israeli name is perfect for congenial and easygoing Sagittarius.

Akando (ah-KAHN-doh) Native American: Ambush. Ruled by Jupiter, the planet of exploration and good luck, and symbolized by the Archer, who represents the thrill of the hunt, Sagittarians are adventure-loving souls who thrive on intrigue and challenge.

Akron (AK-run) African/Ochi: Ninth-born son. Sagittarius is the ninth sign of the zodiac. Variation: *Akon*.

Aladdin (a-LAD-inn) Arabic: Height of faith. This exotic and fitting name from folklore is ideal for the ever-optimistic Sagittarian boy.

Alon (ah-LON) Hebrew: Oak tree. The oak is one of three trees ruled by the sign of Sagittarius. (The other two are the mulberry and the birch.)

Alvin (AL-vin) Old German: Friends to all. Among the most popular people of the zodiac, Sagittarians are renowned for their openhearted and undemanding friendships. Variations: *Albin, Alvie, Alvino, Alwin, Alwyn.*

Aramis (AYRE-a-miss) French: Meaning unknown. While the original meaning of this now famous French name is unknown, *Aramis* originally came to the attention of the reading public as the name of the celebrated swordsman in Alexandre Dumas's swashbuckling classic, *The Three Musketeers.* This intriguing name is a marvelous choice for thrill-seeking Sagittarius.

Archer (AHRCH-ur) Old English: Archer. The Archer is the symbol of the sign of Sagittarius.

Arley (AHR-lee) Old English: Bowman. *Arley* is an appropriate choice for Sagittarius, who is symbolized by the Archer.

Armand (AHR-mund) Old German: Military man. This classic name is suitable for a boy born under Sagittarius, the sign of the hunt. Variations: *Arman, Armin, Armon, Armond.*

Armstrong (AHRM-strong) English: One who has a strong arm. This traditional name connotes the power of the Archer, Sagittarius's symbol. Like the Archer, Sagittarians aim high toward their goals.

Arri (AHR-ee) Greek: Looking for the best outcome. Sagittarians are innately optimistic and cheerful. Variation: *Ari.*

Artemus (AHR-teh-mus) Greek: Belonging to Artemis, the Greek goddess of the hunt. Sagittarius, symbolized by the Archer, is the sign of the hunt. Variations: *Artimas, Artimis.*

Asadel (Ah-sah-del) Arabic: Greatly successful. *Asadel*, a popular name in Muslim countries, is an apt choice for Sagittarians, whose quick minds and determined pursuit of high goals enable them to do anything they focus on.

Azad (uh-ZUHD) Turkish: Born free. One-of-a-kind individuals, Sagittarians dearly cherish their independence and refuse to let anyone's rules restrain them.

Barclay (BAHR-clay) English: Valley of the birches. The birch is one of the trees associated with the sign of Sagittarius. Variations: *Barcley, Barklay, Barkley.*

Barry (BARE-ee) English: Sword. This traditional name suggests the imagery of the hunt, with which Sagittarius is strongly associated. Variations: *Barrie, Barrington.*

Basir (bah-SEER) Turkish: Discerning. *Basir* is a fine choice for inquisitive and insightful Sagittarius.

Bassam (bah-SAHM) Arabic: Smiling. This name is well suited to perpetually happy, fun-loving Sagittarius. Variation: *Basim.*

Belen (BEH-lehn) Greek: Arrow. *Belen* suggests the imagery of the Archer, Sagittarius's symbol.

Berkeley (BUR-klee) Irish: Meadow of birch trees. This traditional name is an apt choice for Sagittarius, who is affiliated with the birch tree. Variations: *Berkley, Berl, Burlin.*

Birch (BURCH) English: For the tree. Birches, mulberries, and oaks are the three trees associated with the sign of Sagittarius.

Birk (BURK) Old English: Beside the birch trees. Sagittarius is strongly associated with the birch tree.

Blaine (BLAYN) Scottish: Sleek. Just as the Archer gracefully and surely points his bow, Sagittarians aim at their goals with a distinct flair. Variations: *Blane, Blaney, Blayne*.

Bogart (BOH-gahrt) French: The strength of a bow. *Bogart* suggests the imagery of the Archer, Sagittarius's symbol. Variations: *Bogey, Bogie*.

Brian (BRYE-an) Irish: He rises. An ever-popular name, *Brian* suggests the way Sagittarius aims high in all things. Variations: *Briano, Briant, Bryan, Bryant, Bryon*.

Broderick (BRAHD-rik) Scottish: Brother. Sincere and kind-hearted Sagittarians make one-of-a-kind friends and companions who give freely of their time and energy, expecting little in return. Variations: *Brodie, Brody*.

Cahil (kah-HIL) Turkish: Ingenuous. Guileless Sagittarians are refreshingly sincere and honest in all things.

Cain (CAYN) Hebrew: Spear. *Cain* suggests the imagery of the hunt, with which Sagittarius is strongly associated.

Cappi (KAHP-pee) English Gypsy: Good luck. This unique name is a suitable choice for naturally lucky Sagittarius.

Chance (CHANS) Middle English: Good luck. Sagittarius's ruling planet of Jupiter governs opportunity and good luck.

Chaney (CHAH-ney; CHAY-nee) Old French: Oak wood. The oak is one of three trees governed by Sagittarius. Variation: *Cheney*.

Chase (CHAYC) Old French: One who hunts. Sagittarius, symbolized by the Archer, is the sign of the hunt. Variations: *Chace, Chaise*.

Chester (CHESS-tur) Old English: Near the army camp. This traditional name is well suited to Sagittarius, who is associated with the hunt. Variations: *Ches, Cheston, Chet*. (Famous Sagittarian: Chet Huntley, news anchor)

Cullen (KULL-ent) Irish: Holly. The holly is one of the flowers associated with the sign of Sagittarius. Variations: *Cullan, Cullin, Cully*.

Dakarai (dah-KAH-rah-ee) African/Zimbabwean: Happiness. One of the key characteristics of Sagittarius is an eternally joyful nature.

Damian (DAYM-yan) Greek: Sweet and harmless. Sagittarians are among the most honest, sincere, and truly guileless children of the zodiac. Variations: *Damien, Damion, Damon*.

Darin (DARE-in) Greek: Precious gift. Sagittarians, who are caring, honest, fun loving, exuberant, free spirited, and endearing, are considered unique and rare blessings by their loved ones. Variations: *Darren, Darrin, Darron*.

Darwin (DAHR-win) Old English: Dear friend. Sagittarius, who freely gives his time and energy to others and asks little in return, makes a true, lifelong friend. Variation: *Dar*.

Demothi (deh-MOH-tee) Native American: He who talks as he walks. *Demothi* connotes both Sagittarius's love of conversation and his inclination to wander.

Deror (deh-ROHR) Hebrew: He who loves freedom. This popular Israeli name is a marvelous choice for a Sagittarian, who prizes freedom and independence above all things. Variations: *Dare, Darrie, Derori*.

Derwin (DUR-win) Old English: Much loved ally. Spirited, kindhearted, and enthusiastic, Sagittarians make sincere and loyal friends.

Dichali (dee-CHAH-lee) Native American: He who talks often. Endowed with excellent communication skills, Sagittarians have a great love of conversation.

Didier (di-DYEH) French: Desired. This name is an ideal choice for exuberant, fun-loving, and good-natured Sagittarius, who makes an appealing friend or mate.

Dirk (DEERK; DURK) Danish: Dagger. *Dirk* is an apt choice for a boy born under Sagittarius, the sign of the hunt.

Dyre (DEE-reh) Scandinavian: Dear heart. This name, popular in Norway, suggests Sagittarius's good nature and genuine interest in others.

Edgar (ED-ger) Old English: Prosperous swordsman. Sagittarius's ruling planet of Jupiter governs good fortune and the hunt. Variations: *Edgard, Edgardo, Edgars.*

Enoch (EE-nok or ay-NOHK) Hebrew: Dedicated. Sagittarius, who cherishes his independence and refuses to compromise his dreams for anyone, devotes his energies to achieving his plans.

Erasmus (e-RAS-mus) Greek: Lovable. Saint Erasmus, also known as Saint Elmo, is the patron saint of sailors. Many Sagittarians, endearing and kindhearted, are drawn to occupations that involve travel. Variations: *Erasme, Erasmo, Ras.*

Ernest (UR-nest) Old German: Vigor. Sagittarius is endowed with enormous energy, vitality, and enthusiasm. Variations: *Earnest, Ernesto, Ernst.*

Evan (EV-un) Old Welsh: Bowman. The Archer is the symbol of the sign of Sagittarius. Variations: *Evin, Ewan, Owen.*

Faris (FAH-rees) Arabic: Horseman. The Horse is the animal associated with the sign of Sagittarius.

Farr (fahr) English: Wayfarer. This name is an ideal choice for Sagittarius, who is especially fond of travel and the adventures it brings.

Feroz (FEE-roos) Persian: Lucky. Jupiter, Sagittarius's ruling planet, governs good fortune and optimistic outcomes.

Fitzgerald (FITZ-jehr-uld or fitz-JERR-ald) Old English: Son of the sword-mighty. *Fitzgerald* is suitable for a boy born under Sagittarius, the sign of the hunt. Variation: *Fitz*.

Fletcher (FLETCH-ur) Middle English: Arrow feather. This thirteenth-century occupational name for an arrow maker is an apt choice for Sagittarius, whose symbol is the Archer. Variation: *Fletch*.

Flint (FLINT) Old English: Strong as a flint stone. This name is an unusual and appropriate choice for Fire sign Sagittarius, who is capable of igniting enthusiasm and passion in all he meets.

Fortuné (for-too-NEH) French: Given to good luck. *Fortuné* is an apt name for Sagittarius, whose ruling planet of Jupiter governs good luck.

Francis (FRAN-sis) Latin: A free man. This classic name, or one of its popular variations, is an ideal choice for unconventional, independence-loving Sagittarius. Variations: *Franc, Franchot, Francisco, Frank, Frans, Franz*. (Famous Sagittarians: Frank Zappa, singer/musician; Frank Sinatra, actor/singer; Francisco Franco, former general and head of Spanish state)

Franklin (FRANK-lin) Old German: Free man. Free-spirited Sagittarius compromises his ideals for no one. Variation: *Frank*.

(Famous Sagittarian: Franklin Pierce, fourteenth president of the U.S.)

Gadi (GAH-dee) Arabic: My fortune. *Gadi*, a popular name in Israel, is a fine choice for Sagittarius, whose ruling planet of Jupiter governs good luck and opportunity.

Garrick (GA-rik) English: He who rules by the sword. This name suggests the imagery of the hunt, with which Sagittarius is closely associated. Variation: *Garrik*.

Gary (GAR-ee) Old German: Spear carrier. *Gary*, a classic and popular name, is a fine choice for Sagittarius, whose symbol is the Archer and who is affiliated with the hunt. Variations: *Garey, Gari, Garry*.

Gerald (JAYR-uld) Old German: He who rules by the spear. This traditional name is an apt choice for a boy born under Sagittarius, the sign of the hunt. Variations: *Geralde, Geraldo, Gerek, Gerhard, Gerry, Girauld, Jerrold, Jerry*.

Gerik (GAY-rik) Polish: Prosperous spearman. *Gerik*, suggesting the hunt and good fortune, is an ideal choice for naturally lucky Sagittarius, whose symbol is the Archer.

Gil (GEEL) Hebrew: Joy. Fun loving, enthusiastic, and optimistic, Sagittarius spreads happiness wherever he goes.

Gyasi (JAH-see) African/Ghanian: Marvelous baby. Like their Libra cousins, Sagittarians are "low-maintenance" children who are happy and easygoing by nature.

Harley (HAHR-lee) Teutonic: Archer. The Archer is the symbol of Sagittarius. Variations: *Arleigh, Arley, Harleigh, Harly*.

Hunter (HUNT-er) Old English: Hunter. Sagittarians, symbolized by the Archer aiming his bow, seem to spend their lives in continual pursuit of some elusive goal.

Huntley (HUNT-lee) Old English: Hunter's field. This traditional name is an apt choice for a boy born under Sagittarius, the sign of the hunt. Variations: *Huntleigh, Huntly*.

Husain (hoo-SAYN) Arabic: Glory child. Others marvel at the tremendous zest for life, truly sincere heart, and unconventional wisdom possessed by Sagittarius. Variations: *Husein, Hussein*.

Igasho (ee-GAH-shoh) Native American: Wanderer. Adventure-loving Sagittarians are renowned for their love of travel and need to experience all that life has to offer.

Isaac (EYE-zak) Hebrew: He laughs. One of the most prominent characteristics of Sagittarius is a fabulous sense of humor. Many comedians are born under the sign of Sagittarius. Variations: *Isaak, Isak, Yitzhak*.

Ivar (EE-vahr or EYE-var) Old Norse: Yew-bow army. *Ivar* connotes the imagery of both the Archer, Sagittarius's symbol, and the hunt, with which the sign is closely associated. Variation: *Ivor*.

Ives (EEVS or EYEVS) Old English: Young archer. The sign of Sagittarius is represented by the Archer, one of the few zodiacal symbols with a human aspect. Variation: *Yves*.

Ivon (EE-vohn or EYE-vohn) Teutonic: Archer. The sign of Sagittarius is symbolized by the Archer. Variation: *Ivan*.

Ixaka (ee-SHAH-kah) Hebrew: Laughter. Sagittarians are known as the most fun-loving, humorous children of the zodiac.

Jal (JAHL) English Gypsy: Wanderer. Restless Sagittarius is happiest when traveling to distant places or exploring new territory.

Jaron (JARE-on) Hebrew: To shout out. The irrepressible exuberance and zest for life possessed by Sagittarians make them exceptionally talkative and outgoing in social situations. Variations: *Gerron, Jaren, Jarin, Jarren, Jarron, Jeran, Jeren, Jeron, Jerron*.

Jarvis (JAHR-vis) Old German: Man who leads with a spear. This classic name is an apt choice for a boy born under Sagittarius, the sign of the hunt. Variation: *Jervis*.

Javas (JAH-vis) Hindu: Swift-footed. Sagittarius, who is plagued by wanderlust, relishes the excitement and adventure afforded by travel.

Jolon (JOH-lohn) Native American: Valley of the dead oaks. The oak is one of three trees affiliated with the sign of Sagittarius.

Jovan (jo-VAHN) Latin: The sky's father. *Jovan* is a suitable choice for Sagittarius, who always sets his goals sky-high. Variations: *Jovi, Jovin*.

Kaemon (kah-AY-mon) Japanese: Joyful. *Kaemon*, an old Samurai name, is ideal for exuberant, fun-loving Sagittarius.

Kaga (KAH-gah) Native American: Writer. This unusual name is an apt choice for Sagittarius, who is endowed with a natural gift for the written word.

Karney (CAHR-nee) Irish: Winner. Sagittarius's ruling planet, Jupiter, governs good luck and opportunity, making Sagittarians naturally fortunate in all things. Variations: *Carney, Carny*.

Keane (KEEN) Old English: Sharp. Highly inquisitive Sagittarius tries to learn as much as possible about the world around him. Variations: *Kean, Keen*.

Kerey (KEH-ree) English Gypsy: Homeward bound. Although Sagittarius adores the adventure of travel, he never stays away from his loved ones for too long. Variations: *Keir, Ker, Keri, Kerry*.

Kerr (KER or KAR) Irish: Spear. *Kerr* connotes the hunt, or chase, associated with the sign of Sagittarius.

Kevin (KEV-in) Irish: Loving and gentle. Sagittarians are among the most kindhearted and sincere children of the zodiac. Variations: *Kevan, Keven*.

Kistur (KEE-stoor) English Gypsy: One who rides well. *Kistur* suggests Sagittarius's close association with the horse.

Kuzih (KOO-zhi) Native American: Great talker. Sagittarius is renowned for his exceptional communication skills.

Kwende (KWEHN-deh) African/Malawi: "Let's go!" Free-spirited Sagittarius is always ready for an adventure or journey.

Lal (LAHL) Hindu: Beloved. Another name for the god Krishna, *Lal* is a fine choice for Sagittarius, whose natural exuberance, kind nature, and refreshing sincerity endear him to all.

Lane (LAYN) Middle English: One from the narrow road. This name suggesting travel suits Sagittarius, whose spirit of adventure frequently leads to journeys to distant lands.

Lap (LAPP) Vietnamese: Independent. Above all, Sagittarians cherish their freedom.

Lee (LEE) Irish: Poet. Free-spirited and imaginative Sagittarians often make exceptionally gifted writers. Variation: *Leigh*. (Famous Sagittarian: Lee Trevino, golf champion)

Leopold (LEE-oh-pohld) Old German: Daring one. Sagittarians possess an intense love for travel, exploration, and adventure. Variation: *Leo*.

Lonato (loh-NAH-toh) Native American: Flint. *Lonato* is an apt name for Fire sign Sagittarius, who seems to ignite the energies of those around him with his enthusiasm and tremendous zest for life.

Lyron (lee-ROHN) Hebrew: Songlike. This whimsical name is a suitable choice for joyful and exuberant Sagittarius. Variation: *Liron.*

Lysander (lye-SAN-der) Greek: He who has come to free. Independence-loving Sagittarius readily gives plenty of freedom to others. Variation: *Lisandro.*

Maimun (mye-MOON) Arabic: Fortunate. Sagittarius's ruling planet of Jupiter governs opportunity and good luck.

Major (MAY-jir) Latin: Better. *Major* connotes the side of Sagittarius that continually strives to gain more knowledge and improve himself. Variations: *Majar, Mayer, Mayor.*

Makalani (mah-kah-LAH-nee) African/Kenyan: Excellent writer. Imaginative and free-spirited Sagittarians are highly gifted at writing. Many writers are born under the sign of Sagittarius.

Manipi (mah-NEE-pee) Native American: Walking wonder. Irrepressible Sagittarians are known for their intense wanderlust and spirit of adventure.

Marnin (mahr-NEEN) Hebrew: He who sings. *Marnin*, a popular name in Israel, is an appropriate choice for exuberant, high-spirited Sagittarius.

Masud (mah-SOOD) Arabic: Lucky. This name, a popular choice in Swahili culture in Africa, is suitable for Sagittarius, whose ruling planet of Jupiter governs good luck.

Menachem (men-AH-kem) Hebrew: Comforting. Completely genuine and down-to-earth, Sagittarians are capable of putting others at ease with their optimism and openhearted ways. Variations: *Menahem, Mendel, Mendeley*.

Mendel (MEHN-del) Yiddish: Scholarly accomplishments. When young, intensely curious Sagittarians are more eager to experience life than read about it. They often pursue higher learning later in life, with exceptional results.

Mestipen (MESS-ti-pen) English Gypsy: Luck. Jupiter, Sagittarius's ruling planet, governs optimism and good luck.

Mohan (MOH-han) Hindu: Wonderful. One of the many names of the god Krishna, *Mohan* suggests the humor, honesty, curiosity, and love possessed by Sagittarius.

Motega (moh-TEH-gah) Native American: A new arrow. This unusual name connotes the imagery of the Archer, Sagittarius's symbol.

Narcisse (nahr-SIS) French: Daffodil. *Narcisse* is the name of the beautiful Greek boy who could only love his own reflection. The narcissus is one of the flowers associated with the sign of Sagittarius. Variations: *Markissos, Narcissus*.

Nestor (NESS-tir) Greek: Sojourner. This name is an appropriate choice for Sagittarius, who possesses an eternal wanderlust.

Newland (NOO-lind) Old English: New land. *Newland* connotes Sagittarius's intense need to travel to distant places.

Newton (NOO-tin) Old English: New town. Sagittarians often satisfy their love of adventure and new experiences through travel.

Nolan (NOH-linn) Irish: Well known. Sagittarians are famously popular owing to their unmatched vitality, exceptional sense of humor, spirit of adventure, and genuine interest in the welfare of others. Variations: *Noelin, Noland, Nolin, Nollan.*

Oakes (OHKS) Old English: Near the grove of oak trees. Sagittarius is strongly associated with the oak tree. Variations: *Oak, Ochs.*

Oakley (OHK-lee) Old English: Field of oaks. This name is an appropriate choice for Sagittarius, who is affiliated with the oak tree. Variations: *Oakleigh, Oakly.*

Odin (OH-dinn) Scandinavian: For the Norse god, *Odin*, the source of all knowledge and the patron of heroes. This name suggests Sagittarius's thirst for learning and love of adventure.

Ogden (OG-dinn) Old English: He who lives near the oak grove. The trees associated with the sign of Sagittarius are the oak, the mulberry, and the birch. Variations: *Ogdan, Ogdon.*

Orrick (OR-ick) Old English: Venerable oak. Sagittarius is strongly affiliated with the oak tree. Variations: *Oreck, Orric.*

Ouray (oh-RAY or OO-ray) Native American: Arrow. This unique name connotes the imagery of the Archer, Sagittarius's symbol.

Owen (OH-wehn) Old English: Young bowman. *Owen* is an apt name for Sagittarius, whose symbol is the Archer. Variation: *Owain.*

Palani (pah-LAH-nee) Hawaiian: Free man. Independence-loving Sagittarius allows nothing to confine him.

Palmer (PAHL-mer) Old English: Pilgrim bearing palms. This traditional name is well suited to Sagittarius, who is happiest when traveling to distant lands.

Pancho (PAHN-choh) Spanish: Free man. Independent-minded Sagittarius compromises his ideals for no one.

Payat (PAY-yaht) Native American: On his way. *Payat* suggests adventure-loving Sagittarius's intense desire to travel and explore. Variations: *Pay, Payatt*.

Payne (PAYN) Latin: Comrade. Enthusiastic, fun loving, free spirited, and genuinely interested in others, Sagittarians make ideal friends and companions. Variation: *Paine*.

Philip (FILL-ip) Greek: Horse lover. This popular and classic name is ideal for Sagittarius, who is strongly associated with the Horse. Variations: *Felipe, Filip, Fischel, Phillip, Phillippe*. (Famous Sagittarian: Phil Donahue, talk-show host)

Pias (PEE-ahs) English Gypsy: Fun. One of the most prominent qualitites of Sagittarius is a marvelous sense of humor.

Radman (RADD-munn) Slavic: Happiness. Sagittarians are famous for their abundant cheer, enthusiasm, and optimism.

Ransom (RAN-som) Old English: Son of the armored one. The sign of Sagittarius is often associated with the imagery of hunting. Variations: *Rance, Ransome, Ranson*.

Rapier (RAYP-ee-air) Middle French: Sharp as a sword. Sagittarius is renowned for his quick, insightful mind and his ongoing thirst for knowledge.

Remus (REE-mus) Latin: Fleet-footed. Adventurous Sagittarians, drawn to travel, often find it difficult to stay in one place for long.

Rider (RYE-der) Old English: Horse rider. The horse is the animal symbol of Sagittarius. Variations: *Ridder, Ryder*. (Famous Sagittarian: Rider Strong, actor)

Riordan (REER-den) Irish: Troubadour. *Riordan* is an ideal choice for Sagittarius, who often entertains others with his humorous tales and imaginative writing. Variations: *Rearden, Reardon.*

Roger (RAH-jer) Old German: Famous swordsman. This classic name suits a boy born under Sagittarius, the sign of the hunt. Variations: *Rodge, Rodger, Rogerio, Ruggero, Rutger.*

Rohin (roh-HEEN) East Indian: On the upward path or sky-bound. Just as their symbol, the Archer, aims his bow toward the sky, Sagittarians always shoot for the stars.

Sachiel (SA-chee-ell) Hebrew: For the archangel of that name. *Sachiel* is the angel who watches over those born under the sign of Sagittarius.

Sarngin (SAHRN-geen) Hindu: Archer. *Sarngin* is another name for Vishnu, the great Hindu god who carries a bow.

Saxon (SAX-un) Old English: Blade. This traditional name is suitable for a boy born under Sagittarius, which is closely associated with the imagery of the hunt. Variations: *Saxe, Saxen.*

Scanlon (SCAN-lun) Irish: Young hunter. Sagittarius is the sign of the hunt. Variations: *Scanlan, Scanlen.*

Seif (say-EEF) Arabic: Religion's saber. This name connotes Sagittarius's constant striving to understand higher beliefs and defend the freedom to explore them.

Sevilen (seh-veh-LEN) Turkish: Much beloved. Sagittarians endear themselves to all with their enthusiasm, good humor, sincerity, unconventional ways, and truly kind nature.

Simcha (SEEM-khah) Hebrew: Joy. Cheerful, ebullient Sagittarius possesses a remarkable zest for life.

Skelly (SKELL-ee) Irish: Storyteller. Endowed with exceptional communication skills, Sagittarians are interesting, delightful, and often humorous conversationalists. They also make gifted writers. Variations: *Skelley, Skellie.*

Sloan (SLOHN) Irish: Warrior. *Sloan* is an apt choice for Sagittarius, the sign of the hunt symbolized by the Archer.

Spear (SPEER) Old English: Swordsman. Sagittarius, whose symbol is the Archer, is associated with the imagery of the hunt. Variations: *Spears, Speer, Speers, Spiers.*

Tai (TAH-ee) Vietnamese: Talent. Sagittarius is gifted in many areas, including writing, communication, and comedy.

Tait (TITE) Swedish: Merry. Lively and cheerful Sagittarius is known for his marvelous sense of humor and great love of laughter.

Thaddeus (THAD-dee-us) Aramaic: Bold. Free-spirited Sagittarians love adventure, compromising their ideals for no one. Variations: *Tad, Tadd, Taddeo, Tade, Tadeas, Tadey, Thaddeo.*

Theron (THAIR-uhn) Greek: Hunter. Symbolized by the Archer and ruled by Jupiter, the planet of adventure, Sagittarians are ardent explorers who love the thrill of the chase.

Tivon (tee-VOHN) Hebrew: Nature lover. Sagittarians are renowned for their love of the outdoors.

Travis (TRA-viss) Old French: From the crossroads. Sagittarius, delighted by all the different choices and opportunities life has to offer, relishes the adventure each path may bring. Variations: *Traver, Travers, Travus.*

Troy (TROY) Irish: Trooper. This classic name is suitable for a boy born under Sagittarius, the sign of the hunt. Variations: *Troi, Troye.*

Tumaini (tu-MAH-nee) African/Kenyan: Hope. One of Sagittarius's most prominent characteristics is eternal optimism.

Victor (VIK-tur) Latin: He who triumphs. Highly intelligent, enthusiastic, and innovative, Sagittarians always achieve the high goals they set their minds to. Variations: *Vic, Vick, Victoire, Victorio, Viktor, Vito, Vitor, Vittorio.*

Vidor (VEE-dohr) Hungarian: Cheerful. Sagittarians are endowed with an eternal joie de vivre.

Wade (WAYD) Old English: From the river crossing. Any name that connotes travel or exploration is ideal for Sagittarius, who relishes all types of adventures.

Wapi (WAH-pee) Native American: Lucky. Jupiter, the planet of good fortune and abundance, rules the sign of Sagittarius.

Wayland (WAY-land) Old English: Near the footpath. Suggesting the route of a journey, *Wayland* is an appropriate choice for adventurous, wandering Sagittarius. Variations: *Way, Waylan, Waylin, Waylon.*

Wen (WEHN) Englisy Gypsy: Born in the winter. Sagittarius is the first zodiac sign of winter.

Whistler (WHIS-ler) Old English: He who whistles. *Whistler* is a delightful choice for Sagittarius, who loves to laugh and always remains in high spirits.

Yagil (yah-GEEL) Hebrew: He who celebrates. This name is an apt choice for Sagittarius, who lives life to the fullest every day.

Zared (zah-RED) Hebrew: Ambush. *Zared* is an appropriate name for a boy born under Sagittarius, the sign of the hunt.

Zeke (ZEEK) Aramaic: Shooting star. Sagittarians, who always aim high, often achieve great success in whatever they set out to do.

Zeki (ze-KYE) Turkish: Smart. Sagittarians, possessed with a burning desire to have the answers to all of life's questions, are quick and eager learners.

Zenos (ZEE-nohs) Greek: Jupiter's gift. The planet Jupiter governs the sign of Sagittarius.

Famous Sagittarians

11-23-1804	Franklin Pierce	11-27-1976	Jaleel White
11-23-1859	Billy the Kid	11-28-1894	Brooks Atkinson
11-23-1887	Boris Karloff	11-28-1929	Berry Gordy, Jr.
11-23-1888	Harpo Marx	11-28-1943	Randy Newman
11-24-1784	Zachary Taylor	11-28-1946	Joe Dante
11-24-1853	Bat Masterson	11-28-1949	Alexander Godunov
11-24-1868	Scott Joplin	11-28-1949	Paul Shaffer
11-24-1888	Dale Carnegie	11-28-1950	Ed Harris
11-24-1925	William F. Buckley, Jr.	11-28-1959	Judd Nelson
11-25-1846	Carry Nation	11-28-1967	Anna Nicole Smith
11-25-1914	Joe DiMaggio	11-29-1832	Louisa May Alcott
11-25-1920	Ricardo Montalban	11-29-1895	Busby Berkeley
11-25-1947	John Larroquette	11-29-1908	Adam Clayton Powell, Jr.
11-25-1960	Amy Grant		
11-25-1960	John F. Kennedy, Jr.	11-29-1927	Vin Scully
11-26-1912	Eugene Ionesco	11-29-1932	Diane Ladd
11-26-1912	Eric Severeid	11-29-1933	John Mayall
11-26-1922	Charles Schulz	11-29-1939	Peter Bergman
11-26-1933	Robert Goulet	11-29-1940	Chuck Mangione
11-26-1938	Rich Little	11-29-1949	Garry Shandling
11-26-1938	Tina Turner	11-29-1955	Howie Mandel
11-27-1909	James Agee	11-29-1956	Jeff Fahey
11-27-1917	"Buffalo" Bob Smith	11-29-1960	Cathy Moriarty
11-27-1940	Bruce Lee	11-30-1667	Jonathan Swift
11-27-1941	Eddie Rabbit	11-30-1835	Mark Twain
11-27-1942	Jimi Hendrix	11-30-1874	Winston Churchill
11-27-1957	Caroline Kennedy	11-30-1923	Efrem Zimbalist, Jr.
11-27-1964	Robin Givens	11-30-1926	Richard Crenna

11-30-1929	Dick Clark	12-06-1936	David Ossman
11-30-1930	G. Gordon Liddy	12-06-1953	Tom Hulce
11-30-1936	Abbie Hoffman	12-06-1955	Steven Wright
11-30-1937	Robert Guillaume	12-07-1915	Eli Wallach, Jr.
11-30-1947	David Mamet	12-07-1923	Ted Knight
11-30-1953	Shuggie Otis	12-07-1932	Ellen Burstyn
11-30-1955	Billy Idol	12-07-1942	Harry Chapin
11-30-1962	Bo Jackson	12-07-1947	Johnny Bench
12-01-1897	Cyril Ritchard	12-07-1956	Larry Bird
12-01-1913	Mary Martin	12-07-1958	Edd Hall
12-01-1935	Woody Allen	12-08-1886	Diego Rivera
12-01-1936	Lou Rawls	12-08-1894	James Thurber
12-01-1939	Lee Trevino	12-08-1911	Lee J. Cobb
12-01-1940	Richard Pryor	12-08-1925	Sammy Davis, Jr.
12-01-1945	Bette Midler	12-08-1930	Maximillian Schell
12-02-1859	George Seurat	12-08-1933	Flip Wilson
12-02-1923	Maria Callas	12-08-1936	David Carradine
12-02-1948	Cathy Lee Crosby	12-08-1939	James Galway
12-02-1962	Tracy Austin	12-08-1943	Jim Morrison
12-02-1973	Monica Seles	12-08-1947	Gregg Allman
12-03-1857	Joseph Conrad	12-08-1953	Kim Basinger
12-03-1930	Jean-Luc Godard	12-08-1964	Teri Hatcher
12-03-1930	Andy Williams	12-08-1966	Sinead O'Connor
12-03-1948	Ozzy Osbourne	12-09-1608	John Milton
12-03-1980	Anna Chlumsky	12-09-1898	Emmett Kelly
12-04-1866	Wassily Kandinsky	12-09-1909	Douglas Fairbanks, Jr.
12-04-1892	Francisco Franco	12-09-1916	Kirk Douglas
12-04-1944	Dennis Wilson	12-09-1922	Redd Foxx
12-04-1949	Jeff Bridges	12-09-1925	Dina Merrill
12-04-1963	Jozef Sabovcik	12-09-1928	Dick Van Patten
12-04-1964	Marisa Tomei	12-09-1930	Buck Henry
12-05-1782	Martin Van Buren	12-09-1941	Beau Bridges
12-05-1839	George Armstrong Custer	12-09-1942	Dick Butkus
12-05-1901	Walt Disney	12-09-1957	Donny Osmond
12-05-1906	Otto Preminger	12-10-1830	Emily Dickinson
12-05-1932	Little Richard	12-10-1911	Chet Huntley
12-05-1947	Jim Messina	12-10-1914	Dorothy Lamour
12-05-1951	Morgan Brittany	12-10-1928	Dan Blocker
12-06-1870	William S. Hart	12-10-1952	Susan Dey
12-06-1886	Joyce Kilmer	12-10-1960	Kenneth Branagh
12-06-1896	Ira Gershwin	12-11-1882	Fiorello La Guardia
12-06-1906	Agnes Moorehead	12-11-1913	Carlo Ponti
12-06-1920	Dave Brubeck	12-11-1931	Rita Moreno
12-06-1924	Wally Cox	12-11-1942	Donna Mills
		12-11-1944	Brenda Lee

12-11-1949	Teri Garr	12-16-1943	Steven Bochco
12-11-1954	Jermaine Jackson	12-16-1946	Benny Andersson
12-11-1979	Rider Strong	12-16-1962	William "Refrigerator"
12-12-1893	Edward G. Robinson		Perry
12-12-1915	Frank Sinatra	12-17-1894	Arthur Fiedler
12-12-1918	Joe Williams	12-17-1929	William Safire
12-12-1923	Bob Barker	12-17-1930	Bob Guccione
12-12-1938	Connie Francis	12-18-1886	Ty Cobb
12-12-1941	Dionne Warwick	12-18-1916	Betty Grable
12-12-1952	Cathy Rigby	12-18-1917	Ossie Davis
12-12-1957	Sheila E.	12-18-1925	Roger Smith
12-12-1975	Mayim Bialik	12-18-1943	Keith Richards
12-13-1913	Archie Moore	12-18-1947	Steven Spielberg
12-13-1925	Dick Van Dyke	12-18-1950	Leonard Maltin
12-13-1927	Christopher Plummer	12-18-1963	Brad Pitt
12-13-1941	John Davidson	12-19-1902	Ralph Richardson
12-13-1948	Ted Nugent	12-19-1920	David Susskind
12-14-1503	Nostradamus	12-19-1933	Cicely Tyson
12-14-1911	Spike Jones	12-19-1934	Al Kaline
12-14-1914	Morey Amsterdam	12-19-1944	Tim Reid
12-14-1919	Shirley Jackson	12-19-1946	Robert Urich
12-14-1932	Charlie Rich	12-19-1960	Daryl Hannah
12-14-1935	Lee Remick	12-19-1963	Jennifer Beals
12-14-1946	Patty Duke	12-19-1972	Alyssa Milano
12-14-1946	Michael Ovitz	12-20-1868	Harvey Firestone
12-15-1892	J. Paul Getty	12-20-1922	George Roy Hill
12-15-1933	Tim Conway	12-20-1946	Uri Geller
12-15-1949	Don Johnson	12-21-1879	Joseph Stalin
12-16-1770	Ludwig van Beethoven	12-21-1922	Paul Winchell
12-16-1775	Jane Austen	12-21-1935	Phil Donahue
12-16-1899	Noel Coward	12-21-1937	Jane Fonda
12-16-1901	Margaret Mead	12-21-1940	Frank Zappa
12-16-1917	Arthur C. Clarke	12-21-1948	Samuel L. Jackson
12-16-1939	Liv Ullmann	12-21-1954	Chris Evert
12-16-1941	Leslie Stahl	12-21-1966	Kiefer Sutherland

CAPRICORN
(December 22–January 20)

GLYPH: ♑

SYMBOL: The Goat

POLARITY: Feminine

QUALITY: Cardinal

ELEMENT: Earth

RULING PLANET: Saturn

BIRTHSTONE: Garnet

SPECIAL COLORS: Deep greens and warm browns of nature

FLOWER: Carnation and ivy

METAL: Lead

ANIMAL: Goat and all other cloven-hoofed animals

MOST LIKEABLE TRAITS: Reliability, diligence, and self-discipline

♑

One of the most misunderstood and underrated of the zodiac's children, Capricorns have been unfairly painted as dark, moody, somber, cold, withdrawn, critical, and self-absorbed. At their best, they are often depicted as unimaginative but hardworking and reliable old souls who never rock the boat. At their worst, they have been decried as viciously self-promoting and Machiavellian in intent, able manipulators of the unsuspecting masses. None of these Capricornian portraits is fair or wholly correct. Capricorn, the least talked-about of astrology's signs, is in fact one of the most deeply complex and potentially great. Like Sagittarius and Gemini, Capricorns have a profoundly dual nature—determinedly grounded in the rational and practical, yet superbly capable of achieving visionary feats of accomplishment. The mature and fully realized Capricorn is that rarest of animals, a dreamer and a doer, capable not only of imagining great things but also of accomplishing them. Helping Capricorn children reconcile their powerful dual natures and realize their greatest dreams is their parents' challenging but privileged task.

General Qualities

Capricorn is a Feminine and Cardinal Earth sign that is ruled by the darkly mysterious planet Saturn. The influence of Saturn in Capricorn is powerfully complex, and an understanding of the myth and history surrounding this planet is key to understanding the complicated nature of Capricorns.

In Roman mythology, Saturn was the god who ruled over harvest time, specifically over the sowing and reaping of grain. Thus one aspect of Saturn's planetary influence is benevolent and associated with fertility, growth, and bounty. Children born under Saturn-ruled Capricorn, an Earth sign, are renowned for their down-to-earth sensibility and their extraordinary dedication to working hard, accomplishing formidable tasks, and achieving great success and material rewards.

In Greek mythology, however, Saturn was known as Kronos, named for the deposed king of the gods who was infamous for eating his own children. Strongly associated with the relentless passage of time (chronos), Kronos/Saturn was frequently depicted as an elderly man carrying a sickle—an image still used today to symbolize Father Time.

In ancient times, Saturn was also the most distant of the known planets, a fact that lent it a dark and mysterious quality, an association that persists today. Many astrologers view Saturn in Jungian terms, calling it the "shadow" planet or the "dark sun"—a receptacle for many of the more somber human emotions and tendencies. Capricorns are thus frequently depicted, often unfairly, as unduly serious, withdrawn, cold, ruthless, and melancholy.

This dual notion of the planet Saturn as associated both with positive, productive qualities and darker, subterranean tendencies makes for one of the most potent planetary influences in astrology. Indeed, most modern astrologers refer to Saturn as the "celestial taskmaster" because it governs such traits as hard work, cautiousness, perseverence, self-discipline, and the overcoming of obstacles and limitations. All of these abilities are strongly present in Capricorns, who are among the most ambitious and success-driven children of the zodiac.

Invariably dedicated to achieving great things—with material wealth frequently being the motivating factor—Capricorns are renowned for their superb organizational and time-management skills, their dogged commitment to hard work, and their practical, conservative, and cautious approach to everything in life. Capricorns are also patient, reserved, self-disciplined, and self-determined. Thus they are able to delay gratification in all forms in deference to their long-range goals of success and wealth.

The Feminine influence in Capricorn is most critical, supporting Capricorn children's driving ambition with great reserves of inner strength, keen intuition about the environment around them, and almost hypnotic personalities that can draw large groups of people into their personal orbit. Elvis Presley, Mao Tse-tung, and Joseph Stalin were famous Capricorns in whom the feminine hypnotic influence was deeply operative.

The Cardinal quality of this sign powerfully amplifies Capricorns' fierce drive to succeed by endowing those born under the sign with considerable initiative, outer-directed energy, and superb leadership skills. The element of Earth deeply grounds Capricorns in the present and supports their practical and conservative natures.

The Capricornian image one might reasonably draw from the preceding descriptions is of a complex and difficult-to-categorize individual who is driven equally by both positive and negative traits: hard work and self-absorption; public magnetism and fiercely personal ambition; intuitiveness and taciturnity; abundant energy and little imagination; outer success and inner isolation. Some Capricorns have been, or have been called, all these things. Indeed, three of modern history's most famous Capricorns are embodiments of these qualities: Richard Nixon, J. Edgar Hoover, and Howard Hughes. But this is a limited and one-sided view of complicated Capricorn, who also includes among its children such extraordinary figures as Martin Luther King, Jr., Albert Schweitzer, Anwar Sadat, Muhammad Ali, Louis Pasteur, and Benjamin Franklin.

While the typical Capricorn's approach to life is decidedly one of seriousness, hard work, rationality, and personal ambition, they also have a richly emotional side, though it is often hidden behind the Capricornian public persona of achievement-driven energy. This deeper aspect of Capricorn is aptly demonstrated in the symbol for the sign, The Goat or Capricornus. No ordinary goat, the Capricornus is in fact a legendary creature, a sea goat with a fantastical appearance: the head, chest, and forelegs of a goat; the hindquarters and tail of a fish.

On the one hand, then, Capricorn is represented by the sure- and swift-footed mountain goat who easily scales rocky terrain, ever upward, determinedly butting its way through any obstacle and challenge that comes along. These qualities of hard-won success are quintessentially Capricornian. But the other half of the Capricornus is a formidable creature of the sea, capable of navigating deep and roily waters. Present in earthy Capricorns, therefore, is a strong Water influence, giving them many of the qualities of the Water signs, Cancer and Pisces. Capricorns are deeply sensitive, empathetic, compassionate, and capable of sharing their considerable powers of reconciliation and healing. Whereas these qualities are very much on the surface in Cancers and Pisces, in Capricorns they often remain below the surface, taking second place to ambition, hard work, and the drive for success. Nevertheless, the Water qualities of Capricorn remain potent influences in Capricorn children's lives, and often surface with maturity to take a compelling first place.

Capricorns who can comfortably and successfully weave together these two diverse sides of their natures are among the most astoundingly successful people of the zodiac, capable of singular achievements and long-lasting influence.

Home

On the surface, Capricorn children can appear so mature and self-possessed that they seem to need little intervention or direction from their parents. From toddlerhood on, they demonstrate a quiet, mature, and decidedly serious approach to the world and the people around them. Remarkably adaptable and accommodating souls, Capricorns are comfortable with and comforted by well-defined rules, routines, and family rituals. They rarely get into trouble, never challenge the status quo, and make devoted, loyal companions who are especially drawn to the older members of their families.

Considerate, thoughtful, and innately self-disciplined, Capricorns are eager helpmates who often prefer to take part in more directed and adult activities, rather than aimlessly playing with their peers or younger siblings. For one thing, many Capricorn children aren't naturally playful, similar to their nearest cousins, Virgos. But whereas fastidious Virgos may avoid play because they can't tolerate messes or getting dirty, achievement-oriented Capricorns often avoid play because they simply don't see the point of it. They find it difficult to join in with unstructured activities that have no useful focus. Instead, from an early age on, Capricorns are drawn to clearly defined tasks and activities that have neat and identifiable beginnings, middles, and ends.

In particular, Capricorns want to feel useful to those around them, so many of their activities involve helping out in the home. They also derive enormous personal satisfaction from accomplishing especially difficult and adult tasks, and the more challenging the task, the harder and more determinedly Capricorns work at it. Unlike Sagittarians, Capricorn children will never abandon a job, however difficult, tedious, or boring. Indeed, anything that remotely resembles work is in fact a joy to achievement-driven Capricorns. Think of the wild mountain goat, so closely associated with this sign: Climbing a nearly vertical and rocky slope is a daunting, frightening, and arduous task, but the sure-footed mountain goat inevitably reaches the summit—often with glee and panache!

Nevertheless, Capricorn children's seriousness, self-possession, and precocious work ethic can be disconcerting at first glance, especially to parents who esteem more creative and imaginative lifestyles. Work is play to young Capricorns—it is how they define themselves, assess their capabilities, and pre-

pare for an adult life dedicated to singular success and achievement. Parents must learn to honor and support this sober but
necessary tendency in their Capricorn children, because many
Capricorns are destined to play key roles in the world.

All the Earth signs—Virgo, Capricorn, and Taurus—are vital
to the ongoing function of the world. They are the workers, the
doers, the accomplishers of the zodiac. They give form and
meaning to the dreams and aspirations of the other signs. Of all
the Earth signs, Capricorn is the most critical to raising a mere
dream to a singular reality. Virgos work hard, but they consciously choose secondary roles. Taureans work hard too, but
they rarely take the initiative and are frequently hampered by
bad tempers and stubbornness. Among the hardworking Earth
signs, only Capricorns are willing to aim for leadership roles,
despite being naturally quiet and unassuming. And they garner
the confidence to aim high by practicing for their adult roles in
childhood.

Another simpler, less obvious reason affects why young Capricorns are often reluctant to play and join in with their peers.
Beneath their cool and self-contained exteriors runs a deep shyness and a terrible vulnerability to criticism. More comfortable
with adults, who have clear and specific expectations of them,
Capricorns who are faced with the raw and unbridled energy of
other children often become reticent with their peers and confused about just how to behave. They are innately quiet, mature,
and self-possessed, and those qualities alone make them less
childlike. Capricorns don't know how to enjoy aimlessness, doing things for the sheer pleasure of doing them: It's simply not
in their nature. Because they are deeply intelligent, intuitive, and
sensitive about how the world works, no one is more aware than
Capricorns themselves of how different from other children their
approach to life is. They know they are ready targets for taunts
and teases, and they want to fit in like any other young child.
Here, the Water element in Capricorn is very strong, resembling
the deeply sensitive and emotionally vulnerable Cancers and Pisces.

One of the greatest gifts parents can give their Capricorn children is to gently teach them how to reconcile their cool, self-

contained, pragmatic, and earth-bound Cardinal qualities with their softer, sensitive, compassionate, and vulnerable Water qualities. Parents should try to honor and support their Capricorn children's self-possession, serious approach, and dedicated commitment to high achievement. However precocious and off-putting these tendencies may sometimes seem in one so young, they are the warp and weft of every successful Capricorn's life and vital to Capricorn's well-being. At the same time, parents must find ways to bolster their Capricorn children's sensitive and compassionate sides by assuring them that vulnerability is not a chink in their achievement-driven armor, but an avenue to understanding the world through the heart as well as the head.

Those Capricorns who never learn to embrace their softer sides run the risk of becoming ruthless and isolated in their drive to succeed; their victories, however great, ultimately ring hollow. If Capricorns' deeply serious and self-directed approach to life is denigrated early on, they may remain forever cast adrift from personal visions that could have great and lasting effects. But Capricorns who succeed in reconciling their hearts and minds are capable of outstanding accomplishments, becoming that rare handful of singular visionaries who make the world a better place.

School and Play

In every way, Capricorns are model students who excel academically and garner high marks for good behavior in the bargain. Their commitment to hard work and success blossoms in an academic setting where achievement is quantifiable and feedback is almost instantaneous. Respectful of authority and comfortable with rules and structure, Capricorns thrive in the ordered environment of the school where expectations are clearly defined and progress is methodically plotted. Initially more comfortable with teachers—with whom they establish an easy rapport—than with their fellow students, Capricorns in time will ease into leadership roles on student councils and in after-school clubs. With maturity, self-confidence replaces Capricorn children's natural reticence with their peers, and they are often viewed as the most dependable and loyal of friends, whose wise and sensible counsel is eagerly sought.

Like Virgos, Capricorns take a practical and conservative approach to their schoolwork, giving themselves plenty of time to plan, organize, and think through assignments. They have a natural aptitude for math and science. As older students, they demonstrate a keen facility for economics. Less adept in the more extemporaneous and creative subjects, they nevertheless work long and hard in these personally challenging areas to prove to themselves—and the world—that they can master anything.

Despite their ambitious and competitive natures, young Capricorns are not drawn to team sports. Instead, when interested in sports at all, they tend to choose individually oriented athletics, such as track and field, or one-on-one competitions such as tennis, wrestling, fencing, and boxing, where they can easily test, retest, and assess their personal limits and achievements on a regular basis.

Play, as discussed earlier, is not the Capricorn child's natural milieu. Capricorns prefer doing "useful" and adult things, often around the home, and certainly this tendency should be encouraged and applauded. However, Capricorn children, like Virgos, run a decided risk of growing old before their time, so they may benefit greatly by being part of a small, organized play group at a young age. In a manageable group of peers, engaged in directed activities, Capricorns may display a surprisingly uninhibited and spontaneous side to their serious natures.

The World

As adults, Capricorns are often consumed with becoming great successes and preeminent leaders in their chosen fields. Furthermore, their drive to succeed is rarely characterized by flamboyance, aggression, and self-absorption, like the more fiery signs of Leo and Aries.

Instead, most Capricorns are that very rare commodity: committed visionaries who are willing to defer gratification and work long and hard to achieve their goals. Mature Capricorns are superbly equipped for great success. Self-motivated, self-disciplined, and self-contained, they are rarely distracted or defeated by obstacles, setbacks, and criticism. Capricorns' approach to achieving success is undramatic, reasonable, and rational. First, they methodically lay out a well-planned and well-organized path. Then they set out on that path, never deviate from the route, and slowly but surely follow the road to ultimate achievement and recognition.

Along the way, Capricorns are renowned for their coolness in the face of difficulties, their clearheadedness in managing problems, and their hardworking commitment to getting a job done superbly and efficiently. They are innately gifted business people who ably manage time, people, and multiple tasks with authority and alacrity. Industry, politics, and high finance are quintessentially Capricornian fields and afford Capricorns ample opportunity to seek and attain the high levels of leadership to which aspire. Science, too, has attracted its fair share of Capricorns, but the creative arts are notably lacking in this sign.

Capricorns are strongly motivated in their endeavors by the need to acquire wealth and material possessions. With Capricorns, however, money is valued less for the things it can buy—the typical Capricorn is conservative and cautious about displaying material wealth—and more for the security it can ensure. Perceptive, rational, and deeply intuitive observers of their environment, Capricorns are well aware that the seemingly orderly affairs of men can be turned topsy-turvy in a heartbeat. Hence, Capricorns spend much of their adult lives accumulating money as a defense against chaos.

The drive to succeed, to lead, and to accumulate wealth and security are the overriding concerns of the public persona of most Capricorns, making them appear somewhat aloof, calculating, and self-absorbed in pursuit of their goals. The private persona, however, can be deeply compassionate and empathetic. In friendship, Capricorns are loyal and dependable comrades, eager to offer their wise counsel and sensitive support in times of trouble. Romantically, Capricorns may also be devoted and ardent spouses, though it is not unusual for them to postpone marriage until late in life, after they have achieved their ambitions and fully reconciled their rational and emotional sides.

The mature Capricorn is a refreshing breeze in a frenetic world—sensible, rational, realistic, and self-confident in the face of almost any dilemma. Possessed of extraordinary inner resources, emotional and physical resiliency, and an unwavering belief in their ability to change the world by virtue of simple hard work, quiet Capricorns seem unlikely candidates for greatness. Yet great they often are, counting among their members some of the genuine visionaries of modern times.

Choosing a Name for Your Capricorn Child

When choosing a name for your Capricorn child, first think about the major attributes and symbols associated with the sign. Capricorn is the sign of hard work, reliability, practicality, hard-won success, leadership, and material wealth. Guided by a strong sense of purpose throughout their lives, Capricorns are committed to achieving great things. They are dedicated, disciplined, and loyal workers who, unlike their Virgo cousins, are not content to work behind the scenes. Capricorns aspire to leadership roles in whatever fields they enter, and they are willing to take the long and methodical road to success, rather than become a flash in the pan.

Along with their penchant for hard work and self-discipline, Capricorns have formidable organizational and time-management skills and are renowned for taking a slow yet incisive approach to strategizing and prioritizing tasks and time. They bring these skills both to school, where they are excellent students, and to business, where they are invariably successes. They are especially adept in mathematics, science, and industry. Wise investors and managers of money, many Capricorns aspire to great wealth and eventually attain it.

Capricorn is a Feminine, Cardinal Earth sign governed by the planet Saturn. Saturn's influence in Capricorn is complex and twofold. On the one hand, Saturn traditionally is connected to nature and governs the sowing and reaping of grain. On the other hand, Saturn is also also associated with both the relentless march of time and the more serious, even dark, human qualities and tendencies, including remoteness, coldness, self-discipline, and caution. Saturn also is associated with overcoming obstacles and limitations. Capricorns are themselves dual natured, having both a deep and fertile connection to the Earth and a more cerebral and driving need to succeed while remaining self-contained and impervious to others' influences.

The Feminine aspect endows Capricorns with tremendous inner strength, intuition, and magnetism. The Cardinal quality energizes Capricorns and makes them outer directed. The Earth grounds Capricorns in the present and encourages their practicality and caution.

Capricorn is the tenth sign of the zodiac, encompassing the winter months of December and January, and often associated with Christmas and snowfalls. The garnet is the sign's official birthstone, and lead is the metal governed by Capricorn. The deep greens and muted browns of nature are the sign's colors. The "flowers" of Capricorn are the carnation and ivy, while the pine, elm, and poplar trees are also strongly associated with the sign. The sign is symbolized by the Goat and also rules all other cloven-hoofed animals.

When you choose a name for your child, also bear in mind some of Capricorn's key personal qualities. They have a deep connection to nature and the natural environment around them. They are poised, self-contained, self-disciplined, and inner directed. Capricorns are ambitious and committed to success, but respectful of rules, regulations, and authority. They can be quite emotionally reserved, but beneath this reserve are richly compassionate souls who are deeply loving and loyal.

For additional inspiration when choosing a name for your Capricorn child—especially a middle name—you may want to browse through the names listed in Capricorn's companion Earth signs, Virgo and Taurus.

Names for Capricorn Girls

A'ishah (ah-ee-SHAH) Arabic: Prosperous. Success and material wealth are primary goals of Capricorn. Variations: *Aishah, Ayesha.*

Abia (ah-BEE-ah) Arabic: Great. Fiercely ambitious, Capricorns aim very high in their career goals and often aspire to leadership roles.

Afra (AH-frah) English: Color of the Earth. Capricorn is one of three Earth signs in the zodiac. (The other two are Virgo and Taurus.) Variations: *Affera, Affra, Aphra.*

Ailaina (a-LAYN-ah) Scottish: Rock. Capricorns are famous for their dependability, practicality, and steadfast loyalty. Variations: *Alaine, Alanis, Elaine.*

Aja (AH-jah) Hindu: Goat. The Goat, or Capricornus, is the animal symbol of the sign of Capricorn.

Allison (AL-lis-sohn) Greek: Truthful. Capricorns are renowned for their virtuous natures and high ethical standards. Variations: *Alison, Allie, Alyson.*

Alta (AHL-tah) Latin: High. Ambitious Capricorns are driven to succeed and often achieve great things.

Amalthea (ah-mahl-THEE-ah) Greek: Mythological mountain goat. Capricorn is symbolized by the mythological sea goat, Capricornus, an animal that was half-goat and half-fish.

Amelia (ah-MEEL-yah) Latin: Hard worker. One of the key characteristics of Capricorn is a remarkable commitment to work. Variations: *Amali, Amalia, Amalie, Amelina, Amelita, Amie, Amilia.*

Anona (ah-NOH-nah) Latin: Seasonal plantings. Capricorn, one of the Earth signs of the zodiac, is ruled by the planet Saturn, which governs reaping and sowing.

Arista (ah-REES-tah) Greek: Harvest. *Arista* is a unique name for Capricorn, whose ruling planet of Saturn is strongly associated with harvest time.

Artha (AHR-tah) Hindu: Tremendous wealth. Capricorn's strong work ethic and dedication to her goals enable her to realize her dreams of financial prosperity.

Arwa (AHR-wah) Arabic: Young goat. Like the surefooted and sturdy Goat that is their symbolic animal, Capricorns are able to butt their way through life's obstacles.

Asiza (ah-SEE-zah) African/Dahomey: Forest spirit. Born under an Earth sign, Capricorns have a special affiliation with their natural environment.

Audra (AWH-drah) English: Noble strength. Capricorns are noted for their extraordinary inner strength. Variations: *Audi, Audrey*.

Ayalah (eye-YAHL-ah) Hebrew: Deer. Capricorn is symbolized by the Goat, but the sign also governs all other cloven-hoofed animals.

Ayoola (ah-YOO-lah) African/Nigerian: Joy in wealth. Capricorn is the sign of material success, and Capricorns are renowned for their excellent management of money.

Azza (AHZ-zah) Arabic: Gazelle. The gazelle is among the cloven-hoofed animals governed by the sign of Capricorn.

Bariah (ba-RYE-ah) Arabic: To succeed. Capricorns are committed to success and material wealth.

Bolade (BOH-lah-deh) African/Nigerian: Honor arrives. Noted for their pristine work ethic, Capricorns place a high value on honesty and fairness.

Bona (boh-NAH) Hebrew: Builder. Capricorns take the slow and steady route to success, methodically laying out a practical strategy for success.

Bryanna (bree-AN-nah) Irish: Fortitude. Capricorns, renowned for their self-discipline, have enormous staying power. Variations: *Brianna, Briona, Bryana, Bryann, Bryanne.*

Bryony (BREE-ah-nee) English: A perennial vine with green flowers. The ivy vine and the color green are strongly associated with the sign of Capricorn. Like a vine, Capricorn's approach to life is steadfast and tenacious.

Carmela (kahr-MAY-lah) Latin: Bountiful orchard. Capricorn is an Earth sign ruled by the planet Saturn, which is named for the ancient Roman god of reaping and sowing. Variations: *Carmel, Carmelita, Carmella, Carmelle.*

Caroline (KARE-oh-lin; KARE-oh-lyne) Latin: Little womanly one. Self-contained and self-disciplined, Capricorns are sagacious and mature beyond their years. Variations: *Cari, Carla, Carleen, Carly, Carol, Carole, Carrie, Cary.*

Ceres (SIR-eez) Latin: Cultivate. *Ceres* was the name of the Roman goddess of agriculture. This name is a lovely choice for Capricorn, one of three Earth signs of the zodiac.

Chantal (shan-TAHL) French: Rocky location. This popular French name is a fitting choice for Capricorn, who is born under an Earth sign and has a special affinity for the natural environment.

Charlotte (SHAHR-lot) French: Little womanly one. Self-contained and respectful of authority, young Capricorns are often wise and sophisticated beyond their years.

Charmaine (shahr-MAYNE) French: Bountiful orchard. The sign of Capricorn is often associated with fertility, growth, and bounty. Variations: *Charmayne, Charmian, Charmine*.

Chasina (hah-SEE-nah) Hebrew: Strong. The Feminine influence in Capricorn, together with the practical qualities of the sign's Earth element, endows Capricorns with great emotional fortitude. Variation: *Hasina*.

Chiara (chee-AHR-rah) Italian: Clear. The Capricorn drive to succeed is always supported by clear-minded and rational goals. Variations: *Clara, Klara*.

Chika (CHEE-kah) Japanese: Intelligence. Capricorn is the sign of practical and rational wisdom. Variation: *Chikako*.

Chloris (KLOH-riss) Greek: Green. *Chloris* is the name of a Roman goddess of vegetation. Capricorn is ruled by Saturn, the planet that governs the harvesting of grain. Green is one of the Earth colors strongly associated with this sign. Variations: *Cloris, Clorissa*.

Christabel (kriss-tah-BELL) Latin: Beautiful Christian. The sign of Capricorn encompasses the Christmas holiday, and many beautiful names reflective of both Christ and the holiday are appropriate choices for a Capricorn girl. Variations: *Cristabel, Cristabella*.

Christina (kriss-TEE-nah) English: Christian. This classic and popular name is suitable for Capricorns born on or near Christmas, the day Jesus Christ was born. Variations: *Christa, Christiane, Christine, Christy, Krista, Kristine*. (Famous Capricorn: Christy Turlington, supermodel)

Christmas (KRISS-miss) Old English: For the holiday. This name, very popular in Colonial America, is a unique choice for a Capricorn born on or near the Christmas holiday.

Constance (KAHN-stintz) Latin: Firm and unwavering. Capricorn's approach to work and life is determined, focused, rational, and conservative. Variations: *Conni, Connie, Constancia, Constanta, Constantia, Costanza.*

Cybele (si-BELL) Greek: Mother. In mythology, *Cybele* was the name of an Asia Minor nature goddess. One of the Earth signs of the zodiac, Capricorn shares a close connection with and concern for her natural environment. Variations: *Cybelle, Sibyl, Sybil, Sybille.*

Dagania (dahg-GAHN-ee-ah) Hebrew: Corn. Saturn, Capricorn's ruling planet, was named for the Roman god who governed the sowing and reaping of grain, including corn. Variations: *Dag, Dagana, Dagi.*

Dallas (DA-liss) Scottish: Of the dales and the meadows. One of the Feminine Earth signs, Capricorns have a strong affinity for the natural environment. Variation: *Dallis.*

Decima (DAY-see-mah) Latin: Tenth. Capricorn is the tenth sign of the zodiac, encompassing the months of December and January.

Delaney (de-LAY-nee) Irish: Child of a competitor. Capricorns are ambitious, committed to success in their chosen fields, and formidable competitors in the public marketplace. Variations: *Delaina, Delaine, Delayna, Delayne.*

Demetria (de-MEE-tree-ah) Greek: Of Demeter, the Greek goddess of corn and the harvest. Capricorn's ruling planet, Saturn, also governs harvest time and the sowing and reaping of corn. Variations: *Demetra, Demi, Demitra, Dimetria.*

Dixie (DIX-ee) French: Tenth. Capricorn is the tenth sign of the zodiac. Variations: *Dix, Dixee.*

Donna (DAHN-ah) Latin: Lady. Mature and self-possessed beyond their years, Capricorn girls are often models of traditional femininity. Variations: *Dahna, Dahnya, Dona, Donelle, Donetta, Donya.* (Famous Capricorn: Donna Summer, singer)

Eartha (UR-thah) Old English: Earth's daughter. This lovely name is suitable for a girl born under the sign of Capricorn, one of the three Earth signs of the zodiac. Variations: *Erta, Hertha.* (Famous Capricorn: Eartha Kitt, actress)

Ebba (EBB-bah) Old English: Fortress of prosperity. Material wealth is a primary goal of Capricorns, who are noted for their wise investment skills.

Edwardine (EDD-wer-deen) Old English: Rich protector. Acquiring wealth is often an overriding concern of Capricorns, who are also devoted and generous friends. Variations: *Edwarda, Edwardeen, Edwardyne.*

Edwina (ed-WEE-nah) Old English: Wealthy friend. Capricorns, who aspire to great wealth, make truly loyal and reliable friends.

Egidia (ee-JID-ee-ah) Scottish: Young goat. Capricorn rules the Goat and all other cloven-hoofed animals.

Ela (EHL-ah) Hindu: Intelligent woman. Intelligence, rationality, and clear thinking are hallmarks of the sign of Capricorn. Variations: *Elakshi, Elee, Elina, Elita, Ella.*

Eldreda (ell-DREY-dah) English: Elderly counselor. Even at very young ages, Capricorns demonstrate a precocious wisdom and firm practicality that inspires others to seek their advice and counsel.

Eliska (EL-izh-kah) Czechoslovakian: Truthful. Capricorns prize honesty and fair-mindedness.

Emily (EM-ah-lee) Gothic: Hard worker. *Emily* is an ideal name for industrious and ambitious Capricorn, who does all she can to achieve her high goals. Variations: *Em, Ema, Emera, Emi, Emie, Emilie, Emlyn, Emma.*

Enola (ay-NOH-lah) Native American: Original meaning is unclear, but many scholars believe this word means "alone" or "solitary." (Backward, it spells *alone.*) The self-contained and inner-directed Capricorn is capable of strong self-sufficiency.

Estefany (ess-STEFF-ah-nee) Spanish: Wealth. Hardworking Capricorn is often motivated by her desire for financial success. Variations: *Estefani, Estefania, Estephanie.*

Fabia (FAH-bee-ah) Latin: She who grows beans. *Fabia*, or one of its beautiful variations, is an apt choice for Capricorn, an Earth sign. Variations: *Fabiana, Fabiane, Fabianna, Fabienne, Fabiola.*

Fauna (FAWN-nah) Latin: To favor. *Fauna* is the name of the Roman goddess of farming, agriculture, and animals, and an alternative name for the goddess *Chloris* (see *Chloris*). Capricorn is ruled by Saturn, the planet that governs sowing and reaping.

Felda (FELL-dah) Old German: From the field. Names that evoke images of nature are wonderful choices for Capricorn, who is closely attuned to the natural environment.

Flora (FLORR-ah) Latin: Flower. An Earth sign with a strong Feminine element, Capricorn is closely associated with nature and the nurturing and growing of food, plants, and flowers. Variations: *Flo, Florence, Flori, Florie, Florrie, Florry.*

Fola (FAW-lah) African/Nigerian: Honor. Virtuous, practical, wise, and sensitive, Capricorns are highly respected by all.

Folayan (faw-LAH-yahn) African/Nigerian: To walk with dignity. Confident and self-possessed, Capricorn strikes a dignified and commanding figure.

Gafna (GAHF-nah) Hebrew: Vine. The ivy vine is strongly associated with the sign of Capricorn.

Gaia (GYE-ah) Greek: The planet Earth. *Gaia* was the name of the mythological Greek goddess of the Earth who gave birth to the seas, the mountains, and the sky. It is a lovely choice for Capricorn, one of three Earth signs. Variations: *Gaea, Gaiea, Gala.*

Ganit (gah-NEET) Hebrew: Garden. Capricorn, one of the Earth signs of the zodiac, is closely attuned to agriculture and the natural environment. Variations: *Gana, Ganice.*

Garnet (GAHR-nitt) Middle English: For the gemstone. The garnet is the birthstone of the sign of Capricorn.

Gazelle (gah-ZELL) Latin: Gazelle. Capricorn rules all cloven-hoofed animals. Variation: *Gazella.*

Georgia (JOR-jah) Latin: She who sows the earth. *Georgia* is an ideal choice for a girl born under the Earth sign of Capricorn. The sign's ruling planet of Saturn is associated with the sowing and reaping of grain. Variations: *Georgeann, Georgeina, Georgene, Georgianna, Georgie, Georgina, Jorgina.*

Gerda (GAIR-dah) Old Norse: Enclosure. This word, originally meaning an enclosure for farm animals, suggests Capricorns' connection to agriculture and various domesticated animals. Variations: *Gerde, Gerta.*

Gilberte (jil-BEHRT) Old German: Shining vow. Serious-minded Capricorns are loyal, dedicated, and committed in all they do. Variations: *Berta, Berty, Gigi, Gilberta, Gilbertina, Gillie.*

Grainne (GRAYN) Irish: From Irish mythology. *Grainne* was the name of the goddess of the grain. The sign of Capricorn is strongly affiliated with the sowing and reaping of grain. Variations: *Grania, Granna.*

Gressa (GRAY-sah) Norwegian: Earthly carpet. This name is an appropriate choice for Capricorn, one of the three Earth signs of the zodiac.

Haidee (HAY-dee) Greek: With propriety. With an intuitive sense of how to behave in any situation, Capricorns are often models of decorum, even at very young ages. Variation: *Haydee.*

Hana (HAH-nah) Japanese: Blossom. *Hana* connotes Capricorn's deep love for her natural environment as well as her ability to reconcile her inner sensitivity, empathy, and compassion with her exterior seriousness, practicality, and discipline as she matures. Variation: *Hanae.*

Heidi (HYE-dee) Swiss: Honorable. Honor, truth, justice, and fair play are key qualities admired by Capricorns. Variations: *Hedie, Heidie, Hydie.*

Hermina (hayre-MEE-nah) Czechoslovakian: Child of the earth. *Hermina* is an ideal choice for Capricorn, one of the three Earth signs of the zodiac. Variation: *Herma.*

Hertha (HUR-thah) Teutonic: Child of the earth. In Teutonic mythology, *Hertha* was a goddess of fertility. Capricorn is an Earth sign that has a deep affinity for the natural environment and for growing crops.

Hinda (HIN-dah) Yiddish: A deer. The deer is among the swift and surefooted cloven-hoofed animals ruled by the sign of Capricorn.

Hola (HOH-lah) Native American: Seed-filled club. The *hola* was a sacred instrument used in Hopi harvest rituals. Capricorn is ruled by Saturn, the planet that governs the sowing and reaping of grain and corn.

Humita (hoo-MEE-tah) Native American: Shelled corn. Capricorn's ruling planet, Saturn, is strongly associated with the sowing and reaping of grains, including corn.

Ida (EYE-dah) Old English: Wealthy. Hardworking and highly disciplined, Capricorns are often motivated by a desire to achieve financial success. Variations: *Idalene, Idalia, Idalina, Ide, Idell, Idelle, Idette, Ita.*

Imala (EE-mah-lah) Native American: Disciplinarian. Enormously self-disciplined and self-possessed, Capricorns expect the same from others and often have little tolerance for what they consider frivolous.

Imara (ee-MAH-rah) African/Swahili: Firm. *Imara* suggests the fiercely determined and strongly disciplined nature of Capricorn.

Irina (ee-REEN-ah) Czechoslovakian: Farmer. Saturn, Capricorn's ruling planet, governs harvest time and the sowing and reaping of crops. Variation: *Jiruska.*

Istas (EE-stahs) Native American: Snow. This unique name is an ideal choice for Capricorns born in the winter months of December and January.

Ivy (EYE-vee) Old English: Climber. *Ivy* is the name of the evergreen climbing vine of the ginseng family, one of Capricorn's two symbolic "flowers." Variations: *Iva, Ivalyn, Ivey, Ivie.*

Jemina (jay-MEE-nuh) Hebrew: Favoring the right side. Capricorns are eminently concerned with doing the right thing at the right time and prize the attributes of honesty, fairness, and practicality. Variations: *Jem, Jemi, Jemma, Jemmi, Jemmy, Mina.*

Jerica (JARE-ah-kah) American: Strong and gifted ruler. This beautiful contemporary name, a blending of *Jeri* and *Erica,* is a fitting choice for a Capricorn girl, known for her superlative leadership skills. Variations: *Jerika, Jerrica, Jerrika.*

Jessica (JESS-sah-kah) Hebrew: Wealthy. This popular name is an ideal choice for Capricorn, whose hard work often pays off in the form of financial success. Variations: *Jess, Jessalyn, Jesseca, Jessi, Jessie, Jesslyn.*

Jethra (JEH-thrah) Hebrew: Abundance. The sign of Capricorn is associated with fertility, growth, and bounty.

Judith (JOO-dith) Hebrew: Glorified one. Capricorns are highly respected for their dedication to hard work, highly ethical natures, compassionate sensitivity, and ability to turn mere ideas into monumental accomplishments that may change the world. Variations: *Giudita, Judi, Judy.*

Kamila (kah-MEE-lah) Arabic: The perfect one. *Kamila* is a lovely and suitable choice for virtuous, dedicated, loyal, wise, and intuitive Capricorn, who is highly esteemed by all and capable of extraordinary achievements. Variations: *Kamilah, Kamilla, Kamillah.*

Kane (KAH-neh) Japanese: Doubly accomplished. Capricornus, the sea goat that symbolizes the sign of Capricorn, was a mythical creature that was half-goat and half-fish. Capricorns possess both the practical and rational qualities of Earth signs and the imaginative and intuitive qualities of Water signs.

Keitha (keth-AH) Gaelic: Woodland. Born under an Earth sign, Capricorns are happiest when surrounded by all of nature's blessings.

Kimberly (KIM-bur-lee) Old English: From the brilliant one's field. Children born under the sign of Capricorn, an Earth sign, are noted for their practical intelligence. Variations: *Kim, Kimberlee, Kimberli, Kimmi, Kym*.

Kira (KEE-rah) Russian: Lady. Reserved, serious, mature, and wise, Capricorns possess a naturally regal bearing. Variations: *Kiran, Kirana, Kiri, Kirra, Kyra*.

Kona (KOH-nah) Hindu: Hard curves. In East Indian mythology, *Kona* was another name for Saturn, an ancient Hindu divinity who governed storytelling and historical lore. Saturn is Capricorn's ruling planet.

Kuni (KOO-nee) Japanese: Country born. Quiet, conservative, and highly appreciative of their natural environments, Capricorns enjoy living in rural areas.

Kuniko (KOO-nee-koh) Japanese: Child from the countryside. Capricorn's ruling planet, Saturn, governs harvest time and the sowing and reaping of crops.

Lahela (lah-HAY-luh) Hawaiian: Sheep. This Hawaiian variation of *Rachel* is an apt choice for Capricorn, who is associated with all cloven-hoofed animals.

Leala (lee-AL-ah) French: Faithful or devoted. Capricorns make extraordinarily loyal and dependable friends who can be counted on in all times of need. Variations: *Lealia, Lealie, Leola*.

Lee (lee) Old English: Meadow. Born under one of the zodiac's Earth signs, Capricorn has a special affinity for her natural environment. Variations: *Lea, Leigh*.

Leotie (lay-OH-tee) Native American: Prairie flower. *Leotie* is an appropriate name for nature-loving Capricorn.

Leya (LAY-yah) Spanish: Loyalty to the law. Virtuous Capricorn never challenges the status quo and rarely gets into any trouble with authority.

Liana (lee-AHN-ah) French: The liana vine. The ivy vine is one of Capricorn's two symbolic "flowers." In their great and single-minded determination to succeed, Capricorns mimic the tenacity and durability of all vinelike plants. Variations: *Lean, Leana, Leane, Leeanne, Liane, Lianna, Lianne.*

Linette (lin-ETTE) Welsh: Honored model. This name is ideal for Capricorn, whose extraordinary achievements and virtuous work ethic make her an individual to emulate. Variations: *Lanette, Linet, Linnet, Linnetta, Lynette.*

Lola (LOH-lah) Hawaiian: Honored. *Lola* is a suitable name for Capricorns, who are known as highly esteemed leaders who work long and hard and reach their goals.

Lomasi (loh-MAH-see) Native American: Pretty flower. *Lomasi* is a unique choice for Capricorn, who is highly appreciative of her natural environment. (The "flowers" associated with the sign of Capricorn are the carnation and the ivy.)

Lotta (LOH-tah) Swedish: Little womanly one. This name suggests Capricorn's qualities of quiet reserve, intuitive sensitivity, and devotion to loved ones. Variations: *Lotte, Lottie.*

Mahalia (mah-HAHL-ee-ah) Aramaic: For calves, lambs, or kids prepared for market. Capricorn governs the Goat and other animals with cloven hooves. Variation: *Mehalia.*

Mahika (mah-HEE-kah) Hindu: Earth. Capricorn is one of the three Earth signs of the zodiac. Variation: *Mahi.*

Malvina (mal-VEE-nah) Irish: Smooth brow. Self-contained, emotionally controlled, and fiercely self-disciplined, Capricorns often present a stoic and cool face to the world.

Martha (MAR-thah) Aramaic: Honored lady. *Martha* is the patron saint of social workers, nurses, and doctors. Capricorns are highly esteemed for their dedication and discipline. Variations: *Marit, Marite, Mart, Marta, Martell, Marthe, Marthena, Marti, Martina, Martita, Matti*.

Matsu (MAHT-soo) Japanese: Pine. The sign of Capricorn is associated with the elm, poplar, and pine trees.

Mema (MAY-mah) Spanish: Hardworking. Among all the practical qualities associated with Capricorns, their extraordinary capacity for hard work is the most renowned.

Michiko (MIH-chih-koh) Japanese: The righteous way. Capricorns are adamant about living life virtuously and using only honest means to achieve their goals. Variation: *Michi*.

Midori (mee-DOH-ree) Japanese: Green. This lovely name is an apt choice for Capricorn, who is strongly associated with the color green.

Mili (MEE-lee; MIL-ee) Hebrew: Virtuous. *Mili* is an appropriate name for hardworking, disciplined, loyal, and determined Capricorn. Variations: *Millie, Milly*.

Mina (MEE-nah) Czechoslovakian: Child of the Earth. Capricorn, one of the three Earth signs of the zodiac, is closely associated with nature. Variations: *Meena, Minette, Minna, Minnette*.

Miyuki (mee-YOO-kee) Japanese: Deep snow. *Miyuki* is a lovely name for a Capricorn born during the winter months of December and January.

Mona (MOH-nah) Greek: Just. Capricorns are among the most virtuous and ethical children of the zodiac.

Moneka (mon-EE-kah; MON-ee-kah) Native American: Earth. Capricorn, which has a deep connection to nature, is one of the three Earth signs of the zodiac. Variation: *Moneca*.

Mura (MOO-rah) Japanese: Countryside. Capricorns often gravitate toward rural places where they can freely enjoy all of nature's gifts.

Natalie (NAT-ah-lee) Latin: Birth day. *Natalie* is a lovely name often given to Capricorns born on or near Christmas Day. Variations: *Naasa, Nat, Natala, Natalina, Nataline, Nathalia, Nathalie, Nati, Natty, Netti, Nettie, Netty, Tillie*.

Neda (NEH-duh) Old English: Prosperous guardian. This unusual name connotes Capricorns' desire to gain financial success with the intention of providing security for their loved ones.

Nediva (neh-DEE-vah) Hebrew: Highborn. Reserved, disciplined, and wealth-conscious, Capricorns possess a regal bearing.

Neema (NEE-mah; neh-EH-mah) African/Swahili: Born during a prosperous time. *Neema* is an apt choice for Capricorn, whose ruling planet, Saturn, governs harvest time.

Netia (NEHT-ee-ah) Hebrew: Vegetation. This popular Israeli name is appropriate for Capricorn, who shares a special connection with nature. Variations: *Neta, Netta, Nettie, Netty*.

Neva (NEH-vah) Spanish: Snowy. *Neva* is a lovely choice for a Capricorn girl born during the winter months of December and January. Variations: *Neiva, Neve*.

Nirel (ni-RAYL) Hebrew: Field of crops. Capricorn's ruling planet, Saturn, is named for the Roman god who governed the sowing and reaping of grain.

Nitara (ni-TAHR-rah) Hindu: Profoundly grounded. *Nitara* is an apt choice for earthy Capricorn, one of the most practical and rational of the zodiac's children.

Nizana (nee-ZAH-nah) Hebrew: Blossom. Capricorn's ruling planet, Saturn, is named for the Roman god of the harvest. Thus, the sign of Capricorn is strongly associated with growth and the glory of nature. Variations: *Nitza, Nitzana, Zana.*

Noelle (noh-ELL) French: Christmas. This popular name, or one of its beautiful variations, is a wonderful choice for a Christmas-born Capricorn. Variations: *Noel, Noël, Noele, Noeline, Noell, Noella, Noleen.*

Nori (NOR-ee) Japanese: Principle. Capricorns are renowned for their remarkable self-control and strict adherence to the high standards they set for themselves.

Odera (oh-DAY-ruh) Hebrew: Plough. Because Capricorn's ruling planet, Saturn, governs harvest time and the sowing and reaping of crops, the sign is often associated with the imagery of farming.

Odette (oh-DETTE) French: Riches. Hardworking and highly disciplined Capricorn is often motivated by her desire to accumulate great wealth. Variation: *Odetta.* (Famous Capricorn: Odetta, folk singer)

Olabunmi (aw-lah-BOON-mee) African/Nigerian: Prize won through honor. This unusual name suggests the way Capricorns strive long, hard, and virtuously to achieve their goals.

Onatah (oh-NAH-tah) Native American: God of corn. Saturn, Capricorn's ruling planet, governs the sowing and reaping of all grains, including corn.

Onida (oh-NEE-dah) Native American: The looked-for one. Dedication to ideals, extraordinary work ethics, great inner strength, and the determination to turn dreams into reality enable Capricorns to accomplish truly singular achievements that may even change the world. Variation: *Oneida..*

Onora (ON-or-ah) Latin: Honor. *Onora* is a suitable name for Capricorn, who never fails to act with dignity and virtue. Variations: *Honor, Honoria, Onoria, Onorine.*

Oprah (OH-prah) Hebrew: Fawn. Symbolized by the Goat, Capricorn also is affiliated with other types of cloven-hoofed animals. Variations: *Ofra, Ofrat, Ophra, Opra, Orpa, Orpha, Orphy.*

Orino (oh-REE-noh) Japanese: Weaver's field. Capricorn, one of the Earth signs of the zodiac, is strongly associated with nature and the outdoors. Variation: *Ori.*

Ornice (or-NEES) Hebrew: Pine tree. The pine is one of three trees governed by the sign of Capricorn. Variations: *Orna, Ornit.*

Papina (pah-PEE-nah) Native American: Crawling ivy. The flowers associated with the sign of Capricorn are the ivy and the carnation.

Patricia (pah-TRI-shah) Latin: Of the nobility. Reserved, serious, and wise, Capricorns often possess a naturally regal bearing. Variations: *Pat, Patrice, Patrizia, Patsy, Patti, Patty, Tricia, Trisha.* (Famous Capricorns: Patti Smith, singer; Pat Benetar, singer; Patricia Neal, actress)

Philomena (fil-oh-MEE-nah) Greek: Lover of strength. *Philomena* is an ideal choice for Capricorn, who is endowed with great inner strength and fierce determination. Variation: *Fila-mena*.

Pilisi (pi-LEE-see) Greek: Green branch. One of the three Earth signs of the zodiac, Capricorn is associated with the deep green colors of nature.

Precious (PRESH-us) English: Of tremendous value. Capricorns are highly esteemed for their extraordinary accomplishments, adherence to high ethical standards, and dependability and sensitivity in relationships. Variations: *Precia, Preciosa*.

Radmilla (RAHD-mel-luh) Slavic: Worker for the people. Industrious Capricorns often achieve great things that make the world a better place. Famous Capricorns who have had a lasting influence on society include Martin Luther King, Jr., Benjamin Franklin, and Louis Pasteur.

Rae (ray) Hebrew: Ewe. The sign of Capricorn, symbolized by the Goat, is affiliated with all cloven-hoofed animals. Variations: *Raeann, Raelene, Raquel, Ray, Raye, Rayette, Raylene*.

Ramah (rah-MAH) Hebrew: High. This name suits high-minded Capricorn, who manages to keep her feet on the ground while accomplishing extraordinary feats.

Rashida (rah-SHEE-dah) Arabic: Righteous. Capricorns are among the most virtuous and ethical of the zodiac's children. Variations: *Rasheeda, Rasheedah*.

Razilee (rah-zi-LEE) Hebrew: My secret. *Razilee* suggests Capricorn's highly sensitive and compassionate inner persona that usually remains hidden behind her protective outer layer. Variation: *Razili*.

Resi (REH-see) German: Reaper. This name is an apt choice for a girl born under Capricorn, whose ruling planet of Saturn is closely associated with the reaping and sowing of grain.

Reza (REHZS-ah) Czechoslovakian: Harvest. Saturn, Capricorn's ruling planet, governs harvest time. Variations: *Rezi, Rezka*.

Rhea (REE-ah) Greek: Earth. Capricorn is one of the three Earth signs of the zodiac. (The other two are Virgo and Taurus.) Variations: *Rea, Rhia, Ria*.

Rima (REE-mah) Arabic: Antelope. *Rima* is an appropriate choice for a girl born under the sign of Capricorn, which is associated with all cloven-hoofed animals.

Rusalka (roo-SAHL-kah) Czechoslovakian: Wood nymph. This unusual name is ideal for nature-loving Capricorns born under one of the three Earth signs of the zodiac. Variation: *Russalka*.

Sabra (SAH-brah) Hebrew: Thorny, or strong as a cactus. Although Capricorns may appear hard and inscrutable on the outside, they possess oft-hidden, highly sensitive, and deeply compassionate hearts. Variation: *Sabrina*.

Sade (shar-DAY) African/Nigerian: She whom honor has made royal. *Sade* suggests the highly esteemed qualities possessed by Capricorn: quiet determination, intuitive wisdom, keen sensitivity, and powerful magnetism. Variations: *Shadae, Shardae, Shardai, Sharday, Sharde*. (Famous Capricorn: Sade, singer)

Shannon (SHAH-nun) Irish Gaelic: Old; wise. Thoughtful, reserved, and intuitive, Capricorns often appear wise beyond their years. Variation: *Shannen*.

Shatara (shah-TAHR-ah) Arabic: Hardworking. One of the most prominent characteristics of Capricorn is the ability to work long and hard, often delaying all types of gratification in order to achieve a long-term goal.

Shika (SHEE-kah) Japanese: Sweet deer. The sign of Capricorn is affiliated with all types of cloven-hoofed creatures.

Shina (SHEE-nah) Japanese: Wealth. The motivation behind Capricorn's drive for success is often the desire for great wealth.

Shizu (SHEE-zoo) Japanese: Clear; quiet. *Shizu* is an ideal name for reserved, practical, and rational Capricorn. Variations: *Shizuka, Shizuko*.

Silivia (see-lee-VEE-uh) Hawaiian: Out of the forest. Truly Earth children, Capricorns possess a deep appreciation for nature and the outdoors. Variation: *Silva*.

Sophia (soh-FEE-ah) Greek: Wisdom. Reserved, intuitive, disciplined, and serious, Capricorns often appear wise beyond their years. Variations: *Sofia, Sophie*. (Famous Capricorn: Sophie Tucker, early recording artist)

Sumi (SOO-mee) Japanese: Clear and refined. Capricorns, who possess great inner strength, dedication, and a fierce drive to succeed, always know exactly what they want and what they must do to achieve their goals.

Sylvia (SILL-vee-yah) Latin: Woods. As one of the zodiac's Earth signs, Capricorn has a strong association with nature. Variations: *Silvia, Sylvana, Sylvie, Sylvina, Sylvonna*.

Tabia (tah-BEE-ah) African/Swahili: Talents. Endowed with keen intelligence, great sensitivity, powerful inner strength, and a fierce drive to succeed, Capricorns are capable of achieving any goal they set for themselves.

Tabitha (TA-bih-thah) Aramaic: Leaping gazelle. The swift-footed gazelle is one of the many cloven-hoofed animals governed by Capricorn, the sign of single-minded success.

Taka (TAH-kah) Japanese: Honorable. *Taka* is an ideal choice for virtuous Capricorn, who prides herself on her extraordinary work ethic.

Takala (TAH-kah-lah) Native American: Corn tassel. Images of the harvest, especially those connected with the sowing, growing, and reaping of grain and corn, are closely associated with the sign of Capricorn.

Talasi (TAH-lah-see) Native American: Corn tassel flower. *Talasi* is a unique choice for nature-loving Capricorn, born under one of the zodiac's Earth signs.

Tallis (TAHL-iss) English: Forest. An Earth sign, Capricorn is associated with the deep greens and warm browns of nature.

Tasha (TAH-shah) Russian: Born on Christmas. *Tasha* is a lovely choice for a Capricorn girl born on or near Christmas Day. Variation: *Natasha*.

Tasso (TAH-sohs) Greek: Reaper. Capricorn's ruling planet, Saturn, is named for the Roman god who governs the sowing and reaping of grain and corn.

Temira (teh-MEE-ruh) Hebrew: Of substantial height. Capricorns keep their feet on the ground while setting their dreams and goals sky-high. Variation: *Timora*.

Thelma (THEL-mah) Greek: Will or willful. *Thelma* connotes Capricorns' fierce determination, great inner strength, and unwavering commitment to their goals. Variation: *Telma*.

Theresa (te-REES-ah) Greek: Reaper. Capricorn's ruling planet, Saturn, governs the sowing and reaping of crops. Variations: *Tera, Teresa, Terese, Teressa, Terri, Terry, Tess, Tessa, Tessie, Therese*.

Tokiwa (toh-KEE-wah) Japanese: Everlastingly constant. *Tokiwa* is an appropriate choice for loyal, dependable, and reliable Capricorn.

Tosia (TOH-shuh) Polish: Inestimable. Capricorn is highly respected for her hard work, loyalty, determination, and innate wisdom.

Tresa (TRESS-uh) German: Reaper. Capricorn's ruling planet, Saturn, governs harvest time and the sowing and reaping of crops.

Trudy (TROO-dee) German: Forcefulness. One of Capricorn's most prominent characteristics is a fierce commitment to achieving her goals. Variations: *Truda, Trude, Trudeliese.*

Tuwa (TOO-wah) Native American: Earth. Capricorn is one of three Earth signs. (Virgo and Taurus are the other two.)

Ushi (oo-SHEE) Chinese: Ox. Capricorn governs the Goat and all other cloven-hoofed animals.

Vandani (vahn-DAHN-ee) Hindu: Honor. Capricorns display virtue and dignity in all they do. Variation: *Vandana.*

Vanika (vahn-EE-kah) Hindu: Small forest. Those born under Capricorn, one of the three Earth signs of the zodiac, have a special connection to nature and feel most at home when surrounded by all of the Earth's natural beauty.

Verity (VER-ih-tee) Latin: Truth or reality. *Verity* connotes the highly virtuous nature possessed by pragmatic Capricorns.

Veronica (ver-RON-ni-kah) Greek: Forerunner of victory. Combining their gifts of intelligence, self-discipline, and determination, Capricorns carefully lay the groundwork for success before moving forward to achieve great things. Variations: *Verenice, Verona, Veronika, Veronique.*

Vidonia (vee-DOHN-ee-ah) Portuguese: Vine branch. The ivy vine is associated with the sign of Capricorn. Variations: *Veedonia, Vidonya.*

Winema (we-NEH-mah) Native American: Woman chief. Winema is an ideal name for female Capricorns, who are noted for achieving great success in leadership roles.

Yepa (YAY-pah) Native American: Snow maiden. Capricorn is a winter sign, encompassing the months of December and January when snowstorms are most frequent.

Yoluta (yoh-LOO-tah) Native American: Seed. Aspects of nature that are linked to the sowing, nurturing, and harvesting of grain are strongly associated with Capricorn.

Yoshi (YOH-shee) Japanese: Respectful. High-minded and comfortable with structure and organization, Capricorns have a keen respect for the status quo. Variations: *Yoshie, Yoshiko.*

Yuki (YOO-kee) Japanese: Snow. This unique name is well suited to Capricorns, who are born in the winter months of December and January. Variations: *Yukie, Yukiko.*

Zea (ZEE-ah; ZAY-ah) Latin: Grain. Capricorn is governed by the planet Saturn, which rules the sowing and reaping of grain. Variation: *Zia.*

Zelenka (ZE-layn-kah) Czechoslovakian: Little green one. The deep greens and muted browns of nature are the colors of the sign of Capricorn.

Names for Capricorn Boys

Abasi (ah-BAH-see) African/Swahili: Stern. Reserved, self-disciplined, and self-composed, Capricorns have a naturally quiet demeanor that is frequently mistaken as coldness or aloofness.

Abi (ah-BEE) Turkish: Elder brother. Wise and precocious beyond their years and always eager to help, Capricorns are often sought for their sage advice.

Abejide (ah-beh-JEE-deh) African/Nigerian: Born in winter. Capricorn is a winter sign encompassing the months of December and January.

Adeben (ah-deh-BEHN) African/Ghanian: Twelfth-born son. *Adeben* is an unusual but fitting name for a Capricorn born in December, the twelfth month of the year.

Adio (ah-DEE-oh) African/Nigerian: Righteous. Capricorn, who sets high ethical standards for himself, is committed to living a virtuous and honorable life.

Akil (ah-KEEL) Arabic: Astute. Capricorns are renowned for their practical and clear-headed approach to problems.

Alden (AHL-din) English: Old and wise. Even as children, Capricorns possess intelligence and self-discipline beyond their years.

Alim (ah-LEEM) Arabic: Wise. *Alim* is an apt name for Capricorn, who possesses great intelligence and keen intuition. Variations: *Aleem, Alem*.

Amin (ah-MEEN) Arabic: Trustworthy. Dependability is a key characteristic of the sign of Capricorn.

Amos (AY-muss) Hebrew: One with many responsibilities. Capricorns willingly seek leadership roles in both school and business and, with their sensible and methodical approach to work, are more than able to juggle many tasks at the same time.

Armstrong (AHRM-strong) English: One with a strong arm. Capricorns can always be depended upon to get even the most tedious of jobs done masterfully and efficiently.

Atman (AHT-muhn) Hindu: The self. This renowned Hindu name is a fitting choice for self-possessed and inner-directed Capricorn.

Baily (BAY-lee) English: Bailiff. During the Middle Ages, a bailiff managed an estate or farm. In addition to keen leadership skills and a great aptitude for business, Capricorns have a life-long affinity for the natural environment. Variations: *Bail, Baillie, Ballie, Bayley.*

Barton (BAHR-tun) English: Field of barley. Capricorn, one of three Earth signs, is ruled by the planet Saturn, which governs the sowing and reaping of grain.

Berger (BUR-ger) French: Shepherd. The sign of Capricorn governs not only the Goat, but all other animals with cloven (split) hooves, such as sheep, cattle, deer, and gazelles. Variation: *Burger.*

Berk (BURK) Turkish: Stable. Levelheaded and dependable Capricorns dislike any type of disorder or chaos, often devoting their lives to ensuring financial security.

Berwin (BUR-win) Middle English: Friend of the harvest. Capricorn's ruling planet, Saturn, is associated with the harvest.

Blair (BLAYR) Irish: Child of the fields. As one of the Earth signs of the zodiac, Capricorn has a deep appreciation for nature and all its beauty.

Boaz (BOH-ahz) Hebrew: Mighty and quick. Capricorns are renowned for their disciplined work habits and formidable organizational and management skills. They are noted for getting any job done quickly and efficiently.

Bond (BOND) Old English: Tiller of the soil. *Bond* is a suitable name for Capricorn, whose ruling planet of Saturn is associated with the Roman god who governed the harvesting of crops. Variations: *Bondon, Bonds*.

Boyce (BOYS) Old French: Son of the forest. Born under one of the zodiac's Earth signs, Capricorns have a special affinity for the natural environment. Variation: *Boice*

Brody (BROH-dee) Russian: Man with an unusual beard. This classic name is a whimsical choice for a boy born under the sign of Capricorn, which is represented by the bearded Goat.

Brent (BRENT) Old English: Steep hill. *Brent* is an apt name for Capricorn, who is renowned for his ability to meet any challenge, no matter how uphill the battle, with his diligence, pragmatism, and hard work. This name also connotes Capricorns' element of Earth and their close relationship with the natural environment.

Buckley (BUCK-lee) English: Field where deer graze. Capricorns, who deeply appreciate the natural environment, are associated with all types of cloven-hoofed animals. Variation: *Bucklie*.

Cadmus (KAD-muss) Greek: One who excels. Like their Virgo cousins, Capricorns are esteemed for their superior work skills.

Calvert (KAL-virt) English: Cow herder. The sign of Capricorn governs all cloven-hoofed animals. Variation: *Calbert*.

Carleton (KAHRL-tin) English: Farmer's land. This classic English surname—recently enjoying popularity as a first name—is a wonderful choice for land-loving Capricorn. Variation: *Carlton*. (Famous Capricorn: Carlton Fisk, professional baseball player)

Casper (KASS-pur) Persian: Master of the treasure. Acquiring wealth can be a consuming passion for Capricorns, who are noted for their keen money management skills. Variations:

Cash, Caspar, Cass, Gaspar, Gaspard, Jasper, Kaspar.

Cassiel (KASS-ee-ell) Hebrew: Name of an archangel. *Cassiel* is the archangel who watches over those born under the sign of Capricorn.

Cham (CHAM) Vietnamese: Hard worker. One of Capricorn's most prominent characteristics is a highly industrious nature.

Chance (CHANSS) Middle English: Good fortune. Capricorns, who rarely leave anything to chance and create their own good fortunes, methodically chart a surefooted road to success.

Chuma (CHOO-mah) African/Zimbabwean: Wealth. The motivation behind Capricorns' hard work is often the desire for financial success and security.

Clay (KLAY) Old English: Of the earth. Capricorn is one of three Earth signs. (The other two are Virgo and Taurus.)

Colman (KOHL-mun) Icelandic: Head man. This classic name suits hard-working Capricorns who are renowned for aspiring to key leadership positions. Variations: *Cole, Coleman.*

Cosmo (KOZ-moh) Greek: Order. Supremely organized, Capricorns are noted for their efficient management of time, tasks, and money. Variations: *Cos, Cosme Cosimo, Kosma, Kosmo.*

Courtland (KORT-lind) English: Farm land. Capricorn's ruling planet, Saturn, governs harvest time and the sowing and reaping of crops. Variation: Cortland.

Dagan (DAH-gahn) East Semitic: Earth. Capricorn is one of the three Earth signs of the zodiac.

Damek (DAH-mik) Czechoslovakian: Earth. One of three Earth signs, eminently practical Capricorns have a keen affinity for the natural world.

Darby (DAHR-bee) Old Norse: One from the deer estate. The sign of Capricorn is closely associated with all cloven-hoofed animals.

Darius (DARE-ee-us) Persian: One who upholds the good. Fierce defenders of the righteous path, Capricorns have a strong sense of morality and justice. Variations: *Dario, Darrio, Darrius*.

Darren (DAHR-in) Greek: Wealthy. *Darren* is an attractive choice for Capricorn, who often strives to reach a high level of financial security. Variations: *Dare, Daren, Darin, Daron*.

Darton (DAHR-tin) English: The place where deer graze. Symbolized by the Goat, Capricorns are closely associated with all cloven-hoofed animals.

Dean (DEEN) Old English: One from the valley. *Dean* is a fitting name for Capricorn, born under an Earth sign and endowed with a deep appreciation for the natural environment. Variations: *Deane, Dino*.

Dearborn (DEER-born) English: River of deer. Capricorn, an Earth sign that shares many of the same Water qualities of Cancer and Scorpio, governs cloven-hoofed animals.

Decha (deh-CHAH) Thai: Strength. One of the greatest gifts bestowed upon Capricorns is fierce inner determination that enables them to accomplish any goal they set for themselves.

Derby (DUR-bee) English: Village with deer. *Derby* is a suitable name for Capricorn, who is affiliated with the Goat and all other cloven-hoofed animals. Variation: *Darby*.

Derward (DUR-wird) English: Deer herder. The sign of Capricorn is associated with all cloven-hoofed animals. Variation: *Durward*.

Devine (dee-VYNE) Irish: Ox. The ox, another animal with cloven hooves, is a deeply symbolic animal in Chinese astrology. It is a sturdy and reliable animal, much like the Goat that symbolizes Capricorn.

Dinos (DYE-nohs) Latin: Firm and constant. *Dinos* is an appropriate name for strong and dependable Capricorn.

Egidio (ee-GEE-dee-oh) Italian: Young goat. Capricorn is represented by the sea goat, or Capricornus, a mythological creature that was half-goat and half-fish.

Elder (ELL-dur) English: Older person. Even as children, Capricorns are serious, intuitive, and success-driven, preferring to spend their free time working rather than playing.

Ellery (EL-luhr-ee) Middle English: Elder of the isle. Quiet and reserved, with a self-possessed personality, Capricorns frequently seem wise beyond their years. Variations: *Ellary, Ellerey*.

Elman (ELL-mahn) German: Elm tree. *Elman* is an appropriate choice for Capricorn, who is closely affiliated with the elm tree.

Elmore (ELL-mor) English: Valley with elm trees. The elm is one of three trees associated with the sign of Capricorn. (The other two are the pine and the poplar.)

Elton (ELL-tun) Old English: Of the ancient village. *Elton* suggests Capricorn's wisdom beyond his years. Variations: *Elden, Elder, Elon, Elson, Elston*.

Emil (AY-meel; ay-MEEL) Latin: Industrious. A classic name, *Emil* personifies hardworking Capricorn. Variations: *Emile, Emilio*.

Ephraim (EFF-ram or eff-RAH-ihm) Hebrew: Very bountiful. The acquisition of money and material possessions is a frequent preoccupation of ambitious Capricorns. Variations: *Efrain, Efrem, Efren, Ephrain*.

Erik (AYRE-ick) Old Norse: External strength. Capricorns are capable of withstanding long periods of work under harsh conditions in order to achieve their goals. Variations: *Erek, Eric, Erick, Ric*.

Ethan (EE-than) Hebrew: Firm and strong. The Feminine influence in Capricorn endows children born under this sign with great reserves of inner strength. Variation: *Etan*.

Eustace (YOOS-tiss) Greek: Bountiful. Saturn, Capricorn's ruling planet, is associated with the Roman god who governed the harvest—a time of abundance and wealth. Variations: *Eustache, Eustachius, Eustasius, Eustazio*.

Ezhno (EHZH-noh) Native American: By oneself. Reserved and self-contained, Capricorns often feel most confident and comfortable when alone.

Fabian (FAY-bee-in) Latin: One who sows beans. Capricorn is ruled by the planet Saturn, associated with the Roman god who governed the sowing and reaping of grain. Variations: *Fabek, Fabiano, Fabien, Fabio, Fabyan*.

Fadey (fah-DAY) Ukrainian: Stouthearted. *Fadey* is a suitable name for dependable, loyal, and reliable Capricorn.

Farley (FAHR-lee) Old English: Sheep's meadow. Symbolized by the Goat, Capricorn is associated with all other cloven-hoofed animals. Variations: *Fairlee, Fairleigh, Fairley, Farlee, Farleigh*.

Fidel (FEE-dehl or fee-DELL) Latin: Faithful and sincere. Despite their ambition and drive to succeed, Capricorns are rarely manipulative and are renowned for their loyalty to friends and coworkers.

Forbes (forbs) Irish: Prosperous one. Capricorn is often rewarded for his long hours of hard work with wealth and security.

Garth (GAHRTH) Old Norse: Enclosure, or from the garden. Capricorns have a special affinity for all of nature's gifts.

George (JORJ) Latin: Farmer. This traditional and ever popular name is an appropriate choice for Capricorn, whose ruling planet Saturn governs harvest time and the sowing and reaping of grain. Variations: *Georg, Georgie, Giorgio, Jorge.* (Famous Capricorns: George Reeves, actor; George Foreman, boxer; George Burns, comedian/actor/entertainer; George Balanchine, ballet choreographer)

Germain (jer-MAYN) Middle English: Sprout or bud. As an Earth sign ruled by Saturn and driven by a strong Feminine influence, Capricorns have a deep connection to nature, particularly to objects and images that suggest fertility, nurturing, and growth. Variations: *Jermain, Jermaine.*

Gil (GEEL) Spanish: Young goat. The sign of Capricorn is symbolized by the Goat.

Gilchrist (GIL-kreest) Irish: Christ's servant. The sign of Capricorn encompasses the Christmas holiday, the traditional celebration of Christ's birth. Parents with a Christmas-born son may find any of the Christ-derived names appropriate choices. Variations: *Gil, Gilley.*

Giles (JYLZ; GYLZ) Greek: Baby goat. The Goat is the animal symbol of the sign of Capricorn.

Glen (glen) Gaelic: Valley. *Glen* is an apt name for Capricorn, born under an Earth sign and strongly connected to the natural environment. Variations: *Glenn, Glynn.* (Famous Capricorn: Glenn Yarborough, singer)

Goran (GOH-ran) Scandinavian: Land worker. Born under one of the zodiac's Earth signs, Capricorns are endowed with a deep appreciation for the natural environment and all of its gifts. *Goran* also connotes Capricorns' commitment to hard work.

Gus (GUSS) Greek: Constant. Capricorns are renowned for sticking with a task to completion, no matter how difficult the job nor how many obstacles are in their path. Variations: *Gustav, Gustave, Gustavo, Gustavus.*

Granger (GRAYN-ger) French: Farmer. Capricorn's ruling planet, Saturn, is associated with the Roman god who governed the sowing and reaping of crops. Variation: *Grainger.*

Halsten (HALL-stun) Scandinavian: Rock and stone. Steadfast, self-determined, and committed to personal achievement, Capricorns are among the most strong-willed children of the zodiac. Variations: *Hallstein, Hallsten, Hallston, Halston.*

Hamidi (hah-MEE-dee) African/Swahili: Commendable. Capricorns are well respected and highly praised for their dedication to hard work, high morals, and determination to succeed.

Hanif (HAH-neef) Arabic: True believer. Capricorns have a tremendous sense of their own self-worth and a deep respect for their personal missions in life. They are rarely distracted from their chosen paths, no matter how slow or arduous the journey to success.

Hart (HAHRT) Old English: Male deer. *Hart* is an appropriate choice for Capricorn, who is symbolized by the Goat and associated with all cloven-hoofed animals. Variations: *Harte, Hartman.*

Hartley (HAHRT-lee) English: Meadow where deer graze. Capricorns, who are closely attuned to their natural environment, are affiliated with animals with cloven hooves. Variations: *Hartlee, Hartleigh.*

Hasad (huh-SUHD) Turkish: Harvest. Capricorn's ruling planet, Saturn, associated with the Roman god of sowing and reaping, is closely associated with harvest time.

Hersh (HURSH) Yiddish: Deer. Capricorn, symbolized by the Goat, also governs all other cloven-hoofed animals. Variations: *Hersch, Herschel, Herzl, Hirsch, Hirschel.*

Hisoka (hee-SOH-kah) Japanese: Reserved. This unusual name is a fitting choice for quiet, self-possessed Capricorn.

Hutchinson (HUTCH-in-sin) English: Thought. Never the ones to act rashly or prematurely, Capricorns are successful in their chosen careers primarily because they take the time to think through and plan a sensible course of action.

Jael (YAH-ehl or yah-ELL) Hebrew: Mountain goat. The Goat symbolizes the sign of Capricorn, and the mountain goat in particular embodies the Capricorn approach to achievement: a methodical but surefooted assent despite any rocky obstacles or rough terrain encountered along the way. Variation: *Yael.*

Jahi (JAH-hee) African/Swahili: Dignity. Capricorns display honor and virtue in all they do.

Jarek (YAH-rek) Polish: Born during the month of January. The sign of Capricorn encompasses the first three weeks of January. Variations: *Janiusz, Januarius.*

Jasper (JASS-per) English: Wealthy. *Jasper* is a suitable choice for money-conscious Capricorn. Variation: *Jaspar.*

Jethro (JEH-throh) Hebrew: Abundance. The sign of Capricorn is associated with growing and harvesting. Variation: *Jeth.*

Joji (JOH-jee) Japanese: One who sows. Saturn, Capricorn's ruling planet, is associated with the Roman god who governs the sowing and reaping of crops.

Julius (JOO-lee-us) Latin: Downy bearded. The softly bearded mountain Goat is the most common symbol of the sign of Capricorn. Variations: *Giuliano, Giulio, Jule, Jules, Julian, Juliano, Julien, Julio.*

Juri (YOO-ree) Estonian: Farm worker. Nature-loving Capricorns have a great appreciation for the Earth's harvest. Capricorn's ruling planet, Saturn, governs the sowing and reaping of crops.

Juro (joo-ROH) Japanese: Tenth son. Capricorn, a Cardinal Earth sign with a Feminine influence, is the tenth sign of the zodiac.

Kadir (KAH-deer) Arabic: Green crop of grain. The sign of Capricorn is associated with the deep green colors of nature. Capricorn's ruling planet is named for the Roman god who governs the sowing and reaping of grain. Variation: *Kadeer.*

Kaj (kah-EE) Greek: Earth. Capricorn is one of the zodiac's three Earth signs. Variation: *Kai.*

Kamil (kah-MEEL) Arabic: Without error. Capricorns strive to approach all tasks with reason and caution—qualities essential to avoiding mistakes. Variation: *Kameel.*

Karmel (KAHR-mell) Hebrew: Vineyard. The ivy vine is one of the "flowers" of Capricorn. Many Capricorns share the vining plants' qualities of durability and tenacity. Variations: *Carmel, Carmello.*

Kasib (KAH-sib or kah-SEEB) Arabic: Earthy and productive. *Kasib* is an apt name for a boy born under the Earth sign of Capricorn. Capricorn's ruling planet, Saturn, governs the sowing and reaping of crops. Variation: *Kaseeb.*

Kedem (KE-dem) Hebrew: Ancient. Self-possessed and practical Capricorns often appear mature beyond their years.

Kemal (KEH-mahl) Turkish: Greatest honor. Hardworking and determined Capricorns strive to be number one in everything they do. Variation: *Kamal*.

Kester (KESS-tur) English: He who carries Christ in his heart. This Old English name is a classic choice for a Capricorn boy born near or on Christmas Day.

Kincaid (kin-KAYD) Celtic: Lead warrior. Capricorn's approach to success and achievement may appear fiercely competitive, but once they have reached their goals, they often make benevolent leaders.

Kit (KITT) Greek: Christ bearer. *Kit* is another Christian-derived name that is appropriate for a Capricorn boy born on or near the Christmas holiday. Variation: *Kitt*.

Kiyoshi (kee-YOH-shee) Japanese: Wordless. Capricorns are known for their quiet demeanor and great sense of propriety. Variation: *Yoshi*.

Kostas (KO-stahs) Greek: Constant. *Kostas* is an apt name for dedicated, loyal, and reliable Capricorn.

Kyros (KEEH-ros or KY-ros) Greek: Master. Invariably successful in whatever field they choose to enter, Capricorns may display extraordinary, even mesmerizing, leadership skills.

Laszlo (LAHZ-loh) Hungarian: Renowned leader. Unlike their Virgo cousins, who work hard but prefer to stay behind the scenes, Capricorns strive to win positions of power and desire recognition for their efforts. Variations: *Laslo, Lazlo*.

Lennox (LEN-icks) Scottish: With many elm trees. The elm, pine, and poplar trees are all governed by the sign of Capricorn. Variations: *Lenox, Lenx*.

Liang (LEE-ahng) Chinese: Well done. *Liang* suggests Capricorns' drive for success, striving for perfection, and dedication to accomplishing the most challenging tasks.

Linfred (LIN-freed) Old German: Calm. From early childhood on, Capricorns are quiet, reserved, and self-possessed, rarely letting their emotions get the better of them.

Loman (LOH-mahn) Serbo-Croatian: Sensitive. Despite their formidable work skills, Capricorns are extremely sensitive to criticism, often reworking and redoing tasks in order to get them just right.

Marar (MAH-rahr) African/Zimbabwean: Earth. Capricorn is one of the three Earth signs of the zodiac.

Maximillian (MAX-ee-MILL-yun) Latin: Supreme quality. Industrious, dedicated, intuitive, and purposeful, Capricorn is capable of achieving extraordinary things that may one day change the world. Variations: *Mac, Mack, Massimo, Max, Maxie, Maxim, Maxime.*

Mayer (MAY-ir) German: Overseer. *Mayer* connotes Capricorn's lifelong aspirations of leadership.

Mayfield (MAY-feeld) Old English: One's field is strong. Steadfast Capricorns have a deep connection to nature, particularly their immediate natural environment.

Maynard (MAY-nahrd) Old English: Hard strength. Endowed with fierce determination and great inner strength, Capricorn is capable of achieving any goal. Variations: *Mayne, Maynhard, Meinhard, Mendar.*

Mimis (MEE-miss) Greek: Belonging to Demeter. Demeter was the Greek goddess of agriculture. Capricorn is ruled by Saturn, the planet named for the ancient god of sowing and reaping.

Nero (NAYR-oh or NEE-roh) Latin: Stern. Capricorn's quiet and cautious public persona is often mistaken for aloofness. Variations: *Neron, Nerone*.

Nevada (ne-VAH-dah) Spanish: Covered in snow. The sign of Capricorn encompasses the snowy months of December and January.

Nitis (NEE-tiss) Native American: Trustworthy. Deeply compassionate, empathetic, and dependable, Capricorns make ideal friends and companions who can always be counted on for advice, help, and comfort.

Noel (NOH-el or noh-ELL) French: Day of Christ's birth; born on Christmas. This name is appropriate for a Capricorn boy or girl born on or near the holiday. Variations: *Nowel, Noël, Nowell*. (Famous Capricorn: Noel Paul Stookey, folk singer [Paul of Peter, Paul and Mary])

Ogano (oh-GAHN-oh) Japanese: Deer pasture. Symbolized by the Goat, Capricorn is also affiliated with all other cloven-hoofed animals.

Ola (AW-lah) African/Nigerian: Wealth or riches. Capricorns, never ones to spend their hard-earned money on extravagant items, desire financial success in order to provide security for their families and themselves.

Oren (OH-ren) Hebrew: Pine tree. The pine is one of the trees strongly associated with the sign of Capricorn. (The other two are the elm and the poplar.) Variations: *Orin, Orren, Orrin*.

Otto (AH-toh) Old German: One with riches. *Otto* is a suitable choice for Capricorn, who aspires to great wealth. Variations: *Odon, Otek, Othon, Otik, Otman*.

Owen (OH-wehn) Greek: Born into fortune. Determined to succeed and equipped with both tremendous work skills and an abundant sense of purpose, Capricorns are destined for achievement in any field they enter. Variations: *Ewan, Ewen, Owain, Owin.*

Oxford (OX-fird) Old English: Oxen crossing the river. Any name suggesting a cloven-hoofed animal is an apt one for Capricorn, who is symbolized by the Goat. Capricorns, like oxen, are determined, strong, and hardworking. Variation: *Ford.*

Parlan (PAHR-lan) Scottish: Son of the earth. *Parlan* is an appropriate choice for Capricorn, one of the zodiac's Earth signs.

Parnell (PAHR-nell) Old French: Little Peter. The original Aramaic meaning of *Peter* is "rock" or "foundation." Capricorns are renowned for their dependability. Variations: *Parnel, Parrnell, Pernel, Pernell.*

Peter (PEE-tur) Greek: Rock or foundation. This classic name is an ideal choice for stalwart, dependable, and strong Capricorn, who can always be counted on in times of need. Variations: *Pedro, Pete, Petey, Petr, Petro, Pierre, Pierrot, Piet, Pieter, Piotr.*

Pierce (PEERSS) Old Anglo-French: Rock. *Pierce* is a handsome name for reliable and disciplined Capricorn, who prides himself on his strict adherence to living virtuously. Variations: *Pearce, Pearson, Piers, Pierson.*

Plato (PLAY-toh) Greek: Strong shoulders. Capricorns, known for their durability and dependability, can shoulder any load and lead others to safe ground. Variation: *Platon.*

Pov (POHV) English Gypsy: Earth. Capricorn is the last of the zodiac's three Earth signs.

Powa (PO-wah) Native American: Wealthy. Hardworking and success-driven Capricorns often achieve great financial success through their efforts.

Rafferty (RAFF-ur-tee) Irish: One who brings riches. *Rafferty* is a wonderfully appropriate choice—with many splendid variations—for the supremely wealth-conscious Capricorn boy. Variations: *Rafe, Rafer, Raferty, Raff, Raffarty, Raffer.*

Raleigh (RAHL-ee) Old English: Meadow of the swift deer. Capricorn, who is closely attuned to his natural environment, is associated with all types of cloven-hoofed animals. Variations: *Lee, Leigh, Rawley, Rawleigh.*

Rashid (rah-SHEED) African/Swahili: One of good council. Levelheaded, intuitive, and compassionate, Capricorns make ideal people to turn to for advice. Variation: *Rasheed.*

Razi (RAH-zee) Aramaic: My secret. Rarely ones to show their feelings, quiet Capricorns can be trusted confidants for friends who need a shoulder to lean on. Variations: *Raz, Raziel.*

Renfred (RENN-frid) English: Strong peace. Calm, reserved, and self-possessed Capricorn possesses great inner strength.

Renton (RENN-ton) English: Deer habitat. Capricorn, a sign with a strong connection to the natural environment, governs the Goat and all other cloven-hoofed animals.

Rock (rock) Old English: From the rock. Born under an Earth sign, Capricorns are famous for their reliability and great strength of character. Variations: *Rocco, Rockie, Rocky.*

Rowell (ROH-ell) English: Deer spring. The sign of Capricorn, associated with all cloven-hoofed animals, also has a profound Water influence.

Sennet (SENN-it) French: Old age. From early on, Capricorns are wise, serious, disciplined, and committed to success.

Shannon (SHA-nun) Irish: Ages old. This classic Irish name is staging a remarkable comeback—for boys *and* girls. *Shannon* is a strong and fitting choice for reserved, cautious, and self-possessed Capricorns, who often appear mature beyond their years. Variations: *Shanan, Shannan, Shannen.*

Shea (shay) Irish: Penetrating. Slow, methodical, cautious, and eminently practical, Capricorns easily cut to the heart of any problem or task, a trait they share with their very similar Virgo cousins. Variations: *Shae, Shai, Shayan, Shaye.*

Snowden (SNOW-den) Old English: Snow-capped mountain. *Snowden* is an apt name for a boy born under the sign of Capricorn, which encompasses the winter months of December and January.

Steadman (STED-man) Old English: Owner of a farm. *Steadman* is an ideal choice for Capricorn, who shares a special connection with the natural world. Saturn, the sign's ruling planet, is associated with the Roman god who governs the sowing and reaping of crops. Variations: *Steadmann, Stedman.*

Sterne (STURN) English: Unyielding. Capricorns' quiet determination to follow their own paths, together with their extreme emotional reserve, can be mistakenly interpreted as rigidity or aloofness. Variations: *Stearn, Stearne, Stern.*

Steel (STEEL) Old English: Implacable. Although Capricorn's reserved and fiercely determined exterior sometimes causes others to think of him as uncompromising and cold, he actually possesses a deeply sensitive and compassionate soul. Variation: *Steele.*

Thad (TADD or THADD) Greek: Courageous and stouthearted. *Thad* is a suitable name for determined, dependable, and ambitious Capricorn, who stops at nothing when it comes to realizing his dreams. Variations: *Tad, Tadd, Tadea, Tades, Thadd, Thaddeus, Thaddy.*

Tomi (TOH-mee) Japanese: Wealthy. Capricorns are often driven by the need to achieve financial prosperity in order to maintain a steady and secure lifestyle.

Vachel (VAY-chel) Old French: Keeper of the cows. Capricorns, deeply attuned to their natural environments, are born under the sign that governs the Goat and all other cloven-hoofed animals.

Vadin (VAH-deen) Hindu: Renowned lecturer. Capricorns can be consummate scholars and speakers when they are deeply interested in a particular subject.

Wakiza (wah-KEE-zah) Native American: Determined warrior. When Capricorn sets his mind to something, nothing and no one can get in his way.

Walden (WAHL-din) Old English: Child of the forest valley. Born under one of the zodiac's Earth signs, Capricorns have a special connection to the natural environment. Variations: *Wald, Waldo, Waldon.*

Wen (WEHN) English Gypsy: Child born in the winter. *Wen* is a fitting choice for Capricorns, who are born during the winter months of December and January.

Wesh (WEHSH) English Gypsy: Child from the woods. Born under one of the zodiac's Earth signs, Capricorn possesses a special affinity for his natural environment.

William (WILL-yum) Old German: Unwavering protector. Beneath their reserved demeanors, Capricorns are deeply empathetic and compassionate, and are among the most loyal and steadfast friends in the zodiac. Variations: *Bill, Bille, Billie,*

Billy, Guglielmo, Guillaume, Guillermo, Will, Willem, Willie, Willis, Willy, Wilson. (Famous Capricorns: William Peter Blatty, screenwriter and novelist; William Bendix, actor)

Winfield (WIN-feeld) Teutonic: Friend of the earth. Born under one of the zodiac's three Earth signs, Capricorns have a strong awareness of their natural environment. Variations: *Win, Winn, Winnfield, Wyn, Wynfield.*

Yarin (yah-REEN) Hebrew: Understand. One of Capricorns' trademark characteristics is to dissect all the angles of any new task or problem before even beginning to work on it. This slow, cautious, and rational approach to problem-solving ensures that Capricorns always find a solution.

Yasar (yah-SAHR or YAH-sar) Arabic: Wealth. Hardworking and self-disciplined Capricorns often accumulate great wealth through their efforts. Variations: *Yaser, Yasser.*

Yazid (YAH-zid) Arabic: He will increase. Capricorns are gifted money managers and have a particular facility for wise investments. Later in life, they often accumulate sizeable estates.

Yukio (yoo-KEE-oh) Japanese: Snow boy. The snowy month of January is governed by the sign of Capricorn. Variations: *Yuki, Yukiko.*

Yule (yool) Old English: Born on Christmas Day. *Yule* is an apt and seasonable choice for a Capricorn born on or near the Christmas holiday. Variation: *Yul.*

Zahid (zah-HEED) Arabic: Self-denying. Capricorns, keenly interested in accumulating wealth, are savers and investors—not spenders.

Zaki (ZAH-kee) Arabic: Intelligent. Capricorn possesses a special type of intuitive wisdom that helps him to turn his dreams into reality.

Famous Capricorns

12-22-1912	Lady Bird Johnson	12-28-1946	Edgar Winter
12-22-1917	Gene Rayburn	12-28-1954	Denzel Washington
12-22-1922	Barbara Billingsley	12-29-1800	Charles Goodyear
12-22-1945	Diane Sawyer	12-29-1808	Andrew Johnson
12-22-1948	Steve Garvey	12-29-1937	Mary Tyler Moore
12-22-1949	Maurice Gibb	12-29-1938	Jon Voight
12-22-1949	Robin Gibb	12-29-1946	Marianne Faithfull
12-23-1862	Connie Mack	12-29-1947	Ted Danson
12-23-1918	Jose Greco	12-29-1954	Ed Autry
12-23-1943	Harry Shearer	12-30-1865	Rudyard Kipling
12-23-1948	Susan Lucci	12-30-1914	Bert Parks
12-23-1971	Corey Haim	12-30-1928	Bo Diddley
12-24-1809	Kit Carson	12-30-1934	Russ Tamblyn
12-24-1905	Howard Hughes	12-30-1935	Sandy Koufax
12-24-1922	Ava Gardner	12-30-1937	Noel Paul Stookey
12-25-1642	Sir Isaac Newton	12-30-1942	Michael Nesmith
12-25-1893	Robert Ripley	12-30-1946	David Jones
12-25-1907	Cab Calloway	12-30-1959	Tracey Ullman
12-25-1918	Anwar Sadat	12-30-1975	Tiger Woods
12-25-1924	Rod Serling	12-31-1869	Henri Matisse
12-25-1946	Jimmy Buffett	12-31-1930	Odetta
12-25-1948	Barbara Mandrell	12-31-1937	Anthony Hopkins
12-25-1949	Sissy Spacek	12-31-1941	Sarah Miles
12-26-1791	Charles Babbage	12-31-1943	John Denver
12-26-1891	Henry Miller	12-31-1943	Ben Kingsley
12-26-1893	Mao Tse-tung	12-31-1945	Barbara Carrera
12-26-1914	Richard Widmark	12-31-1946	Patti Smith
12-26-1921	Steve Allen	12-31-1948	Donna Summer
12-26-1927	Alan King	12-31-1959	Val Kilmer
12-26-1947	Carlton Fisk	01-01-1735	Paul Revere
12-27-1822	Louis Pasteur	01-01-1752	Betsy Ross
12-27-1879	Sydney Greenstreet	01-01-1895	J. Edgar Hoover
12-27-1901	Marlene Dietrich	01-01-1900	Xavier Cugat
12-27-1906	Oscar Levant	01-01-1909	Barry Goldwater
12-27-1939	John Amos	01-01-1919	J. D. Salinger
12-27-1948	Gerard Depardieu	01-01-1943	Don Novello
12-28-1856	Woodrow Wilson	01-02-1904	Sally Rand
12-28-1905	Cliff Arquette	01-02-1939	Jim Bakker
12-28-1905	Earl "Fatha" Hines	01-02-1920	Isaac Asimov
12-28-1908	Lew Ayres	01-02-1936	Roger Miller
12-28-1911	Sam Levenson	01-02-1961	Gabrielle Carteris
12-28-1924	Johnny Otis	01-02-1966	Tia Carrere
12-28-1934	Maggie Smith	01-02-1968	Cuba Gooding, Jr.

01-02-1969	Christy Turlington
01-03-1892	J.R.R. Tolkien
01-03-1897	Marion Davies
01-03-1898	Zazu Pitts
01-03-1905	Ray Milland
01-03-1909	Victor Borge
01-03-1918	Maxene Andrews
01-03-1919	Jesse White
01-03-1932	Dabney Coleman
01-03-1939	Bobby Hull
01-03-1945	Stephen Stills
01-03-1950	Victoria Principal
01-03-1956	Mel Gibson
01-03-1960	Joan Chen
01-03-1975	Danica McKeller
01-04-1809	Louis Braille
01-04-1838	Charles "Tom Thumb" Stratton
01-04-1905	Sterling Holloway
01-04-1914	Jane Wyman
01-04-1935	Floyd Patterson
01-04-1937	Dyan Cannon
01-04-1958	Matt Frewer
01-05-1876	Konrad Adenauer
01-05-1914	George Reeves
01-05-1928	Walter Mondale
01-05-1931	Alvin Ailey
01-05-1931	Robert Duvall
01-05-1938	Juan Carlos I, King of Spain
01-05-1946	Diane Keaton
01-05-1953	Pamela Sue Martin
01-06-1878	Carl Sandburg
01-06-1880	Tom Mix
01-06-1883	Kahlil Gibran
01-06-1912	Danny Thomas
01-06-1913	Loretta Young
01-06-1920	Sun Myung Moon
01-06-1929	Vic Tayback
01-06-1944	Bonnie Franklin
01-06-1955	Rowan Atkinson
01-06-1957	Nancy Lopez
01-07-1800	Millard Fillmore
01-07-1911	Butterfly McQueen
01-07-1912	Charles Addams

01-07-1922	Jean-Pierre Rampal
01-07-1928	William Peter Blatty
01-07-1948	Kenny Loggins
01-07-1957	Katie Couric
01-07-1964	Nicolas Cage
01-07-1971	David Yost
01-08-1912	Jose Ferrer
01-08-1923	Larry Storch
01-08-1924	Ron Moody
01-08-1926	Soupy Sales
01-08-1933	Charles Osgood
01-08-1935	Elvis Presley
01-08-1937	Shirley Bassey
01-08-1939	Yvette Mimieux
01-08-1942	Stephen Hawking
01-08-1947	David Bowie
01-08-1969	Ami Dolenz
01-09-1904	George Balanchine
01-09-1913	Richard Nixon
01-09-1935	Bob Denver
01-09-1941	Joan Baez
01-09-1941	Susannah York
01-09-1944	Jimmy Page
01-09-1951	Crystal Gayle
01-10-1904	Ray Bolger
01-10-1908	Paul Henreid
01-10-1927	Gisele MacKenzie
01-10-1927	Johnnie Ray
01-10-1939	Sal Mineo
01-10-1945	Rod Stewart
01-10-1949	George Foreman
01-10-1953	Pat Benatar
01-11-1755	Alexander Hamilton
01-11-1905	Ellery Queen
01-11-1926	Grant Tinker
01-11-1930	Rod Taylor
01-11-1952	Ben Crenshaw
01-12-1876	Jack London
01-12-1906	Henny Youngman
01-12-1926	Ray Price
01-12-1930	Glenn Yarborough
01-12-1944	Joe Frazier
01-12-1951	Rush Limbaugh
01-12-1954	Howard Stern
01-12-1955	Kirstie Alley

01-13-1832	Horatio Alger	01-17-1927	Eartha Kitt
01-13-1884	Sophie Tucker	01-17-1928	Vidal Sassoon
01-13-1919	Robert Stack	01-17-1931	James Earl Jones
01-13-1925	Gwen Verdon	01-17-1934	Shari Lewis
01-13-1931	Charles Nelson Reilly	01-17-1942	Muhammad Ali
01-13-1943	Richard Moll	01-17-1962	Jim Carrey
01-13-1961	Julia Louis-Dreyfus	01-18-1782	Daniel Webster
01-14-1741	Benedict Arnold	01-18-1882	A. A. Milne
01-14-1875	Albert Schweitzer	01-18-1892	Oliver Hardy
01-14-1892	Hal Roach	01-18-1904	Cary Grant
01-14-1906	William Bendix	01-18-1913	Danny Kaye
01-14-1920	Andy Rooney	01-18-1941	Bobby Goldsboro
01-14-1938	Jack Jones	01-18-1955	Kevin Costner
01-14-1941	Faye Dunaway	01-19-1807	Robert E. Lee
01-14-1969	Jason Bateman	01-19-1809	Edgar Allan Poe
01-15-1906	Aristotle Onassis	01-19-1839	Paul Cezanne
01-15-1913	Lloyd Bridges	01-19-1922	Guy Madison
01-15-1929	Dr. Martin Luther King, Jr.	01-19-1923	Jean Stapleton
		01-19-1931	Tippi Hedren
01-15-1937	Margaret O'Brien	01-19-1939	Phil Everly
01-15-1951	Charo	01-19-1943	Janis Joplin
01-16-1853	Andre Michelin	01-19-1944	Shelley Fabares
01-16-1909	Ethel Merman	01-19-1946	Dolly Parton
01-16-1911	Dizzy Dean	01-19-1953	Desi Arnaz, Jr.
01-16-1935	A. J. Foyt	01-19-1969	Junior Seau
01-16-1944	Ronnie Milsap	01-19-1982	Jodie Sweetin
01-16-1948	John Carpenter	01-20-1896	George Burns
01-16-1950	Debbie Allen	01-20-1920	Federico Fellini
01-16-1959	Sade	01-20-1920	DeForest Kelley
01-16-1974	Kate Moss	01-20-1926	Patricia Neal
01-17-1706	Ben Franklin	01-20-1930	Edwin "Buzz" Aldrin
01-17-1884	Mack Sennett	01-20-1934	Arte Johnson
01-17-1899	Al Capone	01-20-1937	Dorothy Provine
01-17-1922	Betty White	01-20-1946	David Lynch

AQUARIUS
(January 21–February 19)

GLYPH: ♒

SYMBOL: The Waterbearer

POLARITY: Masculine

QUALITY: Fixed

ELEMENT: Air

RULING PLANET: Uranus

BIRTHSTONE: Amethyst

SPECIAL COLORS: Sky blue

FLOWER: Orchid

METAL: Uranium

ANIMAL: Large birds

MOST LIKEABLE TRAITS: Friendliness, independence, and humanitarianism

♒

Aquarius, the sign that was immortalized during the turbulent, provocative, and phantasmagorical 1960s—the most famed Age of Aquarius—is generally considered the most fascinating and challenging of the zodiac's signs. Aquarians are the visionaries, dreamers, and revolutionaries of the zodiac, renowned for their egos, individuality, independence, freethinking, innovation, and eccentricity. Yet despite being the penultimate nonconformists of astrology, Aquarians are also esteemed for their quicksilver intelligence, high ideals, deep empathy for others, and strong humanitarian and philanthropic interests.

Like their nearest cousins, the Capricorns, Aquarians are startlingly complex creatures with two distinct and opposing natures. One is an eccentric and enigmatic loner who eschews convention and hard work and lives, at least metaphorically, on the fringes of mainstream society. The other is a deeply caring and idealistic individual who thrives on the company of others and strives to make the world a better place. Learning to accept, honor, support, and celebrate the Aquarian child's diverse and dramatic personality is an exhilarating challenge.

General Qualities

Aquarius is a Masculine and Fixed Air sign that is ruled by the transformational outer planet of Uranus. Named after the Greek god of the skies, Uranus is the planet of revolution, anarchy, and unconventionalism. Uranus is most strongly identified with the tearing down of established but outmoded social and political systems, and thus it governs sudden, deep, and often cataclysmic change. Uranus also rules stormy weather, modern science and technology, invention, astronomy, and space travel.

The influence of Uranus in the sign of Aquarius is marked and profound. Aquarians are the quintessential free spirits of the zodiac, famed for their individuality, independence, innovation, and originality. Naturally rebellious, Aquarians have a penchant for eccentricity, deliberately flout convention, and have a life-long vested interest in being different from the "madding crowd." They are generally amiable, easygoing, and engaging— as long as their invariably unconventional beliefs and lifestyles aren't challenged.

Above all else, Aquarians prize their freedom and individuality. They will vigorously fight being forced to conform to anyone's predefined notions of correct behavior. They respond to any challenges to their uniqueness with fierce anger and an obstinate determination to be more outrageous than ever. Contrariness is second nature to Aquarians, and they are nearly invulnerable to outside criticism and influence. Their egos are robust, resilient, and highly evolved. Indeed, Aquarians frequently have charmingly inflated notions of their starlike destinies in the world. Uranus-ruled Aquarians are true-blue to their governing planet: quixotic and stubborn mavericks, never content with the status quo, who often are enamored of change merely for change's sake.

Uranus, however, governs another kind of change, one that is deeper, subtler, and more meaningful. This is the planet that rules personal transformation, humanitarianism, and philanthropy. Despite their nonconformist, lone-wolf natures, Aquarians have a keen and heartfelt interest in righting the social and political inequities of the world. They are especially empathetic with victims of social injustice and often ally themselves mightily with the disenfranchised, for whose rights they will vigorously fight. Moreover, Aquarians are great visionaries and frequently the arbiters of complex and profound changes in their respective spheres of influence.

Many astrologers, in fact, consider the roster of famed Aquarians to be the most esteemed in the zodiac. Certainly it contains some of the modern age's most seminal and influential politicians, scientists, thinkers, activists, and creative artists. Just a partial list includes such diverse visionaries as Thomas Paine, Abraham Lincoln, Franklin Roosevelt, Adlai Stevenson, and Ronald Reagan; Galileo, Johannes Gutenberg, and Thomas Edison; Sir Francis Bacon and Charles Darwin; Sinclair Lewis, Susan B. Anthony, and Bess Truman; Edouard Manet and Jackson Pollock; Buzz Aldrin and Charles Lindbergh; Franz Schubert, Wolfgang Amadeus Mozart, and Bertolt Brecht; D. W. Griffith, John Ford, Federico Fellini, and Milos Forman; James Dean, Humphrey Bogart, and Paul Newman; Charles Dickens, Virginia Woolf, Lewis Carroll, Colette, Jules Verne, Gertrude Stein, James Joyce, William Burroughs, Alice Walker, and Toni Morrison.

What differentiates this esteemed group from the fiery "superstars" of Leo or the brilliant "jesters of Sagittarius is emotional character. Leo's movers and shakers and Sagittarius's shining humorists consciously grab the spotlight and are comfortable center stage. Aquarians, on the other hand, try to distance themselves from the public eye. They are emotionally self-contained and coolly intellectual; however profound their public influence, their private personas—with few exceptions— are often enigmatic.

This Aquarian duality is aptly represented by the sign's two distinct symbols. The glyph that represents the sign (♒) is believed to symbolize strong energy impulses that are manifested through the intellect and dispensed as universal wisdom. Here lies the cool and rational side of Aquarians, the side that celebrates the life of the mind and is capable of great visions and strategies. This is where one may find the Aquarian's trademark qualities of free-spiritedness, independence, intuitiveness, and originality.

The Waterbearer symbol of the sign, however, is more involved in the everyday concerns of humanity. He is most often depicted as freely—and equally—bestowing the living waters of creation, sustenance, growth, and healing upon the world. Here lies the concerned and tenderhearted side of Aquarius, the side that celebrates the life of the soul and cares deeply about humanitarian issues. This is where one may find the other Aquarian qualities of high-mindedness, sensitivity, and empathy, together with the consuming belief that the world can be changed for the better.

The origins of the Waterbearer's intriguing duality may be found in Greek mythology. Most astrological scholars believe that the Waterbearer was originally Ganymede, a beloved Greek prince who was famed as the most beautiful mortal on Earth. Zeus, the king of the Greek gods, became enamored of Ganymede and had him kidnapped and flown to Mount Olympus by a great eagle. There, Ganymede became the cupbearer of the gods, but was never happy in his subservient role. Eventually Zeus granted Ganymede a unique but lonely kind of freedom— as the constellation Aquarius. Forever after, Ganymede was to be the universal cupbearer to all humankind, dispensing a never-ending flow of life-sustaining water.

The symbolism of the Waterbearer brings to light yet another Aquarian contradiction. On the one hand, Aquarius is the sign of friendship. Aquarians are cherished companions who derive much stimulation, pleasure, and insight from the company of others. Furthermore, they are able to inspire people to rally together for a great cause and then see it through to its resolution. At the same time, however, Aquarians are emotionally self-protective and self-contained, having difficulty committing to one-on-one intimate relationships. Sooner, rather than later, Aquarians often leave behind the considerable pleasures and stimulations of the crowd, however illustrious the company, to keep solitary company with themselves. An aura of loneliness and even melancholy surrounds many Aquarians. Perhaps this is because they are forever engaged in an eternal tug between their public self, which wants to do great things, and their private self, which wants to do great things—from an emotionally safe distance.

The Masculine and Air influences in this sign endow Aquarians with their hallmark qualities of energy, optimism, idealism, and expansiveness. Their quick minds are constantly devising schemes and strategems for changing the world, and they are remarkably persuasive in rallying large groups of people around a common interest. The Fixed quality of this sign underscores the Aquarian's rigid determination, persistence, and resourcefulness in the face of any challenge, large or small, to their integrity, individuality, and ideals.

Some have said that Aquarians not only march to the sound of their own music, they also compose the songs, play all the instruments, and conduct the orchestra. Certainly Aquarians are among the most intriguing and talented children of the zodiac. Cerebral and emotionally reticent, inclined to prefer their own company, Aquarians are consummate originals, innovative and radical in their approach to life. Yet they invariably manage to overcome their self-imposed isolation and move out into the more dangerous waters of teeming humanity. There they often apply their considerable gifts of innovation, invention, high ideals, and deep empathy to the cause of bettering the lives of those around them.

Home

Parents can expect to be constantly challenged and surprised by their quixotic Aquarian children—and to have their patience tested to the absolute limit. Left alone, Aquarians are generally loving, kind, thoughtful, and considerate. They are supremely comfortable with themselves and have an easygoing approach to life. But Aquarians also live in their own unique and off-kilter worlds where life is explored in a haphazard fashion at their own pace and in their own time. Trying to chart an Aquarian child's development by the preset standards of a baby book is a fruitless task. The Aquarian approach to life and development is start, stop, think, and regroup; then start again, stop again, think again, and perhaps abandon the whole process for a while! Even at a very young age, the Aquarian lifestyle is a fascinating, though sometimes bewildering, work in progress.

Always free spirited and determined to have their way, Aquarians aren't naturally respectful of authority—parental or otherwise—and abhor discipline, rules, and rigid routines. Aquarian children resist any attempt by others to box them in to preconceived notions of how children, boys or girls, should behave. Pushed against the proverbial wall, Aquarians bolt for the nearest exit. Contrariness is second nature to them, so this is the child for whom taking an oppositive tack may help to keep the peace and produce the best results. Instead of making unequivocal demands, parents might try asking for the opposite of what they really want from their young Aquarian, or simply take a deep breath and smile at their child's eccentricities—techniques that often bring contrary Aquarians back to the family fold.

Aquarian children, who are strongly influenced by the element of Air in their signs, require a great deal of mental stimulation. Invariably, they favor the life of the mind over physical play. Yet they are quite resourceful at amusing themselves and take every opportunity to transform a seemingly mundane task or object into a challenging project that engages their talents of imagination, invention, and innovation.

The humanitarian aspect in Aquarians manifests itself early as considerable thoughtfulness and concern for family members and friends. Supremely intuitive, Aquarians are sensitive to others' moods and feelings, a quality this Air sign shares with the Water signs. But rather than emotionally expressed, cool-headed Aquarians' concerns are often intellectualized and rationalized—

they believe there is a logical answer to everything. Thus they are often perceived as insensitive, when in fact they simply aren't comfortable with their feelings. Teaching Aquarian children to acknowledge and accept the "illogic" of deeply felt emotions is an especially meaningful lesson that their parents can pass on to them.

School and Play

Expect Aquarian children to have some trouble in school. Despite their considerable intelligence, reasoning powers, intuition, and energy, they don't find school particularly challenging or stimulating. The academic environment's rules and regulations, restricting classrooms, forced attendance, and mandatory participation in extracurricular events are all anathema to the Aquarian child.

Furthermore, like their near cousins, the Sagittarians, Aquarians tend to work hard only at those subjects that engage their interest; more boring studies are quickly abandoned. And homework feels completely optional to the typical Aquarian. Here a firm parental line must be drawn with Aquarians, so that they learn to understand how critical a strong academic foundation is to realizing their long-range goals, dreams, and visions for the future. Strongly encourage and support Aquarians where they are academically strong—usually in the sciences and in technology. Then get them all the extra help they need to get through their more daunting subjects.

Most Aquarians can take or leave everyday play. Like the other Air signs, they favor mental stimulation over physical stimulation. In the case of Aquarians in particular, their idealistic dreams and far-reaching visions of changing the world take precedence over any school playing field. They are rarely drawn to competitive sports, or even the more solitary realms of track and field.

Aquarians can often be found in after-school computer, science, and math clubs. Alternatively, they may get involved in school politics or neighborhood social causes. Many Aquarians are also gifted writers and speakers, and with their love for argument, they are prestigious additions to any debating club.

Yet outside activities take second place to Aquarian children's need for a great deal of private time and space. Left to their own devices, Aquarians can spend hours aimlessly but vigorously exercising their minds and imaginations with a variety of solitary but challenging tasks. In these quiet times Aquarian children begin to construct the dreams and visions that will dominate their adult years.

Once they've had that time and space, Aquarian children are ready to enjoy being with groups of children who are engaged in exciting and interesting tasks. Like Capricorns, Aquarians aren't interested in aimless play, but take pleasure in rallying their buddies around a common goal. In this type of group play, Aquarians nurture their budding humanitarian interests and learn to trust their emotional instincts.

The World

Aquarians are the great schemers and dreamers of the zodiac. They frequently pursue careers in politics, law, and political and social activism. All three areas provide ample opportunity for Aquarians to give form and energy to their altruistic and humanitarian visions. Their easygoing natures, levelheaded intelligence, and gifts of intuition and oratory make them natural, if reluctant, leaders who are adept at getting others to work for them.

Like Sagittarians, Aquarians often aren't interested in doing the hard work necessary to give substance to their dreams. They burn up a great deal of their energy and staying power in all the mental activity expended on birthing their visions. Once the vision is born, Aquarians often hand over its rearing to their capable followers.

With the powerful influence of Uranus in their sign, Aquarians also are strongly drawn to science and technology, particularly to the areas of invention and innovation. In many ways, the field of science and technology is most suited to Aquarians—if it weren't for their strong humanitarian streak—because it affords them the creative solitude that is their natural milieu. That same solitary creative drive can also be satisfied in the field of writing, as many fine writers are born under the sign of Aquarius.

As noted earlier, Aquarius is the sign of friendship, and Aquarians are among the most delightful and engaging comrades of the zodiac. They are loyal, tenderhearted, fiercely devoted, and never fickle in their affection. They enjoy the company of large groups of people and derive great intellectual and emotional stimulation from interacting with others. In the end, however, Aquarians often leave the party alone. They are most comfortable and most confident when they are alone with their own thoughts, perhaps a legacy of the lonely Ganymede who became the human embodiment of the Waterbearer.

Emotionally guarded and reluctant to let their defenses down, Aquarians may never settle down with one person. If so, they usually do it later in life and usually with another Aquarian. Only another Aquarian can truly understand the complex double nature of the Waterbearers: independent, innovative, eccentric visionaries who care deeply about changing the world but who ultimately want to be left alone. Content to leave the glory that is inherent in their visions in the capable hands of more gregarious others, Aquarians can make a deep and everlasting mark upon the world. Despite the brilliance of their outer achievements, their inner personas remain impenetrable enigmas.

Choosing a Name for Your Aquarius Child

When choosing a name for your Aquarius child, first think about the major attributes and symbols associated with the sign. Aquarius is the sign of friendship, individuality, independence, innovation, and originality. Aquarians are quintessential free spirits who are renowned for their devoted and fiercely loyal friendships, progressive thinking, unconventionalism, eccentricity, assertiveness, strong-mindedness, intellectualism, and rigid thinking. Aquarians are naturally rebellious, flout convention, and have a strong need to be different from the crowd. They are also charming, outgoing, and generally amiable and even-tempered—as long as they are allowed to follow their own unique paths without challenge. Aquarians have well-developed egos and an assured sense of their own starlike destinies in life. They have creative, imaginative, and intuitive intellects and are great seekers of knowledge. Aquarians are frequently drawn to science, technology, astronomy, and law, as well as to the creative arts.

Aquarius is a Masculine, Fixed Air sign governed by the planet Uranus. The Masculine aspect endows Aquarians with physical and intellectual energy, an expansive view of the world, and an extroverted nature. The Fixed quality of the sign is responsible for Aquarians' rigid single-mindedness, determination, consistency, and self-containment. The Air influence supports Aquarians' keen intellectual, communication, and reasoning skills.

Aquarius's ruling planet, Uranus, is the planet of anarchy and unconventional behavior, which governs sudden and dramatic changes, modern technology, revolution, radicalism, independence, individuality, and personal transformation. Uranus also rules all humanitarian and philanthropic activities. Aquarians, renowned for their fierce individuality, their penchant for bucking the status quo, and their need to be different, also have a strong humanitarian streak. They frequently aspire to be the instruments of great social and political change, though they often get others to implement their visions and dreams.

Aquarius is the eleventh sign of the zodiac and encompasses the winter months of January and February. The amethyst is the sign's official birthstone, and uranium is the sign's metal. The bright blue of the sky is the sign's symbolic color. The orchid is the flower of Aquarius, and all fruit-bearing trees are also strongly associated with the sign. The sign of Aquarius rules all large birds, and the archetypical qualities of the bird—playfulness, free-spiritedness, and unfettered access to all the world has to offer—are quintessentially Aquarian.

When you choose a name for your child, bear in mind some of Aquarian children's key personal qualities. They prize freethinking, independence, and equality for all, but they are also rigid and inflexible when it comes to their own opinions and lifestyles. Aquarians defy convention and have a strong, individualistic self-image. Generally easygoing, expansive, energetic, intellectual, and imaginative, they have a great facility for making long and passionate friendships, and for inspiring groups of people to follow them in pursuit of a common ideal.

For additional inspiration when choosing a name for your Aquarius child—especially a middle name—you may want to look through the names listed in Aquarius's companion Air signs, Gemini and Libra.

Names for Aquarius Girls

Adesina (ah-DAY-see-nah) African/Nigerian: Baby who inspires more to follow. Aquarians are idealistic dreamers who are capable of inspiring others to implement their ideas and visions.

Adora (ah-DOR-ah) Latin: Much adored. Aquarians are ardent and flamboyant friends who fiercely defend the rights of others. Variations: *Adoree, Adoria, Adorlee, Dora, Dori, Dorie.*

Aeola (ay-OH-lah) Greek: Goddess of the winds. Aquarius is an air sign whose children are famous for their free-spirited natures.

Ahava (ah-HAH-vah) Hebrew: Cherished one. *Ahava* is a suitable choice for a girl born under Aquarius, the sign of friendship. Variations: *Ahuva, Hava.*

Aimee (AY-mee) French: Loved one. Aquarians are renowned for their passionate friendships. Variation: *Amy.* (Famous Aquarian: Amy Lowell, Pulitzer Prize-winning poet)

Ain (ah-EEN) Arabic: Apple of one's eye. All fruit-bearing trees are ruled by the sign of Aquarius. Aquarians are noted for their outstanding individuality.

Akilina (ah-kee-LEEN-ah) Greek: Eagle. The sign of Aquarius rules all large birds. Variations: *Acquilina, Aquilina.*

Alani (uh-LAH-nuh) Hawaiian: Orange tree. The sign of Aquarius governs all fruit-bearing trees.

Alauda (ah-LAW-dah) Irish: Bird who sings. Birds are ruled by the sign of Aquarius, whose children are naturally exuberant and frequently drawn to the performing arts.

Aldara (ahl-DAHR-ah) Greek: Winged gift. Aquarians, ruled by Uranus, the planet of great and radical change, are often aspired to make a tremendous difference in the world. Variation: *Aldora.*

Alinda (ah-LIN-dah) English: Tender. Aquarians have great empathy for those less fortunate than themselves.

Alleen (ah-LEEN) Dutch: Alone. Aquarians thrive on being innovators of social change, yet they tend to avoid intimate one-on-one relationships and are frequently loners.

Allegra (ah-LEG-rah) Latin: Cheerful. Generally amiable and outgoing, Aquarians are naturally ebullient creatures when allowed to do their own thing.

Alpha (AL-fah) Greek: Leader; superiority. Aquarians are superbly gifted at rallying groups of people to a common cause. Variation: *Alfa.*

Althea (ahl-THEE-ah) Latin: To heal. With a keen empathy for the disenfranchised of society, Aquarians are often driven to right the fundamental wrongs they see around them.

Althena (ahl-THEE-nah) English: Contemporary combination of *Althea* (the healer) and *Athena* (the Greek goddess of wisdom). Aquarians are gifted with keen intelligence and a great desire to heal the social wounds of the world.

Amethyst (AM-ih-thist) Greek: Against intoxication. The amethyst is the birthstone of the sign of Aquarius. In ancient Greece, this gem was believed to protect its wearer against the effects of alcohol.

Amissa (ah-MEE-suh) Hebrew: Friend. Aquarius is the sign of passionate and long-term friendships. Variation: *Amisa*.

Amoke (ah-moh-KEH) African/Nigerian: To know her is to pet her. Aquarians are charming, devoted, and affectionate friends.

Anemone (ah-NEH-moh-nee) Greek: Breath. Aquarius is one of three Air signs. (The other two are Libra and Gemini.) Variations: *Ann-Aymone, Anne-Aymone*.

Ann (ahn) Hebrew: Graceful. Like the birds their sign is associated with, Aquarians seem to glide effortlessly through life. Variations: *Anna, Anne, Annette, Annie, Anushka, Anya, Ayn*. (Famous Aquarians: Anne Jeffreys, actress; Ann Sothern, actress; Ann Jillian, actress; Ayn Rand, writer)

Apara (ah-PAHR-ah) African/Nigerian: Girl who comes and goes. Aquarians prize independence, frequently flout convention, and always reserve their right to change their minds.

Aquene (ah-KAY-neh) Native American: Peace. Peace and justice are frequent goals of progressive Aquarians.

Arlette (ar-LET) English: Eagle. The sign of Aquarius rules all large birds. Variations: *Arlettie, Arletty*.

Avis (AY-viss) English: Bird. This classic and traditional English name embodies the prized Aquarian ideal of unfettered freedom of movement and thought.

Azami (ah-ZAH-mee) Japanese: Thistle flower. In Asia, the thistle symbolizes defiance and surliness. Normally easygoing and free spirited, Aquarians can be astonishingly defiant and rigid when their unconventional lifestyles are challenged.

Baka (BAH-kah) Hindu: Crane. In East Indian mythology, the crane symbolized long life and good health. Large birds are governed by the sign of Aquarius.

Barika (bah-REE-kah) Arabic: Win. Crusading Aquarians are renowned for their dedication to winning tough political and social battles.

Becca (BEK-ah) English: To bind. Bringing disparate groups together to heal and sooth social injustices is a common goal of Aquarians. Variations: *Beck, Beckie, Becky, Bekka, Rebecca.*

Bel (bell) Hindu: For the sacred apple tree. The apple and other fruit trees are governed by Aquarius. Variations: *Bella, Belle.*

Berenice (ber-eh-NEES, BER-eh-nees, or ber-NEES) Greek: She brings victory. Aquarians are noted for their commitment to conquering social injustice. Variation: *Bernice.*

Cam (KAM) Vietnamese: Orange fruit. Fruit-bearing trees are ruled by the sign of Aquarius.

Caprice (kah-PREESE) Italian: Ruled by whim. Unconventional to the extreme, Aquarians are noted for their unusual, even eccentric, lifestyles. Variations: *Capriana, Capricia, Caprie.*

Cari (KAH-ree) Turkish: Flowing like water. The sign of Aquarius is healing water symbolized by the Waterbearer who freely supplies to humanity. Variations: *Carrie, Kari.*

Charity (CHARE-ah-tee) Latin: Love for humankind. All Aquarians have a strong humanitarian streak. Variations: *Carissa, Carita, Chareese, Charissa, Charisse, Charita, Charitee, Charitey, Sharitee.*

Chenoa (chay-NOH-ah) Native American: Bird of peace. Social and political justice are frequent aims of Aquarians, who are associated with the bird as their animal sign. Variations: *Shenandoa, Shenandoah, Shonoa.*

Cheryl (SHER-ill) English: Petite beauty. Free spirited, imaginative, and charming, Aquarius possesses great inner beauty. Variation of *Charlotte*. Variations: *Sherilyn, Sheryl.* (Famous Aquarians: Sheryl Crow, singer; Sherilyn Fenn, actress)

Chesna (CHESS-nah) Slavic: Bringing peace and calm. Aquarians cherish peace, justice, and equanimity for all. Variations: *Chessa, Chessy.*

Chidori (chee-DOR-ee) Japanese: Bird. *Chidori* is an appropriate choice for a girl born under the sign of Aquarius, which is strongly associated with large birds.

Cholena (choh-LAYN-ah) Native American: Bird. Birds, governed by the sign of Aquarius, suggest the freewheeling and unencumbered lifestyles that are quintessentially Aquarian.

Chuma (KOO-mah) Aramaic: Warmth. Naturally happy and easygoing, Aquarians are renowned for their ardent and long-lasting friendships. Variations: *Chumi, Huma, Humi.*

Dalila (dah-LEE-lah) Hebrew: Waterbearer. The Waterbearer is the symbol of the sign of Aquarius. Variations: *Dalice, Dalilah, Delia, Delilah, Lila.*

Dalit (dah-LEET) Hebrew: To draw water. Images of free-flowing water are strongly associated with the sign of Aquarius, which is symbolized by the waterbearer.

Derora (dee-ROH-rah) Hebrew: Independence. Aquarians prize intellectual and physical freedom above all things. Variations: *Derorice, Derorit.*

Dickla (dee-KLAH) Hebrew: Date tree. All fruit-bearing trees are governed by the sign of Aquarius. Variations: *Dikla, Diklice, Diklit.*

Drina (DREE-nah) Spanish: Fighter for justice. Many Aquarians frequently choose careers in the fields of social justice and political activism. Variation: *Dreena.*

Edna (ED-nah) Hebrew: Rejuvenation. Aquarius is ruled by Uranus, the planet of personal transformation. Variation: *Ednah.*

Edwige (ed-WEEJ) French: Pleasing strife. When the goal is social equality or political peace, Aquarians love nothing more than a good battle of the minds. Variations: *Edvig, Edwig, Hedvig, Hedwibe, Hedwig.*

Eira (AYR-ah) Scandinavian: Goddess of medicine. Born under the planet of Uranus, which governs all modern technology, Aquarians often are drawn to scientific fields. Variation: *Eyra.*

Elma (ell-MAH) Turkish: Apple. Fruit trees are symbolic of the sign of Aquarius.

Emmeline (EM-meh-line, EM-meh-leen, or EM-meh-lihn) English: Little rival. Aquarians enjoy opposition and competition when fighting for a good cause. Variations: *Emma, Emmalina, Emmie.*

Falda (FAHL-dah) Icelandic: Folded wings. The image of the bird—free-flying, independent, and unencumbered—is symbolic of the sign of Aquarius.

Fardoos (FAHR-dooz) Arabic: Utopia. The highest of social and political ideals are often the Aquarian's driving concerns. Variation: *Farduz.*

Farica (fahr-IK-ah) German: Leader of peace. Aquarians are gifted visionaries and leaders, deftly able to arouse the hearts and minds of people in support of a common political cause.

Farida (fah-REED-ah) Arabic: Unique. The most unconventional and free spirited of the zodiac's children, Aquarians are truly one-of-a-kind individuals who flout convention at every turn. Variations: *Faridah, Farideh*.

Feige (FAY-gah) Hebrew: Bird. Birds, the symbol of unfettered independence, are emblematic of the sign of Aquarius. Variations: *Faga, Faiga, Faigel, Feiga, Feigel, Feigele*.

Fernanda (fur-NAHN-dah) German: Peace and courage. Aquarians, born under the sign of friendship, often become fearless and tireless champions of the disenfranchised. Variation: *Fernande*.

Fontane (fahn-TAYN) French: Fountain. The image of flowing water—symbolic of the bestowing of free and equal gifts to human kind—is strongly associated with the sign of Aquarius.

Frederika (fred-eh-REE-kah) German: Peaceful ruler. Peace and justice are abiding concerns of Aquarians, who are highly capable of leading others to follow their goals. Variations: *Flicka, Fredericka*.

Gloria (GLAW-ree-ah) Latin: Glory-born. Aquarians, the great dreamers and visionaries of the zodiac, take enormous pride in being the instruments of profound change. Variations: *Gloree, Gloriana, Gloriane, Glorie, Glorria, Glory*.

Halolani (hah-loh-LAHN-ee) Hawaiian: Fly like a bird. Like the birds their sign is associated with, Aquarians are free-spirited, expansive, and powerful.

Harita (hah-REE-tah) Hindu: The wind. Aquarius is one of three Air signs of the zodiac.

Hasana (hah-SAH-nah) African/Nigerian: She who arrives first. This lovely African name is a wonderful choice for an Aquarian born in January, the first month of the calendar year.

Imelda (ee-MAYLD-ah) Italian: Embracing the fight. On the battleground of social justice, Aquarians are incomparable and unstoppable opponents. Variation: *Imalda.*

Imma (EEM-mah; EYE-mah) Akkadian: One who pours water from a jug. *Imma* is another name for the constellation Aquarius, which is symbolized by the Waterbearer, who freely pours out life-giving water to any who want it.

Inam (ee-NAHM) Arabic: Charitable. The Waterbearer, Aquarius's symbol, represents the free and equal distribution of life-enhancing gifts to all humanity. Variation: *Enam.*

Iolana (ee-oh-LAH-nah) Hawaiian: To soar like a hawk. All large birds are governed by the sign of Aquarius.

Janan (jah-NAHN) Arabic: Spirited. Unconventional and individualistic Aquarians remain enthused and unwavering when fighting for their ideals.

Jardena (yahr-DAY-nah) Hebrew: To flow downward. Images of free-flowing water—symbolic of a universal and freely given gift—are strongly associated with the sign of Aquarius.

Jarita (jah-REE-tah) Arabic: Earthen water jug. The Waterbearer, who symbolizes the sign of Aquarius, is depicted holding an ancient water vessel. Artifacts associated with the storage and pouring of water are symbolic of the sign of Aquarius.

Kadiah (KAH-dee-ah) Hebrew: Pitcher. Objects for carrying and pouring water are symbolic of the sign of Aquarius, symbolized by the Waterbearer. Variations: *Kadia, Kadya.*

Kaminari (kah-mee-NAHR-ee) Japanese: Thunder. Aquarius is ruled by Uranus, the planet that governs storms, as well as sudden and earthshaking change.

Kanoa (kah-NOH-ah) Hawaiian: Free one. Independence is the Aquarian child's most treasured possession.

Kapuki (kah-POO-kee) Sudanese: Firstborn daughter. This Middle Eastern name makes an unusual choice for an Aquarian born in January, the first month of the year.

Karisma (kah-RIZ-mah) English: Charisma. Aquarians are renowned for their gifts of persuasion which are mesmerizing when arousing a crowd to a common cause.

Kasmira (kas-MIR-ah) Slavic: Bringing peace. Aquarians are champions of equality, freedom, justice, and peace for all.

Kelalani (keh-lah-LAH-nee) Hawaiian: Limitless sky. Free-spirited and independent-minded Aquarians are strongly influenced by the element of Air in their sign.

Kelsey (KELL-see) English: Island. Despite their gift for friendship and their famous public personas as champions of social change, Aquarians may be romantically reticent loners who prefer their own company. Variations: *Kelcey, Kelci, Kelcie, Kelcy, Kelsa, Kelsea, Kelsee, Kelseigh, Kelsi, Kessie.*

Keola (keh-OH-lah) Hawaiian: One life. Aquarians are extraordinarily passionate and imaginative visionaries, who enlist the help of others in their efforts to create a more equal world for all.

Keshia (KEESH-yah) African: Favorite one. Aquarius, the sign of devoted and passionate friendship, produces many of the most popular of the zodiac's children.

Koko (KOH-koh) Japanese: Stork. Large birds are governed by the sign of Aquarius.

Lani (LAH-nee) Hawaiian: Sky. One of three Air signs, Aquarians are renowned for their all-embracing view of the world.

Latoya (lah-TOY-ah) Spanish: Victorious one. Aquarians are unstoppable—and frequently unbeatable—in their pursuit of political and social equality for all. Variations: *Latoia, Latoyia*.

Laura (LAW-rah) English: Laurel tree. *Laura* is a lovely name for a girl born under the sign of Aquarius, which is associated with all fruit-bearing trees, including the berry-producing laurel. Variations: *Lauren, Laurie, Lora*. (Famous Aquarians: Laura Dern, actress; Laura Ingalls Wilder, writer)

Laverne (lah-VERN) Latin: The Roman goddess of minor criminals. This name is a whimsical choice for unconventional and free-spirited Aquarians who are often drawn to unusual and sometimes unsavory characters. Variations: *Laverine, Lavern, Laverna, LaVerne, Verne*.

Leeba (LEE-bah) Hebrew: Heart. Empathetic and genuinely concerned about the welfare of others, Aquarians are champions of justice and fairness for all.

Leoda (lee-OH-dah) German: Of the people. Deeply empathic and idealistic, Aquarians are known as the humanitarians and philanthropists of the zodiac. Variation: *Leota*.

Liliha (lee-LEE-huh) Hawaiian: Angry disregard. Normally joyful and easygoing, but notoriously rigid in the face of criticism, Aquarians can turn fiercely angry when their lifestyles or beliefs are questioned.

Lirit (lee-RIT) Hebrew: Poetic. Strongly influenced by the element of Air in their sign, Aquarians are immensely creative and imaginative.

Lynn (LINN) Old English: Falling water. The image of pouring water is symbolic of the sign of Aquarius, which is symbolized by the Waterbearer. Variations: *Lin, Linell, Linelle, Linette, Linn, Linne, Lyln, Lyndel, Lyndelle, Lynelie, Lynell, Lynette, Lynna, Lynne.*

Makani (mah-KAH-nee) Hawaiian: Wind. The qualities associated with the wind—sudden and dramatic change, capriciousness, and potential catastrophe—are all quintessentially Aquarian, one of three Air signs.

Makeda (mah-KEE-dah) Hebrew: Vessel or cup. Water vessels are strongly associated with the sign of Aquarius, which is symbolized by the Waterbearer.

Margea (mahr-GEE-ah) Hebrew: Peace. *Margea* is an appropriate name for Aquarius, who prizes justice, equality, and peace for all.

Melora (meh-LOH-rah) Latin: Improve. Aquarians are ruled by Uranus, the planet that governs humanitarianism and philanthropy.

Merima (mer-EE-mah) Hebrew: Uplifted. Aquarians are invariably drawn to champion great political and social change. Variation: *Meroma.*

Milca (MILL-cah) Hebrew: Adviser. Renowned for their devotion to peace and justice, and esteemed for their cool intelligence, Aquarians are sought-after leaders and advisers in the volatile field of social change. Variations: *Milcah, Milka, Milkah.*

Miranda (mer-AN-dah) Latin: To be admired. Naturally gifted leaders, Aquarians are renowned for their ability to sway large groups of people to a common, and sometimes unpopular, cause. Variation: *Meranda.*

Miri (MEE-ree) English Gypsy: My own. Aquarians are passionately protective of their unique and often eccentric lifestyles.

Miriam (MIR-ee-ahm) Hebrew: She who follows her own way. Aquarians, who have a keen sense of their own uniqueness and singular place in life, are rarely dissuaded from following their chosen path, however unconventional it may be. Variations: *Mariam, Mimi, Minni, Minnie, Mirjma, Mitz.*

Moani (moh-AHN-ee) Hawaiian: Light breeze. *Moani* is a lovely and suitable choice for a girl born under Aquarius, one of the zodiac's Air signs.

Mystique (miss-TEEK) French: Intriguing. The most unconventional of the zodiac's children, Aquarians are fascinating and enigmatic creatures. Variations: *Mistique, Mystica.*

Naseem (nah-SEEM) Hindu: Morning breeze. Aquarius is one of three Air signs. (The other two are Libra and Gemini.) Variation: *Nasim.*

Nasya (NAH-see-ah; NAHS-yuh) Hebrew: Divine transformation. Aquarius is ruled by Uranus, the planet of personal transformation. Variation: *Nasia.*

Neci (NEH-see) Latin: Without limits. Absolute freedom—mental, physical, and spiritual—is the Aquarian motto.

Neola (neh-OH-lah) Greek: Youthful soul. Confirmed idealists and unrepentant free spirits, Aquarians are among the most perennially youthful of the zodiac's children.

Nicole (nih-KOHL) French: Victory of the people. Aquarians are the quintessential champions of the common man. Variations: *Niccola, Nichole, Nicki, Nicky, Nicola, Nicolette, Nikki, Nikole.*

Nita (NEE-tah) Hindu: Friendly. Aquarius is the sign of open-hearted and generous friendships. Variations: *Neeta, Nitali*.

Novella (noh-VELL-ah) Spanish: New little thing. Aquarians are the innovators and upstarts of the zodiac.

Olympia (oh-LIMP-ee-ah) Greek: Mount Olympus. Mount Olympus was the mythological home of the Greek gods, the place from which universal justice and retribution were meted out to mankind. *Olympia* is a classic choice for the politically and socially conscious Aquarian. Variations: *Olimpia, Olympya, Pia*.

Onawa (oh-NAH-wah) Native American: Wide awake. Aquarians are renowned for their sharp intelligence and informed intuition.

Ondrea (ohn-DREE-ah, OHN-dree-ah, or ohn-DRAY-ah) Czechoslovakian: Fierce woman. Normally pleasant and easygoing, independent-minded Aquarians can be driven to rage when their unconventional beliefs and lifestyles are seriously challenged. Variations: *Andra, Andrea, Ondra*.

Onida (oh-NEE-dah) Native American: Eagerly awaited. Noted visionaries, Aquarians are much admired—and much followed—leaders of social and political change. Variation: *Oneida*.

Ophelia (oh-FEE-lee-ah) Greek: Help. This classic name from Shakespeare's *Hamlet* is a marvelous choice for humanitarian-minded Aquarians.

Oriole (OR-ee-ohl) English: Bird. Free-spirited Aquarians emulate many of the untethered qualities of the bird. Variations: *Auriel, Orella, Oriel, Oriola*.

Orlenda (or-LEHN-dah) Russian: Female eagle. The powerful, solitary, and enigmatic eagle is quintessentially Aquarian, ruled by the sign that governs large birds.

Orquidea (or-kee-DAY-ah) Spanish: Orchid. The rare and beautiful orchid is the symbolic flower of the sign of Aquarius.

Ozera (oh-ZER-ah) Hebrew: Helper. Empathic and idealistic Aquarians are quick to offer their assistance to others, especially those who are victims of social injustice.

Palila (pah-LEE-lah) Hawaiian: Bird. Aquarius rules all large birds, whose free-spirited, unfettered, and wide-ranging natures are emblematic of the sign.

Paula (PAW-lah) Latin: Small. While they are often the innovators of tiny ideas that eventually lead to great social change, Aquarians rarely allow others to glimpse more than a small part of their inner worlds. Variations: *Paule, Paulette, Paulina, Pauline*.

Pavana (pah-VAHN-ah) Hindu: Wind. This unusual name is an apt choice for a girl born under free-wheeling Aquarius, one of the three Air signs of the zodiac. Variation: *Pavani*.

Pema (PAYM-bah) African: Meteorological power. Aquarius is ruled by Uranus, the planet of storms and sudden, great, and often catastrophic change.

Perry (PEAR-ee) Greek: Pear tree. Fruit-bearing trees are governed by the sign of Aquarius. Variations: *Peri, Perrey, Perri, Perrie*.

Petula (pe-CHOOL-ah) Latin: Sassy. *Petula* is a charming choice for unconventional Aquarius, who bridles at any suggestion that she bow to the status quo. Variations: *Petulah, Petulia*.

Qubilah (ka-BEE-lah) Arabic: Concord. Peace, justice, and social equanimity are common goals of the typical Aquarian.

Rabiah (rah-BEE-ah) Arabic: Breeze. Aquarians, strongly motivated by the element of Air in their sign, have a casual and free-spirited approach to life. Variations: *Rabi, Rabia.*

Raidah (rah-EE-dah) Arabic: Guide. Aquarians, renowned for their singular dreams and visions, have a consummate ability to inspire others to support and implement their goals.

Ramona (rah-MOH-nuh) Spanish: All-knowing defender. So-cially conscious, politically savvy, sharply intelligent, and keenly intuitive, Aquarians are empathetic defenders of the com-mon good.

Reiko (RAY-koh) Japanese: Very pleasant child. Happy, charm-ing, and easygoing, Aquarians are among the most delightful of companions. Variation: *Rei.*

Ritsa (REET-sah) Greek: Defender and helper of mankind. *Ritsa* is an apt name for Aquarius, who eagerly fights for the rights of the disenfranchised.

Rowena (roh-WEE-nah) Old English: Famous friend. Aquarius is the sign that governs friendship.

Sakuna (sah-KOO-nah) East Indian: Bird. The sign of Aquarius is associated with all large birds.

Samantha (sah-MAN-thah) Aramaic: She who listens. The strong element of Air in their sign endows Aquarian children with great communication skills—among them, the more subtle but immensely important ability to be a keen and empathetic listener. Variations: *Sam, Sammi, Sammie, Sammy.*

Sandra (SAN-drah) Greek: Helper of mankind. Aquarians, who possess a strong humanitarian streak, are always willing to fight for the rights of the disenfranchised. Variations: *Sandi, Sandy, Sondra.*

Saril (shuh-RIH) Turkish: Sound of running water. Images of falling, running, and pouring water are strongly associated with

Aquarius, the sign symbolized by the Waterbearer.

Sasona (sah-SOHN-nah) Hebrew: Bliss. Unconventional and free spirited, Aquarians are living embodiments of the modern-day adage, "Follow your bliss."

Selda (SELL-dah) Old English: Companion. Aquarius is the sign of friendship, making imaginative, intuitive, and empathetic Aquarian children esteemed and beloved friends. Variations: *Selde, Zelda.*

Selima (sah-LEEM-ah) Hebrew: Peace. Social and political justice are lifelong concerns of the Aquarian. Variation: *Selimah.*

Shada (SHAH-dah) Native American: Pelican. The sign of Aquarius rules all large birds.

Shalvah (SHAHL-vah) Hebrew: Peace. *Shalvah* suggests Aquarius's desire to bring equality, freedom, and harmony to all. Variation: *Shalva.*

Shani (SHAH-nee) African/Swahili: Marvelous. Eccentric, unconventional, and deeply imaginative, Aquarians are among the most amazing and uniquely gifted children of the zodiac.

Shomera (SHO-mer-ah) Hebrew: Guard. Aquarians are devoted, committed, and protective friends who fiercely guard their personal relationships. Variations: *Shamira, Shomria, Shomriah, Shomrit, Shomriya, Shomrona.*

Simi (SEE-mee) Native American: Wind valley. Freewheeling and unconventional Aquarians are strongly influenced by the quixotic element of Air in their sign.

Sisika (si-SEE-kah) Native American: Singing bird. Aquarians embody many of the qualities traditionally associated with birds: unencumbered flight, unlimited freedom, and carefree joy.

Sloane (SLONE) Irish: A multitude of people. Aquarians are renowned for their ability to rouse a crowd to a common cause. This name is also appropriate for a boy. Variation: *Sloan*.

Solange (soh-LANZH) French: Solitary. Aquarians have expansive, jovial, and encompassing public images, but frequently avoid romantic commitment in their private lives. Variations: *Sola, Soledad*.

Sora (SOH-rah) Native American: Singing bird soars. The sign of Aquarius rules all large birds. Like birds, Aquarians are often free spirited, expansive, and playful.

Stacey (STAY-cee) Contemporary: Derived from *Eustacia*, meaning "she who brings peace." The humanitarians of the zodiac, Aquarians often dedicate their lives to ending social and political injustice and making the world a better place. Variations: *Staci, Stacy*.

Starla (STAR-lah) English: Star. Aquarians ruled by the planet that governs modern technology and science, often choose careers in astronomy and aeronautics. Variations: *Estelle, Estrella, Star, Starleena, Starlena, Starlene, Starlette, Starr, Stella*.

Sunny (SON-ee) English: Bright disposition. Naturally upbeat and easygoing, Aquarians are among the most charming children of zodiac. Variations: *Sunita, Sunni, Sunnie*.

Svetlana (svett-LAH-nah) Russian: Star. Aquarians, who have a deep affinity for the heavens, are frequently drawn to astronomy and space travel. Variations: *Svetla, Svetlanka*.

Tadi (TAH-dee) Native American: Wind. One of three Air signs, Aquarius rules spontaneous and unencumbered change. Variation: *Tadewi*.

Taima (tah-EE-mah) Native American: Thunderbolt. *Taima* is a suitable choice for unconventional, energetic, and powerful

Aquarius, which is ruled by the planet that governs storms.

Taipa (tah-EE-pah) Native American: Wings spread. All of the archetypical images associated with birds have deep resonance for Aquarians, who cherish freedom, independence, and unlimited boundaries.

Tama (TAH-mah) Native American: Thunderbolt. Aquarius's ruling planet, Uranus, governs storms as well as sudden and profound change.

Tami (TAH-mee) Japanese: People. Aquarians are renowned for their deep interest in humanitarian and philanthropic causes. Variations: *Tamie, Tammy*. (Famous Aquarian: Tammy Grimes, actress)

Tamika (TAH-mih-kah) Japanese: Child of the people. Aquarius, the sign of deep and committed friendship, is renowned for the tender and empathetic natures of its children. Variations: *Tamike, Tamiko, Tamiya, Tamiyo*.

Ulima (oo-LEE-mah) Arabic: Wise. Astute intelligence and the desire to acquire knowledge are hallmarks of the sign of Aquarius. Variation: *Ullima*.

Urania (yoor-AYN-ee-ah) Greek: The heavenly one; the sky. In Greek mythology, *Urania* was the muse of astronomy. Aquarians, who are ruled by the planet Uranus, often have a keen interest in astronomy and space exploration.

Utina (oo-TEE-nah) Native American: Female compatriot. Aquarians, passionate about pursuing great and common causes, are adept at rallying a like-minded crowd around them.

Veda (VAY-dah) Hindu: Knowledge. Aquarians, who are strongly influenced by the element of air in their sign, are renowned for their keen intellectual skills and great interest in acquiring knowledge. Variation: *Veeda*.

Vincentia (vin-SENS-ee-ah) Latin: To conquer. Aquarius's ruling planet, Uranus, governs anarchy, revolution, independence, and radicalism. Thus, Aquarians—usually even tempered and amiable—react with fierce and uncompromising determination when the cause of freedom and independence is challenged. Variations: *Vincenta, Vincentena, Vincentina, Vincenza, Vincetta, Vinia, Vinnie.*

Washi (wah-SHEE) Japanese: Eagle. The sign of Aquarius governs all large birds.

Wesesa (weh-seh-SAH) African/Ugandan: Imprudent. Unconventional and free spirited, Aquarians may make rash and impractical personal choices.

Wilfreda (wil-FRAY-dah or will-FREE-dah) English: Peaceful will. Aquarians, who value freedom and equality for all, are often uncompromising and rigid in their own opinions and lifestyle.

Winifred (WIN-i-fred) Welsh: Holy peace. Aquarians consider freedom, equality, and peace to be sacred gifts. Variations: *Win, Winifrede, Winifride, Winne, Winni, Winnie, Wynn.*

Winona (wih-NOH-nah) Native American: Firstborn daughter. *Winona* is a classic American name for an Aquarian girl born in January, the first month of the calendar year. Variation: *Wenona.*

Yeva (YEH-vah) Russian: Life-enhancing. Aquarians prize social and political equality for all.

Yoki (YOH-kee) Native American: Bluebird on the mesa. Bright blue is the color of Aquarius, the sign that rules all large birds.

Zafina (zah-FEEN-ah) Arabic: Triumphant. Aquarians thrill to the challenge of a great social cause.

Zan (ZAN) Chinese: Support. Devoted friends, Aquarians can always be depended on to come through during times of trouble.

Zazu (ZAH-zoo; zah-ZOO) Hebrew: Action. Aquarians are governed by Uranus, the planet of social change, action, and revolution. All Aquarians have a decided penchant for bucking the status quo. Variation: *Zaza*.

Zefiryn (ZEH-fee-reen) Polish: Goddess of the west wind. Aquarius is one of three Air signs.

Zephrya (ZEH-feer-ah) Greek. The west wind. *Zephrya* is a unique choice for a girl born under Aquarius, one of the zodiac's Air signs. Variations: *Zefir, Zefira, Zefiryn, Zephira, Zephyra*.

Zirah (ZIR-ah) Hebrew: Arena. Champions of social and political causes, Aquarians are always ready to do public battle for a noble cause. Variation: *Zira*.

Names for Aquarius Boys

Abel (AYE-bul) Hebrew: Breathing spirit. Aquarius is one of the zodiac's three Air signs. The element of Air combined with the driving Masculine energy in the sign endows Aquarian children with keen intuitive, intellectual, and communication skills.

Adad (ah-DAHD) Assyrian: For the Assyrian-Babylonian god who governed stormy weather. Aquarius is ruled by Uranus, the planet of sudden and cataclysmic change.

Adlai (ADD-lee; ADD-lay) Aramaic: Justice of the Lord. Peace and social justice issues are lifelong concerns of Aquarians. (Famous Aquarian: Adlai E. Stevenson, Jr., politician/former vice president of the United States)

Adler (AD-lur) Old English: Eagle. The sign of Aquarius governs all large birds.

Ahio (ah-HEE-oh) Polynesian: Whirlwind. The qualities associated with the wind—sudden and dramatic change, capriciousness, and potential catastrophe—are all quintessentially Aquarian, one of the three Air signs.

Ahren (AHR-in) Old German: Eagle. The eagle, one of the large birds governed by the sign of Aquarius, embodies many key qualities of Aquarians: fierce and free-spirited independence, strength, and uniqueness.

Akar (ah-KAHR) Turkish: Rushing stream. The image of flowing or rushing water—symbolic of the bestowing of free and equal gifts—is strongly associated with the sign of Aquarius, which is symbolized by the Waterbearer.

Akin (ah-KEEN) African/Nigerian: Heroic. Aquarians, among the great visionaries of the zodiac, take enormous pride in being the instruments of profound change. Variations: *Ahkeen, Akeen.*

Akira (ah-KEE-rah) Japanese: Intelligent. Keen intelligence and cool reasoning skills are hallmarks of the sign of Aquarius.

Alastair (AL-iss-tehr) Greek: One who avenges. This Scottish version of Alexander is fitting for Aquarians, who have a highly developed sense of universal right and wrong, and are mighty defenders of the disenfranchised. Variations: *Alaster, Alisdair, Alister, Allaster, Allister.*

Alexander (al-ehk-ZAN-der) Greek: Protector of humanity. Aquarians, ruled by Uranus, the planet that governs humanitarian and philanthropic endeavors, are fierce defenders of social and political justice. Variations: *Alec, Aleck, Alek, Aleksandr, Alex, Alexandre, Alexis, Sasha.*

Altair (ahl-TAYR) Arabic: Flying eagle. The powerfully independent and indefatigable eagle is emblematic of key Aquarian qualities. Aquarius is also the sign that governs large birds.

Amon (AY-mon) Hebrew: Builder. Aquarians, ruled by the planet of change and personal transformation, frequently challenge outdated norms and practices, actively oppose political and social injustice, and view themselves as essential to building new and equitable futures. Variation: *Ammon*.

Andor (AN-dorr) Scandinavian: Thor. Thor was the great Norse god of thunder and changing weather. Aquarius is ruled by Uranus, the planet of seismic changes. Variation: *Anders*.

Anil (AHN-il) Hindu: Air. Aquarius is one of the zodiac's three Air signs.

Anka (AHN-kah) Turkish: Legendary phoenix. The mythical phoenix, which burned itself to ashes on a sacrificial pyre and then rejuvenated to live another five hundred years, is symbolic of Aquarius, the sign of personal transformation.

Apela (ah-PAYL-ah) Hawaiian: Breathing spirit. *Apela* suggests Aquarius's element of Air and the qualities of powerful vision, deep sensitivity, and life-giving sustenance associated with the sign.

Aren (AR-in) Scandinavian: Eagle. The eagle is one of the large birds of prey governed by the sign of Aquarius.

Arlen (AHR-len) Irish: Oath. Aquarians are committed humanitarians and philanthropists who often dedicate their lives to righting social and political injustices. Variations: *Arlan, Arlin, Arlyn*.

Arliss (AHR-liss) Hebrew: Pledge. *Arliss* connotes the determined energy Aquarius devotes to defending his beliefs. Variations: *Arleigh, Arles, Arley, Arlis, Arly*.

Arnon (AHR-non) Hebrew: Rushing stream. Aquarius is symbolized by the Waterbearer, who freely pours out life-giving water to any who want it.

Arundel (AHR-uhn-dell) English: Valley of the eagle. The powerful, solitary, and enigmatic eagle is quintessentially Aquarian.

Arvid (AHR-vid) Scandinavian: Eagle in a tree. Free-spirited and individualistic Aquarians share many of the untethered qualities of the soaring and skybound eagle.

Avel (AH-vel) Greek: Breath; wind. The qualities associated with the wind—sudden and dramatic change, capriciousness, and potential catastrophe—are all quintessentially Aquarian, one of three Air signs.

Awan (AH-wahn) Native American: Somebody. Aquarians have highly developed egos and a unique self-awareness regarding their worth in the world.

Azim (ah-ZEEM) Arabic: Defender. Endowed with great powers of empathy and genuinely concerned about the welfare of others, Aquarians are keen proponents of justice and equality for all. Variation: *Azeem*.

Baldwin (BAHLD-win) Old German: Bold protector. Aquarians fight vigorously to defend the rights of those who are victims of social injustice.

Barak (BARE-ek; BAHR-rak) Hebrew: Lightning bolt. Aquarius is the sign of storms, as well as swift, unexpected, and profound change. Variation: *Barrak*.

Barnabas (BAHR-nah-bus) Greek: Son of exhortation. Aquarians are singularly gifted at rousing and inspiring large groups of people to follow a common cause. Variation: *Barnaby*.

Bavol (BAH-vohl) English Gypsy: Air. Aquarius, Libra, and Gemini are the zodiac's three Air signs.

Beval (BAY-vahl) English Gypsy: Like the wind. Free spirited and unpredictable, Aquarians are powerfully influenced by the quixotic influence of Air in their sign.

Birtle (BUR-til) English: Hill with birds. Aquarians exemplify many archetypical avian qualities: unfettered and free-wheeling flight, singular independence, and carefree joy.

Boris (BOR-iss) Slavic: Battler. Aquarians are ferocious—and frequently unstoppable—combatants of social inequality. (Famous Aquarians: Boris Spassky, former world chess champion; Boris Pasternak, Nobel Prize-winning writer)

Bram (BRAMM) Welsh: Raven. Aquarians, who cherish unbounded freedom above all things, emulate the unfettered life-styles of the wild bird.

Brede (BREH-deh or BREED) Scandinavian: Iceberg. Aquarius is a Masculine and Fixed Air sign ruled by quixotic Uranus. Aquarian children, who celebrate the life of the mind over the life of the senses, may express strong and rigid opinions, while remaining aloof, emotionally self-contained, and cool.

Brennan (BREN-in) Irish: Raven. *Brennan* is a handsome choice for a boy born under Aquarius, the sign associated with all large birds. Variation: *Brennen*.

Cary (KARE-ee) English: To move or stir. Aquarians are renowned for their innate ability to stir up and motivate a crowd about important social issues. Variation: *Carey*.

Case (KAYSS) English: He who brings peace. Peace, freedom, and social justice are primary concerns of Aquarians.

Cassius (KASS-ee-us) Latin: Narcissistic. Aquarians, who are noted for their healthy egos and developed sense of self-importance, are often their own best admirers.

Chim (JIM) Vietnamese: Bird. All large birds are governed by the sign of Aquarius.

Colin (KOL-in or KILL-ihn) English: Victory of the people. Aquarians are esteemed for their deep commitment to humanitarian and philanthropic issues that benefit all humanity. Variations: *Collin, Collins*.

Conlan (KON-lin) Irish: Hero. Crusading Aquarians are noted for their fierce drive to win tough political and social battles. Variations: *Conlen, Conley, Conlin, Conlon, Connlyn*.

Cosgrove (KOZ-grohv) Irish: Triumphant one. Aquarians have an unshakeable belief in their ability to change the world. Variation: *Cosgrave*.

Daly (DAY-lee) Irish: Gathering. Aquarians are gifted rabble-rousers, capable of rallying a crowd to a common cause. Variation: *Daley*.

Del (DELL) English: Leader of the people. Aquarians are instinctive and empathetic leaders who are adept at inspiring others to realize their dreams and visions.

Dilip (dih-LEEP) Hindu: Protector. Empathetic and intuitive, Aquarians are genuinely concerned about preserving the welfare and rights of others.

Dyami (dee-AH-mee) Native American: Eagle. *Dyami* is a suitable choice for a boy born under Aquarius, the sign that governs all large birds.

Efron (EFF-ron; EE-fron) Hebrew: Bird. Aquarius rules all large birds, whose free-flying, unencumbered, and wide-ranging natures are symbolic of the sign. Variation: *Ephron*.

Elon (AY-lon) African-American: Spirit. Strongly influenced by the element of Air in their sign, Aquarians have a relaxed and free-spirited approach to life.

Elsu (EHL-soo) Native American: Falcon flying high and low. All large birds of prey are governed by the sign of Aquarius.

Ernest (UR-nest) Teutonic: Intent. *Ernest* is an apt name for energetic, determined, and single-minded Aquarius. Variations: *Ernie, Ernesto, Ernst*. (Famous Aquarians: Ernest Borgnine, actor; Ernie Banks, professional baseball player; Tennessee Ernie Ford, country gospel singer; Ernie Kovacs, actor/comedian)

Ethan (EE-thun) Hebrew: Firmness. Aquarians are notorious for their rigid belief systems. Variations: *Eitan, Etan, Eytan*.

Fang (FUNG) Chinese: Wind. Aquarius, one of the zodiac's three Air signs, is ruled by Uranus, the planet of sudden change.

Franklin (FRANK-lin) Middle English: A free man. Aquarians prize political, social, and spiritual freedom. (Famous Aquarian: Franklin D. Roosevelt, twenty-sixth president of the United States)

Freedom (FREE-dom) English: Liberty. *Freedom* is an unusual but apt choice for independence-loving Aquarians.

Freeman (FREE-mon) English: Free man. Aquarians, who dearly cherish their own independence, are great defenders of the freedom of others. Variation: *Freemon*.

Fremont (FREE-mont) English: Protector of freedom. Aquarians are esteemed for protecting the rights of others as fiercely as they protect their own personal freedom.

Frewin (FREE-win) English: Free friend. Devoted and deeply committed friends, Aquarians freely give to others the same liberties they themselves prize. Variation: *Frewen*.

Fulton (FULL-tin) English: Town of the people. Aquarians, born under the sign of friendship, are most comfortable when at the helm of a large group of supportive and adoring friends.

Gavin (GAVV-in) Welsh: White falcon. The falcon is one of the large birds of prey governed by the sign of Aquarius. Variations: *Gavan, Gaven, Gavyn, Gawain, Gawaine, Gawayn.*

Gavril (gahv-REEL or gah-BREEL) Russian: God's hero. *Gavril* is an appropriate name for brave, determined, and empathic Aquarius, who possesses strong humanitarian and philanthropic interests.

Gideon (GIDD-ee-un) Hebrew: Mighty battler. Gideon was a judge who freed the Israelites from captivity. Aquarians are eager and ardent fighters for the rights of the disenfranchised. Variations: *Gedeon, Gideone.*

Gladwin (GLAD-win) English: Happy friend. Aquarians are naturally ebullient and easygoing friends. Variations: *Gladwinn, Gladwyn.*

Goel (go-AYL; JOHL) Hebrew: Redeemer. With their highly developed social and political sensibilities, Aquarians are committed and empathetic fighters for social change and the common good.

Gozal (goh-ZAHL) Hebrew: Soaring. Aquarians embody many of the characteristics typically associated with birds: unfettered flight, freedom, and a carefree and joyful expansiveness.

Guy (GYE) French: Leader or guide. Renowned as the visionaries and revolutionaries of the zodiac, Aquarians possess an extraordinary ability to inspire others to follow them. Variation: *Guido.*

Halil (hah-LEEL) Turkish: Intimate friend. Aquarius is the sign of deep and abiding friendship.

Hamish (HAYM-ish) Scottish: He who removes. Aquarians are renowned for their deep interest in righting social and political inequities.

Harding (HAHR-ding) Old English: Bold man. Eccentric, unconventional, and independent, Aquarius has a strong need to stand out from the crowd.

Hector (HEK-tur) Greek: Holding fast. Free-spirited Aquarians are notoriously defiant and rigid when their unconventional lifestyles and beliefs are challenged. Variations: *Heitor, Hektor.*

Herald (HARE-uld) English: Bearer of news. Aquarians are eloquent speakers who are mightily persuasive in heralding the benefits of peace, justice, and equality.

Homer (HOH-mur) Greek: Pledged. Aquarians often view their commitment to social equality and political peace as a sacred path. Variations: *Homere, Homeros, Homerus, Omer, Omeros.*

Humphrey (HUM-free) Old German: Soldier of peace. Aquarians, who cherish freedom in all forms, willingly fight for the rights of those who have been poorly treated, particularly victims of social injustice.

Ingram (ING-rum) English: Raven. *Ingram* is a classic and handsome name for a boy born under Aquarius, the sign that governs all large birds. Variations: *Ingraham, Ingrim.*

Jacob (JAY-cub) Hebrew: He who supplants. *Jacob* is a classic and ever-popular choice for the Aquarian child who takes great pride in being an instrument of profound change. Variations: *Jake, Jakob, Yakov.*

James (JAYMZ) Hebrew: Supplanting one. This ever popular classic name is well-suited to Aquarius, whose ruling planet Uranus governs revolution, anarchy, radicalism, and sudden and dramatic change. Variations: *Jaime, Jameson, Jamieson, Jami-*

son, Jaymes, Jaymie, Jim, Jimmy, Seamus. (Famous Aquarians: James Joyce, Irish writer; James Dickey, poet/writer; James Michener, author; James Dean, 1950s actor/icon; Jimmy Durante, entertainer/comedian; Jimmy Hoffa, union leader)

Jarek (YAH-rek; JAIR-ik) Polish: Born in January. *Jarek* is an appropriate name for a January-born Aquarian.

Javas (JAH-vahs) Sanskrit: Quick. Strongly influenced by the element of Air in their sign, Aquarians have facile and penetrating intellects.

Javin (jah-VEEN; JAV-in) English: Understanding one. Deeply empathetic, Aquarians are devoted and compassionate comrades.

Jay (jay) Old French: Blue jay. All large birds are governed by the sign of Aquarius.

Job (johb) Hebrew: Oppressed. *Job* suggests Aquarius's ability to assist the disenfranchised and to overcome social injustice in the world. Variations: *Joab, Jobe, Joby.*

Jordan (JOR-din) Hebrew: Flowing downward. The sign of Aquarius is symbolized by the Waterbearer, who freely pours out life-enhancing water to all who need it. Variations: *Jordon, Jori, Jory.*

Kabir (kah-BEER) Hindu: Spiritual leader. Charismatic and idealistic humanitarians, Aquarians have a unique ability to influence others in positive ways.

Kalil (kah-LEEL) Arabic: Good friend. Aquarius is the sign of friendship. Variations: *Kahlil, Khaleel, Khalil.*

Keith (KEETH) Irish: Man from the battleground. Aquarians are great champions of political and social change.

Kele (KEH-lee) Native American: Sparrow hawk. The hawk is one of the large birds of prey governed by Aquarius. Variation: *Kelle*.

Kempton (KEMP-tin) English: Town of fighters. Generally cheerful and relaxed, Aquarians can become charged with fiery, belligerent energy when their unconventional beliefs are challenged or when they witness examples of social injustice in their community.

Khiry (KEER-ee) Arabic: Benevolent. Aquarians are gifted with deep empathy for the plight of others. Variations: *Khiri, Kiri, Kiry*.

Killian (KILL-ee-in) Irish: Conflict. Aquarius is ruled by Uranus, the planet of change, action, and revolution. Aquarians have an innate drive to buck the status quo. Variations: *Kilian, Killy*.

Knoton (NOH-ton) Native American: The wind. Aquarius is one of the three Air signs of the zodiac.

Konni (KOH-nee; KAHN-nee) German: Bold counselor. Intuitive, empathetic, and genuinely concerned about others, Aquarians are much sought-after advisers and counselors.

Lawrence (LOR-ince) Latin: Laurels. *Lawrence* is a fitting name for a boy born under the sign of Aquarius, which is associated with all fruit-bearing trees, including the berry-producing laurel. Variations: *Larne, Larry, Laurence, Laurent, Lonnie, Lorenzo, Lorin, Lorne*. (Famous Aquarians: Lawrence Taylor, professional football player; Larry "Buster" Crabbe, actor)

Leggett (LEG-it) Old French: Representative of the people. Aquarians are ardent and flamboyant defenders of others' rights. Variations: *Leggitt, Liggett*.

Lel (LAYL) English Gypsy: He takes. Aquarians are fiercely protective of their own beliefs and lifestyles.

Liberio (lee-BAYR-ee-oh) Portuguese: Freedom. Free-spirited Aquarians cherish their independence above all else.

Linfred (LINN-frid) German: Gentle peace. Peace and justice are life-long pursuits of Aquarians.

Lyndon (LINN-dun) Old English: From the lime-tree hill. The lime tree is strongly associated with the sign of Aquarius. Variations: *Linden, Lindon, Lindy, Linton, Lynn, Lynton.*

Lysander (lye-SAN-dur) Greek: Liberator. Aquarians are gifted with deep empathy for the plight of others. Variations: *Lisandro, Lissandro.*

Macaulay (mah-KAW-lay) Scottish: Son of righteousness. Generally easygoing and even tempered, Aquarius can become filled with fiery energy when he witnesses acts of social injustice. Variations: *Macauley, Mack, Mackie, Macklin.*

Madison (MA-dih-sun) Old English: Son of the brave soldier. When the prize is social justice, Aquarians love nothing more than a good fight. Variations: *Maddie, Maddy, Madeson.*

Mahir (mah-HEER) Hebrew: Expert. Aquarians are the innovators and visionaries of the zodiac, approaching their efforts with carefully considered strategies to assure success.

Makoto (mah-KOH-toh) Japanese: Good. Aquarians are the quintessential champions of the common good.

Malin (MAY-lin) Old English: Brave, young soldier. *Malin* suggests Aquarius's boldly revolutionary nature and his intense desire to defend his unconventional beliefs. Variations: *Mallin, Mallon, Malon.*

Manco (MAHN-koh) Spanish: High authority. Aquarians are consummate leaders, uniquely gifted at rousing the hearts and minds of others in support of a common cause.

Manton (MAN-tun) Old English: Town of the returning hero. Brave and idealistic Aquarians are renowned as champions of the common people. Variations: *Mannton, Manten.*

Marcellus (mahr-SELL-us) Latin: Young fighter. On the battle-field of political peace, Aquarians are unstoppable foes. Variations: *Marceau, Marcel, Marcelin, Marcellino, Marcello, Marcely.*

Marid (MAH-rid) Arabic: Rebellious. Unconventional, eccentric, single-minded, and free spirited, Aquarians are the noncon-formists of the zodiac.

Matthew (MATH-yu) Hebrew: Divine gift. Free-spirited, idealistic, charming, loyal, and caring, Aquarians are dearly cherished by their friends and family. Variations: *Mathew, Mathias, Mathieu, Matt, Matteo, Matty.* (Famous Aquarians: Matt Dillon, actor; Matt Groening, cartoonist/creator of *The Simpsons*)

Mered (me-REHD) Hebrew: Revolt. Uranus, Aquarius's ruling planet, is associated with revolution, anarchy, and radicalism.

Merlin (MUR-linn) Middle English: Falcon who flies low. All large birds are ruled by Aquarius. Variations: *Marlin, Marlon, Merle, Merlen, Merlinn, Merlyn.*

Modred (MOH-dred) English: Valiant adviser. Empathic, wise, and humanitarian, Aquarians are often drawn to careers in law, politics, and social activism. Variation: *Mordred.*

Mori (MOR-ee) Hebrew: My guide. Aquarians, the revolution-aries and visionaries of the zodiac, possess the ability to influence large groups of people. Variations: *Maury, Morie.*

Nadir (nah-DEER) Hebrew: Pledge. Aquarians, renowned for their singular ideals and visions, can be fiercely committed to making their dreams a reality.

Namid (NAH-meed) Native American: Dances with the lights of heaven. Ruled by Uranus, the planet that governs modern technology and science, Aquarians are frequently fascinated with astronomy and aeronautics.

Nawat (NAH-waht) Native American: On the left. The political bent of most Aquarians is decidedly to the left.

Nicholas (NIC-oh-lahs) Greek: Triumph of the people. This traditional name suits the humanitarian and philanthropic interests, of Aquarians who are quick to come to the defense of the disenfranchised. Variations: *Claus, Cole, Niccolo, Nicol, Nicolai, Nicolas, Nicole, Niklas, Nils.* (Famous Aquarians: Nicholas Copernicus, sixteenth-century astronomer; Nick Nolte, actor)

Nodin (NOH-din) Native American: The wind. Aquarius is one of the zodiac's three Air signs. (The other two are Libra and Gemini.) Variation: *Noton.*

Nusair (noo-SYRE) Arabic: Vulture. Large birds of prey are ruled by Aquarius.

Ohanko (oh-HAHN-koh) Native American: Reckless. Unconventional and even eccentric, Aquarians sometimes make rash and impractical choices.

Oliver (AH-lih-vur) Greek: Peace. Peace and justice are frequent goals of Aquarians, who often come to the defense of victims of social and political injustice. Variations: *Olivier, Ollie.*

Oswin (OZ-win) Old English: Friend of the gods. The mythological Greek and Roman gods were mighty purveyors of justice and retribution, a tendency that is typically Aquarian.

Palladin (PAHL-ah-din) Native American: Fighter. Aquarians are renowned as defenders of the rights of the common man. Variations: *Pallaten, Pallaton.*

Palmer (PAHM-ur) English: Carrying palm branches. The palm branch is an ancient symbol of political peace, an issue of vital concern to Aquarians. Variations: *Pallmer, Palmar.*

Patamon (PAH-tah-mahn; PAT-a-muhn) Native American: Raging. Typically easygoing and charming, free-spirited Aquarians can be moved to rage when their unconventional lives are challenged or critiqued.

Patton (PAT-ton) Old English: Village of warriors. *Patton* suggests Aquarius's fiery anger when he witnesses acts of social injustice. Aquarians are also skilled at rallying groups of people to support causes they strongly believe in. Variations: *Paten, Patin, Paton, Patten, Pattin.*

Paul (pawl) Latin: Small. While they are often the innovators of tiny ideas that eventually lead to great social change, Aquarians rarely allow others to glimpse more than a small part of their inner worlds. (Famous Aquarians: Paul Scofield, actor; Paul Newman, actor) Variations: *Pablo, Paulo, Pavel, Pawel, Pol.*

Paz (PAHZ) Spanish: Peace. True humanitarians, Aquarians crusade for peace, justice, and freedom for all.

Pericles (PARE-ah-kleez) Greek: For the ancient Greek leader who democratized Athens. Political and social justice are hallmark beliefs of the sign of Aquarius.

Perry (PAYR-ee) French: Pear-bearing tree. All fruit-bearing trees are governed by Aquarius. Variations: *Parry, Perrie.*

Peyton (PAY-tuhn) Old English: From the warrior's home. Because their ruling planet, Uranus, governs anarchy, revolution, and radicalism, Aquarians often are associated with war-like imagery. Variations: *Pate, Paton, Payton*.

Pillan (pee-LAHN) Native American: Supreme spirit. *Pillan* is an Araucanian Indian god of stormy weather. Aquarius is ruled by Uranus, the planet of storms and sudden change. Variation: *Pilan*.

Pomeroy (PAHM-e-roy) French: Apple tree grove. Aquarius, the sign that governs fruit-bearing trees, is also the sign of wisdom and the pursuit of knowledge. In Oriental mythology, the apple is a symbol of wisdom.

Pruit (PROO-it) French: Brave little one. Even as children, Aquarians are bold defenders of both their own independence and that of others. Variations: *Prewett, Prewitt, Pruitt*.

Purvis (PURR-viss) English: Purveyor. Aquarians are superbly adept at rallying people to a common cause. Variation: *Purviss*.

Quinlan (KWIN-lan) Irish: Strong man. *Quinlan* is a suitable name for determined, independent, and bold Aquarius. Variations: *Quindlen, Quinley, Quinly*.

Rabi (ra-BEE) Arabic: Breeze. Aquarius is one of three Air signs of the zodiac.

Rahim (rah-HEEM) Hebrew: Compassionate. Deep empathy for the misfortunes of others is a trademark quality of Aquarius. Variations: *Racham, Rachim, Rachmiel, Raham*.

Raiden (RYE-den) Japanese: Thunder god. *Raiden* suggests the sudden and dramatic change associated with the sign of Aquarius, which also governs storms.

Ransley (RANS-lee) Old English: Field of ravens. Birds—whose characteristics are quintessentially Aquarian—are governed by the sign of Aquarius. Variations: *Ransleigh, Ransly*.

Raymond (RAY-mund) Old German: Wise protector. Keenly intuitive and intelligent, Aquarians often devote themselves to humanitarian and philanthropic causes by pursuing successful careers in politics, law, and social activism. Variations: *Raimondo, Raimund, Raimundo, Ramon, Ray, Raymund.*

Remington (REM-ing-tin) English: Family of ravens. The sign of Aquarius rules all large birds. Variations: *Rem, Remee, Remi, Remie, Remmy.*

Rhett (RETT) Welsh: Rash. Aquarians are renowned for their impulsive and quixotic natures.

Rickward (RIK-wurd) English: Powerful guardian. Strong, determined, and deeply humanitarian, Aquarians readily defend victims of social injustice. Variations: *Rickwerd, Rickwood.*

Ringo (RING-goh) Japanese: Apple. The sign of Aquarius governs all fruit-bearing trees. In the Orient, the apple is a symbol of peace, the frequent goal of many Aquarians.

Roderick (ROD-rik) Old German: A leader who is remembered. Aquarian leadership skills are highly esteemed. Variations: *Roddy, Roderic, Rodrich, Rodrick, Rodrigo, Rurik.*

Rohin (roh-HEEN) East Indian: Skybound. Aquarians, who have a deep affinity for the heavens, are often drawn to careers in astronomy and space travel.

Rover (ROH-vir) English: Wanderer. Aquarians, who prize their free-spirited and unencumbered lifestyles, bristle at any suggestion that they settle down.

Sahen (shah-HEHN; SAH-hen) Hindu: Falcon. Large birds of prey are governed by Aquarius.

Sargent (SAHR-gent) Old French: Officer. Aquarians are natural leaders.

Saul (SAWLL) Hebrew: Petitioned. *Saul* is a classic name for peace-loving Aquarians, who are esteemed for their devotion to humanitarian and philanthropic causes.

Sawney (SAW-nee) Scottish: Protector of men. Aquarians are renowned champions of social justice for all. Variations: *Sawnie, Sawny*.

Searle (SURL:) Old English: Shield. Deeply empathetic, Aquarians go out of their way to defend others from social injustice.

Seth (SETH) Hebrew: To support. Aquarians, who possess strong philanthropic and humanitarian interests, are quick to offer help to those who need it.

Shalom (shah-LOHM) Hebrew: Peace. *Shalom* is a suitable name for Aquarians, who strive for freedom, justice, and peace for all. Variation: *Sholom*.

Simen (SYE-min) English Gypsy: Equal. Political and social equality are abiding concerns of typical Aquarians.

Simon (SYE-mun) Hebrew: Heard. Aquarians are renowned for their superb communication skills. Variations: *Shimon, Simeon*.

Skylar (SKY-lur) Dutch: Shield. Aquarians make fiercely protective and devoted friends. Variations: *Schuylar, Schuyler, Skuyler, Skyler*.

Sloane (SLONE) Irish: A multitude of people. Aquarians are renowned for their ability to rouse a crowd to a common cause. This name is also appropriate for a girl. Variation: *Sloan*.

Stig (STEEG) Scandinavian: Wanderer. Aquarians cherish and vigorously defend their unconventional and free-wheeling lifestyles. Variation: *Styge*.

Storm (STORM) Old English: Storm. Aquarius is ruled by Uranus, the planet of storms and sudden and often cataclysmic change.

Tabor (TAY-bor) Hungarian: Coming from the trenches. Aquarians are fierce champions of the common man. Variations: *Taber, Taibor, Tayber, Taybor.*

Tadi (TAH-dee) Native American: Wind. *Tadi* is a suitable name for a boy born under Aquarius, an Air sign.

Tava (TAH-vah) Polynesian: Tree with fruit. The sign of Aquarius governs all fruit-bearing trees.

Tavas (TAH-vas) Hebrew: Peacock. Large birds are governed by Aquarius, and the flamboyant and eccentric peacock is quintessentially Aquarian.

Thomas (TAHM-uss) Greek: Twin. *Thomas* suggests the seemingly dual nature possessed by Aquarians. Outwardly, they are socially active, loyal friends, and social leaders; privately, they spend time alone, avoid intimate relationships, and distance themselves from the public eye. Variations: *Tamas, Thom, Tom, Tommy.* (Famous Aquarians: Tom Brokaw, news anchor; Thomas Alva Edison, inventor; Tom Selleck, actor; Tom Smothers, comedian)

Thorald (THOR-uld) Old Norse: Thor's devotee. Thor, the ancient Norse god of thunder and stormy weather, is closely associated with the sign of Aquarius, which is ruled by Uranus, the planet of storms, as well as swift and powerful change. Variations: *Terrell, Terrill, Thorold, Thorvald, Torald, Tyrell.*

Thorbert (THOR-burt) Old Norse: Thor's brightness. Highly energetic and dramatic Aquarians generally utilize their intensity for good causes. Variation: *Torbert.*

Thorburn (THOR-burn) Old Norse: Thunder's bear. Ferocious combatants on the battlefield of social justice, Aquarians are powerfully influenced by their governing planet, Uranus, ruler of change and transformation.

Thurston (THIRST-in) Scandinavian: Thor's stones. Thor, the ancient Norse god of thunder, is closely affiliated with Aquarius, whose ruling planet Uranus governs sudden and dramatic change. Variations: *Thorstan, Thorstein, Thorsten, Thurstain, Torsten, Torston*.

Tomi (TOH-mee) African/Nigerian: The people. Aquarius is the sign of friendship, and Aquarians are known for believing in peace and equality for all.

Trent (TRENT) Latin: Rapid stream. Images of rushing or pouring water are strongly associated with Aquarius, the sign symbolized by the Waterbearer.

Uriel (YOOR-ee-ell; YOOR-ee-ull) Hebrew: Light of God. *Uriel* is the name of the archangel who protects those born under the sign of Aquarius.

Warner (WARN-ur) Old German: Defending warrior. Aquarius is quick to come to the aid of victims of social injustice. Variations: *Werner, Wernher*.

Wilfred (WIL-frid) Old English: A wish for peace. Aquarians frequently pursue careers in the fields of political and social justice.

Wilny (WILL-nee) Native American: Singing eagle. All large birds are governed by Aquarius, but the eagle—majestic, individualistic, and powerful—is especially emblematic of the Aquarian nature.

Famous Aquarians

01-21-1824	Stonewall Jackson	01-26-1880	Douglas MacArthur
01-21-1922	Paul Scofield	01-26-1923	Anne Jeffreys
01-21-1924	Telly Savalas	01-26-1925	Paul Newman
01-21-1925	Benny Hill	01-26-1929	Jules Feiffer
01-21-1939	Wolfman Jack	01-26-1935	Bob Uecker
01-21-1940	Jack Nicklaus	01-26-1942	Scott Glenn
01-21-1941	Placido Domingo	01-26-1944	Angela Davis
01-21-1942	Mac Davis	01-26-1946	Gene Siskel
01-21-1947	Jill Eikenberry	01-26-1955	Eddie Van Halen
01-21-1956	Robby Benson	01-26-1958	Anita Baker
01-21-1957	Geena Davis	01-26-1958	Ellen DeGeneres
01-21-1963	Hakeem Olajuwon	01-26-1961	Wayne Gretzky
01-22-1561	Sir Francis Bacon	01-27-1756	Wolfgang Amadeus
01-22-1875	D. W. Griffith		Mozart
01-22-1909	Ann Sothern	01-27-1832	Lewis Carroll
01-22-1932	Piper Laurie	01-27-1885	Jerome Kern
01-22-1934	Bill Bixby	01-27-1918	Skitch Henderson
01-22-1937	Joseph Wambaugh	01-27-1921	Donna Reed
01-22-1940	John Hurt	01-27-1936	Troy Donahue
01-22-1959	Linda Blair	01-27-1948	Mikhail Baryshnikov
01-22-1965	Diane Lane	01-27-1964	Bridget Fonda
01-23-1737	John Hancock	01-28-1912	Jackson Pollock
01-23-1832	Edouard Manet	01-28-1936	Alan Alda
01-23-1899	Humphrey Bogart	01-28-1981	Elijah Wood
01-23-1919	Ernie Kovacs	01-29-1843	William McKinley
01-23-1928	Jeanne Moreau	01-29-1880	W. C. Fields
01-23-1933	Chita Rivera	01-29-1885	Huddie "Leadbelly"
01-23-1944	Rutger Hauer		Ledbetter
01-23-1974	Tiffani-Amber Thiessen	01-29-1916	Victor Mature
01-24-1917	Ernest Borgnine	01-29-1918	John Forsythe
01-24-1925	Maria Tallchief	01-29-1942	Katharine Ross
01-24-1941	Neil Diamond	01-29-1945	Tom Selleck
01-24-1949	John Belushi	01-29-1950	Ann Jillian
01-24-1951	Yakov Smirnoff	01-29-1954	Oprah Winfrey
01-24-1960	Nastassia Kinski	01-29-1960	Greg Louganis
01-24-1968	Mary Lou Retton	01-30-1882	Franklin D. Roosevelt
01-25-1759	Robert Burns	01-30-1922	Dick Martin
01-25-1882	Virginia Woolf	01-30-1931	Gene Hackman
01-25-1919	Edwin Newman	01-30-1933	Louis Rukeyser
01-25-1931	Dean Jones	01-30-1934	Tammy Grimes
01-25-1933	Corazon Aquino	01-30-1937	Vanessa Redgrave

01-30-1937	Boris Spassky	02-04-1948	Alice Cooper
01-30-1942	Marty Balin	02-04-1959	Lawrence Taylor
01-30-1951	Phil Collins	02-05-1900	Adlai E. Stevenson, Jr.
01-30-1958	Brett Butler	02-05-1914	William Burroughs
01-31-1915	Garry Moore	02-05-1919	Red Buttons
01-31-1919	Jackie Robinson	02-05-1928	Andrew Greeley
01-31-1921	Mario Lanza	02-05-1934	Henry "Hank" Aaron
01-31-1923	Carol Channing	02-05-1940	H. R. Giger
01-31-1923	Norman Mailer	02-05-1942	Roger Staubach
01-31-1929	Jean Simmons	02-05-1948	Barbara Hershey
01-31-1931	Ernie Banks	02-05-1962	Jennifer Jason Leigh
01-31-1937	Suzanne Pleshette	02-06-1895	Babe Ruth
01-31-1941	Richard Gephardt	02-06-1911	Ronald Reagan
01-31-1947	Nolan Ryan	02-06-1919	Zsa Zsa Gabor
02-01-1895	John Ford	02-06-1931	Rip Torn
02-01-1901	Clark Gable	02-06-1931	Mamie van Doren
02-01-1902	Langston Hughes	02-06-1939	Mike Farrell
02-01-1937	Don Everly	02-06-1940	Tom Brokaw
02-01-1937	Garrett Morris	02-06-1943	Fabian
02-01-1938	Sherman Hemsley	02-06-1944	Michael Tucker
02-01-1965	Sherilyn Fenn	02-06-1945	Bob Marley
02-01-1968	Lisa Marie Presley	02-06-1950	Natalie Cole
02-02-1882	James Joyce	02-06-1962	Axl Rose
02-02-1905	Ayn Rand	02-07-1812	Charles Dickens
02-02-1906	Gale Gordon	02-07-1867	Laura Ingalls Wilder
02-02-1923	James Dickey	02-07-1885	Sinclair Lewis
02-02-1937	Tom Smothers	02-07-1908	Larry "Buster" Crabbe
02-02-1942	Graham Nash	02-07-1920	Eddie Bracken
02-02-1947	Farrah Fawcett	02-07-1962	Garth Brooks
02-02-1954	Christie Brinkley	02-08-1820	Willam Tecumseh Sherman
02-03-1468	Johannes Gutenberg		
02-03-1874	Gertrude Stein	02-08-1828	Jules Verne
02-03-1894	Norman Rockwell	02-08-1902	Lyle Talbot
02-03-1907	James Michener	02-08-1921	Lana Turner
02-03-1918	Joey Bishop	02-08-1924	Audrey Meadows
02-03-1926	Shelley Berman	02-08-1925	Jack Lemmon
02-03-1940	Fran Tarkenton	02-08-1931	James Dean
02-03-1950	Morgan Fairchild	02-08-1932	John Williams
02-04-1902	Charles Lindbergh	02-08-1940	Ted Koppel
02-04-1906	Clyde W. Tombaugh	02-08-1940	Nick Nolte
02-04-1913	Rosa Parks	02-08-1942	Robert Klein
02-04-1918	Ida Lupino	02-08-1968	Gary Coleman
02-04-1921	Betty Friedan	02-09-1773	William H. Harrison
02-04-1945	David Brenner	02-09-1874	Amy Lowell
02-04-1947	Dan Quayle	02-09-1909	Carmen Miranda

02-09-1914	Gypsy Rose Lee	02-13-1944	Jerry Springer
02-09-1923	Brendan Behan	02-13-1944	Peter Tork
02-09-1928	Roger Mudd	02-13-1950	Peter Gabriel
02-09-1942	Carole King	02-14-1894	Jack Benny
02-09-1943	Joe Pesci	02-14-1913	Mel Allen
02-09-1944	Alice Walker	02-14-1913	Jimmy Hoffa
02-09-1945	Mia Farrow	02-14-1921	Hugh Downs
02-10-1890	Boris Pasternak	02-14-1932	Vic Morrow
02-10-1893	Jimmy Durante	02-14-1934	Florence Henderson
02-10-1898	Bertolt Brecht	02-14-1944	Carl Bernstein
02-10-1905	Lon Chaney, Jr.	02-14-1946	Gregory Hines
02-10-1927	Leontyne Price	02-14-1960	Meg Tilly
02-10-1930	Robert Wagner	02-15-1564	Galileo Galilei
02-10-1939	Roberta Flack	02-15-1820	Susan B. Anthony
02-10-1950	Mark Spitz	02-15-1882	John Barrymore
02-10-1955	Greg Norman	02-15-1907	Cesar Romero
02-10-1967	Laura Dern	02-15-1927	Harvey Korman
02-11-1847	Thomas Alva Edison	02-15-1931	Claire Bloom
02-11-1917	Sidney Sheldon	02-15-1951	Melissa Manchester
02-11-1921	Eva Gabor	02-15-1951	Jane Seymour
02-11-1926	Leslie Nielsen	02-15-1954	Matt Groening
02-11-1934	Tina Louise	02-16-1903	Edgar Bergen
02-11-1936	Burt Reynolds	02-16-1909	Hugh Beaumont
02-11-1940	Bobby "Boris" Pickett	02-16-1920	Patty Andrews
02-11-1941	Sergio Mendes	02-16-1935	Sonny Bono
02-11-1963	Sheryl Crow	02-16-1957	LeVar Burton
02-11-1969	Jennifer Aniston	02-16-1958	Ice-T
02-12-1809	Charles Darwin	02-16-1959	John McEnroe
02-12-1809	Abraham Lincoln	02-17-1908	Red Barber
02-12-1904	Ted Mack	02-17-1914	Arthur Kennedy
02-12-1915	Lorne Greene	02-17-1925	Hal Holbrook
02-12-1923	Franco Zeffirelli	02-17-1934	Alan Bates
02-12-1926	Joe Garagiola	02-17-1936	Jim Brown
02-12-1934	Bill Russell	02-17-1954	Rene Russo
02-12-1938	Judy Blume	02-17-1963	Michael Jordan
02-12-1955	Arsenio Hall	02-17-1974	Jerry O'Connell
02-12-1980	Christina Ricci	02-18-1859	Sholom Aleichem
02-13-1885	Bess Truman	02-18-1920	Bill Cullen
02-13-1892	Grant Wood	02-18-1920	Jack Palance
02-13-1919	Tennessee Ernie Ford	02-18-1922	Helen Gurley Brown
02-13-1920	Eileen Farrell	02-18-1925	George Kennedy
02-13-1923	Chuck Yeager	02-18-1930	Gahan Wilson
02-13-1933	Kim Novak	02-18-1931	Toni Morrison
02-13-1934	George Segal	02-18-1932	Milos Forman
02-13-1944	Stockard Channing	02-18-1933	Yoko Ono

02-18-1950	Cybill Shepherd		02-19-1912	Stan Kenton
02-18-1954	John Travolta		02-19-1924	Lee Marvin
02-18-1957	Vanna White		02-19-1940	Smokey Robinson
02-18-1964	Matt Dillon		02-19-1955	Jeff Daniels
02-18-1968	Molly Ringwald		02-19-1955	Margaux Hemingway
02-19-1473	Nicolas Copernicus		02-19-1966	Justine Bateman

PISCES
(February 20–March 20)

GLYPH: ♓

SYMBOL: The Fish

POLARITY: Feminine

QUALITY: Mutable

ELEMENT: Water

PLANET: Neptune

BIRTHSTONE: Aquamarine

SPECIAL COLORS: Blues and greens of the sea

FLOWERS: Jonquil, white poppy, water lily

METAL: Platinum

ANIMAL: Fish

MOST LIKEABLE TRAITS: Compassion, creativity, and sensitivity

♓

Dreamy, mysterious, imaginative, and deeply emotional, Pisceans are among the most intriguing children of the zodiac. Like the double Fish that symbolize their sign, Piscean children have two distinct sides to their characters. Many Pisceans choose to remain emotionally elusive and separate from the "real" world, preferring the dark, subterranean seas of their own richly constructed fantasy worlds. There, submerged and safe in the enveloping waters of the sea, Pisceans are the poetic dreamers of the world, giving lyrical substance to humanity's hopes and dreams through music, poetry, painting, and drama. Other Pisceans make (what is for them) a considerable evolutionary— and emotional—leap from the safety of the sea to the rocky shores of the land, where they often put their great gifts of imagination and empathy to the task of healing the world through charitable work, social action, spirituality, religion, metaphysics, and science.

Encouraging Piscean children in their poetic dreams and visions, or leading them by the hand through the sometimes rocky terrain of the real world, is their parents' pleasurable and enriching task.

General Qualities

Pisces is a Feminine and Mutable Water sign governed by Neptune, the planet of mysticism and mystery. Some astrologers consider Pisces to be co-ruled by Neptune and Jupiter—the planet that rules outgoing Sagittarians and gives its children a decidedly practical streak—but most modern astrologers view Neptune as Pisces's dominant planetary influence.

Neptune, only recently discovered in 1846, is named for the Roman god of the oceans, whose Greek equivalent is Poseidon. Like Uranus, Neptune is a planet of transformation that strongly governs political and social change. Unlike Uranus, however, Neptune-governed change is never sudden and cataclysmic, but always slow, gradual, and steady—much the way the oceans erode the shoreline over time. Neptune is most famously associated with mysticism, mystery, higher consciousness, spiritual union, and visionary dreams. The planet also governs understanding, sacrifice, and simple human kindness.

Pisceans are kind and gentle souls who are famed for their mysterious, otherworldly natures. They are deeply imaginative and sensitive, emotionally fragile, empathetic to the extreme, and forgiving and embracing of all who come into their lives. They trust deeply—and sometimes naïvely—and thus attract a variety of people, good and bad, into their orbits. As well as being sensitive and kindhearted, Pisceans are extremely vulnerable to the influence of others, even becoming chameleonlike in their ability to assume a variety of masks, personalities, and public personas. They also may be easily swayed and taken in by disreputable characters.

The two Fish—tied together but swimming in opposite directions—that symbolize the sign of Pisces are embodiments of a powerful tug of war with which Pisceans grapple throughout their lives. On the one hand, many Pisceans, inspired by their deep empathy for others, feel compelled to make a difference in the world and become instruments of positive change. Very often, they are drawn to hands-on charitable work where they can immediately see and feel the healing effects they have on others. However, this is also terribly painful work for Pisceans, who readily take on the hurts of others and can become emotional sponges for the foibles and failings of any person who comes along. In the process, Pisceans often lose sight of their own worth, individuality, talents, and needs. On the other hand, certain Pisceans are acutely aware of their emotional vulnerability and simply forgo the real world and its potential pain entirely. These Pisceans feel safest and most comfortable in their own private sanctuaries of dreams, fantasies, and humanitarian visions.

Fully developed Pisceans can function quite well in an imaginary landscape of their own creation. There they may reach out to the world, and often have a singularly unique effect on it, through their lush and lyrical creative endeavors. Pisces is the sign of Michelangelo, Auguste Renoir, Piet Mondrian, Maurice Ravel, and Victor Hugo. Other Pisceans channel their creative energies into invention and innovation. This is also the sign of Copernicus, Alexander Graham Bell, Dr. Seuss, and Mr. Fred Rogers.

Underdeveloped Pisceans who cut themselves off from the world, however, run the risk of becoming disillusioned and cynical—other qualities that are strongly governed by Neptune—and of drowning in the tidal waves of their own deep feelings. These Pisceans are prone to emotional instability and to the perilous waters of addiction. More than a fair share of famous Pisceans have had very public battles with alcohol and drugs.

The Feminine influence in this sign further endows Pisceans with powerful imagination and intuition, a deep vulnerability and receptiveness to the feelings of others, and a marked tendency to turn away from the world and retreat into inner fantasy.

The Mutable quality of the sign is responsible for Pisceans' remarkable chameleonlike ability to take on the characteristics and styles of the people and world around them. This gift serves Pisceans well in the performing arts, where they are abundantly represented. Despite their quiet and self-protective tendencies, many Pisceans are very comfortable on stage or in film. Within the dramatic arena, they can indulge their gift of poetic interpretation, their penchant for personal transformation, and their ability to submerge themselves entirely behind another persona.

The Water element in Pisces affects it more strongly than the other two Water signs of Scorpio and Cancer. Its influence feeds Pisceans' profound emotionalism, sensitivity, and spirituality. While sharing these qualities with its companion Water signs, Pisces lacks the emotional resiliency of Scorpio and Cancer. Instead, Pisceans are fragile, thin-skinned, trusting creatures who are vulnerable on all sides to the hurts and incursions, large and small, of everyday life. Along with their deep reserves of kindness, gentility, and sensitivity, Pisceans often have a tinge of melancholy bewilderment running through them. Luckily, gentle-hearted Pisceans are invariably the beneficiaries of devoted and protective friends and mentors who are more than willing to shield these gentle souls from the sometimes harsh realities of life outside the sea.

Home

Pisceans are among the most kind and accommodating of the zodiac's children. They are eager to please, respectful of authority, and willing to play by the rules. They have a remarkable and joyful ability to go with the flow and adapt themselves readily to the texture and tempo of family life.

Young Piscean children are naturally and unconditionally loving, deeply understanding, and astonishingly unselfish and undemanding—rare qualities indeed in young children. Sweet and gentle souls, they are adored by their parents and siblings alike and rarely inspire jealousy or discord. In fact, Pisceans will go out of their way to endear themselves, in unique and varied ways, with each member of the family equally. They have a keen ability to automatically tune in to the emotional tenor, needs, and wants of whomever they are with at any given moment, and have a great capacity to understand, soothe, heal, and protect those they love. Yet their approach is never intrusive—always gentle, patient, and respectful. Piscean children invariably put the needs of others before their own, without resentment or complaint, and they expect little or nothing in return.

These are laudable qualities in any child—or adult—and certainly should be nurtured. However, parents of Piscean children must be mindful of the fact that their children's generous and self-effacing behavior may come at a high price. Because Pisceans are so adept at putting on a pleasant mask, the toll taken may not be readily apparent. That toll is the sacrifice of the Pisceans' own individuality and inner strength, and a tendency to forget that they have their own unique talents, needs, and wants that must be nurtured, filled, and acknowledged. This lack of self-regard is encouraged by the powerful influence of the planet Neptune, which emphasizes personal self-sacrifice in pursuit of a great and higher goal. Thus Pisceans have a precocious awareness of the fact that they and everyone else are merely small parts of a large and more important whole.

Parents need to encourage their Piscean children's kind and humanitarian tendencies, but also need to teach them assertiveness and self-respect at a very young age. Because Pisceans are so sensitive and open to other people's influence, and so eager to please and fit in, they are prime candidates to be taken advantage of by unsavory characters. Additionally, their dreamy, otherworldly, and sometimes naïvely trusting approach to life often makes them unsophisticated flounderers in a pool of potential sharks. They can be swept along into shady, even dangerous, "adventures" without fully realizing what they're getting into. Unsuspecting Pisceans are often made the scapegoats of others' follies.

Left alone, Pisceans are eminently resourceful at amusing themselves. Like Aquarians, their rich imaginations and intricately woven fantasy worlds can engage their hearts and minds for hours at a time. Any toy, piece of music, writing utensil, or article of clothing can be turned into a focal point for intense creative reverie by Pisceans. Indeed, they often get so lost in their world of fantasy and imagination that they need to be summoned back to more mundane tasks like eating and bathing. Pisceans are not only adept at amusing themselves, they are also delightfully entertaining for those around them. With their deft ability to assume whole other personas, Pisceans are natural and inspired performers who derive great pleasure from amusing and moving others.

School and Play

Piscean students are strongest in subjects that call on their extraordinary gifts of creativity, imagination, and interpretation. Thus they shine in English, writing, art, music, languages, and dance. Their accommodating natures also make them popular students with teachers and classmates alike. Never complaining about rules and restrictions, they are happy to go along with the crowd.

In fact, Pisceans' greatest academic challenge often is just learning how to keep their dreamy natures in check and settle down to the hard work and focused attention that school regularly requires. It isn't that they get easily bored with subjects, like Aquarians do; Pisceans are genuinely interested in everyone and everything. They are simply too often the victims of their own rich imaginations. Pisceans are extremely vulnerable to emotional stimulation, whatever the source, and their attention tends to wander, indeed jump, from one thing to another. They often rely on learning by osmosis, but their keen intuition can take them only so far in a daunting and varied academic curriculum. Pisceans benefit much by being in a traditional and structured school environment that has clear and specific academic expectations.

At play, Pisceans are inclined to avoid competitive sports because they just aren't aggressive by nature. They love all water sports, arts and crafts, imaginative board and computer games of any kind. Often they become dedicated readers and diarists.

Innate performers themselves, Pisceans also enjoy attending plays, films, and musical concerts. This is one child who can be taken to the theater at a young age.

Most of all, Pisceans adore the company of other children and are themselves popular and cherished playmates who are always willing to defer to the whims of the group and lend a compassionate and helping hand when necessary.

The World

Pisceans are not driven by ambition, nor are they interested in prestige, wealth, or fame. Satisfying the creative siren call of their rich and imaginative inner lives is their primary urge, which generally leads adult Pisceans one of two ways in the world.

The more emotionally independent and mature Pisceans often choose the creative arts as a life path, and they are particularly drawn to the solitary pursuits of writing, painting, and composing. Those Pisceans that choose to pursue a solitary creative life often live near the sea, the source of their greatest stimulation and comfort. Other creative Pisceans who possess a more assertive streak often choose performance as a career. Either choice allows creative Pisceans to fully explore their gifts of intuition, imagination, and interpretation while still giving them a measure of emotional protection from the world.

Other, more socially minded Pisceans, strongly influenced by Neptune's charitable side, want to exercise their capacity to comfort, heal, and inspire personal change in others. These Pisceans often choose careers in social service, teaching, religion, spirituality, or mysticism. The spiritual side of Pisceans, and their drive toward higher ideals, is a less famous but nevertheless very strong component of this sign. Because Pisces is the last of the zodiac's signs, and thus completes the full astrological circle, many astrologers accord it great metaphysical significance. Thus, Pisces is frequently seen as the sign most deeply linked with higher levels of consciousness, spiritual healing and rebirth, and intimations of immortality and eternity. Indeed, some perceive Pisces as symbolizing a doorway to a greater world beyond this one. Pisceans who pursue the spiritual life never reach the Rasputin-like extremes that their most similar, but more aggressive, Scorpio cousins do. Nevertheless working quietly, empathetically, and compassionately behind the scenes, Pisceans can have a profound effect on the social and spiritual consciences of those around them.

Romantically Pisces is very similar to the other Water signs of Cancer and Scorpio. All three are noted for placing a high premium on loving deeply, passionately, and eternally. But to Pisces must be added the proviso that Pisceans often love too quickly, hence too often and unwisely. Sensitive Pisceans are renowned for being wounded in love—over and over again. Thus they sometimes develop a penchant for serial marriage— trying again until they get it right; or they may postpone marriage until late in life, and then marry another Piscean. What Pisceans miss out on in romantic commitments, however, they more than make up for in the lifelong love, devotion, and protectiveness that they inspire in their friends. Pisceans are among the most sought-after, beloved, and prized companions in the zodiac.

In our hard, lean, and fast-paced culture, which often esteems accomplishment as an end in itself, perhaps too much emphasis is placed upon the doers, the achievers, the acquirers, and the bottom liners of the world. They have their place, of course, but so too do the soft-hearted and gentle dreamers. Every idea and innovation that marches majestically across the marketplace is birthed on the quieter shores of dream and imagination. Pisceans are our penultimate dream catchers, compassionate, creative, and empathetic old souls who hold a gentle but steady line against the crass and the cold.

Choosing a Name for Your Pisces Child

When choosing a name for your Pisces child, first think about the major attributes and symbols associated with the sign: Pisces is the sign of deep emotion, sensitivity, vulnerability, mystery, and mysticism. Pisceans are the most imaginative and sensitive of the zodiac's children—but they are also the most emotionally vulnerable. Pisceans are keenly sensitive to the pain of others, extraordinarily understanding and empathetic, willing to help anyone at any time however unsavory the beneficiaries of their help may be, and renowned for their unselfish generosity.

Pisces is a Feminine, Mutable Water sign governed primarily by the planet Neptune, named for the Roman god of the oceans. It governs mysticism, higher truths, slow but profound change, mystery, illusion, and charity. On its darker side, Neptune also governs deception, cynicism, escapism, and disillusion.

The Feminine aspect in the sign endows Pisceans with powerful imagination and intuition, a deep vulnerability and receptiveness to the feelings of others, and a marked tendency to turn away from the world and retreat into inner fantasies. The Mutable quality of the sign is responsible for Pisceans' remarkable, chameleonlike ability to take on the characteristics and styles of the people and world around them, and their tendency to rapidly adapt to changes in the physical, social, or political environment. The Water element in Pisces feeds the sign's profound emotionalism, sensitivity, and spirituality.

Pisces is the twelfth sign of the zodiac, encompassing the months of February and March. Because Pisces is the last of the zodiac's signs, thus completing the astrological cycle, many astrologers accord it great metaphysical significance, linking the sign to higher planes of consciousness, rebirth, and eternity.

Pisces also heralds the start of spring, and therefore is strongly associated with the annual rebirth of nature, with the rainy season, and with the budding, blossoming, and flowering of trees and plants. Jonquils, water lilies, and white poppies are the flowers associated with Pisces, as are the willow and fig trees. (The willow tree is a traditional symbol of healing.) The sign rules all fish, and the greens and blues of the ocean are Pisces's symbolic colors. The aquamarine is the sign's official birthstone, and platinum is its metal.

When you choose a name for your child, bear in mind some of Piscean children's key personal qualities. They are acutely sensitive, imaginative, intuitive, perceptive, empathetic to a fault, unselfish, and loyal. Pisceans are also dreamy, mysterious, and otherworldly, and often show interest in religion, mysticism, and spiritual healing. They have a profound connection to the sea and its denizens. The mystery, beauty, grace, and extreme vulnerability of the Fish are all emblematic of the Piscean child. Pisceans also have a heightened sense of drama and are renowned for their ability to wear a variety of masks.

For additional inspiration when choosing a name for your Pisces child—especially a middle name—you may want to look through the names listed in Pisces's companion Water signs, Cancer and Scorpio.

Names for Pisces Girls

Adena (ah-DEEN-ah) Hebrew: Sensuous one. Pisceans are endowed with great sensitivity to their external environment. Variations: *Adina, Adine, Dena, Dina.*

Aethra (EE-thra) Greek: From Greek mythology. *Aethra* is the name of a child fathered by one of the Oceanids, children of Oceanus, the god of the Ocean. Pisces is one of the three Water signs of the zodiac.

Aletea (ah-leh-TEH-uh) Spanish: Life's eternal verities. Pisces's ruling planet, Neptune, governs higher truths and, as the last sign of the zodiac, Pisces is associated with eternity. Variations: *Alethea, Althea.*

Alima (ah-LEE-muh) Arabic: She whose heart soars in music and dance; also, sea maiden. In Middle Eastern mythology, *Alima* was the goddess of the oceans. Both of the meanings of this name suit creatively inclined Pisces, one of the zodiac's three Water signs.

Alma (AHL-mah) Latin: Nurturing one. The element of Water in Pisces endows the sign's children with profound empathy and deep compassion for others. Variations: *Allma, Almah.*

Amanda (ah-MAHN-dah) Latin: She who loves deeply. Pisceans are among the most caring, sensitive, and truly loving children of the zodiac. Variations: *Amandine, Amandy, Amata, Manda, Mandaline, Mandie.*

Anahita (ah-nah-HEE-tah) Persian: In Persian mythology, the goddess of the rivers and water. Pisces, a Mutable, Feminine Water sign, is strongly associated with all bodies of water.

Andromeda (ahn-DRAH-mee-dah) Greek: Meditator. In Greek mythology, *Andromeda* was the young woman whom Perseus saved from an angry sea monster. Pisceans, known for their deep thinking and innate mysticism, have a strong connection to the sea. Variations: *Andra, Andrea, Meda.*

Aolani (ow-LAH-nee) Hawaiian: Celestial home. Imaginative, creative, and vulnerable, Pisceans often find refuge in their fantasies and dreams.

April (AYE-prel) Latin: Opening up or blooming; for the calendar month. As the sign which signals the start of spring, Pisces is often associated with the annual rebirth of nature's bounty. Variations: *Aprilette, Aprille, Averil, Averyl, Avril.*

Arabella (ahr-ah-BEHL-ah) Latin: Beautiful altar. Spiritually inclined Pisceans often find refuge from the harshness of the world when spending time in religious environs.

Arizona (air-ee-ZOH-nah) Native American: Little springs. *Arizona* is an appropriate choice for a girl born under Pisces, the sign most closely associated with water.

Astrid (AS-trid) Teutonic: Impulsive in love. Pisceans often fall deeply in love many times before finally settling down with the "right" person.

Aviva (ah-VEE-vah) Hebrew: A joyful spring. This name is traditionally used to refer to the renewal of the earth after winter.

The sign of Pisces heralds the start of spring. Variations: *Avit, Avivah, Avivi, Avrit, Viva.*

Beverly (BEH-ver-lee) English: Stream where the beavers swim. Any name connoting a body of water is suitable for a girl born under Pisces, one of the zodiac's three Water signs. Variations: *Beverelle, Beverley, Bevlyn, Bevvy.*

Bevin (BEV-in) Irish: Melodious one. Creative and lyrical Pisceans are often musically gifted. Variations: *Bevan, Beyvn.*

Blossom (BLOS-sum) Old English: Blossom, flower. *Blossom* is a delightful choice for a girl born under Pisces, the sign that heralds the start of spring and connotes the annual rebirth of nature.

Brooke (brook) Old English: Dweller by the brook. Pisceans are most comfortable and content when near the water. Variations: *Brook, Brooks.*

Cadence (KAY-denz) Latin: Having rhythm. *Cadence* suggests Pisces's natural aptitude for music. Variations: *Cadance, Cadena, Cadenza, Cady.*

Calida (kah-LEE-dah) Spanish: Loving and warm. Pisceans are among the most generous, caring, and kindhearted children of the zodiac. Variations: *Calla, Callista.*

Caresse (kah-RESS) French: Tender touch. Highly sensitive Pisceans, who feel others' pain as deeply as their own, are quick to offer comfort with a hug or a thoughtful word. Variations: *Caress, Caressa.*

Carina (kah-REEN-ah) Latin: Dear, small one. Endearing, kind, and compassionate, Pisceans easily capture the hearts of their loved ones. Variations: *Cara, Carin, Carine, Kara, Karen, Karin.*

Carmen (KAHR-min) Latin: She who sings. Pisces are known for their lyrical talents, leading them to become singers, poets, musicians, and dancers. Variations: *Carmencita, Carmine, Carmita, Karmen.*

Castalia (kah-STAY-lee-ah) Greek: From Greek mythology. *Castalia* was a nymph who was pursued by the god Apollo. To escape him, she threw herself into a spring that later became a sacred fountain of the gods. This unusual name suggests the escapist tendencies associated with Pisces, as well as the Water element of the sign.

Catherine (KAH-thur-inn) Greek: Pure. *Catherine* is a classic and fitting choice for a girl born under Pisces, the purest of the zodiac's three Water signs. Variations: *Cathi, Cathy, Katarina, Kate, Katharine, Katherine, Kathleen, Kathryn, Kathy, Katie, Katina, Katya, Kay.* (Famous Piscean: Kathy Ireland, model)

Charmaine (SHAR-mayn) Latin: Little one's song. Pisceans are attracted to the creative arts, often discovering their natural talents for music, art, writing, and drama at a young age. Variations: *Charmain, Sharmain.*

Chelsea (CHEL-see) Old English: Ship's harbor. *Chelsea*, an increasingly popular name for girls, is a suitable choice for Pisces, born under one of the zodiac's Water signs. Variations: *Chelsa, Chelsi, Chelsie, Chelsy.*

Chiyo (CHEE-yo) Japanese: Eternal. As the last sign of the zodiac, Pisces is often associated with rebirth and eternity.

Choon-Hee (choon-HEE) Korean: Daughter of spring. *Choon-Hee* is an apt name for a girl born under Pisces, the sign that heralds the budding, blossoming, and flowering of trees and plants.

Chun (CHUN) Chinese: Spring. The sign of Pisces, which signals the start of spring, is affiliated with the annual rebirth of nature.

Corazon (kor-ah-ZAHN) Spanish: Heart. This unique name is an appropriate choice for Pisceans, who are renowned for their generous natures and loving ways. Variations: *Cora, Corazana*.

Cordelia (kor-DEEL-ya; kor-DEEL-ee-ya) Welsh: Jewel from the sea. Pisces, one of the three Water signs of the zodiac, is closely associated with the aquamarine gemstone. In Shakespeare's *King Lear*, Cordelia was the forgiving daughter, the only one to remain loyal and loving after her father's downfall. Variation: *Delia*.

Corliss (KOR-liss) Old English: Good-natured. Pisceans are famous for their unselfish ways and perpetually sweet demeanors. Variations: *Colise, Corlie, Corly*.

Cyrena (sye-REEN-ah) Greek: From Cyrene. In Greek mythology, *Cyrena* was a water nymph much beloved by Apollo. Pisces shares a special connection with the ocean and all its creatures. Variations: *Cyrene, Serena*.

Daphne (DAF-nee) Greek: Laurel tree. In Greek mythology, *Daphne* was the daughter of Peneus, the Greek river god. Pisceans, born under a Water sign, are deeply empathetic, unfailingly generous, and prone to sacrificing their own happiness for the benefit of others—qualities suggesting the honor with which the laurel tree is strongly associated. Variation: *Dafna*.

Darlene (dahr-LEEN) Old English: Dear. Pisces is renowned for her ceaseless generosity, deep sensitivity, and universal compassion. Variation: *Darleen*.

Delfina (del-FEEN-ah) Latin: Dolphin. *Delfina* is a lovely name for a girl born under Pisces, the sign that governs all types of fish. Variations: *Delphina, Delphine*.

Delja (DAYL-yah) Polish: Daughter of the sea. Pisces is one of the three Water signs of the zodiac. (Cancer and Scorpio are the other two.)

Delora (day-LOHR-ah) Spanish: From the sea coast. The sign of Pisces is affiliated with the deep blue and green colors of the sea.

Destiny (DESS-tih-nee) English: Fate. Pisces, the last sign of the zodiac, is associated with the themes of rebirth, higher consciousness, and eternity. Variations: *Destina, Destine, Destinee, Destini, Destinie.*

Devan (DEV-an) Irish: Poet. Highly imaginative and lyrical Pisceans often find success in the creative arts. Variations: *Devin, Devina, Devinna, Devinne, Devon, Devona.*

Dooriya (DOO-ree-yuh) Irish: The deep, a reference to the sea. Pensive and sensitive Pisceans often find comfort and inspiration from the ocean. Variation: *Dooya.*

Doris (DOR-iss) Greek: One from the ocean. This traditional name is suitable for a Pisces, born under a Water sign. Variations: *Dori, Doria, Dorice, Dorisa, Dorit, Dorris, Dory.*

Dulcie (DOOL-see) Latin: Sweet one. *Dulcie* is an appropriate choice for generous, compassionate, and loving Pisces. Variations: *Dulce, Dulcine, Dulcinea, Dulsie.*

Dylana (dah-LAHN-ah) Welsh: Ocean-born. Pisces, a Water sign symbolized by the Fish and governed by Neptune, the planet named for the Roman god of the oceans, shares a powerful connection with the dark depths of the ocean.

Easter (EE-stir) Old English: Child born on Easter Day. This unusual name is a charming choice for a girl born on or near the Easter holiday, which typically falls during Pisces's phase (late March to late April).

Edna (ED-nah) Welsh: Purity of soul. Pisces is endowed with tremendous sensitivity, spiritual insight, and emotional depth. Variation: *Enit*.

Euphemia (yoo-FEM-ee-ah, yoo-fem-EE-ah or yoo-FEE-mee-ah) Greek: One who is spoken well of. Imaginative, generous, kind, and endearing, Pisceans are popular and respected. Variations: *Effi, Effie, Effy, Euphenie, Phemie*.

Flora (FLOR-ah) Latin: Flower. In Roman mythology, *Flora* was the name of the goddess of spring and flowers. The sign of Pisces, which accompanies the start of spring, is often associated with the budding, blossoming, and flowering of plants. Variation: *Fleur*.

Fontane (fawn-TAN) French: Source of water. Pisces is one of the three Water signs of the zodiac.

Galatea (gal-ah-TEE-ah; gal-ah-TAY-ah) Greek: From Greek mythology. *Galatea* was a famed sea nymph. Pisceans, born under a Water sign, have a strong attraction to the sea and all its creatures.

Garland (GAHR-lind) Old French: Necklace of flowers. Signaling the start of spring, the sign of Pisces is often associated with the blossoming and flowering of plants. The flowers associated with Pisces are water lilies, white poppies, and jonquils. Variations: *Garlanda, Garlande, Garlandera*.

Glenluan (glen-LOO-in) Welsh: Blessed flood. *Glenluan* is a unique choice for a girl born under Pisces, one of the zodiac's Water signs.

Grace (GRAYSS) Latin: Kindness, mercy, and beauty of form. Highly sensitive and emotional, Pisces is generous, compassionate, and accommodating to the extreme. Variations: *Gracie, Graciella*.

Gudrun (GOOD-ren) Scandinavian: She with secret knowledge of God. Influenced by their ruling planet, Neptune, which governs mysticism and higher truths, many Pisceans have a deep interest in spirituality. Variations: *Gudren, Gudrin, Guro.*

Hallie (HAHL-ee; HAIL-ee) Greek: Thinking of the sea. *Hallie* is a name well suited to Pisces, a pensive daydreamer born under one of the zodiac's Water signs. Variations: *Halli, Hally.*

Hama (HAH-mah) Japanese: Shore. This lovely name connotes Pisceans' desire to find a private haven away from the stormy, unpredictable "real world"—a need that is easily soothed by close proximity to the ocean. Variation: *Hamako.*

Harper (HAHR-pur) Old English: Harp player. Creative Pisceans often pursue careers in the arts—with great success.

Haru (hah-ROO) Japanese: Born in spring. The sign of Pisces heralds the annual rebirth of nature. Variations: *Harue, Haruko, Oharu.*

Haven (HAY-vin) Dutch: Safe harbor. Vulnerable and highly sensitive, Pisceans often seek rest from the pain and harshness of the world in soothing places near the water. Variation: *Hagen.*

Honey (HUN-ee) Old English: Sweet one. Pisces is naturally compassionate, generous, and loving. Variation: *Honi.*

Hortense (HOR-tenz) Latin: She who works in the garden. As the sign that heralds the beginning of spring, Pisces is commonly associated with the budding, blossoming, and flowering of trees and plants. The flowers associated with Pisces are water lilies, white poppies, and jonquils. Variations: *Hortencia, Hortensia, Ortensia.*

Ianthe (ee-AHNTH or ee-AN-thee) Greek: Violet flower. In Greek mythology, *Ianthe* was the daughter of the sea nymph, Oceanus. This lovely name is well-suited to a girl born under the Water sign of Pisces. Variations: *Ianthia, Ianthina, Janthia*.

Irvette (er-VETT) Old English: Friend of the sea. *Irvette* is an apt name for Pisces, who feels a powerful connection to the ocean.

Iwalani (ee-wah-LAH-nee) Hawaiian: Sea bird. Pisceans, born under a Water sign, are affiliated with the sea and all its creatures.

Jalini (jah-LEE-nee) Hindu: She who lives by the water. Emotional and creative Pisceans often choose to make their homes near bodies of water, from which they find great inspiration.

Jennifer (JEN-ee-fir) Old Welsh: White wave. Connoting the imagery of the sea, *Jennifer* is a suitable choice for a girl born under Pisces, a Water sign. Variations: *Genifer, Genn, Ginnifer, Jen, Jenifer, Jenn, Jenny*. (Famous Pisces: Jennifer O'Neill, actress)

Jonquil (JAHN-quil) English: For the flower. The jonquil is the one of the three flowers associated with the sign of Pisces. Variations: *Jonquila, Jonquille*.

Kai (KAY) Hawaiian: Deep blue seas. Pisces, a Water sign, is associated with the deep blue and green colors of the ocean.

Kallan (KAL-in) Scandinavian: Stream. Pisces is one of the three Water signs of the zodiac. (The other two are Cancer and Scorpio.)

Kallirroe (kal-LEE-roh) Greek: Beautiful stream. Artistically inclined Pisceans, born under a Water sign, often find inspiration by spending time near bodies of water.

Kamali (KAH-mah-lee) African/Zimbabwean: Spirit guide. In African mythology, *Kamali* was the protector of newborns. Spiritually inclined and endowed with deep sensitivity, Pisces aspires to help others and make the world a better place. Pisces is also associated with rebirth.

Kamoana (kah-moh-AHN-ah) Hawaiian: Ocean. Pisces's ruling planet of Neptune is named for the Roman god of the oceans.

Keida (KAY-dah) Old Norse: Flowing water. Pisces is one of the three Water signs of the zodiac. Variations: *Keli, Kelie, Kelley, Kelli.*

Kelby (KELL-bee) Scandinavian: Place by the flowing water. Many Pisceans choose to make their homes near a body of water, where they feel most calm and comfortable.

Kelsey (KEL-see) Old English: Victory ship. This unusual name connotes the Piscean penchant for achieving dreams when inspired and surrounded by the imagery of the sea.

Kenda (KEN-dah) English: Child of clear, cool water. The Water element in the sign of Pisces is the strongest of the zodiac's signs, bestowing its children with deep sensitivity, profound spirituality, and intense emotions.

Kishi (KEE-shee) Japanese: Beside the shore. *Kishi* is an appropriate name for a girl born under Pisces, one of the zodiac's three Water signs.

Kismet (KIZ-met) Turkish: Destiny. As the last sign of the zodiac, Pisces is associated with the themes of rebirth, eternity, and higher levels of consciousness.

Kolenya (koh-LAYN-yah) Native American: Coughing fish. Any name connoting the denizens of the sea is an appropriate name for a girl born under Pisces, a Water sign symbolized by the Fish.

Koto (KOH-toh) Japanese: Harp or string jewel. Creatively inclined Pisceans often show great talent in the areas of music, art, and writing.

Kyle (KILE) Scottish: From near the narrow channel. Any name suggesting a body of water is appropriate for a girl born under Pisces, one of the three Water signs of the zodiac. Variations: *Kial, Kile, Kiley, Kyla, Kylie.*

Lexine (lex-EEN) English: She who helps others. The generous nature and keen sensitivity of Pisceans are renowned, drawing many Pisceans to charitable work. Variations: *Lexene, Lexi, Lexy.*

Lian (LEE-an) Chinese: A willow that sways like a dancer. The sign of Pisces is affiliated with the willow tree, a traditional symbol of healing.

Lilia (lee-LEE-uh) Hawaiian: Lilies. The water lily is one of the three flowers associated with the sign of Pisces.

Lillian (LILL-ee-an) Latin: Lily blossom. *Lillian*, or one of its beautiful variations, is a suitable choice for a girl born under Pisces, the sign associated with white poppies, jonquils, and water lilies. Variations: *Lili, Lilian, Liliana, Liliane, Lillianne, Lillyan, Lillyanna.*

Lindsey (LIND-zee) Old English: From the linden tree island. Born under a Water sign, Pisceans have a natural affinity for the ocean, and often choose to live near a body of water. Variations: *Lindsay, Lynsey.*

Lola (LOH-lah) Spanish: Strong woman of sorrows. *Lola* suggests the emotional vulnerability and deep sensitivity found in Pisceans, who often absorb other people's pain. Variations: *Lita, Lolita.*

Lorelei (lor-ah-LYE or LOR-eh-lye) German: The place name of a rock that juts out of the Rhine River. In German mythology, *Lorelei* was a sea siren who sat on the rock and sang a mesmerizing song that drew sailors to an untimely death. Pisceans, born under one of the zodiac's Water signs, are often blessed with enchanting musical gifts. Variations: *Loralee, Loralie, Loralyn, Lura, Lurette, Lurleen, Lurline.*

Lynn (lin) Welsh: Lake. Pisces is one of the Water signs of the zodiac. Variation: *Lyn.* (Famous Piscean: Lynn Redgrave, actress)

Lyra (LEER-ah) Greek: Lyrical one. Sensitive dreamers who are creatively inclined, Pisceans often have great artistic talents. Variations: *Liris, Lirit, Lyris.*

Malila (muh-LEE-lah) Native American: Salmon swimming rapidly up a stream. Pisces is the sign that governs all Fish.

Mana (MAH-nuh) Hawaiian: Psychic gifts. As the last sign of the zodiac, Pisces is deeply linked to higher levels of consciousness and visions of a greater world beyond this one.

Mangena (mahn-GAY-nuh) Hebrew: Song. Creatively inclined Pisceans often are endowed with great musical and lyrical gifts. Variation: *Mangina.*

Marina (mahr-REE-nah) Latin: Sea born. *Marina* is a beautiful and apt name for Pisces, who is happiest when near the ocean. Variations: *Mara, Marena, Marine, Marinna, Marna, Marne, Marni.*

Marissa (mah-RISS-ah) Latin: Sea born. Pisces is one of the zodiac's Water signs. Variations: *Maris, Marisa, Maritza, Mariza, Marysa, Merisa, Merissa.*

Masika (mah-SEE-kah) African/Swahili: Born during the rainy season. Pisces is the sign affiliated with the annual rebirth of nature and the reappearance of the rainy season.

Meena (MEE-nah) Hindu: Fish. In Hindu astrology, *Meena* is a name traditionally given to a child born under the sign of Pisces, which is symbolized by the Fish. Variations: *Meenal, Mina, Minal, Minali, Minisha, Minna.*

Meliora (may-lee-OHR-ah) Latin: To make better. Sensitive and intuitive, Pisceans have a great desire to heal the pain of others. Variation: *Melyora.*

Melody (MEL-oh-dee) Greek: Melody, song. Pisceans are endowed with great appreciation for the arts, including music. Variations: *Mel, Melodia.*

Meredith (MARE-uh-dith) Old Welsh: She who guards the sea. Born under one of the zodiac's Water signs, Pisceans have a great affinity for the sea. Variations: *Meridith, Merri, Merridith, Merrie, Merry.*

Meriel (MARE-ee-el) Gaelic: Brilliant seas. Creatively inclined Pisceans often are inspired by the powerful ocean. Variations: *Merial, Meriol, Merrill, Meryl, Muriel.*

Merla (MER-lah) Welsh: Fortress by the sea. *Merla*, the feminine form of Merlin—the name of the great wizard and seer—suggests both Pisces's tendency to hide away from the world and the sign's powers of vision and higher consciousness. Variation: *Merl.*

Mesi (MAY-see) African/Malawian: Water. Of the three Water signs of the zodiac, Pisces is the most strongly connected to Water.

Misty (MIS-tee) Contemporary: Misty or foggy. *Misty* is a name well suited to dreamy Pisces, born under one of the zodiac's Water signs. Variations: *Misti, Mistie.*

Morgan (MOR-gin) Old Welsh: By the sea. Born under the planet that rules the oceans, Pisces is greatly influenced by the forces of the sea. Variations: *Morgaine, Morgana, Morganne, Morgayne, Morgen.*

Morwenna (mor-WENN-ah) Welsh: Ocean wave. Pisces, more than any other Water sign, is associated with the imagery of the sea.

Mozelle (moh-ZEH-le; moh-ZEL) Hebrew: Taken from the water. *Mozelle*, the feminine variation of *Moses*, is a suitable name for a girl born under the Water sign of Pisces. Variation: *Moselle.*

Muna (MOO-nah) Native American: Freshet. In the Hopi culture, this name is traditionally given to child born during the time the streams rise, making it appropriate for a Pisces girl, born under a Water sign in spring.

Murdina (mir-DEEN-ah) Scottish: Sea warrior. Pisces is governed by the planet Neptune, named for the Roman god who ruled the sea. Variations: *Murdag, Murdann.*

Musetta (moo-SAYT-ah; myu-SAYT-ah) Greek: Source of inspiration. Derived from the Muses of Greek mythology, who govern music, poetry, and the arts, this name suits imaginative and creative Pisceans. Variations: *Muse, Musette.*

Myff (MIFF) Welsh: Child of the water. The Water element in Pisces endows the sign's children with profound emotionalism, sensitivity, and spirituality. Variation: *Myvanwy.*

Nadian (NAHD-ee-an) Hebrew: Pond. Pisces is one of the three Water signs of the zodiac. (The other two are Cancer and Scorpio.)

Naia (nah-EE-ah) Hawaiian: Dolphin. Pisceans, born under the zodiac's Water sign that is symbolized by the Fish, feel a special connection with the creatures of the sea.

Naida (nah-DAH or NAY-dah) Latin: Sea goddess. This lovely name is well suited to Pisces, which is ruled by the planet Neptune, named for the Roman god of the sea.

Nasnan (NAHS-nahn) Native American: Embraced by music. Imaginative and sensitive, Pisceans have a special affinity for the musical arts.

Natasha (nah-TAHSH-ah) Greek: Rebirth. As the last sign of the zodiac, Pisces is often associated with rebirth and eternity. Variations: *Nastasia, Nastassia, Nastassja, Natasia, Natazy, Tasha.*

Nenet (neh-NET) Egyptian: Goddess of the deep. Associated with the sea, Pisces is also known for having a mysterious, unfathomable emotional side.

Nerine (neh-REEN) Greek: Ocean sprite. Associated with the planet that governs the sea, Pisces has an imaginative spirit that enjoys the spontaneity of music and dance. Variations: *Nerice, Nerida.*

Nerissa (ner-RISS-ah) Greek: Ocean's daughter. Born under the planet Neptune, which was named for the Roman god of the sea, Pisceans always show a deep attachment to the ocean. Variations: *Nerisse, Rissa.*

Nessa (NEH-sah) Russian: Reborn from the dead. Pisces, the twelfth and last sign of the zodiac, is often associated with rebirth and eternity.

Nirveli (neer-VAY-lee) Hindu: Child of the deep waters. Pisceans, born under a Water sign, tend to be sensitive and vulnerable deep thinkers who may spend hours wrapped in their own private fantasy world.

Nixie (NIX-ee) German: Water nymph. This enchanting name suits imaginative and mystical Pisces, one of the zodiac's three Water signs.

Noelani (noh-ah-LAH-nee) Hawaiian: Mist of heaven. Pisces, a Water sign, is often associated with spirituality and higher consciousness. Variation: *Noe*.

Oba (OH-buh) African/Nigerian: Goddess who rules the rivers. Born under the planet that governs the ocean, Pisceans maintain a deep connection to all bodies of water.

Oceana (oh-SHAH-nah; oh-see-AHN-ah) Greek: Ocean. In Greek mythology, Oceanus was the god of the ocean. Pisces, a Water sign symbolized by the Fish, is ruled by Neptune, the planet named for the Roman god of the oceans.

Odele (oh-DAYL) Greek: Little ode or song. Pisces are known to have a strong logical bent, showing great talent as poets, singers, and musicians. Variations: *Odelet, Odelette, Odile*.

Oki (OH-kee) Japanese: Ocean depths. Like the bodies of water so closely associated with their sign, Pisceans are deep and mysterious.

Omega (oh-MAYG-ah) Greek: The last child or the end. *Omega*, also the name of the last letter in the Greek alphabet, is a suitable choice for a girl born under Pisces, the last sign of the zodiac.

Ondine (UHN-deen) Latin: Little wave. Any name related to water is well suited to Pisces, the purest of the Water signs. Variations: *Ondina, Ondyne, Undina, Undine*.

Pacifica (pah-SIH-fee-kah) Spanish: To make peace. This unique name is appropriate to Pisces, as it reflects the internal emotional state of those born under the sign and also connotes the ocean that holds such an attraction for typical Pisceans.

Parthenope (pahr-THEN-ah-pee) Greek: From Greek mythology. *Parthenope* was a Greek siren who threw herself into the sea when her singing failed to shipwreck Ulysses and his fleet. Highly sensitive and emotional, Pisceans often use their musical and artistic gifts to shield themselves from the pain of the world.

Pasha (PAH-shah) Greek: From the sea. Pisces, ruled by the planet that governs the oceans, is one of three Water signs of the zodiac. Variations: *Palasha, Pashka.*

Pelagia (peh-lah-HEE-ah) Greek: The ocean. *Pelagia* is an apt choice for a girl born under Pisces, a Water sign whose ruling planet of Neptune was named for the ancient Roman god of the ocean. Variations: *Pelage, Pelagie, Pelegia, Pelgia.*

Penelope (peh-NELL-oh-pee) Greek: She who weaves her dreams. Pisceans are sensitive and highly imaginative, often preferring to remain in the magical world of dreams rather than return to the harshness of reality. Variation: *Penny.*

Persephone (pehr-SEH-foh-nee) Greek: Rebirth or springtime. In Greek mythology, *Persephone* was the goddess of spring. Heralding the start of spring, Pisces is strongly associated with the annual renewal of nature.

Piper (PYE-pur) Old English: A player of pipes. Pisceans are endowed with exceptional musical talents. Variation: *Pip.*

Pirene (pye-REEN-ee) Greek: From Greek mythology. *Pirene* was the daughter of a river god. Pisces is ruled by the planet that governs large bodies of water.

Quintessa (kwin-TAYS-sah) Latin: The essence. This lovely name suggests the profound spirituality and sensitivity linked to the sign of Pisces. Variations: *Tess, Tessa, Tessie.*

Rain (RAYN) English: The water that falls to the earth. *Rain* is a unique choice for a girl born under Pisces, a Water sign associated with the rainy season. Variation: *Rainnie.*

Ren (REN) Japanese: Water lily. The water lily is one of the three flowers associated with the sign of Pisces.

Renee (reh-NAY) French: Reborn. Pisces, the last sign of the zodiac, is commonly associated with rebirth and immortality. Variations: *Rene, René, Renée, Renelle, Reni, Renie, Renisha, Renita, Renni.*

Rhonda (RON-dah) Welsh: Powerful seas. Creatively inclined Pisceans, born under a Water sign, often are inspired by the intensity of the ocean. Variations: *Rhona, Rhonette, Rona, Ronda.*

Ria (REE-ah) Spanish: River's origin. In touch with their deep inner source of creative and artistic inspiration, Pisceans are born under the Water sign that is closely associated with large bodies of water. Variations: *Rea, Rhea, Rie.*

Rilla (RILL-ah) German: Stream. The calm and creative energies of Pisceans flow continuously like a gentle stream. Variations: *Rilletta, Rillette.*

Riva (REE-vah) French: On a river bank. Pisces's renowned ability to create gentle yet continuous change can be compared to a seashore or riverbank, where the flowing water gradually wears away the solid land. Variation: *Reva.*

Rosemary (ROZ-mayr-ee) Latin: Dew of the sea. Children born under the sign of Pisces are the gentle offspring of the planet

Neptune, known as the ruler of the oceans and seas. Variations: *Rosemaria, Rosemarie*.

Ruana (roo-AH-nah) Hindu: Musical string instrument. Creative Pisceans are often drawn to the arts, and many are endowed with musical gifts.

Ryba (REE-bah) Czechoslovakian: Fish. The sign of Pisces is symbolized by the Fish. Variations: *Reba, Riba*.

Sabrina (sah-BREE-nah) Latin: In Celtic mythology, this water nymph lived in England's Severn River. Pisces, one of the zodiac's three Water signs, is known for its mystical and mysterious qualities. Variations: *Brina, Sabreen, Sabreena, Sabrena, Sabrinna*.

Sagara (sah-GAH-rah) Hindu: Ocean. Neptune, Pisces's ruling planet, was named for the Roman god of the ocean.

Sancia (sahn-SEE-ah) Latin: Holy and sacred one. Pisceans frequently are drawn to spirituality and higher levels of consciousness. Variations: *Sancha, Sanchia, Sancie, Sancy*.

Sarila (sah-RIL-ah) Turkish: Rush of the waters. Pisces is one of the three Water signs of the zodiac. (The other two are Cancer and Scorpio.)

Sarita (sah-REE-tah) Hindu: River. This lovely name is well suited to a girl born under Pisces, a Water sign.

Shino (SHEE-noh) Japanese: Slender bamboo, the symbol of fidelity. Generous and understanding, Pisces loves unconditionally.

Shiri (SHEE-ree) Hebrew: Song of my soul. Pisceans, who show a natural affinity for music and art, are among the most sensitive and spiritual children of the zodiac. Variations: *Shira, Shirah*.

Sibyl (SIB-il) Greek: Prophetess. The sign of Pisces is often associated with mysticism, higher consciousness, and visionary dreams. Variations: *Cybele, Cybil, Sibella, Sibyll, Sybil, Sybille*.

Sirena (sye-REEN-ah; sye-RAYN-ah) Greek: One who enchants with song. In Greek mythology, the Sirens lured sailors to their island with their enchanting voices. Highly creative and imaginative Pisceans often are endowed with talents for music, art, and writing. Variation: *Serena*.

Susan (SUZ-en) Hebrew: Graceful lily. This classic name is appropriate for a girl born under the sign of Pisces, which is affiliated with the water lily. Variations: *Sue, Suka, Sukee, Suki, Susanna, Susannah, Susanne, Susetta, Susie, Suzanna, Suzannah, Suze, Suzetta, Suzette*.

Suzamni (soo-ZAHM-nee) Carrier Indian: Graceful lily. The flowers associated with the sign of Pisces are water lilies, white poppies, and jonquils.

Taki (TAH-kee) Japanese: Waterfall returning home. This unique name is well suited to Pisces, whose spirit is always drawn to waterside environs.

Tansy (TANZ-ee) Greek: Immortal one. Because it is the last sign of the zodiac, Pisces is often associated with eternity and rebirth. Variations: *Tandi, Tandy*.

Taura (tah-OO-rah) Japanese: Many rivers. Pisces is the sign governed by Neptune, the planet associated with oceans and other large bodies of water. Variation: *Taurina*.

Teal (TEEL) English: The dark green-blue color. The greens and blues of the ocean are the colors associated with the sign of Pisces. Variation: *Teela*.

Thalassa (thah-LAHS-ah) Greek: She who comes from the sea. Pisces, symbolized by the fish, has a deep connection to water and the sea.

Tiberia (tye-BEER-ee-ah) Latin: The Tiber River. This unique name is a suitable choice for a girl born under Pisces, one of the zodiac's three Water signs. Variations: *Tibbie, Tibby*.

Toby (TOH-bee) Hebrew: God is good. *Toby* connotes Pisces's strong interest in religion and spirituality. Variations: *Tobi, Tobia*.

Tyne (TINE) Old English: River. Pisces, one of the zodiac's Water signs, is associated with all large bodies of water. (Famous Piscean: Tyne Daly, actress)

Ula (OO-lah) Celtic: Jewel of the sea. Pisces, associated with the aquamarine gemstone, is one of the three Water signs of the zodiac. Variation: *Ulla*.

Umiko (OO-mee-koh) Japanese: Child of the sea. The powerful Water element in Pisces endows the sign's children with great sensitivity, deep spirituality, and intensely rich emotions.

Vana (VAH-nah) Polynesian: Sea urchin. Pisces is symbolized by the fish and associated with every aspect of the sea. Variation: *Vanna*.

Verna (VUR-nah) Latin: Springlike. Pisces, the sign that signals the beginning of spring, is often linked to the annual rebirth of nature. Variations: *Vernal, Vernetta, Vernis, Virna*.

Virginia (ver-JIN-yah; ver-JIN-ee-ah) Latin: Springlike and flourishing. Heralding the start of spring, the sign Pisces is commonly associated with the budding, blossoming, and flowering of trees and plants. Variations: *Ginger, Ginny*.

Whitney (WIT-nee) English: Beautiful island. Born under a Water sign, Pisceans have a special affinity for the ocean and usually choose to live near a body of water.

Willow (WILL-oh) Middle English: The willow tree; also, liberated spirit. The sign of Pisces is affiliated with the willow and fig trees.

Xantho (ZAN-thoh) Greek: Golden-haired. In Greek mythology, *Xantho* was a sea nymph. This intriguing name is an ideal choice for a light-complexioned Pisces, born under the planet that governs the sea.

Yoko (YOH-koh) Japanese: Child of the open seas. Freethinking Pisceans often are inspired by the powerful and expansive ocean.

Yuriko (YOO-ree-koh) Japanese: Lily child. The flowers assigned to the sign of Pisces are water lilies, white poppies, and jonquils.

Zanna (ZAN-nah) Hebrew: Lily. *Zanna* is an unusual and lovely choice for a girl born under Pisces, the sign associated with the water lily.

Zarya (ZAHR-yah) Czechoslovakian: In Slavic mythology, *Zarya* was a water priestess. Pisceans, born under one of the zodiac's Water signs, are often attracted to mysticism and spirituality. Variations: *Zara, Zora, Zorya.*

Zelenka (zeh-LENN-keh) Czechoslovakian: Like a budding green plant. Signaling the start of spring, the sign of Pisces is often associated with the budding, blossoming, and flowering of trees and plants.

Zenia (ZEEN-ya; ZEEN-ee-ah) Greek: Charitable one. Sensitive and compassionate Pisceans are renowned for their selflessness and generosity. Variations: *Xenia, Zeni, Zina.*

Names for Pisces Boys

Achelous (ak-ah-LOH-us) Greek: From Greek mythology. *Achelous*, a river god, was the eldest of the three thousand sons of Oceanus. Pisceans delight in streams, rivers, and oceans.

Acheron (AK-eh-run) Greek: Pain. In Greek mythology, the dead were carried through Hades across Acheron, the river of woe. Sympathetic Pisces easily enters the emotional currents of others, and through his natural compassion, brings them safely to the other side.

Adeben (ah-deh-BEHN) African/Ghanian: Twelfth-born son. Pisces is the twelfth sign of the zodiac, making *Adeben* a most fitting choice.

Ahir (uh-HEER) Turkish: End, or last. This exotic name is appropriate for those born under the zodiac's last sign.

Akar (ah-KAHR) Turkish: Flowing water. The Fish is happiest when swimming, sailing, or dreamily floating down the stream.

Alf (alf) Norwegian: One who lives in the world beyond. Famous for their other worldliness, Pisceans often appear to have their minds more in the heavens than on earth.

Alpheus (al-FEE-us) Greek: Transparent being. In Greek mythology, the river god Alpheus was in love with the nymph Arethusa. *Alpheus* is an appropriate name for Pisces who has an affinity for water as well as a deep capacity for love.

Amos (AYE-mis) Hebrew: Burden bearer. Pisces is deeply empathetic to the plight of others, often taking on a friend's pain as his own.

Ansel (AN-sell) Old German: Divine guardian. All aspects of spirituality are of interest to Pisceans, who are blessed with an almost-angelic concern for the welfare of others. Variations: *An-*

cell, Anse, Anselm, Anselmo, Elmo, Hans, Hansel. (Famous Piscean: Ansel Adams, photographer)

Asa (AYZ-ah) Hebrew: Healer. Sensitive, loving, and imaginative, Pisceans have an innate ability to heal the spirit.

Asariel (ah-sah-REE-ell) Hebrew: Prince of God. *Asariel* is the name of the archangel who protects those born under the sign of Pisces, making this name a perfect choice for natives of the sign.

Asher (AH-sher) Hebrew: Felicitous. Pisceans are known for their generally good-natured and endearing temperaments. Variation: *Acher.*

Aukai (AH-oo-KAH-ee) Hawaiian: Seafarer. The mariners of the zodiac, Pisceans are more at home on water than on land.

Aviv (ah-VEEV) Hebrew: Nature's renewal. The sign of Pisces is associated with the start of spring and the natural rejuvenation that it brings.

Baird (BAHRD or BAYRD) Irish: Ballad singer. With their flair for the dramatic, Pisceans can excel at this ancient art. Variations: *Bard, Barr.*

Beck (BECK) Middle English: Brook. All forms of flowing water hold charm for Pisceans.

Botan (boh-TAHN) Japanese: Blossom. The sign of Pisces is identified with springtime and the rebirth of the season's new flowers.

Brede (BREH-deh or BREED) Scandinavian: Iceberg. Pisceans have an affinity for water in all its manifestations.

Brishen (BREE-shen) English Gypsy: Child who brought the rain. Mystical Pisces may appear to have power over the natural elements, especially those that pertain to water.

Brook (brook) English: Running water. The silvery beauty of this gentle stream appeals to Pisceans. Variations: *Brooke, Brooks.*

Caldwell (KAHLD-well) Old English: Cool spring. Powers of intuition and imagination bubble up in Pisceans from the deep spring of the unconscious. Variations: *Cal, Calder.*

Carmine (kahr-MEE-neh; KAHR-mine) Hebrew: Garden. A harbinger of spring, the sign of Pisces is linked to buds, blossoms, and flowering plants.

Carr (KAHR) Scandinavian: From the wetlands. Pisceans feel most comfortable when their home is near water. Variations: *Karr, Kerr.*

Carswell (KAHRS-wel) Old English: One from the watercress spring. All forms of water and the life it contains are affiliated with the sign of Pisces.

Claiborne (KLAY-born) Old English: From the clay-bottomed stream. Wading barefoot in a running stream is bliss for Pisceans. Variations: *Claiborn, Clayborne, Claybourne.*

Corey (KOR-ee) Irish: One who lives by the misty pool. Pisceans prefer to make their home near water. The drama of mist appeals to their love of the unknown. Variations: *Correy, Cory, Korey, Kory.*

Dante (DAHN-tay) Italian: Eternally enduring. Because of its association with rebirth and rejuvenation, Pisces is the sign of the eternal.

Darryl (DAR-ril) Old French: Dear one. Sweet tempered and generous, Pisceans easily endear themselves to others. Variations: *Daren, Darin, Daron, Darrin, Derron.*

Deacon (DEEK-in) Greek: Messenger. With a keen ability to be empathetic and receptive, Pisceans are gifted at relaying information, particularly of a spiritual or inspirational nature, to others.

Delfino (del-FEE-noh) Latin: Dolphin. Pisceans envy and admire dolphins, who are both friend to man and lord of the seas in mythology.

Delmar (DEL-mahr) Latin: Of the sea. The realm of Poseidon holds an intrinsic appeal for the Water sign of Pisces. Variations: *Del, Delmer.*

Deniz (de-NIHZ) Turkish: Flowing seas. This unique name is a fitting choice for Pisceans, who are enchanted by the ocean and the sea.

Devin (DEH-vin) Latin: Heavenly. Pisceans are specially attuned to the realm of the spirit. Variations: *Devinn, Devon, Devyn.*

Dorian (DOR-ee-in) Greek: Child of the sea. Pisceans are never so happy as when frolicking in the sea.

Dukker (DOOK-kuhr) English Gypsy: To foresee the future. Perceptive and intuitive, Pisceans seem to possess the gift of second sight. Variation: *Duke.*

Durriken (DOO-ree-ken) English Gypsy: Prophet. Pisceans, blessed with a gift for metaphysics, may even be able to divine the future.

Dyre (DEE-re; DYRE) Norse: Dear and precious. Their loving spirit makes Pisceans precious to those who are closest to them.

Erasmus (ee-RAZZ-mus) Greek: Loving and well loved. Pisceans, generous of heart, are rewarded in kind by the love of others. Variations: *Eraste, Erastus, Ras, Rastus.*

Fiorello (fee-oh-REHL-oh) Italian: Little flower. *Fiorello* suggests the vulnerability and sensitivity found in every Piscean. Variations: *Fio, Fiorenzo.*

Fiske (FISK) Middle English: Fish. This name is a perfect match for those born under the sign of the Fish. Variation: *Fisk.*

Flint (FLINT) Old English: Brook. Pisceans are enamored of flowing water.

Galeno (gah-LEH-noh) Spanish: Illuminated child. Possessed of metaphysical wisdom, Pisceans are truly enlightened.

Germain (JUR-mayne) Middle English: Sprout or bud. Blossoms, buds, and new growth of any kind are associated with the sign of Pisces. Variations: *Germaine, Jermain, Jermaine, Jermayne.*

Gillie (GIL-ee; JIL-ee) English Gypsy: A song. While gifted in all branches of the arts, Pisceans have a special talent for music.

Hali (HAH-lee) Greek: Sea. Pisces, born under the planet that governs the sea, is one of the three Water signs of the zodiac.

Harith (hah-REETH) Arabic: Cultivator. The sign of Pisces is associated with the budding, blossoming, and flowering of plants and trees.

Hermes (HER-mees) Greek: Messenger. In Greek mythology, *Hermes* was the messenger of the gods and the guardian of souls in the underworld. Pisces, associated with the dark, otherworldly depths of the ocean, is known for revealing a sense of the mystical and mysterious side of life.

Hiroshi (hee-ROH-shee) Japanese: Generous. One of the key characteristics of the sign of Pisces is a truly unselfish and generous nature.

Holbrook (HOHL-brook) Old English: From the brook in the hollows. This name evokes Pisces's image as a deeply hidden and sometimes dark Water sign. Variation: *Holbrooke*.

Holmes (HOHLMZ) Middle English: From the river islands. Pisces's dual nature of creative action and withdrawn dreaming suggest the image of the solid land meeting the ever-changing water.

Horace (HOHR-iss) Latin: Keeper of time. As the final sign in the astrological circle, Pisces is associated with the continual changing and turning of time. Variations: *Horacio, Horatio, Horatius, Orry*.

Howard (HOW-urd) Teutonic: Watchman. Highly aware of their environs and protective of others' emotional states, Pisces are known as keen observers of another, more mysterious world. Variation: *Howie*. (Famous Pisceans: Howard Hesseman, actor; Howard Jones, musician)

Hoyt (HOYT) Middle English: Small boat. Any name suggesting the imagery of water is appropriate for Pisces, considered the purest of the three Water signs. Variations: *Hoit, Hoyle*.

Hurley (HER-lee) Irish: Born from the seas. Pisces, one of the three Water signs of the zodiac, is named for the planet that governs the oceans and seas. Variations: *Hurlee, Hurleigh*.

Irving (UR-ving) Old English: Friend of the ocean. Water-loving Pisceans enjoy an enduring bond with the sea. Variations: *Earvin, Ervin, Irvin, Irvine*.

Jafar (jah-FAHR) Arabic: Little stream. This popular Middle Eastern name is well suited to Pisces, the sign most strongly associated with images of water.

Jarda (YAHR-dah) Slavic: Springtime's beauty. The sign of Pisces is associated with the budding, blossoming, and flowering of plants and trees. Variation: *Jaroslav.*

Jason (JAY-son) Greek: Healer. This popular name is suitable for Pisces, who tries to soothe others' pain at every opportunity. Variations: *Jase, Jasen, Jay, Jayson.*

Jeffrey (JEF-free) Old French: Heavenly peace. Pisceans, known for their high spiritual awareness, tend to have serene outer personas. Variations: *Geoff, Geoffrey, Jeff, Jefferson.*

Kade (KAYD) Scottish: From the wetlands. This interesting name is appropriate for those born under the sign of Pisces, which is associated with water and its mysterious depths.

Kadir (kah-DEER) Arabic: Fresh greening. Pisces, whose special colors are deep greens and blues, is the sign associated with the budding, blossoming, and flowering of trees and plants.

Kaga (KAH-gah) Native American: Scribe. *Kaga* connotes Pisces's natural aptitude for writing and the creative arts.

Kai (KEY) Hawaiian: Seawater. The Water sign of Pisces is governed by the planet Neptune, named for the Roman god of the oceans and seas.

Kell (KELL) Old Norse: From the spring. This name holds a double meaning, as the Water sign of Pisces, is associated with springtime.

Kelsey (KEL-see) Old English: Town of the keels. Referring to ships, this unique name represents Pisces's close connection to all objects of the sea. (Famous Piscean: Kelsey Grammar, actor)

Kelvin (KEL-vin) Celtic: Man of the waters. Pisceans are deeply connected to all bodies of water. Variations: *Kelvan, Kelven, Kelwyn*.

Kendall (KEN-dull) English: Valley of the Kent River. *Kendall* is a traditional place name for a boy born under Pisces, a Water sign. Variations: *Kendal, Kendale, Kendel, Kent*.

Kenn (KEN) Old Welsh: Sweet and clear water. Pisces is considered the purest of the three Water signs of the zodiac. (The other two are Cancer and Scorpio.) Variations: *Ken, Kenneth*.

Kirkwell (KURK-well) Old English: Spring beside the church. *Kirkwell* suggests not only Pisces's element of Water, but the deep spirituality affiliated with the sign.

Kurt (KURT) German: Able counselor. Pisceans, who possess a strong need to help others, often are drawn to charitable work. Variant of *Conrad*. Variations: *Curt, Curtis, Kurtis*. (Famous Pisceans: Kurt Cobain, singer/musician; Kurt Russell, actor)

Lachlan (LOCK-lin) Scottish: From the land of lakes. This unusual name suggests Pisces's unique ability to blend solid information and fluctuating emotions, similar to the way the land meets the water. Variations: *Lachlann, Lachuun, Loughlin*.

Lamar (la-MAHR) Latin: The sea. Pisces, one of the three Water signs of the zodiac, is ruled by the planet that governs the oceans and seas. Variation: *Lamarr*.

Lee (LEE) Irish: Poet. Highly imaginative and sensitive Pisceans are often drawn to the creative arts. Variation: *Leigh*.

Lennor (LEH-nohr) English Gypsy: Springtime. The sign of Pisces is closely affiliated with the yearly rebirth of nature each spring.

Leron (leh-ROHN) Hebrew: This song is mine. Possessed with vivid imaginations and remarkable creativity, Pisceans excel in music, art, writing, and drama. Variations: *Lerone, Liron, Lirone*.

Lincoln (LINK-an) Welsh: Village by the lake. The quintessential Water sign, Pisces oversees individuals who feel most comfortable when residing near the waterfront. Variation: *Linc*.

Lyn (LIN) Welsh: He who lives by the waterfall. This popular name—more commonly seen as *Lynn*—connotes Pisceans' love of living near a source of water. Variations: *Lin, Llyn, Lynn*.

Lynch (LINCH) Irish: Sailor. Born under the sign of mariners, Pisceans feel most comfortable when near the water.

Lyron (lee-ROHN) Hebrew: Songlike. Pisceans are renowned for their lyrical talents, which often inspire them to become poets, singers, and writers. Variation: *Liron*.

MacMurray (mak-MURR-ay) Irish: Sailor's son. Pisceans are born under the planet of Neptune, which governs all aspects of the oceans and seas. Variations: *Mac, Mack, McMurray, Murray*.

Mallory (MAL-lohr-ee) French: Sad. Highly sensitive, vulnerable, and emotional, Pisceans often absorb the pain of people around them and may be prone to melancholy moods. Variations: *Mallery, Malory*.

Malulani (mow-loo-LAHN-ee) Hawaiian: Spiritual peace. Pisceans, known for their high spiritual awareness, tend to have serene outer personas.

Mansfield (MANZ-feeld) English: Field by a river. Pisceans often evoke the image of land meeting water, suggesting their ability to smoothly combine the solid outer world with their emotional inner depths.

Marino (mah-REE-noh) Latin: Of the sea. Pisces, one of the three Water signs of the zodiac, is guided by the planet Neptune, which governs the oceans and seas. Variation: *Marin*.

Marland (MAHR-land) Old English: Settlement near the pond. *Marland* is an apt name for a Pisces, who prefers to live near water, where he feels most comfortable and secure.

Marley (MAHR-lee) Old English: Pasture beside the pond. Creative Pisceans are capable of combining their awareness of the real world with their otherworldly dreams, an image seen in the meeting of land and water.

Marlow (MAHR-loh) Old English: Slope beside the pond. Pisces's favorite place to be is by the water's edge. Variations: *Marley, Marlowe*.

Mart (MAHRT) Turkish: Born in the month of March. *Mart* is an appropriate choice for a Pisces boy born from early to mid-March.

Marwood (MAHR-wood) Old English: Forest pond. This interesting name suggests Pisces's deep, watery roots.

Merrill (MER-il) English: Gleaming water. This classic name evokes the image of those outgoing Pisceans who brilliantly pursue the more "fluid" performing arts of dance and music. Variations: *Meril, Merill, Merrel, Meryl*.

Merton (MUR-ton) Old English: Town near the pond. This unusual name reflects the urge of many Pisceans to live near water, even when surrounded by others.

Mervin (MER-vin) Celtic: Beautiful sea. Pisceans, born under the planet that governs the oceans and seas, are most content and inspired when near these massive bodies of water. Variations: *Marv, Marven, Marvin, Mervyn, Merwin, Merwyn, Murvin*.

Misu (MEE-soo) Native American: Rippling water. This unique name reflects the extreme versatility seen in those born under the Water sign of Pisces.

Monroe (MON-roh; mun-ROH) Irish: Mouth of the Roe River. Pisces, one of the three Water signs of the zodiac, is associated with all large bodies of water. Variations: *Monro, Munro, Munroe.*

Morgan (MORE-gin) Welsh: Gleaming seas. Creatively inclined Pisceans find great inspiration from the sea. Variation: *Morgen.*

Mortimer (MOR-tih-mer) Old French: Calm seas. Associated with the oceans and seas, Pisceans feel great comfort and peace in being near the water. Variations: *Mort, Mortmer, Mortym.*

Morven (MOHR-vin) Scottish: Child of the sea. Pisceans are born under the planet of Neptune, named for the Roman god who governs the oceans and seas.

Moses (MOZ-ez) Hebrew: Saved from the water. Born under the Water sign associated with the oceans and seas, Pisces feel secure and comfortable when close to a source of water. Variation: *Moshe.*

Murdock (MUR-dock) Scottish: Warrior-sailor. Born under the planet of Neptune, which governs the oceans and seas, Pisceans valiantly protect their loved ones and their emotional needs. Variations: *Murdo, Murdoch, Murtagh, Murtaugh.*

Murphy (MUR-fee) Scottish: Man of the sea. Pisceans are in their element when near bodies of water. Variations: *Murph, Murphie.*

Murray (MUR-ray) Scottish: Sailor. Pisceans, born under the Water sign that governs large bodies of water, have a close connection to the oceans and seas.

Nairn (nayrn) Scottish: River. Pisces is one of the three Water signs of the zodiac. Variation: *Nairne*.

Naji (NAH-jee) Arabic: To save. Associated with rebirth and spiritual renewal, Pisceans strive to help others awaken their higher consciousness. Variation: *Naj*.

Nen (NEN) Egyptian: Ancient waters. Pisceans' love of the water is deeply embedded in their natures.

Neptune (NEP-tyoon) Latin: The god of the oceans in Roman mythology. Pisces's ruling planet is Neptune, which in addition to ruling the oceans and seas, also governs mystery, higher levels of consciousness, understanding, and sacrifice.

Nevin (NEH-vinn) Irish: Spiritually significant. As the last sign in the astrological circle, Pisces often is credited with great powers of spiritual renewal and rebirth. Variations: *Nev, Nevan, Nevins, Nevyle*.

Newlin (NOO-lin) Old Welsh: Freshly made lake. This unusual name suits those born under the sign of Pisces, who are known to be wonderfully creative and greatly inspired by proximity to water. Variation: *Newlyn*.

Ocean (OH-shin) English: Ocean. Pisces, one of the three Water signs of the zodiac, is ruled by the planet that governs the oceans. Variation: *Oceanus*.

Okoth (oh-KOTH) African/Ugandan: Born when it was raining. The sign of Pisces, which encompasses the months of February and March, is strongly affiliated with the rainy season.

Oleg (OH-lehg) Russian: Sacred. Pisces's ruling planet, Neptune, governs mysticism, spirituality, and higher consciousness. Variation: *Olezka*.

Omar (OH-mahr) Arabic: Supreme devotee. Easily influenced by others, Pisceans may be extremely loyal and loving to a particular mentor or leader. Variations: *Omarr, Omer*.

Oran (OH-ran) Irish: Green life. The deep greens and blues of the ocean are the colors assigned to the sign of Pisces. Variations: *Oren, Orin, Orran, Orren, Orrin*.

Osbert (OZ-burt) Old English: Luminescent divinity. This rare name suggests Pisces's brilliant awareness of mystical and spiritual worlds.

Osmar (OZ-mahr) Old English: Marvelously sacred. As the final sign in the astrological circle, Pisces is credited with possessing a "doorway" into greater realms of consciousness.

Oswin (OZ-win) Old English: Friend in spirit. Pisceans are renowned for their unfailing generosity, kindness, and compassion. Variations: *Osvin, Oswinn, Oswyn*.

Oved (OH-vehd) Hebrew: Devotee. Trusting and guileless Pisceans are sensitive and receptive to the influence of others.

Oxford (OX-fird) Old English: River's pass. Closely connected to water, Pisces also possesses a gateway for the flowing of artistic and spiritual thoughts.

Panas (PAH-nahs) Greek: Immortal. As the last sign of the zodiac, Pisces is affiliated with the themes of rebirth, eternity, and immortality.

Pascal (PAHS-cull; pahs-CAL) French: Born at Easter or Passover. Pascal is a suitable name for a Pisces boy born around the holidays of Easter or Passover, which typically occur during the sign's phase (from late February until late March).

Pat (PAT) Native American: Fish. The symbol of the sign of Pisces is the Fish.

Peregrine (PER-eh-grin) Latin: Spiritual wanderer. Pisceans are known for their tendency to explore the depths and heights of spiritual consciousness. Variations: *Peregin, Peregryn.*

Phineas (FINN-ee-us) Hebrew: Prophecy. As the last sign of the zodiac, Pisces is often associated with visionary dreams and higher levels of consciousness.

Pontus (PON-tus) Greek: From Greek mythology. *Pontus,* the son of Uranus and Gaia, was an early Greek god of the ocean. Pisces, one of the three Water signs of the zodiac, is ruled by the planet Neptune, the Roman god of the oceans who was called Poseidon by the Greeks. (The other two are Cancer and Scorpio.)

Prescott (PRESS-kaht) Old English: Home of the priest. The sign of Pisces is strongly associated with spirituality and healing. Variations: *Prestcot, Prestcott.*

Presley (PRESS-lee) Old English: Fields of the priest. Compassionate, sensitive, and spiritually inclined, Pisceans often pursue religious vocations.

Preston (PRESS-tun) Old English: Estate owned by the priest. As the final sign in the astrological circle, Pisces is thought to have a special connection, indeed a doorway, into the realm of the divine.

Putnam (PUTT-num) Old English: Beside the lake. This unusual name suggests the Piscean inclination to reside near a large body of water.

Rachim (rah-HEEM) Hebrew: Compassion. One of the key characteristics of Pisces is an unfailing empathetic and compassionate nature. Variations: *Rachmiel, Raham, Rahim.*

Radnor (RAD-ner) English: Red shore. Names connoting the imagery of the sea are appropriate for a boy born under Pisces, a Water sign. Variation: *Radner*.

Rafa (RAH-fah) Hebrew: Cure. *Rafa* connotes Pisces's intense desire to heal the pain of those around him. Many Pisceans are drawn to charitable or religious work. Variations: *Rapha, Rappa*.

Rahman (rah-MAHN) Arabic: Understanding. Pisceans are renowned for their unfailing generosity, compassion, and empathy.

Ralph (RALF) Old English: Protector. *Ralph* is a suitable choice for Pisces, who seeks to shield his loved ones from harm and often sacrifices his own needs for the happiness of others. Variations: *Rafe, Rolf, Rolph*. (Famous Pisceans: Ralph Abernathy, civil rights leader; Ralph Nader, consumer advocate; Ralph Ellison, novelist)

Ranit (rah-NEET) Hebrew: Song. Highly imaginative and creative Pisceans often lose themselves in listening to—and even writing—their own music, wrapped up in their own private fantasy. Variation: *Ronit*.

Ranon (rah-NOHN) Hebrew: To sing. Many Pisceans are endowed with tremendous musical and lyrical gifts. Variation: *Ranen*.

Raviv (rah-VEEV) Hebrew: Mist. This unique name connotes Pisces's ephemeral and imaginative ability as the purest of the Water signs, to transform innovative thought into creative art.

Rene (ruh-NAY) French: Reborn. As the last sign of the zodiac, Pisces is associated with the themes of rebirth, eternity, and immortality. Variations: *Renat, Renato, Renatus, René, Renne, Renny*.

Rio (REE-oh) Spanish: River. This unique name is appropriate for those born under Pisces, the sign that governs oceans, seas, and all large bodies of water. Variation: *Reo*.

River (RIH-ver) Old French: River. The sign of Pisces is deeply connected to all large bodies of water.

Riyad (ree-YAHD) Arabic: Gardens. Pisces, associated with rebirth and rejuvenation, is also connected to the blooming and flowering of plants.

Rockwell (ROCK-well) Old English: From the rocky stream. Pisceans are associated with all types of flowing water.

Roka (ROH-kah) Japanese: Foamy wave. Pisces is ruled by the planet of Neptune, considered to govern all aspects of the oceans and seas.

Romney (ROM-nee) Old Welsh: Curving river. This rare name is well suited to the sign of Pisces, which is associated with flowing water and all large bodies of water.

Ronan (ROH-nen) Irish: Little seal. Born under one of the zodiac's Water signs, Pisceans possess a special connection with the ocean and all of its creatures.

Saville (sah-VEEL) French: Willow town. The sign of Pisces is affiliated with the willow and fig trees. Variations: *Savil, Savill, Savylle*.

Seabert (SEE-burt) Old English: From the bright sea. Those born under the sign of Pisces are inspired by and closely connected to the sea. Variation: *Sebert*.

Seaton (SEE-ton) Old English: From the seaside town. Pisceans often find their homes near a large body of water, where they feel most inspired and content. Variations: *Seeton, Seton*.

Seger (SEE-gir) Old English: Sea warrior. Though not aggressive, those born under the Water sign of Pisces stand firm in their sensibilities and ideas. Variations: *Seager, Seeger, Segar.*

Seldon (SELL-din) English: Valley of willows. The willow tree, a traditional symbol of healing, is one of the trees associated with the sign of Pisces. Variations: *Selden, Sellden.*

Seward (SOO-wahrd) Old English: Protector of the sea. Born under a Water sign, Pisceans are passionate about the ocean. Variation: *Sewerd.*

Sewell (SOO-il) English: Strong at sea. Born under the sign of the god of that governs the sea, Pisceans gain strength and serenity whenever they are near the sea. Variations: *Sewald, Sewall.*

Shen (SHEN) Chinese: Spirit. As the final sign in the astrological circle, Pisces is credited with possessing deep religious and mystical insight.

Sherborn (SHUR-born) Old English: From the clear brook. This old-fashioned name is appropriate for those born under the sign of Pisces, with their effervescent insight and close connection to water. Variations: *Sherborne, Sherbrooke, Sherburn, Sherburne.*

Skip (SKIP) Scandinavian: Ship's authority; skipper. Any image of the sea suggests an appropriate name for those born under the sign of Pisces, which is ruled by the planet that governs the oceans and seas. Variations: *Skipp, Skipper, Skippy.*

Sorley (SORR-lee) Irish: Summer sailor. This unusual name is appropriate to Pisceans, who are born under the sign of mariners.

Spiro (SPEER-oh) Greek: Full of soul. With their keen intuition and strong religious insight, Pisceans are considered to have great spiritual depth. Variations: *Spire, Spiridon, Spyro.*

Strom (strahm) German: Stream. Considered the purest of Water signs, Pisces is associated with all types of flowing water.

Struthers (STRUHTH-ers) Irish: Brook. This traditional name evokes the water imagery that is common to all Pisceans.

Taggart (TAG-gurt) Irish: Priest's heir. *Taggart* connotes the deep spirituality associated with the sign of Pisces. Variation: *Taggert.*

Tal (TAL) Hebrew: Rain. Encompassing the months of February and March, the Water sign of Pisces is often affiliated with the rainy season of spring.

Teague (TEEG) Irish: Poet or philosopher. Either of the meanings of this name is suitable for deep-thinking and highly creative Pisces. Variations: *Tadhg, Taogh, Teigue.*

Toru (TOH-roo) Japanese: Sea. *Toru* is an appropriate name for a boy born under Pisces, a Water sign associated with the oceans and seas.

Trent (TRENT) Latin: Flowing rivers. This handsome name is well suited to the watery Pisces, which is known as extremely versatile and accommodating. Variations: *Trenten, Trentin, Trenton.*

Varil (var-IL) Hindu: Water. Pisces is considered the purest of the zodiac's three Water signs.

Varun (var-OON) Hindu: God of water. Born under the planet that reigns over the oceans and seas, Pisces holds a high position of honor in the zodiacal realm of Water signs. Variations: *Varin, Varoon.*

Vasant (vah-SANT) Hindu: Spring. The sign of Pisces is associated with the annual rebirth of nature.

Verlin (VUR-lin) American: Spring. Associated with transformation and renewal, Pisces is the sign that oversees the season of greatest rejuvenation. Variations: *Verle, Verlon, Virle.*

Vernon (VUR-nen) Latin: Like spring. The sign of Pisces is closely connected to the rejuvenation of nature in the season of spring. Variation: *Verne.*

Virgil (VURR-jill) Latin: Flourishing. Born under the sign that rules spring and the budding and flowering of plants, Pisces's children can be creatively gifted and emotionally giving. Variations: *Verge, Vergil, Virgilio.*

Wade (WAYD) Old English: Ford in the river. Those born under the sign of Pisces are closely linked to bodies of water and to places where land and water meet.

Welby (WELL-bee) English: Waterside farm. Pisceans often make their homes near a body of water, where they feel most comfortable and content. Variations: *Welbey, Wellbey.*

Weldon (WELL-dun) Old English: From the estate with a spring. This traditional place name is appropriate for Pisceans, who typically prefer to have a solid home base, but always want to live near a source of water. Variation: *Welton.*

Wells (WELLZ) Old English: From the spring. Like the flowing water with which their sign is associated, Pisceans always demonstrate a deep inner source of innovative and intuitive energy.

Westbrook (WEST-bruk) English: Western stream. Any name connoting a body of water is suitable for a boy born under the Water sign of Pisces. Variations: *West, Westbrooke.*

Wilford (WIL-ford) Old English: Ford by the willows. The trees associated with the sign of Pisces are willows and figs.

Willoughby (WIL-oh-bee) Old English: Farm of willows. The willow tree, a traditional sign of healing, is strongly affiliated with the sign of Pisces. Variation: *Willoughbie*.

Zale (ZAYL) Greek: Strength from the sea. Creatively inclined Pisceans are often inspired by the powerful and unpredictable ocean. Variation: *Zayle*.

Zamir (zah-MEER) Hebrew: Song. Pisces often expresses his intense emotions through creative means, such as a song, painting, or poem. Variation: *Zemer*.

Zeeman (ZEE-mun) Dutch: Seaman. *Zeeman* is an apt choice for a boy born under the sign of Pisces, one of the three Water signs of the zodiac and protector of all mariners.

Zerika (zayr-EE-kah) Hebrew: Rain shower. Pisces, a Water sign, is often associated with the rainy season.

Famous Pisceans

02-20-1902	Ansel Adams	02-21-1893	Andres Segovia
02-20-1924	Sidney Poitier	02-21-1925	Sam Peckinpah
02-20-1924	Gloria Vanderbilt	02-21-1927	Erma Bombeck
02-20-1925	Robert Altman	02-21-1933	Nina Simone
02-20-1934	Bobby Unser	02-21-1935	Rue McClanahan
02-20-1937	Nancy Wilson	02-21-1936	Barbara Jordan
02-20-1941	Buffy Sainte-Marie	02-21-1943	David Geffen
02-20-1946	Sandy Duncan	02-21-1946	Tyne Daly
02-20-1948	Jennifer O'Neill	02-21-1955	Kelsey Grammer
02-20-1949	Ivana Trump	02-21-1958	Alan Trammell
02-20-1954	Patty Hearst	02-22-1732	George Washington
02-20-1963	Charles Barkley	02-22-1900	Luis Buñuel
02-20-1966	Cindy Crawford	02-22-1907	Sheldon Leonard
02-20-1967	Kurt Cobain	02-22-1907	Robert Young
02-20-1967	Andrew Shue	02-22-1908	John Mills

02-22-1932	Edward M. Kennedy	02-28-1942	Brian Jones
02-22-1950	Julius Erving	02-28-1948	Bernadette Peters
02-22-1975	Drew Barrymore	02-29-1860	Herman Hollerith
02-23-1685	George Frederic Handel	02-29-1896	William Wellman
02-23-1868	W.E.B. DuBois	02-29-1904	Jimmy Dorsey
02-23-1939	Peter Fonda	03-01-1904	Glenn Miller
02-23-1944	Johnny Winter	03-01-1910	David Niven
02-23-1955	Howard Jones	03-01-1914	Ralph Ellison
02-24-1873	Enrico Caruso	03-01-1917	Dinah Shore
02-24-1921	Abe Vigoda	03-01-1926	Pete Rozelle
02-24-1932	Michel Legrand	03-01-1927	Harry Belafonte
02-24-1947	Edward James Olmos	03-01-1935	Robert Conrad
02-24-1955	Steven Jobs	03-01-1944	Roger Daltrey
02-25-1841	Pierre Auguste Renoir	03-01-1947	Alan Thicke
02-25-1904	Adelle Davis	03-01-1954	Ron Howard
02-25-1913	Jim Backus	03-01-1958	Nik Kershaw
02-25-1917	Anthony Burgess	03-02-1904	Dr. Seuss
02-25-1943	George Harrison	03-02-1917	Desi Arnaz
02-25-1943	Sally Jessy Raphael	03-02-1931	Mikhail Gorbachev
02-26-1802	Victor Hugo	03-02-1944	Lou Reed
02-26-1846	William "Buffalo Bill" Cody	03-02-1952	Laraine Newman
		03-02-1962	Jon Bon Jovi
02-26-1887	William Frawley	03-03-1847	Alexander Graham Bell
02-26-1906	Madeleine Carroll	03-03-1911	Jean Harlow
02-26-1922	Margaret Leighton	03-03-1962	Jackie Joyner-Kersee
02-26-1916	Jackie Gleason	03-03-1962	Herschel Walker
02-26-1920	Tony Randall	03-04-1888	Knute Rockne
02-26-1921	Betty Hutton	03-04-1932	Miriam Makeba
02-26-1928	Fats Domino	03-04-1939	Paula Prentiss
02-26-1932	Johnny Cash	03-04-1948	Chris Squire
02-26-1953	Michael Bolton	03-04-1969	Chastity Bono
02-27-1897	Marian Anderson	03-05-1908	Rex Harrison
02-27-1902	John Steinbeck	03-05-1922	James Noble
02-27-1930	Joanne Woodward	03-05-1936	Dean Stockwell
02-27-1932	Elizabeth Taylor	03-05-1939	Samantha Eggar
02-27-1934	Ralph Nader	03-05-1946	Michael Warren
02-27-1940	Howard Hesseman	03-05-1958	Andy Gibb
02-27-1943	Mary Frann	03-05-1975	Niki Taylor
02-28-1901	Linus Pauling	03-06-1475	Michelangelo Buonarroti
02-28-1907	Earl Scheib		
02-28-1915	Zero Mostel	03-06-1906	Lou Costello
02-28-1923	Charles Durning	03-06-1923	Ed McMahon
02-28-1930	Gavin MacLeod	03-06-1930	Lorin Maazel
02-28-1939	Tommy Tune	03-06-1936	Marion Barry
02-28-1940	Mario Andretti	03-06-1941	Willie Stargell

03-06-1944	Kiri Te Kanawa	03-14-1879	Albert Einstein
03-06-1945	Rob Reiner	03-14-1912	Les Brown
03-06-1959	Tom Arnold	03-14-1920	Hank Ketcham
03-06-1972	Shaquille O'Neal	03-14-1928	Frank Borman
03-07-1849	Luther Burbank	03-14-1933	Michael Caine
03-07-1872	Piet Mondrian	03-14-1933	Quincy Jones
03-07-1875	Maurice Ravel	03-14-1947	Billy Crystal
03-07-1930	Lord Snowdon	03-15-1767	Andrew Jackson
03-07-1934	Willard Scott	03-15-1912	Samuel "Lightnin' "
03-07-1940	Daniel J. Travanti		Hopkins
03-07-1942	Tammy Faye Bakker	03-15-1913	Macdonald Carey
03-08-1909	Claire Trevor	03-15-1916	Harry James
03-08-1923	Cyd Charisse	03-15-1935	Judd Hirsch
03-08-1943	Lynn Redgrave	03-15-1940	Phil Lesh
03-08-1945	Mickey Dolenz	03-15-1944	Sly Stone
03-08-1959	Aidan Quinn	03-15-1961	Fabio
03-08-1963	Kathy Ireland	03-16-1751	James Madison
03-09-1918	Mickey Spillane	03-16-1912	Pat Nixon
03-09-1926	Irene Papas	03-16-1926	Jerry Lewis
03-09-1932	Keely Smith	03-16-1940	Bernardo Bertolucci
03-09-1936	Mickey Gilley	03-16-1949	Erik Estrada
03-09-1940	Raul Julia	03-17-1895	Shemp Howard
03-09-1943	Bobby Fischer	03-17-1918	Mercedes
03-09-1971	Emmanuel Lewis		McCambridge
03-10-1903	Bix Beiderbecke	03-17-1919	Nat "King" Cole
03-10-1918	Pamela Mason	03-17-1938	Rudolf Nureyev
03-10-1940	Chuck Norris	03-17-1944	John Sebastian
03-10-1958	Sharon Stone	03-17-1949	Patrick Duffy
03-11-1903	Lawrence Welk	03-17-1951	Kurt Russell
03-11-1926	Ralph Abernathy	03-17-1955	Gary Sinise
03-11-1931	Rupert Murdoch	03-17-1964	Rob Lowe
03-11-1934	Sam Donaldson	03-18-1837	Grover Cleveland
03-12-1921	Gordon MacRae	03-18-1886	Edward Everett Horton
03-12-1922	Jack Kerouac	03-18-1926	Peter Graves
03-12-1928	Edward Albee	03-18-1927	George Plimpton
03-12-1932	Andrew Young	03-18-1932	John Updike
03-12-1940	Al Jarreau	03-18-1938	Charlie Pride
03-12-1941	Barbara Feldon	03-18-1941	Wilson Pickett
03-12-1942	Paul Kantner	03-18-1959	Irene Cara
03-12-1946	Liza Minnelli	03-18-1963	Vanessa Williams
03-12-1948	James Taylor	03-18-1964	Bonnie Blair
03-13-1855	Percival Lowell	03-18-1970	Queen Latifah
03-13-1911	L. Ron Hubbard	03-19-1848	Wyatt Earp
03-13-1913	William Casey	03-19-1928	Patrick McGoohan
03-13-1939	Neil Sedaka	03-19-1935	Phyllis Newman

03-19-1936	Ursula Andress	03-20-1928	Mr. Fred Rogers
03-19-1947	Glenn Close	03-20-1931	Hal Linden
03-19-1955	Bruce Willis	03-20-1945	Pat Riley
03-20-1904	B. F. Skinner	03-20-1950	William Hurt
03-20-1906	Ozzie Nelson	03-20-1957	Spike Lee
03-20-1922	Carl Reiner	03-20-1958	Holly Hunter

APPENDIX

A Ten-Minute Method for
Casting Your Baby's Birth Chart

Basically there are two types of birth charts that you can cast: a *natal birth chart* and a *solar birth chart*. Of the two, the natal chart is the more individualistic and specific about personality traits, family, work, and relationships. It requires that you calculate the newborn's *ascendant* or *rising sign* using a complicated mathematical system that incorporates both the time of your child's birth and the latitude and longitude of the birth place. Unfortunately, calculating the ascendant requires charts and equations that are beyond the scope of this book. However, all the books listed under "Further Reading" provide charts and instructions for calculating your child's ascendant. Many people also use the fine astrological charting services provided on the Internet. Of these, Astrolabe, at astrolabe.com, is an excellent resource. You provide them with your child's time, date, and place of birth, and, for a minimal fee, they will provide you with a complete birth chart.

The other type of birth chart, the solar chart, which is based on the child's Sun (or astrological) sign, is less specific than a natal chart (anyone born on the same day has the same solar chart), but still provides valuable information about the child's general personality traits and potential approach to work, relationships, and family. Here we provide you with simple instructions for calculating your newborn's solar birth chart.

Calculating Your Child's Solar Birth Chart

To cast your newborn's solar chart, you'll need this book, some paper and colored pencils, and the date of your child's birth. The example used here is the author's nephew, born on March 8, 1998.

First, draw a large circle and then divide the circle into twelve equal segments as illustrated in Chart 1. Starting at the "9 o'clock" position and, going counterclockwise around the circle, number the outside of each segment 1 through 12. These are the twelve houses of the zodiac that represent specific areas or interests in an individual's life. As shown in Chart 1, write the names of the houses alongside each number: (1) personality; (2) possessions and wealth; (3) education and communication; (4) family and home; (5) creativity, arts, and leisure; (6) work, health, and service; (7) partnership and marriage; (8) sexuality, death, rebirth, and occult; (9) religion, philosophy, and travel; (10) career; (11) social relationships, dreams, ambitions, and politics; and (12) mysticism, secrets, sorrows, and personal trials.

Second, write your newborn's Sun sign in segment 1, as illustrated in Chart 2. In our example, for March 8, 1998, the child's Sun sign is Pisces. To refresh your memory, the list of Sun signs with their respective dates can be found in the Introduction on pages xii and xiii.

Third, going counterclockwise around the circle and starting with segment 2, write in the signs of the zodiac in the exact order that they would follow your child's Sun sign (in segment 1). As a reminder, the order of the zodiac signs is: Aries, Taurus, Gemini, Cancer, Leo, Virgo, Libra, Scorpio, Sagittarius, Capricorn, Aquarius, and Pisces. See our example in Chart 2. The first sign, Pisces (the child's Sun sign) in the first house, is followed by Aries, Taurus, Gemini, Cancer, etc., with Aquarius being the last sign written in the twelfth house.

Fourth, using the Planetary Tables that begin on page 627, determine what signs the Sun, Moon, and other eight planets were in on the day your child was born. Write the planets down in their respective signs. In Chart 3—our example of a completed solar chart—on March 8, 1998, the Sun and Jupiter were

Chart 1

irthdate: March 8, 1998

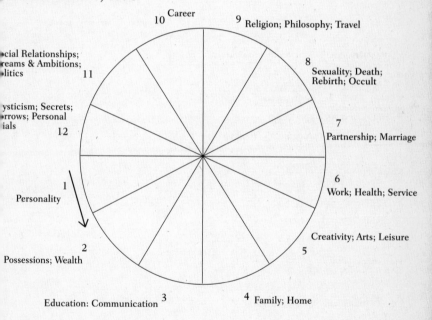

Chart 2

Birthdate: *March 8, 1998*

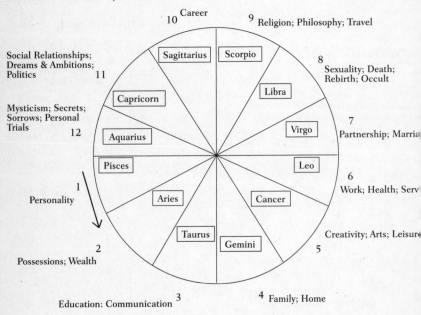

Chart 3

Birthdate: March 8, 1998

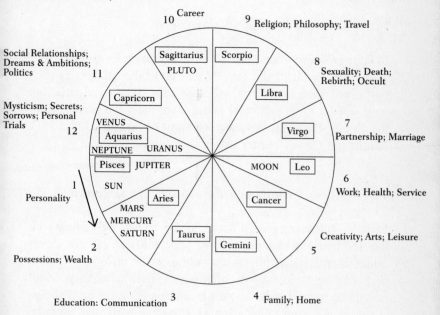

in Pisces in the first house (Ex. the Sun's position was determined to be in Pisces because March 8 falls between February 18 and March 20, lines 2 and 3 of the 1998 Sun Table); Mars, Mercury, and Saturn were in Aries in the second house; the Moon was in Leo in the sixth house; Pluto was in Sagittarius in the tenth house; and Venus, Uranus, and Neptune were in Aquarius in the twelfth house.

Once you have filled in the planets, your newborn's solar chart is complete! Now, what does it all mean?

Interpreting Your Baby's Solar Chart

In your newborn's solar chart, you will want to look particularly at the placement of the Sun, Moon, and other planets in each house and each sign. You will also want to look at each sign with respect to its particular house, especially the placement of the Ruling Sign—in this case, Neptune. You should also look at how the planets cluster within the chart.

The Signs and Planets in the Houses of the Zodiac

Start by considering each house of the zodiac, beginning with the first house, which governs the personality or ego and determines character and physical appearance. To understand how a particular sign relates to or influences a specific house, you will now have to read over the profiles in this book for each zodiac sign, not just your child's Sun sign, paying particular attention to personality traits, work, relationships, and the discussion of the planetary influences in the sign. You may also wish to refer back to the Introduction, where a brief description is given of each sign and each planet.

As we pointed out earlier, no individual can be characterized by just one sign. Rather, three or four zodiac signs often have a strong influence in a person's life, and indeed, we all live out aspects of all twelve of the signs.

First House.

This is especially true of our example of a boy born on March 8, 1998 (see Chart 3). This child is a Pisces, classically the most otherworldly of the zodiac signs, deeply emotional and vulnerable, drawn to mysticism or religion, scornful of wealth and material possessions, and frequently shunning the spotlight of success to live in an isolated world of fantasy. Pisceans often quietly pursue creative work behind the scenes. But here, the influence of the Sun in Pisces in the first house strengthens this boy's ego, makes him more emotionally resilient and capable of pursuing larger goals singlemindedly. Jupiter is an excellent partner with the Sun, endowing the normally shy Pisces with an outgoing, enthusiastic, and upbeat nature, even to the point of overconfidence, a very non-Piscean trait! Jupiter, however, formerly a ruling planet of Pisces, does suggest that this child may have problems staying active and focused if he doesn't consistently follow through on plans or is overly confident. Jupiter also suggests a tendency toward self-indulgence in drugs, alcohol, or religion.

Second House.

The non-Piscean trend in this chart continues in the second house of wealth and material possessions, where fiery, confident, and headstrong Aries dominates the house, supported by three strong planetary influences—Mars, Mercury, and Saturn. Mars, the planet of action, energy, and self-determination, is also the ruling planet of Aries, thus intensifying the Arian qualities of assertiveness and drive. Unlike traditional Pisceans, this boy seems inevitably headed toward a highly successful career where acquiring wealth and material possessions are of paramount importance. Mercury favors great communication skills, a facile mind, and a natural talent for understanding what people want and need. Sales, manufacturing, or publishing, therefore, may be careers of choice, though this Piscean may have to learn to control a sharp tongue, quick temper, and need to control subordinates and work situations. Sports, as an outlet for his surplus of both physical and mental energy as well as his aggressive tendencies, may figure prominently in this Piscean's life. Saturn is an important sobering influence, adding the tendency to worry about finances, which will spur this Piscean ever onward in his quest for wealth. Saturn also suggests that this boy may be a late bloomer in terms of career success if he can't learn to control his ferocious energies, appetites, and interests.

Third, Fourth, and Fifth Houses.

The next three houses are conspicuously devoid of planetary influences and thus the sign in each house is the predominating influence on the respective area of life. Taurus, in the third house of education and communication, is a welcome omen, tempering the more ferocious aspects of the Arian influence and suggesting that this Piscean will learn how to direct his emotions and energies constructively in the service of others. A love of beautiful things, and a quick temper are also suggested here, as they are in the first house.

However successful this Piscean may be, freedom-loving Gemini in the fourth house of family and home suggests that he may well be a loner when it comes to intimate relationships, though he will enjoy an abundance of friends through work and social activities. Cancer, in the fifth house of creativity, seems to imply that this Piscean will enjoy success and wealth in one of the more creative fields, perhaps publishing, and will most likely start his own business which may take the place of family in his life.

Sixth House.

Leo, in the sixth house of service, and ruled by the same Sun that influences the first house of personality, suggests again that this boy is no typical Piscean. He has a well-developed ego, enjoys the limelight, is nearly invulnerable to criticism, and naturally assumes a leadership role in all endeavors. The Moon in this house, together with Leo, is a critically needed influence. On the one hand, it underscores this Piscean's drive and tenacity when it comes to achieving his goals. On the other hand, the Moon's maternal and compassionate influences temper this unque Piscean's tendency toward aggressiveness, egotism, and self-absorption.

Seventh, Eighth, and Ninth Houses.

These three houses are also devoid of any planetary presence, and thus their respective signs are the primary influence in these particular areas of our young Piscean's life. Virgo, in the seventh house of partnership and marriage, suggests great success in business, which is in keeping with the overall trend of this chart. Sensible and analytical Virgo also keeps a check on the more fiery Arian qualities.

Libra, in the eighth house of sexuality, death, rebirth, and the occult, has a strong positive and negative presence in this chart. On the positive side, Libra is the sign of harmonious partnership, immediately confirming the success in business, perhaps through a fortuitous partnership, indicated by Virgo in the previous house. On the negative side, Librans, represented by the scales of justice, continually struggle with all the choices that life has to offer. In fact, they may take so long to make a decision about those choices that they wind up doing nothing at all. This is also a trait of Pisceans, and while this boy does seem headed for success, he may grapple for quite some time about just what path he takes there. Libra in this house also suggests that this Piscean may be a late bloomer, as mentioned earlier. He may have several careers before he hits his stride, or he may be sidetracked entirely in his younger years by more Piscean interests.

Scorpio, in the ninth house of religion, philosophy, and travel, seems to confirm Libra's warning. Scorpio is the darkest and most profound of the zodiac's signs, denoting an interest in things that are hidden, mystical, or occult. This Scorpion tendency is doubled by the sign's appearance in the ninth house, which represents journeys—actual and metaphysical—of the body, mind, and soul to some greater union or connection with the universe. These darker and more mystical tendencies in this

Piscean's chart are in direct contrast to the more direct, success-oriented qualities observed earlier. This Piscean may be a late bloomer because he spends his youth delving into mysticism and the occult, or in traveling the globe.

Tenth House.

Sagittarius in the tenth house of career echoes the influence of Scorpio in possibly sidetracking this Piscean's quest for career success, wealth, and material possessions. Sagittarians are also prone to wanderlust, travel to exotic places, and metaphysical journeys of the mind and soul. On the other hand, they are not dark souls, like so many Scorpions are, but are characteristically upbeat and optimistic, qualities that are in keeping with the general trend of this chart. It may well be that this individual channels his wanderlust into a highly successful import/export business that requires him to travel extensively. Pluto's planetary influence in this house again suggests that this Piscean may be a late-blooming success, after he gets his wanderlust under control, and that he possesses a true gift for business.

Eleventh House.

Capricorn in the eleventh house of relationships, dreams, ambitions, and politics, without any planetary influence, in many ways suggests this Piscean at full maturity, well on his way to success and wealth. Capricorns are gifted in business and in making money. In fact, they will often sacrifice friendships and other humanitarian concerns to succeed and must be cautious about being too self-serving. This latter tendency is often offset by the "water" side of Capricorn (the capricorn is a mythical beast that is half goat and half fish). The water element in Capricorn lends a deep emotionality to the sign which is almost Piscean in its power. Again, this Piscean boy may spend many years learning to channel and focus his Piscean/Capricorn feelings and Arian energies into constructive work that will ultimately bring the material success he craves.

Twelfth House.

The twelfth house of mysticism, secrets, sorrows, and personal trials completes the zodiac circle and theoretically embodies or ties together all that has been learned, both good and bad, in the previous eleven houses. Deep mysticism and a desire for unity characterize the twelfth house. In this chart, Aquarius, appropriately enough, is the twelfth house's sign. Aquarius is one of the more complex of the zodiac's signs, largely because of its dual nature. On the one hand, Aquarius represents order and practicality. On the other hand, Aquarius also rules anarchy and impracticality, new and radical ideas that may never see fruition. Aquarians are great dreamers, but often can't put their dreams into actions because of their impractical bents. They are loners, as well, and often push away the very people who could help them realize their dreams.

For our Piscean boy, the warning here is the same one echoed throughout his chart: This unusual Piscean will only realize his dreams for success when he learns to channel his abundant physical and mental energies and harness his deep and mystic tendencies in constructive ways that embrace rather than alienate the people who can help him further his goals. This is the only way he will achieve the wealth and material possessions he so ardently desires.

The three strong planetary influences in this last house seem to underscore this warning, but also suggest counteractive characteristics this Piscean can employ. Uranus suggests a need for meditation and relaxation techniques to offset the fiery Arian qualities and a tendency to overwork. Uranus also suggests that success will come by tearing down old, traditional concepts of what is valuable and what is not. This Piscean may be an innovator in whatever field he enters.

Venus alone in this house would normally suggest a shy person who lacks self-confidence and is easily influenced by the attention of others. But the co-influence of Aquarius in the twelfth house with Venus denotes a person who is naturally outgoing and forceful, perhaps even a rebel. He is good with money and with people and able to exert a strong influence on those around him.

Neptune, the third planet in the twelfth sign of this birth chart, is also the ruling planet of the chart and deserves special mention on its own.

The Ruling Planet

The ruling planet of any birth chart is the planet that traditionally governs the zodiac sign appearing in the first house of personality. In our example, Pisces appears in the first house, and is ruled by Neptune. Thus, Neptune is the ruling planet of this birth chart, and its appearance in the twelfth house tellingly brings the birth chart of this unique Piscean full circle to his metaphysical roots.

Neptune is the planet of deep transformations and slow, continual change. The planet is associated with mysticism, spirituality, the seeking of higher truths, and the desire for unity with a higher power. Those influenced by Neptune can be both sensitive and emotional, self-serving and cynical, and Pisceans in particular are adept at hiding their true selves under various social masks either to protect themselves or to further their aims. Put to positive use, the collective talents of Neptune-influenced people may produce born leaders who inspire their subordinates to great change. Put to negative use, these same talents may produce ruthless despots. The appearance of strong-willed but upbeat and humanitarian-minded Aquarius with Neptune in this Piscean's twelfth house will temper Neptune's more negative influences, certainly by the time this boy becomes an adult, and suggests that he will be a one-of-a-kind success who marries deep feelings and ambitions to strong actions in the social arena, actions that may not only bring him wealth and success, but also better the lives of those around him. A unique combination indeed!

I hope you've enjoyed this introduction to the rich and exciting world of astrology, and that you will be encouraged to learn more about this fascinating and rewarding view into human behavior. Happy parenting! And glorious stargazing!

Sun Table

	1998	1999	2000	2001	2002	2003
JAN	20 AQU	20 AQU	21 AQU	20 AQU	20 AQU	20 AQU
FEB	18 PIS	19 PIS	19 PIS	19 PIS	19 PIS	19 PIS
MAR	20 ARI	21 AIR	20 ARI	21 ARI	21 ARI	21 ARI
APR	20 TAU	20 TAU	20 TAU	20 TAU	20 TAU	20 TAU
MAY	21 GEM	21 GEM	21 GEM	21 GEM	21 GEM	21 GEM
JUN	21 CAN	21 CAN	21 CAN	21 CAN	22 CAN	22 CAN
JUL	23 LEO	23 LEO	23 LEO	23 LEO	23 LEO	23 LEO
AUG	23 VIR	23 VIR	23 VIR	23 VIR	23 VIR	24 VIR
SEP	23 LIB	23 LIB	23 LIB	23 LIB	23 LIB	23 LIB
OCT	23 SCO	23 SCO	23 SCO	23 SCO	24 SCO	24 SCO
NOV	22 SAG	22 SAG	22 SAG	22 SAG	22 SAG	23 SAG
DEC	22 CAP	22 CAP	22 CAP	22 CAP	22 CAP	22 CAP

	2004	2005	2006	2007	2008	2009
JAN	21 AQU	20 AQU	20 AQU	20 AQU	21 AQU	20 AQU
FEB	19 PIS	19 PIS	19 PIS	19 PIS	19 PIS	19 PIS
MAR	20 ARI	21 ARI	21 ARI	21 ARI	20 ARI	20 ARI
APR	20 TAU	20 TAU	20 TAU	20 TAU	20 TAU	20 TAU
MAY	21 GEM	21 GEM	21 GEM	21 GEM	21 GEM	21 GEM
JUN	21 CAN	21 CAN	22 CAN	22 CAN	21 CAN	21 CAN
JUL	22 LEO	23 LEO	23 LEO	23 LEO	22 LEO	23 LEO
AUG	23 VIR	23 VIR	23 VIR	24 VIR	23 VIR	23 VIR
SEP	23 LIB	23 LIB	23 LIB	23 LIB	23 LIB	23 LIB
OCT	23 SCO	23 SCO	24 SCO	24 SCO	23 SCO	23 SCO
NOV	22 SAG	22 SAG	22 SAG	23 SAG	22 SAG	22 SAG
DEC	22 CAP	22 CAP	22 CAP	22 CAP	22 CAP	22 CAP

	2010
JAN	20 AQU
FEB	19 PIS
MAR	20 ARI
APR	20 TAU
MAY	21 GEM
JUN	21 CAN
JUL	23 LEO
AUG	23 VIR
SEP	23 LIB
OCT	23 SCO
NOV	22 SAG
DEC	22 CAP

Moon Tables

1998

JAN	FEB	MAR	APR	MAY	JUN
2 PIS	2 TAU	2 TAU	2 CAN	2 LEO	1 VIR
4 ARI	5 GEM	4 GEM	5 LEO	4 VIR	3 LIB
6 TAU	7 CAN	6 CAN	7 VIR	7 LIB	6 SCO
8 GEM	9 LEO	8 LEO	10 LIB	9 SCO	8 SAG
11 CAN	12 VIR	11 VIR	12 SCO	12 SAG	11 CAP
13 LEO	14 LIB	13 LIB	15 SAG	14 CAP	13 AQU
15 VIR	17 SCO	16 SCO	17 CAP	17 AQU	15 PIS
18 LIB	19 SAG	18 SAG	19 AQU	19 PIS	17 ARI
20 SCO	21 CAP	21 CAP	22 PIS	21 ARI	19 TAU
23 SAG	24 AQU	23 AQU	24 ARI	23 TAU	21 GEM
25 CAP	26 PIS	25 PIS	26 TAU	25 GEM	23 CAN
27 AQU	28 ARI	27 ARI	28 GEM	27 CAN	26 LEO
29 PIS		29 TAU	30 CAN	29 LEO	28 VIR
31 ARI		31 GEM			30 LIB

JUL	AUG	SEP	OCT	NOV	DEC
3 SCO	2 SAG	1 CAP	2 PIS	1 ARI	2 GEM
5 SAG	4 CAP	3 AQU	5 ARI	3 TAU	4 CAN
8 CAP	6 AQU	5 PIS	6 TAU	5 GEM	6 LEO
10 AQU	9 PIS	7 ARI	8 GEM	7 CAN	9 VIR
12 PIS	11 ARI	9 TAU	11 CAN	9 LEO	11 LIB
14 ARI	13 TAU	11 GEM	13 LEO	11 VIR	14 SCO
17 TAU	15 GEM	13 CAN	15 VIR	14 LIB	16 SAG
19 GEM	17 CAN	16 LEO	18 LIB	16 SCO	19 CAP
21 CAN	19 LEO	18 VIR	20 SCO	19 SAG	21 AQU
23 LEO	22 VIR	20 LIB	23 SAG	21 CAP	23 PIS
25 VIR	24 LIB	23 SCO	25 CAP	24 AQU	26 ARI
28 LIB	27 SCO	25 SAG	28 AQU	26 PIS	28 TAU
30 SCO	29 SAG	28 CAP	30 PIS	28 ARI	30 GEM
		30 AQU		30 TAU	

1999

JAN	FEB	MAR	APR	MAY	JUN
1 CAN	2 VIR	1 VIR	2 SCO	2 SAG	1 CAP
3 LEO	4 LIB	3 LIB	5 SAG	4 CAP	3 AQU
5 VIR	6 SCO	6 SCO	7 CAP	7 AQU	5 PIS
8 LIB	9 SAG	8 SAG	10 AQU	9 PIS	8 ARI
10 SCO	11 CAP	11 CAP	12 PIS	11 ARI	10 TAU
13 SAG	14 AQU	13 AQU	14 ARI	13 TAU	12 GEM
15 CAP	16 PIS	15 PIS	16 TAU	15 GEM	14 CAN
17 AQU	18 ARI	18 ARI	18 VIR	17 CAN	16 LEO
20 PIS	20 TAU	20 TAU	20 CAN	19 LEO	18 VIR
22 ARI	22 GEM	22 GEM	22 LEO	22 VIR	20 LIB
24 TAU	24 CAN	24 CAN	24 VIR	24 LIB	23 SCO

629

JAN	FEB	MAR	APR	MAY	JUN
26 GEM	27 LEO	26 LEO	27 LIB	27 SCO	25 SAG
28 CAN		28 VIR	29 SCO	29 SAG	28 CAP
30 LEO		31 LIB			30 AQU

JUL	AUG	SEP	OCT	NOV	DEC
3 PIS	1 ARI	2 GEM	1 CAN	2 VIR	1 LIB
5 ARI	3 TAU	4 CAN	3 LEO	4 LIB	4 SCO
7 TAU	5 GEM	6 LEO	5 VIR	6 SCO	6 SAG
9 GEM	8 CAN	8 VIR	8 LIB	9 SAG	9 CAP
11 CAN	10 LEO	10 LIB	10 SCO	11 CAP	11 AQU
13 LEO	12 VIR	13 SCO	13 SAG	14 AQU	14 PIS
15 VIR	14 LIB	15 SAG	15 CAP	16 PIS	16 ARI
18 LIB	16 SCO	18 CAP	18 AQU	19 ARI	20 GEM
20 SCO	19 SAG	20 AQU	20 PIS	21 TAU	22 CAN
23 SAG	21 CAP	23 PIS	22 ARI	23 GEM	24 LEO
25 CAP	24 AQU	25 ARI	24 TAU	25 CAN	26 VIR
28 AQU	26 PIS	27 TAU	26 GEM	27 LEO	29 LIB
30 PIS	28 ARI	29 GEM	28 CAN	29 VIR	31 SCO
	31 TAU		30 LEO		

2000

JAN	FEB	MAR	APR	MAY	JUN
3 SAG	2 CAP	3 AQU	1 PIS	1 ARI	2 GEM
5 CAP	2 AQU	5 PIS	4 ARI	3 TAU	4 CAN
8 AQU	7 PIS	7 ARI	6 TAU	5 GEM	6 LEO
10 PIS	9 ARI	9 TAU	8 GEM	7 CAN	8 VIR
13 ARI	11 TAU	12 GEM	10 CAN	9 LEO	10 LIB
15 TAU	13 GEM	14 CAN	12 LEO	12 VIR	12 SCO
17 GEM	16 CAN	16 LEO	14 VIR	14 LIB	15 SAG
19 CAN	18 LEO	18 VIR	17 LIB	16 SCO	17 CAP
21 LEO	20 VIR	22 SCO	19 SCO	19 SAG	20 AQU
23 VIR	22 LIB	25 SAG	21 SAG	21 CAP	22 PIS
25 LIB	24 SCO	27 CAP	24 CAP	24 AQU	25 ARI
28 SCO	27 SAG	30 AQU	26 AQU	26 PIS	27 TAU
30 SAG	29 CAP		29 PIS	28 ARI	29 GEM
				31 TAU	

JUL	AUG	SEP	OCT	NOV	DEC
1 CAN	2 VIR	2 SCO	2 SAG	1 CAP	1 AQU
3 LEO	4 LIB	5 SAG	4 CAP	3 AQU	3 PIS
5 VIR	6 SCO	7 CAP	7 AQU	6 PIS	6 ARI
7 LIB	8 SAG	10 AQU	9 PIS	8 ARI	8 TAU
10 SCO	11 CAP	12 PIS	12 ARI	10 TAU	10 GEM
12 SAG	13 AQU	15 ARI	14 TAU	13 GEM	12 CAN
15 CAP	16 PIS	17 TAU	16 GEM	15 CAN	14 LEO
17 AQU	18 ARI	19 GEM	18 CAN	17 LEO	16 VIR
20 PIS	21 TAU	21 CAN	21 LEO	19 VIR	18 LIB
22 ARI	23 GEM	23 LEO	23 VIR	21 LIB	21 SCO
24 TAU	25 CAN	25 VIR	25 LIB	23 SCO	23 SAG
27 GEM	27 LEO	27 LIB	27 SCO	26 SAG	25 CAP
29 CAN	29 VIR	30 SCO	29 SAG	28 CAP	28 AQU
31 LEO	31 LIB				30 PIS

2001

JAN	FEB	MAR	APR	MAY	JUN
2 ARI	1 TAU	2 GEM	1 CAN	2 VIR	3 SCO
4 TAU	3 GEM	4 CAN	3 LEO	4 LIB	5 SAG
6 GEM	5 CAN	6 LEO	5 VIR	6 SCO	7 CAP
9 CAN	7 LEO	8 VIR	7 LIB	9 SAG	10 AQU
11 LEO	9 VIR	10 LIB	9 SCO	11 CAP	12 PIS
13 VIR	11 LIB	13 SCO	11 SAG	13 AQU	15 ARI
15 LIB	13 SCO	15 SAG	14 CAP	16 PIC	17 TAU
17 SCO	15 SAG	17 CAP	16 AQU	18 ARI	19 GEM
19 SAG	18 CAP	20 AQU	19 PIS	21 TAU	21 CAN
22 CAP	20 AQU	22 PIS	21 ARI	23 GEM	24 LEO
24 AQU	23 PIS	25 ARI	23 TAU	25 CAN	26 VIR
27 PIS	25 ARI	27 TAU	26 GEM	27 LEO	28 LIB
29 ARI	28 TAU	29 GEM	28 CAN	29 VIR	30 SCO
			30 LEO	31 LIB	

JUL	AUG	SEP	OCT	NOV	DEC
2 SAG	1 CAP	2 PIC	2 ARI	1 TAU	2 CAN
5 CAP	3 AQU	5 ARI	4 TAU	3 GEM	5 LEO
7 AQU	6 PIS	7 TAU	7 GEM	5 CAN	7 VIR
10 PIS	8 ARI	9 GEM	9 CAN	7 LEO	9 LIB
12 ARI	11 TAU	12 CAN	11 LEO	9 VIR	11 SCO
14 TAU	13 GEM	14 LEO	13 VIR	12 LIB	13 SAG
17 GEM	15 CAN	16 VIR	15 LIB	14 SCO	15 CAP
19 CAN	17 LEO	18 LIB	17 SCO	16 SAG	18 AQU
21 LEO	19 VIR	20 SCO	19 SAG	18 CAP	20 PIS
23 VIR	21 LIB	22 SAG	22 CAP	20 AQU	23 ARI
25 LIB	23 SCO	24 CAP	24 AQU	23 PIS	25 TAU
27 SCO	26 SAG	27 AQU	27 PIS	25 ARI	28 GEM
29 SAG	28 CAP	29 PIS	29 ARI	28 TAU	30 CAN
	30 AQU			30 GEM	

2002

JAN	FEB	MAR	APR	MAY	JUN
1 LEO	1 LIB	1 LIB	1 SAG	1 CAP	2 PIS
3 VIR	3 SCO	3 SCO	3 CAP	3 AQU	4 ARI
5 LIB	6 SAG	5 SAG	6 AQU	6 PIS	7 TAU
7 SCO	8 CAP	7 CAP	8 PIS	8 ARI	9 GEM
9 SAG	10 AQU	10 AQU	11 ARI	11 TAU	12 CAN
12 CAP	13 PIS	12 PIS	13 TAU	13 GEM	14 LEO
14 AQU	15 ARI	15 ARI	16 GEM	15 CAN	16 VIR
17 PIS	18 TAU	17 TAU	18 CAN	18 LEO	18 LIB
19 ARI	20 GEM	20 GEM	21 LEO	20 VIR	20 SCO
22 TAU	23 CAN	22 CAN	23 VIR	22 LIB	22 SAG
24 GEM	25 LEO	24 LEO	25 LIB	24 SCO	25 CAP
26 CAN	27 VIR	26 VIR	27 SCO	26 SAG	27 AQU
28 LEO		28 LIB	29 SAG	28 CAP	29 PIS
30 VIR		30 SCO		31 AQU	

JUL	AUG	SEP	OCT	NOV	DEC
2 ARI	1 TAU	2 CAN	1 LEO	2 LIB	1 SCO
4 TAU	3 GEM	4 LEO	4 VIR	4 SCO	4 SAG
7 GEM	6 CAN	6 VIR	6 LIB	6 SAG	6 CAP
9 CAN	8 LEO	8 LIB	8 SCO	8 CAP	8 AQU
11 LEO	10 VIR	10 SCO	10 SAG	10 AQU	10 PIS
13 VIR	12 LIB	12 SAG	12 CAP	13 PIS	13 ARI
15 LIB	14 SCO	14 CAP	14 AQU	15 ARI	15 TAU
18 SCO	16 SAG	17 AQU	16 PIS	18 TAU	18 GEM
20 SAG	18 CAP	19 PIS	19 ARI	20 GEM	20 CAN
22 CAP	21 AQU	22 ARI	21 TAU	23 CAN	22 LEO
24 AQU	23 PIS	24 TAU	24 GEM	25 LEO	25 VIR
27 PIS	25 ARI	27 GEM	26 CAN	27 VIR	27 LIB
29 ARI	28 TAU	29 CAN	29 LEO	29 LIB	29 SCO
	30 GEM		31 VIR		31 SAG

2003

JAN	FEB	MAR	APR	MAY	JUN
2 CAP	1 AQU	2 PIS	1 ARI	1 TAU	2 CAN
4 AQU	3 PIS	5 ARI	3 TAU	4 GEM	4 LEO
6 PIS	5 ARI	7 TAU	6 GEM	6 CAN	7 VIR
9 ARI	8 TAU	10 GEM	8 CAN	8 LEO	9 LIB
11 TAU	10 GEM	12 CAN	11 LEO	10 VIR	11 SCO
14 GEM	13 CAN	14 LEO	13 VIR	12 LIB	13 SAG
16 CAN	15 LEO	17 VIR	15 LIB	15 SCO	15 CAP
19 LEO	17 VIR	19 LIB	17 SCO	16 SAG	17 AQU
21 VIR	19 LIB	21 SCO	19 SAG	19 CAP	19 PIS
23 LIB	21 SCO	23 SAG	21 CAP	21 AQU	22 ARI
25 SCO	23 SAG	25 CAP	23 AQU	23 PIS	24 TAU
27 SAG	26 CAP	27 AQU	26 PIS	25 ARI	27 GEM
29 CAP	28 AQU	29 PIS	28 ARI	28 TAU	29 CAN
				30 GEM	

JUL	AUG	SEP	OCT	NOV	DEC
2 LEO	2 LIB	1 SCO	2 CAP	1 AQU	2 ARI
4 VIR	4 SCO	3 SAG	4 AQU	3 PIS	5 TAU
6 LIB	7 SAG	5 CAP	7 PIS	5 ARI	7 GEM
8 SCO	9 CAP	7 AQU	9 ARI	8 TAU	10 CAN
10 SAG	11 AQU	9 PIS	11 TAU	10 GEM	12 LEO
12 CAP	13 PIS	12 ARI	14 GEM	13 CAN	15 VIR
14 AQU	15 ARI	14 TAU	16 CAN	15 LEO	17 LIB
17 PIS	18 TAU	17 GEM	19 LEO	18 VIR	19 SCO
19 ARI	20 GEM	19 CAN	21 VIR	20 LIB	21 SAG
21 TAU	23 CAN	22 LEO	23 LIB	22 SCO	23 CAP
24 GEM	25 LEO	24 VIR	25 SCO	24 SAG	25 AQU
26 CAN	27 VIR	26 LIB	27 SAG	26 CAP	27 PIS
29 LEO	30 LIB	28 SCO	29 CAP	28 AQU	30 ARI
31 VIR		30 SAG		30 PIS	

2004

JAN	FEB	MAR	APR	MAY	JUN
1 TAU	3 CAN	1 CAN	2 VIR	2 LIB	2 SAG
4 GEM	5 LEO	3 LEO	4 LIB	4 SCO	4 CAP
6 CAN	7 VIR	6 VIR	6 SCO	6 SAG	6 AQU
9 LEO	10 LIB	8 LIB	8 SAG	8 CAP	8 PIS
11 VIR	12 SCO	10 SCO	11 CAP	10 AQU	11 ARI
13 LIB	14 SAG	12 SAG	13 AQU	12 PIS	13 TAU
16 SCO	16 CAP	14 CAP	15 PIS	14 ARI	16 GEM
18 SAG	18 AQU	16 AQU	17 ARI	17 TAU	18 CAN
20 CAP	20 PIS	19 PIS	20 TAU	19 GEM	21 LEO
22 AQU	23 ARI	21 ARI	22 GEM	22 CAN	23 VIR
24 PIS	25 TAU	23 TAU	25 CAN	24 LEO	25 LIB
26 ARI	27 GEM	26 GEM	27 LEO	27 VIR	28 SCO
29 TAU		28 CAN	30 VIR	29 LIB	30 SAG
31 GEM		31 LEO		31 SCO	

JUL	AUG	SEP	OCT	NOV	DEC
2 CAP	2 PIS	1 ARI	3 GEM	2 CAN	1 LEO
4 AQU	4 ARI	3 TAU	5 CAN	4 LEO	4 VIR
6 PIS	7 TAU	5 GEM	8 LEO	7 VIR	6 LIB
8 ARI	9 GEM	8 CAN	10 VIR	9 LIB	9 SCO
10 TAU	12 CAN	10 LEO	13 LIB	11 SCO	11 SAG
13 GEM	14 LEO	13 VIR	15 SCO	13 SAG	13 CAP
15 CAN	17 VIR	15 LIB	17 SAG	15 CAP	15 AQU
18 LEO	19 LIB	17 SCO	19 CAP	17 AQU	17 PIS
20 VIR	21 SCO	20 SAG	21 AQU	19 PIS	19 ARI
23 LIB	23 SAG	22 CAP	23 PIS	22 ARI	21 TAU
25 SCO	25 CAP	24 AQU	25 ARI	24 TAU	24 GEM
27 SAG	28 AQU	26 PIS	28 TAU	26 GEM	26 CAN
29 CAP	30 PIS	28 ARI	30 GEM	29 CAN	29 LEO
31 AQU		30 TAU			31 VIR

2005

JAN	FEB	MAR	APR	MAY	JUN
3 LIB	1 SCO	1 SCO	1 CAP	3 PIS	1 ARI
5 SCO	4 SAG	3 SAG	3 AQU	5 ARI	3 TAU
7 SAG	6 CAP	5 CAP	5 PIS	7 TAU	6 GEM
9 CAP	8 AQU	7 AQU	7 ARI	9 GEM	8 CAN
11 AQU	10 PIS	9 PIS	10 TAU	12 CAN	11 LEO
13 PIS	12 ARI	11 ARI	12 GEM	14 LEO	13 VIR
15 ARI	14 TAU	13 TAU	14 CAN	17 VIR	16 LIB
18 TAU	16 GEM	16 GEM	17 LEO	19 LIB	18 SCO
20 GEM	19 CAN	18 CAN	19 VIR	21 SCO	20 SAG
22 CAN	21 LEO	21 LEO	22 LIB	24 SAG	22 CAP
25 LEO	24 VIR	23 VIR	24 SCO	26 CAP	24 AQU
27 VIR	26 LIB	25 LIB	26 SAG	28 AQU	26 PIS
30 LIB		28 SCO	28 CAP	30 PIS	28 ARI
		30 SAG	30 AQU		30 TAU

JUL	AUG	SEP	OCT	NOV	DEC
3 GEM	2 CAN	3 VIR	3 LIB	1 SCO	1 SAG
5 CAN	4 LEO	5 LIB	5 SCO	4 SAG	3 CAP
8 LEO	7 VIR	8 SCO	7 SAG	6 CAP	5 AQU
10 VIR	9 LIB	10 SAG	10 CAP	8 AQU	7 PIS
13 LIB	12 SCO	12 CAP	12 AQU	10 PIS	9 ARI
15 SCO	14 SAG	14 AQU	14 PIS	12 ARI	12 TAU
17 SAG	16 CAP	16 PIS	16 ARI	14 TAU	14 GEM
20 CAP	18 AQU	18 ARI	18 TAU	17 GEM	16 CAN
22 AQU	20 PIS	20 TAU	20 GEM	19 CAN	19 LEO
24 PIS	22 ARI	23 GEM	22 CAN	21 LEO	21 VIR
26 ARI	24 TAU	25 CAN	25 LEO	24 VIR	24 LIB
28 TAU	26 GEM	28 LEO	27 VIR	26 LIB	26 SCO
30 GEM	29 CAN	30 VIR	30 LIB	29 SCO	28 SAG
	31 LEO				30 CAP

2006

JAN	FEB	MAR	APR	MAY	JUN
2 AQU	2 ARI	1 ARI	2 GEM	2 CAN	3 VIR
4 PIS	4 TAU	3 TAU	4 CAN	4 LEO	5 LIB
6 ARI	6 GEM	6 GEM	7 LEO	7 VIR	8 SCO
8 TAU	9 CAN	8 CAN	9 VIR	9 LIB	10 SAG
10 GEM	11 LEO	10 LEO	12 LIB	12 SCO	12 CAP
12 CAN	14 VIR	13 VIR	14 SCO	14 SAG	15 AQU
15 LEO	16 LIB	15 LIB	17 SAG	16 CAP	17 PIS
17 VIR	19 SCO	18 SCO	19 CAP	18 AQU	19 ARI
20 LIB	21 SAG	20 SAG	21 AQU	20 PIS	21 TAU
22 SCO	23 CAP	23 CAP	23 PIS	23 ARI	23 GEM
25 SAG	25 AQU	25 AQU	25 ARI	25 TAU	25 CAN
27 CAP	27 PIS	27 PIS	27 TAU	27 GEM	28 LEO
29 AQU		29 ARI	29 GEM	29 CAN	30 VIR
31 PIS		31 TAU		31 LEO	

JUL	AUG	SEP	OCT	NOV	DEC
3 LIB	2 SCO	3 CAP	2 AQU	1 PIS	2 TAU
5 SCO	4 SAG	5 AQU	4 PIS	3 ARI	4 GEM
8 SAG	6 CAP	7 PIS	6 ARI	5 TAU	6 CAN
10 CAP	8 AQU	9 ARI	8 TAU	7 GEM	8 LEO
12 AQU	10 PIS	11 TAU	10 GEM	9 CAN	11 VIR
14 PIS	12 ARI	13 GEM	12 CAN	11 LEO	13 LIB
16 ARI	14 TAU	15 CAN	15 LEO	14 VIR	16 SCO
18 TAU	17 GEM	18 LEO	17 VIR	16 LIB	18 SAG
20 GEM	19 CAN	20 VIR	20 LIB	19 SCO	21 CAP
23 CAN	21 LEO	23 LIB	22 SCO	21 SAG	23 AQU
25 LEO	24 VIR	25 SCO	25 SAG	23 CAP	25 PIS
27 VIR	26 LIB	28 SAG	27 CAP	26 AQU	27 ARI
30 LIB	29 SCO	30 CAP	29 AQU	28 PIS	29 TAU
	31 SAG			30 ARI	31 GEM

2007

JAN	FEB	MAR	APR	MAY	JUN
3 CAN	1 LEO	3 VIR	2 LIB	1 SCO	3 CAP
5 LEO	4 VIR	5 LIB	4 SCO	4 SAG	5 AQU
7 VIR	6 LIB	8 SCO	7 SAG	6 CAP	7 PIS
10 LIB	9 SCO	10 SAG	9 CAP	9 AQU	9 ARI
12 SCO	11 SAG	13 CAP	11 AQU	11 PIS	11 TAU
15 SAG	13 CAP	15 AQU	14 PIS	13 ARI	14 GEM
17 CAP	16 AQU	17 PIS	16 ARI	15 TAU	16 CAN
19 AQU	18 PIS	19 ARI	18 TAU	17 GEM	18 LEO
21 PIS	20 ARI	21 TAU	20 GEM	19 CAN	20 VIR
23 ARI	22 TAU	23 GEM	22 CAN	21 LEO	22 LIB
26 TAU	24 GEM	25 CAN	24 LEO	24 VIR	25 SCO
28 GEM	26 CAN	28 LEO	26 VIR	26 LIB	28 SAG
30 CAN	28 LEO	30 VIR	29 LIB	29 SCO	30 CAP
				31 SAG	

JUL	AUG	SEP	OCT	NOV	DEC
2 AQU	1 PIS	1 TAU	1 GEM	1 LEO	1 VIR
4 PIS	3 ARI	3 GEM	3 CAN	4 VIR	3 LIB
7 ARI	5 TAU	5 CAN	5 LEO	6 LIB	6 SCO
9 TAU	7 GEM	8 LEO	7 VIR	9 SCO	8 SAG
11 GEM	9 CAN	10 VIR	10 LIB	11 SAG	11 CAP
13 CAN	11 LEO	12 LIB	12 SCO	14 CAP	13 AQU
15 LEO	14 VIR	15 SCO	15 SAG	16 AQU	16 PIS
17 VIR	16 LIB	18 SAG	17 CAP	18 PIS	18 ARI
20 LIB	19 SCO	20 CAP	20 AQU	20 ARI	20 TAU
22 SCO	21 SAG	22 AQU	22 PIS	23 TAU	22 GEM
25 SAG	24 CAP	25 PIS	24 ARI	24 GEM	24 CAN
27 CAP	26 AQU	27 ARI	26 TAU	26 CAN	26 LEO
30 AQU	28 PIS	29 TAU	28 GEM	29 LEO	28 VIR
	30 ARI		30 CAN		31 LIB

2008

JAN	FEB	MAR	APR	MAY	JUN
2 SCO	1 SAG	2 CAP	1 AQU	2 ARI	1 TAU
5 SAG	3 CAP	4 AQU	3 PIS	4 TAU	3 GEM
7 CAP	6 AQU	6 PIS	5 ARI	6 GEM	5 CAN
9 AQU	8 PIS	9 ARI	7 TAU	8 CAN	7 LEO
12 PIS	10 ARI	11 TAU	9 GEM	11 LEO	9 VIR
14 ARI	12 TAU	13 GEM	11 CAN	13 VIR	11 LIB
16 TAU	15 GEM	15 CAN	13 LEO	15 LIB	14 SCO
18 GEM	17 CAN	17 LEO	16 VIR	18 SCO	16 SAG
20 CAN	19 LEO	19 VIR	18 LIB	20 SAG	19 CAP
22 LEO	21 VIR	22 LIB	20 SCO	23 CAP	21 AQU
25 VIR	23 LIB	24 SCO	23 SAG	25 AQU	24 PIS
27 LIB	26 SCO	27 SAG	25 CAP	28 PIS	26 ARI
29 SCO	28 SAG	29 CAP	28 AQU	30 ARI	28 TAU
			30 PIS		30 GEM

JUL	AUG	SEP	OCT	NOV	DEC
2 CAN	1 LEO	1 LIB	1 SCO	2 CAP	2 AQU
4 LEO	3 VIR	4 SCO	4 SAG	5 AQU	5 PIS
6 VIR	5 LIB	6 SAG	6 CAP	7 PIS	7 ARI
9 LIB	7 SCO	9 CAP	9 AQU	10 ARI	9 TAU
11 SCO	10 SAG	11 AQU	11 PIS	12 TAU	11 GEM
14 SAG	12 CAP	14 PIS	13 ARI	14 GEM	13 CAN
16 CAP	15 AQU	16 ARI	15 TAU	16 CAN	15 LEO
19 AQU	17 PIS	18 TAU	17 GEM	18 LEO	17 VIR
21 PIS	20 ARI	20 GEM	19 CAN	20 VIR	20 LIB
23 ARI	22 TAU	22 CAN	22 LEO	22 LIB	22 SCO
26 TAU	24 GEM	24 LEO	24 VIR	25 SCO	24 SAG
28 GEM	26 CAN	27 VIR	26 LIB	27 SAG	27 CAP
30 CAN	28 LEO	29 LIB	28 SCO	30 CAP	30 AQU
	30 VIR		31 SAG		

2009

JAN	FEB	MAR	APR	MAY	JUN
1 PIS	2 TAU	1 TAU	2 CAN	1 LEO	2 LIB
3 ARI	4 GEM	3 GEM	4 LEO	3 VIR	4 SCO
6 TAU	6 CAN	5 CAN	6 VIR	5 LIB	6 SAG
8 GEM	8 LEO	8 LEO	8 LIB	8 SCO	9 CAP
10 CAN	10 VIR	10 VIR	10 SCO	10 SAG	11 AQU
12 LEO	12 LIB	12 LIB	13 SAG	13 CAP	14 PIS
14 VIR	15 SCO	14 SCO	15 CAP	15 AQU	16 ARI
16 LIB	17 SAG	16 SAG	18 AQU	18 PIS	19 TAU
18 SCO	20 CAP	19 CAP	20 PIS	20 ARI	21 GEM
21 SAG	22 AQU	21 AQU	23 ARI	22 TAU	23 CAN
23 CAP	25 PIS	24 PIS	25 TAU	24 GEM	25 LEO
26 AQU	27 ARI	26 ARI	27 GEM	26 CAN	27 VIR
28 PIS		28 TAU	29 CAN	28 LEO	29 LIB
31 ARI		31 GEM		30 VIR	

JUL	AUG	SEP	OCT	NOV	DEC
1 SCO	2 CAP	1 AQU	1 PIS	2 TAU	2 GEM
4 SAG	5 AQU	4 PIS	3 ARI	4 GEM	4 CAN
6 CAP	7 PIS	6 ARI	6 TAU	6 CAN	6 LEO
9 AQU	10 ARI	8 TAU	8 GEM	8 LEO	8 VIR
11 PIS	12 TAU	11 GEM	10 CAN	11 VIR	10 LIB
14 ARI	14 GEM	13 CAN	12 LEO	13 LIB	12 SCO
16 TAU	17 CAN	15 LEO	14 VIR	15 SCO	15 SAG
18 GEM	19 LEO	17 VIR	16 LIB	17 SAG	17 CAP
20 CAN	21 VIR	19 LIB	19 SCO	20 CAP	19 AQU
22 LEO	23 LIB	21 SCO	21 SAG	22 AQU	22 PIS
24 VIR	25 SCO	23 SAG	23 CAP	25 PIS	24 ARI
26 LIB	27 SAG	26 CAP	26 AQU	27 ARI	27 TAU
28 SCO	30 CAP	28 AQU	28 PIS	29 TAU	29 GEM
31 SAG			31 ARI		31 CAN

2010

JAN	FEB	MAR	APR	MAY	JUN
3 LEO	1 VIR	1 VIR	1 SCO	1 SAG	2 AQU
5 VIR	3 LIB	3 LIB	3 SAG	3 CAP	4 PIS
7 LIB	5 SCO	5 SCO	6 CAP	5 AQU	7 ARI
9 SCO	8 SAG	7 SAG	8 AQU	8 PIS	9 TAU
11 SAG	10 CAP	9 CAP	11 PIS	10 ARI	11 GEM
14 CAP	12 AQU	12 AQU	13 ARI	13 TAU	14 CAN
16 AQU	15 PIS	14 PIS	15 TAU	15 GEM	16 LEO
19 PIS	18 ARI	17 ARI	18 GEM	17 CAN	18 VIR
21 ARI	20 TAU	19 TAU	20 CAN	19 LEO	20 LIB
24 TAU	22 GEM	22 GEM	22 LEO	21 VIR	22 SCO
26 GEM	24 CAN	24 CAN	24 VIR	24 LIB	24 SAG
28 CAN	27 LEO	26 LEO	26 LIB	26 SCO	27 CAP
30 LEO	28 VIR	28 VIR	28 SCO	28 SAG	29 AQU
		30 LIB		30 CAP	

JUL	AUG	SEP	OCT	NOV	DEC
2 PIS	3 TAU	2 GEM	1 CAN	2 VIR	1 LIB
4 ARI	5 GEM	4 CAN	3 LEO	4 LIB	3 SCO
7 TAU	7 CAN	6 LEO	5 VIR	6 SCO	5 SAG
9 GEM	9 LEO	8 VIR	7 LIB	8 SAG	7 CAP
11 CAN	11 VIR	10 LIB	9 SCO	10 CAP	10 AQU
13 LEO	13 LIB	12 SCO	11 SAG	12 AQU	12 PIS
15 VIR	16 SCO	14 SAG	14 CAP	15 PIS	15 ARI
17 LIB	18 SAG	16 CAP	16 AQU	17 ARI	17 TAU
19 SCO	20 CAP	19 AQU	19 PIS	20 TAU	20 GEM
21 SAG	23 AQU	21 PIS	21 ARI	22 GEM	22 CAN
24 CAP	25 PIS	24 ARI	24 TAU	25 CAN	24 LEO
26 AQU	28 ARI	26 TAU	26 GEM	27 LEO	26 VIR
29 PIS	30 TAU	29 GEM	28 CAN	29 VIR	28 LIB
31 ARI			31 LEO		30 SCO

Mercury Tables

	1998	1999	2000	2001	2002	2003
JAN	12 CAP	7 CAP 26 AQU	19 AQU	11 AQU	4 AQU	CAP
FEB	2 AQU 20 PIS	12 PIS	5 PIS	1 PIS 7 AQU	4 CAP 14 AQU	13 AQU
MAR	8 ARI	2 ARI 18 PIS	PIS	17 PIS	12 PIS 30 ARI	5 PIS 22 ARI
APR	ARI	17 ARI	13 ARI 30 TAU	6 ARI 22 TAU	13 TAU 30 TAU	6 TAU
MAY	15 TAU	8 TAU 23 GEM	14 GEM 30 CAN	6 GEM	TAU	TAU
JUN	1 GEM 15 CAN 30 LEO	6 CAN 26 LEO	CAN	GEM	TAU	13 GEM 29 CAN
JUL	LEO	31 CAN	CAN	13 CAN 30 LEO	7 CAN 22 LEO	14 LEO 31 VIR
AUG	LEO	11 LEO 31 VIR	7 LEO 22 VIR	14 VIR	6 VIR 27 LIB	VIR
SEP	8 VIR 24 LIB	16 LIB	8 LIB 29 SCO	1 LIB	LIB	VIR
OCT	12 SCO	5 SCO 30 SAG	SCO	LIB	2 VIR 11 LIB	7 LIB 24 SCO
NOV	1 SAG	9 SCO	7 LIB 9 SCO	8 SCO 27 SAG	1 SCO 19 SAG	12 SAG
DEC	SAG	11 SAG	4 SAG 23 CAP	16 CAP	9 CAP	3 CAP 31 SAG

Mercury (cont'd)

	2004	2005	2006	2007	2008	2009
JAN	14 CAP 30 AQU	10 CAP 23 AQU	4 CAP	15 AQU	8 AQU	21 CAP
FEB	7 AQU 26 PIS	17 PIS	9 PIS	2 PIS 27 AQU	AQU	15 AQU
MAR	12 ARI	5 ARI	PIS	18 PIS	15 PIS	9 PIS 26 ARI
APR	1 TAU 13 ARI	ARI	17 ARI	11 ARI 27 TAU	3 ARI 18 TAU	10 TAU
MAY	16 TAU	12 TAU 28 GEM	5 TAU 20 GEM	11 GEM 29 CAN	3 GEM	1 GEM 14 TAU
JUN	6 GEM 20 CAN	11 CAN 28 LEO	3 CAN 29 LEO	CAN	GEM	14 GEM
JUL	5 LEO 26 VIR	LEO	11 CAN	CAN	11 CAN 26 LEO	4 CAN 18 LEO
AUG	25 LEO	LEO	11 LEO 28 VIR	5 LEO 20 VIR	10 VIR 29 LIB	3 VIR 26 LIB
SEP	10 VIR 29 LIB	5 VIR 21 LIB	13 LIB	6 LIB 28 SCO	LIB	18 VIR
OCT	16 SCO	9 SCO 30 SAG	2 SCO	24 LIB	LIB	10 LIB 28 SCO
NOV	5 SAG	26 SCO	SCO	11 SCO	5 SCO 23 SAG	16 SAG
DEC	SAG	13 SAG	8 SAG 28 CAP	2 SAG 21 CAP	12 CAP	6 CAP

Mercury (cont'd)

		2010
JAN		CAP
FEB	11	AQU
MAR	2	PIS
	18	ARI
APR	3	TAU
MAY		TAU
JUN	11	GEM
	26	CAN
JUL	10	LEO
	28	VIR
AUG		VIR
SEP		VIR
OCT	4	LIB
	21	SCO
NOV	9	SAG
DEC	2	CAP
	19	SAG

Venus Tables

	1998	1999	2000	2001	2002	2003
JAN	AQU 9 CAP	CAP 4 AQU 28 PIS	1 SAG 25 CAP	4 PIS	19 AQU	8 SAG
FEB	CAP	21 ARI	18 AQU	3 ARI	12 PIS	5 CAP
MAR	4 AQU	18 TAU	13 PIS	ARI	8 ARI	3 AQU 28 PIS
APR	6 PIS	12 GEM	7 ARI	ARI	1 TAU 26 GEM	22 ARI
MAY	3 ARI 29 TAU	8 CAN	1 TAU 26 GEM	ARI	21 CAN	16 TAU
JUN	24 GEM	5 LEO	19 CAN	6 TAU	15 LEO	10 GEM
JUL	19 CAN	12 VIR	13 LEO	6 GEM	11 VIR	5 CAN 29 LEO
AUG	13 LEO	15 LEO	7 VIR 31 LIB	2 CAN 27 LEO	7 LIB	22 VIR
SEP	6 VIR 30 LIB	LEO	25 SCO	21 VIR	8 SCO	16 LIB
OCT	24 SCO	7 VIR	19 SAG	15 LIB	SCO	10 SCO
NOV	17 SAG	9 LIB	13 CAP	9 SCO	SCO	3 SAG 27 CAP
DEC	11 CAP	5 SCO	8 AQU	2 SAG 26 CAP	SCO	21 AQU

Venus (cont'd)

	2004	2005	2006	2007	2008	2009
JAN	15 PIS	10 CAP	2 CAP	4 AQU	24 CAP	4 PIS
				28 PIS		
FEB	9 ARI	3 AQU	CAP	21 ARI	18 AQU	3 ARI
		27 PIS				
MAR	6 TAU	23 ARI	5 AQU	18 TAU	13 PIS	ARI
APR	4 GEM	16 TAU	6 PIS	12 GEM	6 ARI	12 PIS
						24 ARI
MAY	GEM	10 GEM	3 ARI	8 CAN	1 TAU	ARI
			30 TAU		25 GEM	
JUN	GEM	4 CAN	24 GEM	6 LEO	18 CAN	6 TAU
		28 LEO				
JUL	GEM	23 VIR	19 CAN	15 VIR	13 LEO	5 GEM
AUG	7 CAN	17 LIB	13 LEO	9 LEO	6 VIR	1 CAN
					31 LIB	27 LEO
SEP	7 LEO	12 SCO	6 VIR	LEO	24 SCO	21 VIR
			30 LIB			
OCT	4 VIR	8 SAG	24 SCO	8 VIR	19 SAG	15 LIB
	29 LIB					
NOV	23 SCO	5 CAP	17 SAG	9 LIB	13 CAP	8 SCO
DEC	17 SAG	16 AQU	11 CAP	6 SCO	8 AQU	2 SAG
				31 SAG		26 CAP

	2010
JAN	19 AQU
FEB	12 PIS
MAR	8 ARI
APR	1 TAU
	26 GEM
MAY	21 CAN
JUN	15 LEO
JUL	11 VIR
AUG	8 LIB
SEP	9 SCO
OCT	SCO
NOV	9 LIB
DEC	1 SCO

Mars Tables

	1998	1999	2000	2001	2002	2003
JAN	AQU	26 SCO	4 PIS	SCO	19 ARI	17 SAG
	25 PIS					
FEB	PIS	SCO	12 ARI	15 SAG	ARI	SAG
MAR	4 ARI	SCO	23 TAU	SAG	2 TAU	5 CAP
APR	13 TAU	SCO	TAU	SAG	14 GEM	22 AQU
MAY	24 GEM	5 LIB	4 GEM	SAG	28 CAN	AQU
JUN	GEM	LIB	17 CAN	SAG	CAN	17 PIS
JUL	6 CAN	5 SCO	CAN	SAG	14 LEO	PIS
AUG	20 LEO	SCO	1 LEO	SAG	30 VIR	PIS
SEP	LEO	2 SAG	17 VIR	9 CAP	VIR	PIS
OCT	7 VIR	17 CAP	VIR	28 AQU	16 LIB	PIS
NOV	27 LIB	26 AQU	4 LIB	AQU	LIB	PIS
DEC	LIB	AQU	24 SCO	9 PIS	2 SCO	17 ARI

Mars (cont'd)

	2004	2005	2006	2007	2008	2009
JAN	ARI	SAG	TAU	17 CAP	1 GEM	CAP
FEB	3 TAU	7 CAP	18 GEM	26 AQU	GEM	5 AQU
MAR	21 GEM	21 AQU	GEM	AQU	4 CAN	15 PIS
APR	GEM	AQU	14 CAN	6 PIS	CAN	23 ARI
MAY	7 CAN	1 PIS	CAN	16 ARI	10 LEO	ARI
JUN	24 LEO	12 ARI	4 LEO	25 TAU	LEO	1 TAU
JUL	LEO	28 TAU	23 VIR	TAU	2 VIR	12 GEM
AUG	10 VIR	TAU	VIR	7 GEM	19 LIB	26 CAN
SEP	26 LIB	TAU	8 LIB	29 CAN	LIB	CAN
OCT	LIB	TAU	24 SCO	CAN	4 SCO	17 LEO
NOV	11 SCO	TAU	SCO	CAN	16 SAG	LEO
DEC	26 SAG	TAU	6 SAG	CAN	27 CAP	LEO

	2010
JAN	LEO
FEB	LEO
MAR	LEO
APR	LEO
MAY	LEO
JUN	8 VIR
JUL	30 LIB
AUG	LIB
SEP	15 SCO
OCT	29 SAG
NOV	SAG
DEC	8 CAP

Jupiter Tables

1998	JAN	1 – FEB	3	AQU
	FEB	4 – DEC	31	PIS
1999	JAN	1 – FEB	12	PIS
	FEB	13 – JUN	27	ARI
	JUN	28 – OCT	22	TAU
	OCT	23 – DEC	31	ARI
2000	JAN	1 – FEB	14	ARI
	FEB	15 – JUN	29	TAU
	JUN	30 – DEC	31	GEM
2001	JAN	1 – JUL	12	GEM
	JUL	13 – DEC	31	CAN
2002	JAN	1 – AUG	1	CAN
	AUG	2 – DEC	31	LEO
2003	JAN	1 – AUG	26	LEO
	AUG	27 – DEC	31	VIR

2004	JAN	1 – SEP	24	VIR
	SEP	25 – DEC	31	LIB
2005	JAN	1 – OCT	25	LIB
	OCT	26 – DEC	31	SCO
2006	JAN	1 – NOV	23	SCO
	NOV	24 – DEC	31	SAG
2007	JAN	1 – DEC	18	SAG
	DEC	19 – DEC	31	CAP
2008	JAN	1 – DEC	31	CAP
2009	JAN	1 – JAN	5	CAP
	JAN	6 – DEC	31	AQU
2010	JAN	1 – JAN	18	AQU
	JAN	19 – JUN	6	PIS
	JUN	7 – SEP	9	ARI
	SEP	10 – DEC	31	PIS

Saturn Tables

1998	JAN	1 – JUN	8	ARI	**2004**	JAN	1 – DEC 31	CAN
	JUN	9 – OCT	24	TAU				
	OCT	25 – DEC	31	ARI	**2005**	JAN	1 – JUL 16	CAN
						JUL	17 – DEC 31	LEO
1999	JAN	1 – FEB	28	ARI				
	MAR	1 – DEC	31	TAU	**2006**	JAN	1 – DEC 31	LEO
2000	JAN	1 – AUG	9	TAU	**2007**	JAN	1 – SEP 2	LEO
	AUG	10 – OCT	15	GEM		SEP	3 – DEC 31	VIR
	OCT	16 – DEC	31	TAU				
					2008	JAN	1 – DEC 31	VIR
2001	JAN	1 – APR	20	TAU				
	APR	21 – DEC	31	GEM	**2009**	JAN	1 – OCT 29	VIR
						OCT	30 – DEC 31	LIB
2002	JAN	1 – DEC	31	GEM				
					2010	JAN	1 – APR 7	LIB
2003	JAN	1 – JUN	3	GEM		APR	8 – JUL 21	VIR
	JUN	4 – DEC	31	CAN		JUL	22 – DEC 31	LIB

Uranus Tables

1998	JAN	1 – DEC 31	AQU	**2004**	JAN	1 – DEC 31	PIS
1999	JAN	1 – DEC 31	AQU	**2005**	JAN	1 – DEC 31	PIS
2000	JAN	1 – DEC 31	AQU	**2006**	JAN	1 – DEC 31	PIS
2001	JAN	1 – DEC 31	AQU	**2007**	JAN	1 – DEC 31	PIS
2002	JAN	1 – DEC 31	AQU	**2008**	JAN	1 – DEC 31	PIS
2003	JAN	1 – MAR 10	AQU	**2009**	JAN	1 – DEC 31	PIS
	MAR	11 – SEP 14	PIS				
	SEP	15 – DEC 29	AQU	**2010**	JAN	1 – MAY 28	PIS
	DEC	31 –	PIS		MAY	29 – AUG 13	ARI
					AUG	15 – DEC 31	PIS

Neptune Tables

1998	JAN	1 – JAN	28	CAP	**2004**	JAN	1 – DEC 31	AQU
	JAN	29 – AUG	22	AQU				
	AUG	23 –		CAP	**2005**	JAN	1 – DEC 31	AQU
		NOV	26					
	NOV	27 – DEC	31	AQU	**2006**	JAN	1 – DEC 31	AQU
1999	JAN	1 – DEC	31	AQU	**2007**	JAN	1 – DEC 31	AQU
2000	JAN	1 – DEC	31	AQU	**2008**	JAN	1 – DEC 31	AQU
2001	JAN	1 – DEC	31	AQU	**2009**	JAN	1 – DEC 31	AQU
2002	JAN	1 – DEC	31	AQU	**2010**	JAN	1 – DEC 31	AQU
2003	JAN	1 – DEC	31	AQU				

Pluto Tables

1998	JAN	1 – DEC 31	SAG	**2005**	JAN	1 – DEC	31	SAG
1999	JAN	1 – DEC 31	SAG	**2006**	JAN	1 – DEC	31	SAG
2000	JAN	1 – DEC 31	SAG	**2007**	JAN	1 – DEC	31	SAG
2001	JAN	1 – DEC 31	SAG	**2008**	JAN	1 – JAN	25	SAG
					JAN	26 – JUN	13	CAP
2002	JAN	1 – DEC 31	SAG		JUN	14 – NOV	26	SAG
					NOV	27 – DEC	31	CAP
2003	JAN	1 – DEC 31	SAG	**2009**	JAN	1 – DEC	31	CAP
2004	JAN	1 – DEC 31	SAG	**2010**	JAN	1 – DEC	31	CAP

FURTHER READING

Campion, Nicholas. *The Practical Astrologer*. New York: Harry N. Abrams, Inc., 1987.

Frank, Debbie. *Baby Signs: How to Discover Your Child's Personality Through the Stars*. New York: Pocket Books, 1996.

Griffon, T. Wynne, ed. *The Illustrated Guide to Astrology*. New York: Mallard Press, 1990.

Lynch, John, ed. *The Coffee Table Book of Astrology*. New York: Viking Press, 1967.

Rachleff, Owen S. *Sky Diamonds: The New Astrology*. New York: Hawthorn Books, Inc., 1973.

Woolfolk, Joanna Martine. *The Only Astrology Book You'll Ever Need*. Lanham, Maryland: Scarborough House, 1990.

ABOUT THE AUTHOR

Nancy Burke is a writer and freelance editor. Her other books include *Teachers Are Special, Meditations on Health: Thoughts and Quotations on Healing and Wellness, St. John's Wort: The Miracle Medicine*, co-authored with Dr. Alan H. Pressman, and *The American Association of Oriental Medicine's Complete Guide to Chinese Herbal Medicine*, co-authored with David Molony. Her writing frequently appears in *BodyMindSpirit* and *New Age Journal* magazine. She lives with her daughter in New England.